For selected older vintages, refer to the chart...

ITALY										
Barolo, Barbaresco	8									
Chianti Classico Ris.	8									
Brunello	8			8	7	9	8	5	9	8
Amarone	7	9	6	8	5	9	8	5	7	9
SPAIN										
Ribera del Duero	8	5	5	6	9	8	8	5	8	7
Rioja (red)	8	7	6	6	9	9	7	6	8	8
PORTUGAL										
South	7	8	8	7	8	8	6	5	8	9
North	8	8	8	5	8	8	8	7	8	9
Port	7	8	10	7	8	8	9	5	7	9
USA										
California Cabernet	9	8	9	9	8	8	7	7	8	6
California Chardonnay	10	8	9	8	7	8	9	8	8	7
Oregon Pinot Noir	7	8	6	8	7	8	8	8	7	9
Wash. State Cabernet	8	8	8	8	8	7	8	7	8	9
AUSTRALIA										
Coonawarra Cabernet	9	8	6	9	10	8	8	9	9	6
Hunter Semillon	9	7	8	8	9	8	8	7	8	9
Barossa Shiraz	8	9	6	8	10	8	7	10	9	8
Marg. River Cabernet	9	9	9	6	10	9	8	7	10	8
NEW ZEALAND										
M'lborough Sauvignon	8	5	9	9	7	8	8	6	9	9
H'kes Bay Cab/Merlot	9	8	9	8	7	8	5	9	6	8
SOUTH AFRICA										
Stellenbosch Cabernet	10	9	9	8	7	8	9	5	9	8
S'bosch Chardonnay	10	8	9	8	8	9	8	6	7	7

Numerals (1–10) represent an overall rating for each year.
◗ *Not ready* ◕ *Just ready* ● *At peak* ◐ *Past best* ○ *Not generally declared*

OZ CLARKE

POCKET WINE BOOK 2011

PAVILION

This edition first published in 2010 by Pavilion Books

An imprint of
Anova Books Company Ltd
10 Southcombe Street
London W14 0RA

www.anovabooks.com
www.ozclarke.com

Editor Maggie Ramsay
Cartographer Andrew Thompson
Photography Michael Wicks
Desktop Publishing Jayne Clementson
Proofreader Julie Ross
Indexer Angie Hipkin

19th edition. First published in 1992.
Revised editions published annually.

ISBN 978-1-862-05895-8

Printed and bound by Imago in China

Keep up to date with Oz on his website **www.ozclarke.com**. Here you can
find information about his books, wine recommendations, recipes, wine and
food matching, event details, competitions, special offers and lots more...

Thanks are due to the following people for their invaluable help with the
2011 edition and the generous spirit in which they have shared their knowl-
edge: Sarah Ahmed, Tony Aspler, Nicolas Belfrage MW, Dan Berger,
Stephen Brook, Bob Campbell MW, Michael Cox, Giles Fallowfield,
James Forbes, Peter Forrestal, Elizabeth Gabay MW, Rosemary George
MW, Natasha Hughes, James Lawther MW, John Livingstone-
Learmonth, Angela Lloyd, Wink Lorch, Dan McCarthy, Dave McIntyre,
Charles Metcalfe, Adam Montefiore, Jasper Morris MW, Victor de la
Serna, Stephen Skelton MW, Paul Strang, Stuart Walton.

CONTENTS

HOW TO USE THIS BOOK

The **World of Wine** section, starting on page 20, gives an overview of all the world's significant wine-producing countries. The most important countries are followed by a full list of the relevant entries in the A–Z section. Remember that regional A–Z entries guide you to further recommended producers in each region or appellation.

The A–Z section starts on page 58 and includes over 1600 entries on wines, producers, grapes and wine regions from all over the world. It is followed on page 322 by a **Glossary** of winemaking terms.

Detailed **Vintage Charts**, with information on which of the world's top wines are ready for drinking in 2011, can be found on the inside front and back covers; the front chart features vintages back to 2000; the back chart covers a selection of older vintages for premium wines.

Glass Symbols   These indicate the wines produced.

🍷 Red wine   🍷 Rosé wine   🍷 White wine

The order of the glasses reflects the importance of the wines in terms of volume produced. For example:

🍷 White followed by rosé wine

🍷 Red followed by rosé, then white wine

Grape Symbols   These identify entries on grape varieties.

⣿ Red grape   ⣿ White grape

Star Symbols   These indicate wines and producers that are highly rated by the author.
- ★   A particularly good wine or producer in its category
- ★★   An excellent wine or producer in its category – one especially worth seeking out
- ★★★   An exceptional, world-class wine or producer

Best years   Recommended vintages are listed for many producer and appellation entries. Those listed in bold, e.g. **2009, 05**, indicate wines that are ready for drinking now, although they may not necessarily be at their best; those appearing in brackets, e.g. **(2008), (06)**, are preliminary assessments of wines that are not released at the time of going to press.

Cross References   Wine names, producers and regions that have their own entries elsewhere in the A–Z are indicated by SMALL CAPITALS. **Grape varieties** are not cross-referred in this way, but more than 70 varieties, from Albariño to Zinfandel, are included.

Special Features   The A–Z section includes special 2-page features on the world's most important wine styles, regions and grape varieties. These features include recommended vintages and producers, as well as lists of related entries elsewhere in the A–Z.

Index   The Index contains over 4000 recommended producers. Some of the world's most famous brand names are also included.

INTRODUCTION

Prohibitionism is a pernicious movement. It moves surreptitiously in dark and unsuspected places. It slides and slithers beneath our consciousness, along unnoticed parallel avenues until suddenly we find we are sleep-walking into a state where alcohol becomes generally perceived as a demon, and the popular will accepts the political determination to restrict and even to ban its use. And yes, wine-drinkers – friendly, sociable, morally responsible wine-drinkers – I'm talking to you. Legislators simply see alcohol as alcohol. We see wine as something entirely superior, but wine contains alcohol, often lots of it, and despite the fact that we protest that we don't attack policemen, break into cars and generally harm both society and our own health, legislators look at alcohol as alcohol, and alcohol abuse as alcohol abuse. They look at statistics detailing hospital admissions, criminal charges, days off work, they tot up the damage and they take action. Against alcohol. Against alcohol abuse. And because we love wine, and wine isn't possible without alcohol - against us.

I'm not saying this hellish situation is with us - yet. But nobody thought it was with America in 1919, when prohibition was voted in. It just crept up on the nation. The first Dry Law was enacted in Indiana in 1816, more than a century before National Prohibition. By the 1840s towns and counties throughout the nation were voting themselves dry and, beginning with Kansas in 1880, whole states began to go dry, and a sense of mass guilt about alcohol led to 33 states voting against alcohol by 1914. National Prohibition in 1919 became a formality. And all the while, the wine folk thought that they'd be all right because wine was nutritious, wholesome, stimulating, biblical even. Wine was good for you. They wouldn't ban that. They did.

Until a few years ago, modern medical opinion was broadly in favour of wine. It may still be, of course, but the medical opinion that now hits the newspaper headlines, which influences politicians, and which will influence the national mood of countries as diverse as France, Britain, Australia and the USA has become increasingly hostile to alcohol. The stories about red wine being good for your cholesterol, Champagne being a welcome stimulant for older people – you know, attractive commonsense tales that we loved seeing in the papers – are now thin on the ground. But they do still exist. Just.

Ladies, take heart – if you're a red wine drinker you will gain less weight than if you were a non-drinker. It's true. I read it in the newspapers. I also read that red wine 'could help you think'. What? That you'd like another glass? I read that two glasses of red wine a day may help prevent lung cancer. I read…oh, it goes on and on. The good news is there, along with the headlines trumpeting the dangers of drink. But the balance in the argument seems to have gone. Drinking too much is bad for you, we all know that. Binge-drinking is bad for you and those around you. But do we, as regular wine-drinkers, fit into these categories? Some fit into the first category, obviously, but the second category, I'd say not at all.

As to what is too much – I repeat, it used to be a matter of common sense. Now it's about units, whatever they are, and however many we should allow ourselves a week. The recommended weekly consumption of alcohol in France is four times higher than it is in Poland. A unit of alcohol in Japan is nearly two-and-a-half times bigger than it is in Britain. So which unit is more accurate? I had a friend who was a liver expert who'd been consulted about units of alcohol when the British Government decided to introduce drinking guidelines. 'There's no such thing as a unit of alcohol,' he said. So I asked him what he had advised, and he said they just plucked the unit out of the air. A glass of wine. Half a pint of beer. Whatever. 10% is a nice round figure for the alcoholic strength – and they did drink a lot of weak Liebfraumilch in those days – out of 125ml glasses. So that was it. A small glass of 10% wine. We now normally drink out of 175ml glasses and our wine is normally near 13% alcohol, and very often more. So if the government was making the rule today, would a unit be a 175ml glass of 13% wine? We still wouldn't be anywhere near a Japanese unit, but we'd be a lot closer to a realistic appraisal of what we think of as harmless, possibly health-giving, social wine-drinking which, by the way, makes most of us happier, nicer people. Isn't that worth something?

And with that in mind, I shall happily, enthusiastically, partake of a wide variety of wines this year, and I'm going to be adventurous. I've had some lovely, vivacious **Luxembourg** wines already, I've drunk delightful **Croatian** Malvasias, Welschrieslings and Gewürztraminers, piquant **Slovenian** Pinot Gris and Furmint, ripe, sturdy **Jordanian** Cabernet Sauvignon and powerfully scented mouthfuls of Öküzgözü and Bogazkere from **Turkey**. New pleasurable, I'll have more of them.

I've begun to rediscover Chardonnay – fabulous examples above all from **Australia**, **New Zealand**, **California** and **Canada** showing a restrained brilliance – now I remember why we used to love the grape so much. And cool-climate Syrah. What a wonderful, fragrant, silky wine that is. The **North Island** of **New Zealand**, the chillier corners of **Victoria** in **Australia**, the northern vineyard valleys of **Chile**. Give me more. Well, give me more of most of Chile's wines. **Argentina** has finally worked out how to make the best of unctuously scented white Torrontés, a perfect partner to the lush red crowd-pleaser Malbec.

My most thrilling discovery in the USA this year has been the wine from vineyards spread around Washington DC, in particular those of **Virginia** whose sumptuous, scented Viogniers are world class. A perfect partner for the leaner, racier delights of **New York State**. In **California** I'm going to revel in the gorgeous Pinot Noirs and Chardonnays of **Sonoma Coast**, and old-vine pre-Prohibition oddities of every kind from further inland, and after a few years of being exasperated by their high alcohol and baked fruit, **Napa Valley** reds seem to be rediscovering how to mix power and beauty. I'll be giving them another go.

In **France**, I'm looking for a bit less power and a bit more beauty. 2009 is proving to be a cracker of a vintage, and I'll be stocking up on some **Bordeaux** and **Rhône** wines to enjoy in a few years' time. But there's also fabulous 2009 stuff to drink now. When was the last time you drank a **Beaujolais**? The 2009s are juicy and gorgeous. The red wines from the **Loire Valley** are crunchy fruit heaven, for drinking now or holding on to for a generation.

Further south I'll be drinking pink and white **Rioja** from **Spain**, white **Rías Baixas** and lush, herb-scented red **Garnacha** from **Aragón**. And I'll be drinking even more Portuguese wine. Thrilling, tangy real **Vinho Verde** can do the Sauvignon job at lower alcohol levels and the reds from **Dão**, **Douro**, **Tejo** and **Alentejo** are ripe, scented and increasingly less oaked. And in **Italy**, I know I shouldn't be starting on the great 2004 Piedmont reds yet, but they're so good. I'll wash away the tannins with white Verdicchio, Falanghina, Fiano and Arneis – or maybe **Austrian Grüner Veltliner** and **German Riesling** from further north.

Or, of course, from much further north, **English fizz**, just over the channel from Champagne and year by year mounting a serious challenge by the simple expedient of tasting better.

SOME OF MY FAVOURITES

The following are some of the wines I've enjoyed most this year. They're not definitive lists of 'best wines', but all the wines, regions and producers mentioned here are on an exciting roll in terms of quality. Some are easy to find; others are very rare or expensive, but if you get the chance to try them, grab it! You can find out more about them in the A–Z on pages 58 to 321: the cross-references in SMALL CAPITALS will guide you to the relevant entries.

WORLD-CLASS WINES THAT DON'T COST THE EARTH
- Tim ADAMS Shiraz, Australia
- ATA RANGI Célèbre, New Zealand
- BOEKENHOUTSKLOOF Syrah, South Africa
- BROWN BROTHERS Heathcote Shiraz
- CARMEN Nativa Cabernet Sauvignon, Chile
- GRAHAM Crusted Port
- Viña Leyda, Cahuil Pinot Noir, SAN ANTONIO, Chile
- MAN O'WAR Syrah, New Zealand
- MCWILLIAM'S Mount Pleasant Lovedale Semillon, Australia
- PLANETA, Santa Cecilia, Sicily, Italy
- ROC DE CAMBES, France
- Ch. SOCIANDO-MALLET, France
- Tokara White, STELLENBOSCH, South Africa
- VALDESPINO Fino Inocente, Spain
- VILLA MARIA Reserve Merlot, Hawkes Bay, New Zealand

BEST LOOKALIKES TO THE CLASSICS
Bordeaux-style red wines
- CULLEN Cabernet Sauvignon-Merlot, Australia
- OPUS ONE, California
- VERGELEGEN, South Africa

Burgundy-style white wines
- CULLEN, Kevin John Chardonnay, Australia
- HAMILTON RUSSELL Chardonnay, South Africa
- LEEUWIN ESTATE Art Series Chardonnay, Australia
- RAMEY, Chardonnay, California

Champagne-style wines
- CAMEL VALLEY, Pinot Noir rosé, England
- Jansz (Vintage), YALUMBA, Australia
- ROEDERER ESTATE L'Ermitage, California

TOP-VALUE WINES
- AGUSTINOS, Chile
- ALENTEJO, Portugal
- COLOMÉ, Torrontés, Argentina
- CÔTES DE GASCOGNE whites, France
- DOÑA PAULA, Argentina
- Old-vines Garnacha reds from CALATAYUD and CAMPO DE BORJA, Spain
- Hungarian whites
- Peter LEHMANN whites, Australia
- MAJELLA The Musician, Australia
- White RIOJA, Spain
- Seigneurs d'Aiguilhe, CÔTES DE CASTILLON, France

REGIONS TO WATCH
- ARAGÓN, Spain
- AWATERE VALLEY, New Zealand
- Brazil, for sparkling wine
- CÔTES DE CASTILLON, France
- DÃO, Portugal
- Darling, South Africa
- ELQUI, Chile
- HEATHCOTE, Australia
- Leyda, SAN ANTONIO, Chile
- PATAGONIA, Argentina
- Santa Lucia Highlands, MONTEREY COUNTY, California
- SICILY, Italy
- Sussex, England

PRODUCERS TO WATCH
- ASTROLABE, New Zealand
- CASA MARÍN, San Antonio, Chile
- Larry CHERUBINO, Australia
- Collector, CANBERRA, Australia
- FALERNIA, Elqui, Chile
- NOEMIA, Patagonia, Argentina
- S C PANNELL, South Australia
- Perrin & Fils (see Ch. de BEAUCASTEL), Rhône Valley, France
- Philip SHAW, New South Wales, Australia

AUSTRALIA
- BROKENWOOD Semillon and Graveyard Shiraz
- Burge Family Garnacha, BAROSSA
- Henschke HILL OF GRACE Shiraz
- LEEUWIN ESTATE Art Series Chardonnay
- Charles MELTON Shiraz
- MOUNT HORROCKS Watervale Riesling
- PARKER COONAWARRA First Growth
- PRIMO ESTATE Moda Cabernet-Merlot
- ROCKFORD Basket Press Shiraz
- SKILLOGALEE Shiraz
- TYRRELL'S Vat 1 Semillon

RED BORDEAUX
- Ch. ANGÉLUS
- Ch. AUSONE
- Ch. CANON-LA-GAFFELIÈRE
- Ch. GRAND-PUY-LACOSTE
- Ch. Feytit-Clinet
- Les Forts de LATOUR
- Ch. LÉOVILLE-BARTON
- Ch. LÉOVILLE-POYFERRÉ
- Ch. LYNCH-BAGES
- Ch. la MISSION-HAUT-BRION
- Ch. PÉTRUS
- Ch. PICHON-LONGUEVILLE
- Ch. PICHON-LONGUEVILLE-LALANDE
- TERTRE-RÔTEBOEUF

BURGUNDY
- CARILLON, Bienvenues-Bâtard-Montrachet (white)
- R Chevillon, NUITS-ST-GEORGES (red)
- COCHE-DURY, Corton-Charlemagne (white)
- B Dugat-Py, Charmes-CHAMBERTIN (red)
- J-N GAGNARD, Bâtard-Montrachet (white)
- Anne GROS, Clos de Vougeot (red)
- LAFON, Volnay Santenots (red)
- Dom. LEROY, Nuits-St-Georges les Boudots (red)
- M Rollin, CORTON-CHARLEMAGNE (white)
- E Rouget, ÉCHÉZEAUX (red)
- Villaine La Digoine BOURGOGNE-CÔTE CHALONNAISE (red)

CALIFORNIA
- Cline Cellars, Bridgehead ZINFANDEL, Contra Costa County
- DIAMOND CREEK
- Lang & Reed Cabernet Franc, NAPA VALLEY
- Long Meadow Ranch, NAPA VALLEY
- NEWTON The Puzzle
- RAMEY, Hyde Vineyard Chardonnay
- RIDGE Geyserville
- ST SUPÉRY, Dollarhide Cabernet Sauvignon
- SHAFER Hillside Select Cabernet Sauvignon
- Sean Thackrey, Orion Rossi Vineyard Syrah, NAPA VALLEY
- Viader, NAPA VALLEY

ITALIAN REDS
- ALLEGRINI Amarone and La Poja
- BOSCARELLI
- Giacomo CONTERNO, Barolo, Cascina Francia
- Firriato Harmonium Nero d'Avola, SICILY
- GAJA, Langhe, Sperss
- Illuminati Zanna, MONTEPULCIANO d'Abruzzo
- ISOLE E OLENA Cepparello
- Mormoreto, FRESCOBALDI
- ORNELLAIA Masseto
- PLANETA Santa Cecilia
- POLIZIANO Le Stanze
- SASSICAIA
- SELVAPIANA Chianti Rufina, Riserva Bucerchiale

RHÔNE VALLEY
- Ch. de BEAUCASTEL Roussanne Vieilles Vignes (white)
- CLAPE Cornas
- Dom. du Colombier, CROZES-HERMITAGE and HERMITAGE
- Clos du Caillou, CHÂTEAUNEUF-DU-PAPE
- Clos du Joncuas, GIGONDAS
- CUILLERON, Condrieu les Chaillets
- Pierre Gaillard, CONDRIEU
- GRAILLOT, Crozes-Hermitage
- JAMET, Côte-Rôtie
- Dom. de la Janasse, CHÂTEAUNEUF-DU-PAPE Vieilles Vignes

CABERNET SAUVIGNON
- BALNAVES, Australia
- HENSCHKE, Cyril Henschke, Australia
- Ladera, HOWELL MOUNTAIN, California
- Long Meadow Ranch, NAPA VALLEY, California
- PENLEY ESTATE, Australia
- RIDGE Monte Bello, California
- SANTA RITA Floresta, Chile
- STAG'S LEAP WINE CELLARS Fay, California
- TERRAZAS DE LOS ANDES Cheval des Andes, Argentina
- Miguel TORRES Manso de Velasco, Chile

CHARDONNAY
- CONCHA Y TORO Amelia, Chile
- Diamond Valley Vineyards, YARRA VALLEY, Australia
- Dog Point, MARLBOROUGH, New Zealand
- FELTON ROAD, New Zealand
- FLOWERS Camp Meeting Ridge, California
- GIACONDA, Australia
- HAMILTON RUSSELL, South Africa
- KUMEU RIVER, New Zealand
- Littorai, Mays Canyon RUSSIAN RIVER VALLEY, California

- NEWTON Unfiltered, California
- RIDGE Monte Bello, California
- SAINTSBURY, Carneros, California
- SHAW & SMITH M3, Australia
- TABALÍ Reserva Especial, Chile

MERLOT

- ANDREW WILL, Washington State
- STEENBERG, South Africa
- CASABLANCA Nimbus Estate, Chile
- CONO SUR 20 Barrels, Chile
- CRAGGY RANGE, New Zealand
- Fermoy Estate, MARGARET RIVER, Australia
- LEONETTI CELLAR, Washington State
- Sacred Hill Broken Stone, HAWKES BAY, New Zealand
- VILLA MARIA Reserve, New Zealand
- WOODWARD CANYON, Washington State

PINOT NOIR

- ATA RANGI, New Zealand
- Bass Philip Reserve, GIPPSLAND, Australia
- DRY RIVER, New Zealand
- ELK COVE Reserve, Oregon
- Escarpment, MARTINBOROUGH, New Zealand
- FELTON ROAD, New Zealand
- FLOWERS Camp Meeting Ridge, California
- Freycinet, TASMANIA, Australia
- Kusuda, MARTINBOROUGH, New Zealand
- Viña Leyda, Lot 21, SAN ANTONIO, Chile
- SAINTSBURY Carneros, California

RIESLING

- Tim ADAMS, Clare Valley, Australia
- H DONNHOFF Oberhäuser Brücke, Nahe, Germany
- F X PICHLER, Wachau, Austria
- GROSSET, Clare Valley, Australia
- Fritz HAAG Brauneberger Juffer Sonnenuhr, Mosel, Germany
- Dr LOOSEN, Mosel, Germany
- MOUNT HORROCKS, Australia
- PEGASUS BAY, New Zealand
- Horst SAUER Escherndorfer Lump, Franken, Germany
- Martin Schaetzel, Kaefferkopf, ALSACE, France

SAUVIGNON BLANC

- CASAS DEL BOSQUE, Chile
- Ch. DOISY-DAËNE Sec, France
- Neil ELLIS Groenekloof, South Africa

- Ch. MALARTIC-LAGRAVIÈRE, France
- O:TU, AWATERE VALLEY, New Zealand
- SAINT CLAIR Block 4 Sawcut, New Zealand
- Ch. SMITH-HAUT-LAFITTE, France
- TE MATA Cape Crest, New Zealand
- VAVASOUR, New Zealand
- VERGELEGEN, South Africa
- VILLA MARIA Reserve Clifford Bay, New Zealand

SYRAH/SHIRAZ

- Tim ADAMS, Australia
- ALBAN, EdnaValley, California
- BROKENWOOD Graveyard Vineyard, Australia
- CAYUSE Cailloux Vineyard, Washington State
- CLONAKILLA, Australia
- CRAGGY RANGE Le Sol, New Zealand
- FALERNIA Reserve, Elqui, Chile
- Heathcote Winery Slaughterhouse, HEATHCOTE, Australia
- Jamsheed Silvan, YARRA VALLEY, Australia
- Peter LEHMANN Stonewell, Australia
- TRINITY HILL Homage, New Zealand
- Two Hands, BAROSSA, Australia

FORTIFIED WINE

- Buller Fine Old Muscat, RUTHERGLEN
- Cossart Gordon Vintage Bual, MADEIRA WINE COMPANY
- CHAMBERS Rutherglen Muscat
- GONZALEZ BYASS Noé Pedro Ximénez
- GRAHAM Vintage Port
- HENRIQUES & HENRIQUES 15-year-old Madeira
- HIDALGO La Gitana Manzanilla
- NIEPOORT Vintage Port
- PENFOLDS Great Grandfather Grand Old Liqueur Tawny

SPARKLING WINE

- BILLECART-SALMON Cuvée N-F Billecart Champagne
- CAMEL VALLEY Pinot Noir, England
- CLOUDY BAY Pelorus, New Zealand
- Delamotte Blanc de Blancs Champagne
- DEUTZ Prestige Cuvée, New Zealand
- Alfred GRATIEN Vintage Champagne
- Charles HEIDSIECK Champagne
- Jansz, YALUMBA, Australia
- Charles MELTON Sparkling Red, Australia
- Le Mesnil Blanc de Blancs CHAMPAGNE
- QUARTZ REEF Vintage, New Zealand

MODERN WINE STYLES

Not so long ago, if I were to have outlined the basic wine styles, the list would have been strongly biased towards the classics – Bordeaux, Burgundy, Sancerre, Mosel Riesling, Champagne. But the classics have, over time, become expensive and unreliable – giving other regions the chance to offer us wines that may or may not owe anything to the originals. *These* are the flavours to which ambitious winemakers the world over now aspire.

WHITE WINES

Ripe, up-front, spicy Chardonnay is the main grape and fruit is the key: apricot, peach, melon, pineapple and tropical fruits, spiced up with the vanilla and butterscotch richness of some new oak to make a delicious, approachable, fruit cocktail of taste. Australia, South Africa and Chile are best at this style, but all have begun to tone down the richness. Oak-aged Chenin from South Africa, Semillon from Australia and Semillon-Sauvignon from South-West France can have similar characteristics.

Green and tangy New Zealand Sauvignon was the originator of this style – zingy lime zest, nettles and asparagus and passionfruit – and South Africa now has its own tangy, super-fresh examples. Chile's San Antonio and Casablanca regions produce something similar, and there are good, less expensive versions from southern France and Hungary. Bordeaux and the Loire are the original sources of dry Sauvignon wines, and an expanding band of modern producers are matching clean fruit with zippy green tang. Spain's Rueda is zesty. Riesling in Australia is usually lean and limy.

Bone-dry, neutral The most famous, and most appetizing, examples are from Chablis. Producers of unoaked Chardonnay in cool parts of Australia, New Zealand and the USA are doing a good, but fruitier, impression. Many Italian and Greek whites from indigenous varieties fit this bill. Southern French wines are often like this, as are many basic wines from Bordeaux, South-West France, Muscadet and Anjou. Modern young Spanish whites and dry Portuguese Vinho Verdes are good examples. I don't like seeing too much neutrality in New World wines, but cheap South African and California whites are 'superneutral'. More interesting are Verdelhos and Chenins from Australia.

White Burgundy By this I mean the nutty, oatmealy-ripe but dry, subtly oaked styles of villages like Meursault at their best. Few people do it well, even in Burgundy itself, and it's a difficult style to emulate. California makes the most effort. Washington, Oregon, New York State and British Columbia each have occasional successes, as do top Australian, South African and New Zealand Chardonnays.

Perfumy, off-dry Gewurztraminer, Muscat and Pinot Gris from Alsace will give you this style and in southern Germany Gewürztraminer, Scheurebe, Grauburgunder (Pinot Gris) and occasionally Riesling may also do it. In New Zealand, Riesling, Pinot Gris and Gewürztraminer can be excellent. Irsai Olivér from Hungary and Torrontés from Argentina are both heady and perfumed. Albariño in Spain is leaner but heady with citrus scent. Viognier is apricotty and scented in southern Europe, Australia, Chile, California, South Africa and New Zealand.

Mouthfuls of luscious gold Good sweet wines are difficult to make. Sauternes is the most famous, but the Loire, and sometimes Alsace, can also come up with rich, intensely sweet wines that can live for decades. Top sweeties from Germany and Austria are stunning. Hungarian Tokaji has a wonderful sweet-sour smoky flavour. Australia, California and New Zealand have some exciting examples and there are a few rare but excellent sweeties from South Africa and the USA.

RED WINES

Spicy, warm-hearted Australia is out in front at the moment through the ebullient brashness of her Shiraz reds – ripe, almost sweet, sinfully easy to enjoy. France's southern Rhône Valley is also motoring, and the traditional appellations in the far south of France are looking good. In Italy, Piedmont is producing delicious beefy Barbera and juicy exotic Dolcetto, Puglia has chocolaty Negroamaro and Sicily has Nero d'Avola. Portugal's Tejo and Alentejo also deliver the goods, as does Malbec in Argentina. California Zinfandel made in its most powerful style is spicy and rich; Lebanese reds have the succulent scent of the kasbah.

Juicy, fruity Beaujolais can be the perfect example, but leafy, raspberryish Loire reds, and Grenache and Syrah vins de pays are often better bets. Modern Spanish reds from Valdepeñas, Bierzo and La Mancha, and old-vine Garnachas from Campo de Borja and Calatayud, do the trick, as do unoaked Douros from Portugal and young Valpolicella and Teroldego in Italy. Young Chilean Merlots are juicy, and Argentina has some good examples from Bonarda, Tempranillo, Sangiovese and Barbera.

Deep and blackcurranty Chile has climbed back to the top of the Cabernet tree, though good producers in cooler parts of Australia produce Cabernets of thrilling blackcurranty intensity. New Zealand Merlot and Cabernet Franc are dense and rich yet dry. California too frequently overripens its Cabernet and Merlot, though restrained examples can be terrific. Top Bordeaux is on a rich blackcurranty roll since 2000: it's expensive but exciting – as is top Tuscan Cabernet.

Tough, tannic long-haul boys Bordeaux leads this field, and the best wines are really good after 10 years or so – but, except in years like 2005, minor properties won't age in the same way. It's the same in Tuscany and Piedmont – only the top wines last well – especially Brunello di Montalcino, Vino Nobile di Montepulciano, some IGT and DOCG wines from Chianti Classico, Barolo and Barbaresco. Portugal has some increasingly good Dão and Douro reds, and Spain's Toro and Ribera del Duero reds need aging.

Soft, strawberryish charmers Good Burgundy definitely tops this group. Rioja in Spain can sometimes get there, as can Navarra and Valdepeñas. Pinot Noir in California, Oregon, Chile and New Zealand is frequently delicious, and South Africa and Australia increasingly get it right too. Germany can hit the spot with Spätburgunder (Pinot Noir). Over in Bordeaux, of all places, St-Émilion, Pomerol and Blaye can do the business.

Rosé There's been a surge in rosé's popularity, probably led by California's blush Zinfandel and Grenache. But far better, drier rosés are also becoming popular, with Spain and France leading the way for drier styles and Chile, New Zealand and Australia the best for fuller pinks.

SPARKLING AND FORTIFIED WINES

Fizz This can be white, pink or red, dry or sweet, and I sometimes think it doesn't matter what it tastes like as long as it's cold enough and there's enough of it. Champagne can be best, but frequently isn't – and there are lots of new-wave winemakers making good-value lookalikes. Australia is tops for tasty bargains, followed by California, New Zealand and England. Spain pumps out oceans of good basic stuff.

Fortified wines There's nothing to beat the top ports and sherries in the deep, rich, sticky stakes – though Australia, California and South Africa have their own versions. The Portuguese island of Madeira produces fortifieds with rich, brown smoky flavours and a startling acid bite – and luscious Muscats are made all round the Mediterranean and in Rutherglen, Australia.

MATCHING FOOD AND WINE

Give me a rule, I'll break it – well, bend it anyway. So when I see the proliferation of publications laying down rules as to what wine to drink with what food, I get very uneasy and have to quell a burning desire to slosh back a Grand Cru Burgundy with my chilli con carne.

The pleasures of eating and drinking operate on so many levels that hard and fast rules make no sense. What about mood? If I'm in the mood for Champagne, Champagne it shall be, whatever I'm eating. What about company? An old friend, a lover, a bank manager – each of these companions would probably be best served by quite different wines. What about place? If I'm sitting gazing out across the shimmering Mediterranean, hand me anything, just as long as it's local – it'll be perfect.

Even so, there are some things that simply don't go well with wine: artichokes, asparagus, spinach, kippers and mackerel, chilli, salsas and vinegars, chocolate, all flatten the flavours of wines. The general rule here is avoid tannic red wines and go for juicy young reds, or whites with plenty of fruit and fresh acidity. And for chocolate, liqueur Muscats, raisiny Banyuls or Italy's grapy, frothy Asti all work, but some people like powerful Italian reds such as Barolo or Amarone. Don't be afraid to experiment. Who would guess that salty Roquefort cheese and rich, sweet Sauternes would go together? But they do, and it's a match made in heaven. So, with these factors in mind, the following pairings are not rules – just my recommendations.

FISH

Grilled or baked white fish White Burgundy or other fine Chardonnay, white Bordeaux, Viognier, Australian and New Zealand Riesling and Sauvignon, South African Chenin.

Grilled or baked oily or 'meaty' fish (e.g. salmon, tuna, swordfish) Alsace or Austrian Riesling, Grüner Veltliner, fruity New World Chardonnay or Semillon; reds such as Chinon or Bourgueil, Grenache/Garnacha, or New World Pinot Noir or Cabernet Franc.

Fried/battered fish Simple, fresh whites, e.g. Soave, Mâcon-Villages, Verdelho, Vinho Verde, Pinot Gris, white Bordeaux, or a Riesling Spätlese from the Pfalz.

Shellfish Chablis or unoaked Chardonnay, Sauvignon Blanc, Pinot Blanc; *clams and oysters* Albariño, Aligoté, Vinho Verde, Seyval Blanc; *crab* Riesling, Viognier; *lobster, scallops* fine Chardonnay, Champagne, Viognier; *mussels* Muscadet, Pinot Grigio.

Smoked fish Ice-cold basic fizz, manzanilla or fino sherry, Riesling, Sauvignon Blanc, Alsace Gewurztraminer or Pinot Gris.

MEAT

Beef and lamb are perfect with just about any red wine.

Beef/steak *Plain roasted or grilled* tannic reds, Bordeaux, New World Cabernet Sauvignon, Ribera del Duero, Chianti Classico, Pinotage.

Lamb *Plain roasted or grilled* red Burgundy, red Bordeaux, especially Pauillac or St-Julien, Rioja Reserva, New World Pinot Noir, Merlot or Malbec.

Pork *Plain roasted or grilled* full, spicy dry whites, e.g. Alsace Pinot Gris, lightly oaked Chardonnay; smooth reds, e.g. Rioja, Alentejo; *ham, bacon, sausages, salami* young, fruity reds, e.g. Beaujolais, Lambrusco, Teroldego, unoaked Tempranillo or Garnacha, New World Malbec, Merlot, Zinfandel/Primitivo, Pinotage.

Veal *Plain roasted or grilled* full-bodied whites, e.g. Pinot Gris, Grüner Veltliner, white Rioja; soft reds, e.g. mature Rioja or Pinot Noir; *with cream-based sauce* full, ripe whites, e.g. Alsace Pinot Blanc or Pinot Gris, Vouvray, oaked New World Chardonnay; *with rich red-wine sauce (e.g. osso buco)* young Italian reds, Zinfandel.

Venison *Plain roasted or grilled*
Barolo, St-Estèphe, Pomerol,
Côte de Nuits, Hermitage, big
Zinfandel, Alsace or German
Pinot Gris; *with red-wine sauce*
Piedmont and Portuguese reds,
Pomerol, St-Émilion, Priorat, New
World Syrah/Shiraz or Pinotage.
Chicken and turkey Most red
and white wines go with these
meats – much depends on the
sauce or accompaniments. Try
red or white Burgundy, red
Rioja Reserva, New World
Chardonnay.
Duck Pomerol, St-Émilion, Côte
de Nuits or Rhône reds, New World
Syrah/Shiraz (including sparkling)
or Merlot; also full, soft whites from
Austria and southern Germany.
Game birds *Plain roasted or grilled*
top reds from Burgundy, Rhône,
Tuscany, Piedmont, Ribera del
Duero, New World Cabernet or
Merlot; also full whites such as
oaked New World Semillon.
Casseroles and stews Generally
uncomplicated, full-flavoured
reds. The thicker the sauce, the
fuller the wine. If wine is used in
the preparation, match the colour.
For strong tomato flavours
see Pasta.

HIGHLY SPICED FOOD
Chinese Riesling, Sauvignon,
Pinot Gris, Gewürztraminer,
unoaked New World Chardonnay
or Semillon; fruity rosé; light Pinot
Noir.
Indian Aromatic whites,
e.g. Riesling, Sauvignon Blanc,
Gewürztraminer, Viognier;
non-tannic reds, e.g. Valpolicella,
Rioja, Grenache.
Mexican Fruity reds, e.g. Merlot,
Cabernet Franc, Grenache,
Syrah/Shiraz, Zinfandel.
Thai/South-East Asian Spicy
or tangy whites, e.g. Riesling,
Gewürztraminer, New World
Sauvignon Blanc, dry Alsace
Muscat. Coconut is tricky: New
World Chardonnay may work.

EGG DISHES
Champagne and traditional-method
fizz; light, fresh reds such as
Beaujolais or Chinon; full, dry
unoaked whites; New World rosé.

PASTA, PIZZA
With tomato sauce Barbera,
Valpolicella, Soave, Verdicchio,
New World Sauvignon Blanc; *with
meat-based sauce* north or central
Italian reds, French or New World
Syrah/Shiraz, Zinfandel; *with cream-
or cheese-based sauce* gently oaked
Chardonnay, though the Italians
would drink unoaked whites from
northern Italy; Valpolicella or soft
Merlot; *with seafood/fish* dry, tangy
whites, e.g. Verdicchio, Vermentino,
Grüner Veltliner, Muscadet;
with pesto New World Sauvignon
Blanc, Dolcetto, Languedoc reds.
*Basic pizza, with tomato, mozzarella
and oregano* juicy young reds, e.g.
Grenache/Garnacha, Valpolicella,
Austrian reds, Languedoc reds.

SALADS
Sharp-edged whites, e.g. New
World Sauvignon Blanc, Chenin
Blanc, dry Riesling, Vinho Verde.

CHEESES
Hard Full reds from Italy, France
or Spain, New World Merlot or
Zinfandel, dry oloroso sherry,
tawny port.
Soft LBV port, Zinfandel, Alsace
Pinot Gris, Gewürztraminer.
Blue Botrytized sweet whites such
as Sauternes, vintage port, old
oloroso sherry, Malmsey Madeira.
Goats' Sancerre, Pouilly-Fumé,
New World Sauvignon Blanc,
Chinon, Saumur-Champigny.

DESSERTS
Chocolate Asti, Australian Liqueur
Muscat, Banyuls, Canadian
Cabernet Franc Icewine.
Fruit-based Sauternes, Eiswein,
fortified European Muscats.
Christmas pudding Asti,
Australian Liqueur Muscat.

MATCHING WINE AND FOOD

With very special bottles, when you have found an irresistible bargain or when you are casting around for culinary inspiration, it can be a good idea to let the wine dictate the choice of food.

Although I said earlier that rules in this area are made to be bent, if not broken, there are certain points to remember when matching wine and food. Before you make specific choices, think about some basic characteristics and see how thinking in terms of grape varieties and wine styles can point you in the right direction.

In many cases, the local food and wine combinations that have evolved over the years simply cannot be bettered (think of ripe Burgundy with *coq au vin* or *boeuf bourguignon*; Chianti Riserva with *bistecca alla Fiorentina*; Muscadet and Breton oysters). Yet the world of food and wine is moving so fast that it would be madness to be restricted by the old tenets. Californian cuisine, fusion food, and the infiltration of innumerable ethnic influences coupled with the re-invigoration of traditional wines, continuous experiment with new methods and blends and the opening up of completely new wine areas mean that the search for perfect food and wine partners is, and will remain, very much an on-going process.

Here are some of the characteristics you need to consider, plus a summary of the main grape varieties and their best food matches.

Body/weight As well as considering the taste of the wine you need to match the body or weight of the wine to the intensity of the food's flavour. A heavy alcoholic wine will not suit a delicate dish, and *vice versa*.

Acidity The acidity of a dish should balance the acidity of a wine. High-acid flavours, such as tomato, lemon or vinegar, should need matching acidity in their accompanying wines, but, almost by mistake, I've tried a few reds with salad dressing and the wine's fruit was enhanced, not wrecked. Was I lucky? More research needed, I think. Use acidity in wine to cut through the richness of a dish – but for this to work, make sure the wine is full in flavour.

Sweetness Sweet food makes dry wine taste unpleasantly lean and acidic. With desserts and puddings, find a wine that is at least as sweet as the food (sweeter than the food is fine). However, many savoury foods, such as carrots, onions and parsnips, taste slightly sweet and dishes in which they feature prominently will go best with ripe, fruity wines that have a touch of sweetness.

Salt Salty foods, such as blue cheese, and sweet wines match. Salty foods and tannin are definitely best avoided.

Age/maturity The bouquet of a wine is only acquired over time and should be savoured and appreciated: with age, many red wines acquire complex flavours and perfumes and a relative simplicity in the flavour of the food is often a good idea.

Tannin Red meat, when cooked rare, can have the effect of softening tannic wine. Mature hard cheeses can make rough wine seem gentle. Avoid eggs and fish with tannic wines.

Oak Oak flavours in wine vary from the satisfyingly subtle to positively strident. This latter end of the scale can conflict with food, although it may be suitable for smoked fish (white wines only) or full-flavoured meat or game.

Wine in the food If you want to use wine in cooking it is best to use the same style of wine as the one you are going to drink with the meal (it can be an inferior version though).

14

RED GRAPES

Barbera Wines made to be drunk young have high acidity that can hold their own with sausages, salami, ham, and tomato sauces. Complex, older or oak-aged wines from the top growers need to be matched with rich food such as beef casseroles and game dishes.

Cabernet Franc Best drunk with plain rather than sauced meat dishes, or, slightly chilled, with grilled or baked salmon or trout.

Cabernet Sauvignon All over the world the Cabernet Sauvignon makes full-flavoured reliable red wine: the ideal food wine. Cabernet Sauvignon seems to have a particular affinity with lamb, but it partners all plain roast or grilled meats and game well and would be an excellent choice for many sauced meat dishes such as beef casserole, steak and kidney pie or rabbit stew and substantial dishes made with mushrooms.

Dolcetto Dolcetto produces fruity purple wines that go beautifully with hearty meat dishes such as calves' liver and onions or casseroled pork, beef or game.

Gamay The grape of red Beaujolais, Gamay makes wine you can drink whenever, wherever, however and with whatever you want – although it's particularly good lightly chilled on hot summer days. It goes well with pâtés, bacon and sausages because its acidity provides a satisfying foil to their richness. It would be a good choice for many vegetarian dishes.

Grenache/Garnacha Frequently blended with other grapes, Grenache nonetheless dominates, with its high alcoholic strength and rich, spicy flavours. These are wines readily matched with food: barbecues and casseroles for heavier wines; almost anything for lighter reds and rosés – vegetarian dishes, charcuterie, picnics, grills, and even meaty fish such as tuna and salmon.

Merlot Merlot makes soft, rounded, fruity wines that are some of the easiest red wines to enjoy without food, yet are also a good choice with many kinds of food. Spicier game dishes, herby terrines and pâtés, pheasant, pigeon, duck or goose all team well with Merlot; substantial casseroles made with wine are excellent with Pomerols and St-Émilions; and the soft fruitiness of the wines is perfect for pork, liver, turkey, and savoury foods with a hint of sweetness such as Iberico, Parma or honey-roast ham.

Nebbiolo Lean but fragrant, early-drinking styles of Nebbiolo wine are best with Italian salami, pâtés, *bresaola* and lighter meat dishes. Top Barolos and Barbarescos need substantial food: *bollito misto*, rich hare or beef casseroles and *brasato al Barolo* (a large piece of beef marinated then braised slowly in Barolo) are just the job in Piedmont, or anywhere else for that matter.

Pinot Noir The great grape of Burgundy has taken its food-friendly complexity all over the wine world. However, nothing can beat the marriage of great wine with sublime local food that is Burgundy's heritage, and it is Burgundian dishes that spring to mind as perfect partners for the Pinot Noir: *coq au vin*, *boeuf bourguignon*, rabbit with mustard, braised ham, chicken with tarragon, *entrecôtes* from prized Charolais cattle with a rich red-wine sauce … the list is endless.

Pinot Noir's subtle flavours make it a natural choice for complex meat dishes, but it is also excellent with plain grills and roasts. New World Pinots are often richer and fruitier – excellent with grills and roasts and a good match for salmon or tuna.

In spite of the prevalence of superb cheese in Burgundy, the best Pinot Noir red wines are wasted on cheese.

Sangiovese Tuscany is where Sangiovese best expresses the qualities that can lead it, in the right circumstances, to be numbered among the great grapes of the world. And Tuscany is very much 'food with wine' territory. Sangiovese wines such as Chianti, Rosso di Montalcino, Vino Nobile di Montepulciano and the biggest of them all, Brunello, positively demand to be drunk with food. Drink them with *bistecca alla Fiorentina*, roast meats and game, calves' liver, casseroles, hearty pasta sauces, *porcini* mushrooms and Pecorino cheese.

Syrah/Shiraz Whether from France (the Rhône Valley and Languedoc), Australia, California, South America or South Africa, this grape always makes powerful, rich, full-bodied wines that are superb with full-flavoured food. The classic barbecue wine when drunk young, Shiraz/Syrah also goes with roasts, game, hearty casseroles and charcuterie. It can be good with tangy cheeses such as Manchego or Cheshire.

Tempranillo Spain's best native red grape makes juicy wines for drinking young, and matures well in a rich (usually) oaky style. Tempranillo is good with game, cured hams and sausages, casseroles and meat grilled with herbs; it is particularly good with roast lamb. It can partner some Indian and Mexican dishes.

Zinfandel California's much-planted, most versatile grape is used for a bewildering variety of wine styles from bland, slightly sweet pinks to rich, succulent, fruity reds. And the good red Zinfandels themselves may vary greatly in style,

from relatively soft and light to big and beefy, but they're always ripe and ready for spicy, smoky, unsubtle food: barbecued meat, haunches of lamb, venison or beef, game casseroles, sausages, Tex-Mex, the Beach Boys, The Eagles – anything rowdy – Zin copes with them all. The pale blush style of Zinfandel goes well with tomato-based dishes, such as pizza and pasta, as well as with hamburgers.

WHITE GRAPES

Albariño Light, crisp, aromatic in a grapefruity way, this goes well with crab and prawn dishes as well as Chinese-style chicken dishes.

Aligoté This Burgundian grape can, at its best, make very versatile food wine. It goes well with many fish and seafood dishes, smoked fish, salads and snails in garlic and butter.

Chardonnay More than almost any other grape, Chardonnay responds to different climatic conditions and to the winemaker's art. This, plus the relative ease with which it can be grown, accounts for the marked gradation of flavours and styles: from steely, cool-climate austerity to almost tropical lusciousness. The relatively sharp end of the spectrum is one of the best choices for simple fish dishes; most Chardonnays are superb with roast chicken or other white meat; the really full, rich, New World blockbusters need rich fish and seafood dishes. Oaky Chardonnays are, surprisingly, a good choice for smoked fish.

Chenin Blanc One of the most versatile of grapes, Chenin Blanc makes wines ranging from averagely quaffable dry whites to the great sweet whites of the Loire. The lighter wines can be good as aperitifs or with light fish dishes or salads while the medium-sweet versions usually retain enough of their acidity to counteract the richness of creamy chicken and meat dishes. The sweet wines are superb with foie gras or blue cheese, and with fruit puddings – especially those made with slightly tart fruit.

Gewürztraminer Spicy and perfumed, Gewürztraminer has the weight and flavour to go with such hard-to-match dishes as *choucroute* and smoked fish. It is also a good choice for Chinese or any lightly spiced Oriental food, with its use of lemongrass, coriander and ginger, and pungent soft cheeses, such as Munster from Alsace.

Grüner Veltliner In its lightest form, this makes a peppery, refreshing aperitif. Riper, more structured versions keep the pepper but add peach and apple fruit, and are particularly good with grilled or baked fish.

Marsanne These rich, fat wines are a bit short of acidity, so match them with simply prepared chicken, pork, fish or vegetables.

Muscadet The dry, light Muscadet grape (best wines are *sur lie*) is perfect with seafood.

Muscat Fragrant, grapy wines coming in a multitude of styles, from delicate to downright syrupy. The drier ones are more difficult to pair with food, but can be delightful with Oriental cuisines; the sweeties really come into their own with most desserts. Sweet Moscato d'Asti, delicious by itself, goes well with rich Christmas pudding or mince pies.

Pinot Blanc Clean, bright and appley, Pinot Blanc is very food-friendly. Classic fish and chicken dishes, modern vegetarian food, pasta and pizza all match up well.

Pinot Gris In Alsace, this makes rich, fat wines that need rich, fat food: *choucroute, confit de canard*, rich pork and fish dishes. Italian Pinot Grigio wines are light quaffers. New World Pinot Gris is often delightfully fragrant and ideal with grilled fish.

Riesling Good dry Rieslings are excellent with spicy cuisine. Sweet Rieslings are best enjoyed for their own lusciousness but are suitable partners to fruit-based desserts. In between, those with a fresh acid bite and some residual sweetness can counteract the richness of, say, goose or duck, and the fuller examples can be good with Oriental food and otherwise hard-to-match salads.

Sauvignon Blanc Tangy green flavours and high acidity are the hallmarks of this grape. Led by New Zealand, New World Sauvignons are some of the snappiest, tastiest whites around and make good, thirst-quenching aperitifs. Brilliant with seafood and Oriental cuisine, they also go well with tomato dishes, salads and goats' cheese.

Sémillon Dry Bordeaux Blancs are excellent with fish and shellfish; fuller, riper New World Semillons are equal to spicy food and rich sauces, often going even better with meat than with fish; sweet Sémillons can partner many puddings, especially rich, creamy ones. Sémillon also goes well with many cheeses, and Sauternes with Roquefort is a classic combination.

Viognier Fresh, young Viognier is at its best drunk as an aperitif. It can also go well with mildly spiced Indian dishes or chicken in a creamy sauce. The apricot aroma that typifies even inexpensive Viognier suggests another good pairing – pork or chicken dishes with apricot stuffing.

MAKING THE MOST OF WINE

Most wine is pretty hardy stuff and can put up with a fair amount of rough handling. Young red wines can knock about in the back of a car for a day or two and be lugged from garage to kitchen to dinner table without coming to too much harm. Serving young white wines when well chilled can cover up all kinds of ill-treatment – a couple of hours in the fridge should do the trick. Even so, there are some conditions that are better than others for storing your wines, especially if they are on the mature side. And there are certain ways of serving wines which will emphasize any flavours or perfumes they have.

STORING

Most wines are sold ready for drinking, and it will be hard to ruin them if you store them for a few months before you pull the cork. Don't stand them next to the central heating or the cooker, though, nor on a sunny windowsill, as too much warmth will flatten the flavour and give a 'baked' taste.

Light and extremes of temperature are also the things to worry about if you are storing wine long-term. Some wines, Chardonnay for instance, are particularly sensitive to exposure to light over several months, and the damage will be worse if the bottle is made of pale-coloured glass. The warmer the wine, the quicker it will age, and really high temperatures can spoil wine quite quickly. Beware in the winter of garages and outhouses, too, a very cold snap – say –4°C (25°F) or below – will freeze your wine, push out the corks and crack the bottles. An underground cellar is ideal, with a fairly constant temperature of 10°–12°C (50°–53°F). And bottles really do need to lie on their sides, so that the cork stays damp and swollen, and keeps out the air.

TEMPERATURE

The person who thought up the rule that red wine should be served at room temperature certainly didn't live in a modern, centrally heated flat. It's no great sin to serve a big, beefy red at the temperature of your central heating, but I prefer most reds just a touch cooler. Over-heated wine tastes flabby and may lose some of its more volatile aromas. In general, the lighter the red, the cooler it can be. Really light, refreshing reds, such as Beaujolais, are nice lightly chilled. Ideally, I'd serve Burgundy and other Pinot Noir wines at larder temperature (about 15°C/59°F), Bordeaux and Rioja a bit warmer (18°C/64°F), Rhône wines and New World Cabernet at a comfortable room temperature, but no more than 20°C (68°F).

Chilling white wines makes them taste fresher, emphasizing their acidity. White wines with low acidity especially benefit from chilling, and it's vital for sparkling wines if you want to avoid exploding corks and a tableful of froth. Drastic chilling also subdues flavours, however – a useful ruse if you're serving basic wine, but a shame if the wine is very good. A good guide for whites is to give the cheapest and lightest a spell in the fridge, but serve bigger and better wines – Australian Chardonnays or top white Burgundies – perhaps half-way between fridge and central-heating temperature. If you're undecided, err on the cooler side, for whites or reds. To chill wine quickly and to keep it cool, an ice bucket is more efficient if filled with a mixture of ice and water, rather than ice alone.

OPENING THE BOTTLE

There's no corkscrew to beat the Screwpull, and the Spinhandle Screwpull is especially easy to use. Don't worry if bits of cork crumble into the wine – just fish them out of your glass. Tight corks that refuse to budge might be

18

loosened if you run hot water over the bottle neck to expand the glass. If the cork is loose and falls in, push it right in and don't worry about it.

Opening sparkling wines is a serious business – point the cork away from people! Once you've started, never take your hand off the cork until it's safely out. Remove the foil, loosen the wire, hold the wire and cork firmly and twist the bottle. If the wine froths, hold the bottle at an angle of 45 degrees, and have a glass at hand.

AIRING AND DECANTING
Scientists have proved that opening young to middle-aged red wines an hour before serving makes no difference whatsoever. The surface area of wine in contact with air in the bottle neck is too tiny to be significant. Decanting is a different matter, because sloshing the wine from bottle to jug or decanter mixes it up quite thoroughly with the air. The only wines that really need to be decanted are those that have a sediment which would cloud the wine if they were poured directly – mature red Bordeaux, Burgundy and vintage port are the most common examples. Ideally, if you are able to plan that far in advance, you need to stand the bottle upright for a day or two to let the sediment settle in the bottom. Draw the cork extremely gently. As you tip the bottle, shine a bright light through from underneath as you pour in a single steady movement. Stop pouring when you see the sediment approaching the bottle neck.

Contrary to many wine buffs' practice, I would decant a mature wine only just before serving; elderly wines often fade rapidly once they meet with air, and an hour in the decanter could kill off what little fruit they had left. By contrast, a good-quality young white wine can benefit from decanting.

GLASSES
If you want to taste wine at its best, to enjoy all its flavours and aromas, to admire its colours and texture, choose glasses designed for the purpose and show the wine a bit of respect. The ideal wine glass is a fairly large tulip shape, made of fine, clear glass, with a slender stem. When you pour the wine, fill the glass no more than halfway to allow space for aromas. For sparkling wines choose a tall, slender glass, as it helps the bubbles to last longer.

KEEPING LEFTOVERS
Leftover white wine keeps better than red, since the tannin and colouring matter in red wine is easily attacked by the air. Any wine, red or white, keeps better in the fridge than in a warm kitchen. And most wines, if well made in the first place, will be perfectly acceptable, if not pristine, after 2 or 3 days re-corked in the fridge. But for better results it's best to use one of the gadgets sold for this purpose. The ones that work by blanketing the wine with heavier-than-air inert gas are much better than those that create a vacuum in the air space in the bottle.

FRANCE

I've visited most of the wine-producing countries of the world, but the one I come back to again and again, with my enthusiasm undimmed by time, is France. The sheer range of its wine flavours, the number of wine styles produced, and indeed the quality differences, from very best to very nearly worst, continue to enthral me, and as each year's vintage nears, I find myself itching to leap into the car and head for the vineyards of Champagne, of Burgundy, of Bordeaux and the Loire. France is currently going through a difficult period – aware that the New World is making tremendous strides and is the master of innovation and technology, yet unwilling to admit to the quality and character of this new breed of wines. But the best French producers learn from the newcomers while proudly defining their Frenchness.

CLIMATE AND SOIL

France lies between the 40th and 50th parallels north, and the climate runs from the distinctly chilly and almost too cool to ripen grapes in the far north near the English Channel, right through to the swelteringly hot and almost too torrid to avoid grapes overripening in the far south on the Mediterranean shores. In the north, the most refined and delicate sparkling wine is made in Champagne. In the south, rich, luscious dessert Muscats and fortified wines dominate. In between is just about every sort of wine you could wish for.

The factors that influence a wine's flavour are the grape variety, the soil and climate, and the winemaker's techniques. Most of the great wine grapes, like the red Cabernet Sauvignon, Merlot, Pinot Noir and Syrah, and the white Chardonnay, Sauvignon Blanc, Sémillon and Viognier, find conditions in France where they can ripen slowly but reliably – and slow, even ripening always gives the best flavours to a wine. Since grapes have been grown for over 2000 years in France, the most suitable varieties for the different soils and mesoclimates have naturally evolved. And since winemaking was brought to France by the Romans, generation upon generation of winemakers have refined their techniques to produce the best possible results from their different grape types. The great wines of areas like Bordeaux and Burgundy are the results of centuries of experience and of trial and error, which winemakers from other countries of the world now use as role models in their attempts to create good wine.

WINE REGIONS

White grapes generally ripen more easily than red grapes and they dominate the northern regions. Even so, the chilly Champagne region barely manages to ripen its red or white grapes on its chalky soil. But the resultant acid wine is the ideal base for sparkling wine: with good winemaking and a few years' maturing, the young still wine can transform into a golden honeyed sparkling wine of incomparable finesse.

Alsace, on the German border, is warmer and drier than Champagne (the vineyards sit in a rain shadow created by the Vosges mountains that rise above the Rhine Valley) but still produces mainly dry white wines, from grapes such as Riesling, Pinot Gris and Gewurztraminer that are seldom encountered elsewhere in France. With its clear blue skies, Alsace can provide ripeness, and therefore the higher alcoholic strength of the warm south, but also the perfume and fragrance of the cool north.

South-east of Paris, heading into limestone country, Chablis marks the northernmost tip of the Burgundy region, and the Chardonnay grape here produces very dry wines, usually with a streak of green acidity and minerality, but nowadays with a fuller softer texture to subdue any harshness.

It's a good 2 hours' drive further south to the heart of Burgundy – the Côte d'Or, which runs between Dijon and Chagny. World-famous villages such as Gevrey-Chambertin and Vosne-Romanée (where the red Pinot Noir dominates) and Meursault and Puligny-Montrachet (where Chardonnay reigns) here produce the great Burgundies that have given the region renown over the centuries. Lesser Burgundies – but they're still good – are produced further south in the Côte Chalonnaise, while between Mâcon and Lyon are the Mâconnais white wine villages (Pouilly-Fuissé and St-Véran are particularly tasty) and the villages of Beaujolais, famous for bright, easy-going red wine from the Gamay grape. The 10 Beaujolais Crus or 'growths' are the most important communes and should produce wine with more character and structure.

East of Burgundy, Jura makes unusual whites, good sparkling and light reds; Savoie, further south, has crisp whites and light, spicy reds.

South of Lyon, in the Rhône Valley, red wines begin to dominate. The Syrah grape makes great fine wine at Côte-Rôtie and Hermitage in the north, while in the south the Grenache and a host of supporting grapes (most southern Rhône reds will add at least Syrah, Mourvèdre or Cinsaut to their blends) make full, satisfying reds, of which Châteauneuf-du-Pape is the richest, most famous and most expensive. The white Viognier makes lovely wine at Condrieu and Château-Grillet in the north.

The whole of the south of France has undergone considerable change over the last 20 years. Despite the financial woes of growers who over-extended themselves in the late 1990s, new ownership and a new generation are

producing exciting wines from previously unpromising lands. The traditional Provence, Languedoc and Roussillon vineyards make increasingly impressive reds from Grenache, Syrah, Mourvèdre and Carignan, as well as Cabernet Sauvignon (although it is declining in Provence) and some surprisingly fragrant whites. And with the new Languedoc appellation (covering the whole of Languedoc and Roussillon), the possibilities and freedom to improve by blending will be extended. Many of the tastiest and most affordable wines are vins de pays. Roussillon also makes fine sweet Muscats and Grenache-based fortifieds.

The south-west of France is dominated by the wines of Bordeaux, but has many idiosyncratic gems representing amazing value for money. Dry whites from Gascony and Bergerac can be exciting. Gaillac in the Tarn and Jurançon in the foothills of the Pyrenees produce some remarkable dry and sweet wines, while Madiran, Cahors, Fronton, Gaillac and Bergerac produce some top-quality reds. Monbazillac and Saussignac make some of the finest of all French sweet wines.

But Bordeaux is the king here. Cabernet Sauvignon and Merlot are the chief grapes, the Cabernet dominating the production of deep reds from the Médoc peninsula and its famous villages of Margaux, St-Julien, Pauillac and St-Estèphe on the left bank of the Gironde river. Round the city of Bordeaux are Pessac-Léognan and Graves, where Cabernet and Merlot blend to produce fragrant refined reds. On the right bank of the Gironde estuary, the Merlot is most important in the plump rich reds of St-Émilion and Pomerol. Sweet whites from Sémillon and Sauvignon Blanc are made in Sauternes, with increasingly good dry whites produced in the Entre-Deux-Mers, and especially in Graves and Pessac-Léognan.

The Loire Valley is the most northerly of France's Atlantic wine regions but, since the river rises in the heart of France not far from the Rhône, styles vary widely. Sancerre and Pouilly in the east produce tangy, *terroir*-influenced Sauvignon whites and some surprisingly good Pinot Noir reds. Along the river Cher, which joins the Loire at Tours, the best varieties are Sauvignon and Romorantin for whites, Gamay and Côt/Malbec for reds. In central Touraine, Saumur and Anjou the focus is squarely on Chenin Blanc in styles which range from bone dry to lusciously sweet, even sparkling and, for the reds, Cabernet Franc with a little Cabernet Sauvignon. Down at the mouth of the river, as it slips past Nantes into the Atlantic swell, the vineyards of Muscadet produce dry whites that take on the salty notes of the sea. At the vanguard of the natural wine movement – some 2415 hectares (6000 acres) are cultivated organically – the Loire Valley is teeming with producers working as naturally as possible both in the vineyard and winery, the best of whom make highly characterful wines – look out for ambitious vins de France

CLASSIFICATIONS

Not for the first time, France has made an attempt to simplify its wine classification system, this time in partnership with general changes in the EU wine industry. The basic Vin de Table category will now become **Vin de France** and will be able to show both grape variety and vintage for the first time. The middle-ranking **Vin de Pays** category has been morphed into a pretty similar **IGP** (Indication Géographique Protégée) category. For instance, Vin de Pays d'Oc will now appear with Pays d'Oc IGP on the label. It'll taste exactly the same, but there'll be another gaggle of contented bureaucrrats somewhere in Europe. The top quality classification is Appellation d'Origine Protégée, or **AOP**. It used to be **AC** (Appellation d'Origine Contrôlée). A small category of **VDQS** wines (Vin Délimité de

Qualité Supérieure) will be absorbed into the AOP classification. These changes will mostly start affecting wines from the 2010 vintage onwards.

2009 VINTAGE REPORT

Another vintage of the century in Bordeaux? Forgive me asking, but wasn't the last one only four years ago in 2005? And aren't there another 90 years to come in the 21st century? I'd like to scoff, but I can't. 2009 is shaping up to be another humdinger. Ripening conditions were ideal: a cold winter, damp spring, hot, dry summer and rain when it was needed in September. Weather during the harvest was generally warm, balmy and fine, the top Médoc estates finished by 9 October, the late harvesters still picking two weeks later. The reds are big, rich and powerful with relatively high alcohol degrees but with smooth, ripe tannins and in gorgeous balance for producers who didn't interfere too much with nature. Dry whites are full but fresh and even Sauternes producers are delighted, particularly after the difficulties (frost and ragged vintage) in 2008. The only people you have to feel sorry for are the growers hit by hailstorms in May (parts of Bourg, Blaye, Castillon, St-Émilion and the Entre-Deux-Mers), some with the crop virtually wiped out. As to the price, let's hope the success of the vintage doesn't go too much to producers' heads! Gosh. Did you see that pig fly by?

Growers in South-West France are over the moon. The vintage of the decade? Almost certainly. Perfect weather all the way from budburst to harvest: hot dry periods punctuated by showery patches. Localized hail spoilt the picture for some, but on the whole few complained, except perhaps those who picked very late for their sweetest wines (Jurançon, Monbazillac), some of whom suffered from November rains.

After two difficult years, Burgundy growers were desperate for a change and, in due course, their wishes were granted. The early season was mixed but a superb August with dry weather continuing through September set up a potentially brilliant vintage. The wines are full of fruit, with totally ripe tannins, while relatively low acid levels suggest they will be approachable early.

Beaujolais experienced near-ideal climatic conditions over the course of 2009. After a cold winter, temperatures in March to July remained high, although heavy rains fell in June. The harvest, which was moderate in yield, took place under sunny skies. Quality overall is high, with a good balance of fruit and acidity, although alcohol levels may be somewhat higher than usual.

A hot, very dry summer in the Rhône resulted in intensely ripe grapes, low yields, and dark wines packed with big fruit, muscular flavours, lots of extract. Better balance in the cooler northern Rhône. Southern reds are full and heady, and will be expressive straight away. Sound whites, but low acidity suggests early drinking.

In Provence, good weather conditions meant the harvest took place a week earlier than in 2008. A rainy winter – ideal for building up water resources – a fair spring and a dry summer all contributed to good vineyard development. A hot summer resulted in healthy vines and grapes of excellent quality, although many producers noted that yields were significantly lower than usual.

Languedoc and Roussillon had another wet spring and a slow start to the summer. A warm September made for elegant wines from unstressed vines. Low yields in some areas.

After two nail-biting vintages, the Loire Valley got the summer it deserved. Apart from hail, which devastated pockets of the central vineyards (especially Menetou-Salon), it was dry and sunny right through to harvest in September and October. Volume is up and, across the board, wines are clean, ripe and fruity, drawing comparison with great vintages like 1989, 1990 and

2005. Unlike 2005, when drought conditions prevailed, winter rains helped replenish soils, making for exceptionally fine, balanced reds, the best of which will age beautifully. Whites will be less ageworthy than in classic years, but they are eminently drinkable. And there's good news for sweet wine lovers – the quality of *moelleux* Chenin Blanc is high, from entry level up.

One of Alsace's premier growers, André Ostertag, commented at the end of 2009 that it had been 'a real vintage with real seasons, like in the old days'. What he meant was that a cold, dry winter was followed by a balmy spring, with hot, sunny days through the summer months. Picking began in the first half of September. Good acidity, excellent fruit definition and appreciable maturity characterized the harvest, with the Pinots Gris and Blanc showing particularly well, and the chance of some fine, ripe Pinot Noir reds. Sweet wines may be thinner on the ground. A splendid vintage.

After a warm and unusually dry summer from mid-July onwards, the 2009 Champagne harvest looks to be generally good in quality with some producers comparing it with top-class vintages like 1982 and 1989. Ripeness levels were high and while acidity was slightly lower than average, the crop was exceptionally healthy, even better than in 2008. Pinot Noir looks like being the pick of the crop. A difficult flowering reduced yields for Chardonnay in some areas, but average yields across the appellation were close to the maximum allowed. The only thing likely to limit widespread production of vintage Champagne is the weak market.

French entries in the A–Z section (pages 58–321), by region.

Latour
Latour-Martillac
Latour-à-Pomerol
Laville-Haut-Brion
Léoville-Barton
Léoville-Las-Cases
Léoville-Poyferré
la Louvière
Lynch-Bages
Magdelaine
Malartic-Lagravière
Malescot St-
  Exupéry
Margaux
Maucaillou
Meyney
la Mission-Haut-
  Brion

Monbousquet
Montrose
Moueix, J P
Mouton-Cadet
Mouton-
  Rothschild
Nairac
Palmer
Pape-Clément
Pavie
Pavie-Macquin
Petit-Village
Pétrus
de Pez
Pichon-Longueville
Pichon-Longueville-
  Lalande
le Pin

Pontet-Canet
Potensac
Poujeaux
Prieuré-Lichine
Rauzan-Ségla
Reynon
Rieussec
Roc de Cambes
St-Pierre
Siran
Smith-Haut-Lafitte
Sociando-Mallet
Suduiraut
Talbot
Tertre-Rôteboeuf
la Tour Blanche
Troplong-Mondot
Trotanoy

Valandraud
Vieux-Château-
  Certan
d'Yquem

SEE ALSO
Bordeaux Red
  Wines
Bordeaux White
  Wines
St-Émilion Premier
  Grand Cru Classé

**BURGUNDY AND
BEAUJOLAIS**
ACs
Aloxe-Corton
Auxey-Duresses
Bâtard-Montrachet
Beaujolais
Beaujolais-Villages
Beaune
Blagny
Bonnes-Mares
Bourgogne
Bourgogne-Côte
  Chalonnaise
Bourgogne-Hautes-
  Côtes de Beaune
Bourgogne-Hautes-
  Côtes de Nuits
Brouilly
Chablis
Chablis Grand Cru
Chambertin
Chambolle-Musigny
Chassagne-
  Montrachet
Chénas
Chiroubles
Chorey-lès-Beaune
Clos des Lambrays
Clos de la Roche
Clos St-Denis
Clos de Tart
Clos de Vougeot
Corton
Corton-Charlemagne
Côte de Beaune
Côte de Beaune-
  Villages
Côte de Brouilly
Côte de Nuits-
  Villages

Coteaux du
  Lyonnais
Crémant de
  Bourgogne
Échézeaux
Fixin
Fleurie
Gevrey-Chambertin
Givry
Irancy
Juliénas
Ladoix
Mâcon
Mâcon-Villages
Maranges
Marsannay
Mercurey
Meursault
Montagny
Monthelie
Montrachet
Morey-St-Denis
Morgon
Moulin-à-Vent
Musigny
Nuits-St-Georges
Pernand-Vergelesses
Pommard
Pouilly-Fuissé
Pouilly-Vinzelles
Puligny-Montrachet
Régnié
Richebourg
la Romanée
la Romanée-Conti
Romanée-St-Vivant
Rully
St-Amour
St-Aubin
St-Bris
St-Romain

St-Véran
Santenay
Savigny-lès-Beaune
la Tâche
Viré-Clessé
Volnay
Vosne-Romanée
Vougeot

PRODUCERS
d'Angerville,
  Marquis
Boisset
Bouchard Père et
  Fils
Bouzereau
Brocard, Jean-Marc
Buxynoise, La
Carillon & Fils, Louis
Cathiard, Sylvain
Chablisienne, La
Chandon de Briailles
Clair, Bruno
Coche-Dury, J-F
Dauvissat, René &
  Vincent
Drouhin, Joseph
Duboeuf, Georges
Dujac
Durup, Jean
Faiveley, Joseph
Gagnard, Jean-Noël
Girardin, Vincent
Gouges, Henri
Grivot, Jean
Gros
Hospices de Beaune
Jadot, Louis
Lafarge, Michel
Lafon
Laroche, Dom.

Latour, Louis
Leflaive, Dom.
Leflaive, Olivier
Leroy, Dom.
Liger-Belair
Méo-Camuzet
Montille, Dom. de
Mortet, Denis
Mugnier, J-F
Potel, Nicolas
Ramonet
Raveneau, Jean-
  Marie
Rion
Rodet, Antonin
Romanée-Conti,
  Dom. de la
Roumier, Georges
Rousseau, Armand
Sauzet
Tollot-Beaut
Verget
Vogüé, Comte
  Georges de
Vougeraie, Dom.
  de la

SEE ALSO
Aligoté
Beaujolais Nouveau
Burgundy Red
  Wines
Burgundy White
  Wines
Côte de Beaune
Côte de Nuits
Côte d'Or

25

CHAMPAGNE
Champagne AC
Champagne Rosé
Coteaux
 Champenois AC
Rosé des Riceys AC

PRODUCERS
Billecart-Salmon
Bollinger
Deutz
Duval-Leroy
Gratien, Alfred
Gosset
Heidsieck, Charles
Henriot
Jacquesson
Krug
Lanson
Laurent-Perrier
Moët & Chandon
Mumm, G H
Paillard, Bruno
Perrier, Joseph
Perrier-Jouët
Philipponnat
Piper-Heidsieck
Pol Roger
Pommery
Roederer, Louis
Ruinart
Taittinger
Veuve Clicquot

**JURA AND
 SAVOIE**
Arbois AC
Bugey
Château-Chalon AC
Côtes du Jura AC
Crémant du Jura
 AC
l'Étoile AC
Savoie

LOIRE VALLEY
ACs
Anjou Blanc
Anjou Rouge
Anjou-Villages
Bonnezeaux
Bourgueil
Cabernet d'Anjou
Cheverny
Chinon
Côte Roannaise
Coteaux de
 l'Aubance
Coteaux du Layon
Crémant de Loire
Gros Plant du Pays
 Nantais VDQS
Jasnières
Menetou-Salon
Montlouis-sur-Loire
Muscadet
Pouilly-Fumé
Pouilly-sur-Loire
Quarts de Chaume
Quincy
Reuilly
Rosé de Loire
St-Nicolas-de-
 Bourgueil
Sancerre
Saumur
Saumur-Champigny
Saumur Mousseux
Savennières
Touraine
Val de Loire, Vin de
 Pays du
Vouvray

PRODUCERS
Baudry, Bernard
Baumard, Dom. des
Blot, Jacky
Bourgeois, Dom.
 Henri
Chidaine, François
Clos de la Coulée-
 de-Serrant
Clos Naudin, Dom.
 du
Dagueneau, Didier
Druet, Pierre-
 Jacques
l'Ecu, Dom. de
Huet
Hureau, Ch. du
Mabileau, Frédéric
Mellot, Alphonse
Pierre-Bise, Ch.
Ragotière, Ch. de la
Roches Neuves,
 Dom. des
Vacheron, Dom.
Villeneuve, Ch. de

RHÔNE VALLEY
ACs
Beaumes-de-Venise
Château-Grillet
Châteauneuf-du-
 Pape
Clairette de Die
Collines
 Rhodaniennes,
 Vin de Pays des
Condrieu
Cornas
Costières de Nîmes
Côte-Rôtie
Coteaux de
 l'Ardèche, Vin de
 Pays des
Coteaux du
 Tricastin
Côtes du Rhône
Côtes du Rhône-
 Villages
Côtes du Vivarais
Crémant de Die
Crozes-Hermitage
Gigondas
Hermitage
Lirac
Lubéron
Muscat de
 Beaumes-de-
 Venise
Rasteau
St-Joseph
St-Péray
Tavel
Vacqueyras
Ventoux
Vinsobres

PRODUCERS
Allemand, Thiérry
Beaucastel,
 Ch. de
Chapoutier, M
Chave, Jean-Louis
Clape, A
Clos des Papes
Colombo, Jean-Luc
Coursodon, Pierre
Cuilleron, Yves
Delas Frères
Font de Michelle,
 Dom.
Graillot, Alain
Guigal
Jaboulet Aîné, Paul
Jamet
Oratoire St-Martin,
 Dom.
Perret, André
Rayas, Ch.
Réméjeanne,
 Dom. la
Rostaing, Réné
St-Gayan, Dom.
Sang des Cailloux,
 Dom. le
Tain, Cave de
Vieux Télégraphe,
 Dom. du

SEE ALSO
Cairanne

SOUTHERN FRANCE

SOUTH-WEST

ACs
Béarn
Bergerac
Buzet
Cahors
Coteaux du Quercy
Côtes de Duras
Côtes de Gascogne,
Vin de Pays
Côtes du
Marmandais
Fronton
Gaillac
Irouléguy
Jurançon
Madiran
Marcillac
Monbazillac
Montravel
Pacherenc du Vic-
Bilh
Pécharmant
St-Mont
Tursan VDQS

PRODUCERS
l'Ancienne Cure,
Dom. de
Arretxea, Dom.
Aydie, Ch. d'
Berthoumieu, Dom.
Cauhapé, Dom.
Causse Marines,
Dom. de
Cèdre, Ch. du
Chapelle Lenclos
Clos de Gamot
Clos Triguedina
Clos Uroulat
Cosse-Maisonneuve,
Dom.
Elian da Ros, Dom.
Laffitte-Teston, Ch.
Montus, Ch.
Pech, Dom. du
Plageoles, Robert
Plaimont,
Producteurs
Plaisance, Ch.
Ramaye, Dom. de la
Rotier, Dom.
Tariquet, Ch. du
Tirecul la Gravière,
Ch.
Tour des Gendres,
Ch.
Verdots, Vignoble
des

LANGUEDOC-ROUSSILLON

ACs
Banyuls
Blanquette de
Limoux
Cabardès
Collioure
Corbières
Coteaux du
Languedoc
Côtes Catalanes,
Vin de Pays des
Côtes du Roussillon
Côtes du
Roussillon-Villages
Côtes de Thongue,
Vin de Pays des
Crémant de Limoux
Faugères
Fitou
Gard, Vin de Pays du
Hérault, Vin de Pays
de l'
Limoux
Maury
Minervois
Muscat de
Frontignan
Muscat de
Rivesaltes
Muscat de St-Jean-
de-Minervois
Oc, Vin de Pays d'
Rivesaltes
St-Chinian

PRODUCERS
Alquier, Dom. Jean-
Michel
Antugnac, Dom. d'
Borie la Vitarèle
Canet-Valette,
Dom.
Casenove, Ch. la
Cazes, Dom.
Clos de l'Anhel
Clos Bagatelle
Clos Centeilles
Clos Marie
Clot de l'Oum
Denois, J-L
Estanilles, Ch. des
Gauby, Dom.
Grange des Pères,
Dom. de la
Hecht & Bannier
l'Hortus, Dom. de
l'Hospitalet, Ch.
Mas Blanc, Dom. du
Mas Bruguière
Mas la Chevalière
Mas de Daumas
Gassac
Mont Tauch
Nizas, Dom. de
Peyre Rose, Dom.
Prieuré de St-Jean
de Bébian
Sieur d'Arques, les
Vignerons du
Skalli-Fortant de
France
Tour Boisée, Ch.
Val d'Orbieu, les
Vignerons du
Voulte-Gasparets,
Ch. la

SEE ALSO
Clape, La
Pic St-Loup
Roussillon

PROVENCE

ACs
Bandol
les Baux-de-
Provence
Bellet
Bouches-du-Rhône,
Vin de Pays des
Cassis
Coteaux d'Aix-en-
Provence
Coteaux Varois
Côtes de Provence
Palette

PRODUCERS
d'Eole, Dom.
Esclans, Ch. d'
Pibarnon, Ch. de
Richeaume, Dom.
Romanin, Dom.
Sorin, Dom.
Trévallon, Dom. de
Vannières, Ch.

CORSICA

Arena, Dom.
Antoine
Corse AC, Vin de

ITALY

Despite having fallen to a low ebb for around a century from the 1870s, due to vine disease and problems of an economic and political nature, Italy can boast by far the world's longest continuous wine-producing tradition. Organized viticulture may, as we are told, have originated in Asia Minor, but religious strictures, even in Ottoman-occupied Greece, destroyed or at least seriously interrupted the vinous flow. As for Christian lands to Italy's north and west – France, Spain, Iberia, Germany – they didn't receive viticulture for a millennium after Italy, and then from the Italians themselves, known as Romans. So the revolutionaries of the 1970s on, men like Piero Antinori and Angelo Gaja, had a deep-rooted base to build on, even though much of it was in shambles. Over the past 40 years these pioneers, and their increasingly numerous followers, have turned Italian wine around, so that today Italy stands ready to reclaim her historic place at the head of the league of enological nations.

GRAPE VARIETIES AND WINE REGIONS

The most important of all Italy's wine traditions is its amazing diversity of grapes, with each region, province, zone and sub-zone seeming to have its own type of fruit, in the form of different varieties, different sub-varieties or different clones. The north-west, especially Piedmont, is the home of many of the best Italian red grapes, like Nebbiolo (the grape of Barolo and Barbaresco), Dolcetto and Barbera, while the north-east (Friuli-Venezia

Giulia, Trentino-Alto Adige and the Veneto) is more noted for the success of native white varieties like Garganega (Soave) and Prosecco (now re-named Glera), reds like Corvina and Corvinone, and imports like Pinot Grigio, Chardonnay and Sauvignon Blanc. The Po Valley is Lambrusco country west of Bologna, while Sangiovese – aka Sangioveto in Chianti Classico, Brunello in Montalcino and Morellino in the Maremma – rules in Romagna and Tuscany. The east coast boasts versatile white Verdicchio and deep-coloured Montepulciano, as well as, farther south in Puglia, full reds Negroamaro and Primitivo. Campania (also Basilicata) has elegant red Aglianico plus perfumed whites Fiano and Greco, to name a few. Sicily makes its best red wines from Nero d'Avola, with whites from Inzolia. Sardinia claims white Vermentino as well as reds Cannonau and Carignano.

CLASSIFICATIONS

Vino da Tavola, 'table wine', is used for wine that is produced either outside the existing laws, or in an area where no delimited zone exists. Both cheap, basic wines and inspired innovative creations like Tignanello, Sassicaia and other so-called Super-Tuscans used to fall into this anonymous category. Now the fancy wines have become either DOC (particularly in Piedmont with its Langhe and Piemonte DOCs) or IGT (particularly in Tuscany, or Toscana). Remaining Vini da Tavola are labelled simply as bianco, rosso or rosato without vintages or varietal or geographical indications.

IGT (Indicazione Geografica Tipica) began taking effect in the mid-1990s to identify wines from certain areas as an equivalent of the French Vin de Pays. A great swathe of both ordinary and premium wines traded their Vino da Tavola status for a regional IGT, of which there are now over 120.

DOC (Denominazione di Origine Controllata) is the main classification for wines from designated zones made following traditions that were historically valid but often outdated. Recently the laws have become more flexible, bringing quality wines under new appellations that allow for recognition of communes, estates and single vineyards. If anything, the problem today is a surfeit of DOCs. There are now well over 350, a good number of which are unnecessary or repetitive.

DOCG (Denominazione di Origine Controllata e Garantita) was conceived as a 'super-league' for DOCs that promised high class but didn't always provide it. Wines are made under stricter standards that have favoured improvements, but the best guarantee of quality remains the producer's name. Currently DOCGs number almost 40.

What Italy's denominations need is a good pruning, which is what the EU would like to give them. The plan from Brussels was to reduce the total number of DOCGs, DOCs and IGTs to just 182 DOPs and IGPs: **DOP** and **IGP** (Denominazione di Origine Protetta and Indicazione Geografica Protetta; *protetta* = protected). These were indeed introduced from August 2009, but with an open-ended option to carry on using the old designations. The result, of course, is more names and greater confusion than ever. Or so it would be, except for the fact that no one in Italy is paying a blind bit of notice to the EU's new categories. Indeed, they are creating new IGTs, DOCs and DOCGs as if the EU didn't exist.

2009 VINTAGE REPORT

2009 continued the trend toward ever less volume production – down 10% on the average of the preceding 10 years (1999–2008). From the centre northward a reasonably rain-free vintage period followed a very hot and mainly dry summer. The result was big crops of good, some very good and some top-class wine from Piedmont, Veneto and, especially, Tuscany. On the east coast, from Friuli right down to Puglia, there were adverse weather conditions leading to reduced production and a compromised level of quality especially for later-picked varieties. Sicily and Sardinia suffered rain-wise after mid-September. All in all, though, a good year with points of excellence.

Italian entries in the A–Z section (pages 58–321).

GERMANY

The dull semi-sweet wines with names like Liebfraumilch and Niersteiner Gutes Domtal that used to dominate the export market, are rapidly vanishing off all but the most basic radar screens. Instead, we are seeing a better range of single-estate wines of fine quality, although the choice, except at specialist wine merchants, remains limited. Throughout Germany, both red and white wines are year by year, region by region, grower by grower, becoming fuller, better balanced and drier.

GRAPE VARIETIES

Riesling makes the best wines, at least in northerly regions such as the Mosel and Rheingau, in styles ranging from dry to intensely sweet. Other white wines come from Grauburgunder/Ruländer (Pinot Gris), Weissburgunder (Pinot Blanc), Gewürztraminer, Silvaner, Scheurebe and Rieslaner, although Müller-Thurgau produces much of the simpler wine. Plantings of red grape varieties now account for 36% of the nation's vineyard. Good reds are being made in the south of the country from Spätburgunder (Pinot Noir) and Lemberger.

WINE REGIONS

Many of the most delectable Rieslings come from villages such as Bernkastel, Brauneberg, Ürzig and Wehlen on the Mosel, and Kiedrich, Johannisberg and Rüdesheim in the Rheingau. Characterful dry Mosel Rieslings are the speciality of villages such as Winningen near Koblenz. The Nahe makes superb Rieslings in Schlossböckelheim and Traisen, and Niederhausen has the region's best vineyards. Rheinhessen's top wines are the excellent racy Rieslings produced on steep riverside slopes in Nackenheim and Nierstein, but growers such as Keller and Wittmann are showing the real potential of some inland sites. Franken is the one place the Silvaner grape excels, often made in a powerful, dry, earthy style. The Pfalz is climatically similar to Alsace and has a similar potential for well-rounded, dry whites, plus rapidly improving reds. Baden also produces fully ripe wine styles, which, were they better marketed, should appeal to an international market accustomed to rich, dry wines. In Württemberg many red wines are thin and dull, but a few producers understand the need for weight and flavour. The other smaller wine regions make little wine and little is exported, although the Ahr has a growing reputation for Pinot Noir.

CLASSIFICATIONS

Germany's classification system is based on the ripeness of the grapes and therefore their potential alcohol level.

Deutscher Tafelwein (table wine) is the most basic term, used for any blended wine; it accounts for only a tiny percentage of production and will be eliminated from 2012 onwards.

Landwein (country wine) is a slightly more up-market version, linked to 19 regional areas. These must be Trocken (dry) or Halbtrocken (medium-dry).

QbA (Qualitätswein bestimmter Anbaugebiete) is 'quality' wine from one of 13 designated regions, but the grapes don't have to be very ripe, and sugar can be added to the juice to increase alcoholic content.

QmP (Qualitätswein mit Prädikat) or 'quality wine with distinction' is the top level; in 2007 the term was replaced by ' Prädikatswein'. There are 6 levels of QmP (in ascending order of ripeness): Kabinett, Spätlese, Auslese, Beerenauslese, Eiswein, Trockenbeerenauslese (TBA). The addition of sugar is forbidden.

Since 2000, there have been 2 designations for varietal dry wines: **Classic** for 'good' wines and **Selection** for 'top-quality' wines, but they haven't really caught on. And an increasing number of good estates use single-vineyard names only on their top selections.

The Rheingau has introduced an official classification – Erstes Gewächs (First Growth) – for its best sites. Other regions have evolved a widely adopted classification called Grosses Gewächs.

2009 VINTAGE REPORT

The summer got off to a slow start but most of August and September was warm and sunny, leading to an early and successful harvest of Chardonnay and Pinot varieties in the south. Fine weather continued into October, allowing Riesling to ripen fully too. Early indications suggest a vintage that could equal the excellent 2007. A full range of wines could be made, from dry to nobly sweet, but the crop was 25% smaller than in 2008. However, quality was consistently fine throughout Germany.

German entries in the A–Z section (pages 58–321).

AUSTRIA

can't think of a European nation where the wine culture has changed so dramatically over a generation as it has in Austria. Austria still makes great sweet wines, but a new order based on world-class medium- and full-bodied dry whites and increasingly fine reds has emerged.

WINE REGIONS AND GRAPE VARIETIES

The Danube runs through Niederösterreich, scene of much of Austria's viticulture. The Wachau produces great Riesling and excellent pepper-dry Grüner Veltliner. The Riesling is powerful and ripe, closer in style to Alsace than Germany. Next up the Danube are Kremstal and Kamptal, rapidly improving as fine dry white regions with a few good reds. The Weinviertel, in the north-east, produces large quantities of decent reds and Grüner Veltliner whites. Burgenland, south-east of Vienna, produces the best reds, mostly from local varieties Zweigelt, Blaufränkisch and St-Laurent. Also, around the shores of the Neusiedler See, especially near the towns of Rust and Illmitz, Burgenland produces some superb dessert wines. Further south, in Steiermark (Styria), Chardonnay and Sauvignon are increasingly oak-aged, though many drinkers still prefer the racy unoaked 'classic' wines from these varieties.

33

CLASSIFICATIONS

Wine categories are similar to those in Germany. **Qualitätswein** must come from one of the 16 main wine-producing regions. Like German wines, quality wines may additionally have a special category: Kabinett, Spätlese, Auslese, Beerenauslese, Ausbruch, Trockenbeerenauslese. Since most Austrian wine are either dry or nobly sweet, these categories count for less than in Germany. The Wachau has its own ripeness scale for dry whites: Steinfeder wines are made for early drinking, Federspiel wines can last three years or so and the most powerful wines are known as Smaragd. Over recent years Austria has developed its own geographical appellation system called DAC, but it comes with stylistic constraints. Thus the Leithaberg DAC comes from the Burgenland but the red wine must be mostly from Blaufränkisch. It seems unlikely that the system is understood outside Austria. I'll say.

2009 VINTAGE REPORT

As in 2007, the summer was wet and often stormy, alternating with dry spells. Heavy mid-September rain along the Danube provoked more rot, but then dry weather set in until the second week of October. The crop was reduced and selection was essential, but quality in Kremstal, Kamptal and the Wachau was surprisingly good. The Burgenland had drier weather and, despite outbreaks of hail, Steiermark produced excellent whites. A good year for sweet wines too.

Austrian entries in the A–Z section (pages 58–321).

SPAIN

The technical makeover of Spain's long-dormant wine scene was largely complete by 2000. Since that date, we have witnessed a progressive refinement of the wines, as increasing numbers of producers eschewed the over-oaking and ultra-powerful style that had been a hallmark of this country's revolution. Not coincidentally, forgotten regions and forgotten native grape varieties have now come to the fore.

WINE REGIONS

Galicia in the green, hilly north-west grows Spain's most aromatic whites. The heartland of the great Spanish reds, Rioja, Navarra and Ribera del Duero, is situated between the central plateau and the northern coast. Further west along the Duero, Rueda produces fresh whites and Toro good chunky reds. Cataluña is principally white wine country (much of it sparkling Cava), though there are some great reds in Priorat and increasingly in Terra Alta, Empordà-Costa Brava, Costers del Segre and Montsant. Aragón's reds and whites are looking good too, with an impressive relaunch of Aragón's great (but neglected for too long) native grape Garnacha. The central plateau of La Mancha makes mainly cheap reds and whites, though smaller private estates are improving spectacularly and neighbouring Manchuela is on the march with beefy reds. Valencia, known for inexpensive and unmemorable wines, is now producing, with neighbouring Murcia, increasingly ambitious and rich reds. Andalucía's specialities are the fortified wines – sherry, Montilla and Málaga. There has been a notable rebirth of viticulture and winemaking in both the Balearics and the Canary Islands.

CLASSIFICATIONS

Vino de Mesa (table wine) is the lowest level. For a while, it was used for some non-DO 'Super-Spanish'. Under new European regulations, this may be optionally changed to, simply, Vino.

Vino de la Tierra (country wine) followed by a geographical designation. Under new regulations, wines may be labelled Indicación Geográfica Protegida (IGP).

35

DO (Denominación de Origen) is the main classification for wines from designated zones, which are subject to various regulations. In Castilla-La Mancha and Navarra, this category now encompasses single-estate DOs (Denominación de Origen **Vino de Pago**). Under new European regulations, wines may be labelled Denominación de Origen Protegida (DOP).

DOCa (Denominación de Origen Calificada) is a super-category. Only two regions (Rioja and Priorat) have been promoted.

2009 VINTAGE REPORT

There were two very different stories in Spain after a harsh summer that was overall drier and hotter than 2003. In the early-ripening Mediterranean regions the conditions created havoc, with vine stress resulting in unripe grapes becoming raisined on the plant; only rigorous grape selection produced good wines and total output plunged. In Atlantic-influenced Spain, from Navarra to Galicia, the welcome September rains enabled most vineyards to recover and regions such as Ribera del Duero had a remarkable vintage. Overall in Spain, production was lower than in 2008.

Spanish entries in the A–Z section (pages 58–321).

PORTUGAL

Investment and imagination are paying off in this attractive country, with climates that vary from the mild, damp Minho region in the north-west to the subtropical island of Madeira. Use of native grapes, occasionally blended with international varieties, means that Portugal is now a rich source of characterful wines of ever-increasing quality.

WINE REGIONS

The lush Vinho Verde country in the north-west gives very different wine from the parched valleys of the neighbouring Douro, with its drier, more continental climate. The Douro, home of port, is also the source of some of Portugal's best unfortified red wines. In Beiras, which includes Bairrada and Dão, soil types are crucial in determining the character of the wines. Lisboa and Tejo (formerly known as Estremadura and Ribatejo) use native and international varieties in regions influenced either by the maritime climate or by the river Tagus. South of Lisbon, the Península de Setúbal (ex-Terras do Sado) and Alentejo produce some exciting table wines – and the Algarve is waking up. Madeira is unique, a volcanic island 850km (530 miles) out in the Atlantic Ocean.

CLASSIFICATIONS

Vinho de Mesa is the lowest level, but commercially important as so much off-dry to medium-dry rosé is exported in this category.

Vinho Regional, or Indicação Geográfica Protegida (IGP), is the next level, with laws and permitted varieties much freer than for IPR and DOC.

IPR (Indicação de Proveniência Regulamentada) is the intermediate step for wine regions hoping to move up to DOC status. Many have been promoted, leaving just 4 IPRs, not all of which will definitely become DOCs.

DOC/DOP (Denominação de Origem Controlada/Protegida) is the most strictly regulated; there are now 27 DOC/DOPs.

2009 VINTAGE REPORT

The 2008/2009 winter was cold and wet in the north, with snow in the Douro and Dão. Rain during flowering in May and June slightly lowered yields all over the country. Apart from this rain, the rest of the year was dry and sunny, and very hot in the Douro and Alentejo, where some grapes had to be picked before they had fully mature tannins. In the Douro, higher, cooler vineyards gave better reds and, probably, ports. The summer heat of the Alentejo was too much for some vineyards, although early-pickers made some good wines. In Vinho Verde, Bairrada and Dão it was a great year for whites, and in Bairrada for reds also; Dão reds were not so consistent. In Lisboa and the Tejo, whites were good, reds less so. Madeira's promising crop was ruined by rain that started in mid-August and continued right through harvest.

Portuguese entries in the A–Z section (pages 58–321).

REGIONS	Setúbal	Ferreira	Roques, Quinta dos
Alentejo	Vinho Verde	Fonseca	Rosa, Quinta de la
Algarve		Fonseca, José Maria	Sandeman
Beiras	PRODUCERS	da	Santos Lima, Casa
Lisboa	Aliança	Graham	São João, Caves
Península de Setúbal	Bacalhôa Vinhos de	Henriques &	Smith Woodhouse
Tejo	Portugal	Henriques	Sogrape
Trás-os-Montes	Burmester	Madeira Wine	Taylor
	Churchill	Company	Vesúvio, Quinta do
DOC	Cockburn	Malhadinha Nova,	Warre
Alenquer	Cortes de Cima	Herdade de	
Bairrada	Côtto, Quinta do	Niepoort	SEE ALSO
Bucelas	Crasto, Quinta do	Noval, Quinta da	Albariño
Dão	Croft	Pato, Luís	Baga
Douro	D F J Vinhos	Ramos, Joao	Graciano
Madeira	Dow	Portugal	Tempranillo
Port	Esporão	Ramos Pinto	Touriga Nacional

USA

The United States has more varied growing conditions for grapes than any other country in the world, which isn't so surprising when you consider that the 50 states of the Union cover an area that is larger than Western Europe and although Alaska doesn't grow grapes in the icy far north, Washington State does in the north-west, as does Texas in the south and New York State in the north-east, and even Hawaii, lost in the pounding surf of the Pacific Ocean, manages to grow grapes and make wine. Every state, including Alaska (thanks to salmonberry and fireweed), now produces wine of some sort or another; it ranges from some pretty dire offerings, which would have been far better distilled into brandy, to some of the greatest and most original wines to be found in the world today.

GRAPE VARIETIES AND WINE REGIONS

California is far and away the most important state for wine production. In its determination to match the best red Bordeaux and white Burgundy, California proved that it was possible to successfully re-interpret the classic European role models in an area thousands of miles away from their home. However, there is more to California than this. The Central Valley produces the majority of the simple beverage wines that still dominate the American market, but the northern end around Lodi is proving that real quality is possible here. Napa and Sonoma Counties north of San Francisco Bay do produce great Cabernet and Chardonnay, but grapes like Zinfandel and

Merlot also make their mark and the Carneros, Russian River Valley and Sonoma Coast areas are highly successful for Pinot Noir, Chardonnay and sparkling wines. In the north, Mendocino and Lake Counties produce good grapes and Anderson Valley is superb for fizz. South of San Francisco, in the cool, foggy valleys between Santa Cruz and Santa Barbara, and the Santa Lucia Highlands in Monterey County, Chardonnay, Pinot Noir and Syrah are producing exciting cool-climate but ripe-flavoured wines.

Oregon, with a cooler and more capricious climate than most of California, perseveres with Pinot Noir, Chardonnay, Pinot Gris, Pinot Blanc and Riesling with patchy success. Washington, so chilly and misty on the coast

38

becomes virtual desert east of the Cascade Mountains and it is here, in irrigated vineyards, that superb reds and whites can be made, with thrillingly focused fruit.

In New York, winemakers in the Finger Lakes are creating a regional style and national reputation for dry Riesling. Long Island continues to impress with classically styled Merlot, Cabernet Sauvignon and Cabernet Franc, as well as Chardonnay to pair with the local lobster. Improved vineyard practices have enabled growers to cope with the vagaries of the region's inconsistent weather, resulting in an overall increase in quality from year to year.

Other states have seen dramatic growth in the wine industry over the past decade. Established industries in Virginia, Maryland, Pennsylvania, Texas and Missouri have led the way, but look also for new growth in North Carolina, Georgia, Ohio and Michigan.

CLASSIFICATIONS

The AVA (American Viticultural Area) system was introduced in the 1980s. It does not guarantee a quality standard, but merely requires that at least 85% of grapes in a wine come from the specified AVA. There are over 190 AVAs, more than 100 of which are in California. AVAs come in all shapes and sizes, varying from the largest, Upper Mississippi Valley, which spans an area of 77,477 sq km (29,914 sq miles) to the smallest, Cole Ranch, which covers a little less than a quarter of a square mile.

2009 VINTAGE REPORT

In California, spring was early and mild, and berry set was good; a large crop developed. The weather remained mild through the growing season and summer was cool, with only a few days of heat. Flavours developed early and most growers picked early; others waited and were hit with rain on 5 October. Some didn't pick their red grapes until after the first rain and colours were diluted. A second storm on 11 October brought plenty more rain, and it stayed foggy and humid for many days. Most whites are reportedly spectacular; reds are dependent on when they were picked. Napa and Sonoma generally look good.

In Washington, wind and cool weather during flowering resulted in a variable fruit set. Midsummer weather was brutally hot, breaking records in many AVAs; some vine damage occurred. The heat spell broke in August and the weather returned to perfect growing conditions. Veraison began in the first week of August. Due to the early summer heat, harvest was earlier than usual, yielding wines with high acidity, dark colour and high potential alcohol. A hard freeze on 8 October, followed by intermittent rain, caused the season to end early for many growers. The combination of cold, wet weather and the grape shrivel from the July heat spike required careful sorting to avoid rotten and overripe fruit from being processed. There are brightly flavoured whites and zesty reds, and the best will be outstanding.

In Oregon, the growing season was characterized by week-to-week variations in temperature. Cooler than expected weather in late September and early October led to a vintage with a record long hang time for the fruit. A few rain sessions followed by warm periods preserved the fresh quality of the fruit and prevented desiccation of the berries. The red wines are balanced in alcohol and acidity, and many ripe and showy Pinot Noirs with intense fruit flavour were produced. The white wines are crisp and also lower in alcohol than usual.

The Eastern US recorded a strong vintage, with a relatively cool summer and prolonged harvest, keeping acidity and ripeness in balance.

AUSTRALIA

Australia finds itself at a bit of a crossroads nowadays. Its reputation, which soared sky-high on a relatively small volume of wine produced, has begun to teeter as volumes have mushroomed. Its ability to overdeliver quality at a fair price, which fuelled the New World wine revolution, has been undermined by the need to soak up large amounts of excess production from poorly thought-out expansion of vineyards. And despite the fact that its winemakers, especially those of independent companies and estates, are creating some of Australia's best-ever wine, the country has increasingly been saddled with the downmarket reputation of 'critter' brands, based on whatever marsupial had not yet featured on a label, and deep-discounted junk. These are wines to avoid. Now is the time to rediscover Australia's genius, sometimes rough and ready, but frequently finely balanced and sublime, and unlike the wines of any other country in the world.

GRAPE VARIETIES

Varietal wines remain more prized than blends. Shiraz has long been a key varietal and is more fashionable than Cabernet Sauvignon, especially in its ever-increasing cool-climate manifestations. Renewed respect for old-vine Grenache and Mourvèdre has seen these former workhorse varieties transformed into sought-after stars. Merlot and – in cooler-climate regions – Pinot Noir lead the pack of alternative red varieties and Australia's endless appetite for experiment has found prospective new stars in Petit Verdot, Tempranillo, Nebbiolo and Sangiovese. Among white grapes the position of Chardonnay has been challenged by the upstart Sauvignon Blanc, despite the fact that modern Australian Chardonnay is some of the best in the world. Sales of Sauvignon (70% of which comes from New Zealand) have exceeded

Chardonnay in Australia and although one in four of the whites Australians drink is Chardonnay, its popularity has declined by about 7% per year: a serious problem when one realizes how much is produced. Semillon and Riesling follow, with the Rhône varieties Marsanne and Viognier (now fashionably included in blends with Shiraz) both impressing; Verdelho and Pinot Gris are making a strong case for themselves as alternatives to Chardonnay. Sweet whites are produced from Semillon and Muscat – both the top-class Brown Muscat (a sub-variety of Muscat Blanc à Petits Grains) and the more workaday Muscat Gordo Blanco.

WINE REGIONS

South Australia dominates the wine scene – it grows the most grapes, makes the most wine and is home to most of the nation's biggest wine companies. There is more to it, however, than attractive, undemanding, gluggable wine. The Clare Valley produces outstanding cool-climate Riesling, as well as excellent Shiraz and Cabernet. The Barossa is home to some of the planet's oldest vines, particularly Shiraz and Grenache.

Victoria was Australia's major producer for most of the 19th century until her vineyards were devastated by phylloxera. It's only recently that Victoria has regained her position as provider of some of the most startling wine styles in the country: stunning liqueur Muscats; thrilling dark reds from Central Victoria; urbane Yarra Valley and Mornington Peninsula reds and whites.

New South Wales was home to the revolution that propelled Australia to the front of the world wine stage (in the Hunter Valley, an area that remains a dominant force). However, the state is a major bulk producer in Riverina, and a clutch of new regions in the Central Ranges are grabbing headlines.

Western Australia is a vast state, virtually desert except for its south-western coastal strip. The sun-baked region near Perth is best suited to throaty reds and fortified wines, yet winery and vineyard expertise has become more sophisticated and decent aromatic dry whites are now being made. The most exciting wines, both red and white, come from Margaret River and Great Southern down toward the coast.

Tasmania, with its cooler climate, is attracting attention for top-quality Pinot Noirs and Champagne-method sparkling wines – and there is excellent potential for Riesling, Pinot Gris and Gewürztraminer.

CLASSIFICATIONS

Formal appellation control, restricting certain grapes to certain regions, is virtually unknown; regulations are more of a guarantee of authenticity than a guide to quality. In a country so keen on inter-regional blending for its commercial brands, a system resembling France's AC could be problematic. However, the Label Integrity Program (LIP) guarantees all claims made on labels and the Geographical Indications (GI) committee is busy clarifying zones, regions and sub-regions – albeit with plenty of lively, at times acrimonious, debate about where some regional borders should go.

2010 VINTAGE REPORT

This has been an amazing vintage in Australia because, for once, all regions have been somewhere on the continuum from happy to ecstatic with the quality of their wines. Yields have been about average. Where they have been down, there has still been compensatory high quality. Although it is difficult to generalize, most regions had abundant winter rainfall, a generally cool growing season with few extremes of heat, rain at the right times and dry weather for picking.

The irrigated areas of the Riverina and Riverland benefited from additional water allocation and excellent conditions, in spite of a November heatwave which was moderated by rains later in the month. The Hunter Valley had an early harvest following excellent growing conditions, although yields were reduced by hail. Orange and the Canberra District faced rot problems following summer rains, but the most experienced producers were able to deal with this.

It will be a great year for Rutherglen fortified and red wines, and for the Italian varietals in the King Valley in north-east Victoria. The Yarra Valley, Mornington Peninsula and Tasmania are buoyant about their Chardonnay and Pinot Noir, and the quality of the sparkling wine base from Tasmania, the Yarra and Tumbarumba in New South Wales looks particularly promising.

In South Australia, the harvest was excellent in the Barossa, Coonawarra, the Clare Valley, McLaren Vale (except for Grenache) and Adelaide Hills, in spite of difficult weather conditions. Fortune continued to favour Western Australia with ideal growing conditions in most regions: superb whites – especially Chardonnays – will come from Margaret River. Rain late in the season affected some producers in Margaret River and may have impacted on quality, but most believe the Cabernets will be very good to outstanding.

Australian entries in the A–Z section (pages 58–321).

NEW ZEALAND

New Zealand's wines, though diverse in style, are characterized by intens[e] fruit flavours, zesty acidity and pungent aromas – the product of cool growin[g] conditions and high-tech winemaking.

GRAPE VARIETIES

New Zealand is a small, cool-climate wine-producing country which has don[e] a brilliant job of selling itself on rarity, exclusivity, high quality and high price[.] Its fame was based firmly on Sauvignon Blanc – deservedly so, becaus[e] Sauvignon's explosion onto the world's consciousness during the 1980s an[d] 1990s changed forever our views of how tangy and refreshing a white win[e] could be. Sauvignon Blanc is still the Kiwi flagwaver – too much so, since fo[r] the first time we are now seeing discounted cheap examples of Marlboroug[h] Sauvignon Blanc around the world as sales fail to keep up with excessiv[e] planting. Unless things quickly get back into balance, New Zealand'[s] reputation for producing only high-quality, high-price wine is seriously a[t] risk. That would be a tragedy, since the country also produces superb, full-bodied, oatmealy Chardonnay, succulent Pinot Gris, fragrant Riesling an[d] Gewürztraminer and excellent fizz.

For a long time thought of as too cool for high-quality reds, New Zealand is now creating sensational, scented Pinot Noir, dark, serious Bordeaux-style blends usually based on Merlot and Cabernet Sauvignon, and a small amount of exquisite Syrah. Wines of such quality are rare and should be high-priced. The flood of cheap Sauvignon Blanc threatens the country's hard-won reputation.

NORTH ISLAND
Matakana

AUCKLAND
Kumeu/Huapai
Henderson
Auckland

Waiheke Island

BAY OF PLENTY

WAIKATO

GISBORN[E]

HAWKES BAY

WELLINGTON
Wairarapa
Martinborough

Nelson
NELSON
Blenheim Wellington
MARLBOROUGH

CANTERBURY
Waipara
Christchurch

SOUTH ISLAND

OTAGO
Dunedin

Main vineyard areas

0   100   200 km

0   100 miles

WINE REGIONS

Nearly 1600km (1000 miles) separate New Zealand's northernmost wine region from the country's (and the world's) most southerly wine region, Central Otago. In terms of wine styles it is useful to divide the country into two parts. The warmer climate of Hawkes Bay and one or two pockets around Auckland produce the best Cabernet Sauvignon, Merlot and Cabernet Franc as well as increasingly good Syrah. Waiheke Island and Hawkes Bay's Gimblett Gravels have some of the most exciting red wine vineyards. Martinborough and Wairarapa are noted for Pinot Noir. In the South Island, Nelson is good for Pinot Noir and aromatic whites, while Marlborough is the hub of the industry, famous for Sauvignon Blanc, but also excellent for fizz, Chardonnay, Riesling and Pinot Noir. Waipara is small but produces very characterful reds and whites, while Central Otago produces fabulous Pinot Noir, vibrant Riesling and an increasing amount of flavoursome Pinot Gris.

CLASSIFICATIONS

Labels guarantee geographic origin. The broadest designation is New Zealand, followed by North or South Island. Next come the 10 or so regions. Labels may also name specific localities and individual vineyards.

2010 VINTAGE REPORT

New Zealand's 2010 vintage was a reminder that the country's wine regions span a lengthy latitude of more than 1500km (1000 miles), with significant variation likely from one region to another. Auckland, for example, enjoyed the warmest, driest summer and autumn weather anyone can remember, while further south the weather was cooler and often wetter. Wet, cool summer weather had Gisborne and Hawkes Bay winemakers worried by mid-March but the long, hot spell that followed got ripening back on track. Nonetheless, later-ripening varieties, including most of the red grape varieties, are generally better than early-ripeners such as Chardonnay. Marlborough had a cool, slow start to the vintage although the region was less affected by rain. Following two bountiful harvests most Sauvignon Blanc growers pruned their vines hard to reduce yield. Low bunch weights reduced cropping levels even further, although low yields made a significant contribution to generally very high quality. Other South Island regions report a drop in quantity with good quality wines overall. Central Otago Pinot Noir is likely to produce best results in warmer sites such as Bannockburn, Bendigo and Alexandra.

New Zealand entries in the A–Z section (pages 58–321).

REGIONS	PRODUCERS		
Auckland	Astrolabe	Hunter's	Pask, C J
Awatere Valley	Ata Rangi	Jackson Estate	Pegasus Bay
Canterbury	Babich	Kumeu River	Quartz Reef
Central Otago	Church Road	Man O' War	Saint Clair
Gisborne	Cloudy Bay	Martinborough	Seresin
Hawkes Bay	Coopers Creek	Vineyard	Stonyridge
Kumeu/Huapai	Craggy Range	Matua Valley	Te Mata
Marlborough	Delegat's	Millton	Trinity Hill
Martinborough/	Dry River	Montana	Vavasour
Wairarapa	Felton Road	Neudorf	Villa Maria
Nelson	Framingham	Ngatarawa	Wither Hills
Waiheke Island	Fromm	Nobilo	
		Palliser Estate	

SOUTH AMERICA

ARGENTINA

The revolution in Argentine wine is complete. A decade of foreign investment combined with a large crop of young and well-travelled home grown talent has turned a slumbering, old-fashioned industry into a dynamic modern world force, with the little-known French grape variety Malbec becoming the national standard-bearer. At its most ordinary, Malbec can be attractive, juicy and damsony; at its best thrilling, perfumed, complex and long lived. The best hail from Mendoza, in particular the Upper Mendoza River region and the Uco Valley in the shadows of the Andes mountains. The cooler regions of Neuquén and Río Negro in Patagonia are noted for minerally, deep Malbecs, while the extreme altitude vineyards of Salta in the north produce the most dense and powerful expressions. Malbec is not the only fruit, however; red varieties such as Bonarda and Tempranillo are full of potential, and the aromatic, perfumed white Torrontés (a uniquely Argentine speciality) finds its spiritual home in Salta.

CHILE

A vibrant economy and a stable government continue to make Chile the dynamic leader of Latin America, and its wine is impressing consumers worldwide. The dark, rich, savoury flavours of Carmenère are increasingly evident, especially from numerous established vineyard sites in the Rapel and Aconcagua Valleys. Cabernet Sauvignon and Merlot, from Maipo and elsewhere, are still Chile's best-known wines, but superb, fragrant Pinot Noir is appearing from coastal areas such as San Antonio, and excellent Syrah is being made in cool areas like Limarí and Elqui as well as the warmer Colchagua Valley. Chile's fruity Chardonnay is some of the New World's best balanced, with exciting Sauvignon Blanc, Riesling and Gewürztraminer from the coastal Leyda Valley and southerly regions such as Bío Bío. Maule is experiencing a revival.

URUGUAY

Most of the vines are on clay soils in the Canelones region around Montevideo, which has high rainfall in a relatively cool climate: the thick-skinned, rot-resistant black Tannat grape from South-West France is the leading variety. A clutch of modern wineries are working hard to soften the tannic Tannat; they are also producing snappy Sauvignon Blanc and fresh Cabernet Franc and Merlot. Best producers: Bouza, Carrau, Castillo Viejo, Filgueira, Juanicó, PISANO, Stagnari, Toscanini, Viñedo de los Vientos.

BRAZIL

Look at Brazil, how vast it is. Yet in all this expanse, running from 33° South to 5° North, there's nowhere ideal to site a vineyard. Aridity is the problem in the north, humidity in the south. Even so, they do manage to make some very attractive wines, and vineyards in the far south-east are promising. The Vale de São Francisco in the far north is an ambitious tropical undertaking, producing two harvests a year. Sparkling wine is the most consistent Brazilian style.

OTHER COUNTRIES

Peru has seemingly good vineyard sites in the Ica Valley south of Lima. Bolivia has few vineyards, but they're incredibly high. Venezuela's chief claim to fame is that some of her subtropical vines give three crops a year!

2010 VINTAGE REPORT

High quality, small crop – sums up the vintage in Argentina. Late frosts and golfball-sized hail led to 10% fewer grapes than normal. What survived – naturally concentrated and benefiting from otherwise perfect growing conditions – looks to be one of the best vintages this century.

On 27 February Chile suffered a massive earthquake. Many of Chile's more southerly wine-growing regions were affected, but miraculously the vineyards and wineries largely came through unscathed. Owing to early spring frosts and a cool summer growing season, the grape harvest was running about 2–3 weeks late in many regions and the harvest commenced in mid-March. Early indications show that the overall quality is very high, but the cooler conditions will result in total yields being about 15% down on the record 2009 levels.

South American entries in the A–Z section (pages 58–321).

ARGENTINA	Terrazas de Los	PRODUCERS	Luis Felipe Edwards
Mendoza	Andes	Agustinos	Matetic Vineyards
Patagonia	Trapiche	Almaviva	Montes
La Rioja	Zuccardi	Anakena	Pérez Cruz
Salta		Carmen	San Pedro Tarapacá
San Juan	CHILE	Casa Lapostolle	Santa Rita
	Aconcagua	Casa Marín	Seña
	Bío Bío	Casa Silva	Tabalí
PRODUCERS	Casablanca	Casablanca, Viña	Torres, Miguel
Achaval Ferrer	Central Valley	Casas del Bosque	Undurraga
Catena Zapata	Colchagua	Concha y Toro	Valdivieso
Cobos	Curicó	Cono Sur	Ventisquero
Colomé	Elqui	Cousiño Macul	von Siebenthal
Dominio del Plata	Limarí	De Martino	
Doña Paula	Maipo	Emiliana Orgánico	SEE ALSO
Fabre Montmayou	Maule	Errázuriz	Carmenère
Fournier, O	Rapel	Falernia	Malbec
Las Moras	San Antonio	Foumier, O	
Noemía	(Leyda)	Haras de Pirque	
Norton		La Rosa, Viña	
Pascual Toso			

SOUTH AFRICA

South Africa celebrated its wine industry's 350th birthday year with an exceptional harvest in 2009. Destructive spring floods in some regions and summer fires – particularly a five-week-long blaze around Stellenbosch – put a dampener on quality and quantity for some unfortunate producers, but on the whole, winemakers couldn't have wished for a better year for both whites and reds. The good news continued with a healthy upward trend in exports: close to 390 million litres left South Africa's shores in 2009. The UK remains the biggest export destination, where South Africa continues to rank as the fastest-growing wine category. More encouraging still is the increase of sales at higher price points. Less healthy is the pressure on grape prices at the lower end of the market; for some growers the situation is becoming untenable. But as new, quality producers from across the winelands enter the market, the increasing diversity of variety and style makes South African wine one of the most exciting categories to choose from.

GRAPE VARIETIES AND WINE REGIONS

The Cape's winelands run roughly 400km (250 miles) north and east of Cape Town, although small pockets of new vineyards are taking the winelands way outside their traditional territory. Wine, albeit in tiny quantities, is now being produced from grapes grown in the mountains above the Eastern Cape town of Plettenberg Bay, better known for its holidaymakers than its vines, and from vineyards in the Drakensberg region of KwaZulu-Natal. Plantings generally continue to decrease, though achieving the right balance between white and red varieties, according to demand, appears to be an unending journey; red wine is currently in short supply, so new plantings are likely to increase again. The current share of vineyard area is 54% in favour of whites. Major white varieties are Chenin Blanc, Sauvignon Blanc, Colombard and

Chardonnay, with Cabernet Sauvignon and Shiraz leading reds, though Pinotage was the most planted red according to the 2008 statistics. But Rhône varieties still generate most excitement: as well as Syrah/Shiraz, there's Grenache, Cinsaut and Mourvèdre for reds, and Viognier, Grenache Blanc and Roussanne for whites.

With the major grape varieties being planted over the entire Western Cape winelands, there is little typicity of origin, although some areas are historically associated with specific varieties or styles. Stellenbosch lays claim to some of the best red wines; maritime-influenced Constantia, and Cape Point on the other side of the Peninsula mountain chain, produce exhilarating Sauvignon Blanc, a variety also showing great promise in other coastal areas, right from Upper Langkloof, a ward in the eastern part of Klein Karoo, to Durbanville and Darling on the west coast and even further north to Doring Bay near Vredendal in the Olifants River region, as well as upland Elgin in the Overberg district. Many of these areas are also producing distinctive blends of Semillon and Sauvignon Blanc. Other cool areas include Walker Bay, where the focus is Pinot Noir. Chardonnay, long associated with inland Robertson, is now making its mark with Cap Classique sparkling wines as well as citrous, nutty still wines. This warmer area is also recognized for fortifieds, mainly Muscadel (Muscat). Further to the east, Calitzdorp makes some highly regarded port styles. Inland areas such as Swartland along the west coast have good affinity with Shiraz and other Rhône varieties; white blends including Chenin, Chardonnay and Viognier are starting to create waves.

CLASSIFICATIONS

The Wine of Origin (WO) system divides wine-producing areas into regions, districts, wards and single vineyards. Varietal, vintaged wines must be made from at least 85% of the named grape and vintage.

2010 VINTAGE REPORT

A year that produced much better quality than an inclement spring might have suggested. Ferocious wind at the end of October followed by an unusually prolonged wet and cold spell adversely affected both flowering and the young vine shoots. High disease pressure also had to be controlled. Cool, dry conditions through early summer allowed for long ripening with fruit high in natural acid, intense flavours and full ripeness at lower sugars. A longer and more extreme heatwave in early March was a negative for fruit still on the vines, but generally producers are happy they have at least some wonderful wines in the cellar; their tears are spared for a low crop, anything between 20% and 60%, with some vineyards even worse affected.

South African entries in the A–Z section (pages 58–321).

WINE REGIONS	Boekenhoutskloof	Hamilton Russell	Saxenburg
Constantia WO	Bouchard Finlayson	Hartenberg Estate	Simonsig
Durbanville WO	Buitenverwachting	Jordan	Spice Route
Elgin WO	Cape Chamonix	Kanonkop	Springfield Estate
Franschhoek WO	Cape Point	Klein Constantia	Steenberg
Paarl WO	Cluver, Paul	KWV	Thelema
Robertson WO	De Trafford	L'Avenir	Veenwouden
Stellenbosch WO	Distell	Meerlust	Vergelegen
Walker Bay WO	Ellis, Neil	Morgenhof	Villiera
	Els, Ernie	Mulderbosch	Warwick
PRODUCERS	Fairview	Rust en Vrede	
Beck, Graham	Glen Carlou	Rustenberg	SEE ALSO
Beyerskloof	Grangehurst	Sadie Family	Pinotage

OTHER WINE COUNTRIES

ALGERIA With many vines over 40 years old, there should be grea
potential here, but political uncertainty hinders progress despite governmen
support. The western coastal province of Oran produces three-quarters o
Algeria's wine, including the soft but muscular Coteaux de Tlemcen wine
and dark, beefy reds of the Coteaux de Mascara.

BELGIUM Belgium's vineyards were established by the Romans, but it i
only within the past 20 years that climate change has once again allowed vine
to thrive, and the country now has a budding wine industry, admittedly on
very small scale. There are about 20 commercial producers, many of whom ar
based in an area known as Hageland, east of Brussels. Pitting itself against on
of the strongest, most varied beer and food cultures in the world, Belgian win
is rising to the challenge and finding a place on restaurant lists. Pinot Noi
and Chardonnay are grown for sparkling and still wines, most notably som
Chablis-like Chardonnay.

BULGARIA After success in the 1980s and disarray in the 90s, som
progress followed the introduction of new wine legislation in 2001, an
investment in new vineyards is beginning to gather pace. Entry into the EI
in 2007 has encouraged a more positive attitude in the vineyards, and ther
are signs of single-estate wines emerging, although in some regions there is
shortage of vineyard workers as they seek employment in wealthier EU state
New World influences are having some effect, although few wines shine
Cabernet Sauvignon and Merlot dominate, but local grapes – plumm
Mavrud, meaty Gamza, deep Melnik, fruity white Dimiat and Misket – ca
be good. Established wineries such as Boyar Estates, Khan Krum an
Suhindol are being joined by new operations every year, some finance
locally, others with international backing. Stork Nest and Bessa Valley ar
two of the largest, and anyone doubting Bulgaria's potential should taste th
eminently affordable and excellent Enira wines from Bessa Valley (owned b
Stephan von Neipperg of Ch. CANON-LA-GAFFELIÈRE in St-Emilion in France).

CANADA The strict VQA (Vintners Quality Alliance) maintains hig
standards in British Columbia and Ontario, and there is continuing progres
in the 2 most important regions – OKANAGAN VALLEY in British Columbia an
the NIAGARA PENINSULA in Ontario. Also jutting into Lake Ontario is the up
and-coming PRINCE EDWARD COUNTY. Sweet Icewine, made primarily fron
Vidal and Riesling, but occasionally from Cabernet Franc and other varietals
is still Canada's trump card. But producers have realized they also mak
world-class Chardonnay and have begun to market Canadian Chardonna
more aggressively. Pinot Gris, Riesling, Sauvignon Blanc an
Gewurztraminer also do well; Merlot, Cabernet Franc, Cabernet Sauvignon
even Syrah in British Columbia and Pinot Noir in Ontario, are producin
tasty red wines.

CHINA Though China officially promotes wine (especially red), it
potential remains unfulfilled as the majority of Chinese are reluctant to drin
it. This isn't surprising when you consider the relative incompatibility o
much Chinese cuisine with the dry, slightly bitter flavours of much red wine
Aromatic and zesty whites suit the food much better, but red is the luck
colour in China and it's red that every producer wants to push. However, a
the Chinese economy expands, demand for its wines is increasing
particularly in the cities. Home-grown premium wines are emerging an

reign investment proceeds apace with continual improvements in ticulture and winemaking. Exactly what effect Ch. LAFITE-ROTHSCHILD's cision to create a wine estate there will have isn't clear. But one thing is ear: Lafite-Rothschild is the most clamoured-for of the top French reds. nything local with the Lafite imprimatur *will* sell and *won't* be cheap. hina's vineyards are increasing rapidly; it now has the fourth-largest area der vine, with massive new plantings every year – mainly international apes such as Chardonnay and Cabernet Sauvignon, with some traditional hinese, German and Russian varieties. There are now over well over 400 ineries. Major producers include Changyu, Dynasty, Great Wall, HUADONG d Xintian. One of China's biggest problems is where to plant grapes with e potential for top quality. The most popular region is Shandong on the stern coast, but persistent summer rains and wet autumns mean it's difficult achieve top-quality reds. Ningsha, 2000km (1240 miles) inland from handong, with a continental climate and long dry autumns, is the latest hot p for reds. The south-west province of Yunnan has become popular with owers and several new wineries have been established here, despite pretty treme conditions.

ROATIA Croatia has a strong viticultural heritage and an undercurrent of sing potential: bulk whites dominate but small private producers are nerging. What the country needs now is more investment, more technology the vineyard and winery and a fair price for the grapes; planned embership of the EU will undoubtedly help. Tourism is flourishing and this ould help popularize the wines – so long as foreigners can pronounce them. he most established red vineyards are on the Dalmatian coast – much of the d Yugoslav red used to come from here – where international varieties are ing planted alongside gutsy indigenous grapes: deep, tannic Plavac Mali – lated to Zinfandel – has long produced the best-known red wines, but there e several other indigenous varieties at least as good. The original site for infandel (locally known as Crljenak, and down to just half a dozen vines) has een replanted and should become a shrine for Zinheads. The most popular hite grapes are Malvazija (Malvasia) from Istria up towards the Italian order and Grasevina (Welschriesling) in the centre of the country. Style and uality vary widely but the best are light and fresh. On the Serbian border at nska Gora, there is excellent Traminac (Traminer). GRGICH of California has winery on the Peljesac peninsula. Frano Milos (also on the Peljesac ninsula) and Kozlovic and Matosevic in Istria are other names to look for.

YPRUS Modernization and quality are coming to Cyprus. Large wineries ch as Sodap (now Kamanterena) and Keo have moved to the Troodos ountains. Small wineries such as Argyrides, Kyperounda, Tsiakkas, lassides and Zambartas show real promise. Good reds from the indigenous aratheftiko grape, and Lefkada is useful in blends; Xynisteri is capable of esh whites if grown at altitude. Rich, treacly COMMANDARIA has been famous nce the Crusades.

HE CZECH REPUBLIC The vineyards of Bohemia in the north-west and loravia in the south-east are mainly planted with white varieties – Grüner eltliner, Müller-Thurgau, Riesling, Pinot Blanc, Pinot Gris – with pockets red such as St-Laurent and Lemberger (Blaufränkisch). Beer is far more iportant than wine in the Czech culture, but in a world where too many ines are becoming excessively oaky and alcoholic, the fragile, scented, low-coholic charms of Czech wine become more and more attractive.

DENMARK Grapes shouldn't grow this far north: Copenhagen, li▮ Edinburgh in Scotland, is just below the 56th parallel. But as global warmi▮ pushes the threshold for viticulture ever northward and new grape varieties a▮ developed to thrive here, the EU permitted commercial wine production ▮ 2000. The industry is still tiny, with about 40 growers taking advantage of t▮ long hours of sunshine to ripen their grapes. Neighbouring southern Swede▮ with very similar conditions, is also getting in on the act.

ENGLAND The UK's winegrowing industry has celebrated more th▮ 50 vintages since the 'revival' of commercial vineyards in the early 195▮ However, with around 1,350 ha (3,334 acres) of vines, 450 vineyards (ma▮ very small), 120 wineries and an average annual output of around 2.2 milli▮ bottles, it is still pretty small. Nevertheless, producers have learnt whi▮ varieties are successful (Bacchus, Schönburger and Seyval Blanc for white▮ Rondo, Regent, Dornfelder and Pinot Noir for reds; but above a▮ Chardonnay, Pinot Noir and Pinot Meunier for quality sparklers), how ▮ train and trellis them to cope with the (usually) cool summers and – mo▮ importantly – how to make sound, sometimes excellent, wines. In particul▮ sparkling wines have shown they can equal CHAMPAGNE in quality and t▮ area planted to the classic Champagne varieties is now approaching 50% ▮ the UK total and almost all new plantings are of the Champagne varieti▮ The quality is likely to be excellent, but I fear there'll be a glut of grapes in▮ few years time. Growers from Champagne are taking notice and seve▮ famous houses have been looking for sites; a producer of very go▮ Champagne from Avize has planted 4ha (10 acres) in Hampshire and mo▮ are sure to follow. Regulations now require growers to submit their wines f▮ testing before they can label them 'English'; wines labelled 'UK table win▮ should be avoided.

The most popular winemaking counties are: West Sussex (NYETIMBE▮ RIDGEVIEW), Kent (Balfour, Biddenden, CHAPEL DOWN, Sandhurst), Surr▮ (DENBIES), Essex (New Hall), Hampshire, (Wickham), East Sussex (BREA▮ BOTTOM, Davenport), Devon (SHARPHAM, Yearlstone), Gloucestershire (THR▮ CHOIRS), Berkshire (STANLAKE PARK) and Cornwall (CAMEL VALLEY). 2007 a▮ 2008 were both difficult years for growers, with poor flowering conditio▮ leading to small harvests. What was picked was good, though. 2009 was ▮ amazing year and without any doubt, *the* best year that UK vineyards ha▮ ever had. With potential alcohol levels for hitherto difficult to ripen varieti▮ such as Chardonnay and Pinot Noir in the 11%-13% level, the UK really ▮ becoming the new Chablis, or Champagne, or Sancerre or… well, Sancer▮ isn't so wishful. A new vineyard is being planted on Sark (Channel Islanc▮ and the consultant has stated rather optimistically that Sark is on the sam▮ latitude as the Loire Valley! With this in mind, he's planting Cheni▮ Chardonnay and Pinot Gris – but so far no Sauvignon. For that you'll have ▮ wait for Denbies' new experimental plot to crop.

GEORGIA Georgia faces many challenges – lack of regulatio▮ counterfeiting, and a recent ban on exports to Russia, its biggest market – b▮ its diverse climates (from subtropical to moderate continental) and soils cou▮ produce every style imaginable. The tourist industry is vibrant and helpi▮ introduce Georgian wines to a wider audience. International and indigeno▮ varieties abound; the peppery, powerful red Saperavi could be a world-beat▮ Most wine is still pretty rustic, but investment is beginning to have an effe▮ with GWS (Georgian Wines & Spirits Company, 75% owned by Pern▮ Ricard) leading the way, and dozens more wine producers keen to excel.

REECE The reputation, distribution and sales of Greek wines, both red d white, continue to improve, particularly in the US, but the Greek ancial crisis has badly affected their domestic market. The new generation f winemakers and grape growers, many of them trained in France, Australia e California, have a clear vision of the flavours they want to achieve and their ines are modern but marvellously original too. Polarization between cheap lk and expensive boutique wines continues, but large companies such as outari, Kourtaki and Tsantali are upping the quality stakes and flavours prove every vintage. More vineyard and marketing work – many labels are ill difficult to understand – is needed. International plantings have led to rprising and successful blends with indigenous varieties such as the red giorgitiko, Limnio and Xynomavro, and white Assyrtiko (often blended ith Sémillon), Malagousia, Moschofilero and Roditis. Quality areas: Naousa d Nemea for reds, Santorini for whites, SAMOS for sweet Muscats, Patras for essert Mavrodaphne. Wineries to watch include: Aidarinis, Argyros, NTONOPOULOS, Gentilini, GEROVASSILIOU, Hatzimichalis, Kyr Yianni, Domaine osta LAZARIDI, Mercouri, Papaïoannou, Strofilia and Tselepos.

UNGARY Hungary makes remarkably good whites, improving reds and utstanding sweet wines, and has joined the EU, yet few of us have much ea about her as a wine country. Stringent regulations and vestment/advice from Australian and western European companies and onsultants – for example at the BALATONBOGLÁR winery – have put Hungary ack on the international wine map. There is renewed interest in native rieties such as Furmint, Hárslevelü and Irsai Olivér for whites, Kékfrankos 3laufränkisch) and Kadarka (the traditional grape used in BIKAVÉR) for reds, d top Hungarian winemakers – Akos Kamocsay (at HILLTOP), Vilmos hummerer, Attila Gere and others – are now a solid force. But price and putation remain low and many vineyards are being abandoned out of esperation. TOKAJI in particular has yet to develop the world-class reputation s wines deserve.

NDIA India's climate is generally unsuitable for wine production: only a nall percentage of the 68,000ha (170,000 acres) of vines is used for wine; oth international varieties and ancient Indian ones, such as Arkesham and rkavati, are planted. Wine consumption is increasing rapidly and with unitive import duties on foreign bottles the potential for growth is evident. HATEAU INDAGE, with vineyards in the Maharashtra hills east of Mumbai 3ombay), dominates the market and produces still and sparkling wines. Sula ineyards is leading the way with screwcaps on all its wines – bright, fresh, ositively cool-climate flavours are the result – and is planning to bring its rea under vines up to 650ha (1600 acres). Advice from international wine uru Michel Rolland put Grover Vineyards in Bangalore on the map. There'll e a lot more in the future, but growth will be a stop-start affair.

RAEL Coastal Israel is hot and humid, so vineyards are being planted in he cooler, higher-altitude Upper Galilee, Golan Heights and Judean Hills. uality is good and improving, but high-alcohol wines are becoming idespread. Thankfully wineries such as CASTEL, Carmel, Flam and Chillag are edicated to producing wines in a more elegant style. The best rated wines are abernet Sauvignon and Bordeaux-style blends, so it is a pleasure to also find dgier wines like old-vine Carignan, Petite Sirah and some very good Shiraz. Vineries leading the way range from the giants Golan Heights and Carmel, o the smaller CASTEL, Clos de Gat, Margalit and YATIR.

53

Kosher wine, necessary for observant Jews and usually suitable for vega and vegetarians, is common in Israel, even though not all Israeli wines a kosher. Regular winemaking methods are used, but there has to be a religio Jewish workforce and winemaking materials have to be certified as kosh Some kosher wines are genuinely international quality, like Castel, Yatir an Yarden from Israel, Covenant and Herzog from California. Several t French wineries – such as LAURENT-PERRIER, POMMERY, Ch. LÉOVILLE-POYFERR Ch. PONTET-CANET, Ch. SMITH-HAUT-LAFITTE, and Ch. VALANDRAUD – and sor big brands such as SKALLI-FORTANT DE FRANCE and MOUTON-CADET have made kosher cuvée.

JAPAN As long as there is confusion between which wines are 100% loca grown and which are multi-country blends (which most are), Japanese win especially those made from indigenous varieties such as Koshu, will nev really be appreciated by an international audience, though 2010 did see Koshu export drive hit Europe. One has to assume that the present situati suits most producers, who sell almost all their wines locally. However, t Japanese are increasingly interested in wine, and their national wine sho now attracts entries from around the world. Despite humid conditions, wi is produced in almost every province. SUNTORY is in the best regic Yamanashi, and is expanding its vineyards. Other main players are Mercia Sapporo, Manns and the unpromising-sounding Domaine Sogga.

LEBANON Very good reds with the full fruit of the Lebanese sun a spiciness of the eastern Mediterranean. Most wineries lie in the Bekaa Valle CHATEAU MUSAR, for years unchallenged, now has some quality rivals: C Kefraya and Ch. Ksara have made good wine for a while; they have be joined by Massaya, Clos St Thomas, Dom. Wardy and Dom. des Tourell Latest development is a number of new, highly individual boutique wineri including Karam, Ch. Belle-Vue, Dom. de Baal, Ch. Marsyas and Ch. Kou:

LUXEMBOURG With one of the world's highest levels of wi consumption per capita, very little wine is exported. Co-operatives domina here and quality is about what you would expect. Plantings of Elbling an Rivaner (Müller-Thurgau) are in decline, and are being replaced with quali varietals such as Riesling, Pinot Noir, Chardonnay and Gewürztramin *Crémant* (sparkling) wines continue to increase in quality and popularity.

MALTA The first impression of Malta is of an arid rocky island squeezed f of people and with barely enough soil to grow basic food crops. And it *nev* seems to rain. Well, it does rain, and its limestone rock is able to absorb a hold a significant amount of water in reserve. Even so, water is scarce, but t vine doesn't need much – often the morning and evening dews from the s breezes is enough to keep it going. Most wines used to be made fro imported Italian grapes, and they weren't bad. But, especially on the sm island of Gozo – famous locally for being green, but green is a relative term Malta – serious vineyards are being developed and attractive wines are no available from 100% Maltese grapes. They're good, but you can taste the su

MEXICO In the far north-west of Mexico, in Baja California, some go reds are made by L A CETTO as well as by smaller companies such as Mor Xanic and Casa de Piedra. In the rest of the country, only high-altitude are such as the Parras Valley and Zacatecas have the potential for quality win Casa Madero, in the Parras Valley, has some success with Cabernet Sauvigno

Other promising grape varieties include Nebbiolo, Petite Sirah, Tempranillo, Zinfandel and Barbera, with Viognier and Chardonnay also planted.

MOLDOVA Moldovan winegrowers suffered a major setback in 2006 when their main export market, Russia, banned imports of their wines. Standards of winemaking and equipment leave much to be desired, but fruit quality is good, and international players, including PENFOLDS and winemakers Jacques Lurton, Hugh Ryman and Alain Thiénot, have worked with local wineries. However, chaotic social conditions have led to many attempts being abandoned.

MONTENEGRO This red-wine-dominated part of the former Yugoslavia shows some potential in the beefy Vranac grape with its bitter cherry flavours - but the worst wines are really poor.

MOROCCO Known for big, sweet-fruited reds that once found a ready blending market in France. France is still the biggest export market, but the wines have improved dramatically since the 1990s and domestic consumption is increasing, especially among young urban professionals. Massive investment by Castel Frères kickstarted the renaissance, and quality is on the rise at Morocco's leading producer, Celliers de Meknès. Domaine el Baraka and Domaine Larroque are promising, and French producers Bernard Magrez (sometimes in harness with Gérard Depardieu) and Alain GRAILLOT are making some good wines here, especially from Syrah.

NETHERLANDS The vineyard area is expanding rapidly: there are currently around 175ha (430 acres), in the hands of more than 150 commercial growers, most of whom sell all their wines locally. The best vineyards are in the southern part of the country, in the rolling hills of Limburg. Chardonnay is the most promising grape variety. Growers have set themselves the additional challenge of living up to Holland's 'green' image, and are looking into what can be achieved organically. Good luck.

ROMANIA The huge vineyard area has declined somewhat in recent years as hybrid grape varieties are pulled up, to be replanted with *Vitis vinifera* grapes such as Pinot Noir, Cabernet Sauvignon, Merlot and the native Feteasca Negra for reds, Pinot Gris and Chardonnay for whites. International-backed ventures such as Cramele Recas, Halewood (Prahova Valley) and Carl Reh are a sign of the mini-revolution, but challenges remain. The appellation system is of limited value, although Dealul Mare, Murfatlar and Cotnari all have ancient reputations. Accession to the EU in 2007 has done little to help the fortunes of Romanian growers as there is now a shortage of labour to work the vineyards and there has been an increase in the amount of wine being imported into Romania from Spain and Italy.

SLOVAKIA The eastern part of the old Czechoslovakia, with its cool-climate vineyards, is dominated by white varieties – Pinot Blanc, Riesling, Grüner Veltliner, Irsai Olivér – with the occasional fruity Frankovka (Blaufränkisch) red. Western investment is rapidly improving the quality.

SLOVENIA Many of the old Yugoslav Federation's best vineyards are here. Potential is considerable, and some interesting wines are emerging, with whites generally better than reds. A simplified appellation system and the increasing popularity of Slovenia as a holiday and second-home region should increase availability. On the Italian border, Brda and Vipava have go-ahead co-operatives, and Kraski Teran is a red wine of repute. The Movia range, from the Kristancic family, looks promising.

SWITZERLAND Fendant (Chasselas) is the main grape for spritzy but neutral whites from the VALAIS and VAUD. Like the fruity DÔLE reds, they are best drunk very young. German-speaking cantons produce whites from Müller-Thurgau and mostly light reds and rosés from Pinot Noir (Blauburgunder); top producers, such as Daniel GANTENBEIN, make more powerful versions. Italian-speaking TICINO concentrates on Merlots, which have been increasingly impressive since 2000. Serious wines, especially in Valais, use Syrah, Chardonnay, Marsanne and traditional varieties like Amigne and Petite Arvine. Indeed, the traditional varieties, of which there are many, are undergoing a revival. Pinot Noir from the Valais is greatly improved. See also NEUCHÂTEL.

THAILAND I first tasted Thai wine a few years ago: it was a light and fruity red and impressive for what I thought of as subtropical conditions. Since then serious Shiraz and Chenin Blanc wines have shown that Thailand's high altitude vineyards are capable of some tasty offerings. The once-common practice of blending local and imported wines (without declaring it on the label) is lessening.

TUNISIA Ancient wine traditions have had an injection of new life from international investment, and results so far are encouraging. Tourism soaks up most of the production and little is exported.

TURKEY The world's sixth-largest grape producer, where there is enormous potential and variety, but only 2–4% ends up as wine. Wine growers have a difficult time in Turkey, but suddenly there are major investments in quality by existing large wineries and new small ones. Already there are significant regional differences emerging with the European Thrace vineyards and those down the Aegean coast growing good international grapes as well as some as yet obscure local varieties. Central and south-eastern Anatolia have very ancient vineyards, mostly planted with ancient varieties like the white Emir and Narince and the fascinating reds Kalecik Karasi, Öküzgözü (which hold the world record for most umlauts in a single grape variety) and the muscular yet scented Bogazkere from the tribal lands in the east. There are several large companies, led by Kavaklidere, Doluca and Kayra – all making some seriously good wines. Promising new wineries include Pamukkale, Baküs Butik, Corvus, Turnsan, Kocabag, Likya, Prodom, Umurbey, Idol and Buyülübag.

UKRAINE The Crimea's vineyards are the most important, producing hearty reds, sweet and sparkling wines; there's a surprisingly good sweet red sparkler, and sweet Muscatels are considered to be a cause for national pride, especially the Massandra brand. The Odessa region is successful with its sparkling wines, the best-known facilities being the Inkerman winery, Novy Svet and Zolota Balka. European investment is said to be in the pipeline.

A–Z

OF WINES, PRODUCERS, GRAPES & WINE REGIONS

In the following pages there are over
1600 entries covering the world's top wines, as well as leading
producers, main wine regions and grape
varieties, followed on page 322 by a glossary of wine terms
and classifications.

*On page 4 you will find a full explanation of
How to Use the A–Z. On page 331 there is an index
of all wine producers in the book, to help you find the
world's best wines.*

AALTO *Ribera del Duero DO, Castilla y León, Spain* Former VEGA SICILIA wine
maker Mariano García and ex-RIBERA DEL DUERO appellation boss Javier
Zaccagnini created this winery in 1999. From the outset, they have
challenged top Spanish producers with their dense but elegant reds.
Aalto★★ and old vines cuvée Aalto PS★★. Best years: (2007) 06 05 04 03
01 00 99.

ABACELA *Umpqua Valley AVA, Oregon, USA* Earl and Hilda Jones planted the
first Tempranillo vines in the Pacific Northwest, in the Umpqua Valley
southern OREGON, in 1995. Today they produce Tempranillo, Syrah,
Merlot, Dolcetto, Malbec, Grenache and Albariño. the Tempranillo
(Reserve★★) has been the most successful wine; the Albariño★★ is
surprisingly similar to those of GALICIA. Best years: (2009) (08) 07 06 05.

ABEJA *Walla Walla Valley AVA, Washington State, USA* Located in a century-old
farmstead in the foothills of the Blue Mountains, Abeja is a state-of-the-
art facility in a romantic setting. Winemaker John Abbott produces crisp
Viognier★★ in small quantities, rich and concentrated Chardonnay★,
spicy Syrah★, supple Merlot and fine Cabernet Sauvignon★★. A tiny
amount of Cabernet Sauvignon Reserve★★ is assembled from select
barrels. Best years: (Cabernet Sauvignon) (2008) 07 06 05.

ABRUZZO-MOLISE *Italy* Abruzzo, with its (viniculturally speaking)
satellite Molise, is part maritime, part mountainous. White Trebbiano
d'Abruzzo DOC is usually dry and neutral; tastier whites come from the
Pecorino grape. The fruity, full-coloured Montepulciano d'Abruzzo DOC,
despite high production, can be a red of real character, as can its rosé partner
Cerasuolo. Training techniques are being revised to favour quality over
quantity, and new DOCs and DOCGs are being introduced. Good producers
include Contesa★★, Illuminati★★, Marramiero★★, Masciarelli★★, Orlandi
Contucci Ponno★, Tollo★, Valentini★★★.

ACACIA *Carneros AVA, California, USA* Leading producer of Chardonnay and
Pinot Noir from CARNEROS. The regular Carneros Chardonnay★ is
restrained but attractive. Pinot Noirs include Carneros★ and a number of
very good single-vineyard examples (Beckstoffer Vineyard★★). Best
years: (Pinot Noir) (2008) 07 06 05 03 02 01 00.

ACHAVAL FERRER *Mendoza, Argentina* A former garage winery created in
1998, and now one of Argentina's most sought-after labels. 80-year-old
vines in the La Consulta area of Uco Valley produce Finca
Altamira★★★, a Malbec bursting with personality. Also superb single-
vineyard Malbecs Bella Vista★★★ and Mirador★★★ as well as more
approachable red blend Quimera★ and regular Malbec★. Best years: 2007
06 05 04 03 02.

ACONCAGUA *Chile* A warm region and home to some of Chile's best
reds, from Cabernet Sauvignon, Syrah and Carmenère. Recent
vineyard developments in the Aconcagua Costa region, close to the sea,
are proving very exciting for Sauvignon Blanc. Best producers:
ERRÁZURIZ★★, SEÑA★★, VON SIEBENTHAL★.

JEAN-BAPTISTE ADAM *Alsace AC, Alsace, France* Long-established family
vineyard in Ammerschwihr with a reputation for luscious, classically
perfumed Gewurztraminer★★ from the recently created Kaefferkopf
Grand Cru, as well as concentrated Riesling★★, herbaceous Pinot Gris★
and an exciting Pinot Noir★★ given 18 months in oak. Best years:
(Kaefferkopf Gewurztraminer) (2009) 08 07 05 04 02 01 00 99 98 97 95.

TIM ADAMS *Clare Valley, South Australia* Important maker of fine, traditional wine whose need to buy in grapes may disappear since his bargain purchase of 75ha (185 acres) of vines from LEASINGHAM. Classic dry Riesling★★, oaky Semillon★★ and rich, opulent Shiraz★★ (both sometimes ★★★), Cabernet★★ and Cabernet-Merlot★★. The Fergus★★ can be a glorious Grenache-based blend, and minty, peppery Aberfeldy Shiraz★★★ is a remarkable, at times unnerving, mouthful of brilliance from 100-year-old vines. The botrytis Semillon★ can be super. Best years: (Aberfeldy Shiraz) (2009) 08 06 05 04 03 02 01 **00 99 98 96 94**.

Tim Adams

2008
RIESLING
CLARE VALLEY

WINE OF AUSTRALIA
MADE BY TIM ADAMS WINES, WAREHOUSE RD CLARE, STH. AUST.
750mL 11.5% Vol.

ADELAIDE HILLS *South Australia* Small, exciting region 30 minutes' drive from Adelaide. High altitude affords a cool, moist climate ideal for fine table wines and superb sparkling wine. Consistently good Sauvignon Blanc and Chardonnay, promising Pinot Noir and increasingly exciting, fleshy Shiraz from warmer southern vineyards. Best producers: Ashton Hills★, Barratt, Bird in Hand★, HENSCHKE★★, The Lane★, Longview★, Nepenthe★★, PETALUMA★★, Riposte★, SHAW & SMITH★★, Geoff WEAVER★★.

ADELSHEIM VINEYARD *Willamette Valley AVA, Oregon, USA* Over the past 3 decades, Adelsheim has established a reputation for excellent, generally unfiltered, Pinot Noir – especially cherry-scented Elizabeth's Reserve★ and Bryan Creek Vineyard★ – and for rich Chardonnay Caitlin's Reserve★. Also a bright, minerally Pinot Gris★. Best years: (Elizabeth's Reserve) (2008) 07 06 **05** 04 03 02.

AGLIANICO DEL VULTURE DOC *Basilicata, Italy* Red wine from the Aglianico grape (considered by some as among the top 3 red varieties of Italy) grown on the steep slopes of extinct volcano Mt Vulture. Despite the zone's location almost on the same latitude as Naples, the harvest here is sometimes later than in BAROLO, 750km (470 miles) to the north-west, because the Aglianico grape ripens very late at altitude. The best wines are structured, complex and long-lived. Best producers: Basilium★, Bisceglia★, D'Angelo★★, Elena Fucci★, Cantine del Notaio★★, Tenuta del Portale, Le Querce★, Consorzio Viticoltori Associati del Vulture (Carpe Diem★). Best years: (2009) (08) 07 06 **05** 04 03 01 00 98 97.

AGUSTINOS *Aconcagua and Bío Bío, Chile* Organic producer of elegant Pinot Noir★ and Malbec★, as well as whites. The BÍO BÍO estate is impressive. Agustinos is part of the VC Family Estates group – along with Gracia, Porta and Veranda – which owns the majority of the fledgling Pinot Noir plantings in this promising region, as well as vineyards in Argentina.

AHR *Germany* The Ahr Valley is a small 558ha (1380-acre) mainly red wine region south of Bonn. Chief grape varieties are the Spätburgunder (Pinot Noir) and Portugieser. Adeneur★, Deutzerhof★, Meyer-Näkel★★ and Stodden★ are the best of a growing band of serious producers.

AIRÉN Spain's – and indeed the world's – most planted white grape can make fresh, modern, but generally neutral-flavoured wines, with some eye-opening exceptions, such as Ercavio's stunning old-vines white from Toledo. Airén is grown all over the centre and south of Spain, especially in La MANCHA, VALDEPEÑAS and ANDALUCIA (where it's called Lairén).

ALBAN *San Luis Obispo County, California, USA* Based in the cool Arroyo Grande district of Edna Valley, John Alban is a RHÔNE specialist. He offers 2 Viogniers (Estate★★, Central Coast★★) and a Roussanne★★ laden with honey notes. There are 3 Syrahs (Reva★★★, Lorraine★★ and Seymour's Vineyard★★), intense Grenache★★ and Pandora★★, a blend of about 60% Grenache, 40% Syrah. These are some of America's purest expressions of Rhône varietals, despite some extremely high alcohol levels. Best years: (Syrah) 2006 **05 04 03 02 01 00 99**.

ALBARIÑO Possibly Spain's most characterful white grape. It is a speciality of RIAS BAIXAS in Galicia in Spain's rainy north-west and, as Alvarinho, in Portugal's VINHO VERDE region. When well made, Albariño wines have fascinating flavours of apricot, peach, grapefruit and Muscat grapes, refreshingly high acidity, highish alcohol – and unrefreshingly high prices. The ever-present danger to quality is excessive yields.

ALENQUER DOC *Lisboa, Portugal* Maritime-influenced hills north of Lisbon, producing wines from (mostly) local grape varieties such as Castelão (Periquita) and Trincadeira, but also from Cabernet, Syrah and Chardonnay. Many wines are simply labelled LISBOA (ex-Estremadura). Best producers: Quinta do Carneiro, Quinta de Chocapalha★, Quinta da Cortezia, Quinta do Monte d'Oiro★★, Casa SANTOS LIMA★. Best years: (reds) 2009 **07 05 04 03 01 00**.

ALENTEJO *Portugal* A large chunk of southern Portugal south and east of Lisbon and, along with the DOURO, one of Portugal's fastest improving red wine regions. Potential is far from realized, but already some of Portugal's finest reds come from here. Vinho Regional wines are labelled Alentejano. Best producers: (reds) Quinta da Terrugem★★/ALIANCA, BACALHOA★ (Tinto da Ânfora Grande Escolha★★), Borba co-op★, CORTES DE CIMA★, Dona Maria★, ESPORAO★★, Fita Preta, Fundação Eugénio de Almeida (Cartuxa★, Pera-Manca★★), Paulo Laureano Vinus★, MALHADINHA NOVA★★, Monte da Penha, Mouchão★★, Quinta do Mouro★, João Portugal RAMOS★★, Herdade de São Miguel, SOGRAPE★, José de Sousa★, Terras de Alter. Best years: (reds) 2008 07 **05 04 01 00**.

ALEXANDER VALLEY AVA *Sonoma County, California, USA* AVA centred on the northern Russian River, which is fairly warm, with only patchy summer fog. Cabernet Sauvignon is highly successful here, with lovely, juicy fruit not marred by an excess of tannin. Chardonnay may also be good but is often overproduced and lacking in ripe, round flavours. Merlot and old-vine Zinfandel can be outstanding from hillside vineyards. Best producers: Alexander Valley Vineyards★, CLOS DU BOIS★, De Lorimier★, GEYSER PEAK★, JORDAN★, Murphy-Goode★★, RIDGE (Geyserville★★), SEGHESIO★★, SILVER OAK★★, SIMI★, Trentadue★★. See also RUSSIAN RIVER VALLEY AVA, SONOMA COUNTY. Best years: (reds) 2008 07 06 04 03 **02 01 99 97 95 91 90**.

ALGARVE *Portugal* Holiday region with mostly red wines in 4 DOCs: Lagoa, Lagos, Portimão and Tavira. Look out for reds and rosés from Sir Cliff Richard's Vida Nova, Quinta do Barranco Longo and Morgado da Torre.

ALIANÇA *Beira Litoral, Portugal* Aliança makes crisp, fresh whites and soft, approachable red BAIRRADAS★. Also made, either from its own vineyards or bought-in grapes or wines, are reds from the DÃO (Quinta da

Garrida★) and ALENTEJO (Quinta da Terrugem★★). Quinta dos Quatro Ventos★★ from the DOURO is the top red, a blend of Tinta Roriz, Touriga Franca and Touriga Nacional.

ALIGOTÉ French grape, found mainly in Burgundy, whose basic characteristic is a lemony tartness. It can make extremely refreshing wine, especially from old vines, but is generally rather dull and lean. The best comes from the village of Bouzeron in the CÔTE CHALONNAISE, where Aligoté has its own appellation. Occasionally also found in Moldova and Bulgaria. Drink young. Best producers: (Burgundy) COCHE-DURY★, A Ente★, J-H Goisot★, D MORTET★, les Temps Perdus, TOLLOT-BEAUT, Villaine★.

ALLEGRINI *Valpolicella DOC, Veneto, Italy* High-profile producer in VALPOLICELLA Classico, making single-vineyard IGTs La Grola★★ (Corvina with a bit of Syrah) and La Poja★★★ (100% Corvina) wines which show the great potential that exists for Veronese red as a table wine. Outstanding AMARONE★★★ and RECIOTO Giovanni Allegrini★★. Best years: (Amarone) (2009) (08) 07 **06 04 03 01 00 97 95**.

THIÉRRY ALLEMAND *Cornas AC, Rhône Valley, France* Thiérry Allemand has 5ha (12 acres) of high-quality hillside vines. He keeps yields low, uses little sulphur and makes top-class wines with clear fruit and very good depth. He produces 2 unfiltered expressions of CORNAS at its intense and powerful best: Chaillot★★ is marginally the lighter; Reynard★★★ is from a parcel of very old Syrah. Best years: (Reynard) 2009 08 07 06 05 04 03 01 00 99 98 96 95 94 91 90.

ALLENDE *Rioja DOCa, Rioja, Spain* One of the most admired new names in RIOJA making a mix of single-vineyard (*pago*) and high-quality blends. Scented, uncompromisingly concentrated reds include Aurus★★★, Calvario★★ and fresh, vibrant Allende★★. There is also a marvellous, scented white★★. Best years: (reds) (2007) 06 05 04 **03 02 01 00 99**.

ALMAVIVA★★★ *Maipo, Chile* State-of-the-art joint venture between CONCHA Y TORO and the Baron Philippe de Rothschild company (see MOUTON-ROTHSCHILD), located in MAIPO Valley's Tocornal vineyard at the foot of the Andes. A memorably powerful red from old Cabernet Sauvignon vines planted in alluvial, stony soils; it can be drunk at 5 years but should age for 10. Best years: 2007 06 **05 04 03 02 01**.

ALOXE-CORTON AC *Côte de Beaune, Burgundy, France* An important village at the northern end of the CÔTE DE BEAUNE producing mostly red wines from Pinot Noir. Its reputation is based on the 2 Grands Crus, CORTON (mainly red) and CORTON-CHARLEMAGNE (white only). Other vineyards in Aloxe-Corton used to be a source of tasty, good-value Burgundy, but nowadays the reds rarely exhibit their former characteristic blend of ripe fruit and appetizing savoury dryness. Almost all the white wine is classified as Grand Cru. Best producers: d'Ardhuy★, CHANDON DE BRIAILLES★, M Chapuis★, Marius Delarche★, Dubreuil-Fontaine★, Follin-Arbelet★, Camille Giroud★, Antonin Guyon★, JADOT★, Mallard, Rapet★, Comte Senard★, TOLLOT-BEAUT★★. Best years: (reds) (2009) 08 **07** 06 05 **03 02 99 96 95**.

DOM. JEAN-MICHEL ALQUIER *Faugères AC, Languedoc, France* This estate shows how good FAUGÈRES can be. Barrel aging of all wines, and low yields for the special cuvées, Les Bastides★★ and La Maison Jaune★. Also a good white blend of Marsanne and Grenache Blanc. Best years: (Bastides) 2008 07 06 **05 04 03 01 00**.

ALSACE AC *Alsace, France* Tucked away on France's eastern border with Germany, Alsace produces some of the most individual white wines of all, rich in aroma and full of ripe, distinctive flavours. Alsace is almost as far north as CHAMPAGNE, but its climate is considerably warmer and drier. Wines from the 51 best vineyard sites can call themselves Alsace Grand Cru AC and account for 4% of production; quality regulations are more

stringent and many individual crus have further tightened the rules. Riesling, Muscat, Gewurztraminer and Pinot Gris are generally considered the finest varieties in Alsace and were originally the only ones permitted for Grand Cru wines, although Sylvaner is now legal in Zotzenberg and further changes will follow. Pinot Blanc can produce good wines too. Reds from Pinot Noir are improving fitfully. Alsace labels its wines by grape variety and, apart from the Edelzwicker blends and CREMANT D'ALSACE fizz, nearly all Alsace wines are made from a single variety, although blends from certain Grand Cru sites, such as Altenberg de Bergheim and Kaefferkopf, are now recognized. Medium or sweeter wines are labelled *moelleux*. Vendange Tardive means 'late-harvest'; the grapes (Riesling, Muscat, Pinot Gris or Gewurztraminer) are picked late and almost overripe, giving higher sugar levels and potentially more intense flavours. The resulting wines are usually rich and mouthfilling and often need 5 years or more to show their personality. Sélection de Grains Nobles – late-harvest wines made from superripe grapes of the same varieties – are invariably sweet and usually affected by noble rot; they are among Alsace's finest, but are very expensive to produce (and to buy). Best producers: J-B ADAM★★, Lucien Albrecht★, Barmès-Buecher★, Becker, Léon Beyer★, P BLANCK★★, Bott-Geyl★★, A Boxler★, Ernest Burn★★, DEISS★★, Dirler-Cadé★★, Pierre Frick★, Rémy Gresser★, HUGEL★, Josmeyer★★, Kientzler★, Klur, Kreydenweiss★★, Seppi Landmann★, A MANN★★, Meyer-Fonné★, Mittnacht Frères, MURE★★, Ostertag★★, Pfaffenheim co-op, Ribeauvillé co-op, Rieflé★, Rolly Gassmann★, Martin Schaetzel★★, Charles Schléret, Schlumberger★, SCHOFFIT★, Louis Sipp★, Bruno Sorg★, Marc Tempé, TRIMBACH★★, TURCKHEIM co-op★, WEINBACH★★, Paul Zinck★, ZIND-HUMBRECHT★★★. Best years: 2009 08 **07 05 04 02 01 00 98 97 96 95**.

ALTARE *Barolo DOCG, Piedmont, Italy* Elio Altare led the winemaking revolution in traditionalist Alba, drastically shortening maceration times for Nebbiolo and other grapes. Though a professed modernist, Elio's wines are intense, full and structured while young, but with clearly discernible fruit flavours, thanks to an almost fanatical diligence in the vineyard. He makes outstanding BAROLO Arborina★★★ and Brunate★★★ and 3 barrique-aged wines under the LANGHE DOC: Arborina★★★ (Nebbiolo), Larigi★★★ (Barbera) and La Villa★★ (Nebbiolo-Barbera). Best years: (Barolo) (2009) (08) (07) 06 **04 03** 01 00 99 98 96 95.

ALTO ADIGE *Trentino-Alto Adige, Italy* A largely German-speaking province, originally called Südtirol. The DOC covers dozens of different types of wine. Reds range from light and perfumed when made from the ubiquitous (but diminishing in importance) Schiava grape, to fruity and more structured when made from Cabernet or Merlot, to dark and velvety if Lagrein is used. Oak aging, once inclined to excess, is being handled ever better. Whites nclude Chardonnay, Gewürztraminer, Pinot Grigio, Riesling and Sauvignon, among others, and world appreciation is increasing for the steely, minerally and potentially long-lived Pinot Bianco wines (aka Weiss-burgunder). There is also some good sparkling wine. Production is dominated by well-run co-ops, although there are excellent individual producers. Sub-zones include the previously independent DOCs of Santa Maddalena and Terlano. Best producers: Abbazia di Novacella★, Casòn Hirschprunn★, Peter Dipoli★★, Egger-Ramer★, Franz Gojer★, Franz Haas★★, Haderburg★★, Hofstätter★★, Kränzl★, LAGEDER★★, Laimburg★, Loacker★, Josephus Mayr★, Muri-Gries★★, Josef Niedermayr★, Ignaz Niedriest★, Plattner Waldgries★, Peter Pliger-Kuenhof★, Hans Rottensteiner★, Heinrich Rottensteiner★, TIEFENBRUNNER★★, Elena Walch★, Baron Widmann★; (co-ops) Caldaro★, Colterenzio★★, Girlan-Cornaiano★, Gries★★, Nals-Margreid★★, Prima & Nuova/Erste & Neue★, San Michele Appiano★★, Santa Maddalena★, Terlano★★★, Termeno★★.

ALVARINHO See ALBARINO.

ALYSIAN *Russian River Valley, Sonoma County, California, USA* Joint venture between Gary Farrell and investor William Hambrecht, started in 2007, has released a string of superb Pinot Noirs★★ that emulate the delicate, balanced style that Farrell pioneered at his own Russian River outfit.

CASTELLO DI AMA *Chianti Classico DOCG, Tuscany, Italy* Model estate of CHIANTI CLASSICO, with outstanding Chianti Classico★★, plus single-vineyard Riservas★★★ (Bellavista and La Casuccia). L'Apparita★★★ is one of Italy's best Merlots. Also good Chardonnay Al Poggio★. Best years: (Chianti Classico) (2009) (08) 07 06 **04 03 01** 00 99 97 95.

AMARONE DELLA VALPOLICELLA DOC *Veneto, Italy* A brilliantly individual, bitter-sweet style of VALPOLICELLA made from grapes shrivelled on mats for months after harvest. The wine, which can reach 16% of alcohol and more, differs from the sweet RECIOTO DELLA VALPOLICELLA in that it is fermented to near-dryness. Wines from the Classico zone are generally the best, with exceptions from DAL FORNO, Corte Sant'Alda and Roccolo Grassi; and more recently from Pra's La Morandina. Best producers: Accordini★★, ALLEGRINI★★★, Bertani★★, Brigaldara★, Brunelli★, BUSSOLA★★★, Michele Castellani★★, Corte Sant'Alda★★, Valentina Cubi★★, DAL FORNO★★★, Guerrieri-Rizzardi★★, MASI★★, QUINTARELLI★★★, Le Ragose★★, Roccolo Grassi★, Le Salette★★, Serègo Alighieri★, Speri★★, Tedeschi★★, Tommasi★, Villa Monteleone★★, VIVIANI★★, Zenato★★. Best years: (2009) (08) 06 **04 03 01** 00 97.

AMIGNE Ancient Swiss grape variety that is virtually limited to 40ha (100 acres) around Vétroz in the VALAIS. The wine has an earthy, nutty intensity and benefits from a few years' aging. Best producers: Bonvin, Cottagnoud★, A Fontannaz, Jean-René Germanier★, Labuthe.

ANAKENA *Cachapoal, Rapel, Chile* A modern winery resulting from a collaboration between Felipe Ibáñez and Jorge Gutiérrez. Produces one of Chile's best Viogniers★★, Ona Pinot Noir★ and the unusual Ona white blend of Riesling, Viognier and Chardonnay★.

DOM. DE L'ANCIENNE CURE *Bergerac AC and Monbazillac AC, South-West France* Christian Roche exemplifies the best of BERGERAC, with textured elegant reds★, crisp dry whites★ and balanced, luscious sweet MONBAZILLAC★★. Top cuvées L'Abbaye★ and L'Extase★★ for both reds and whites. Best years: (reds) (2009) 08 **06 05 04**.

ANDALUCÍA *Spain* Fortified wines, or wines naturally so strong in alcohol that they don't need fortifying, are the speciality of this southern stretch of Spain. Apart from sherry (JEREZ / MANZANILLA DO), there are the lesser, sherry-like wines of Condado de Huelva DO and MONTILLA-MORILES DO, and the rich sweet wines of MÁLAGA DO. These regions also make some modern but bland dry whites; the best are from Condado de Huelva. Red wine and unfortified white wines are now appearing from producers in Málaga, Cádiz, Seville, Granada and Almería provinces.

ANDERSON VALLEY AVA *California, USA* Small appellation (less than 245ha/600 acres) in western MENDOCINO COUNTY that produces brilliant wines. Most vineyards are within 15 miles of the Pacific Ocean, making this one of the coldest AVAs in California. Delicate Pinot Noirs and Chardonnays, and one of the few places in the state for first-rate Gewürztraminer and Riesling. Superb sparkling wines with healthy acidity and creamy yeast are highlights as well. Best producers: Brutocao★, Goldeneye★, Greenwood Ridge★, HANDLEY★★, Lazy Creek★, Littorai★, NAVARRO★★★, ROEDERER ESTATE★★, SCHARFFENBERGER CELLARS★.

ANDREW WILL WINERY *Washington State, USA* Winemaker Chris Camarda makes delicious blends of BORDEAUX varietals from a range of older WASHINGTON vineyards. At the top are the complex Champoux Vineyard★★★ and the opulent Ciel du Cheval★★★. Wine from the estate vineyard, Two Blondes Vineyard★, shows young vine character. Sorella★★, a blend of the best barrels each vintage, can be outstanding with age. Best years: (reds) (2008) 07 06 05 04 03 01 00.

CH. ANGÉLUS★★★ *St-Émilion Grand Cru AC, 1er Grand Cru Classé, Bordeaux, France* One of the best-known ST-ÉMILION Grands Crus, with an energetic owner and talented winemaker. Rich, dark, spicy, modern St-Émilion. Promoted to Premier Grand Cru Classé in 1996 and still on top form. Best years: 2008 07 06 05 **04** 03 02 01 00 99 98 96 95 93 92 90 89.

MARQUIS D'ANGERVILLE *Volnay, Côte de Beaune, Burgundy, France* The late Jacques d'Angerville for half a century produced an exemplary range of elegant Premiers Crus from VOLNAY, the subtlest of the CÔTE DE BEAUNE's red wine appellations. Quality continues to improve. Clos des Ducs and Taillepieds are ★★★. All should be kept for at least 5 years. Best years: (top reds) (2009) 08 07 06 05 03 **02** 99 98 96 95 91 90.

CH. D'ANGLUDET★ *Margaux AC, Haut-Médoc, Bordeaux, France* This English-owned château makes a gentle, charming style that has been getting better and better in the last decade. It ages well for at least a decade. Best years: 2008 06 **05** 04 03 02 00 **98** 96 95 94 90.

ANJOU BLANC AC *Loire Valley, France* Ill-defined AC; ranges from bone dry to sweet, from excellent to dreadful; the best are dry. Up to 20% Chardonnay or Sauvignon can be added, but many of the leading producers – some preferring the Vin de Pays du VAL DE LOIRE label – use 100% Chenin from top sites once dedicated to sweet COTEAUX DU LAYON. Best producers: M Angeli/Sansonnière★★, S Bernaudeau, des Chesnaies★, P Delesvaux★, Fesles★, Dom. F L, La Grange aux Belles, de Juchepie★, Richard Leroy★, Montgilet/V Lebreton, Mosse★, Ogereau★, PIERRE-BISE★, Pithon-Paillé★, Richou★, Roulerie★, Soucherie★. Best years: (top wines) 2009 08 07 06 05 04 03 02.

ANJOU ROUGE AC *Loire Valley, France* Anjou reds (from Cabernet Sauvignon and Franc or Pineau d'Aunis) are increasingly successful. Usually fruity, easy-drinking wine, with less tannin than ANJOU-VILLAGES.

Wines made from Gamay are sold as Anjou Gamay. **Best producers:** Brizé★, B Courault, La Grange aux Belles, PIERRE-BISE (Anjou Gamay), Pithon-Paillé, Putille, Richou★, Roulerie, Sablonnettes. **Best years: (top wines) (2009) 08 06 05 04 03 02 01.**

ANJOU-VILLAGES AC *Loire Valley, France* Superior Anjou red from 46 villages, and made from Cabernet Franc and Cabernet Sauvignon. Anjou-Villages Brissac's schist-dominated soils produce particularly firmly structured wines which reward aging. **Best producers:** Bablut/Daviau★★, P Baudouin, Brizé★, de Conquessac, P Delesvaux★, Deux Arcs, Haute Perche, Montgilet/V Lebreton★, de la Motte, Ogereau★, PIERRE-BISE★★, Putille★, Richou★★, Rochelles★★, Sauveroy, la Varière/Beaujeau★. **Best years: (2009) 08 06 05 04 03 02 01 97 96.**

ANSELMI *Veneto, Italy* Roberto Anselmi (with PIEROPAN) has shown that the once much-maligned SOAVE can have real personality when carefully made. Using ultra-modern methods he has honed the fruit flavours of his San Vincenzo★★ and Capitel Foscarino★★ and introduced small-barrel-aging for single-vineyard Capitel Croce★★ and luscious, SAUTERNES-like I Capitelli★★ (sometimes ★★★), as well as the Cabernet Sauvignon Realdà. All sold under the regional IGT rather than Soave DOC. **Best years: (I Capitelli) (2009) (08) 07 05 04 03 01 00.**

ANTHONY ROAD *Finger Lakes AVA, New York State, USA* Located on the west edge of Seneca Lake, Anthony Road specializes in dry★, semi-dry★ and sweet Rieslings, as well as an Alsace-styled Gewurztraminer. The winery is part of a group effort to define the region's style of dry Riesling.

ANTINORI *Tuscany, Italy* World-famous Florentine family firm that has been involved in wine since 1385, but it is Piero Antinori, the current head, who has made the Antinori name synonymous with quality and innovation. CHIANTI CLASSICO wines like Badia a Passignano★ (Riserva★★), Pèppoli★ and Tenute Marchese Antinori Riserva★★ are consistently good, but it was Antinori's development of the 'Super-Tuscan' concept of superior wines outside the DOC that launched a quality revolution during the 1970s: TIGNANELLO★★ (sometimes ★★★) and, especially, SOLAIA★★★ can be great wines. Other Tuscan wines include VINO NOBILE La Braccesca★★, Bramasole Syrah from Cortona DOC, BRUNELLO DI MONTALCINO Pian delle Vigne★★ and BOLGHERI's Guado al Tasso★★ (a Cabernet-Merlot blend; also a Vermentino white). Interests further afield include PRUNOTTO in Piedmont, Tormaresca in PUGLIA, FRANCIACORTA's Montenisa, Bátaapáti in Hungary and Albis in Chile. A joint venture with CHATEAU STE MICHELLE in the USA acquired STAG'S LEAP WINE CELLARS in 2007. **Best years: (reds) (2009) (08) 07 06 04 03 01 00 99 97.** See also Castello della SALA.

ANTONOPOULOS *Patras AO, Peloponnese, Greece* Boutique winery with a range that includes barrel-fermented Chardonnay★★, Cabernet Nea Dris (New Oak)★ and Private Collection★, a promising red blend.

DOM. D'ANTUGNAC *Limoux AC, Languedoc, France* Two young Burgundians, Jean-Luc Terrier and Christian Collovray, are producing impressive Pinot Noir and Chardonnay in the cool LIMOUX region. Côté Pierre Lys is the Pinot Noir, with finesse and complexity. Chardonnay Les Gravas★ is barrel-fermented and aged, balancing richness with apples and cream freshness. **Best years: (Les Gravas) 2008 07 06 05 04 01.**

ARAGÓN *Spain* Aragón stretches south from the Pyrenees to Spain's central plateau. Winemaking has improved markedly, first of all in the cooler, hilly, northern SOMONTANO DO, and now also further south, in CAMPO DE BORJA

DO, CALATAYUD DO and CARINENA DO; these 3 areas have the potential to be a major budget-price force in a world mad for beefy but juicy reds.

ARAUJO *Napa Valley AVA, California, USA* Boutique winery whose great coup was to buy the Eisele vineyard, traditionally a source of superb Cabernet. Araujo Cabernet Sauvignon★★★ is one of California's most sought-after reds, combining great fruit intensity with powerful but digestible tannins. Impressive Syrah★★ and attractively zesty Sauvignon Blanc★★.

ARBOIS AC *Jura, France* The largest of the ACs in the Jura region, with the sub-appellation Pupillin. All the Jura styles are made here, including sparkling CRÉMANT DU JURA and the region's best reds, from Trousseau and Poulsard. Most widely seen outside the region are the whites, from Chardonnay or the local Savagnin. Some have a sherry-like flavour that is most concentrated in *vin jaune*; others are fruity or more 'Burgundian' and mineral. There is also a rare, sweet *vin de paille*. **Best producers:** Fruitière Vinicole d'Arbois, L Aviet★, Dugois★, Ligier, F Lornet★, H Maire, l'Octavin, Overnoy/Houillon★, la Pinte★, J Puffeney★★, Renardière, Rijckaert★, Rolet, A & M Tissot★★, J Tissot★, Tournelle★. **Best years:** (2008) 07 **06 05 04 02**.

DOM. ANTOINE ARENA *Patrimonio AC, Corsica, France* Family-owned bio-dynamic vineyard in Patrimonio, which specializes in white wines based on Vermentino, white Bianco Gentile (a local grape which had fallen into disuse) and stunning reds under the Carco, Grotte di Sole★ and Morta Maio labels. **Best years:** (Grotte di Sole) 2005 **04 03 01 00**.

ARGIOLAS *Sardinia, Italy* Sardinian star making DOC wines Cannonau (Costera★), Monica (Perdera) and Vermentino (Costamolino★) di Sardegna and IGT Isola dei Nuraghi blends: Turriga★★ and Korem★ are powerful, spicy reds; Angialis★★ is a golden, sweet white.

ARGYLE *Willamette Valley AVA, Oregon, USA* In 1987, Brian Croser and Rollin Soles planned a world-class New World sparkling wine firm; the cool WILLAMETTE VALLEY was ideal for late-ripened Pinot Noir and Chardonnay. Argyle sparkling wine★ was soon followed by barrel-fermented Chardonnay★ and Pinot Noir★. The Reserve★★, Nuthouse★★ and Spirithouse★★ bottlings show just how much potential this large winery possesses. **Best years:** (Pinot Noir) (2008) 07 06 **05 04 03 02**.

ARNEIS Italian grape grown in the ROERO hills in PIEDMONT. Arneis is DOCG in Roero, producing dry white wines which, at best, have an attractive appley, herbal perfume. Good ones can be expensive, but cheaper versions rarely work. COOPERS CREEK and TRINITY HILL make good ones in New Zealand. **Best producers:** Brovia★, Cascina Chicco★, Correggia★, Deltetto★, GIACOSA★, Malvirà★, Angelo Negro★, PRUNOTTO★, Sorilaria★, Vietti★, Gianni Voerzio★.

DOM. ARRETXEA *Irouléguy AC, South-West France* Michel and Thérèse Riouspeyrous are the growers to look out for in IROULÉGUY. Whites are crisp, full and dry; the rosé is directly pressed rather than drawn off the red juice. Good reds, with top Cuvée Haitza★★ rather like a refined MADIRAN in style, but still gutsy and macho. **Best years:** (2009) 08 **06 05** 04.

CH. L'ARROSÉE★ *St-Émilion Grand Cru AC, Grand Cru Classé, Bordeaux, France* This small property, just south-west of the historic town of ST-ÉMILION, makes really exciting wine: rich, chewy and wonderfully luscious, with a comparatively high proportion (40%) of Cabernet. New investment from 2002. Drink after 5 years, but may be cellared for 10 or more. **Best years:** 2008 07 06 05 **04 03 02 00 98 96 95 90**.

RROWOOD *Sonoma Valley AVA, California, USA*   Richard Arrowood started his winery in 1986. The wines have mostly been tip-top – beautifully balanced Cabernet★★, superb Merlot★★, deeply fruity Syrah (Saralee's★★, Le Beau Mélange★), lovely, velvety Chardonnay★ (Alary Vineyards★) and fragrant Viognier★★. In 2006 the winery was acquired by Jackson Family Wines. Founder Arrowood now divides his time between this property and a new brand, Amapola Creek. Best years: (Cabernet Sauvignon) (2006) 05 04 03 **02 01 00** 99 97 96 95 94 91 90.

RTADI *Rioja DOCa, País Vasco, Spain*   This former co-op is now producing some of RIOJA's deepest, most ambitious reds, but they in no way overshadow the delightful, floral Joven★ and the excellent, scented and fairly priced Viñas de Gain★★. Blockbusters include Grandes Añadas★★★, superlative Viña El Pisón★★★ and fascinating, richly ripe Pagos Viejos★★. Best years: (2007) 06 05 04 **03 01 00** 98 96 95 94.

STI DOCG *Piedmont, Italy*   Asti Spumante, the world's best-selling sweet sparkling wine, was long derided as light and cheap, though promotion to DOCG signalled an upturn in quality. Made in the province of Asti, under a denomination which includes the rarer MOSCATO D'ASTI, the wine is now called simply Asti. Its light sweetness and refreshing sparkle make it ideal with fruit and a wide range of sweet dishes. Drink young. Best producers: Araldica, Bera★, Cinzano★, Contero, Giuseppe Contratto★, Cascina Fonda★, FONTANAFREDDA, Gancia★, Martini & Rossi★, Cascina Pian d'Or★.

STROLABE *Marlborough, South Island, New Zealand* High-flying winery launched in 2001. The Voyage range includes a powerful Sauvignon Blanc★★, taut dry Riesling★ and subtly oaked Chardonnay. The Discovery range showcases MARLBOROUGH sub-regions and includes two excellent Sauvignon Blancs, from AWATERE★★ and Kekerengu★★. The Experience range is restricted to tiny parcels of experimental wines. Best years: (Sauvignon Blanc) **2009** 07 06.

TA RANGI *Martinborough, North Island, New Zealand*   Small, high-quality winery. Stylish, concentrated reds include seductively perfumed cherry/plum Pinot Noir★★★, and an impressive Cabernet-Merlot-Syrah blend called Célèbre★★. Whites include big, rich Craighall Chardonnay★, delicately luscious Lismore Pinot Gris★★ and a concentrated, mouthwatering Sauvignon Blanc★. A succulent Kahu Botrytis Riesling is made when vintage conditions allow. Best years: (Pinot Noir) (2009) 08 **07 06 03 01 00**.

TLAS PEAK *Atlas Peak AVA, Napa, California, USA*   Established in 1987 by ANTINORI of Italy, this mountaintop winery in the south-east corner of the NAPA VALLEY was a leader in Californian Sangiovese without ever achieving a consistent style. The brand is now owned by Ascentia Wines and is focused entirely on Cabernet Sauvignon from 4 specific mountain vineyards, although other wineries do still buy the Sangiovese grapes. Best years: 2005 **02 01** 99.

U BON CLIMAT *Santa Maria Valley AVA, California, USA*   Pace-setting winery in this cool region, run by talented, ebullient Jim Clendenen, whose early inspiration was BURGUNDY. The result is a range of lush Chardonnays★★ and intense Pinot Noirs★★ from SANTA MARIA or SANTA BARBARA fruit (Isabelle Morgan and Knox Alexander bottlings can be ★★★). He also makes BORDEAUX-style reds, Italian varietals (both red and white) and some exotic sweeties. Cold Heaven Viognier is made by Clendenen's wife, Morgan. Best years: (Pinot Noir) 2006 **05 04 03 02 01 00** 99 98 97 96 95; (Chardonnay) 2007 **06 05 04 03 02 01**.

AUCKLAND *North Island, New Zealand* Vineyards in this region a
concentrated in the districts of Henderson, KUMEU/HUAPAI, Matakana an
WAIHEKE ISLAND. Clevedon, south of Auckland, is a fledgling area that show
promise. Best years: (Cabernet Sauvignon) (2009) 08 **07 06 05 04 02 00 99**.

CH. AUSONE★★★ *St-Émilion Grand Cru AC, 1er Grand Cru Classé, Bordeaux, Franc*
This beautiful property is situated on what are perhaps the best slopes i
ST-ÉMILION. Owner Alain Vauthier has taken it to new heights since 199
and the wines now display stunning texture and depth and the promise o
memorable maturity. A high proportion (50%) of Cabernet Franc bee
up the Merlot. Second wine: La Chapelle d'Ausone. Best years: 2008 07 0
05 04 03 **02 01 00 99 98 97 96 95 90 89 88**.

AUXEY-DURESSES AC *Côte de Beaune, Burgundy, France* Auxey-Duresses
a backwater village up a valley behind MEURSAULT. The reds should be ligh
and fresh but can lack ripeness. At its best, and at 3–5 years, the white
dry, soft, nutty and hinting at the creaminess of a good Meursault, but a
much lower prices. Of the Premiers Crus, Les Duresses is the mo
consistent. Best producers: (reds) Comte Armand★★, J-P Diconne★, Maiso
Leroy, M Prunier★, P Prunier★; (whites) M Ampeau★, d'Auvenay (Don
LEROY)★★, J-P Diconne★, J-P Fichet★, Gras, Olivier LEFLAIVE★, Maison Leroy★
M Prunier★. Best years: (reds) (2009) 08 **07 06** 05 **03 02 99**; (whites) (2009) 0
07 06 05 04.

AVIGNONESI *Vino Nobile di Montepulciano DOCG,*
Tuscany, Italy Ex-proprietors the Falvo
brothers brought a revolutionary viticultural
system to Tuscany with their high-density,
bush-trained training system known as
settone. VINO NOBILE is their top wine,
especially the Riserva Grandi Annate★★★,

but they also produce fine Cortona DOC varietals from Chardonnay (
Marzocco)★, Merlot (Desiderio)★ and Sauvignon. Their most sough
after wine is Vin Santo★★★, with its partner (from Sangiovese) Occhi
di Pernice★★★. Best years: (Vino Nobile) (2009) (08) 07 06 **04 01**.

AWATERE VALLEY *Marlborough, South Island, New Zealand* MARLBOROUGH sul
region that's cooler than the better-known Wairau Valley. In terms
vineyard area Awatere is larger than HAWKES BAY. Awatere Sauvignon offers
concentrated Marlborough style with nettle, tomato leaf and gree
capsicum characters, while Chardonnay is taut and mineral. Pinot Noir ca
be good but may lack ripeness in cool vintages. Best producer
ASTROLABE★★, Clifford Bay★, Clos Marguerite★, O:TU★, Tohu★, VAVASOUR★
VILLA MARIA★, Yealands★. Best years: (Sauvignon Blanc) **2009 07 06**.

CH. D'AYDIE *Madiran AC, South-West France* The Laplace family owns th
well-known MADIRAN château, whose top wine is a full-blown Tanna
based Madiran★★ named after the château; softer Madiran cuvées calle
Ode d'Aydie★ and Autour du Fruit blend Tannat with a little Cabern
Also simple, fruity Aramis Vin de Pays du Comté Tolosan. Oak-age
white PACHERENCS★ are excellent. Best years: (reds) (2009) 08 06 **05 04 0
01**; (sweet whites) **2009 06 05 04 03**.

BABICH *Henderson, North Island, New Zealand* Family-run winery with prim
vineyard land in MARLBOROUGH and HAWKES BAY. Irongate Chardonnay★
an intense, steely wine that needs plenty of cellaring, while full-flavoure
reds under the Winemakers' Reserve label show even greater potenti
for development. Flagship wine The Patriarch★★ is a red BORDEAU

blend from Hawkes Bay. Marlborough whites include stylish Sauvignon Blanc★, tangy Riesling and light, fruity Pinot Gris. Best years: (premium Hawkes Bay reds) 2009 **08 07 06 05 04**.

ACALHÔA VINHOS DE PORTUGAL *Península de Setúbal, Portugal* Forward-looking operation, using Portuguese and foreign grapes with equal ease. Quinta da Bacalhôa★ is an oaky, meaty Cabernet-Merlot blend, Palácio da Bacalhôa★★ even better; Tinto da Ânfora★ a rich and figgy ALENTEJO red (Grande Escolha★★ version is powerful and cedary); and Cova da Ursa★ a toasty, rich Chardonnay. Portugal's finest sparkling wine, vintage-dated Loridos★, is a decent CHAMPAGNE lookalike. Só Syrah ('só' means 'only' in Portuguese) is characterful if atypical. Also excellent 20-year-old Moscatel de SETÚBAL★★.

AD DÜRKHEIM *Pfalz, Germany* This spa town has some good vineyards and is the headquarters of the dependable Vier Jahreszeiten co-op. Best producers: Darting, Fitz-Ritter, Hensel★, Karl Schaefer★, Egon Schmitt. Best years: (2009) 08 **07 04 03 02 01 99 98**.

ADEN *Germany* Very large, 16,000ha (39,540-acre), wine region stretching from FRANKEN to the Bodensee (Lake Constance). Its dry whites and reds show off the fuller, softer flavours Germany can produce in the warmer climate of its southerly regions. Many of the best non-Riesling German wines come from here, as well as many good barrel-fermented and barrel-aged wines. Germany's best co-operatives are located here, but the number of quality-oriented private estates is growing. See also KAISERSTUHL, ORTENAU.

AGA Important red grape in BAIRRADA. Also planted in smaller quantities in DÃO and the TEJO. It can give deep, complex, blackberryish wine, but aggressive tannin is a continuing problem.

AIRRADA DOC *Beira Litoral, Portugal* Bairrada, along with the DOURO, DÃO and ALENTEJO, can be the source of many of Portugal's best red wines. These can brim over with intense raspberry and blackberry fruit, though with austere tannins that take quite a few years to soften. Traditionally made from a minimum of 50% of the tannic Baga grape; rules changed in 2003 to admit a load of 'international' grapes into the Bairrada fold. The whites are coming on fast with modern vinification methods. With an Atlantic climate, vintages can be very variable. Best producers: (reds) ALIANÇA★, Quinta das Bágeiras★, Quinta de Baixo★, Campolargo★, Cantanhede co-op, Quinta do Encontro, Caves do Freixo, Caves Messias (Quinta do Valdoeiro Reserva★), Casa de Saima★★, Caves SÃO JOÃO★★, SOGRAPE, Sidónio de Sousa★, (whites) Caves SÃO JOÃO★★, SOGRAPE (Reserva★). Best years: (reds) 2009 08 **05 04 03 01 00 97**.

ALATONBOGLÁR WINERY *Transdanubia, Hungary* Premium winery in the Lake Balaton region, which has benefited from heavy investment and the expertise of viticulturist Dr Richard Smart and wine consultant Kym Milne, but still needs to work to improve quality, particularly in the inexpensive but dumbed-down range sold under the Chapel Hill label.

BALEARIC ISLANDS *Spain* Medium-bodied reds and soft rosés were the mainstays of Mallorca's 2 DO areas, Binissalem and Plà i Llevant, until Anima Negra began making impressive, deep reds from the native Callet grape. Best producers: 4 Kilos Vinícola★★, Anima Negra★★, Hereus de Ribas, Miquel Gelabert★, Toni Gelabert★, Miquel Oliver, Son Bordils★.

BALNAVES *Coonawarra, South Australia* Long-term residents of COONAWARRA the grape-growing Balnaves family decided to become involved i making wine in the mid-1990s. With the talented Pete Bissell a winemaker, Balnaves is now among the best producers in the regio Reserve Cabernet The Tally★★★ is complex, wonderfully structured an deeply flavoured; the regular Cabernet★ is well priced and an exceller example of Coonawarra style.

BANDOL AC *Provence, France* A lovely fishing port with vineyards hig above the Mediterranean, producing some of the best reds and rosés i Provence. The Mourvèdre grape gives Bandol its character – dens colour, warm, smoky black fruit and a herby fragrance. The reds happil age for 10 years, sometimes more, but can be very good at 3–4. The rosé delicious and spicy but often too pricey, should be drunk young. Also small amount of neutral, overpriced white. Best producers: la Bastid Blanche★, la Bégude★, Bunan★, Frégate★, le Galantin★, J P Gaussen★★, Gro Noré★, l'Hermitage★, Lafran-Veyrolles★, la Laidière★, Mas Redorne★ la Noblesse★, PIBARNON★★, Pradeaux★★, Ray-Jane★, Roche Redonne★ Ste-Anne★, Salettes★, SORIN, la Suffrène, Tempier★, Terrebrune★, la Tour d Bon★, VANNIERES★★. Best years: 2008 07 06 05 **03 01 00 99 98 97**.

BANFI *Brunello di Montalcino DOCG, Tuscany, Italy* American-owned firm whic got rich on LAMBRUSCO in the 1970s and invested in this huge estate i iconic Montalcino. Despite many awards and much work on Sangioves clones, their BRUNELLOS (Poggio all'Oro★, Poggio alle Mura★) remain bit stodgy, if potent, and are exceeded, quality-wise, by their Summus★★ and Excelsus★★. Also have cellars in PIEDMONT for GAVI and fizz. Bes years: (top reds) (2009) (08) (07) (06) 05 04 **01 00 09**.

BANNOCKBURN *Geelong, Victoria, Australia* The Hooper family has 27h (67 acres) of mature vines, from which all the estate's wines are sourced Most notable are Sauvignon Blanc★★, Chardonnay★★, Pinot Noir★ and Shiraz★, and 4 limited-release wines: my favourite, the complex an classy Alain GRAILLOT-influenced Range Shiraz★★; MEURSAULT-like SRI Chardonnay★★; powerful, gamy Serre Pinot Noir★★; and dense, tightl coiled yet elegant Stuart Pinot★★. Best years: (Shiraz) (2008) 06 05 04 03 0 **01 00 99 98 97 96 94 92 91**.

BANYULS AC *Roussillon, France* One of the best *vins doux naturels*, mad mainly from Grenache, with a strong plum and raisin flavour. *Rimage* vintaged early bottlings – and *rancio* tawny styles are the best. Best drun after dinner, though often served as an apéritif in France. Best producer Cellier des Templiers★, CHAPOUTIER, Clos de Paulilles★, la Coume du Roy★ l'Étoile★, MAS BLANC★★, la Rectorie★★, la Tour Vieille★, Vial Magnères★.

BARBADILLO *Jerez y Manzanilla DO, Andalucía, Spain* The largest sherr company in the coastal town of Sanlúcar de Barrameda makes a wid range of good to excellent wines, in particular salty, dry manzanilla style (Solear★★, En Rama unfiltered★★★) and intense, nutty, but dr amontillados and olorosos (Amontillado Príncipe★★, Oloroso Cuco★★) Neutral dry white Castillo de San Diego is a bestseller in Spain.

BARBARESCO DOCG *Piedmont, Italy* This prestigious red wine, grown i the LANGHE hills south-east of Turin, is often twinned with its neighbou BAROLO to demonstrate the nobility of the Nebbiolo grape. Barbaresc can be a shade softer and less powerful, and is not required by law to ag as long (2 years minimum compared with 3), but at the top level is ofte indistinguishable from Barolo. As in Barolo, traditionalists excel, led b Bruno GIACOSA. Even though the area is relatively compact (575ha/142 acres), styles can differ significantly between vineyards and producers. Best vineyards: Asili, Bricco di Neive, Crichet Pajè, Gallina, Marcorino, Martinenga, Messoirano, Moccagatta, Montestefano, Ovello, Pora, Rabajà, Rio Sordo, Santo Stefano, Serraboella, Sorì Paitin. Best producers: Barbaresco co-op★★, CERETTO★★, Cigliuti★★, Stefano Farina★★, Fontanabianca★★, GAJA★★★, GIACOSA★★★, Lano★, Marchesi di Gresy★★, Moccagatta★★, Fiorenzo Nada★★, Castello di Neive★★, Oddero★, Paitin★★, Pelissero★★, Pio Cesare★★, PRUNOTTO★, Rizzi★, Albino Rocca★★, Bruno Rocca★★, Sottimano★★, La Spinetta★★, Castello di Verduno★★, Vietti★★. Best years: (2009) (08) 07 06 **04 03 01** 00 99 98 97 96 95.

BARBERA A native of north-west Italy, Barbera vies with Sangiovese as the most widely planted red grape in the country. When grown for high yields its natural acidity shows through, producing vibrant quaffers. Low yields from the top PIEDMONT estates create intensely rich and complex wines. Oaked versions can be stunning. Significant plantings in California, Argentina and Australia.

BARBERA D'ALBA DOC *Piedmont, Italy* Some outstanding Barbera, much of it barrique-aged, comes from this appellation. The most modern examples are supple and generous and can be drunk almost at once. More intense, dark-fruited versions require at least 3 years' age, but might improve for as much as 8. Best producers: G Alessandria★★, ALTARE★, Azelia★★, Boglietti★★, Brovia★, Burlotto★★, CERETTO★, Cascina Chicco★, Cigliuti★, CLERICO★, Elvio Cogno★★, Aldo CONTERNO★★, Giacomo CONTERNO★★, Conterno-Fantino★, Corino★, Correggia★★, Elio Grasso★, Giuseppe MASCARELLO★, Moccagatta★, M Molino★, Monfalletto-Cordero di Montezemolo★, Oberto★★, Parusso★, Pelissero★, F Principiano★★, PRUNOTTO★★, RATTI★, Albino Rocca★★, Bruno Rocca★, SANDRONE★★, P Scavino★★, La Spinetta★★, Vajra★★, Mauro Veglio★★, Vietti★★, Gianni Voerzio★★, Roberto VOERZIO★★★. Best years: (2009) (08) 07 **06** 04 03 01.

BARBERA D'ASTI DOC *Piedmont, Italy* While BARBERA D'ALBA plays second fiddle to Nebbiolo in the vineyard, in Asti Barbera is king. Unoaked versions are fruity and intense, while barrique-aged examples can rival the best Barbera d'Alba and even some of the better Nebbiolo-based reds. Best examples can be kept for 5–6 years, occasionally longer. Best producers: Araldica/Alasia★, La Barbatella★★, Pietro Barbero★★, Bava★, Bertelli★★, Braida★★, Cascina Castlèt★, Coppo★★, Hastae (Quorum★), Martinetti★★, Il Mongetto★, PRUNOTTO★★, La Spinetta★★, Vietti★★, Vinchio-Vaglio Serra co-op★. Best years: (2009) 08 **07 06** 04 03 01.

BARBOURSVILLE VINEYARDS *Virginia, USA* Founded by Italy's Zonin winemaking family in 1976, on property that features the ruins of a mansion designed by Thomas Jefferson for his friend, James Barbour. Under winemaker Luca Paschina since 1990, the wines have shown consistent improvement. There's an enticing range of French and Italian styles: minerally, scented Viognier★ is lean but delicious; Cabernet Franc Reserve and Octagon★, a flagship BORDEAUX blend based on Merlot, are good.

BARDOLINO DOC *Veneto, Italy* Zone centred on Lake Garda, giving, at best, light, scented red and rosé (*chiaretto*) wines to be drunk young, from the same grape mix as neighbouring VALPOLICELLA. Bardolino Superiore is DOCG. Best producers: ALLEGRINI★, Cavalchina★, Corte Gardoni★, Guerrieri-Rizzardi★, Le Fraghe, MASI, Le Vigne di San Pietro★, Zeni.

BAROSSA

South Australia

The Barossa Valley, an hour or so's drive north of Adelaide in South Australia, is the heart of the Australian wine industry. The giants of the industry have their major wineries here – Jacob's Creek, Wolf Blass, Penfolds and Yalumba – alongside around 50 or so smaller wineries, producing or processing up to 60% of the nation's wine. However, this percentage is based mostly on grapes trucked in from other regions, because the Barossa's vineyards themselves grow less than 10% of Australia's grapes. Yet Barossa-grown grapes, once rejected as uneconomical for their low yields, are now increasingly prized for those same low yields.

Why? Well, it's highly likely that the world's oldest wine vines are in the Barossa. The valley was settled in the 1840s by Lutheran immigrants from Silesia, who brought with them vines from Europe: most importantly, as it turned out, cuttings from the Syrah (or Shiraz) variety of France's Rhône Valley. And because Barossa has never been affected by the phylloxera louse, which destroyed most of the world's vineyards in the late 19th century, today you can still see gnarled, twisted old vines sporting just a few tiny bunches of priceless fruit that were planted by refugees from Europe all of a century and a half ago, and are still tended by their descendants. A new wave of winemakers has taken up the cause of the Barossa vines with much zeal and no small amount of national pride, and they now produce from them some of the deepest, most fascinating wines, not just in Australia, but in the world.

GRAPE VARIETIES

Shiraz is prized above all other Barossa grapes, able to conjure headswirling, palate-dousing flavours. Barossa is the main source of Shiraz grapes for Penfolds Grange, the wine that began the revolution in Australian red wine in the 1950s. Cabernet Sauvignon can be very good in the best years and similarly potent, as are the Rhône varieties of heady Grenache and deliciously earthy Mourvèdre; some of the most exciting examples are from the original vines planted in the 19th century. All these varieties are largely grown on the hot, dry, valley floor, but just to the east lie the Barossa Ranges, and in these higher, cooler vineyards, especially in those of the neighbouring Eden Valley, some of Australia's best and most fashionable Rieslings are grown, prized for their steely attack and lime fragrance. But even here you can't get away from Shiraz, and some thrilling examples come from the hills, not least Henschke's Hill of Grace and Mount Edelstone.

CLASSIFICATIONS

The Barossa was among the first zones to be ratified within the Australian system of Geographical Indications and comprises the regions of Barossa Valley and Eden Valley. The Barossa lies within South Australia's collective 'super zone' of Adelaide.

See also GRANGE, SOUTH AUSTRALIA; and individual producers.

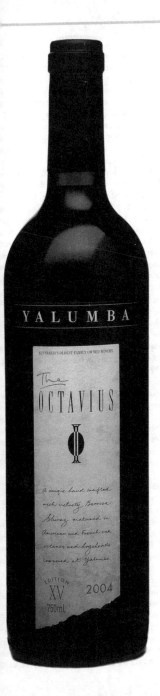

BEST YEARS

(Barossa Valley Shiraz) (2009) 08
06 05 **04 03 02 01 00 99 98 97
96 94 91 90 86**;
(Eden Valley Riesling) **2009** 08 07
06 05 **04 03 02 01 00 99 98 97
96 95**

BEST PRODUCERS

Shiraz-based reds
BAROSSA VALLEY ESTATE, Bethany,
Rolf BINDER, Grant BURGE, Burge
Family, Chateau Tanunda,
Dutschke, John DUVAL, Elderton
(Command), GLAETZER, Greenock
Creek (Block Shiraz, Seven Acre),
HENSCHKE, Hentley Farm,
Heritage, Hewitson, JACOB'S CREEK
(Centenary Hill), Jenke, Trevor
Jones, Kaesler, Kalleske, Langmeil,
Peter LEHMANN, Maverick, Charles
MELTON, Murray Street, PENFOLDS
(RWT, GRANGE), Chris Ringland,
ROCKFORD, ST HALLETT, Tim Smith,
Spinifex, Teusner, Thorn Clarke,
TORBRECK, Torzi Matthews,
Turkey Flat, Two Hands,
The Willows, YALUMBA (Octavius).

Riesling
Bethany, Wolf BLASS (Gold Label),
Grant BURGE, Leo Buring
(Leonay), HENSCHKE, Hewitson,
JACOB'S CREEK (Steingarten),
Peter LEHMANN, McLean, Mesh,
Radford, ROCKFORD, Ross Estate,
ST HALLETT, Thorn Clarke, Torzi
Matthews, YALUMBA (Heggies,
Pewsey Vale).

**Cabernet Sauvignon-based
reds**
Rolf BINDER, Grant BURGE,
Greenock Creek, HENSCHKE,
Peter LEHMANN, ST HALLETT,
The Willows.

**Other reds (Grenache,
Mourvèdre, Shiraz)**
Rolf BINDER, Grant BURGE, Burge
Family (Garnacha, Olive Hill),
Charles Cimicky, Elderton (Ode
to Lorraine), HENSCHKE, Jenke
(Mourvèdre), Kalleske, Langmeil,
Peter LEHMANN, Charles MELTON,
PENFOLDS (Bin 138), Teusner,
TORBRECK, Turkey Flat,
Two Hands.

Semillon
Grant BURGE, HENSCHKE, Heritage,
Jenke, Peter LEHMANN, ROCKFORD,
Turkey Flat, The Willows.

BAROLO DOCG *Piedmont, Italy*   Renowned red wine, named after a villa͏ south-west of Alba, from the Nebbiolo grape grown in around 1500͏ (3700 acres) of vineyards on the steep LANGHE hills, the best coming fro͏ near the top (*bricco*) of those hills. Having in the post-WWII period go͏ to excesses of austerity, Barolo in the 1990s almost threatened to go too ͏ in the other direction, its subtle floral/wild fruit aromas being drowned ͏ too often under expensive but irrelevant oak smells of vanilla and toa͏ Thankfully 21st-century producers are finding their way back to the '͏ and roses' of the grape while managing to keep Nebbiolo's fierce tanni͏ and biting acidity under control. The villages of Barolo and La Morra a͏ said to make the most perfumed wines; Monforte and Serralunga the mo͏ structured. Barolo is frequently labelled by vineyard, though the produce͏ reputation often carries more weight. Best vineyards: Arione, Bricco de͏ Viole, Brunate, Bussia Soprana, Cannubi, Cerequio, Con͏ dell'Annunziata, Fiasco, Francia, Gavarini, Ginestra, Monfallett͏ Monprivato, Rocche dell'Annunziata, Rocche di Castiglione, San͏ Stefano di Perno, La Serra, Vigna Rionda, Villero. Best producers: Alario★★, G Alessandria★★, ALTARE★★, Azelia★★, Boglietti★★, Bongiovanni★ Brovia★★, Burlotto★★, Cappellano★★, CERETTO★★, Chiarlo★, Ciabot Berton͏ CLERICO★★★, Aldo CONTERNO★★, Giacomo CONTERNO★★★, Paulo Conterno★ Conterno-Fantino★★, Corino★★, Luigi Einaudi★★, GIACOSA★★★, Elio Grasso★ M Marengo★★, Bartolo MASCARELLO★★★, Giuseppe MASCARELLO★★★, Monfallett͏ Cordero di Montezemolo★★, Oberto★★, Oddero★★, Parusso★★, Pio Cesare͏ Pira★★, E Pira & Figli★★, F Principiano★, PRUNOTTO★★, Renato RATTI★, Revello★ Giuseppe Rinaldi★★, Rocche dei Manzoni★★, SANDRONE★★★, P Scavino★ M Sebaste★★, Vajra★★, Mauro Veglio★★, Castello di Verduno★★, Vietti★★, Vig͏ Rionda★★, Gianni Voerzio★★, Roberto VOERZIO★★★. Best years: (2009) (08) (0͏ 06 04 01 00 99 98 97 96 95 90 89 88.

BAROSSA VALLEY See pages 72–3.

BAROSSA VALLEY ESTATE *Barossa, South Australia*   Half owned by loc͏ growers, with some of the best-sited vineyards in BAROSSA, and half ͏ industry giant Constellation. Flagship reds are huge, gutsy Baros͏ beauties E&E Black Pepper Shiraz★★★, Ebenezer Shiraz★★ and E&͏ Sparkling Shiraz★★, all of them bursting with ripe plum fruit, spic͏ pepper and vanilla oak. Excellent value in the E Bass Shiraz and budge͏ priced E Minor range. Best years: (E&E Black Pepper Shiraz) (2009) (08) (0͏ 05 04 02 01 99 98 96 94.

JIM BARRY *Clare Valley, South Australia*   After buying Australia's famo͏ Riesling vineyard in 1986, they had to wait until 2005 for the tradema͏ to expire. Now Jim Barry has a flagship wine, The Florita★, to head ͏ quartet of classy, perfumed Rieslings (Watervale★, Lodge Hill★͏ Medium-priced Lodge Hill Shiraz★ is impressive, but the winery is be͏ known for its rich, fruity McRae Wood Shiraz★★ and heady, palat͏ busting Armagh Shiraz★. Best years: (Armagh Shiraz) (2009) 06 05 04 0͏ 01 99 98 96 95 92 89.

BARSAC AC *Bordeaux, France*   Barsac, lying close to the river Garonne ar͏ with the little river Ciron running along its eastern boundary, is the large͏ of the 5 communes in the SAUTERNES AC, and also has its own AC, which͏ used by most, but by no means all, of the top properties. In general, th͏ wines are a little less luscious than other Sauternes, but from good estate͏ they can be marvellous. Best producers: CLIMENS★★★, COUTET★★, DOIS͏ DAÊNE★★, Doisy-Dubroca★, DOISY-VEDRINES★★, Myrat★, NAIRAC★, Piac͏ Suau★. Best years: (2009) 07 05 03 02 01 99 98 97 96 95 90 89 88 86 8͏

BASILICATA *Italy* Southern Italian region best known for one wine, the potentially excellent, gutsy red called AGLIANICO DEL VULTURE.

BASSERMANN-JORDAN *Deidesheim, Pfalz, Germany* Since 1996, this famous estate has been making rich yet elegant Rieslings★★ from Deidesheim and FORST. Best years: (2009) 08 07 06 **05 04 03 02 01 99 98 97**.

CH. BATAILLEY★ *Pauillac AC, 5ème Cru Classé, Haut-Médoc, Bordeaux, France* A byword for reliability and value for money among the PAUILLAC Classed Growth estates. Marked by a full, obvious blackcurrant fruit, not too much tannin and a luscious overlay of creamy vanilla. Lovely to drink at only 5 years old, the wine continues to age well for at least 15 years. Best years: 2008 06 05 **04 03 02 00 98 96 95 90 89**.

BÂTARD-MONTRACHET AC *Grand Cru, Côte de Beaune, Burgundy, France* This Grand Cru produces some of the world's greatest whites – full, rich and balanced, with a powerful mineral intensity of fruit and fresh acidity. There are 2 associated Grands Crus: Bienvenues-Bâtard-Montrachet and the minuscule Criots-Bâtard-Montrachet. All should be able to age for a decade. Best producers: Blain-Gagnard★★, CARILLON★★★, DROUHIN★★, Fontaine-Gagnard★★, J-N GAGNARD★★★, JADOT★★★, Louis LATOUR★★, Dom. LEFLAIVE★★★, Olivier LEFLAIVE★★, Marc Morey★★★, Pierre Morey★★★, RAMONET★★★, SAUZET★★★, VERGET★★. Best years: (2009) 08 07 06 05 04 **03 02 01 00 99**.

BERNARD BAUDRY *Chinon, Loire Valley, France* Baudry, recently joined by his son Matthieu, crafts supple, elegant Cabernet Franc. Aspect and soil type differentiate four site-specific CHINON cuvées: Les Granges (sand/gravel) and Les Grézeaux★ (gravel/clay) are for earlier drinking while Le Clos Guillot★★ (limestone/clay/tuffeau) and La Croix Boissée★★ (clay/limestone) reward patience. Good dry white and rosé too. Best years: (top reds) (2009) 08 06 05 **04 03 02 01 00**.

DOM. DES BAUMARD *Coteaux du Layon, Loire Valley, France* Well-sited vineyards produce sensational QUARTS DE CHAUME★★★ that requires aging, as well as rich, honeyed, impeccably balanced COTEAUX DU LAYON Clos de Ste-Catherine★★. Also fine steely, mineral-scented SAVENNIÈRES Clos du Papillon★★ and Clos St-Yves★★, with a late-harvest Trie Spéciale★★ in top years. Idiosyncratic Vert de l'Or Verdelho varies in sweetness according to vintage. Good CREMANT DE LOIRE★ and sound ANJOU reds. Unusually for France, wines are bottled under screwcap. Best years: (Quarts de Chaume) (2009) 07 06 **05 03 02 01 99 97 96 95 90 89**.

LES BAUX-DE-PROVENCE AC *Provence, France* This AC has proved that organic and biodynamic farming can produce spectacular results in a warm dry climate. Good fruit and intelligent winemaking produce some of the more easily enjoyable reds in Provence. Best producers: Hauvette★, Lauzières★, Mas de la Dame★, Mas de Gourgonnier★, Mas Ste-Berthe★, ROMANIN★, Terres Blanches★. Best years: 2008 07 **06 05 04 03 02 01 00 99 98**.

BAY OF FIRES *Tasmania, Australia* The Tasmanian arm of Constellation has become more important in the past decade as HARDYS' chief sparkling winemaker, Ed Carr, has concentrated on the region's ultra-cool climate. He's making brilliant wines★★, but Constellation doesn't seem to be able to decide what to call them – Bay of Fires, Arras, even House of Arras. There's a renewed focus on table wines, especially the complex, minerally Chardonnay and smooth, tightly structured, ageworthy Pinot Noir★. Bay of Fires also produce a sublime Riesling, impressive Pinot Gris and an intense, steely Sauvignon Blanc.

BÉARN AC *South-West France*   Since 2000, there seems to have been an improvement in quality of wines of all three colours, but I'm still waiting to be gobsmacked. Best producers: CAUHAPÉ, Guilhemas, Lapeyre★, Nigri.

CH. DE BEAUCASTEL *Châteauneuf-du-Pape AC, Rhône Valley, France*   The Perrin family makes some of the richest, most profound reds in CHÂTEAUNEUF-DU-PAPE★★, with an unusually high percentage of Mourvèdre (Hommage à Jacques Perrin★★★ is 60% Mourvèdre), which can take at least a decade to show their best, though their gamy character can sometimes make them an acquired taste. The white Roussanne Vieille Vignes★★★ is classy, exquisite and long-lived. They also produce red★★ and white★ CÔTES DU RHÔNE Coudoulet de Beaucastel and GIGONDAS Dom. des Tourelles★★. Under the Perrin & Fils label there are splendid authentic southern reds, including RASTEAU★ and VINSOBRES★. Best years (reds) 2009 08 07 06 05 **04 03 01 00 99 98 97 96 95 94 90 89 88 86 85** (whites) 2009 08 07 06 **05 04 03 01 00 99 98 97 96 95 94 90 89.**

BEAUJOLAIS AC *Beaujolais, Burgundy, France*   Wine region in the beautiful hills that stretch down from Mâcon to Lyon, producing predominantly red wine from the Gamay grape. Beaujolais is best known for BEAUJOLAIS NOUVEAU, which accounts for around 40% of the production. The better quality reds, each having their own appellation, come from the north of the region and are BEAUJOLAIS-VILLAGES and the 10 single Cru villages: from north to south these are ST-AMOUR, JULIENAS, MOULIN-A-VENT, CHENAS, FLEURIE, CHIROUBLES, MORGON, REGNIE, BROUILLY and CÔTE DE BROUILLY. There is growing buzz about the area: standards have improved dramatically in recent years as a new wave of producers (a younger generation of locals and winemakers from both Burgundy in the north and the Rhône in the south) have begun investing here. Growing consumer demand for food friendly wines with lower alcohol levels may help to spark renewed interest in the area. In good vintages simple Beaujolais is light, fresh, aromatic and delicious to drink, but in poorer vintages the wine can be drab and acidic. A little rosé is also made from Gamay, and a small quantity of Beaujolais Blanc is made from Chardonnay. Best producers: J-P Brun/Terres Dorées★, A Chatoux★, Coquard, H Fessy, J-F Garlon★.

BEAUJOLAIS NOUVEAU *Beaujolais AC, Burgundy, France*   Also known as Beaujolais Primeur, this is the first release of bouncy, fruity Beaujolais on the third Thursday of November after the harvest. Once a simple celebration of the new vintage, nouveau was badly over-hyped and, as a result, is nowhere near as popular as it once was. Quality is generally reasonable and the wine can be delicious until Christmas and the New Year, but thereafter is likely to throw a slight sediment and soon loses the vivacious fresh fruit that made it so appealing in its youth.

BEAUJOLAIS-VILLAGES AC *Beaujolais, Burgundy, France*   Beaujolais-Villages can come from one of 38 villages in the north of the region. Top examples rival the BEAUJOLAIS Crus, having more body, character, complexity and elegance than simple Beaujolais and representing all the pleasure of the Gamay grape at its best. Best villages are Lancié, Quincié and Perréon. Best producers: Ch. de Belleverne★, Ch. Cambon★, DUBOEUF, Ch. du Pavé★, JADOT (Combe aux Jacques), Gilles Roux/de la Plaigne★.

BEAUMES-DE-VENISE AC *Rhône Valley, France*   Area famous for its scented, honeyed sweet wine, MUSCAT DE BEAUMES-DE-VENISE. The red wine is also good, full of smoky dark fruit and crisp tannins and can show well for 8–10 years. Best producers: (reds) Beaumalric, Bernardins, Cassan★, Durban★, Fenouillet, Ferme Saint-Martin, les Goubert, Ch. Redortier.

BEAUNE AC *Côte de Beaune, Burgundy, France* Most of the wines are red, with delicious, soft red-fruits ripeness. There are no Grands Crus but some excellent Premiers Crus, especially Boucherottes, Bressandes, Clos des Mouches, Fèves, Grèves, Marconnets, Teurons, Vignes Franches. White-wine production is increasing – DROUHIN makes outstanding, creamy, nutty Clos des Mouches★★★. Best producers: (growers) de Bellene★, Croix★, Germain/Ch. de Chorey★★, LAFARGE★★, de MONTILLE★, Albert Morot★, Rateau, TOLLOT-BEAUT★★; (merchants) BOUCHARD PÈRE ET FILS★★, Champy★★, Chanson★, DROUHIN★★, Camille Giroud★★, JADOT★★. Best years: (reds) (2009) 08 07 **06** 05 **03** 02 99; (whites) (2009) 08 07 **06** 05 04 02.

CH. BEAU-SÉJOUR BÉCOT★★ *St-Émilion Grand Cru AC, 1er Grand Cru Classé, Bordeaux, France* Demoted from Premier Grand Cru Classé in 1986 and promoted again in 1996, this estate is on top form. Brothers Gérard and Dominique Bécot produce firm, ripe, richly textured wines that need at least 8–10 years to develop. Best years: 2008 07 06 05 **04** 03 02 01 00 99 98 96 95 90 89.

BEAUX FRÈRES *Willamette Valley AVA, Oregon, USA* The goal here is to make ripe, unfiltered Pinot Noir★★ that expresses the essence of their 10ha (24-acre) vineyard atop Ribbon Ridge in the Chehalem Valley. A parcel known as The Upper Terrace★★★ yields exceptional fruit from Dijon clones. Best years: (2008) 07 **06** 05 04 03 02.

GRAHAM BECK WINES *Robertson WO, South Africa* A 2-cellar operation, overseen by Pieter Ferreira. ROBERTSON's potential for Cap Classique sparkling is realized in a range led by the new, Chardonnay-based Cuvée Clive★★ with 5 years on the lees; there's also a rich NV Brut★ and toastily fragrant, creamy, barrel-fermented and ageworthy Blanc de Blancs★. Single-vineyard duo The Ridge Syrah★ and

flavoursome, succulent Lonehill Chardonnay★ lead the Robertson table wines. Viognier is good too. Top wines from FRANSCHHOEK include Old Road Pinotage★, The Joshua Shiraz-Viognier★★, DURBANVILLE-sourced Pheasants' Run Sauvignon Blanc★★ and single-vineyard Coffestone Cabernet★. The William★, a Cabernet Sauvignon-Pinotage blend, shows promise and aging potential.

BEDELL CELLARS *Long Island, New York State, USA* Winemaker Kip Bedell helped establish LONG ISLAND's reputation with his Bordeaux-styled Merlot★ (Reserve★★) and red blends. The wines have continued to improve under new ownership, with Bedell still chief winemaker. Sister winery Corey Creek produces a noteworthy Gewürztraminer.

BEECHWORTH *Victoria, Australia* Beechworth was best known as Ned Kelly country before Rick Kinzbrunner planted the slopes of sub-Alpine north-east Victoria and started making wines at GIACONDA. Now boutique wineries produce tiny volumes at high prices and are on a steep learning curve. BROKENWOOD has a major new vineyard here, called Indigo. Best producers: Amulet (Shiraz★★), BROKENWOOD, Castanga★ (Shiraz★★), Cow Hill★, GIACONDA★★★, Savaterre (Chardonnay★★), Sorrenberg★.

BEIRAS *Portugal* This large Portuguese province includes the DOCs of DÃO, BAIRRADA, Távora-Varosa and Beira Interior. Vinho Regional wines use

Portuguese red and white varieties along with international grapes such a
Cabernet Sauvignon and Chardonnay. Best producers: ALIANÇA, Quinta de
Cardo★, Quinta dos Cozinheiros, Quinta dos Currais, Figueira de Castelo Rodrigo co
op, Quinta de Foz de Arouce★, Filipa Pato★, Luís PATO★★, Rogenda, Caves SÃO JOÃO
(Quinta do Poço do Lobo), Quinta dos Termos. Best years: 2008 05 **04 03 01 00**.

CH. BELAIR-MONANGE★★ *St-Émilion Grand Cru AC, 1er Grand Cru Classé*
Bordeaux, France   Used to be simply Belair until renamed by new owne
négociant J-P MOUEIX in 2008. The soft, supremely stylish wines are
drinkable at 5–6 years, but also capable of long aging. Best years: 2008 06
05 **04** 03 02 01 00 99 98 95 90 89 88 86.

BELLAVISTA *Franciacorta DOCG, Lombardy, Italy*   Specialist in FRANCIACORTA
sparkling wines, with a very good Cuvée Brut★★ and 4 distinctive Gra
Cuvées★★ (including an excellent rosé). Vittorio Moretti★★ is made in
exceptional years. Also produces lovely still wines, including white blend
Convento dell'Annunciata★★★, Chardonnay Uccellanda★★ and red
Casotte★ (Pinot Nero) and Solesine★★ (Cabernet-Merlot).

BELLET AC *Provence, France*   Tiny AC in the hills behind Nice; the wine i
nearly equally divided between red, white and rosé, and is usually highly
priced, although domaines such as Toasc are now producing cheaper vir
de pays from young vines. Best producers: Ch. de Bellet★, Clos St Vincent★
Ch. de Crémat, de la Source, Toasc. Best years: (2009) **08 07 06 05 04**.

BENDIGO *Central Victoria, Australia*   Warm, dry, former gold-mining region
which is now home to about 40 small-scale, high-quality wineries. The
best wines are rich, ripe, distinctively minty Shiraz and Cabernet. Bes
producers: Balgownie, Blackjack★, Bress, Chateau Leamon, Passing Clouds
PONDALOWIE★, Turner's Crossing★, Water Wheel. Best years: (Shiraz) 2008 06
05 04 **03** 02 01 00 99 98 97 95 94 93 91 90.

BERCHER *Burkheim, Baden, Germany*   A top KAISERSTUHL estate. High point
are the powerful oak-aged Spätburgunder★★ (Pinot Noir) reds, Grau-
burgunder★★ (Pinot Gris) and Chardonnay★ dry whites, which marry
richness with perfect balance, and dry Muskateller★, which is firm
elegant and tangy. Best years: (whites) (2009) 08 07 **05 04 03**; (reds) (2009)
08 07 06 05 **04 03**.

BERGERAC AC *South-West France*   The Bergerac vineyards are an eastern
extension of Bordeaux, using the same grape varieties as those used in the
BORDEAUX ACs. The reds are generally like a light, fresh claret, with a good
raw blackcurrant fruit and hint of earth. Côtes de Bergerac AC is one
step up, and its wines are usually aged in wood. The better reds can age
for at least 3–5 years. The fresh dry whites for early drinking. Swee
whites are more ambitious and generally produced under their own more
specific appellations: MONBAZILLAC, Saussignac, MONTRAVEL and Rosette.
Best producers: l'ANCIENNE CURE★★, Bélingard★, la Colline★, Eyssards
Fontenelles★, la Jaubertie, Marnières★, les Miaudoux★, Monestier-la-Tour★
TOUR DES GENDRES★★, VERDOTS★. Best years: (reds) (2009) 08 **06 05 01 00**.

BERGSTRÖM *Willamette Valley AVA, Oregon, USA*   The Bergström family uses
biodynamic farming to bring out the best character from the *terroir* of
their 9ha (23-acre) estate vineyard. The primary focus is on Pinot Noir,
with Bergström Vineyard★★ and de Lancellotti Vineyard★★ forming
the greater part of the production. Cumberland Reserve★★★ is a multi-
vineyard blend that can rival many fine Burgundies in its complexity.
Also small amounts of Chardonnay★ and Riesling★★. Best years: (reds)
2008 07 06 **05 04**.

ERINGER *Napa Valley AVA, California, USA* Beringer, part of the Foster's Wine Group, mass-produces some fairly average varietal labels, but also offers a serious range of top-class Cabernet Sauvignons. The Private Reserve Cabernet can be ★★★ and is one of NAPA VALLEY's finest yet most approachable; the Chabot Vineyard★★ can be equally impressive. The Knight's Valley Cabernet Sauvignon★ is made in a lighter style and is good value. Beringer also makes red★★ and white★ Alluvium (meritage wines) from Knight's Valley. The powerful Private Reserve Chardonnay★★ is ripe and toasty. Bancroft Ranch Merlot★★ from HOWELL MOUNTAIN is also very good. Best years: (Cabernet Sauvignon) (2006) **05 03 02 01 00 99 98 97 96 95 94 93 91 90** 87 86.

ERNKASTEL *Mosel, Germany* Both a historic wine town in the Middle MOSEL and a large Bereich. Top wines, however, come only from vineyard sites around the town – the most famous of these is the overpriced Doctor vineyard. Wines from the Graben and Lay sites are often as good and cost a fraction of the price. Best producers: Dr LOOSEN★★, MOLITOR★, Pauly-Bergweiler★, JJ PRÜM★★, S A PRÜM★, SELBACH-OSTER★★, Studert-Prüm, Dr H Thanisch★, WEGELER★★. Best years: (2009) 08 07 **06 05 04 02 01 99 98**.

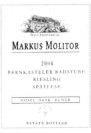

MARKUS MOLITOR

2004

BERNKASTELER BADSTUBE
RIESLING
SPÄTLESE

MOSEL · SAAR · RUWER

ESTATE BOTTLED

OM. BERTHOUMIEU *Madiran AC and Pacherenc du Vic-Bilh AC, South-West France* Didier Barré's wines dead-heat with a small handful of others for top place in these appellations. The top red Cuvée Charles de Batz★★ (the real name of d'Artagnan, fictionalized in *The Three Musketeers*) is outstanding. His best PACHERENCS★ are almost as good. Best years: (reds) (2009) (08) **06 05 04**; (Pacherenc) (2009) **07 05 03**.

EST'S *Grampians, Victoria, Australia* Viv and Chris Thomson run this historic winery, with vineyards dating back to 1868. There have been more recent plantings in the GRAMPIANS and at Lake Boga in the Murray Darling region. The premium range is called Great Western, with superb fleshy Bin No. 0 Shiraz★★★, good Cabernet★ and a fresh, citrus Riesling★. The Thomson Family Shiraz★★ is an outstanding cool-climate Shiraz. Best years: (Thomson Family Shiraz) (2008) 06 05 04 **01 99 98 97 95 94 93 91 90**.

ETZ FAMILY WINERY *Columbia Valley AVA, Washington State, USA* Bob Betz MW spent decades travelling the wine world promoting Washington wines before staking a claim in the goldrush of this young industry. Since 1997, he has crafted wines of uniquely stylish character. Two BORDEAUX-style red blends: Clos de Betz★ and ageworthy, powerful Cabernet Sauvignon-based Père de Famille★★. The Syrah La Côte Rousse★, named for its Red Mountain origin, is opulent; Syrah La Serenne★★ shows more polish and finesse. Best years: (2008) 07 06 **05 04**.

H. BEYCHEVELLE★ *St-Julien AC, 4ème Cru Classé, Haut-Médoc, Bordeaux, France* This beautiful château can make wine of Second Growth quality. It has a charming softness even when young, but takes at least a decade to mature into ST-JULIEN's famous cedarwood and blackcurrant flavour. Over the years, it's given me as much pleasure as any Bordeaux – I drank an awful lot of the 1961 at university with a monumentally indulgent tutor. Then it became inconsistent, but during the last decade has begun to regain its enticing, scented form. Second wine: Amiral de Beychevelle. Best years: 2008 07 06 05 **04 03 02 00 99 98 96 95 89 86**.

BEYERSKLOOF *Stellenbosch WO, South Africa* Variations on the Pinota theme abound at maestro Beyers Truter's property: the new, plus Pinot-like Diesel★★ (named for a loved dog) sets the standard, with th succulent Cabernet-Pinotage-Merlot Synergy (Reserve★) close its heels. Pinotage also contributes to good fizz and a tradition vintage port style. There's also the striking Cabernet Sauvignon-base Field Blend★★ (previously named Beyerskloof). Best years: (Fie Blend/Beyerskloof) 2005 04 03 01 00 99 98 97 96 95.

BIANCO DI CUSTOZA DOC *Veneto, Italy* Dry white wine from the shor of Lake Garda, made from a blend of grapes including SOAV Garganega. Drink young. Best producers: Cavalchina★, Gorgo Montresor★, Le Vigne di San Pietro★, Zeni★.

BIDDENDEN *Kent, England* Established in 1969, this is one of the olde UK vineyards and produces good wines using the little known Orte grape. Also great apple juices and ciders. Best years: 2009 08.

BIENVENUES-BÂTARD-MONTRACHET AC See BÂTARD-MONTRACHET.

BIERZO DO *Castilla y León, Spain* Sandwiched between the rainy mountai of GALICIA and the arid plains of CASTILLA Y LEON. The arrival of Alva PALACIOS, of PRIORAT fame, and his nephew Ricardo Pérez Palacios, wi their inspired Corullón★★ red, shed an entirely new and exciting light the potential of the Mencía grape. Best producers: Bodega del Abad Casar de Burbia★, Castro Ventosa★, Estefanía, Luna Beberide★, Paixar★ Descendientes de José Palacios★★, Peique★, Raúl Pérez★★, Pittacum★, Pra a Tope, Dominio de Tares★, Valtuille★★.

BIKAVÉR *Hungary* Formerly known by its anglicized name, Bull's Bloo Kékfrankos (Blaufränkisch) grapes sometimes replace robust Kadarka the blend; some producers include Cabernet Sauvignon, Kékoporto Merlot. New regulations should improve the quality of Bikavér in the permitted regions, Eger and Szekszárd. Winemakers such as Vilm Thummerer are working hard on this front.

BILLECART-SALMON *Champagne AC, Champagne, France* High-quali family-controlled CHAMPAGNE house which makes extremely elega wines that become irresistible with age. Greatly increased volumes ha sadly dumbed down the non-vintage Brut★, but non-vintage Br Rosé★, Blanc de Blancs★★★, vintage Cuvée Nicolas Franço Billecart★★★ and Cuvée Elisabeth Salmon Rosé★★ are all exceller Clos Saint-Hilaire★★★ is a single-vineyard vintage Blanc de Noirs. Be years: 2004 (02) 00 (99) 98 97 96 95 90 89 88 86 85 82.

ROLF BINDER *Barossa, South Australia* Rolf and Christa Binder's fami winery was known as Veritas until 2004, when the name was changed avoid confusion with a Veritas winery in the US. The motto *In vi veritas* – In wine there is truth – still holds true. There's certainly truth the bottom of a bottle of Hanisch Shiraz★★★ or Heysen Shiraz★★ The Shiraz-Mataro Pressings★★ (known locally as Bull's Blood) ar 'Heinrich' Shiraz-Grenache-Mataro★★ blends are lovely big red Cabernet-Merlot★★ also impresses, as does Riesling★. Under th Christa Rolf label, Shiraz-Grenache★ is good and spicy with attractiv forward black fruit.

BINGEN *Rheinhessen, Germany* A small town and also a Bereich, th vineyards of which fall in both the NAHE and RHEINHESSEN. The be vineyard is the Scharlachberg, which produces some exciting wine stinging with racy acidity and the whiff of minerals. Best producer Kruger-Rumpf, Villa Sachsen. Best years: (2009) 08 07 06 05 04 02.

ÍO BÍO *Chile* One of Chile's most southerly vineyard regions. Cool and wet, but showing promise for Riesling, Pinot Noir and Gewürztraminer. Agustinos, Porta and Veranda (all part of VC Family Estates) are making excellent Pinot with help from Burgundian winemakers. Best producers: AGUSTINOS★, CONCHA Y TORO, CONO SUR, Porta, Veranda.

BIONDI-SANTI *Brunello di Montalcino DOCG, Tuscany, Italy* Franco Biondi-Santi's Greppo estate has created both a legend and an international standing for BRUNELLO DI MONTALCINO. The Biondi-Santi style has remained deeply traditional, while that of other producers has moved on. The very expensive Riserva★★, with formidable levels of tannin and acidity, deserves a minimum 10 years' further aging after release before serious judgement is passed on it. Franco's son, Jacopo, has created his own range of wines at Castello di Montepò, including Sassoalloro★★, a barrique-aged Sangiovese, and Sangiovese-Cabernet-Merlot blend Schidione★★. Best years: (Riserva) (2009) (08) (07) (06) (04) 01 99 **97 95 90 88 85 83 82 75 64 55 45.**

BLAGNY AC *Côte de Beaune, Burgundy, France* The red wine from this tiny hamlet above MEURSAULT and PULIGNY-MONTRACHET can be fair value, if you like a rustic Burgundy. Actually much more Chardonnay than Pinot Noir is grown here, but this is sold as Puligny-Montrachet, Meursault Premier Cru or Meursault-Blagny. Best producers: R Ampeau★, Lamy-Pillot★, Martelet de Cherisey, Matrot★. Best years: (2008) 07 06 05 **04 03 02 99.**

DOM. PAUL BLANCK *Alsace AC, Alsace, France* One of ALSACE's most interesting and reliable domaines, although real character only shows in the Grand Cru wines. Riesling★★ and Vieilles Vignes Gewurztraminer★★ from the Furstentum Grand Cru (also the source of super-rich Pinot Gris SGN★★★) stand out. Riesling Schlossberg★★ and Pinot Gris Altenbourg★★ offer depth and finesse. Best years: (Grand Cru Riesling) 2007 **05 04 02 01 00 98 97 96 95.**

BLANQUETTE DE LIMOUX AC *Languedoc-Roussillon, France* Refreshing fizz from the Mauzac grape, which makes up a minimum 90% of the wine and gives it its striking 'green apple skin' flavour – the balance is made up of Chardonnay and Chenin Blanc. The traditional (CHAMPAGNE) method is used. The more rustic *méthode rurale*, finishing off the original fermentation inside the bottle, is used under a separate appellation, Blanquette Méthode Ancestrale. Best producers: Collin, Fourn★, Guinot, Martinolles★, Rives-Blanques★, SIEUR D'ARQUES★. See also CREMANT DE LIMOUX AC and pages 288–9.

WOLF BLASS *Barossa Valley, South Australia* Wolf Blass, with its huge range, remains a cornerstone (with PENFOLDS) of Australia's largest wine company, the Foster's Wine Group. The wines do still faintly reflect the founder's dictum that they must be easy to enjoy, though I long for them to do better. The reds show overt oak, sometimes clumsy, and occasionally capture the traditional Blass mint and blackcurrant charm. Whites are on the oaky side, except for the Rieslings, which are good, though sweeter and less vibrant than they used to be, including Gold Label Riesling★. White Label Riesling and Chardonnay, released at 5 years of age, has lifted the bar at the top end. Black Label★, a red blend released at 4 years old, is expensive but good. Ultra-expensive Platinum Label Shiraz★ is quite impressive. Regional varietals under the Blass label reflect the winemaking style rather than regional taste. The Eaglehawk range is reliable. Best years: (Black Label) (2009) 08 06 **03 02 01 99 98 97 96 95 91 90 88 86**; (Platinum Shiraz) (2008) 06 05 04 03 02 01 **99 98.**

BORDEAUX RED WINES

Bordeaux, France

 This large area of South-West France, centred on the historic city of Bordeaux, produces a larger volume of fine red wine than any other French region. Wonderful Bordeaux-style wines are produced in California, Australia, South Africa and South America, but the home team's top performers still just about keep the upstarts at bay. Around 560 million bottles of red wine a year are produced here. The best wines, known as the Classed Growths, account for a tiny percentage of this figure, but some of their lustre rubs off on the lesser names, making this one of the most popular wine styles.

GRAPE VARIETIES

Bordeaux's reds are commonly divided into 'right' and 'left' bank wines. On the left bank of the Gironde estuary, the red wines are dominated by the Cabernet Sauvignon grape, with varying proportions of Cabernet Franc, Merlot and Petit Verdot. At best they are austere but perfumed with blackcurrant and cedarwood. The most important left bank areas are the Haut-Médoc (especially the communes of Margaux, St-Julien, Pauillac and St-Estèphe), and, south of the city of Bordeaux, Pessac-Léognan and Graves. On the right bank, Merlot is the predominant grape, which generally makes the resulting wines more supple and fleshy than those of the left bank. The key areas for Merlot-based wines are St-Émilion, Pomerol, Fronsac and Côtes de Castillon.

CLASSIFICATIONS

At its most basic, the wine is simply labelled Bordeaux or Bordeaux Supérieur. Above this are the more specific ACs covering sub-areas (such as the Haut-Médoc) and individual communes (such as Pomerol, St Émilion or Margaux). Single-estate Crus Bourgeois (although, after legal challenge, this is no longer a classification but as of 2008 a certificate awarded on a yearly basis) are the next rung up on the quality ladder, followed by the Crus Classés (Classed Growths) of the Médoc, Graves and St-Émilion. The famous classification of 1855 ranked the top red wines of the Médoc (plus one from Graves) into 5 tiers, from First to Fifth Growths (Crus); there has been only one change, in 1973, promoting Château Mouton-Rothschild to First Growth status. Since the 1950s the Graves/Pessac-Léognan region has had its own classification for red and white wines. St-Émilion's classification (for red wines only) has been revised several times, the last modification being in 2006 (but once again lawyers interfered and the 1996 version was reinstated with the 2006 promotions added); the possibility of re-grading can help to maintain quality, but not if you can't also get relegated. Curiously, Pomerol, home of Château Pétrus, arguably the most famous red wine in the world, has no official pecking order. Many top châteaux make 'second wines', which are cheaper versions of their Grands Vins.

See also BORDEAUX, BORDEAUX-CÔTES DE FRANCS, BORDEAUX SUPERIEUR, CANON-FRONSAC, CÔTES DE BOURG, CÔTES DE CASTILLON, FRONSAC, GRAVES, HAUT-MEDOC, LALANDE-DE-POMEROL, LISTRAC-MEDOC, LUSSAC-ST-EMILION, MARGAUX, MEDOC, MONTAGNE-ST-EMILION, MOULIS, PAUILLAC, PESSAC-LEOGNAN, POMEROL, PREMIÈRES CÔTES DE BLAYE, PREMIÈRES CÔTES DE BORDEAUX, PUISSEGUIN-ST-EMILION, ST-EMILION, ST-ESTÈPHE, ST-GEORGES-ST-EMILION, ST-JULIEN; and individual châteaux.

BEST YEARS

(2009) 08 06 05 **04 03 01 00
98 96 95 90 89 88 86 85 83
82 70 66 61**

BEST PRODUCERS

Graves, Pessac-Léognan
Carbonnieux, Dom. de
CHEVALIER, HAUT-BAILLY, HAUT-
BRION, la LOUVIERE, MALARTIC-
LAGRAVIERE, la MISSION-HAUT-
BRION, PAPE-CLEMENT, SMITH-
HAUT-LAFITTE.

Margaux BRANE-CANTENAC,
FERRIÈRE, MALESCOT ST-EXUPERY,
MARGAUX, PALMER, RAUZAN-SEGLA,
SIRAN, du Tertre.

Pauillac GRAND-PUY-LACOSTE,
HAUT-BAGES-LIBERAL, LAFITE-
ROTHSCHILD, LATOUR, LYNCH-
BAGES, MOUTON-ROTHSCHILD,
PICHON-LONGUEVILLE, PICHON-
LONGUEVILLE-LALANDE, PONTET-
CANET.

Pomerol le BON PASTEUR,
Certan-de-May, Clinet, la
CONSEILLANTE, l'EGLISE-CLINET,
l'EVANGILE, la FLEUR-PETRUS,
GAZIN, Hosanna, LAFLEUR,
LATOUR-A-POMEROL, PETIT-
VILLAGE, PETRUS, le PIN,
TROTANOY, VIEUX-CHATEAU-
CERTAN.

St-Émilion ANGELUS, AUSONE,
BEAU-SEJOUR BECOT, BELAIR-
MONANGE, CANON, CANON-LA-
GAFFELIERE, CHEVAL BLANC, Clos
Fourtet, la Dominique, FIGEAC,
Grand Mayne, Larcis-Ducasse,
MAGDELAINE, MONBOUSQUET, La
Mondotte, PAVIE, PAVIE-MACQUIN,
Rol Valentin, TERTRE-ROTEBOEUF,
TROPLONG-MONDOT,
VALANDRAUD.

St-Estèphe CALON-SEGUR, COS
D'ESTOURNEL, HAUT-MARBUZET,
LAFON-ROCHET, MONTROSE, les
Ormes de Pez.

St-Julien BEYCHEVELLE,
BRANAIRE-DUCRU, DUCRU-
BEAUCAILLOU, GRUAUD-LAROSE,
LAGRANGE, LANGOA-BARTON,
LEOVILLE-BARTON, LEOVILLE-LAS-
CASES, LEOVILLE-POYFERRE, ST-
PIERRE, TALBOT.

BORDEAUX WHITE WINES

Bordeaux, France

 This is France's largest fine wine region but, except f[or] the sweet wines of Sauternes and Barsac, Bordeau[x] international reputation is based almost entirely on [its] reds. From 52% of the vineyard area in 1970, white win[e] now represent only 11% of the present 120,000[ha] (296,500 acres) of vines. Given the size of the region, the diversity [of] Bordeaux's white wines should come as no surprise. There are dr[y] medium and sweet styles, ranging from dreary to some of the mo[st] sublime white wines of all. Bordeaux's temperate southern climate moderated by the influence of the Atlantic and of two rivers, t[he] Dordogne and the Garonne – is ideal for white wine productio[n] particularly south of the city along the banks of the Garonne.

GRAPE VARIETIES

Sauvignon Blanc and Sémillon, the most important white grapes, a[re] both varieties of considerable character and are usually blended togethe[r] They are backed up by smaller quantities of other grapes, the mo[st] notable of which is Muscadelle (unrelated to Muscat), which len[ds] perfume to sweet wines and spiciness to dry.

DRY WINES

With the introduction of new technology and new ideas, many of the[m] influenced by the New World, Bordeaux has become one of France[s] most exciting white wine areas. There are both oaked and unoake[d] styles. The unoaked are leafy, tangy and stony-dry. The barrel-fermente[d] styles are delightfully rich yet dry, custard-cream softness mellowir[g] leafy acidity and peach and nectarine fruit.

SWEET WINES

Bordeaux's most famous whites are its sweet wines made from grape[s] affected by noble rot, particularly those from Sauternes and Barsac. Th[e] noble rot concentrates the flavours, producing rich, honeyed wine[s] replete with pineapple and peach flavours, and which develop a lanoli[n] and beeswax depth and a barley sugar and honey richness with age. O[n] the other side of the Garonne river, Cadillac, Loupiac and Ste-Croi[x] du-Mont also make sweet wines; these rarely attain the richness [or] complexity of a top Sauternes, but they are considerably less expensive.

CLASSIFICATIONS

The two largest dry white wine ACs in Bordeaux are Bordeaux Blan[c] and Entre-Deux-Mers. There are plenty of good dry wines in the Grav[es] and Pessac-Léognan regions; the Pessac-Léognan AC, created in 198[7] contains all the dry white Classed Growths. The great sweet wines [of] Sauternes and Barsac were classified as First or Second Growths in 185[5.]

See also BARSAC, BORDEAUX, BORDEAUX-CÔTES DE FRANCS, BORDEAUX SUPERIEUR, CADILLAC, CERONS, CÔTES DE BOURG, ENTRE-DEUX-MERS, GRAVES, LOUPIAC, PESSAC-LEOGNAN, PREMIÈRES CÔTES DE BLAYE, PREMIÈRES CÔTES DE BORDEAUX, STE-CROIX-DU-MONT, SAUTERNES; and individual châteaux.

BEST PRODUCERS

Dry wines

Pessac-Léognan Dom. de
CHEVALIER, Couhins-Lurton,
FIEUZAL, HAUT-BRION, LATOUR-
MARTILLAC, LAVILLE-HAUT-BRION,
la LOUVIERE, MALARTIC-LAGRAVIERE,
SMITH-HAUT-LAFITTE;
Graves Archambeau, Ardennes,
Brondelle, Chantegrive, Clos
Floridène, Magneau, Rahoul,
Respide-Médeville, St-Robert
(Cuvée Poncet-Deville), Vieux-
Ch.-Gaubert, Villa Bel Air.

Entre-Deux-Mers BONNET,
de Fontenille, Landereau,
Marjosse, Nardique-la-Gravière,
Ste-Marie, Toutigeac, Turcaud.

Bordeaux AC l'Abbaye de Ste-
Ferme, Bauduc, DOISY-DAENE
(Sec), LYNCH-BAGES,
Ch. MARGAUX (Pavillon Blanc),
MONBOUSQUET, REYNON,
Roquefort, TALBOT, Thieuley,
Tour de Mirambeau.

Premières Côtes de Blaye Charron
(Acacia), Haut-Bertinerie, Cave
des Hauts de Gironde co-op
(Chapelle de Tutiac), Tourtes
(Prestige).

Sweet wines

Sauternes and Barsac CLIMENS,
Clos Haut-Peyraguey, COUTET,
DOISY-DAENE, DOISY-VEDRINES,
FARGUES, GILETTE, GUIRAUD,
LAFAURIE-PEYRAGUEY, NAIRAC,
Raymond-Lafon, RIEUSSEC,
Sigalas-Rabaud, SUDUIRAUT,
la TOUR BLANCHE, YQUEM.

Cadillac Fayau, Manos,
Mémoires.

Cérons Ch. de Cérons, Grand
Enclos du Ch. de Cérons.

Loupiac Clos Jean, Cros,
Mémoires, Noble.

Ste-Croix-du-Mont Loubens,
Pavillon, la Rame.

BLAUBURGUNDER See PINOT NOIR.
BLAUER LEMBERGER See BLAUFRÄNKISCH.

BLAUFRÄNKISCH Good Blaufränkisch, when not blasted with new oa
has a taste similar to raspberries and white pepper or even beetro
Hungarian in origin, it does well in Austria, where it is the principal r
grape of BURGENLAND. The Hungarian vineyards (where it is call
Kékfrankos) are mostly just across the border on the other side of t
Neusiedlersee. Called Lemberger in Germany, where almost all of it
grown in WÜRTTEMBERG. Also successful in NEW YORK STATE and (
Lemberger) in WASHINGTON STATE (getting better with global warming

BLAYE See PREMIÈRES CÔTES DE BLAYE AC.
JACKY BLOT *Loire Valley, France* When he created Domaine de la Taille a
Loups in MONTLOUIS-SUR-LOIRE and VOUVRAY in 1988, Jacky Blot's use
barrel fermentation and new oak caused controversy. However, rigoro
selection of pristine, ripe grapes produces sparkling, dry and sweet whit
with tremendous fruit purity. Top Montlouis-sur-Loire cuvées Rém
(*sec*)★★ and Romulus (*liquoreux*)★★ are groundbreaking – wi
staggeringly good 'Plus' versions in exceptional vintages. Since 2002 B
makes four powerful, well-structured reds at Domaine de la Butte★★
BOURGUEIL AC from separate parcels of south-facing vineyards. Best yea
(whites) (sec) 2008 07 **06**; (moelleux) (2009) 05 **03 02 97 96 95 90**.

BOEKENHOUTSKLOOF *Franschhoek WO, South Africa* Perched high in t
FRANSCHHOEK mountains, this small winery is named after the surroundi
Cape beech trees. The flagship trio comprises punchy, savoury Syrah★
deep, long-lived Cabernet Sauvignon★★, and sophisticated Semillon★
partly from 100-year-old vines. Burly, expressive Chocolate Block★★
a Shiraz-Grenache-Cabernet Sauvignon blend with splashes of Cinsa
and Viognier. Also fruit-focused, good-value Porcupine Ridge★ ran
and The Wolftrap. Best years: (premium reds) 2007 **06 05 04 03 02 01**
99 98 97.

BOIREANN *Queensland, Australia* Peter and Therese Stark establish
Boireann in 1995 as a retirement project to specialize in red wines, wi
400 Cabernet vines. It's now QUEENSLAND's most impressive winery, wi
a 1.5ha (3.5-acre) vineyard planted to 10 red varieties plus Viognier f
the flagship fragrant, plush Shiraz-Viognier★★. Other stunning re
include: Merlot★★, Cabernet Sauvignon★ and, from 2008, the seducti
Lurnea blend (Merlot, Cabernets Sauvignon and Franc and Pe
Verdot).

BOISSET *Burgundy, France* Jean-Claude Boisset bought his first vineyards
1964 and began a *négociant* company whose extraordinary success h
enabled him to swallow up many other long-established names such
Jaffelin, Ponelle, Ropiteau and Héritier Guyot in the CÔTE D'OR, Morea
in CHABLIS, Cellier des Samsons and Mommessin in BEAUJOLAIS and mo
recently RODET in Côte Chalonnaise. Most of these companies a
designed to produce commercially successful rather than fine win
excepting Domaine de la VOUGERAIE and now the Boisset label itself. Als
projects in California, Canada, Chile and Uruguay.

BOLGHERI DOC *Tuscany, Italy* Zone named after an arty village in t
northern MAREMMA with, originally, simple white and rosé wines, lat
major reds based on Cabernet, Merlot and/or Syrah. There is a speci
sub-zone for SASSICAIA. Best producers: Argentiera, Ca' Marcanda★ (GAJA

Grattamacco★★, Guado al Tasso★★ (ANTINORI), Le MACCHIOLE★★, ORNELLAIA★★ (Masseto★★★), Poggio al Tesoro★, Michele Satta★★. Best years: (reds) (2008) (07) (06) **05 04 03 01 00 99 98 97**.

BOLLINGER *Champagne AC, Champagne, France* One of the great CHAMPAGNE houses, with good non-vintage (Special Cuvée★) and vintage wines (Grande Année★★★), made in a full, rich, rather old-fashioned style. (Bollinger is one of the few houses to ferment its base wine in barrels.) It also produces a range of rarer vintages, including Vintage RD★★★, and a Vieilles Vignes Françaises Blanc de Noirs★★ from ancient, ungrafted Pinot Noir vines. New delightfully soft, creamy non-vintage Brut Rosé. Bollinger bought Champagne Ayala, a neighbour in Aÿ, in 2005. Best years: (Grande Année) (2002) 00 **99 97** 96 **95 92 90 89 88 85 82 79**.

CH. LE BON PASTEUR★★ *Pomerol AC, Bordeaux, France* Owned by Michel Rolland, Bordeaux's most famous winemaker. The wines are expensive, but they are always deliciously soft and full of lush fruit. Best years: 2008 06 05 **04 03 02 01** 00 **99 98** 96 **95 90 89 88**.

BONNES-MARES AC *Grand Cru, Côte de Nuits, Burgundy, France* A large Grand Cru straddling the communes of CHAMBOLLE-MUSIGNY and MOREY-ST-DENIS, commendably consistent over the last few decades. Bonnes-Mares generally has a deep, ripe, smoky plum fruit, which starts rich and chewy and matures over 10–20 years. Best producers: d'Auvenay (Dom. LEROY)★★★, BOUCHARD PÈRE ET FILS★★, DROUHIN★★★, Drouhin-Laroze★★, DUJAC★★★, Robert Groffier★★★, JADOT★★★, D Laurent★★, ROUMIER★★★, de VOGÜÉ★★★, VOUGERAIE★★★. Best years: (2009) 08 07 06 05 03 02 **01** 99 98 96 95 93 90.

CH. BONNET *Entre-Deux-Mers AC, Bordeaux, France* This region's pioneering estate for quality and consistency. Large volumes of good, fruity, affordable ENTRE-DEUX-MERS★ and BORDEAUX AC rosé and red, particularly the barrel-aged Réserve★. Drink this at 3–4 years and the others young. Also a special cuvée, Divinus★. Owner André Lurton is also the proprietor of Ch. La LOUVIERE and other properties in PESSAC-LEOGNAN.

BONNEZEAUX AC *Loire Valley, France* One of France's great sweet wines, Bonnezeaux is a zone within the COTEAUX DU LAYON AC. Quality is variable, but top wines are world class. It can age very well in good vintages. Best producers: M Angeli/Sansonnière★★, Fesles★★★, Godineau★★, Les Grandes Vignes★★, Petit Val★★, la Petite Croix, Petits Quarts★★, Terrebrune★★, la Varière★★. Best years: (2009) 07 06 **05 04 03 02 01 99 97** 96 95 90 89.

BONNY DOON *Santa Cruz Mountains AVA, California, USA* Randall Grahm has a particular love for Rhône and Italian varietals: Le Cigare Volant★★ is a blend of Grenache and Syrah and is Grahm's homage to CHÂTEAUNEUF-DU-PAPE. Cigar Blanc★ is lush yet dry. His Ca' del Solo wines are delightful, particularly the Albariño★. Grahm's PACIFIC RIM winery in Washington focuses entirely on Riesling.

BORDEAUX AC *Bordeaux, France* One of the most important ACs in France, covering reds, rosés and the dry, medium and sweet white wines of the entire Gironde region. Most of the best wines are allowed specific district or commune ACs (such as MARGAUX or SAUTERNES) but a vast amount of Bordeaux's wine – delicious, atrocious and everything in between – is sold as Bordeaux AC. At its best, straight red Bordeaux is marked by bone-dry leafy fruit and an attractive earthy edge, but far more frequently the wines are tannic and raw – and often overpriced. Good examples usually benefit from a year or so of aging. Bordeaux Blanc has

87

joined the modern world with an increasing number of refreshing pleasant wines. These may be labelled as Bordeaux Sauvignon. Drin young. Bordeaux Clairet is a pale red wine, virtually rosé but with a littl more substance. Best producers: (reds) BONNET★, Dourthe (Numéro ┃ Ducla, d:vin★, Fontenille★, Gadras, Sirius, Thieuley★, Tour de Mirambea (whites) l'Abbaye de Ste-Ferme★, Bauduc★, DOISY-DAËNE★, Dourthe (Numér I★), LYNCH-BAGES★, MARGAUX (Pavillon Blanc★★), MONBOUSQUET★, REYNON★ Roquefort★, TALBOT★, Thieuley★, Tour de Mirambeau★. See also pages 82–5

BORDEAUX-CÔTES DE FRANCS AC *Bordeaux, France* Tiny area east c ST-ÉMILION for reds and a little white; part of new Côtes de Bordeaux AC from 2008; the top wines are good value. The Thienpont famil (Ch. Puygueraud) is the driving force. Best producers: les Charmes Godard★, Franc-Cardinal, Francs (Les Cerisiers★★), Laclaverie★, Marsau★ Nardou, Pelan★, la Prade★, Puygueraud★★, Vieux Saule. Best years: **(2009)** 0 05 04 03 01 00.

BORDEAUX SUPÉRIEUR AC *Bordeaux, France* Covers the same area as th BORDEAUX AC but the wines must have an extra 0.5% of alcohol, a lowe yield and a longer period of maturation. Many of the best petits château are labelled Bordeaux Supérieur. Best producers: (reds) Barreyre★, Beaulie Comtes des Tastes★, de Bouillerot★, des Chapelains, de Courteillac★, Gran Village★, Parenchère★, Penin★, Pey la Tour★, le Pin Beausoleil★, Reignac★ Thieuley (Réserve Francis Courselle★), Tire-Pé★.

BORIE LA VITARÈLE *St-Chinian AC, Languedoc, France* The Izarn famil produces several ST-CHINIANS, as well as Vin de Pays des Coteaux d Murviel, which express the different soils of their organic vineyard: Le Crès★, dominated by Syrah, is spicy and warm; Les Schistes, with mor Grenache, is ripe and concentrated. Best years: 2008 07 06 05 04 03 01 00

BOSCARELLI *Vino Nobile di Montepulciano DOCG, Tuscany, Italy* Arguabl Montepulciano's best producer, crafting rich and stylish reds witl guidance from star enologist Maurizio Castelli. VINO NOBILE★★, Riserv del Nocio★★ and the barrique-aged Boscarelli★★ are all brilliant. Bes years: (2009) (08) (07) 06 04 03 01 00 99 97.

BOUCHARD FINLAYSON *Walker Bay WO, South Africa* Pinotphile Pete Finlayson produces classy Pinot Noir (Galpin Peak★ and occasional Têt de Cuvée★★). His love of Italian varieties is reflected in Hannibal★★, a multi-cultural mix led by Sangiovese with Pinot Noir, Nebbiolo, Barbera and Shiraz. Chardonnays (Kaaimansgaat/Crocodile's Lair★ – now fresher, more citrusy and less obviously oaky – and full, nutty home-grown Missionvale★) are plausibly Burgundian. Sauvignon Blanc★ i tangy and fresh. Best years: (Pinot Noir) 2008 07 06 05 04 03 02 01 00.

BOUCHARD PÈRE & FILS *Beaune, Burgundy, France* Important merchan with superb holdings such as Chevalier-Montrachet★★, le MONTRACHET★★★, BEAUNE Grèves Vigne de l'Enfant Jésus, as well as a blend labelled Beaune du Château. Reds and whites equally good. Bes years: (top reds) (2009) 08 07 06 05 02 99.

BOUCHES-DU-RHÔNE, VIN DE PAYS DES *Provence, France* Wines from 3 areas: the coast, a zone around Aix-en-Provence and the Camargue. Mainly full-bodied, spicy reds, with estates like Trevallon making use of the vin de pays status to use a high percentage of Cabernet Sauvignon. Unusual varieties include Caladoc (Grenache x Malbec) at la Michelle and Arinaroa (Merlot x Petit Verdot) at St-Pierre. Rosé can be good too. Best producers: Ch. Bas, l'Île St-Pierre, Mas de Rey, la Michelle, TREVALLON★★ Best years: (reds) **2008** 07 06 05.

OM. HENRI BOURGEOIS *Sancerre AC, Loire Valley, France* A major presence with 67ha (166 acres) of domaine vineyards and a substantial *négociant* business extending into POUILLY-FUMÉ, MENETOU-SALON, QUINCY and Coteaux du Giennois, plus Clos Henri label in New Zealand; consistently high quality. The Monts Damnés cuvées★ from a precipitously steep slope have bags of mineral character. Ageworthy old-vine, soil-specific bottlings Jadis★★, d'Antan★★ and the rare barrel-fermented Étienne Henri★★ are among the finest in Sancerre. Good red Sancerre too. Best years: (top wines) 2009 08 **07** 06 05 04 02.

OURGOGNE AC *Burgundy, France* Bourgogne is the French name anglicized as 'Burgundy'. This generic AC mops up all the Burgundian wine with no AC of its own, resulting in massive differences in style and quality. The best wines will usually come from a single grower's vineyards just outside the main village ACs of the COTE D'OR; such wines may be the only way we can afford the joys of fine Burgundy. If the wine is from a grower, the flavours should follow a regional or local style. However, if the address on the label is that of a *négociant*, the wine could be from anywhere in Burgundy. Pinot Noir is the main red grape, but Gamay from a declassified BEAUJOLAIS Cru is, absurdly, allowed. Red Bourgogne is usually light, fruity in an upfront strawberry and cherry way, and should be drunk within 2–3 years. The rosé (Pinot Noir) can be pleasant, but little is produced. Bourgogne Blanc is a usually bone-dry Chardonnay wine and most should be drunk within 2 years. Bourgogne Passe-tout-Grains is made from Gamay with a minimum 33% of Pinot Noir, while the oxymoronically named Bourgogne Grand Ordinaire is rarely more than a quaffing wine, drunk in local bars. Best producers: (reds/growers) G Barthod★★, Dugat-Py★★, Germain/Ch. de Chorey★, LAFARGE★, MEO-CAMUZET★★, P RION★★, ROUMIER★, VOUGERAIE; (reds/merchants) DROUHIN★, GIRARDIN★, JADOT★, Maison Leroy★★, N POTEL★★; (reds/co-ops) BUXYNOISE★, Caves des Hautes-Côtes★; (whites/growers) M BOUZEREAU★, Boyer-Martenot★, J-M BROCARD★, COCHE-DURY★★, J-P Fichet★, P Javillier★★, Ch. de Meursault★, Pierre Morey★, Guy Roulot★; (whites/merchants) DROUHIN★, FAIVELEY, JADOT★, Olivier LEFLAIVE, RODET★; (whites/co-ops) BUXYNOISE, Caves des Hautes-Côtes. Best years: (reds) (2009) **08 07** 05; (whites) 2009 **08 07**. See also pages 90–3.

OURGOGNE ALIGOTÉ AC See ALIGOTE.

OURGOGNE-CÔTE CHALONNAISE AC *Burgundy, France* AC for vineyards to the west of Chalon-sur-Saône around the villages of Bouzeron, RULLY, MERCUREY, GIVRY and MONTAGNY. Best producers: X Besson, Villaine (La Digoine★). Best years: (reds) (2009) **08 07** 05; (whites) (2009) 08 **07**.

OURGOGNE-HAUTES-CÔTES DE BEAUNE AC *Burgundy, France* The hills behind the great CÔTE DE BEAUNE are a good source of affordable Burgundy. The red wines are lean but drinkable, as is the slightly sharp Chardonnay. Best producers: Caves des Hautes-Côtes★, J-Y Devevey★, L Jacob★, J-L Joillot★, Ch. de Mercey★/RODET, Naudin-Ferrand★, C Nouveau★. Best years: (reds) (2009) 08 **07 06** 05; (whites) 2009 **08 07 06** 05.

OURGOGNE-HAUTES-CÔTES DE NUITS AC *Burgundy, France* Attractive, lightweight wines from the hills behind the CÔTE DE NUITS. The reds are best, with an attractive cherry and plum flavour. The whites tend to be rather dry and flinty. Best producers: (reds) D Duband★, FAIVELEY★, A-F GROS★, M GROS★, A Guyon★, Caves des Hautes-Côtes★, Jayer-Gilles★, T LIGER-BELAIR★, A Verdet★; (whites) Caves des Hautes-Côtes★, Champy★, Jayer-Gilles★★, Thévenot-le-Brun★. Best years: (reds) (2009) 08 **07** 06 05; (whites) 2009 **08 07** 06 05.

BURGUNDY RED WINES

Burgundy, France

Rich in history and gastronomic tradition, the region of Burgundy (Bourgogne in French) covers a vast tract of eastern France, running from Auxerre, south-east of Paris, down to the city of Mâcon. As with its white wines, Burgundy's red wines are extremely diverse. The explanation for this lies partly in the fickle nature of Pinot Noir, the area's principal red grape, and partly in the historical imbalance of supply and demand between growers – who grow the grapes and make and bottle much of the best wine – and merchants, whose efforts originally established the reputation of the wines internationally.

WINE STYLES

Pinot Noir shows many different flavour profiles according to climate, soil and winemaking. The reds from around Auxerre (Épineuil, Irancy) in the north will be light, chalky and strawberry-flavoured. Also light though more rustic and earthy, are the reds of the Mâconnais in the south, while the Côte Chalonnaise offers solid reds from Givry and Mercurey.

The top reds come from the Côte d'Or, the heartland of Burgundy. Flavours sweep through strawberry, raspberry, damson and cherry – in young wines – to a wild, magnificent maturity of Oriental spices, chocolate, mushrooms and truffles. The greatest of all – the world-famous Grand Cru vineyards such as Chambertin, Musigny, Richebourg and Clos de Vougeot – are in the Côte de Nuits, the northern part of the Côte d'Or from Nuits-St-Georges up towards Dijon. Other fine reds, especially Volnay, Pommard and Corton, come from the Côte de Beaune. Some villages tend towards a fine and elegant style (Chambolle-Musigny, Volnay), others towards a firmer, more tannic structure (Gevrey-Chambertin, Pommard).

The Beaujolais should really be considered as a separate region, growing Gamay on granitic soils rather than Pinot Noir on limestone, though a small amount of Gamay has also crept north to be included in the lesser wines of Burgundy.

CLASSIFICATIONS

Most of Burgundy has 5 increasingly specific levels of classification: regional ACs (e.g. Bourgogne), specified ACs covering groups of villages (e.g. Côte de Nuits-Villages), village wines taking the village name (Pommard, Vosne-Romanée), Premiers Crus (good village vineyard sites) and Grands Crus (the best individual vineyard sites). At village level, vineyard names in small letters are called *lieux-dits*.

See also ALOXE-CORTON, AUXEY-DURESSES, BEAUJOLAIS, BEAUNE, BLAGNY, BONNES-MARES, BOURGOGNE, BOURGOGNE-COTE CHALONNAISE, BOURGOGNE-HAUTES-COTES DE BEAUNE/NUITS, CHAMBERTIN, CHAMBOLLE-MUSIGNY, CHASSAGNE-MONTRACHET, CHOREY-LÈS-BEAUNE, CLOS DE LA ROCHE, CLOS ST-DENIS, CLOS DE VOUGEOT, CORTON, CÔTE DE BEAUNE, CÔTE DE NUITS, CÔTE D'OR, CRÉMANT DE BOURGOGNE, ÉCHÉZEAUX, FIXIN, GEVREY-CHAMBERTIN, GIVRY, IRANCY, LADOIX, MÂCON, MARANGES, MARSANNAY, MERCUREY, MONTHELIE, MOREY-ST-DENIS, MUSIGNY, NUITS-ST-GEORGES, PERNAND-VERGELESSES, POMMARD, RICHEBOURG, la ROMANÉE-CONTI, ROMANÉE-ST-VIVANT, RULLY, ST-AUBIN, ST-ROMAIN, SANTENAY, SAVIGNY-LÈS-BEAUNE, la TÂCHE, VOLNAY, VOSNE-ROMANÉE, VOUGEOT; and individual producers.

BEST YEARS

(2009) 08 07 06 05 **03 02 01 99 98** 96 95 90

BEST PRODUCERS

Côte de Nuits B Ambroise, Arlaud, l'Arlot, Robert Arnoux, Denis Bachelet, G Barthod, A Burguet, Cacheux-Sirugue, S CATHIARD, Charlopin, J Chauvenet, R Chevillon, Chopin-Groffier, B CLAIR, CLOS DES LAMBRAYS, CLOS DE TART, J-J Confuron, P Damoy, Drouhin-Laroze, C Dugat, B Dugat-Py, DUJAC, Sylvie Esmonin, Fourrier, Geantet-Pansiot, H GOUGES, GRIVOT, R Groffier, GROS, Hudelot-Noëllat, Jayer-Gilles, F Lamarche, Lechenaut, Philippe Leclerc, Dom. LEROY, LIGER-BELAIR, H Lignier, MEO-CAMUZET, Denis MORTET, Mugneret, Mugneret-Gibourg, J-F MUGNIER, Perrot-Minot, Ponsot, RION, Dom. de la ROMANÉE-CONTI, Rossignol-Trapet, Roty, E Rouget, ROUMIER, ROUSSEAU, Sérafin, Taupenot-Merme, J & J-L Trapet, de VOGÜE, VOUGERAIE.

Côte de Beaune M Ampeau, d'ANGERVILLE, Comte Armand, Bize, H Boillot, J-M Boillot, CHANDON DE BRIAILLES, Courcel, Germain/Ch. de Chorey, Michel LAFARGE, LAFON, de MONTILLE, J Prieur, N Rossignol, TOLLOT-BEAUT.

Côte Chalonnaise Joblot, M Juillot, Lorenzon, Raquillet, de Suremain, Villaine.

Merchants BOUCHARD PÈRE ET FILS, Champy, DROUHIN, FAIVELEY, V GIRARDIN, Camille Giroud, JADOT, D Laurent, Maison Leroy, Nicolas POTEL, RODET.

Co-ops BUXYNOISE, Caves des Hautes-Côtes.

91

BURGUNDY WHITE WINES

Burgundy, France

White Burgundy has for generations been thought of as the world's leading dry white wine. The top wines have a remarkable succulent richness of honey and hazelnut, melted butter and sprinkled spice, yet are totally dry. Such wines are all from the Chardonnay grape and the finest are generally produced in the Côte de Beaune, the southern part of the Côte d'Or, in the communes of Aloxe-Corton, Meursault, Puligny-Montrachet, Chassagne-Montrachet and St-Aubin, where limestone soils and the aspect of the vineyard provide perfect conditions for even ripening of grapes. However, Burgundy encompasses many more wine styles than this, even if no single one quite attains the peaks of quality of those 5 villages on the Côte de Beaune.

WINE STYLES

Chablis in the north traditionally produces very good steely wines, aggressive and lean when young, but nutty and rounded – though still very dry – after a few years. Modern Chablis is frequently a softer, milder wine, easy to drink young, and sometimes enriched (or denatured) by aging in new oak barrels.

There is no doubt that Meursault and the other Côte de Beaune villages can produce stupendous wine, but it is in such demand that unscrupulous producers are often tempted to maximize yields and cut corners on quality. Consequently white Burgundy from these famous villages must be approached with caution. Lesser-known villages such as Pernand-Vergelesses and St-Aubin often provide good wine at lower prices. There are also good wines from some villages in the Côte de Nuits, such as Morey-St-Denis, Nuits-St-Georges and Vougeot, though amounts are tiny compared with the Côte de Beaune.

South of the Côte d'Or, the Côte Chalonnaise is becoming more interesting for quality white wine now that better equipment for temperature control is becoming more widespread and oak barrels are being used more often for aging. Rully and Montagny are the most important villages, though Givry and Mercurey can produce nice white, too. The minor Aligoté grape makes some attractive, if acidic, wine, especially in Bouzeron.

Further south, the Mâconnais is a large region, two-thirds planted with Chardonnay. There is some fair sparkling Crémant de Bourgogne, and some very good vineyard sites, in particular in St-Véran and in Pouilly-Fuissé. Increasingly stunning wines can now be found, though there's still a lot of dross.

See also ALOXE-CORTON, AUXEY-DURESSES, BÂTARD-MONTRACHET, BEAUJOLAIS, BEAUNE, BOURGOGNE, BOURGOGNE-CÔTE CHALONNAISE, BOURGOGNE-HAUTES-COTES DE BEAUNE/NUITS, CHABLIS, CHASSAGNE-MONTRACHET, CORTON, CORTON-CHARLEMAGNE, CÔTE DE BEAUNE, CÔTE DE NUITS, CÔTE D'OR, CRÉMANT DE BOURGOGNE, FIXIN, GIVRY, LADOIX, MÂCON, MÂCON-VILLAGES, MARANGES, MARSANNAY, MERCUREY, MEURSAULT, MONTAGNY, MONTHELIE, MONTRACHET, MOREY-ST-DENIS, MUSIGNY, NUITS-ST-GEORGES, PERNAND-VERGELESSES, POUILLY-FUISSÉ, POUILLY-VINZELLES, PULIGNY-MONTRACHET, RULLY, ST-AUBIN, ST-ROMAIN, ST-VERAN, SANTENAY, SAVIGNY-LÈS-BEAUNE, VIRÉ-CLESSÉ, VOUGEOT; and individual producers.

BEST YEARS

(2009) 08 **07 06 05 04 02 00 99**

BEST PRODUCERS

Chablis Barat, J-C Bessin, Billaud-Simon, P Bouchard, A & F Boudin, J-M BROCARD, D Dampt, R & V DAUVISSAT, D-E Defaix, Droin, DURUP, W Fèvre, J-H Goisot, J-P Grossot, LAROCHE, Long-Depaquit, Malandes, Louis Michel, Christian Moreau, Moreau-Naudet, Picq, Pinson, RAVENEAU, Vocoret.

Côte d'Or (Côte de Beaune) M Ampeau, d'Auvenay (LEROY), Blain-Gagnard, H Boillot, J-M Boillot, Bonneau du Martray, M BOUZEREAU, Boyer-Martenot, CARILLON, CHANDON DE BRIAILLES, Coche-Debord, COCHE-DURY, Marc Colin, Dancer, Arnaud Ente, J-P Fichet, Fontaine-Gagnard, J-N GAGNARD, A Gras, P Javillier, F Jobard, R Jobard, LAFON, H Lamy, Dom. LEFLAIVE, Matrot, several Moreys, M Niellon, P Pernot, J & J-M Pillot, RAMONET, M Rollin, G Roulot, SAUZET, VERGET, VOUGERAIE.

Côte Chalonnaise S Aladame, H & P Jacqueson.

Mâconnais D & M Barraud, A Bonhomme, Bret Brothers, Cordier, Corsin, Deux Roches, J-A Ferret, Ch. Fuissé, Guffens-Heynen/VERGET, Guillot-Broux, O Merlin, Robert-Denogent, Ch. des Rontets, Saumaize-Michelin, la Soufrandière, J Thévenet.

Merchants BOUCHARD PÈRE ET FILS, Champy, Chanson, DROUHIN, FAIVELEY, V GIRARDIN, JADOT, Louis LATOUR, Olivier LEFLAIVE, Maison Leroy, Rijckaert, RODET, VERGET.

Co-ops la BUXYNOISE, la CHABLISIENNE, Lugny, Viré.

BOURGUEIL AC *Loire Valley, France* Fine red wine from between Tours and Angers, made with Cabernet Franc, sometimes with a little Cabernet Sauvignon. A concerted quality drive, together with a good run of vintages, is shedding its reputation for rusticity; expect plump raspberry and plum fruit. Best producers: Y Amirault★★, Audebert (estate wines★), la Butte★★/BLOT, T Boucard★, P Breton★★, la Chevalerie★, Clos de l'Abbaye/la Dîme★, L et M Cognard-Taluau, DRUET★★, Forges★, S Guion★, Lamé-Delisle-Boucard★, la Lande/Delaunay★, F MABILEAU★, Nau Frères★, Ouches★, Les Pins/Pitault-Landry, Raguenières★. Best years: (2009) 08 **06 05** 04 03 02 01 99 97 96. See also ST-NICOLAS-DE-BOURGUEIL.

BOUZEREAU *Meursault, Côte de Beaune, Burgundy, France* An extended family of vignerons, all making a range of whites from MEURSAULT and neighbouring villages, plus some less interesting CÔTE DE BEAUNE reds. Best at the moment are Dom. Michel Bouzereau & Fils★ and Vincent Bouzereau★. Best years: (whites) (2009) 08 **07** 06 05.

BRACHETTO An unusual Italian grape native to Piedmont, Brachetto makes every style from dry and still to rich, sweet passito and sweet, frothy light red wines with a Muscat-like perfume, as exemplified by Brachetto d'Acqui DOCG. Best producers: (dry) Contero, Correggia★, Scarpa★; (Brachetto d'Acqui) BANFI★, Braida★, G Marenco★.

CH. BRANAIRE-DUCRU★★ *St-Julien AC, 4ème Cru Classé, Haut-Médoc, Bordeaux, France* After a period of mediocrity, 1994 and subsequent vintages have confirmed a return to full, soft, chocolatey form, with some added muscle in recent vintages. Best years: 2008 07 06 05 **04 03 02 01 00** 99 98 96 95 94.

BRAND'S *Coonawarra, South Australia* COONAWARRA firm, owned by MCWILLIAM'S, with 100ha (250 acres) of new vineyards as well as some ancient vines planted in 1893. Ripe Laira Cabernet★ is increasingly attractive; Patron's Reserve★★ (Cabernet with Shiraz and Merlot) is excellent. New life has been breathed into Shiraz★, and the opulent Stentiford's Reserve★★ (from 100-year-old vines) shows how good Coonawarra Shiraz can be. Merlot★ is among Australia's best examples of the variety. Best years: (reds) (2009) 08 06 05 **04 03** 02 01 00 99 98 97 96 94 90.

CH. BRANE-CANTENAC★★ *Margaux AC, 2ème Cru Classé, Haut-Médoc, Bordeaux, France* After a drab period, Brane-Cantenac returned to form during the late 1990s. Henri Lurton has taken over the family property and is making some lovely wines, particularly the 2000, 2005 and 2008, although don't expect flavours to be mainstream – 2002 and 2003 are tasty but wild. Best years: 2008 07 06 05 **04 03** 02 01 00 99 98 96 95 89.

BRAUNEBERG *Mosel, Germany* Small village with 2 famous vineyard sites, Juffer and (especially) Juffer Sonnenuhr, whose wines have a honeyed richness and creaminess rare in the Mosel. Best producers: Bastgen, Fritz HAAG★★★, Willi Haag★, Paulinshof★, M F RICHTER★★, SCHLOSS LIESER★★. Best years: (2009) 08 07 06 **05 04 03** 02 01 99.

BREAKY BOTTOM *Sussex, England* Small vineyard in the South Downs near Lewes. Peter Hall is a quirky, passionate grower, making delicious sparkling wines, principally from Seyval Blanc★, which continue to improve. Newer plantings include Chardonnay and Pinot Noir.

GEORG BREUER *Rüdesheim, Rheingau, Germany* Intense dry Riesling from RÜDESHEIM Berg Schlossberg★★★, Berg Rottland★ and RAUENTHAL Nonnenberg★★. Also a remarkable Sekt★. Best years: (Berg Schlossberg) (2009) 08 07 06 **05 04 03** 02 01 00 99 98.

AN-MARC BROCARD *Chablis, Burgundy, France* Dynamic winemaker who has built up this 80ha (200-acre) domaine almost from scratch, and is now one of Chablis' most reliable producers. The Premiers Crus (including Montée de Tonnerre★★, Montmains★★) and slow-evolving Grands Crus (les Clos★★★) are tremendous, while the basic Chablis, especially Vieilles Vignes★★, are some of the best on the market. Brocard also produces a range of BOURGOGNE Blancs★ from different soil types. Now adopting an increasingly organic – and in some cases biodynamic – approach to his vineyards. Best years: (2009) **08 07 06 05**.

ROKENWOOD *Hunter Valley, New South Wales, Australia* High-profile winery celebrating its 40th anniversary. Has delicious traditional unoaked HUNTER Semillon★★ (ILR Reserve ★★★). Very good Shiraz★★; best wine is classic Hunter Graveyard Vineyard Shiraz★★★. Cricket Pitch reds and whites are cheerful, fruity ready-drinkers. The Indigo vineyard at BEECHWORTH is making very promising Chardonnay, Viognier and Pinot Noir. Also excellent Forest Edge Chardonnay★★ from ORANGE. Best years: (Graveyard Vineyard Shiraz) (2009) 07 05 04 03 02 **00 99 98 96 95 94 93 91 90 89 88 86**.

RONCO WINE CO. *California, USA* Maker of the Charles Shaw range of wines – known as 'Two-Buck Chuck' because of their $2 price tag. There's now a $5 Napa Cabernet Sauvignon. The company is run by maverick Fred Franzia, who famously said 'wine's too damned expensive'. He is grand-nephew of the late Ernest GALLO, and he owns 14,000ha (35,000 acres) of California vineyard land, marketing 10 million cases of wine under more than a dozen brands.

ROUILLY AC *Beaujolais, Burgundy, France* Largest of the 10 BEAUJOLAIS Crus; at its best, the wine is soft, fruity, rich and brightly coloured. Best producers: Ch. de la Chaize, DUBOEUF (Ch. de Nervers), H Fessy★, J-C Lapalu★★, A Michaud★, Point du Jour (Les Bruyères★), Ch. Thivin★★. Best years: **2009 08**.

ROWN BROTHERS *North-East Victoria, Australia* Highly successful family winery, producing a huge range of varietal wines, which have improved significantly in recent years. Loves to dabble in 'new' grapes such as Tarrango and Cienna. Good fizz and fine stickies★★. Top-of-the-range Patricia wines (Cabernet★★, sparkling Pinot-Chardonnay★★) are Brown's best yet. Premium grapes are from cool King Valley, mountain-top Whitlands and a new vineyard at HEATHCOTE, producing potentially ★★★Shiraz.

RÜNDLMAYER *Kamptal, Niederösterreich, Austria* Willi Bründlmayer makes wine in a variety of Austrian and international styles, but his outstanding dry Riesling (Alte Reben★★★) from the great Heiligenstein vineyard and superb, ageworthy Grüner Veltliner (Ried Lamm★★★) are the best; high alcohol is matched by superlative fruit and mineral flavours. Also excellent Chardonnay★★ and good Sekt★. Best years: (Zöbinger Heiligenstein Riesling) (2009) 08 07 **06 05 04 02 01 00 99**.

RUNELLO DI MONTALCINO DOCG *Tuscany, Italy* Iconic, full but elegant red 'created' by BIONDI-SANTI in the late 19th century. The number of producers soared in the late 20th century as the price of the wine (and land) took off, but the 'Brunellogate' scandal of the early 21st century (some big-name producers were accused of blending French grapes in with what is supposed to be a 100% Sangiovese wine) put a damper on sales, especially in the US, Brunello's main market. Released 4 years or more after vintage. Best producers: Agostina Pieri★★, Altesino★

(Montosoli★★), BANFI★ (Riserva★★), Barbi★, BIONDI-SANTI★★, Gian Brunelli★★, Camigliano★★, La Campana★, Caparzo★ (La Casa★★), Casano di Neri★★, Casanuova delle Cerbaie★★, CASE BASSE★★ Castelgiocondo/FRESCOBALDI (Riserva★), Centolani★ (Pietranera★ Cerbaiona★★, Ciacci Piccolomini d'Aragona★, Donatella Cinelli Colombini★ Col d'Orcia★★, COSTANTI★★, Fuligni★★, La Gerla★★, Le Gode★★, Gorel Due Portine★, Greppone Mazzi★, Maurizio Lambardi★★, Lisini★ Mastrojanni★★ (Schiena d'Asino★★★), Siro Pacenti★★★, Pian dell'Orino★★ Pian delle Vigne★★/ANTINORI, Piancornello★★, Pieve Santa Restituta★★, I Poderina★, Poggio Antico★★, Poggio San Polo★★, il POGGIONE★ (Riserva★★★), Le Potazzine★★, Salvioni★★, Livio Sassetti-Pertimali★★ Talenti★★, La Togata★★, Valdicava★★, Villa Le Prata★★. Best years: (200 (07) (06) 04 **03** 01 **00** 99 98 97 95 90 88 85.

BUCELAS DOC *Lisboa, Portugal* A tiny but historic DOC. The wines ar
♀ whites based on the Arinto grape (noted for its high acidity). Fc attractive, modern examples try Quinta da Murta or Quinta da Romei (Morgado de Santa Catherina★).

BUGEY *France* In the hills between the Jura (see ARBOIS, CÔTES DU JURA) an SAVOIE regions, east of Lyon, Bugey has grape varieties from both region mainly Chardonnay and Altesse for whites; Gamay, Mondeuse, Pinot No and Poulsard for light reds. The wines were elevated to Bugey AC in 2009. A speciality is Bugey-Cerdon, a semi-sweet pink sparkling wine made fron Gamay and Poulsard in the *méthode ancestrale*. Best producers: Angelot, Bartucc Charlin, Lingot-Martin, Monin.

VON BUHL *Deidesheim, Pfalz, Germany* Large estate, sold in 2005 to Achir
♀ Niederberger, the new owner of BASSERMANN-JORDAN. Top Rieslings no invariably ★★. Best years: (Grosses Gewächs Rieslings) (2009) 08 07 **06** 05 0 03 02 01.

BUITENVERWACHTING *Constantia WO, South Africa* Beautiful old propert
♀ part of the Cape's original CONSTANTIA wine farm. Sauvignon Blanc★ penetrating and zesty; Husseys Vlei Sauvignon Blanc★ is bigger an more pungent. Ripe, fruit-laden Chardonnay★ and elegant, subtl Husseys Vlei★★ version. These and a light racy Riesling can improv with a little aging. New, virus-free vines allow for more expressiv though still classically-styled reds, headed by the aristocrati Christine★★, which remains one of the Cape's most accurate BORDEAU lookalikes. Best years: (Christine) 2006 **05** 04 03 02 01 00 99 98 97.

BULL'S BLOOD See BIKAVÉR.

GRANT BURGE *Barossa Valley, South Australia* A leading producer in th
♀ BAROSSA, with extensive vineyard holdings and a wide range, includin chocolaty Filsell Shiraz★ and rich Meshach Shiraz★★, Cameron Val Cabernet★ and Shadrach Cabernet★ (now sourced entirely from Baross fruit), RHÔNE-style Grenache-Shiraz-Mourvèdre blend Holy Trinity★, fres Thorn Riesling★, oaky Zerk Semillon-Viognier, and the excellent-valu Barossa Vines range. Recent vintages have shown a welcome reduction i oak. Best years: (Meshach) (2009) (08) (06) (05) 04 02 **99** 98 96 95 94 91.

BURGENLAND *Austria* 4 regions: Neusiedlersee, including Seewinkel fc sweet wines; Neusiedlersee-Hügelland, famous for sweet wines, now also bi reds and fruity dry whites; Mittelburgenland, for robust Blaufränkisch red and Südburgenland, for good reds. Best producers: Paul Achs★, FEILER

RTINGER★★, Gesellmann★, Gernot Heinrich★★, Juris★, Kerschbaum★, ollwentz★★, KRACHER★★★, KRUTZLER★★, Helmut Lang★★, A & H Nittnaus★★, PITZ★, Pöckl★★, Prieler★, Schröck★, Ernst Triebaumer★★, Tschida★, MATHUM★★, VELICH★★.

URGUNDY See BOURGOGNE AC and pages 90–3.

ÜRKLIN-WOLF *Wachenheim, Pfalz, Germany* One of Germany's largest privately owned estates, with 86ha (212 acres) of vineyards. Since the mid-1990s it has been in the first rank of the PFALZ's producers. Biodynamic since 2005. The powerful, spicy dry Rieslings are ★★ to ★★★. Best years: (Grosses Gewächs Rieslings) (2009) 08 07 **06** 05 04 03 02 01.

URMESTER *Port DOC, Douro, Portugal* Shipper established in 1730, and now owned by the Galician firm Sogevinus, which also owns Cálem, Barros and Kopke. Burmester vintage PORT has improved. As well as refined 10- and 20-year-old tawnies★, there are some outstanding old colheitas★★ which extend back over 100 years. Also decent Late Bottled Vintage and oak-aged DOURO red, Casa Burmester. Gilberts is a range of ports aimed at younger drinkers. Best years: (Vintage) 2007 **03** 00 97 95 94.

OMMASO BUSSOLA *Valpolicella DOC, Veneto, Italy* Tommaso Bussola's AMARONE Vigneto Alto★★★ combines elegance with stunning power. Amarone Classico TB★★ is similar with slightly less finesse, and even the basic Amarone★ is a challenge to the palate. The Ripasso VALPOLICELLA Classico Superiore TB★★ is one of the best of its genre, and the RECIOTO TB★★★ is consistently excellent. Best years: (2009) (08) (07) 06 **04** 03 01 00 99 97 95.

A BUXYNOISE *Côte Chalonnaise, Burgundy, France* One of Burgundy's top co-operatives, producing affordable, well-made Chardonnay and Pinot Noir. The light, oak-aged BOURGOGNE Pinot Noir★ and the red and white Clos de Chenôves★, as well as the nutty white MONTAGNY★, are all good, reasonably priced, and best with 2–3 years' age.

UZET AC *South-West France* Good BORDEAUX-style red wines from the same mix of grapes, at a lower price. There is very little rosé and the whites are rarely exciting. Best producers: Buzet co-op, Dom. du PECH★. Best years: (reds) (2009) **08** 06 05.

A' DEL BOSCO *Franciacorta DOCG, Lombardy, Italy* Model estate, headed by Maurizio Zanella, making some of Italy's finest and most expensive international-style wines: outstanding sparklers in FRANCIACORTA Brut★★, Dosage Zero★, Satén★★ and Cuvée Annamaria Clementi★★★. Still wines include excellent Terre di Franciacorta, Chardonnay★★★, Pinero★★ (Pinot Noir) and BORDEAUX blend Maurizio Zanella★★★. Also varietal Carmenère, Carmenero★.

ABARDÈS AC *Languedoc, France* Next door to MINERVOIS. Cabernet Sauvignon and Merlot are allowed, as well as French Mediterranean grape varieties such as Syrah and Grenache. At best, full-bodied, chewy and rustically attractive – and attractively priced. Best producers: Cabrol★, Jouclary, Pennautier★. Best years: 2008 07 06 **05** 04 03.

ABERNET D'ANJOU AC *Loire Valley, France* Rosé made from both Cabernets; generally medium dry or semi-sweet. Rosé d'un Jour is an alternative vin de France rosé, a riposte to commercial wines, made by several rebellious growers led by Mark Angeli; it is picked overripe and not chaptalized. Drink young. Best producers: M Angeli/Sansonnière, Hautes-Ouches, Ogereau, Petites Grouas, Terrebrune.

CABERNET SAUVIGNON

Wine made from Cabernet Sauvignon in places like Australi; California, Chile, Bulgaria, even in parts of southern Franc; has become so popular that many people may not realize wher it all started – and how Cabernet became the great, omnipresen red wine grape of the world.

WINE STYLES

Bordeaux Cabernet It all began in Bordeaux. With the exception of lively bunch of Merlot-based beauties in St-Émilion and Pomerol, th greatest red Bordeaux wines are based on Cabernet Sauvignon, wit varying amounts of Merlot, Cabernet Franc and possibly Petit Verdo blended in. The blending is necessary because by itself Cabernet make such a strong, powerful, aggressive and assertive wine. Dark and tann; when young, the great Bordeaux wines need 10–20 years for th aggression to fade, the fruit becoming as sweet and perfumed as fres blackcurrants, with a fragrance of cedarwood, of cigar boxes, minglin magically among the fruit. It is this character that has made red Bordeau famous for at least two centuries.

Cabernet worldwide When winemakers in other parts of the worl sought role models to try to improve their wines, most of the; automatically thought of Bordeaux and chose Cabernet Sauvignon. was lucky that they did, because not only is this variety easy to grow i almost all conditions – cool or warm, dry or damp – but that unstoppabl personality always powers through. The cheaper wines are general; made to accentuate the blackcurrant fruit and the slightly earthy tannin They are drinkable young, but able to age surprisingly well. The mo; ambitious wines are aged in oak barrels, often new ones, to enhance th tannin yet also to add spice and richness capable of developing over decade or more. Sometimes the Cabernet is blended – usually wit Merlot, sometimes with Cabernet Franc, and occasionally with othe grapes: Shiraz in Australia, Sangiovese in Italy, Tempranillo in Spain.

Europe Many vineyards in southern France now produce goo affordable Cabernet Sauvignon. Spain has produced some goo Cabernet blends, as has Portugal. Italy's red wine quality revolution w sparked off by the success of Cabernet in Tuscany, and all the leadin regions now grow it. Eastern Europe grows lots of Cabernet, but c widely varying quality, while the Eastern Mediterranean and Nor Africa are beginning to produce tasty examples.

New World There is a general move toward darker, denser, more serio; Cabernets, even in countries like Chile and Australia, whose Cabern triumphs have until now been based on gorgeous blackcurrant fruit. hope they don't ditch too much of the fruit, but I have to say that a lot c these new contenders are excellent. Argentina is also pitching in wit some powerful stuff. California's reputation was created by its stron; weighty Cabernets; it's at a bit of a crossroads right now, with som producers going to superhuman lengths to concentrate and overripe their wines, while others show increasing restraint. It should be possib to exhibit power with balance, since thudding tannins, excess alcohol an low acid fruit defeat Cabernet's purpose and what might have been; great wine descends into soup. Some Napa producers are well aware this and are creating marvellous wines of a gaudy, ferocious beaut; increasingly aided by judicious blending with other varieties. Othe more self-indulgent, producers need to be reminded – less is more.

BEST PRODUCERS

France

Bordeaux CALON-SÉGUR, Dom. de CHEVALIER, COS D'ESTOURNEL, GRAND-PUY-LACOSTE, GRUAUD-LAROSE, LAFITE-ROTHSCHILD, LATOUR, LÉOVILLE-BARTON, LÉOVILLE-LAS-CASES, LÉOVILLE-POYFERRÉ, LYNCH-BAGES, Ch. MARGAUX, MOUTON-ROTHSCHILD, PICHON-LONGUEVILLE, PONTET-CANET, RAUZAN-SEGLA; *Provence* TREVALLON.

Other European Cabernets

Italy CA' DEL BOSCO, GAJA, ISOLE E OLENA, LAGEDER, MACULAN, ORNELLAIA, Castello dei RAMPOLLA, SAN LEONARDO, SASSICAIA, SOLAIA, TASCA D'ALMERITA, Castello del TERRICCIO, TUA RITA. *Spain* Blecua, Enate, Jané Ventura, MARQUES DE GRIÑON, TORRES.

New World Cabernets

Australia BALNAVES, CAPE MENTELLE, CULLEN, Fraser Gallop, HARDYS (Thomas Hardy), HENSCHKE, HOUGHTON (Jack Mann, Gladstones), HOWARD PARK, LEEUWIN, MAJELLA, MOSS WOOD, PARKER COONAWARRA ESTATE, PENFOLDS (Bin 707), PENLEY ESTATE, SANDALFORD, VASSE FELIX (Heytesbury), WENDOUREE, The Willows, WIRRA WIRRA, Woodlands, WYNNS, Zema.

New Zealand BABICH, CRAGGY RANGE, Esk Valley, Goldwater, STONYRIDGE, TE MATA, Vidal, VILLA MARIA.

USA (California) ARAUJO, BERINGER, Bryant Family, Cakebread, CAYMUS, CHIMNEY ROCK, DALLA VALLE, DIAMOND CREEK, DOMINUS, DUNN, Freemark, Grace Family, HARLAN, HARTWELL, Honig, Ladera, LAUREL GLEN, Long Meadow Ranch, Peter MICHAEL, MINER, MONDAVI, NEWTON, PHELPS, RIDGE, ST SUPÉRY, SCREAMING EAGLE, SHAFER, SILVER OAK, SPOTTSWOODE, STAG'S LEAP, Viader; *(Washington)* ANDREW WILL, CADENCE, DELILLE CELLARS, DUNHAM, Fidelitas, LEONETTI, QUILCEDA CREEK, Three Rivers, WOODWARD CANYON.

Chile ALMAVIVA, Altaïr, CARMEN, CASABLANCA, CONCHA Y TORO, ERRÁZURIZ, HARAS DE PIRQUE, SANTA RITA, Miguel TORRES.

Argentina CATENA, TERRAZAS DE LOS ANDES.

South Africa BEYERSKLOOF, BOEKEN-HOUTSKLOOF, BUITENVERWACHTING, Neil ELLIS, GRANGEHURST, KANONKOP, Le Riche, RUSTENBERG, SAXENBURG, THELEMA, VERGELEGEN.

CABERNET FRANC Often unfairly dismissed as an inferior Cabern Sauvignon, Cabernet Franc comes into its own in cool zones or are where the soil is damp and heavy. It can have a leafy freshness linked raw but tasty blackcurrant-raspberry fruit; lighter wines drink w slightly chilled. In France it thrives in the LOIRE VALLEY, where sing varietal wines are the norm. It is blended with Cabernet Sauvignon a Merlot in BORDEAUX, especially ST-ÉMILION (AUSONE, CHEVAL BLANC) ar POMEROL (LAFLEUR). Moderately successful where not overproduced northern Italy, especially ALTO ADIGE and FRIULI, although some plantin here have turned out to be Carmenère, and increasingly preferred Cabernet Sauvignon in Tuscany (Le MACCHIOLE's Paleo Rosso is a outstanding example of pure Cabernet Franc). It is the red of choice f many winemakers in the eastern US, performing especially well in th FINGER LAKES and VIRGINIA. Experiments with Cabernet Franc WASHINGTON STATE and on CALIFORNIA's North Coast show promise and i at last gaining some respect in NAPA VALLEY. There are also some goo South African, Chilean and Australian examples.

CABERNET SAUVIGNON See pages 98–9.

CADENCE *Red Mountain AVA, Washington State, USA* A range of vineyar specific reds. Tapteil Vineyard★★★, a powerful Cabernet Sauvigno dominated blend, is the flagship; Ciel du Cheval Vineyard★★★ is mo forward and juicy. Bel Canto★, a Cabernet Franc-Merlot-domina blend, and Camerata★★, based on Cabernet Sauvignon, are both fro the estate Cara Mia Vineyard. Best years: (2008) 07 06 **05 04 03 02**.

CADILLAC AC *Bordeaux, France* Sweet wine from the southern half of t PREMIÈRES CÔTES DE BORDEAUX. Styles vary from fresh, semi-sweet to rich botrytized. The wines have greatly improved in recent vintages. Drir young. Best producers: Fayau (Cuvée Grains Nobles★), Ch. du Juge, Manos Mémoires★, REYNON★. Best years: (2009) **07 05 03 02 01 99 98**.

CAHORS AC *South-West France* Important South-West red wine regio This dark, traditionally tannic wine is made from at least 70% Auxerro (Malbec or Côt) and has an unforgettable, rich plum and tobacco flavo when ripe and well made. Standards are rising rapidly. The best nee ageing. Best producers: la Caminade★, le CÈDRE★★, Clos la Coutale★, CL DE GAMOT★★, CLOS TRIGUEDINA★★, COSSE-MAISONNEUVE★★, Gaudou, Hau Monplaisir, Haute-Serre, Lamartine★, Latuc, la Reyne★, les Rigalets★. Be years: (2009) 06 **05 04 01 98**.

CAIRANNE *Rhône Valley, France* The top village entitled to the CÔTES RHÔNE-VILLAGES appellation, home of full, herb-scented reds and sol whites. Best producers: Alary★★, Ameillaud★, Armand, Berthet-Rayr Brusset★, Cave de Cairanne★, les Hautes Cances★, ORATOIRE ST-MARTIN★ Présidente★, Rabasse-Charavin★, M Richaud★★. Best years: (reds) 2009 07 (**05 04 03 01**.

CALABRIA *Italy* Italy's poorest, most backward and most corru region. CIRÒ, Donnici, Savuto and Scavigna DOC reds from the nati Gaglioppo grape, and whites from Greco, are much improved thanks greater winemaking expertise. In a very restricted field the two leadir producers remain Librandi – with reds Duca San Felice★ (Gaglioppe and Magno Megonio★★, from once endangered Magliocco, and whi Efeso★★ from Mantonico – and Odoardi, with their excellent Scavigr Vigna Garrone★.

ALATAYUD DO *Aragón, Spain* Over 5000ha (12,500 acres) of old Grenache vines on schistose slopes in the mountains between Madrid and Zaragoza: this is a recipe for vinous success that for too long went ignored as local co-ops made mostly bulk wines. Now, more ambitious Spanish and foreign winemakers are making juicy, herb-scented reds which show some depth. Best producers: Albada★, Ateca★, Escocés Volante, Bodegas y Viñedos del Jalón★, Langa, San Alejandro★, San Gregorio★.

ALERA *San Benito, California, USA* A pace-setter for California Pinot Noir with 5 estate wines: Reed★★, Selleck★★, Jensen★★, Mills★★ and Ryan★. They are complex, fascinating wines, capable of aging. Mt Harlan Chardonnay★★ is excitingly original too. CENTRAL COAST Chardonnay★ and Pinot Noir★ are good value. Small amounts of Viognier★★ are succulent with sensuous fruit. Best years: (Pinot Noir) 2007 06 05 04 **03 02 01 00 99 97 96 95**; (Chardonnay) 2007 06 **05** 04 03 02 01 00 99.

ALIFORNIA *USA* California's importance is not simply in being the ourth largest wine producer in the world (behind France, Italy and Spain). Iost of the revolutions in technology and style that have transformed the xpectations and achievements of winemakers in every country of the world – ncluding France – were born in the ambitions of a band of Californian inemakers during the 1960s and 70s. They challenged the old order, with its egulated, self-serving elitism, and democratized the world of fine wine, to the enefit of every wine drinker. This revolutionary fervour is less evident now. nd there are times when Californians seem too intent on establishing their wn particular New World old order. A few figures: there are around 94,000ha (480,000 acres) of wine grape vineyards, producing around 20 illion hectolitres (500 million gallons) of wine annually, about 90% of all ine made in the US. A large proportion (more than 75%) comes from the ot, inland CENTRAL VALLEY. See also CENTRAL COAST, MENDOCINO COUNTY, ONTEREY COUNTY, NAPA VALLEY, SAN LUIS OBISPO COUNTY, SANTA BARBARA COUNTY, ERRA FOOTHILLS, SONOMA COUNTY.

H. CALON-SÉGUR★★ *St-Estèphe AC, 3ème Cru Classé, Haut-Médoc, Bordeaux, France* Long considered one of ST-ESTÈPHE's leading châteaux, but in the mid-1980s the wines were not as good as they should have been. Vintages from the mid-1990s have been more impressive, with better fruit and a suppler texture, with another leap in quality from 2006. Second wine: Marquis de Calon. Best years: 2008 07 06 05 04 03 **02 01 00 98 96 95 90 89 86.**

AMEL VALLEY *Cornwall, England* Sparkling wine specialists who favour Seyval Blanc and Reichensteiner over CHAMPAGNE varieties; the result is the quintessentially English Camel Valley Brut★. Sparkling Pinot Noir★★ (white and rosé) is also excellent, and still wines (dry white Bacchus★, Rosé★) are fragrant and tasty. Best years: (sparkling) **2007 06**; (still) **2008 07**.

AMPANIA *Italy* Three regions – PUGLIA, SICILY and Campania – lead the evolution in Italy's south. Campania has made excellent progress in the hite department, with varietals from Greco di Tufo, Fiano, Falanghina and everal other native grapes; Feudi di San Gregorio★★ have a particularly ood range of whites. On the red side, other producers besides the venerable ASTROBERARDINO have begun to realize the potential of Campania's soil, limate and grapes, especially with the red Aglianico. The leading red wines re Montevetrano★★★ (Cabernet-Merlot-Aglianico) and Galardi's Terra di

Lavoro★★★ (Aglianico-Piedirosso), but also look for top Aglianicos fro
Antonio Caggiano★★, De Conciliis★, Feudi di San Gregorio★★, Lui
Maffini★, Michele Moio★, Salvatore Molettieri★, Orazio Rillo★, San Pao
and co-operatives Cantina del Taburno★ and La Guardiense★. DOC(G
of note are FALERNO DEL MASSICO, Fiano di Avellino, Greco di Tufo, Ischi
TAURASI and Vesuvio.

CAMPILLO *Rioja DOCa, País Vasco, Spain*   An upmarket subsidiary of Bodega
FAUSTINO, producing some exciting new red RIOJAS★. The wines are ofte
Tempranillo-Cabernet Sauvignon blends, with masses of ripe, velve
fruit. Best years: (Reserva) 2005 **04 03 01 99 98 96 95 94**.

CAMPO DE BORJA *Aragón, Spain*   Located to the south-east of 2 bette
known appellations, RIOJA and NAVARRA, Campo de Borja boasts that i
native clones of Grenache are the finest in all of Spain. This viticultur
treasure trove produced little more than hefty, cheap reds until quality
minded producers led by the innovative Borsao co-op changed all tha
Best producers: Alto Moncayo★★, Aragonesas, Borsao★, Pagos del Moncay

CAMPO DI SASSO *Tuscany, Italy*   Brothers Piero and Lodovico ANTINORI
venture in the commune of Bibbona, near BOLGHERI, with plantings
Cabernet Franc, Petit Verdot and Merlot. Wines include Insoglio d
Cinghiale★★, Il Pino di Biserno and Biserno (from 2010).

CAMPO VIEJO *Rioja DOCa, Rioja, Spain*   The largest producer of RIOJA
owned by Pernod Ricard. Reservas★ and Gran Reservas★ are reliabl
good, as are the elegant, all-Tempranillo Reserva Viña Alcorta and th
barrel-fermented white Viña Alcorta. Albor Tempranillo is a goo
modern young Rioja, packed with fresh, pastilley fruit. Best year
(Reserva) 2005 **04 03 01 98 96 95 94**.

CANARY ISLANDS *Spain*   The Canaries have a treasure trove of pre
phylloxera vines, and a total of 9 DOs. The sweet Malvasia from Lanzaro
DO and La Palma DO is worth a try, and there are a couple of remarkabl
fresh dry whites; otherwise stick with the young reds. Best producers: El Grif
Monje, Viña Norte, Tacande★, Tanajara★, Teneguía★, Viñátigo★.

CANBERRA DISTRICT *New South Wales, Australia*   Cool, high altitud
(800m/2600ft) may sound good, but excessive cold and frost can b
problematic. Even so, with global warming kicking in the smart mone
is on Canberra really shining in the next decade or so. Lark Hill an
Helm make exciting Riesling, Lark Hill and Brindabella Hills som
smart Cabernet blends, and Clonakilla sublime Shiraz. Best producer
Brindabella Hills★, CLONAKILLA★★★, Collector★★, Doonkuna★, Helm
Lake George★, Lark Hill★, Madew★, Mount Majura.

DOM. CANET-VALETTE *St-Chinian AC, Languedoc, France*   Marc Valette
uncompromising in his quest to make great wine: organic cultivation
low yields and traditional *pigeage* (foot-stomping) are just some of h
methods. The wines offer an enticingly rich expression of ST-CHINIAN
grape varieties and clay-limestone soils. Cuvées include Une et Mil
Nuits (1001 Nights)★ and the elegant, complex Syrah-Mourvèdr
Maghani★★. Best years: (Maghani) 2006 05 **04 03 01 00**.

CANNONAU   Sardinian name of Spain's Garnacha and France's Grenach
Noir. In SARDINIA it produces deep, tannic reds, but lighter, modern, dr
red wines are gaining in popularity, although traditional sweet an

fortified styles can still be found. Best producers: (modern reds) ARGIOLAS, SELLA & MOSCA; Dolianova, Dorgali, Jerzu, Alberto Loi, Ogliastra, Oliena, Santa Maria La Palma and Trexenta co-ops.

CH. CANON★★ *St-Émilion Grand Cru AC, 1er Grand Cru Classé, Bordeaux, France* Canon can make some of the richest, most concentrated ST-ÉMILIONS, but was in decline before being purchased in 1996 by Chanel (also owns RAUZAN-SEGLA). Following extensive work on the vineyard and cellars it's now back on succulent form. In good vintages the wine is tannic and rich at first but is well worth aging 10–15 years – my 1985 is only just ready. Second wine: Clos Canon. Best years: 2008 07 06 05 **04 03 02** 01 **00 98 89** 88.

CANON-FRONSAC AC *Bordeaux, France* This AC is the heart of the FRONSAC region. The wines are quite sturdy when young but can age for 10 years or more. Best producers: Barrabaque (Prestige★), Cassagne Haut-Canon (La Trufière★), la Fleur Cailleau, Gaby★, Grand-Renouil★, Haut-Mazeris, Moulin Pey-Labrie★★, Pavillon, Vrai Canon Bouché. Best years: (2009) 08 06 **05** 03 01 **00 98 96 95** 90.

CH. CANON-LA-GAFFELIÈRE ★★ *St-Émilion Grand Cru AC, Grand Cru Classé, Bordeaux, France* Owner Stephan von Neipperg has put this property at the top of the list of ST-ÉMILION GRAND CRU CLASSÉS. The wines are firm, rich and concentrated. He also owns Clos de l'Oratoire★★, Ch. l'Aiguilhe★★ in the CÔTES DE CASTILLON, and the remarkable micro-cuvée La Mondotte★★. Best years: 2008 07 06 05 **04 03 02** 01 **00 99 98 96 95**.

CH. CANTEMERLE★ *Haut-Médoc AC, 5ème Cru Classé, Bordeaux, France* With La LAGUNE, the most southerly of the Crus Classés. The wines are delicate in style and delightful in ripe vintages. Second wine: Les Allées de Cantemerle. Best years: 2008 07 06 05 **04 03** 01 **00 98 96 95**.

CANTERBURY *South Island, New Zealand* The long, cool ripening season of the arid central coast of South Island favours white varieties, particularly Chardonnay, Pinot Gris, Sauvignon Blanc and Riesling, as well as Pinot Noir. The northerly Waipara district produces Canterbury's most exciting wines, especially from Riesling and Pinot Noir. Best producers: Bell Hill★, Greystone, Mountford★, Muddy Water, Omihi Road, PEGASUS BAY★★, Waipara West★. Best years: (Pinot Noir) (2009) **08 07 06 03** 02; (Riesling) 2009 **08 07** 06.

CAPE CHAMONIX *Franschhoek WO, South Africa* High-lying FRANSCHHOEK property with talented winemaker, Gottfried Mocke. Best known for his seamlessly oaked, naturally fermented Chardonnays: citrus/creamy standard★; Reserve★★ with lengthy maturation. Barrel-fermented Sauvignon Blanc Reserve★ shows both richness and cool minerals. Pure-fruited, silky-textured Pinot Noir Reserve★★ gains in complexity with every vintage. Best years: (Chardonnay) 2009 **08 07 06 05 04** 03 02 01.

CAPE MENTELLE *Margaret River, Western Australia* Leading MARGARET RIVER winery, owned by LVMH. Superb, cedary gamy Cabernet★★, impressive Shiraz★★ and Chardonnay★★, tangy Semillon-Sauvignon Blanc★★ and wonderfully chewy Zinfandel★★. Wallcliffe wines include taut Sauvignon Blanc-Semillon★ and concentrated Shiraz★★. All wines benefit from cellaring – whites up to 5 years, reds 8–15. Best years: (Cabernet Sauvignon) (2009) (08) (07) 05 **04 03 02** 01 94.

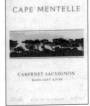

CAPE POINT VINEYARDS *Cape Point WO, South Africa* Pioneering proper▌influenced by bracing Atlantic breezes. Sauvignon Blanc★★ ▌astonishing, ocean-fresh and original. Partially barrel-fermente▌Semillon★★ tantalizes with tangerine and lemongrass intensity, whi▌Isliedh★★★, a barrel-fermented blend of both varieties, combines powe▌with subtlety. Early reds, from a warmer site, also show promise. Bes▌years: (whites) 2009 **08 07 06 05 04 03 02 01**.

CAPEL VALE *Geographe, Western Australia* The Pratten family's winer▌sources fruit from its own vineyards in Geographe, Mount Barke▌PEMBERTON and MARGARET RIVER. After an erratic history, this is now▌winery very much on the up, using only the best varieties from eac▌region. Cheap and cheerful Debut range includes velvety Merlot★ an▌easy-drinking Pinot Noir. There's an impressive Regional Series, an▌two single-vineyard wines: intense yet fine Whispering Hill Riesling★★▌and elegant, beautifully structured Whispering Hill Shiraz★★. Best years▌(Whispering Hill Riesling) 2009 **08 07 06 04 03 02 01 00 98 97**.

CARIGNAN The dominant red grape in the south of France is responsibl▌for much boring, cheap, harsh wine. But when made gently or b▌carbonic maceration, the wine can have delicious spicy fruit. Old vine▌are capable of dense, rich, impressive reds, as shown by the odd success i▌France, California, Chile, Lebanon and Israel. In South Africa it i▌mainly used in Rhône-style blends. Although initially a Spanish grap▌(as Cariñena or Mazuelo), it is not that widespread there, but is useful fo▌adding colour and acidity in RIOJA and CATALUÑA, and has gaine▌unexpected respect in PRIORAT.

CARIGNANO DEL SULCIS DOC *Sardinia, Italy* Carignano is now▌producing wines of quite startling quality. Rocca Rubia★, a barrique▌aged Riserva from the Santadi co-op, with rich, fleshy and chocolat▌fruit, is one of SARDINIA's best reds. Baie Rosse★★ is a step up; even bette▌is the more structured and concentrated Terre Brune★★. Best producer▌Santadi co-op. Best years: (2009) (08) 07 06 **05 04 03 01 00**.

LOUIS CARILLON & FILS *Puligny-Montrachet, Côte de Beaune, Burgundy, France*▌Excellent family-owned estate in PULIGNY-MONTRACHET. The emphasis i▌on traditional, finely balanced whites of great concentration, rather thar▌new oak. Look out for Premiers Crus les Referts★★, Champs Canet★★▌and les Perrières★★★, and the tiny but exquisite production o▌Bienvenues-BÂTARD-MONTRACHET★★★. Reds from CHASSAGNE▌MONTRACHET★, ST-AUBIN★ and MERCUREY★ are good, too. Best years: (whites)▌(2009) 08 07 **06 05 04 02**.

CARIÑENA DO *Aragón, Spain* The largest DO of ARAGÓN, baking under the▌mercilessly hot sun in inland eastern Spain, Cariñena has traditionally▌been a land of cheap, deep red, alcoholic wines from the Garnacha grape▌(Confusingly the Carignan grape is called Cariñena in Spain, but is▌practically absent from the Cariñena region.) Since the late 1990s▌however, temperature-controlled fermentation has been working wonders▌with the Garnacha, and Tempranillo and international grape varieties like▌Cabernet Sauvignon have been planted widely. Best producers: Añadas★▌San Valero (Monte Ducay, Don Mendo), Solar de Urbezo★, Victoria★.

CARLEI *Victoria, Australia* Outstanding biodynamic producer, with▌Chardonnay★★ and Pinot Noir★ from YARRA VALLEY and Shiraz★★ from▌HEATHCOTE. Sergio Carlei's signature blends are Tre Rossi★ (Shiraz-

Barbera-Nebbiolo), Tre Amici (Sangiovese-Cabernet-Merlot) and Tre Bianchi (Sauvignon with small amounts of Semillon and Chardonnay). The modestly priced Green Vineyards range offers very good regional varietals: Chardonnay and Pinot Noir from the Yarra, Heathcote Shiraz, Central Victorian Cabernet and Cardinia Ranges Pinot Gris.

CARMEN *Maipo, Chile* Some of the best reds in MAIPO, including Gold Reserve★★, a limited release made with Carmen's oldest Cabernet Sauvignon vines, Reserve Carmenère-Cabernet★★ and Merlot★★, balanced, complex Wine Maker's Reserve★★ and organic Nativa Cabernet Sauvignon★★. Best years: (reds) 2007 05 04 03 02 01 00 99.

CARMENÈRE An important but forgotten constituent of BORDEAUX blends in the 19th century, historically known as Grande Vidure. Widely planted in Chile, where it thrives on the warm climate and long growing season, it is sold under its own name or mixed with Merlot to greatly improve the blend. When ripe and made with care, it has rich blackberry, plum and spice flavours, with an unexpected but delicious bunch of savoury characters – grilled meat, soy sauce, celery, coffee – thrown in. A true original. Also found in northern Italy, where it has been confused with Cabernet Franc, Argentina and China. Being replanted experimentally in Bordeaux.

CARMIGNANO DOCG *Tuscany, Italy* Red wine from the west of Florence, renowned since the 16th century and revived in the 1970s by Capezzana. The blend (Sangiovese, plus 10–20% Cabernet) gives one of Tuscany's more refined wines and can be quite long-lived. Although Carmignano is DOCG, DOC applies to a lighter red Barco Reale, rosé Vin Ruspo and fine VIN SANTO. Best producers: Ambra★ (Vigne Alte★★), Artimino★, Capezzana★★, Piaggia★★, Pratesi★, Villa di Trefiano★. Best years: (2009) (08) (07) 06 04 03 02 01 00 99 98 97.

CARNEROS AVA *California, USA* Hugging the northern edge of San Francisco Bay, Carneros includes parts of NAPA and SONOMA Counties. Cool and windswept with morning fog off the Bay, it is a top temperate area, suitable for Chardonnay and Pinot Noir as table wine and as a base for sparkling wine. Merlot and Syrah are also coming on well. Best producers: ACACIA★, Buena Vista★, Carneros Creek★, DOMAINE CARNEROS★, Gloria Ferrer, HdV★★, Ramey★★, RASMUSSEN★★, SAINTSBURY★★, Tor (Las Madres Syrah★★), Truchard★★. Best years: (Pinot Noir) 2007 06 05 04 03 02 01 99 98.

CARNUNTUM *Niederösterreich, Austria* 950ha (2350-acre) region south of the Danube and east of Vienna, with sturdy Grüner Veltliner and a strong red wine tradition. Best producers: Artner★, Glatzer, G Markowitsch★, Pitnauer★.

CASA LAPOSTOLLE *Rapel, Chile* Owned by Marnier-Lapostolle of France, with consultancy from leading BORDEAUX winemaker Michel Rolland. Cuvée Alexandre Merlot★★, from the acclaimed Apalta area in COLCHAGUA, was its first hit back in 1994, now eclipsed by red blend Clos Apalta★★★. Also rich, creamy Cuvée Alexandre Chardonnay★ from the CASABLANCA Valley and BoRoBo (Bordeaux, Rhône, Bourgogne), a blend of Pinot Noir, Carmenère, Cabernet Sauvignon, Syrah and Merlot.

CASA MARÍN *San Antonio, Chile* Impressive whites, led by single-vineyard Sauvignon Blancs: Laurel★★ is powerful, full of mineral and intense chilli and fruit flavours, while Cipreses★★★ shows the influence of the Pacific

Ocean in its haunting citrus and stony aromas. Casona Vineyar Gewürztraminer★, Miramar Riesling★ and Estero Sauvignon Gris★ are delightful, too – and there's juicy, cool-climate Pinot Noir★ as well a the outstanding new Miramar Syrah★★★.

CASA SILVA *Colchagua, Chile* Well-run family dynasty heavily involved in th local *huaso* (horsemen) culture and protectors of COLCHAGUA style, especiall with Carmenère. Much development in sub-regions such as Los Lingue Lolol and, more recently, Paredones near the coast. Best wines are Lo Lingues Gran Reserva Carmenère★ and Quinta Generación★.

CASABLANCA *Chile* Coastal valley with a cool-climate personality that i powerful proof of Chile's ability to do regional style. Whites dominate with best results from Sauvignon Blanc, Chardonnay an Gewürztraminer. That said, the Pinot Noir is some of Chile's best, an some producers (Casas del Bosque, Kingston, Loma Larga) make top quality cool-climate Syrah. **Best producers:** Viña CASABLANCA★, CASAS DE BOSQUE★, CONCHA Y TORO★★, CONO SUR★★, EMILIANA★, ERRÁZURIZ★ Kingston★★, Loma Larga★★, MONTES★, Quintay★, Veramonte. **Best years** (2010) 09 08 **07 06 05 04**.

VIÑA CASABLANCA *Casablanca, Chile* Cool CASABLANCA vineyards are th source of some top wines under the Nimbus Estate label: quince-edge Chardonnay★, rose- and lychee-filled Gewürztraminer★, tangy, intens Sauvignon Blanc★, inky-black Cabernet Sauvignon★ and scente Merlot★★. Flagship red blend Neblus★ is made in the best years.

CASAS DEL BOSQUE *Casablanca, Chile* This winery, located in the coo westerly part of CASABLANCA, has a special focus on Sauvignon Blan (Reserva★). The reds are good too, especially the red blend Estat Selection★, and Gran Reserva Syrah★ and Pinot Noir★. **Best years** (whites) **2009** 08 07 06 05 04.

CASE BASSE *Brunello di Montalcino DOCG, Tuscany, Italy* Gianfranco Solder unblushingly proclaims his BRUNELLO DI MONTALCINO★★★ and Brunello d Montalcino Riserva★★★ wines (the latter usually under the Intistier label) to be the best of their genre and, maddeningly, he's pretty muc right. A fanatical biodynamist, Soldera believes perfect grapes are all yo need to make great wine. He ages his wines for a minimum of 5 years i large old (and hence neutral) oak barrels; the result is a wine of brillian colour and an amazing intensity and complexity of perfumes. **Best years** (2009) (08) (07) (06) (04) 01 **99 98 97 95 93 90 88 85.**

CH. LA CASENOVE *Côtes du Roussillon AC, Roussillon, France* Forme photojournalist Étienne Montès, with consultant enologist Jean-Lu COLOMBO, has developed an impressive range, including a perfumed whit vin de pays made from Macabeu and Torbat, MUSCAT DE RIVESALTES★ RIVESALTES★ and 2 predominantly Syrah CÔTES DU ROUSSILLON reds: L Garrigue★★ and Commandant François Jaubert★★. Drink the latte with at least 5 years' bottle age. **Best years:** (François Jaubert) 2005 04 00

CASSIS AC *Provence, France* A picturesque fishing port near Marseille. Th white wine, based on Ugni Blanc and Clairette, is overpriced but can b good if fresh. Light red wine; the rosé can be pleasant. **Best producers:** Bagnol★, Caillol, Clos Ste-Magdelaine★, la Ferme Blanche★, Fontblanche, Ch de Fontcreuse, Mas de Boudard. **Best years:** (white) (2009) **08 07 06 05 04**

DOM. DU CASTEL *Judean Hills, Israel* Israel's leading quality winery Complex Grand Vin★★ is made from 5 BORDEAUX varieties. Blanc d Castel is a barrel-fermented Chardonnay★ with good acidity from th Jerusalem Hills. **Best years:** (reds) 2007 06 05 04 **03 02 00 97.**

CASTEL DEL MONTE DOC *Puglia, Italy* An arid, hilly zone, and an ideal habitat for the Uva di Troia grape, producing long-lived red wine of astonishing character. There is also varietal Aglianico, some good rosé, and the whites produced from international varieties are improving. Best producers: Rivera★, Santa Lucia, Tormaresca★/ANTINORI, Torrevento★. Best years: (2009) (08) **07 06 04 03 01**.

CASTELL *Castell, Franken, Germany* Since medieval times the Castell family has owned the town of that name and its vineyards. Inconsistent in the past, the dry Silvaners and Rieslings are now exemplary, especially from Casteller Schlossberg★★. Powerful TBA★★ too. Best years: (2009) 08 07 **06 05 04**.

CASTELLARE *Chianti Classico DOCG, Tuscany, Italy* Fine estate with excellent CHIANTI CLASSICO★ and deeper, richer Riserva★★. Coniale★★ (Cabernet Sauvignon), Canonico★ (Chardonnay) and Spartito★ (Sauvignon Blanc) are all ripe and fruity. Top wine I Sodi di San Niccolò★★ is an unusual Sangiovese-Malvasia Nera blend, intense but finely perfumed.

CASTILLA-LA MANCHA *Spain* The DOs of the central plateau, LA MANCHA and VALDEPEÑAS, make white wines from the Airén grape, and some good reds from the Cencibel (Tempranillo). Méntrida DO, MANCHUELA DO, Ribera del Júcar DO, Almansa DO and the new Uclés DO, as well as several single-estate (*pago*) appellations, make fast-improving reds and whites. The most ambitious single-estate wines made here are those from MARQUES DE GRIÑON's Dominio de Valdepusa★ estate near the Tagus river and the Dehesa del Carrizal and Pago de Vallegarcía★ estates, both in the Toledo mountains, and Manuel Manzaneque's Cabernet-based reds★ and Chardonnay★ from Sierra de Alcaraz in Albacete province. Manzaneque now has his own DO, Finca Élez, as do the Dominio de Valdepusa and Dehesa del  Carrizal. Other top wines are Uribes Madero's Calzadilla★ in Cuenca province, Ercavio★ and La Plazuela★★ from Toledo, Adaras from Almansa, Arrayán★ and Jiménez-Landi★★ from Méntrida. See also MANCHUELA.

CASTILLA Y LEÓN *Spain* This is Spain's harsh, high plateau, with long cold winters and hot summers (but always cool nights). A few rivers, notably the Duero, temper this climate and afford fine conditions for viticulture. After many decades of winemaking ignorance, with a few exceptions like VEGA SICILIA, the situation has changed radically for the better in all of the region's DOs. In addition to RIBERA DEL DUERO, RUEDA, BIERZO, Cigales and TORO, there is now a bevy of new appellations which were approved in 2009, in coincidence with new EU regulations, covering quality viticultural areas formerly lumped together under the vino de la tierra umbrella: Arlanza, Arribes, Tierra de León, Tierra del Vino de Zamora, Valles de Benavente and Valtiendas. Dynamic winemakers such as Telmo RODRIGUEZ and Mariano García (AALTO and MAURO) have won huge critical acclaim for the region.

CATALUÑA *Spain* Standards vary among the region's DOs. PENEDÈS, between Barcelona and Tarragona, has the greatest number of technically equipped wineries in Spain, but doesn't make a commensurate number of superior wines. In the south, mountainous PRIORAT has become a new icon for its heady, raging reds, and the neighbouring DOs of Montsant and Terra Alt are following in its footsteps, albeit more affordably, with top wines from Acústic, Joan d'Anguera★, Celler de Capçanes★, Europvin Falset★, Ven La Universal★ (Montsant) and Bàrbara Forés and Celler Piñol★★ (Ter Alta). Inland COSTERS DEL SEGRE and Conca de Barberá make potential excellent reds and whites. Up the coast, Alella makes attractive whites an Empordá-Costa Brava, by the French border, is improving noticeabl. Cataluña also makes most of Spain's CAVA sparkling wines. The Cataluny DO allows (generally) inexpensive blends from anywhere in the region.

CATENA ZAPATA *Mendoza, Argentina* Patriarchal owner Nicolás Caten has almost single-handedly dragged Argentina's wine industry into th modern era and Catena Zapata is perhaps the most successful exporter o all. The winery owns some of the best vineyards in the best *terroirs* o MENDOZA, where fruit for the creamy, Meursault-like Alt Chardonnay★★ and perfumed, thrilling Alta Malbec★★ is grow. Nicolás Catena Zapata★★ is a masterpiece based on Cabernet an. recent releases of Malbec Argentino★★★ have set pulses racin among wine lovers the world over. Various inexpensive wines are well made and ripe.

SYLVAIN CATHIARD *Vosne-Romanée, Côte de Nuits, Burgundy, France* Sylvai Cathiard achieved international recognition in the late 1990s and ha made brilliant wines even in difficult vintages since then. The stars ar VOSNE-ROMANÉE Aux Malconsorts★★★ and ROMANÉE-ST-VIVANT★★★ bu his village Vosne-Romanée★★ and NUITS-ST-GEORGES Aux Murgers★★ ar excellent too. Best years: (2009) 08 07 **06** 05 03 **02** 00 99.

DOM. CAUHAPÉ *Jurançon AC, South-West France* Henri Ramonteu has been major influence in JURANÇON, proving that the area can make complex dr. whites as well as more traditional sweet wines. Chant des Vignes★ i. dry, unoaked Jurançon Sec; the oaked version is Sève d'Automne★. To. wines are dry La Canopée★★, sweet Noblesse du Temps★★ and barrel fermented Quintessence★★★. Best years: (sweet) **2007** 05 04 03 00 97.

DOM. DE CAUSSE MARINES *Gaillac AC, South-West France* Patric. Lescarret makes some of the most eccentric but most admired wines i. the GAILLAC area, especially his dry white Les Greilles★ and a range o. splendid but expensive sweet wines★★ deriving from the rare Onden grape. Best years: **2007** 05 03.

CAVA DO *Spain* Cava, the Catalan name for CHAMPAGNE-method fizz, i. made throughout Spain, but most comes from CATALUÑA. Grapes are th. local trio of Parellada, Macabeo and Xarel-lo, although some good Cava. in Cataluña as well as VALENCIA include Chardonnay and Pinot Noir i. their blends. The best-value, fruitiest Cavas are generally the youngest. with no more than the minimum 9 months' aging. A number of top. quality wines are now produced but are seldom seen abroad, since thei. prices are too close to those of Champagne to attract internationa. customers. Best producers: Can Feixes, Can Ràfols dels Caus★, Castell d. Vilarnau, Castellblanch, CODORNÍU★, Colet★, FREIXENET, Gramona★★, Juve. Camps, Marqués de Monistrol, Parxet★, RAÏMAT, Raventós i Blanc, Recaredo★. Rovellats, Signat★, Agustí Torelló★, Dominio de la Vega, Jané Ventura.

CAYMUS VINEYARDS *Napa Valley AVA, California, USA* Caymus Caberne. Sauvignon★ is ripe, intense and generally tannic; it can be outstanding a. a Special Selection★★★. Conundrum★ (sometimes ★★) is an exotic. full-flavoured white blend. Also successful MONTEREY Chardonnay unde.

the Mer Soleil★ label. **Best years:** (Special Selection) 2006 05 04 03 **02 01 00** 99 98 97 95 94 91 90 87 86 84.

CAYUSE VINEYARDS *Walla Walla Valley AVA, Washington State, USA* Winemaker Christophe Baron has created a cult label here. His superb Viognier★★★ is crisp, floral and spicy, yet he is best known for his Syrahs. Using French clones, he farms a vineyard reminiscent of some in CHATEAUNEUF-DU-PAPE for its large stones. Vineyard-designated Syrahs include Cailloux★★, with a distinctive mineral flavour and chocolate depth, and En Cerise★★, with more cherry and raspberry flavour but equal richness. The Bionic Frog★★ sports a cartoon label but is a serious Syrah, reminding me of a northern RHÔNE version. Camaspelo★ is a fascinating Cabernet-based red. **Best years:** (Syrah) (2008) 07 06 **05 04 03** 02.

DOM. CAZES *Rivesaltes, Roussillon, France* The Cazes brothers make outstanding MUSCAT DE RIVESALTES★★, RIVESALTES Tuilé★★ and superb RIVESALTES Aimé Cazes★★, and also produce a range of table wines. Soft red, white and rosé Le Canon du Maréchal★ are good, as are the CÔTES DU ROUSSILLON-VILLAGES Syrah-Grenache-Mourvèdre blends Ego★, Alter★ and Le Credo★★. Also intriguing white Libre Expression★ from Macabeo.

CH. DU CÈDRE *Cahors AC, South-West France* Pascal Verhaeghe leads the new generation of CAHORS winemakers. His wines are dark, richly textured, with a generous coating of chocolaty oak. There are 3 special cuvées: Le Prestige★★; the 100% Auxerrois (Malbec) Le Cèdre★, which is aged in new oak barrels for 20 months; and Cuvée GC★, which is fermented and aged in oak. All benefit from at least 5–6 years' bottle age. **Best years:** (Le Cèdre) (2009) 06 **05 04 01**.

CENCIBEL See TEMPRANILLO.

CENTRAL COAST AVA *California, USA* Huge AVA covering virtually every vineyard between San Francisco and Los Angeles, with a number of sub-AVAs, such as SANTA CRUZ MOUNTAINS, Santa Ynez Valley, SANTA MARIA VALLEY and Monterey. There is superb potential for Pinot Noir and Syrah in Santa Lucia Highlands in MONTEREY COUNTY. See also SAN LUIS OBISPO COUNTY, SANTA BARBARA COUNTY.

CENTRAL OTAGO *South Island, New Zealand* The only wine region in New Zealand with a continental rather than maritime climate. Technically the ripening season is long and cool, suiting Pinot Noir, Gewürztraminer, Chardonnay and Pinot Gris, but there are usually periods of considerable heat during the summer to intensify flavour. Long autumns have produced some excellent Rieslings. There are already nearly 100 wineries and an explosion of plantings, both in good areas like Bannockburn and Lowburn, and in marginal zones. Latest expansion is to the Waitaki Valley in northern Otago. **Best producers:** Akarua★, Carrick★, Chard Farm★, FELTON ROAD★★★, Gibbston
Valley★, Kawarau Estate★, Mt Difficulty★★, Mount Edward★★, Mount Maude, Nevis Bluff★, Peregrine★★, Pisa Range★, QUARTZ REEF★★, Rippon★★, Tarras★, Two Paddocks★, Wild Earth★. **Best years:** (Pinot Noir) (2009) **08 07 06 05 03** 02.

CENTRAL VALLEY *California, USA* This vast area grows 70% of California's wine grapes, used mostly for cheaper wine, along with brandies and grape concentrate. It is a hot area, where irrigated vineyards tend to produce excess tonnages of grapes. It is often said that it is virtually impossible t produce exciting wine in the Central Valley, but in fact the climati conditions in the northern half are not unlike those in many parts o Spain and southern France and, viewed overall, quality has improved i recent years. Vineyards in the Lodi AVA have expanded to aroun 40,000ha (over 90,000 acres), making Lodi the value for money quali leader for Chardonnay, Merlot, Zinfandel and Cabernet; Lodi Zinfande shows most potential. Other sub-regions with claims to quality are th Sacramento Valley and the Delta area. Best producers: (Lodi) Ironstone★ Jessie's Grove★, McManis★, Mettler Family★, Michael-David★, RAVENSWOO (Lodi★), Woodbridge/MONDAVI.

CENTRAL VALLEY *Chile* (Bottles in Europe may have Valle Central o the label.) The heart of Chile's wine industry, and an *appellatio* encompassing the valleys of MAIPO, RAPEL, CURICÓ and MAULE; most majo producers are located here. The key factor determining mesoclimat differences is the distance relative to the Coastal Ranges and the Ande Mountains: the closer you get to the mountains, the cooler you are.

CENTRAL VICTORIA *Victoria, Australia* This zone comprises the region of BENDIGO, HEATHCOTE, Goulburn Valley and the cooler Strathbog Ranges and Upper Goulburn. Central Victoria, with its mostly warr conditions, produces powerful and individual wines. The few wineries o the banks of the Goulburn River feature fine Shiraz and Marsanne; red from the high country are rich but scented and dry, with Heathcot excelling for texture and taste; whites are delicate and scented. Bes producers: Heathcote Winery★★, Jasper Hill★★★, Mitchelton★, Pa Osicka★, PONDALOWIE★, TAHBILK★, Wild Duck Creek★.

CERETTO *Piedmont, Italy* This merchant house was one of the chief moder producers in BAROLO in the 1970s and 80s. Today, Barolo (Bricc Rocche★★, Brunate★ and Prapò★), BARBARESCO (Bricco Asili★), BARBER D'ALBA Piana★ and white Arneis Blangè, while still good, are bein overtaken by smaller, more specialist growers. Ceretto also produces a oak-aged LANGHE red, Monsordo★, from Cabernet, Merlot, Pinot Ner and Nebbiolo. An unusual white counterpart, Arbarei, is 100% Riesling A good fizz, La Bernardina, is made from Chardonnay and Pinot Noir

CÉRONS AC *Bordeaux, France* Sweet, soft, mildly honeyed wine from th GRAVES region of Bordeaux – not quite as sweet as SAUTERNES and not s well known, nor so highly priced. Most producers now make dry win under the Graves AC. Best producers: Ch. de Cérons★, Chantegrive★ Grand Enclos du Château de Cérons★, Haura, Seuil. Best years: (2009) 07 **0 03 02 01 99 98 97 96 95**.

L A CETTO *Baja California, Mexico* One of Mexico's most successful winerie (Monte Xanic is also excellent) relies on mists and cooling Pacific breeze to temper the heat of the Valle de Guadalupe in the northern part of Baj California. Italian Camillo Magoni makes ripe, fleshy Petite Sirah★ oak-aged Cabernet Sauvignon, Zinfandel and Nebbiolo. Whites, led b Chardonnay and Chenin, are greatly improved. Also good fizz.

CHABLAIS *Vaud, Switzerland* A sub-region of the VAUD, south-east of Lak Geneva along the right bank of the Rhône. Most of the vineyards lie o the alluvial plains, but 2 villages, Yvorne and Aigle, benefit from muc steeper slopes. Most of the thirst-quenchingly dry whites are made from Chasselas. The reds are from Pinot Noir, as is a rosé speciality, Oeil d Perdrix. Drink whites and rosés young. Best producers: Badoux, I Baudelière, Conne, J & P Testuz★.

CHABLIS AC *Burgundy, France* Chablis, lying closer to CHAMPAGNE than to the COTE D'OR, is Burgundy's northernmost outpost. When not destroyed by frost or hail, the Chardonnay grape makes a crisp, dry white wine with a steely mineral fruit which can be delicious. Several producers have taken to barrel-aging for their better wines, resulting in some full, toasty, positively rich dry whites. Others are intentionally producing a soft, creamy, early-drinking style, which is nice but not really typical Chablis. Outlying vineyards come under the Petit Chablis AC and these wines should be drunk young. The better straight Chablis AC should be drunk at 2–4 years, while a good vintage of a leading Chablis Premier Cru may take 5 years to show its full potential. About a quarter of Chablis is designated as Premier Cru, the best vineyards on the rolling limestone slopes being Fourchaume, Mont de Milieu, Montmains, Montée de Tonnerre and Vaillons. Best producers: Barat★, J-C Bessin (Fourchaume★★), Billaud-Simon★ (Mont de Milieu★★), Pascal Bouchard★, A & F Boudin★, BROCARD★★, la CHABLISIENNE★, Collet★, D Dampt★, R & V DAUVISSAT★, D-E Defaix★, Droin★, DROUHIN★, DURUP★ (Montée de Tonnerre★★), W Fèvre★★, J-P Grossot (Côte de Troesme★★), LAROCHE★★, Long-Depaquit, Malandes (Côte de Léchêt★★), Louis Michel★★, de Moor★, Christian Moreau★★, Moreau-Naudet★, Picq (Vaucoupin★★), Pinson★, RAVENEAU★★, les Temps Perdus, Vocoret★★. Best years: (Chablis Premier Cru) (2009) 08 07 **06 05 02** 00.

CHABLIS GRAND CRU AC *Burgundy, France* The 7 Grands Crus (Bougros, les Preuses, Vaudésir, Grenouilles, Valmur, les Clos and les Blanchots) facing south-west across the town of Chablis are the heart of the Chablis vineyards. Oak barrelaging takes the edge off taut flavours, adding a rich warmth to these fine wines. Droin and Fèvre are the most enthusiastic users of new oak, but use it less than they used to. Never drink young: 5–10 years are needed before you can see why you spent your money. Best producers: J-C Bessin★★, Billaud-Simon★★★, Pascal Bouchard★, BROCARD★★, la CHABLISIENNE★★, R & V DAUVISSAT★★★, Droin★★, W Fèvre★★★, LAROCHE★★, Long-Depaquit★★, Louis Michel★★, Christian Moreau★★★, Moreau-Naudet★★, Pinson★★, RAVENEAU★★★, Servin★, Vocoret★★. Best years: (2009) 08 07 06 05 **02 00** 99 98 96 90.

LA CHABLISIENNE *Chablis, Burgundy, France* Substantial co-op producing nearly a third of all CHABLIS. The wines are reliable and can aspire to something much better. The best are the oaky Grands Crus – especially les Preuses★★ and Grenouilles (sold as Ch. Grenouilles★★) – but the basic unoaked Chablis★, the Vieilles Vignes★★ and the numerous Premiers Crus★ are good, as is the red BOURGOGNE Épineuil. Best years: (whites) (2009) 08 07 **06 05** 02.

CHADDSFORD WINERY *Pennsylvania, USA* This winery in south-eastern PENNSYLVANIA produces 25,000 cases annually and has gained a following across the US since its founding in 1982. Winemaker Eric Miller uses primarily Cabernet Sauvignon and Merlot, both as varietals and for red blend Merican; he also produces Sangiovese and a juicy picnic red from Chambourcin. Single-vineyard Chardonnays★ can be powerful and elegant.

CHAMBERS *Rutherglen, Victoria, Australia* Legendary family winery making sheer nectar in the form of Muscat and Muscadelle (Tokay). The secret is their ability to draw on ancient stocks put down in wood by earlier generations. The Grand★★ and Rare★★★ blends are national treasures. The Cabernet and Shiraz table wines are good, the whites pedestrian.

CHAMPAGNE AC

Champagne, France

The Champagne region produces the most celebrate sparkling wines in the world. It is the most northerly A in France – a place where (even with the advent of glob warming) grapes struggle to ripen fully, but provide th perfect base wine to make fizz. Champagne is divide into 5 distinct areas – the best are the Montagne de Reims, where th Pinot Noir grape performs brilliantly, and the Chardonnay-dominate Côte des Blancs, south of Épernay. In addition to Chardonnay and Pin Noir, the other main grape permitted for the production of Champagi is Pinot Meunier.

The wines undergo a second fermentation in the bottle, producir carbon dioxide which dissolves in the wine under pressure. Through th method Champagne acquires its crisp, long-lasting bubbles and distinctive yeasty, toasty dimension to its flavour, becoming one of th most delightfully exhilarating wines of all.

That's the theory anyway, and for 150 years or so the Champeno have persuaded us that their product is second to none. It can be, to except when it is released too young or sweetened to cover up a so unripeness. When that periodically happens you know that, once agai the powers of marketing have triumphed over the wisdom and skills the winemaker. But Champagne expertise now turns out excellent fizz a around the globe – especially in California, Australia, New Zealand an England. With a recession weakening demand, there has never been better time for Champagne producers to remind us their suprem marketing is matched by excellent quality.

The Champagne trade is dominated by large companies or house called négociants-manipulants, recognized by the letters NM on th label. The récoltants-manipulants (RM) are growers who make the own wine, and they are becoming increasingly important for drinke seeking characterful Champagne.

STYLES OF CHAMPAGNE

Non-vintage Most Champagne is a blend of 2 or more vintages. Quali varies enormously, depending on who has made the wine and how lor it has been aged. Brut is a dry, but rarely bone-dry, style. Mor completely dry styles – called things like Brut Zéro, Brut Sauvage Extra Brut – are appearing and tasting good, primarily because climat change is providing riper grapes that don't need sugar to hide the rawness. Strangely, Extra Dry denotes a style less dry than Brut.

Vintage Denotes Champagne made with grapes from a single vintag As a rule, it is made only in the best years, but far too many medioc years were declared in the 1990s.

Blanc de Blancs A lighter, and at best highly elegant, style Champagne made solely from the Chardonnay grape.

Blanc de Noirs White Champagne made entirely from black grape either Pinot Noir, Pinot Meunier, or a combination of the two.

Rosé Pink Champagne, made either from black grapes or (more usuall by mixing a little still red wine into white Champagne.

De luxe cuvée In theory the finest Champagne and certainly always th most expensive, residing in the fanciest bottles.

See also **CHAMPAGNE ROSE**; and individual producers.

BEST PRODUCERS

Houses BILLECART-SALMON, BOLLINGER, Cattier, Delamotte, DEUTZ, Drappier, DUVAL-LEROY, GOSSET, Alfred GRATIEN, Charles HEIDSIECK, HENRIOT, JACQUESSON, KRUG, LANSON, LAURENT-PERRIER, Bruno PAILLARD, Joseph PERRIER, PERRIER-JOUET, PHILIPPONNAT, PIPER-HEIDSIECK, POL ROGER, POMMERY, Louis ROEDERER, RUINART, Salon, TAITTINGER, VEUVE CLICQUOT.

Growers Agrapart & Fils, Michel Arnould, Paul Bara, Barnaut, Beaufort, Bérèche & Fils, Franck Bonville, Roger Brun, Claude Cazals, Chartogne-Taillet, Dehours, Paul Déthune, Diebolt Vallois, Egly-Ouriet, René Geoffroy, Gimonnet, H Goutorbe, André Jacquart, Larmandier, Larmandier-Bernier, Maillart, Margaine, Serge Mathieu, Moncuit, Jérôme Prévost, Alain Robert, Selosse, Tarlant, Vilmart.

Co-ops Beaumont des Crayères, H Blin, Nicolas Feuillatte, Jacquart, Mailly, Le Mesnil, Union Champagne.

De luxe cuvées Belle Époque (PERRIER-JOUET), N-F Billecart (BILLECART-SALMON), Blanc de Millénaires (Charles HEIDSIECK), Celebris (GOSSET), Clos des Goisses (PHILIPPONNAT), Clos de Mesnil (KRUG), Comtes de Champagne (TAITTINGER), Cristal (Louis ROEDERER), Cuvée Josephine (Joseph PERRIER), Cuvée Sir Winston Churchill (POL ROGER), Cuvée William Deutz (DEUTZ), Dom Pérignon (MOËT & CHANDON), Dom Ruinart (RUINART), Femme (DUVAL-LEROY) Grand Siècle (LAURENT-PERRIER), Grande Dame (VEUVE CLICQUOT), Noble Cuvée (LANSON), Vintage RD (BOLLINGER).

CHAMBERTIN AC *Grand Cru, Côte de Nuits, Burgundy, France*   The village
GEVREY-CHAMBERTIN, the largest CÔTE DE NUITS commune, has no fewer th
9 Grands Crus (Chambertin, Chambertin-Clos-de-Bèze, Chapell
Chambertin, Charmes-Chambertin, Griotte-Chambertin, Latricière
Chambertin, Mazis-Chambertin, Ruchottes-Chambertin and the rare
seen Mazoyères-Chambertin), which can produce some of Burgund
greatest and most intense red wine. Its rough-hewn fruit, seeming to w
with fragrant perfumes for its first few years, creates remarkable flavou
as the wine ages. Chambertin and Chambertin-Clos-de-Bèze a
neighbours on the slope above the village and the two greatest sites, b
overproduction is a recurrent problem with some producers. Be
producers: Denis Bachelet★★ (Charmes), BOUCHARD PÈRE ET FILS★
Charlopin★, B CLAIR★★, P Damoy★★, DROUHIN★★, Drouhin-Laroze★
C Dugat★★★, B Dugat-Py★★★, FAIVELEY★★ (★★★ since 2005), JADOT★
D Laurent★★, Dom. LEROY★★★, Denis MORTET★★★, H Perrot-Minot★
Ponsot★, Rossignol-Trapet★★, J Roty★★ (Charmes), ROUMIER★
(Ruchottes), ROUSSEAU★★★, J & J-L Trapet★★, VOUGERAIE★. Best yea
(2009) 08 07 06 05 03 02 **01 00 99 98 97 96 95 93 90**.

CHAMBOLLE-MUSIGNY AC *Côte de Nuits, Burgundy, France*   AC with t
potential to produce the most fragrant, perfumed red Burgundy, wh
not over-cropped. Encouragingly, more young producers are no
bottling their own wines. Best producers: Amiot-Servelle★, G Barthod★
J-J Confuron★, DROUHIN★★, DUJAC★★, R Groffier★★, Hudelot-Baillet
Hudelot-Noëllat★, JADOT★★, Dom. LEROY★★, F Magnien★, Marchar
Grillot★, D MORTET★, J-F MUGNIER★★, RION★★, ROUMIER★★, de VOGÜÉ★
Best years: (2009) 08 07 06 05 03 **02 01 00 99 98 96 95 93 90**.

CHAMPAGNE See pages 112–13.

CHAMPAGNE ROSÉ *Champagne AC, France*   Good pink CHAMPAGNE – usua
a little weightier than white – has a delicious fragrance of cherries a
raspberries. The top wines can age well, but most rosé Champagne shou
be drunk on release, as young as possible. Best producers: (vinta
BILLECART-SALMON★★, BOLLINGER★★, GOSSET★★, Charles HEIDSIECK★
JACQUESSON★★, LAURENT-PERRIER (Grand Siècle Alexandra★★★), MOËT
CHANDON★★ (Dom Pérignon★★★), PERRIER-JOUET (Belle Époque★), F
ROGER★★, POMMERY (Louise★★), Louis ROEDERER★ (Cristal★★★), RUINA
(Dom Ruinart★★), TAITTINGER (Comtes de Champagne★★★), VEU
CLICQUOT★★ (Grande Dame★★★); (non-vintage) Paul Bara★, E Barnaut★
Beaumont des Crayères★, BILLECART-SALMON★★, Egly-Ouriet★★, He
Giraud★, Jacquart★, KRUG★★, LANSON★, LAURENT-PERRIER★, MOËT & CHANDC
RUINART★, TAITTINGER, Vilmart★. Best years: 2005 04 03 **02 00 99 98 96 95
89 88 85 82**. See also pages 112–13.

CHANDON DE BRIAILLES *Savigny-lès-Beaune, Côte de Beaune, Burgundy, Fra*
The de Nicolays – François and his sister Claude – combine mode
sophistication with traditional values to produce refined, savoury re
notably PERNAND-VERGELESSES★ (Premier Cru Île des Vergelesses★★) a
CORTON★★, and an equally good range of whites from Pernan
Vergelesses★, Corton★★ and CORTON-CHARLEMAGNE★★. Best years: (re
(2009) 07 **06 05 03 02 99 98 96**.

CHANNING DAUGHTERS *Long Island, New York State, USA*   A bouti
winery in LONG ISLAND's Hamptons AVA that produces exciting but ha
to-find wines, including a racy Sauvignon Blanc★, a Muscat-based ble
called Sylvanus★ and a juicy Blaufränkisch★.

CHAPEL DOWN *Kent, England* The UK's largest winery, producing around 500,000 bottles a year. Most grapes are grown under contract, although 30ha (74 acres) of Chardonnay and Pinot Noir were planted in 2008 on a site in Kent. Good to very good wines, especially non-vintage Chapel Down Brut, Pinot Reserve Sparkling★ and still Bacchus★ and Rosé. Best years: (sparkling) 2004 02 00; (still) 2009 07 06.

CHAPEL HILL *McLaren Vale, South Australia* Chief winemaker Michael Fragos's efforts and some exceptional vintages have added a further dimension to the powerful, classy reds of Chapel Hill. The Cabernet Sauvignon★★ is a blend of mature MCLAREN VALE and COONAWARRA fruit, while the Shiraz★★ is all McLaren Vale; The Vicar★★ is a top reserve Shiraz. Good Bush Vine Grenache★, Unwooded Chardonnay★ and fascinating, bone-dry, honey-scented Verdelho★★, as well as Savagnin★. Best years: (Shiraz) (2008) 06 05 04 02 01 98 97 96 95 94 93 91.

CHAPELLE-CHAMBERTIN AC See CHAMBERTIN AC.

CHAPELLE LENCLOS *Madiran AC, South-West France* A leading name in MADIRAN, Patrick Ducournau invented the technique of micro-oxygenation. More recently he has switched his interest to the marketing of oak chips and has delegated to his Laplace cousins at Ch. d'AYDIE the making of his Chapelle Lenclos★★ and Dom. Mouréou★, legendary, ripe, concentrated reds, which need at least 5 years to mature. Best years: (2009) (08) 06 05 04 01 00.

CHAPOUTIER *Rhône Valley, France* The house of Chapoutier is a big mover in the world of biodynamic viticulture, and is producing serious, exciting wines. The HERMITAGE la Sizeranne★★ and special plot-specific Ermitages (les Greffieux★★, l'Ermite★★, le Méal★★★, le Pavillon★★★), rich white Hermitage (de l'Orée★★, l'Ermite★★★ and Vin de Paille★★), CROZES-HERMITAGE les Varonniers★, ST-JOSEPH les Granits★ (red and white), and CHÂTEAUNEUF-DU-PAPE Barbe Rac★ and Croix de Bois★ are all good, but some reds show excess extraction and oak. Large-volume Crozes-Hermitage les Meysonniers and CÔTES DU RHÔNE Belleruche are good value. Also BANYULS, COTEAUX DU TRICASTIN and Australian joint ventures. Best years: (la Sizeranne) 2009 07 06 05 04 03 01 00 99 98 95 94 91 90 89 88.

CHARDONNAY See pages 116–17.

CHARMES-CHAMBERTIN AC See CHAMBERTIN AC.

CHASSAGNE-MONTRACHET AC *Côte de Beaune, Burgundy, France* Some of Burgundy's greatest white wine vineyards (part of le MONTRACHET and BÂTARD-MONTRACHET, all of Criots-Bâtard-Montrachet) are within the village boundary. The white Chassagne Premiers Crus are not as well known, but can offer nutty, toasty wines, especially if aged for 4–8 years; Blanchots Dessus, Caillerets, Romanée, Ruchottes and Morgeots are among the best. Ordinary white Chassagne-Montrachet is usually enjoyable; the red is a little earthy, peppery and plummy and can be an acquired taste. Look out for reds from the following Premiers Crus: Clos de la Boudriotte, Clos St-Jean and Clos de la Chapelle. Best producers: (whites) Blain-Gagnard★★, B Colin, M Colin★★, P Colin★, J-N GAGNARD★, V GIRARDIN★★, V & F Jouard★, H Lamy★, B Moreau, M Morey★, T Morey★★, V Morey★★, Morey-Coffinet, M Niellon★★, J & J-M Pillot★★, P Pillot★, RAMONET★★; (reds) CARILLON★, V GIRARDIN★★, V Morey★★, RAMONET★★. Best years: (whites) (2009) 08 07 06 05 02 01 00 99; (reds) (2009) 08 07 06 05 03 02 99.

CHARDONNAY

I never thought I'd see myself write this. Yes, we are gettin bored with Chardonnay. Not all Chardonnay: there's probabl more top Chardonnay being produced right now than eve before. And for millions of wine drinkers the Chardonna revolution (easy to pronounce, easy to swallow) has only ju begun. But in the heart of the wine world – the middle market, wher people care about flavour but also care about price – we're getting fed u Far too much sugary, over-oaked, unrefreshing junk has been dumpe into our laps recently, from countries and producers who should kno better. Add to this the increasingly desperate dirt-cheap offerings at th rump end of the market, and you'll see why I think the great golde goose of Chardonnay has the carving knife of cynicism and greed firml held against its neck. The next few years will show whether it wishes t be the supremely versatile all-rounder or the sloppy jack of all trades an master of none.

WINE STYLES

France Although a relatively neutral variety if left alone (this is wh makes it so suitable as a base wine for top-quality Champagne-meth sparkling wine), the grape can ripen in a surprising range of condition developing a subtle gradation of flavours going from the sharp apple-co greenness of Chardonnay grown in Champagne or the Loire Vall through the exciting, bone-dry yet succulent flavours of white Burgund to a round, tropical flavour in Languedoc-Roussillon.

Other regions Italy produces Chardonnay that can be bone dry and le or fat, spicy and lush. Spain does much the same. California a Australia virtually created their reputations on great, viscous, almo syrupy, tropical fruits and spice-flavoured Chardonnays, but these sty are becoming rarer as both producers re-focus on top-quality full-bodie oatmealy styles. Some of the best New World Chardonnays, dry but rip fresh and subtly oaked, are coming from South Africa. Unoaked versio from more mature vines offer increasingly characterful, food-friend drinking. New Zealand is producing beautifully balanced Chardonnay their fragrant fruit only subtly oaked, while Chile and Argentina a rapidly learning how to make fine wine from it too. Add German Austria, Canada, New York State, Greece, Portugal, Slovenia, Moldov Romania, England, Belgium, even China, and you'll see it can perfor almost anywhere.

Using oak The reason for all these different flavours lies in Chardonnay wonderful susceptibility to the winemaker's aspirations and skills. T most important manipulation is the use of the oak barrel for fermenti and aging the wine. Chardonnay is the grape of the great whi Burgundies and these are fermented and matured in oak (not necessar new oak); the effect is to give a marvellous round, nutty richness to wine that is yet savoury and dry. This is enriched still further by aging t wine on its lees.

The New World winemakers sought to emulate the gre Burgundies, planting Chardonnay and employing thousands of o barrels (mostly new), and their success has caused winemak everywhere else to see Chardonnay as the perfect variety – easy to gro easy to turn into wine and easy to sell to an adoring public. But as in things, familiarity can breed contempt.

BEST PRODUCERS

France *Chablis* Billaud-Simon, DAUVISSAT, Droin, Fèvre, Louis Michel, C Moreau, RAVENEAU; *Côte d'Or* R Ampeau, H Boillot, J-M Boillot, Bonneau du Martray, BOUCHARD, CARILLON, COCHE-DURY, M Colin, DROUHIN, A Ente, J-P Fichet, J-N GAGNARD, V GIRARDIN, JADOT, F Jobard, LAFON, H Lamy, Dom. LEFLAIVE, several Moreys, M Niellon, RAMONET, G Roulot, SAUZET; *Mâconnais* D & M Barraud, Bret, Guffens-Heynen/VERGET, O Merlin, Saumaize-Michelin, J Thévenet.

Other European Chardonnays
Austria BRÜNDLMAYER, Kollwentz, TEMENT, VELICH, WIENINGER; *Germany* HUBER, JOHNER, REBHOLZ, WITTMANN; *Italy* Castello di AMA, BELLAVISTA, CA' DEL BOSCO, GAJA, ISOLE E OLENA, LAGEDER, Lis Neris, Pomino Benefizio/FRESCOBALDI, Castello della SALA, TIEFENBRUNNER (Linticlarus), Vie di Romans; *Spain* CHIVITE, ENATE, Manzaneque, Muñoz, Nekeas, Palacio de Muruzabal, Señorío de Otazu, TORRES.

New World Chardonnays
Australia BANNOCKBURN, Bindi (Quartz), Brookland Valley, CAPE MENTELLE, Chapman Grove (Atticus), CULLEN, Curly Flat, By FARR, GIACONDA, GROSSET, HOWARD PARK, LEEUWIN, Marchand & Burch, Moorooduc, OAKRIDGE (864), PENFOLDS, PETALUMA, PIERRO, Savaterre, SHAW & SMITH, TAPANAPPA, TARRAWARRA, TYRRELL'S, VOYAGER, Woodlands, Yering Station (Reserve).

New Zealand Bell Hill, CHURCH ROAD, CLOUDY BAY, CRAGGY RANGE, DRY RIVER, Escarpment, FELTON ROAD, FROMM, KUMEU RIVER, MATUA VALLEY, MONTANA, MORTON ESTATE, NEUDORF, PALLISER, PEGASUS BAY, Peregrine, SAINT CLAIR, SERESIN, TRINITY HILL, VAVASOUR, Vidal, VILLA MARIA.

USA ARROWOOD, AU BON CLIMAT, CALERA, CHATEAU ST JEAN, DOMAINE DROUHIN OREGON, DUTTON GOLDFIELD, FLOWERS, HdV, IRON HORSE, KISTLER, Littorai, MARCASSIN, MATANZAS CREEK, MERRYVALE, Peter MICHAEL, NEWTON, RAMEY, RIDGE, SAINTSBURY, SANFORD, SHAFER, STEELE, STONY HILL, TALBOTT.

South Africa Ataraxia, BUITEN-VERWACHTING, CAPE CHAMONIX, ELLIS, HAMILTON RUSSELL, JORDAN, MULDERBOSCH, THELEMA, VERGELEGEN, Waterford.

South America Aquitania (Sol de Sol), CATENA, CONCHA Y TORO, CONO SUR, DE MARTINO, ERRÁZURIZ, Viña Leyda, Maycas del Limarí (CONCHA Y TORO), MONTES, TABALÍ.

CHASSELAS Chasselas is considered a table grape worldwide. Only in BADEN (where it is called Gutedel) and Switzerland (called FENDANT) is it thought to make decent light, dry wines with a slight prickle. A few Swiss examples, notably from CHABLAIS and DEZALEY, rise above this.

CH. CHASSE-SPLEEN★ *Moulis AC, Haut-Médoc, Bordeaux, France* Chasse-Spleen is not a Classed Growth – but during the 1980s it built a tremendous reputation for ripe, concentrated and powerful wines under the late proprietor, Bernadette Villars. The château is now run by Villars' daughter Céline, and recent vintages are approaching the form of the old days. Second wine: l'Ermitage de Chasse-Spleen. Best years: 2008 07 06 05 04 03 02 01 00 99 96 95 90 89.

CHÂTEAU-CHALON AC *Jura, France* The most prized – and pricey – *vin jaune*, it is bottled exclusively in the 62cl *clavelin*. If you find a bottle, beware – the awesome flavour will shock your tastebuds like no other French wine. Made from the Savagnin grape and aged like sherry under a yeast *flor*, but in old barrels, it is not released until 6 years after the vintage and can be kept for decades. Best producers: Baud★, Berthet-Bondet★★, Bourdy★★, Butin★, J-C Crédoz★, Durand-Perron★, J Macle★★, H Maire, F Mossu★. Best years: (2002) 00 99 98 97 96 95 93 92 90 89 88.

CHÂTEAU-GRILLET AC★★ *Rhône Valley, France* This rare and very expensive RHÔNE white from a 3.4ha (8-acre) terraced vineyard, made from Viognier and aged in used oak, has magic wisps of orchard fruit and harvest bloom when young but is best drunk after 5 years, and decanted. More reserved, more refined than CONDRIEU, and recently improved. Best years: 2009 08 07 06 05 04 03 01 00 98 95.

CHATEAU INDAGE *Maharashtra, India* India's first traditional-method sparkling wine appeared in the 1980s, with technical assistance from Champagne's PIPER-HEIDSIECK. Dry sparklers are firm, fresh and chunky though quality is somewhat erratic. Omar Khayyám is produced from a blend of Chardonnay, Ugni Blanc, Pinot Noir and Pinot Meunier; there's also a demi-sec and a good pink fizz. Red and white table wines use both international and indigenous Indian grape varieties such as Bangalore Purple and Arkavati.

CHATEAU MONTELENA *Napa Valley AVA, California, USA* NAPA winery producing classic California Chardonnay★★ and an estate Cabernet★ that are impressive, if slow to develop. The Napa Valley Cabernet★ is a more elegant wine for younger consumption. Best years: (Chardonnay) 2007 06 05 04 03 02 01; (Cabernet) (2006) 05 03 02 01 00 99 98 91 90.

CHATEAU MUSAR *Ghazir, Lebanon* Founded by Gaston Hochar in the 1930s, managed for many years by his Bordeaux-trained son Serge; now the winery is gradually being passed to the next generation. From a unlikely blend of primarily Cabernet Sauvignon, old-vine Carignan and Cinsaut comes a wine of real, if wildly exotic, character, with sweet dried fruits and good aging potential: Hochar says that red Ch. Musar★ 'should be drunk at 15 years'. Style oscillates between classic Bordeaux and spicy Rhône. Hochar Père & Fils and Cuvée Musar are less complex, more fruit-forward alternatives. White★ is made from indigenous Obaideh (like Chardonnay) and Merwah (similar to Semillon). Best years: (red) 2002 01 00 97 95 94 91 88.

CHATEAU ST JEAN *Sonoma Valley AVA, California, USA* Once known almost entirely for its range of Chardonnays (Belle Terre★★, Robert Young★★), St Jean has emerged as a producer of delicious reds including a BORDEAUX-style blend called Cinq Cépages★★ and a Reserve Merlot★★. Now owned by the Foster's Group. Best years: (Chardonnay) 2006 **05** 04 03 02 01 00 99; (reds) (2006) 05 04 03 **02 01 99 97 95 94**.

CHATEAU STE MICHELLE *Washington State, USA* Pioneering winery with an enormous range of wines, including several attractive vineyard-designated Chardonnays★ (some ★★), Cabernet Sauvignons★ and Merlots★, especially Cold Creek Vineyard★★ and Indian Wells★★. Good Riesling, both dry and sweet, and increasingly interesting red Meritage★. Partnership with Italy's ANTINORI and Germany's Ernst LOOSEN has produced dark, powerful Tuscan-style red Col Solare★★, attractive Riesling Eroica★ and a thrilling sweet version, Single Berry Select★★★, made in tiny quantities. Quality generally seems to be moving upward. Best years: (premium reds) (2008) 07 06 **05** 04.

CHÂTEAUNEUF-DU-PAPE AC *Rhône Valley, France* A large (3350ha/8275-acre) vineyard area between Orange and Avignon. The sweetly fruited red wine is based on Grenache, plus Syrah and Mourvèdre (10 other varieties are also allowed). It should be fine rather than heady and powerful. Always choose Châteauneuf from a single estate, denoted by the papal coat of arms or mitre embossed on the bottle neck. Top reds, particularly old-vine cuvées, will age for 10 years or more, but don't feel you have to pay extra for 'prestige' cuvées: from a good estate, the normal release will be far cheaper, less dense and often more enjoyable. Only 5% of Châteauneuf is white; made mainly from Grenache Blanc, Bourboulenc, Clairette and Roussanne, these wines can be surprisingly good. Many whites are best young. Best producers: (reds) L Barrot★, BEAUCASTEL★★★, Beaurenard★★, Bois de Boursan★★, H Bonneau★★, Bosquet des Papes★★, les Cailloux★★, Chante-Perdrix★, CHAPOUTIER★, la Charbonnière★★, L Charvin★, Clos du Caillou★, Clos du Mont Olivet★★, CLOS DES PAPES★★★, Clos St-Jean★, Cristia★, Font du Loup★, FONT DE MICHELLE★★, Fortia★★, la Gardine★★, Gigognan★, Giraud★, Grand Tinel★, Grand Veneur★, la Janasse★★, Marcoux★★, Mathieu★, Monpertuis★★, Mont-Redon★★, la Nerthe★★, Pégaü★★, RAYAS★★★, Roquette★, Roger Sabon★★, St-Siffrein★, Solitude★★, Tardieu-Laurent★, P Usseglio★★, Vieille Julienne★, Le Vieux Donjon★★, VIEUX TÉLÉGRAPHE★★; (whites) BEAUCASTEL★★★, CLOS DES PAPES★★, FONT DE MICHELLE★★, Grand Veneur★★, Marcoux★★, RAYAS★★, St-Cosme★★, VIEUX TÉLÉGRAPHE★★. Best years: (reds) 2009 07 **06** 05 **04** 03 01 **00 99 98 96 95 90 89 88**.

JEAN-LOUIS CHAVE *Rhône Valley, France* Jean-Louis Chave's red HERMITAGE★★★ is one of the world's great wines, a supreme Syrah, surpassed only by the cellar-selected Cathelin★★★, produced in exceptional years. His wonderful, richly flavoured white Hermitage★★★ (from Marsanne with some Roussanne) sometimes outlasts the reds, as it moves towards its honeyed, nutty zenith. Also a small amount of excellent red ST-JOSEPH★★ and an occasional stunning traditional sweet Vin de Paille★★. Expensive, but worth the money. *Négociant* business makes well-fruited CÔTES DU RHÔNE Mon Coeur and St-Joseph Offerus. Best years: (reds) 2009 07 06 05 04 **03 01 00 99 98 97 96 95 94 92 91 90 89 88 86 85 83 82 79 78**; (whites) 2009 08 07 06 05 **04** 03 01 **00 99 98 97 96 95 94 93 92 91 90 89 88 85 83**.

CHÉNAS AC *Beaujolais, Burgundy, France* The smallest BEAUJOLAIS Cru, Chénas offers styles ranging from light and elegant to austere and needing time to develop Burgundian tones. Best producers: Champagnon★, DUBOEUF, H Lapierre★, Piron & Lafont (Quartz★★), B Santé★. Best years: **2009** 08 07.

CHENIN BLANC One of the most underrated and versatile white wi grapes in the world. In the LOIRE VALLEY, where it is also called Pineau la Loire, it is responsible for sweet, medium, dry and sparkling wine The great sweet wines of COTEAUX DU LAYON, QUARTS DE CHAU BONNEZEAUX and VOUVRAY are some of the longest-lived of all wines. The is an increasing emphasis on barrel-fermented and aged dry wine especially in ANJOU and now in TOURAINE, the best of which are revelation. In South Africa, Chenin Blanc remains both the most plant and most uprooted variety, but total plantings are now fairly stable: sty range from sparkling through easy-drinking, dryish wines and mode barrel-fermented versions to botrytized dessert wines. Chenin is a influential in quality white blends. New Zealand and Australia ha produced good varietal examples, and it is also grown in California (D CREEK VINEYARD, Graziano) and Argentina.

LARRY CHERUBINO *Western Australia* Larry Cherubino has a flair winemaking and an intimate knowledge of the vineyards of WESTE AUSTRALIA that he gained as chief winemaker at HOUGHTON. After leaving the corporate life in 2003, he established a consultancy business and began making wine for his family company. There are 3 ranges: the good-value Ad Hoc; regional single-site wines labelled The Yard (Riesling★);

and small-volume Cherubino Margaret River Cabernet, Frankland Riv Shiraz★★, Pemberton Sauvignon Blanc★ and Mount Barker Riesling★

CH. CHEVAL BLANC★★★ *St-Émilion Grand Cru AC, 1er Grand Cru Clas Bordeaux, France* Along with AUSONE, the leading ST-ÉMILION estate. Rig on the border with POMEROL, it seems to share some of its sturdy richne but with an extra spice and purity of fruit that is impressive recognizably unique. An unusually high percentage (60%) of Caberr Franc is often used in the blend. Gorgeous when young, yet with remarkable ability to age for many decades. Best years: 2008 07 06 05 **04 02 01 00 99 98 96 95 90 89 88 86 85**.

CHEVALIER-MONTRACHET AC See MONTRACHET AC.

DOM. DE CHEVALIER *Pessac-Léognan AC, Cru Classé de Graves, Bordeaux, Fran* Some of Bordeaux's finest wines. The red★★ starts out firm and reserv but over 10–20 years gains heavenly cedar, tobacco and blackcurra flavour. Recent vintages have greater purity of fruit. The brillia white★★★ is both fermented and aged in oak barrels; in the best vintag it will still be improving at 15–20 years but 2006 and 2007 were irresistible I'd be surprised if there's any left now, let alone in 15 yea Best years: (reds) 2008 07 06 05 **04 03 02 01 00 99 98 96 90 89 88**; (whit **2008** 07 06 05 04 02 01 00 99 98 96 90 89 88 87 86.

CHEVERNY AC *Loire Valley, France* A little-known area south of Blois. T local speciality is the white Romorantin grape, which makes a bone-d wine under the AC Cour-Cheverny, but the best whites are fro Chardonnay. Also pleasant Sauvignon, Pinot Noir, Gamay and braci CRÉMANT DE LOIRE. Drink young. Best producers: Cazin★, Chever co-op, de la Gaudronnière, Gendrier/Huards★, Maison, H Marionnet, Montcy★, du Moulin, Salvard, Sauger, C Tessier/la Desoucherie, Tue-Boeuf

CHIANTI DOCG *Tuscany, Italy* The most famous of all Italian wines, b there are many styles, depending on what grapes are used, where they a grown, and by which producer. It can be a light, fresh, easy-drinking r wine with a characteristic hint of bitterness, or it can be an intense, structured yet sleek wine in the same league as fine BORDEAUX. The vineyards are scattered over central Tuscany, either simply as 'Chianti' or Chianti plus the name of one of the 7 sub-zones: Colli Aretini, Colli Fiorentini, Colli Senesi, Colline Pisane, Montalbano, Montespertoli and Rufina. Sangiovese is the main grape; traditionally it was blended with the red Canaiolo and white Malvasia and Trebbiano. Modern wine-makers often make Chianti from Sangiovese alone or blended with 20% of Cabernet, Merlot, Syrah or, increasingly, with native grapes like Colorino. See also CHIANTI CLASSICO, CHIANTI RUFINA. Best producers: (Chianti Colli Fiorentini) Baggiolino★, Le Calvane, Il Corno, Corzano e Paterno★, Lanciola★, Malenchini★, Pasolini dall'Onda★, Poppiano★, La Querce, Sammontana; (Chianti Colli Senesi) Carpineta Fontalpino★, Casabianca, Casale-Falchini★, Farnetella★, Ficomontanino★, Pacina★, Paradiso★, Pietraserena.

CHIANTI CLASSICO DOCG *Tuscany, Italy* The historic CHIANTI zone in the hilly heart of Tuscany between Florence and Siena. Since the 1996 vintage Classico can be made entirely from Sangiovese, though most winemakers still tend to blend, together with the minimum of 80% Sangiovese, other grapes including 'internationals' (see CHIANTI). Riserva must be aged at least 27 months (usually in barrel) and, like Chianti Classico *normale*, must use only red grapes. The finest Riserva wines can improve for a decade or more. Many of the estates also offer regular bottlings of red wine, round and fruity, for drinking about 2–5 years after the harvest. Best producers (Riserva or top cru): Castello di AMA★★★, ANTINORI★ (Riserva★★), Badia a Coltibuono★, Il Borghetto★★, Brancaia★, Cacchiano★★, Capaccia★★, Carpineto★, Casaloste★★, CASTELLARE★, Castell'in Villa★, Collelungo★, Colombaio di Cencio★, Dievole★, Casa Emma★★, FELSINA★★, Le Filigare★, FONTERUTOLI★★, FONTODI★★, ISOLE E OLENA★★, Il Mandorlo★★, Melini★, MONSANTO★★★, Monteraponi★★, Il Palazzino★★, Paneretta★★, Panzanello★★, Poggerino★★, Poggiopiano★★, Poggio al Sole (Casasilia★★★), Querceto★, QUERCIABELLA★★, Castello dei RAMPOLLA★★, RICASOLI (Castello di Brolio★★), RIECINE★★, Rignana★★, Rocca di Castagnoli★★, San Felice★★, San Giusto a Rentennano★★, San Polo in Rosso★, Casa Sola★★, Terrabianca★, Vecchie Terre di Montefili★★, Verrazzano★, Vignamaggio★, Villa Cafaggio★★, VOLPAIA★★. Best years: (2009) (08) 07 06 **04 03 01 99 97 95 90**.

CHIANTI RUFINA DOCG *Tuscany, Italy* Smallest of the CHIANTI sub-zones, an enclave of the Apennine foothills to the east of Florence, where wines were noted for exceptional structure and longevity long before they joined the ranks of Chianti. Today the wines, particularly the long-lived Riserva Bucerchiale from SELVAPIANA and FRESCOBALDI's Montesodi, match the best of CHIANTI CLASSICO. Pomino DOC is a higher zone almost entirely surrounded by Chianti Rufina; dominated by Frescobaldi, it makes greater use of French varieties such as Merlot, Cabernet and Chardonnay. Best producers: (Rufina Riservas) Basciano★, Tenuta di Bossi★, Colognole★, Frascole★, FRESCOBALDI★★, Grati/Villa di Vetrice★, Grignano★, Lavacchio★, SELVAPIANA★★★, Castello del Trebbio★. Best years: (2009) (08) 07 06 **04 03 01 99 97 95**.

FRANÇOIS CHIDAINE *Montlouis-sur-Loire AC, Vouvray AC, Loire Valley, France* Together with Jacky BLOT, François Chidaine has inspired a new generation of MONTLOUIS-SUR-LOIRE vignerons with wines of wonderful purity, precision and length, with a dozen wines differentiated by soil type (clay, silex and limestone) and aspect sourced from Montlouis-sur-

Loire and VOUVRAY including, since 2006, Prince Poniatowski's famou
vineyard, Le Clos Baudoin. Dry wines account for 80% of Chidaine'
range. Montlouis Les Lys★★, a *moëlleux* Sélection de Grains Nobles, i
made only in exceptional vintages. Almost from the outset (1989)
cultivation has been organic (biodynamic since 1999). Best years:
(sec/demi-sec) 2008 07 **06**; (moelleux) **2003 97**.

CHIMNEY ROCK *Stags Leap District AVA, California, USA* Powerful ye
elegantly sculpted Cabernet Sauvignon★★ (Reserve★★) and a meritage
blend called Elevage★★. There's also an ageworthy Elevage Blanc★ (a
blend of Sauvignons Blanc and Gris) and a tangy Fumé Blanc★. Best
years: (Elevage) 2005 04 03 **02 01 00 99 98 97 96 95**.

CHINON AC *Loire Valley, France* Best red wine of the LOIRE VALLEY, made
mainly from Cabernet Franc with an occasional dash of Caberne
Sauvignon. Lovely light reds full of raspberry fruit and fresh summer
earth to drink young, and heavyweights for keeping; always worth buying
a single-estate wine. Best producers: P Alliet★★, B BAUDRY★★, Baudry-
Dutour★, P Breton★, Coulaine★, Couly-Dutheil★, DRUET★, Grosbois
C Joguet★★, la Noblaie★, de Pallus/B Sourdais★★, Wilfrid Rousse
P Sourdais★. Best years: (2009) 08 **06** 05 04 03 02 01 97 96.

CHIROUBLES AC *Beaujolais, Burgundy, France* The highest in altitude of the
BEAUJOLAIS Crus, producing a light, fragrant, delicious Gamay wine
exhibiting all the attractions of a youthful Cru. Best producers
Cheysson★, la Combe au Loup★, D Desvignes★, la Grosse Pierre★, Ch. de
Javernand. Best years: **2009 08 07**.

CHIVITE *Navarra DO, Navarra, Spain* Longtime leader in exports from
NAVARRA. The Gran Feudo★ red and rosé are very good easy drinkers and
unoaked Chardonnay★ is excellent. The more upmarket reds have
improved steadily in a restrained, claret-like style. The top range, called
Colección 125, includes a red Reserva★ (sometimes ★★), classy white
Blanco★★ (barrel-fermented Chardonnay) and a characterful sweet
Vendimia Tardía★★ from Moscatel de Grano Menudo (Muscat Blanc à
Petits Grains). Chivite's northerly estate, Pago de Arínzano★★, received
a separate Vino de Pago appellation in 2008.

CHOREY-LÈS-BEAUNE AC *Côte de Beaune, Burgundy, France* One of those
tiny, forgotten villages that make good, if not great, Burgundy at prices
most of us can afford, with some committed producers too. Can age for
5–8 years. Best producers: Arnoux★, DROUHIN★, Germain/Ch. de Chorey★,
Maillard★, TOLLOT-BEAUT★★. Best years: (2009) 08 **07** 05 03 02 99.

CHURCH ROAD *Hawkes Bay, North Island, New Zealand* A premium-wine
project owned by Pernod Ricard. The reds seem a bit Bordeaux-
obsessed, although Reserve wines, made in the best years, can be very
good. Reserve Chardonnay★★ leapt in quality in recent years to become
one of the country's best. Best years: (reds) (2009) **08** 07 06 04 02.

CHURCHILL *Port DOC, Douro, Portugal* Established in 1981, it was the first
new PORT shipper for 50 years. The wines can be good, notably Vintage★,
LBV★, Crusted★, single-quinta Gricha★ and a well-aged, nutty dry
white port★, and are much more consistent since Quinta da Gricha was
bought in 1999. Churchill Estates is an unfortified DOURO red. Best years:
(Vintage) **2003** 00 97 94 91 85; (Quinta da Gricha) 2007 **03** 01 99.

CINSAUT Also spelt Cinsault. Found mainly in France's southern RHÔNE
VALLEY, PROVENCE and LANGUEDOC-ROUSSILLON. Ideal for rosé wine. In
blends, Cinsaut's low alcohol calms high-degree Grenache. Rare as a

single varietal, but Capitelle de Centeilles from CLOS CENTEILLES is a fine example. Mainstay of the blend for Lebanon's CHATEAU MUSAR. Popular as a bulk blender in South Africa, it is being adopted by enthusiasts of the Rhône style.

IRÒ DOC *Calabria, Italy* Cirò Rosso, a Gaglioppo-based wine of ancient pedigree, went through a quality dip in the late 20th century but has improved remarkably of late. Non-DOC Gaglioppo-based IGTs, like Librandi's Gravello★★ (an oak-aged blend with Cabernet), may be genuinely exciting. The DOC also covers a dry white from Greco and a rare dry rosé. Best producers: Caparra & Siciliani★, Librandi★ (Riserva★★), San Francesco★. Best years: (reds) (2009) (08) 07 06 **05 04 03 01 00**.

RUNO CLAIR *Marsannay, Côte de Nuits, Burgundy, France* Top producer from MARSANNAY with several single-vineyard cuvées there and an impressive range from other top vineyards including CHAMBERTIN Clos de Bèze★★ and Gevrey-Chambertin Clos St-Jacques★★. Also good-value SAVIGNY La Dominode★★ and a delicious Marsannay rosé★. Best years: (top reds) (2009) 08 07 06 05 03 **02 01 99 98 96 90**.

CLAIRETTE DE DIE AC *Rhône Valley, France* Underrated sparkling wine made from a minimum of 75% Muscat: off-dry, with a creamy bubble and a honeyed, grapy, orchard-fresh fragrance. The *méthode Dioise* is used, which preserves the Muscat scent. An ideal light aperitif. Drink young. Best producers: Achard-Vincent★, Clairette de Die co-op, D Cornillon, Jacques Faure, J-C Raspail★. See also CRÉMANT DE DIE.

A CLAPE *Cornas, Rhône Valley, France* Leading estate in CORNAS. Usually dense, tannic wines that reward patient cellaring, full of rich, roasted fruit – though occasionally, as in 2004, scented and sublime – consistently excellent and often ★★★. Younger vine Renaissance★ is good lower-key Cornas. Clape also makes fine red CÔTES DU RHÔNE★ and decent ST-PÉRAY★. Best years: (Cornas) 2009 08 07 06 05 04 **03 02 01 00 99 98 97 96 95 94 91 90 89 88 85 83**.

A CLAPE *Coteaux du Languedoc AC, Languedoc, France* The mountain of La Clape rises above the flat coastal fields south-east of Narbonne; its vineyards produce some excellent whites from Bourboulenc and Clairette, plus fine, herb-scented reds and rosés, mainly from Grenache, Syrah and Mourvèdre. Whites and reds can age. Best producers: Camplazens★★, Capitoul, l'HOSPITALET★, Mire l'Étang, Moyau★, Négly, Pech-Céleyran★, Pech Redon★, Ricardelle★. Best years: (reds) (2009) 08 07 06 **05 04 03 01 00**.

CLARE VALLEY *South Australia* This historic upland region to the north of Adelaide has a deceptively moderate climate and is able to grow both hot-climate and cool-climate grapes successfully, including fine, aromatic Riesling, marvellously textured Semillon, scented Viognier, rich, robust Shiraz and Cabernet blends, and peppery but voluptuous Grenache. Best producers: (whites) Tim ADAMS★★★, Jim BARRY★, Wolf BLASS (Gold Label★), Leo Buring (Leonay★★), Crabtree★, GROSSET★★★, Kilikanoon★★, KNAPPSTEIN★★, KT and the Falcon★, LEASINGHAM★, MITCHELL★, MOUNT HORROCKS★★, O'Leary Walker★★, PETALUMA★★★, Pikes★, SKILLOGALEE★, Taylors/Wakefield★; (reds) Tim ADAMS★★★, Jim BARRY★★, GROSSET★★, Kilikanoon★, KNAPPSTEIN★, LEASINGHAM★, MITCHELL★, O'Leary Walker★, Pikes★, SKILLOGALEE★, Taylors/ Wakefield, WENDOUREE★★★. Best years: (Shiraz) 2009 08 06 05 **04 03 02 01 99 98 97 96 94 92 91 90**; (Riesling) **2008 06 05 04 03 02 01 99 98 97 96 95**.

CLARENDON HILLS *McLaren Vale, South Australia* Winery with a name f
high-priced, highly extracted, unfined, unfiltered and unobtainable red
Single-vineyard Astralis★★ is a hugely concentrated Syrah from ol
vines, aged in 100% French new oak. Other Syrah ★★ labels off
slightly better value, while Merlot★ and Cabernet Sauvignon★ aim t
rub shoulders with great red BORDEAUX – although I'm not sure whic
ones. Several cuvées of Old Vines Grenache★★ are marked by saturate
black cherry fruit and high alcohol. Best years: (Astralis) (2008) (06) (05) (
03 02 01 00 **98 96 95 94**.

CH. CLARKE★ *Listrac-Médoc AC, Bordeaux, France* This property had millio
spent on it by the late Baron Edmond de Rothschild during the lat
1970s, and from the 98 vintage leading Bordeaux winemaker Mich
Rolland has been consultant enologist. The wines can have an attractiv
blackcurrant fruit and now a lot more Merlot (70%) is giving them mor
ripeness and polish. With a name like Clarke, how could they possibl
fail to seduce? There is also a small production of dry white wine,
Merle Blanc★. Best years: 2008 **07 06 05 04 03 01 00 99 98**.

DOMENICO CLERICO *Barolo DOCG, Piedmont, Italy* Domenico Cleric
produces, in his recently finished new cantina, consistently superlativ
BAROLO (Ciabot Mentin Ginestra★★★, Pajana★★★, Per Cristina★★
and excellent BARBERA D'ALBA★ (Trevigne★★), all wonderfully balance
His range also includes LANGHE Arte★★, a barrique-aged blend o
Nebbiolo and Barbera. Best years: (Barolo) (2009) (08) (07) (06) 04 **01 00 9
98 97 96 95**.

CH. CLIMENS★★★ *Barsac AC, 1er Cru Classé, Bordeaux, France* The leadin
estate in BARSAC, with a deserved reputation for fabulous, sensuous wine
rich and succulent yet streaked with lively lemon acidity. Easy to drink a
5 years, but a good vintage will be richer and more satisfying after 10–1
years. Second wine: les Cyprès (also delicious). Best years: 2007 06 05 0
03 02 01 00 99 98 97 96 95 90 89 88.

CLONAKILLA *Canberra,   Australia* Small
family winery, whose flagship Shiraz-
Viognier★★★ is the benchmark for the
style in Australia: elegant, lavender-
scented, fleshily textured and complex,
with the structure to age beautifully.
Tim Kirk also produces increasingly
impressive   Riesling★,   sublime
Viognier★ and a new Semillon-
Sauvignon Blanc. More modestly priced

O'Riada Shiraz★ (from local growers) and HILLTOPS Shiraz (from th
nearby region).

CLOS DE L'ANHEL *Corbières AC, Languedoc, France* In just a few years, Soph
Guiraudon and Philippe Mathias have started to produce remarkabl
wines with a power unusual even for the CORBIÈRES. Top wine is smooth
rich Les Dimanches★★; also Les Terrassettes★ and Les Autres. Bes
years: (Les Dimanches) (2009) 08 07 06 **05 04 03 01 00**.

CLOS BAGATELLE *St-Chinian AC, Languedoc-Roussillon, France* Siblings Lu
and Christine Simon produce various ST-CHINIANS: top wine La Gloire d
Mon Père★ is made from Syrah, Mourvèdre and Grenache, and aged i
100% new oak barrels. Also unoaked, fruit-driven Mathieu et Marie★
Cuvée Camille et Juliette, with spicy, herbal aromas, and a MUSCAT D
ST-JEAN-DE-MINERVOIS.

LOS DU BOIS *Alexander Valley AVA, Sonoma County, California, USA* I've always been partial to the house style here: gentle, fruit-dominated SONOMA Chardonnay, Merlot and Cabernet. Top vineyard selections can be exciting: Calcaire Chardonnay★★, rich, strong Briarcrest Cabernet Sauvignon★★ and Marlstone★★, a red BORDEAUX-style blend. Riesling is the latest project. Now owned by Constellation. Best years: (reds) 2005 04 03 **02 01 00 99 97 96 95**.

CLOS CENTEILLES *Minervois AC, Languedoc-Roussillon, France* Excellent MINERVOIS La Livinière and innovative vins de pays. Impressive Clos Centeilles★★ is the top wine; Capitelle de Centeilles★ and Carignanissime★ are 100% Cinsaut and 100% Carignan respectively. Best years: (2009) 08 07 06 **05 04 03 02 01 00**.

CLOS DE LA COULÉE-DE-SERRANT *Savennières AC, Loire Valley, France* Nicolas Joly is biodynamics' most vocal proponent and, with his winemaker daughter Virginie, produces powerfully concentrated, distinctive and ageworthy SAVENNIÈRES wines with atypically high degrees of alcohol. Eponymous top cuvée hails from monopole Clos de la Coulée de Serrant★★, a steep, walled 7ha (17-acre) vineyard with its own subappellation. Savennières Clos de la Bergerie★★ and Les Vieux Clos★ also impressive. Best years: (2008) 07 06 05 **04 03 02 01 00 97 96 95 90 89**.

CLOS ERASMUS★★★ *Priorat DOCa, Cataluña, Spain* Daphne Glorian's tiny estate turns out one of the most profound and personal reds in the fashionable region of PRIORAT. Her small winery (formerly that of Alvaro PALACIOS) also makes a convincing second wine, Laurel★. Best years: (2008) 07 05 04 **03 02 01 00 99 98 97 96 94**.

CLOS DE GAMOT *Cahors AC, South-West France* In the same family for 400 years, this is benchmark CAHORS★★, which increases in subtlety and complexity with aging. Also outstanding cuvée Clos Saint-Jean★★ and in exceptional years a special cuvée from centenarian vines★★. Best years: (2009) 06 **05 02 01 98**.

LE CLOS JORDANNE *Niagara Peninsula VQA, Ontario, Canada* A joint venture between Canadian giant Vincor (owned by Constellation) and Burgundy's BOISSET, producing convincing Burgundy-style Pinot Noir★ and Chardonnay★★ under BURGUNDY-style designations. At the top end Le Grand Clos echoes Burgundy's Grand Cru; the single-vineyard wines show distinctive *terroir* differences; and the Village Reserve wines are from vineyards in the village of Jordan. All organic.

CLOS DES LAMBRAYS AC★★★ *Grand Cru, Côte de Nuits, Burgundy, France* This 8.8ha (22-acre) Grand Cru vineyard in MOREY-ST-DENIS is almost entirely owned by the domaine of the same name, though Taupenot-Merme also has a few rows, not quite enough to make a barrel a year. Thierry Brouin, manager at the Dom. des Lambrays, has raised his game in recent years by a more severe selection of fruit for the Grand Cru, now using only old vines. Best years: (2009) 08 07 06 05 **03 02 00**.

CLOS MARIE *Pic Saint-Loup, Coteaux du Languedoc AC, Languedoc, France* Since 1995, Christophe Peyrus has been making 4 powerful red wines, blends dominated by Syrah, that regularly wow tasters: Glorieuses★, L'Olivette★, Simon★ and Métairies du Clos★. Also white cuvée Manon. Best years: (2008) 07 06 **05 03 01 00**.

CLOS MOGADOR★★★ *Priorat DOCa, Cataluña, Spain* René Barbier Ferrer was one of the pioneers who relaunched the reputation of PRIORAT in the 1980s. The wine is a ripe, intense, brooding monster built to age. Best years: (2008) 07 06 05 04 **03 01 00 99 98 97 96 95 94**.

DOM. DU CLOS NAUDIN *Vouvray AC, Loire Valley, France*   Philippe Forea
runs this first-rate 11.5ha (28 acre) VOUVRAY domaine. Depending on th
vintage, he produces a range of styles: dry★★, medium-dry★★ an
sweet★★ (rare Réserve★★★), as well as a sparkling Mousseux★★ whic
accounts for 40% of production. The wines are supremely ageworthy. A
with HUET, in 2006, 2007 and 2008 the emphasis is on drier wines. Be
years: (Moelleux Réserve) (2009) 05 **03 97 96 95 90 89**.

CLOS DES PAPES *Châteauneuf-du-Pape AC, Rhône Valley, France*   The re
CHÂTEAUNEUF-DU-PAPE★★★ has a high 20% of Mourvèdre, which giv
structure, complexity and potential longevity. More ample and head
recently, with enough Grenache to ensure the wine's approachability in i
youth and provide an initial blast of fruit. The refined, long-live
white★★ takes on the nutty character of aged Burgundy after 5 or 6 year
Best years: (red) 2009 08 07 06 05 **04 03 01 00 99 98 97 96 95 94 90 89 8**

CLOS DE LA ROCHE AC *Grand Cru, Côte de Nuits, Burgundy, France*   Th
biggest and often best of the 5 MOREY-ST-DENIS Grands Crus. The wine ha
a lovely, bright, red-fruits flavour when young, and should become rich
chocolaty or gamy with age. Best producers: DROUHIN★★★, DUJAC★★
Léchenaut★★, Dom. LEROY★★★, H Lignier★★, Perrot-Minot★
Ponsot★★★, ROUSSEAU★★. Best years: (2009) 08 07 06 05 03 **02 01 99 98 9
95 93 90**.

CLOS ST-DENIS AC *Grand Cru, Côte de Nuits, Burgundy, France*   This sma
(6.5ha/16-acre) Grand Cru, which gave its name to the village of MORE
ST-DENIS, produces wines which are sometimes light, but should b
wonderfully silky, with the texture that only great Burgundy can regular
achieve. Best after 10 years or more. Best producers: Arlaud★★
Charlopin★★, DUJAC★★★, JADOT★★, Ponsot★★★. Best years: (2009) 08 0
06 05 03 **02 01 99 98 96 95 93 90**.

CLOS DE TART AC★★★ *Grand Cru, Côte de Nuits, Burgundy, France*   7.5h
(18-acre) Grand Cru, a monopoly of the Mommessin family, run b
Sylvain Pitiot. Intense, concentrated wines made by traditional method
with a modern result. Now exceptional quality – and price! Best year
(2009) 08 07 06 05 **03 02 01 00 99 96 95 90**.

CLOS TRIGUEDINA *Cahors AC, South-West France*   Jean-Luc Baldès mak
some of the best-known and admired CAHORS★. In top cuvée Princ
Probus★★ he unites the strength of Cahors with elegance. Best year
(2009) 06 **05 02 01 98**.

CLOS UROULAT *Jurançon AC, South-West France*   Charles Hours makes tin
quantities of stunningly good JURANÇON. Fermented mostly in old barrel
dry Cuvée Marie★★ has ripe fruit yet a deliciously refreshing finish. I
ages just as well as the rich sweet Jurançon★★, which pulls togethe
lemon, lime, honey and apricot: enjoyable young, but ages magnificentl
Best years: **2007 05 04 03 00**.

CLOS DU VAL *Napa Valley AVA, California, USA*   Elegant Cabernet Sauvignon
(STAGS LEAP DISTRICT★★), Chardonnay★, Merlot★, Pinot Noir★ an
Zinfandel★. Reserve Cabernet★ can age well. Best years: (Reserv
Cabernet) (2006) 05 04 03 **02 01 00 99 97 96 95 94 91 90**.

CLOS DE VOUGEOT AC *Grand Cru, Côte de Nuits, Burgundy, France*   Enclose
by Cistercian monks in the 14th century, and today a considerable touris
attraction, this large (50ha/125-acre) vineyard is now divided among 80
owners. As a result of this division, Clos de Vougeot is one of the les
reliable Grand Cru Burgundies; the better wine tends to come from th
upper and middle parts. When it is good it is wonderfully fleshy, turning

deep and exotic after 10 years or more. Best producers: B Ambroise★★, Chopin★★, J-J Confuron★★★, Eugénie★★★ (formerly Engel), FAIVELEY★, GRIVOT★★★, Anne GROS★★★, JADOT★★★, Dom. LEROY★★★, T LIGER-BELAIR★★, MEO-CAMUZET★★★, Denis MORTET★★★, Mugneret-Gibourg★★★, Ch. de la Tour★★, VOUGERAIE★★. Best years: (2009) 08 07 06 05 03 **02 01 00 99** 98 96 95 93 90.

CLOT DE L'OUM *Côtes du Roussillon-Villages AC, Roussillon, France* Eric Monné has been making powerful, dense wines since 2001, from 18ha (45 acres) of vines north of Perpignan, which he works organically. Wines include La Compagnie des Papillons★, Saint Bart Vieilles Vignes★ and top wine Numéro Uno★★, from Syrah and a little Carignan grown on granite.

CLOUDY BAY *Marlborough, South Island, New Zealand* New Zealand's most successful winery, Cloudy Bay achieved cult status with the first release of its zesty, herbaceous Sauvignon Blanc in 1985. After a dip in the early 2000s, the winery is getting back on form despite high production levels. Sauvignon Blanc★ has regained a lot of its leafy zest. Sauvignon Blanc Te Koko★★ is very different: rich, creamy, oak-matured and bottle-aged. Cloudy Bay also makes Chardonnay★★, superb Alsace-style Gewurztraminer★★ and Riesling★★ (late-harvest Riesling★★) and very good Pinot Noir★★. Vintage Pelorus★★ is a high-quality old-style CHAMPAGNE-method fizz and non-vintage Pelorus★★ is excellent too. Best years: (Sauvignon Blanc) **2009** 08 06 04.

PAUL CLUVER *Elgin WO, South Africa* Cool-loving varieties respond well in ELGIN: Sauvignon Blanc shows mineral refinement, Chardonnay★ is compact and layered, subtle Gewurztraminer★★, an often vibrant, dryish Riesling★ and thrilling Noble Late Harvest botrytis dessert★★ version. Pinot Noir improves each vintage: standard Pinot Noir★ is silky and refreshing; the ethereal charm of single-vineyard Seven Flags★★ belies its complexity and ageworthiness. Best years: (whites) **2009** 08 07 06.

COBB WINES *Sonoma Coast AVA, California, USA* Small, prestigious Pinot Noir producer in one of the coolest areas of SONOMA COUNTY. Most wines are under 14% alcohol, light in colour, but brilliantly scented and structured (Coastlands: Diane Cobb★★, Emmaline★★). Best years: 2006 **05**.

COBOS *Mendoza, Argentina* Small operation owned by Andrea Marchiori, Luis Barraud and American Paul Hobbs. Voluptuous single-vineyard Malbec★★ from old vines in the Marchiori vineyard in the Perdriel district of MENDOZA. Bramare Cabernet Sauvignon★ and Malbec★★ are similarly ripe and succulent, while Felino Malbec★ offers simple, fresher flavours and great quality for its price.

J-F COCHE-DURY *Meursault, Côte de Beaune, Burgundy, France* Jean-François Coche-Dury, now joined by his son Raphaël, is a modest superstar, quietly turning out some of the finest wines on the CÔTE DE BEAUNE. His best wines are his CORTON-CHARLEMAGNE★★★ and MEURSAULT Perrières★★★, but even his BOURGOGNE Blanc★★ is excellent. His red wines, from VOLNAY★★ and MONTHELIE★ are delicious to drink even when young. Best years: (whites) (2009) 08 07 06 05 **04 02 01 00 99** 95.

COCKBURN *Port DOC, Douro, Portugal* Best known for Special Reserve ruby port; also stylish Vintage★ and Quinta dos Canais★. Cockburn ports are now made by Symington Family Estates. Best years: (Vintage) 2007 **03 00** 97 94 91 70 63 60 55; (dos Canais) 2007 **03 01 00** 95 92.

CODORNÍU *Cava DO, Cataluña, Spain* The biggest CHAMPAGNE-method sparkling wine company in the world. Anna de Codorníu★ and Jaume Codorníu★ are especially good, but all the sparklers are better than the

CAVA average. Drink young for freshness. Codorníu also owns RAÏMAT i COSTERS DEL SEGRE, Masía Bach in the PENEDES and Bodegas Bilbaínas i RIOJA, and has a stake in Scala Dei in PRIORAT.

COLCHAGUA *Rapel, Chile* RAPEL sub-region and home to several excitin estates, such as the Apalta hillside vineyard, where CASA LAPOSTOLL MONTES and others have plantings. Syrah and Carmenère do very we here. Chimbarongo and Los Lingues to the east are cooler due to th influence of the Andes, while Palmilla and Santa Cruz are much warme New vineyards toward the coast in Lolol and Marchíhüe are deliverin exciting reds and whites, especially Syrah and Viognier. New coast region Paredones is showing great promise for salty Sauvignon Blanc Best producers: CASA LAPOSTOLLE★★, CASA SILVA★, CONO SUR★★, EMILIANA★★ Hacienda Araucano/Lurton★, Koyle, Los Vascos, LUIS FELIPE EDWARDS★ MONTES★★, MontGras, Neyen★★, VENTISQUERO★ (Pangea★★), Viu Manent★

COLDSTREAM HILLS *Yarra Valley, Victoria, Australia* Founded by Australia wine guru James Halliday; owned by Foster's since 2005. Pinot Noir (Reserve★★) is usually good: sappy and smoky with cherry fruit an clever use of all-French oak. Chardonnay★ (Reserve★★) has subtlety an delicacy but real depth as well. Reserve Cabernet★ can be very goo though not always ripe; Merlot★★ ripens more successfully. Best year (Reserve Pinot Noir) (2008) 06 **05 04 02 00 98 97 96**.

COLLI ORIENTALI DEL FRIULI DOC *Friuli-Venezia Giulia, Italy* This DOC covers 20 types of wine. Best known are the sweet whites from Verduzzo in the Ramandolo sub-zone and the delicate Picolit, but it is the reds – from the indigenous Refosco and Schioppettino, as well as imports like Cabernet – and dry whites, from Friulano, Ribolla, Pinot Bianco, Pinot Grigio and Malvasia Istriana, that show how exciting the wines can be. Prices are high. Best producers: Ca' Ronesca★, Dario Coos★, Dorigo★, Dri★ (Ramandolo★★), Le Due Terre★★, Livio FELLUGA★★, Walter Filiputti★ Adriano Gigante★★, Livon★, Meroi★, Miani★★, Davide Moschioni★★, Rocc Bernarda★, Rodaro★, Ronchi di Cialla★, Ronchi di Manzano★★, Ronco d Gnemiz★★, Scubla★, Sirch★, Specogna★, Le Vigne di Zamò★★, Zof★ Best years: (whites) (2009) 08 **07 06 04 02 01 00 99 98 97**.

Ronco del Gnemiz
colli orientali del Friuli
denominazione di origine controllata
Pinot Grigio
2007

COLLI PIACENTINI DOC *Emilia-Romagna, Italy* Home to some of EMILI ROMAGNA's best wines, this DOC covers 11 different types, the best o which are Cabernet Sauvignon and the red Gutturnio (a blend of Barber and Bonarda) as well as the medium-sweet white and bubbly Malvasia Best producers: Luretta★, Lusenti, Castello di Luzzano/Fugazza★ Il Poggiarello★, La Stoppa★, Torre Fornello★, La Tosa (Cabernet Sauvignon★ Best years: (reds) (2009) 08 **07 06 04 03 01 00**.

COLLINES RHODANIENNES, VIN DE PAYS DES *Rhône Valley, Franc* Exciting granite/schist hillside region between Vienne and Valenc includes the new vineyard of Seyssuel. The best wines are Syrah, althoug there are some good juicy Merlots and Gamays, too. Best producer P & C Bonnefond★, COLOMBO★, CUILLERON (Viognier★), P Gaillard★, J-M Géri (Viognier), JAMET★★, P Jasmin, Monteillet, S Ogier★★, A PERRET, TAIN CO-op G Vernay★, Vins de Vienne (Coteaux de Seyssuel Sotanum★★). Best year (reds) **2009 07 06 05 03**.

COLLIO DOC *Friuli-Venezia Giulia, Italy* Some of Italy's best and most expensive dry white wines are from these hills on the Slovenian border. There are 19 types of wine, from local (Tocai) Friulano and Malvasia Istriana to international varieties. The best are ageworthy. **Best producers:** Borgo Conventi★, Borgo del Tiglio★★, La Castellada★, Damijan★, Livio FELLUGA★★, Marco Felluga★, Fiegl★, GRAVNER★★, JERMANN★★, Edi Keber★, Renato Keber★★, Livon★, Primosic★, Princic★, Puiatti★, Roncùs★★, Russiz Superiore★, SCHIOPETTO★★, Matijaz Tercic★★, Venica & Venica★★, Villa Russiz★★, Villanova★, Zuani★★. **Best years:** (whites) (2009) 08 07 **06 04 02 01 00**.

COLLIOURE AC *Roussillon, France* This tiny fishing port tucked away in the Pyrenean foothills makes a throat-warming red wine that is capable of aging for a decade but is marvellously rip-roaring when young. **Best producers:** (reds) Abbé Rous, Baillaury★, Clos de Paulilles★, MAS BLANC★★, la Rectorie★★, la Tour Vieille★, Vial Magnères★. **Best years:** (2009) 08 07 06 **05 04 03 01 00 99 98**.

COLOMBARD In France, Colombard traditionally has been distilled to make Armagnac and Cognac, but has now emerged as a table wine grape in its own right, notably as a Vin de Pays des CÔTES DE GASCOGNE. At its best, it has a lovely, crisp acidity and fresh, aromatic fruit. The largest plantings of the grape are in California, where it generally produces rather less distinguished wines, although French winemaker Yannick Rousseau of NAPA VALLEY makes a superb dry version from old vines in RUSSIAN RIVER VALLEY. South Africa can produce attractive refreshing wines, though much is used in brandy production. Australia also has some bright-eyed examples (especially PRIMO ESTATE).

JEAN-LUC COLOMBO *Cornas AC, Rhône Valley, France* Colombo has long decried traditional methods. His sweet, rich CORNAS is more opulent and has far less tannic grip than some. Top cuvées are les Ruchets★★ and the lush old-vines la Louvée★★, made in tiny quantities. Among his *négociant* wines, CONDRIEU Amour de Dieu★★, CHÂTEAUNEUF-DU-PAPE les Bartavelles★ and red and white HERMITAGE le Rouet★ stand out, although some offerings don't always seem fully ripe. Also produces full, fragrant ST-PÉRAY la Belle de Mai★, good red and white CÔTES DU RHÔNE★ and vins de pays from the RHÔNE, PROVENCE and ROUSSILLON. **Best years:** (Cornas) 2009 **07 06 05 04 03 01 00 99 98 95**.

COLOMÉ *Salta, Argentina* Established in the early 19th century, Colomé is one of the oldest, most remote and beautiful wineries in South America. As well as a 5-star boutique hotel, Swiss billionaire owner Donald HESS has invested in a state-of-the-art winery and has been renovating and planting vineyards at extreme altitude. Altura Maxima at just over 3000m (10,000ft) above sea level is the world's highest commercial vineyard. The conversion to biodynamic practices is complete. The Estate Red★★, a blend of Malbec with Cabernet Sauvignon and Tannat, is a masterful, aromatic, wild, herby wine. The Torrontés★ is thrillingly lush and scented. **Best years:** 2007 **06 05 04 03**.

COLORADO *USA* With their high altitudes, many regions in the Rocky Mountains seem perfect to grow wine grapes, but arid conditions, soil anomalies and cold winters make much of Colorado unsuitable. As a result 90% of the fruit used by Colorado's 80 wineries come from one of the two appellations: the warmer Grand Valley AVA and the slightly cooler (and higher in altitude) West Elks AVA. Most vineyards are at 1200–2100 (4000–7000ft). Best producers: Balistreri, BookCliff Vineyards★, Boulder Creek Canyon Wind★★, Carlson, Colorado Cellars, Alfred Eames Cellars★, Garfie Estates★, Infinite Monkey Theorem, Jack Rabbit Hill★, Plum Creek★, Sutclif Terror Creek★, Two Rivers★, Winery at Holy Cross Abbey★.

COLUMBIA CREST *Washington State, USA* An offshoot of CHATEAU S MICHELLE, and now the largest winery in Washington State, producil top-calibre wines at everyday prices. Two Vines budget label is goo Grand Estates Shiraz★ and Grand Estates Chardonnay★ are stro suits, as is the new H3★ label for Horse Heaven Hills fruit; these a good young but will age for several years. Reserve Syrah★ can be heavi oaked but has impressive style. Best years: (reds) (2008) 07 06 **05 04**.

COLUMBIA VALLEY AVA *Washington State, USA* The largest of WASHINGTON viticultural regions, covering a third of the state's landmass a encompassing both the YAKIMA VALLEY and WALLA WALLA VALLEY, as well the newer AVAs of Red Mountain, Wahluke Slope, Rattlesnake Hil Horse Heaven Hills, Snipes Mountain, Columbia Gorge and La Chelan. It produces 98% of the state's wine grapes: Merlot, Caberr Sauvignon and Chardonnay are the most widely planted varieties. Be producers: ANDREW WILL★★, BETZ★, CADENCE★★, CHATEAU STE MICHELLE COLUMBIA CREST★, DELILLE CELLARS★★, DUNHAM CELLARS★, Goose Rid HEDGES★, JANUIK★, L'ECOLE NO 41★★, LONG SHADOWS VINTNERS★★, Matthe Cellars★, QUILCEDA CREEK★★★, SYNCLINE★, WOODWARD CANYON★★. Be years: (reds) (2008) 07 06 **05 04 03 02**.

COMMANDARIA *Cyprus* Amber, treacly wine made from red Mavro a white Xynisteri grapes, sun-dried before vinification and solera agin Potentially one of the world's great rich wines. Etko's Centurion wonderful; Keo's St John is the best of the commercial brands, many which are disappointing.

CONCHA Y TORO *Maipo, Chile* Chile's biggest wine company, Concha Toro has around 6000ha (15,000 acres) of vineyards and a talented grou of winemakers led by Marcelo Papa. Casillero del Diablo★ is t excellent 'international' label and Marqués de Casa Concha★ is the ne step up (reds can be ★★). Higher up, Trio★ and Terrunyo★★ are go labels for reds and whites. LIMARI and CASABLANCA-sourced Amelia★★ the top Chardonnay and small amounts of various excellent reds co out under the Winemaker's Lot label (usually ★★). The classic Caberr Sauvignon-based Don Melchor★★★ is impressively velvety and compl in recent releases. The related Maycas del Limarí winery offers cri Sauvignon Blanc★, ripe, scented yet dense Syrah★★ and tangy, mine Chardonnay★★. New Palo Alto from MAULE. Trivento is an importa Argentinian project. See also ALMAVIVA, CONO SUR.

CONDRIEU AC *Rhône Valley, France* The home of Viognier. Wonderfu fragrant but expensive wine. Ranges from scented, full and opulent sweet, late-harvested; the best have a mineral streak. Quality varies, choose a good producer. Best drunk young. Best producers: G Barge P & C Bonnefond★★, CHAPOUTIER★, du Chêne★★, L Chèze★★, COLOMBO★ CUILLERON★★★, DELAS★★, C Facchin★, Faury★★, P Gaillard★ Y Gangloff★★, J-M Gérin, GUIGAL★★, F Merlin★★, Monteillet★★, Mouton R Niéro★, A Paret★★, A PERRET★★★, C Pichon★★, ROSTAING★ St-Cosme★★, G Vernay★★★, F Villard★★★.

CONERO DOCG See ROSSO CONERO DOC.

CONO SUR *Colchagua, Chile* Dynamic sister winery to CONCHA Y TORO, whose Pinot Noir put the grape on the Chilean map. Basic releases are reliably attractive. The CASABLANCA-sourced 20 Barrels Pinot Noir★★ is rich and perfumed; top-of-the-range Ocio★★ is positively unctuous, yet refreshing. Minerally, crunchy 20 Barrels Sauvignon Blanc★★ is from one of Casablanca's coolest sites. Chardonnay★★, Merlot★★ and Cabernet Sauvignon★★, under 20 Barrels and Visión labels, are excellent, as are the Visión Riesling★★, Gewürztraminer★ and Viognier★. Isla Negra is a budget label.

CH. LA CONSEILLANTE★★ *Pomerol AC, Bordeaux, France* Elegant, exotic, velvety wine that blossoms beautifully after 5–6 years but can age much longer. Second wine: Duo de Conseillante (from 2007). Best years: 2008 07 06 05 **04 03 02 01 00 99 98 96 95 90 89**.

CONSTANTIA WO *South Africa* The historic heart of South African wine, covering much of Simon van der Stel's original 1685 land grant. Today 9 properties stretch along the Constantiaberg, from STEENBERG in the south to Constantia Glen in the north. Sauvignon Blanc thrust this cool-climate area into the limelight, but wines such as the pure-fruited, supple Eagles' Nest Shiraz★ and Steenberg's Merlot★★ show reds too have a promising future. Constantia Uitsig's elegant, flavoursome Constantia White★ reflects an increasing trend for the Semillon-Sauvignon blend. Cap Classique sparkling wines are also gaining in popularity. Best producers: BUITENVERWACHTING★, Constantia Glen★, Constantia Uitsig★, Eagles' Nest★, Groot Constantia (since 2004), High Constantia, KLEIN CONSTANTIA★, STEENBERG★★. Best years: (whites) 2009 **08 07 06 05 04 03 02 01**.

ALDO CONTERNO *Barolo DOCG, Piedmont, Italy* One of BAROLO's finest traditionalist producers. He makes good Dolcetto d'Alba★, excellent BARBERA D'ALBA Conca Tre Pile★★, a barrique-aged LANGHE Nebbiolo Il Favot★★, red blend Quartetto★★ and 2 Langhe Chardonnays: unoaked Printaniè and Bussiador★, fermented and aged in new wood. Pride of the range, though, are his Barolos from the hill of Bussia. In top vintages he produces Vigna Colonnello★★★, Vigna Cicala★★★ and excellent Granbussia★★★, as well as a regular Barolo called Bussia Soprana★★. All these Barolos, though accessible when young, need several years to show their true majesty, but retain a remarkable freshness. Best years: (Barolo) (2009) (08) (07) 06 04 **03 01 00 99 98 97 96 95 90 89 88**.

GIACOMO CONTERNO *Barolo DOCG, Piedmont, Italy* Aldo's late elder brother Giovanni, now followed by his son Roberto, took an even more traditional approach to winemaking. The flagship wine is BAROLO Monfortino★★★ (only released after some 5 or 6 years in large oak barrels) but Barolo Cascina Francia★★★ is also superb. Also excellent traditional BARBERA D'ALBA★★. Best years: (Monfortino) (2009) (08) (07) (06) 04 02 01 **00 99 98 97 96 95 90 89 88 85 82 71**.

CONTINO *Rioja DOCa, Rioja, Spain* An estate on some of the finest RIOJA land, half-owned by CVNE but run with passion and skill as a boutique operation. The wines include a beautifully balanced Reserva★★, a scented single-vineyard Viña del Olivo★★ (sometimes ★★★) and a remarkable, piercing Graciano★★. These wines all age beautifully. The 2007 vintage saw a first experimental white★. Best years: (Reserva) (2005) 04 03 02 **01 00 99 98 96 95 94 86 85**.

COONAWARRA *South Australia* On a flat limestone belt thinly veneered with terra rossa soil, Coonawarra can produce sublime Cabernet with leafy blackcurrant flavours yet real depth, and spicy Shiraz that age for years. Merlot can be good, too. An export-led boom fuelled significant new plantings, much of it outside the legendary terra rossa strip, and saw the production of disappointing light reds. An awareness of the risk to the region's reputation has seen substantial changes to viticultural practice over

the past decade, accompanied by huge investment in revitalizing the vineyards. Best producers: BALNAVES★★, Bowen, BRAND'S★★, Hollick★, JACOB'S CREEK/Orlando★★, KATNOOK★★, Ladbroke Grove, Leconfield★, LINDEMANS, MAJELLA★★★, Murdock, PARKER★★, PENFOLDS★★, PENLEY★★, PETALUMA★★, WYNNS★★, Zema★★. Best years: (Cabernet Sauvignon) (2009) 08 06 05 **04 03 02 01 99 98 97 96 94 91 90 86**.

COOPERS CREEK *Auckland, North Island, New Zealand* Successful HAWKES BAY Chardonnay★ and tangy MARLBOROUGH Sauvignon Blanc★. GISBORNE Arneis★, Marlborough Riesling★ and Late Harvest Riesling★ are also good. A smart range of Reserve reds from Hawkes Bay includes powerful Syrah★ and complex Merlot★ and Cabernet Sauvignon blends★. Best years: (Chardonnay) (2008) 07 06 04.

FRANCIS FORD COPPOLA *Rutherford AVA, California, USA* Movie director Francis Ford Coppola, now a serious wine producer, with volume approaching 1 million cases, has split his winemaking activities between luxury and lifestyle brands. The historic Inglenook Niebaum winery, an elaborate NAPA tourist destination, has been renamed Rubicon Estate. Rubicon★★, a BORDEAUX blend, lacked grace in early vintages but has now taken on a more exciting personality. It still needs 5–6 years of aging. Coppola also offers Cask Cabernet★★, Edizione Pennino★ (Zinfandel), RC Reserve Syrah★ and tiny amounts of Merlot★★ and Cabernet Franc★★, as well as super-premium white blend Blancaneaux★. Coppola has also acquired the former Chateau Souverain winery in SONOMA COUNTY, where brands include Sofia bubblies and good-value Coppola Diamond Collection varietals. Best years: (Rubicon) 2006 05 04 0 **02 01 00 99 97 96 95 94 91 86**.

CORBIÈRES AC *Languedoc, France* This huge region, with its recently recognized cru of Boutenac, produces some of the best reds in the LANGUEDOC, with juicy fruit and more than a hint of wild hillside herbs. Excellent young, but wines from the best estates can age for years. White Corbières can be tasty – usually drink as young as possible. Best producers: (reds) Baillat★, Caraguilhes★, Cascadais★, CLOS DE L'ANHEL★★, Embres-et-Castelmaure★, Étang des Colombes★, Fontsainte★, Grand Crès★, Grand Moulin★, Haut-Gléon★, Hélène★, l'Ille★, Lastours★, Mansenoble★, Ollieux★, les Palais★, St-Auriol★, VOULTE-GASPARETS★★. Best years: (reds) (2009) 08 07 0 **05 04 03 01 00**.

CORNAS AC *Rhône Valley, France* Pure Syrah wines with improved fruit and balance in the past 10 years; attractive alternatives to pricey neighbours HERMITAGE and CÔTE-RÔTIE. When young, the wines are dark red, with brooding dark fruit aromas; the fruit comes with a mineral tang. Best producers: ALLEMAND★★, F Balthazar★★, CLAPE★★★, COLOMBO★, Courbis★★, DELAS★, E & J Durand★★, Equis, JABOULET, J Lemenicier★, J Michel★, V Paris★★, TAIN co-op★, Tardieu-Laurent★★, Tunnel★, A Voge★★. Best years: 2009 07 06 05 04 03 01 00 99 98 97 96 95 94 91 90 89 88 85 83.

CORSE AC, VIN DE *Corsica, France* Overall AC for CORSICA with 5 superior sub-regions: Calvi, Cap Corse, Figari, Porto Vecchio and Sartène. Ajaccio and Patrimonio are entitled to their own ACs. The most distinctive wines, mainly red, come from local grapes: Nielluccio (thought to be related to SANGIOVESE) and Sciacarello for reds; Vermentino (known locally as Vermentinu or MALVASIA) for whites. There are some rich sweet Muscats – especially from Muscat du Cap Corse AC. **Best producers:** ARENA★, Canarelli★, Clos d'Alzeto★, Clos Capitoro, Clos Culombu★, Clos Landry★, Clos Nicrosi★, Gentile, Leccia, Maestracci★, Comte Peraldi★, Renucci★, Saparale, Signadore, Torraccia★.

CORSICA *France* This Mediterranean island has seen a welcome trend toward quality in the last 15 years, with co-ops and local growers investing in equipment and planting varieties such as Syrah, Merlot, Cabernet Sauvignon and Mourvèdre for reds, and Chardonnay and Sauvignon Blanc for whites – to complement the local reds Nielluccio, Sciacarello, Aleatico, and whites Barbarossa and Vermentino. Whites and rosés are pleasant for drinking young; reds are more exciting and can age for 3–4 years. See also CORSE AC.

CORTES DE CIMA *Alentejo, Portugal* Excellent modern Portuguese reds. Blends of Aragonez (Tempranillo) and Syrah with Portuguese grapes such as Trincadeira and Touriga Nacional are used for spicy, fruity Chaminé★, oaked red Cortes de Cima★ and a splendid dark, smoky Reserva★★. Touriga Nacional★★ makes an aromatic varietal red and Incógnito★★ is a gutsy, black-fruited blockbuster Syrah. **Best years:** (2009) 08 **05 04 03 01 00.**

CORTESE White grape variety of south-eastern PIEDMONT in Italy; it can produce good, fairly acidic, dry whites. Sometimes labelled simply as Cortese Piemonte DOC, its main purpose is as the principal grape in GAVI.

CORTON AC *Grand Cru, Côte de Beaune, Burgundy, France* The only red Grand Cru in the CÔTE DE BEAUNE; ideally the wines should have the burliness and savoury power of the top CÔTE DE NUITS wines, combined with the seductively perfumed fruit of Côte de Beaune. Red Corton should take 10 years to mature, but many modern examples never get there. New excitement with participation of Dom. de la ROMANÉE-CONTI from 2009. Very little white Corton is made. **Best producers:** B Ambroise★★, d'Ardhuy★★, Bonneau du Martray★★, CHANDON DE BRIAILLES★★, Dubreuil-Fontaine★★, FAIVELEY★★★, Camille Giroud★★, Guyon★★, JADOT★★★, Dom. LEROY★★★, MEO-CAMUZET★★★, Senard★, TOLLOT-BEAUT★★★. **Best years:** (reds) (2009) 08 07 06 05 03 **02 01 99 98 96 95 90.**

CORTON-CHARLEMAGNE AC *Grand Cru, Côte de Beaune, Burgundy, France* Corton-Charlemagne, on the west and south-west flanks and at the top of the famous CORTON hill, is the largest of Burgundy's white Grands Crus. It can produce some of the most impressive white Burgundies – richly textured yet with a fine mineral quality. The best should show their real worth only at 10 years or more. **Best producers:** Bonneau du Martray★★★, BOUCHARD PÈRE ET FILS★★, Champy★★, CHANDON DE BRIAILLES★★, COCHE-DURY★★★, DROUHIN★★, FAIVELEY★★, V GIRARDIN★★★, JADOT★★★, P Javillier★★, Louis LATOUR★★, Rapet★★, M Rollin★★, ROUMIER★★, TOLLOT-BEAUT★★★, VOUGERAIE★★. **Best years:** (2009) 08 07 06 05 **04 03 02 00 99 97 95.**

CH. COS D'ESTOURNEL★★★ *St-Estèphe AC, 2ème Cru Classé, Haut-Médoc, Bordeaux, France* One of the leading châteaux of BORDEAUX. The wine is classically made for aging and usually needs 10 years to show really well. Used to have a high proportion of Merlot (around 40%) but from 2007 Cabernet Sauvignon has been on the increase (75–85%). Recent vintages have been dark, brooding, powerful and, but for a wobble in 1998 and 99, of the highest order. Small production of white from 2005 and new state-of-the-art winery in 2009. Second wine: les Pagodes de Cos. Best years: 2008 07 06 05 04 03 **02 01 00 96 95 94 90 89 88 86**.

DOM. COSSE-MAISONNEUVE *Cahors AC, South-West France* Mathieu Cosse and Catherine Maisonneuve have become the cult growers of CAHORS, combining the best of the traditional and modern styles into very personal interpretations. From the fruity Le Combal★, move up through Le Petit Sid★★ to Les Laquets★★ and finally Le Sid★★, which reflects the iron that underlies the soil. Best years: (2009) 06 **05 04 01**.

COSTANTI *Brunello di Montalcino DOCG, Tuscany, Italy* One of the original highly respected Montalcino estates making fine BRUNELLO★★ (Riserva★★) and Rosso★, as well as Vermiglio★, a tasty partially barrique-aged Sangiovese. Calbello, a Merlot-Cabernet blend, is one of Montalcino's best 'international' style wines. Best years: (Brunello) (2009) (08) (07) (06) 04 **03 01 99 97 95 90 88 85 82**.

COSTERS DEL SEGRE DO *Cataluña, Spain* DO on the 'banks of the Segre' in western CATALUÑA, with a great array of grape varieties, generally good quality and moderate prices. Best producers: Castell de Remei★, Celler de Cérvoles★★, Tomás Cusiné★, RAÏMAT★. Best years: (reds) 2007 06 05 **04 03 01 00**.

COSTIÈRES DE NÎMES AC *Rhône Valley, France* Quality region west of Avignon. Reds are bright, spicy and perfumed, the best are substantial; rosés are good young gluggers; whites are tasty versions of Marsanne and Roussanne. Best producers: l'Amarine★, Amphoux, Grande Cassagne★, Lamargue, Mas des Bressades★, Mas Carlot, Mas Neuf, Mourgues du Grès★, Nages★, d'Or et de Gueules, la Patience, Roubaud, Tardieu-Laurent, la Tour de Beraud★, la Tuilerie, Vieux-Relais★. Best years: **2009 07 05**.

CÔTE DE BEAUNE *Côte d'Or, Burgundy, France* Southern part of the CÔTE D'OR; beginning at the hill of CORTON, north of the town of BEAUNE, the Côte de Beaune progresses south as far as MARANGES, with white wines gradually taking over from red.

CÔTE DE BEAUNE AC *Côte de Beaune, Burgundy, France* Small AC, high on the hill above the town of Beaune, named to ensure maximum confusion with the title for the whole region. Best producers: DROUHIN★, Giboulot, VOUGERAIE★. Best years: (2009) 08 **07 05**.

CÔTE DE BEAUNE-VILLAGES AC *Côte de Beaune, Burgundy, France* Red wine AC covering 16 villages, such as AUXEY-DURESSES, LADOIX, MARANGES. If the wine is a blend from several villages it is sold as Côte de Beaune-Villages. It can also cover the red wine production of mainly white wine villages such as MEURSAULT. Best producers: DROUHIN★, JADOT★. Best years: (2009) 08 **07 05**.

CÔTE DE BROUILLY AC *Beaujolais, Burgundy, France* Wine from the higher slopes of Mont Brouilly, a small but abrupt volcanic mountain in the south of the BEAUJOLAIS Crus area. The wine is deeper in colour and fruit and has more intensity than that of BROUILLY. Best producers: O Ravier★, Roches Bleues/Lacondemine★, Ch. Thivin★ (La Chapelle★★, Zaccharie★★), Viornery★. Best years: **2009 08 07**.

CÔTE CHALONNAISE See BOURGOGNE-CÔTE CHALONNAISE.

CÔTE DE NUITS *Côte d'Or, Burgundy, France* This is the northern part of the great CÔTE D'OR and is *not* an AC. Almost entirely red wine country, the vineyards start in the southern suburbs of Dijon and continue south in a narrow swathe to below the town of NUITS-ST-GEORGES. The villages are some of the greatest wine names in the world – GEVREY-CHAMBERTIN, VOUGEOT and VOSNE-ROMANÉE etc.

CÔTE DE NUITS-VILLAGES AC *Côte de Nuits, Burgundy, France* Although not much seen, the wines (mostly red) are often good, not very deep in colour but with a nice cherry fruit. Best producers: (reds) D Bachelet★, Chopin-Groffier★, J-J Confuron, Gille, JADOT, Jourdan★, Loichet. Best years: (reds) (2009) 08 **07 06 05 03 02**.

CÔTE D'OR *Burgundy, France* Europe's most northern great red wine area and also the home of some of the world's best dry white wines. The name, meaning 'golden slope', refers to a 48km (30-mile) stretch between Dijon and Chagny which divides into the CÔTE DE NUITS in the north and the CÔTE DE BEAUNE in the south.

CÔTE ROANNAISE AC *Loire Valley, France* Small, improving AC in the upper LOIRE producing Gamay reds and rosés; the best are of BEAUJOLAIS-VILLAGES standard. Vin de pays whites can be good. Best producers: A Baillon, V Giraudon, de la Paroisse, M Piat, R Sérol★.

CÔTE-RÔTIE AC *Rhône Valley, France* The Côte-Rôtie, or 'roasted slope', produces one of France's finest red wines. On its steep, slippery slopes, the Syrah balances full ripeness with freshness, and the small amount of white Viognier sometimes included gives an unexpected exotic or violet fragrance. Lovely young, it is better aged for 5–8 years. Best producers: G Barge★★, Bernard★, Billon, P & C Bonnefond★★, Bonserine★, B Burgaud★, Clusel-Roch★★, CUILLERON★★, DELAS★★, Duclaux★★, Garon★, J-M Gérin★★, GUIGAL★★, JAMET★★★, P Jasmin★★, Levet, S Ogier★★, Rosiers, ROSTAING★★, J-M Stéphan★, Tardieu-Laurent★★, Vidal-Fleury★, F Villard★, Vins de Vienne★★. Best years: 2009 07 06 **05 04 03 01 00 99 98 95 94 91 90 89 88 85**.

COTEAUX D'AIX-EN-PROVENCE AC *Provence, France* The first AC in the south to acknowledge that Cabernet Sauvignon can enormously enhance the traditional local grape varieties such as Grenache, Cinsaut, Mourvèdre, Syrah and Carignan. The reds can age. Some quite good fresh rosé is made, while the whites, mostly still traditionally made, are pleasant but hardly riveting. Best producers: Ch. Bas★, les Bastides★, les Béates★★, Beaupré★, Calissanne★, J-L COLOMBO (Côte Bleue★★), d'EOLE★, Fonscolombe, Revelette★, Valdition, Vignelaure★. Best years: (reds) 2008 07 **06 05 04 03 01 00**.

COTEAUX DE L'ARDÈCHE, VIN DE PAYS DES *Rhône Valley, France* Increasingly good, lively red wines made from Cabernet Sauvignon, Syrah, Merlot or Gamay and dry, fresh whites from Chardonnay, Viognier or Sauvignon Blanc. Best producers: Vignerons Ardechois, Colombier, DUBOEUF, G Flacher, Louis LATOUR★, Mas de Libian (Viognier), Pradel, Vigier.

COTEAUX DE L'AUBANCE AC *Loire Valley, France* Smallish AC north of COTEAUX DU LAYON AC for sweet or semi-sweet white wines made from Chenin Blanc. Top sweet wines are labelled Sélection de Grains Nobles, as in ALSACE. Best producers: Bablut★★/Daviau, Dittière, Giraudières, Haute Perche★, Montgilet★★/V Lebreton, Princé, Richou★★, Rochelles★/ J-Y Lebreton. Best years: (2009) 08 07 **06 05 04 03 02 01 99 97 96**.

COTEAUX CHAMPENOIS AC *Champagne, France* Still wines from Champagne. Fairly acid with a few exceptions, notably from Bouzy and Aÿ. The best age for 5 years or more. **Best producers: Pa** Bara★, BOLLINGER★, Egly-Ouriet★, Geoffroy★, H Goutorbe, LAURENT-PERRIER Joseph PERRIER, Ch. de Saran★/MOËT & CHANDON. **Best years: 2008 04 03 02 00**

COTEAUX DU LANGUEDOC AC *Languedoc, France* Large and increasingly successful region situated between Nîmes and Narbonne producing around 50 million bottles of beefy red, tasty rosé and surprisingly characterful whites. Twelve 'crus', including Montpeyrou Quatourze and Cabrières, have historically been allowed to append their names to the AC – these are in the process of being delineated by climate and soil type. La CLAPE, Grès de Montpellier, Terrasses du Larzac, PIC ST-LOUP and Picpoul de Pinet have already been officially recognized. This appellation will gradually be replaced by the larger Languedoc AC (see LANGUEDOC-ROUSSILLON). **Best** producers: l'Aiguelière★, Aupilhac★, Calage★,

Mas des Chimères
2006
COTEAUX DU LANGUEDOC

Clavel★, CLOS MARIE★, la Coste★, Grès St-Paul★, Lacroix-Vanel★, Mas Ca Demoura, Mas des Chimères★, Mas Jullien★, Mas de Martin, PEYRE ROSE★★ Poujol★, PRIEURE DE ST-JEAN DE BÉBIAN★★, Puech-Haut★, St-Martin de l Garrigue★, Terre Megère★. **Best years: (2009) 08 07 06 05 04 03 01 00.**

COTEAUX DU LAYON AC *Loire Valley, France* Sweet wine from the Layon Valley, south of Angers. The wine is made from Chenin Blanc grapes that, ideally, are attacked by noble rot or, for intense but fresher styles dried by warm, autumnal breezes that concentrate grape sugars. In great years like 2007, and from a talented grower, this can be one of the world's exceptional sweet wines. Top wines are labelled Sélection de Grains Nobles. Six villages are entitled to use the Coteaux du Layon-Village AC which provides for lower yields; the village name appears on th label. Three sub-areas, BONNEZEAUX, QUARTS DE CHAUME (both regarded a Grand Cru sites) and Chaume have their own ACs that stipulate even lower yields. **Best producers:** P Aguilas★★, P Baudouin★★, BAUMARD★★ Bergerie★★, Cady★★, P Delesvaux★★, Dom. F L, Forges★, de Juchepie★ Ogereau★★, Passavant★, PIERRE-BISE★★★, Pithon-Paillé★, Quarres★ J Renou★★, Roulerie★★, Sablonnettes★★, Sauveroy★, Soucherie★★. **Bes** years: (2009) 07 06 **05 04 03 02 01 99 97 96 95 90 89**.

COTEAUX DU LOIR AC See JASNIÈRES AC.

COTEAUX DU LYONNAIS AC *Beaujolais, Burgundy, France* Good, light BEAUJOLAIS-style reds and a few whites and rosés from scattered vineyards between Villefranche and Lyon. Drink young.

COTEAUX DU QUERCY AC *South-West France* A newly-promoted Cabernet Franc-based vineyard area adjoining CAHORS to the south Fruity food-friendly wines of originality and character, best kept for 3 or 4 years. **Best producers** (2009) (08) **06 05 04**.

COTEAUX DU TRICASTIN AC *Rhône Valley, France* Bad publicity about the local nuclear plant has hit this mid-Rhône region. Direct, sometimes full reds and rosés with juicy fruit. The nutty dry white is worth a look. Drink young. **Best producers:** Décelle, Grangeneuve★, Lônes, St-Luc★ la Tour d'Elyssas, Vieux Micocoulier. **Best years: 2009 07 06 05**.

COTEAUX VAROIS AC *Provence, France* North of Toulon and stretching inland where it is notably cooler than the coast, this is an area to watch, with new plantings of classic grapes to improve quality. Best producers: Alysses★, Calisse★, Deffends★, Garbelle, Margüi★, Miraval★, Routas★, St-Estève, St-Jean-le-Vieux, Triennes★. Best years: 2008 **07 06 05 04 03**.

CÔTES DE BERGERAC AC See BERGERAC AC.

CÔTES DE BOURG AC *Bordeaux, France* The best red wines are earthy but blackcurranty and can age for 6–10 years. Very little white is made; most of it is dry and dull. Best producers: Brulesécaille★, Bujan★, FALFAS★, Fougas (Maldoror★), Garreau, Haut-Guiraud, Haut-Macô★, Haut-Mondésir★, Macay, Mercier, Nodoz★, ROC DE CAMBES★★, Tayac, Tour de Guiet★. Best years: (2009) **08 05 03 02 01 00 99 98**.

CÔTES DE CASTILLON AC *Bordeaux, France* Area east of ST-ÉMILION that has surged in quality recently; part of new Côtes de Bordeaux AC from 2008. Good value, but prices are beginning to climb. The best wines are full and firm, yet have the lushness of St-Émilion. Best producers: Dom. de l'A★★, Aiguilhe★★, Belcier, Cap-de-Faugères★, la Clarière Laithwaite, Clos l'Eglise★, Clos Les Lunelles★ (from 2001), Clos Puy Arnaud★★, Côte-Montpezat★, Joanin Bécot★, Poupille★, Robin★, Veyry★, Vieux-Ch.-Champs-de-Mars★. Best years: (2009) **08 06 05 04 03 02 01 00 99 98**.

CÔTES CATALANES, VIN DE PAYS DES *Roussillon, France* Covering much the same area as the CÔTES DU ROUSSILLON AC; co-ops dominate production but there is a growing number of talented individual producers, especially in the Fenouillèdes hills, benefiting from outside investment. Warm, rich, spicy reds, often from old-vines Grenache Noir and Carignan, plus Syrah; full-bodied minerally whites from Grenache Blanc and Gris and Macabeo. Best producers: la CASENOVE, CAZES, GAUBY/ le Soula, Matassa, Pertuisane, O Pithon, Preceptorie de Centenach, Soulanes.

CÔTES DE DURAS AC *South-West France* Between ENTRE-DEUX-MERS and BERGERAC, with good, fresh, leafy reds and whites from traditional BORDEAUX grapes. Drink young. Best producers: Chater★, Condom-Perceval (sweet white★★), Grand Mayne, Lafon, Laulan, Mouthes le Bihan★, Petit Malromé★. Best years: (reds) (2009) **08 06 05**.

CÔTES DE FRANCS See BORDEAUX-CÔTES DE FRANCS.

CÔTES DE GASCOGNE, VIN DE PAYS DES *South-West France* This is Armagnac country, but the tangy-fresh, fruity white table wines outsell everything else from the South-West put together. Drink young. Best producers: Arton, Brumont★, Cassagnoles, de Joy, Lauroux, Millet★, Pellehaut, Producteurs PLAIMONT★, San de Guilhem★, Sédouprat, TARIQUET★.

CÔTES DU JURA AC *Jura, France* This AC includes a variety of ageworthy wines, including specialities *vin jaune* and *vin de paille*. Savagnin makes strong-tasting whites, often sherry-like; some Chardonnay is made in this style, others are dry and mineral, reminiscent of good MÂCON. Distinctive reds and rosés from local Poulsard and Trousseau and also from Pinot Noir. See also CRÉMANT DU JURA AC. Best producers: Ch. d'Arlay★★, Baud★, Berthet-Bondet★, Boilley, Bourdy★, Chalandard, Ganevat★, Grand, A Labet★★, J Macle★, Pignier★★, Reverchon★, Rijckaert★★, Rolet, A & M Tissot★. Best years: (2008) 07 **06 05 04 02**.

CÔTES DU MARMANDAIS AC *South-West France* The addition of grapes such as Abouriou, Cot, Fer Servadou, Gamay and Syrah to Merlot and Cabernet blends distinguishes these wines from those of downstream BORDEAUX. Best producers: Beaulieu★, Bonnet & Laborde, ELIAN DA ROS★★. Best years: (reds) (2009) 08 **06 05 04**.

CÔTES DE PROVENCE AC *Provence, France* Large AC mainly for fruit
reds and rosés to drink young. Whites have improved. Best producer
Barbanau★, la Bernarde★, Clos d'Alari, Clos de la Procure, Commanderie d
Peyrassol★, la Courtade★, Coussin Ste-Victoire★, Cressonnière★
d'ESCLANS★, Féraud★, Fontlade, Galoupet, Gavoty★, Jale, Mauvanne★
Minuty★, Ott★, Réal Martin★, RICHEAUME★, Rimauresq★★, Roquefort★
St-André de Figuière, Sarrins★, SORIN★, Élie Sumeire★, Les Valentines.

CÔTES DU RHÔNE AC *Rhône Valley, France* AC for the whole RHÔN
VALLEY. Over 90% is red and rosé, mainly Grenache, with some Cinsau
Syrah, Carignan and Mourvèdre to add warm southern personalit
Modern winemaking has improved many wines, which are general
juicy, spicy and easy to drink, ideally within 5 years. Most wine is mad
by co-ops. Best producers: (reds) Amouriers★, d'Andézon★, les Aphillanthes★
A Brunel★, L Charvin★★, CLAPE★, COLOMBO★, Coudoulet de BEAUCASTEL★★
Cros de la Mûre★★, DELAS, Espiers★, Estézargues co-op★, Fonsalette★★, FON
DE MICHELLE★, Gramenon★, Grand Moulas★, Grand Prébois★, GUIGAL★
Haut Musiel, Hugues★, JABOULET★, la Janasse★, J-M Lombard★, Mas de Libian★
Mont-Redon, la Mordorée★, la RÉMÉJEANNE★, M Richaud★, Romarins, Roug
Garance, St-Estève d'Uchaux, St-Etienne, ST-GAYAN★, Ste-Anne★, Santa Duc★
Tardieu-Laurent★, Tours★, Vieille Julienne★, Vieux-Chêne★; (whites) Cassa
Coudoulet de BEAUCASTEL★, P Gaillard★, la RÉMÉJEANNE★, Ste-Anne★, S
Maurice. Best years: (reds) **2009 07**.

CÔTES DU RHÔNE-VILLAGES AC *Rhône Valley, France* AC covering 1
villages in the southern CÔTES DU RHÔNE that have traditionally mad
superior wine (especially CAIRANNE, RASTEAU, Laudun, Massif d'Uchau
Séguret, Valréas, Sablet, Visan). Best are spicy, food-friendly reds that ca
age well. Best producers: Achiary★, Amouriers★, Beaurenard★, Boissan★
Bramadou, Bressy-Masson★, de Cabasse★, Cabotte★, Chapoton★, D Charavin★
la Charbonnière★, Chaume-Arnaud★, Combe★, Coriançon★, Coste Chaud
Cros de la Mûre★, Durieu★, Espigouette★, Estézargues co-op★, Florane, le
Goubert, Gourt de Mautens★★, Gramenon★, Grand Moulas★, Grand Veneur★
Gravennes, la Janasse★, Jérôme★, Lucena, Mourchon★, Pélaquié★, Piaugier★
Rabasse-Charavin★, Rasteau co-op★, la RÉMÉJEANNE★, Roche-Audran, ST-GAYAN★
St-Maurice, St-Pierre, St-Siffrein, Ste-Anne★, Saladin, la Soumade★, Trapadis★
Valériane, Viret★. Best years: (reds) **2009 07 06 05 03**.

CÔTES DU ROUSSILLON AC *Roussillon, France* ROUSSILLON's catch-all AC
dominated by co-ops. It's a hot area, and much of the wine is baked an
dull. But there's a lively bunch of estates making exciting reds and doin
surprisingly good things with whites. Best producers: (reds) la CASENOVE★★
Vignerons Catalans, CAZES★, Chênes★, J-L COLOMBO★, Ferrer-Ribière★, Forç
Réal, Joliette, Laporte★, Mas Crémat★, Mossé, Olivier Pithon★, Rivesalte
co-op, Sarda-Malet★. Best years: (reds) (2009) 08 07 06 **05 04 03 01 00**.

CÔTES DU ROUSSILLON-VILLAGES AC *Roussillon, France* Wines fro
the best sites in the northern CÔTES DU ROUSSILLON. Villages Caraman
Latour-de-France, Lesquerde and Tautavel may add their own nam
Best producers: Calvet-Thunevin, Vignerons Catalans, CAZES★, Chênes★, Cl
des Fées★, CLOT DE L'OUM★★, Fontanel★, Força Réal, Gardiés★, GAUBY★★
Jau, Mas Amiel★, Mas Crémat★, Roc des Anges, Schistes★. Best years: (red
(2009) 08 07 06 **05 04 03 01 00 99**.

CÔTES DE THONGUE, VIN DE PAYS DES *Languedoc, France* Zon
north-east of Béziers. More character than most vins de pays, and som
dynamic estates are producing excellent results. Best producers: l'Arjolle★
les Chemins de Bassac, La Croix Belle, Magellan, Monplézy.

ÔTES DU VIVARAIS AC *Rhône Valley, France* Southern Rhône grapes (Grenache, Syrah, Cinsaut, Carignan) produce light, fresh reds and rosés for drinking young. Whites from Marsanne and Grenache Blanc. Uneven quality. **Best producers:** Vignerons Ardechois, Gallety★, Vigier.

UINTA DO CÔTTO *Douro DOC and Port DOC, Douro, Portugal* Unfortified DOURO wine expert. Quinta do Côtto red and creamy Paço de Teixeró white are good, and Grande Escolha★★ can be excellent: oaky and powerful when young, rich and cedary when mature. **Best years:** (Grande Escolha) 2001 **00 97 95 94 90 87 85**.

ERRE COURSODON *St-Joseph AC, Rhône Valley, France* Family-owned, 17ha (42-acre) domaine producing rich, oaked ST-JOSEPH★ from very old vines. The red wines need up to 4 years before they show their magnificent cassis and truffle and violet richness, especially the top wine, La Sensonne★★, aged in new oak. Whites, especially Paradis St Pierre★ from the Marsanne grape, are good, too. **Best years:** (reds) 2009 **07 06 05 04 03 01 00 99 98**.

OUSIÑO MACUL *Maipo, Chile* Chile's oldest winery still in the hands of the founding family, established in 1856 and run by the sixth generation of the Cousiño family. The old Macul winery and cellars near the centre of Santiago are a draw for tourists but the wines are now made in a modern facility further south in Alto Maipo. Best known for Antiguas Reservas★ and premium wines such as Lota★ and Finis Terrae★, but they also make an unusual Sauvignon Gris and a Riesling.

H. COUTET★★ *Barsac AC, 1er Cru Classé, Bordeaux, France* BARSAC's largest Classed Growth property has been in great form in recent years, and with its finesse and balance is once again a classic Barsac. Extraordinarily intense Cuvée Madame★★★ is made in certain exceptional years (last released vintage 1995). **Best years:** 2007 06 05 **04 03 02 01 00 99 98 97 96 95 90 89**.

RAGGY RANGE *Hawkes Bay and Martinborough, North Island, New Zealand* Ambitious winery whose style becomes more attractive and more impressive with each vintage. Premium HAWKES BAY wines include stylish Les Beaux Cailloux Chardonnay★★, a bold Cabernet blend called The Quarry★★, a rich Merlot blend known as Sophia★★ and the flagship Le Sol Syrah★★★. Also elegant Seven Poplars Chardonnay★ and Gimblett Gravels Merlot★★ from Hawkes Bay; fine Te Muna Road Pinot Noir★★ and Riesling★ from MARTINBOROUGH; restrained yet intense Avery Sauvignon Blanc★ and tangy Rapaura Road Riesling★ from MARLBOROUGH. **Best years:** (Syrah) (2009) **08 07 06 04**.

UINTA DO CRASTO *Douro DOC and Port DOC, Douro, Portugal* Well-situated property with very good traditional LBV★★ and Vintage★★ PORT and massively enjoyable juicy red DOURO★★ and oaky but excellent Touriga Nacional★★. Flagship reds Vinha da Ponte★★ and Maria Teresa★★ can reach ★★★. Austere Douro red Xisto★ is a joint venture with Jean-Michel Cazes of Ch. LYNCH-BAGES of Bordeaux. **Best years:** (Vintage port) 2004 **03 00 99 97 95 94**; (Touriga Nacional) 2005 **04 03 01**; (Ponte) **2004 00**; (Maria Teresa) 2005 **03 01 98**.

RÉMANT D'ALSACE AC *Alsace, France* Good CHAMPAGNE-method sparkling wine from ALSACE, usually made from Pinot Blanc and/or Pinot Gris. Reasonable quality, if not great value for money. **Best producers:** J-B ADAM★, P BLANCK★, Cave de Cleebourg, Dopff & Irion, Dopff au Moulin★, J Gross★, Kuentz-Bas, MURÉ★, Ostertag★, Pfaffenheim co-op, P Sparr★, A Stoffel★, TURCKHEIM co-op★.

CRÉMANT DE BOURGOGNE AC *Burgundy, France* Most Burgund
Crémant is white and is made either from Chardonnay alone or blend
with Pinot Noir. The result, especially in ripe years, can be full, so
almost honey-flavoured – if you give the wine the 2–3 years' ag
needed for mellowness to develop. **Best producers:** Chevrot, A Delor
Simonnet-Febvre, A Sounit, Veuve Ambal; and the co-ops at Bailly (the best
rosé★), Lugny★, St-Gengoux-de-Scissé and Viré.

CRÉMANT DE DIE AC *Rhône Valley, France* AC for traditional-method
made entirely from the Clairette Blanche grape. Less aromatic th
CLAIRETTE DE DIE. **Best producers:** Jacques Faure, J-C Raspail.

CRÉMANT DU JURA AC *Jura, France* AC for fizz from all over Jura, wh
accounts for nearly a quarter of the region's production. Larg
Chardonnay-based, with Poulsard, a pale red grape, for the pinks. B
producers: Fruitière Vinicole d'Arbois, Ch. de l'Étoile★, Grand★, La Mais
des Vignerons (Marcel Cabelier), Montbourgeau★, Rolet★, A & M Tissot★.

CRÉMANT DE LIMOUX AC *Languedoc, France* Sparkling wine made fr
a blend of Chardonnay, Chenin Blanc, Mauzac and Pinot Noir; w
wines generally have more complexity than BLANQUETTE DE LIMOUX. Dri
young. **Best producers:** l'Aigle★, Antech, Fourn, Guinot, Lauren
Martinolles★, SIEUR D'ARQUES.

CRÉMANT DE LOIRE AC *Loire Valley, France* Sparkling wine in Anjou a
Touraine, with more fruit and yeast character than those of VOUVRAY a
SAUMUR; increasingly Chardonnay is added to Loire stalwarts Che
Blanc and Cabernet Franc, giving fresh, elegant fruit. Good to drink
soon as it is released. **Best producers:** l'Aulée★, BAUMARD★, Bouvet-Ladubay
Brizé★, Fardeau★, Gratien & Meyer★, Lambert★, Langlois-Château
des Liards★/Berger, Michaud★, Nerleux/Régis Neau, Passavant★, Varinelles

CRIOTS-BÂTARD-MONTRACHET AC See BÂTARD-MONTRACHET AC.

CROFT *Port DOC, Douro, Portugal* Owned by the Fladgate Partnership (alo
with TAYLOR and FONSECA) since 2001, these wines are showing disti
improvements, especially at basic level. Vintage ports★★ ha
traditionally been elegant, rather than thunderous. Single-quinta Quin
da Roêda★ is pretty good in recent vintages. **Best years:** (Vintage) 2007
03 00 94 91 77 70 66 63 55 45; (Roêda) 2005 04 **97 95**.

CROZES-HERMITAGE AC *Rhône Valley, France* The largest of the north
Rhône ACs. Ideally, the pure Syrah reds should have a full colour an
strong, clear, black fruit flavour. You can drink them young, but in r
years from a hillside site the wine improves greatly for 2–5 years. T
much clumsy oak on the more expensive wines can obscure the fruit. T
best whites are fresh and florally scented, and should be drunk young. B
producers: (reds) A Belle★★, R Betton, Bruyères★★, CHAPOUTIER★, Y Chave
Colombier★ (Cuvée Gaby★★), Combier★ (Clos des Grives★
E Darnaud★★, DELAS★ (Le Clos★★, Dom. des Grands Chemins★
O Dumaine★, Entrefaux★, Fayolle Fils & Fille★★, Ferraton★, GRAILLOT★★, F
JABOULET, P & V Jaboulet, Murinais★, Pavillon-Mercurol★, Pochon★ (
Curson★, Remizières★★, G Robin★, Rousset (Picaudières★★), St-Clair, Tar
co-op, Tardieu-Laurent★, Vins de Vienne★; (whites) Y Chave★, Colombie
Combier★, Dard & Ribo★, DELAS★, O Dumaine★, Entrefaux★ (Cuvée
Pends★★), Fayolle Fils & Fille★★, Ferraton★, GRAILLOT★, Mucyn, Poch
Remizières★, M Sorrel★★. **Best years:** (reds) **2009 07 06 05 04 03 01 00**

YVES CUILLERON *Condrieu AC, Rhône Valley, France* With wines l
Cuilleron's you can understand CONDRIEU's fame and high prices. L
Chaillets★★★, from old vines, is everything wine made from Viogn

should be: rich and sensual, with perfumed honey and apricot aromas. La Petite Côte★★ and 18-month-aged Vertige★★ are also exceptional, and the late-harvest Ayguets★★★ is an extraordinary sweet whirl of dried apricots, honey and barley sugar. Cuilleron also makes ST-JOSEPH reds★★ and whites★, ST-PÉRAY★ and limited amounts of ripe, dark, oaked, spicy CÔTE-RÔTIE★★. A joint venture, les Vins de Vienne, with Pierre Gaillard, François Villard and Pierre-Jean Villa, produces Vin de Pays des COLLINES RHODANIENNES Sotanum★★ (100% Syrah) and Taburnum★ (100% Viognier). Best years: (Condrieu) 2009 08 07 06 05 04.

ULLEN *Margaret River, Western Australia* One of the original and best MARGARET RIVER vineyards, established by Diana and Kevin Cullen and now run by their talented winemaker daughter Vanya. Superb Kevin John Chardonnay★★★ is complex and satisfying; Sauvignon-Semillon★★ marries nectarines with melon and nuts. Diana Madeline Cabernet Sauvignon-Merlot★★★ is gloriously soft, deep and scented – and one of Australia's greats. Mangan Malbec-Petit Verdot-Merlot★★ is wild and delicious. Best years: (Cabernet Sauvignon-Merlot) (2009) 08 07 05 04 03 02 01 00 99 98 97 96 95 94 92 91 90.

URICÓ *Chile* Most of the big producers here have planted Cabernet Sauvignon, Merlot, Carmenère, Chardonnay and Sauvignon Blanc. It's a bit warm for whites, except in the coastal regions, but the long growing season provides good fruit concentration for reds. Best producers: Echeverría★★, SAN PEDRO★, Miguel TORRES★★, VALDIVIESO★.

VNE *Rioja DOCa, Rioja, Spain* Compañía Vinícola del Norte de España is the full name of this firm, usually known as 'coonay'. Viña Real★ is one of RIOJA's few remaining well-oaked whites. Viña Real Reserva★ (sometimes ★★) and Gran Reserva★ reds can be rich and meaty, and easily surpass the rather commercial Crianzas. The Viña Real branch has been spun out to a new facility in Rioja Alavesa, using only Alavesa fruit. Imperial Reserva★ (can be ★★) is balanced and delightful; Gran Reserva★★★ is long-lived and impressive. Premium red Real de Asúa★. Best years: (reds) (2006) 05 04 03 02 01 98 96 95 94 91 90 89 87 86 85.

IDIER DAGUENEAU *Pouilly-Fumé AC, Loire Valley, France* This much-needed innovator died in 2008 and is succeeded by his son, Benjamin. Vintages made under the new regime preserve the intensely pure yet complex style and, if anything, are a little more polished. The range starts with Blanc Fumé★★ and moves up through flinty Buisson Renard★★ to barrel-fermented Silex★★ and Pur Sang★★. Wines benefit from 4–5 years' aging. Since 2004, also making a sweet JURANÇON, Les Jardins de Babylone★. Best years: (2009) 08 07 06 05 04 03 02 01.

OMANO DAL FORNO *Valpolicella DOC, Veneto, Italy* VALPOLICELLA Superiore★★★ from Monte Lodoletta vineyard, outside the Valpolicella Classico area, is a model of power and grace; AMARONE★★★ and RECIOTO DELLA VALPOLICELLA★★★, from the same source, are even more voluptuous. Best years: (Amarone) (2009) (08) (07) 06 04 03 01 00 97 96 95.

ENIMENTI LUIGI D'ALESSANDRO *Cortona DOC, Tuscany, Italy* Syrah specialists in Sangiovese country, this estate has benefited from massive investment, today making 2 varietal wines (Migliara★★ and Il Bosco★★, as well as a basic Syrah. The white Fontarca, principally from Viognier, extends the Rhône theme. Best years: (2009) (08) 07 06 04 03 01 00.

ALLA VALLE *Napa Valley AVA, California, USA* Stunning hillside winery, producing some of NAPA's most irresistible Cabernets. Maya★★★ is a magnificent blend of Cabernet Sauvignon and Cabernet Franc; the

straight Cabernet Sauvignon★★★ is almost as rich and brillian
balanced. The wines drink well at 10 years, but will keep for 20 or mo
Best years: (Maya) 2005 02 01 00 **99 98 97 96 95 94 91 90**.

DÃO DOC *Beira Alta, Portugal* Dão has steep slopes ideal for vineyards, anc
great climate for growing local grape varieties, yet it's only just beginni
to realize its potential for characterful, scented, austerely satisfying r
and white wines. Best producers: (reds) ALIANCA (Quinta da Garrida★), Bc
Quintas (Quinta Fonte do Ouro★), Quinta de Cabriz★, Quinta das Maias
Pape★★, Quinta da Pellada★★, Quinta do Perdigão, Quinta da Ponte Pedrinh
Quinta dos ROQUES★★, Quinta de Sães★, Caves SÃO JOÃO★, SOGRAPE★ (Quir
dos Carvalhais★), Quinta da Vegia★★; (whites) Quinta de Cabriz, Quinta c
Maias★, Quinta dos ROQUES★, Quinta de Sães★, SOGRAPE★. Best years: (rec
(2009) 08 **05 04 03 01 00 99 97 96 95**.

D'ARENBERG *McLaren Vale, South Australia* Chester Osborn makes bloc
buster Dead Arm Shiraz★★, Ironstone Pressings Grenache-Shira
Mourvèdre★★, Custodian Grenache★, Coppermine Road Cabern
Sauvignon★★ and numerous other blends from low-yielding old vin
These are big, brash, character-filled wines, and are continually bei
joined by more new ideas – Cenosilicaphobic Cat Sagrantino-Cinsau
anyone? Whites mustn't be overlooked: Money Spider★ (Roussann
and Hermit Crab★ (Viognier-Marsanne) are lush and waxy. Best year
(Dead Arm Shiraz) (2008) 06 05 04 **03 02 01 00 97 96 95**.

RENÉ & VINCENT DAUVISSAT *Chablis, Burgundy, France* CHABLIS at its mo
complex – refreshing, seductive and beautifully structured, with the fru
balancing the subtle influence of mostly older oak. Look for La Forest★★
the more aromatic Vaillons★★★ and the powerful Les Clos★★
Best years: (2009) 08 07 **06 05 03 02 00 99 95**.

MARCO DE BARTOLI *Sicily, Italy* Marco De Bartoli is most noted for a dr
unfortified MARSALA-style wine called Vecchio Samperi – his idea of wh
Marsala was before the English merchant, John Woodhouse, fir
fortified it for export. Particularly fine is the 20-year-old Ventennale★
– dry, intense and redolent of candied citrus peel, dates and old, o
raisins. Also excellent MOSCATO PASSITO DI PANTELLERIA Bukkuram★★.

DE BORTOLI *Riverina, New South Wales/Yarra, Victoria, Australia* Large, family
owned company currently producing some of Australia's most interestir
wines. Some top stuff from the YARRA VALLEY: Sauvignon★
Chardonnay★★, Shiraz★★, Cabernet★ and Pinot Noir★, and thre
Melba Cabernet blends★. The RIVERINA winery first gained prominenc
for its sublime, world-class botrytized Semillon (Noble One★★★) but i
recent times has had consumers smiling because of the quality of i
budget-priced labels – Sacred Hill, Deen and Montage. VICTORIA-base
quaffers in the Sero, Windy Peak and Gulf Station ranges can be goo
too. Best years: (Noble One) (2008) (07) 06 04 03 02 **00 98 96 95 94 93 9C**

DE LOACH VINEYARDS *Russian River Valley AVA, California, USA* Revitalize
under new owner BOISSET of France and run by Jean-Charles Boisset, th
property makes an array of stylish Pinot Noirs★ and soft nutt
Chardonnays★ from estate fruit. Best years: 2007 **06 05 04 03 01**.

DE MARTINO *Maipo, Chile* Old-established winery enjoying a renaissance
producing robust, concentrated red wines in the hands of talente
winemaker and *terroir* expert Marcelo Retamal. Single Vineyar
Carmenère★★, and Single Vineyard Chardonnay★★ from LIMARÍ, ar
among Chile's best examples of these grapes; Gran Familia Caberne
Sauvignon★★ is dense and complex.

E TRAFFORD *Stellenbosch WO, South Africa* David Trafford's boutique-size range shows commendable consistency. His new-wave Chenin Blanc★, from venerable Helderberg vines and barrel fermented on its own yeast, is rich and ageworthy; the Straw Wine★★ is honey-tinged and succulent. Among the reds, both Cabernet Sauvignon★ and Merlot★, alone and with Shiraz in Elevation 393★, are classically styled and built to age. Shiraz★★, brimming with spicy richness, remains remarkably elegant for its size. Best years: (reds) 2008 07 **06 05 04 03 02 01 00** 99.

EHLINGER *Russian River Valley AVA, California, USA* Outstanding Pinot Noir★★★ from vineyards in the cool RUSSIAN RIVER VALLEY, best at 5–10 years old. Also mouthfilling Chardonnay★★ and bold, peppery Syrah★★. Recent vintages of Cabernet Sauvignon★★ reflect a surge in quality. Best years: (Pinot Noir) (2007) 06 05 **04 03 02 01 00**.

MARCEL DEISS *Alsace AC, Alsace, France* Jean-Michel Deiss is fanatical about distinctions of *terroir* and, controversially for ALSACE, his top wines are now blends, named according to the vineyard – Grands Crus Altenberg, Mambourg and Schoenenbourg are all ★★★. These are outstanding wines of huge character, often with some residual sugar. Pinot Noir Burlenburg★★ is vibrant and delicious. Even basic Riesling St-Hippolyte★ and Pinot Blanc Bergheim are delightful. Best years: (Grand Cru blends) (2009) 08 **07 05 04 03 02 01 00** 99.

DELAS FRÈRES *Rhône Valley, France* Up-market merchant (owned by ROEDERER) selling wines from the whole RHÔNE VALLEY, but with its own vineyards in the northern Rhône. Single-vineyard wines include dense, powerful red HERMITAGE★★ (Les Bessards★★★), which needs a decade or more to reach its peak, perfumed CÔTE-RÔTIE La Landonne★★ and complex ST-JOSEPH Ste-Épine★★; CROZES-HERMITAGE Le Clos★★ is good, too. CÔTES DU RHÔNE St-Esprit is value for money. Look out for the aromatic CONDRIEU Clos Boucher★★. Best years: (premium reds) 2009 07 06 **05 04 03 01 00** 99 98 97 96 95 94 91 90 89 88 78.

DELEGAT'S *Henderson, Auckland, North Island, New Zealand* One of New Zealand's largest family-run wineries and getting larger by the second as Oyster Bay becomes a major brand and its MARLBOROUGH fruit style becomes less evident. Delegat's Chardonnay (Reserve★), Cabernet and Merlot (Reserve★) are from HAWKES BAY.

DELILLE CELLARS *Columbia Valley AVA, Washington State, USA* BORDEAUX-style wines from some of the better vineyards in YAKIMA VALLEY. Chaleur Estate Red★★ is a powerful, ageworthy blend of Cabernet and Merlot. Chaleur Estate Blanc★ (Semillon-Sauvignon Blanc) has a GRAVES-like character, albeit with a tad more alcohol. The second wine, D2★★, short for Deuxième, is an early-drinking red. Doyenne Syrah★★ shows great potential. Best years: (Chaleur Estate Red) (2008) 07 06 **05 04 03 02 01**.

DENBIES *Surrey, England* UK's largest single vineyard with 107ha (265 acres) of vines, planted on chalky slopes outside Dorking. Wines have been erratic over the years but have now reached a new plateau of quality with remarkably attractive whites, lively, refreshing rosé and decent to excellent fizz (Greenfields★). Pinot Noir-based Redlands can be good too. Best years: (still) **2007 06**.

JEAN-LOUIS DENOIS *Vin de Pays d'Oc, Languedoc, France* Maverick produce based in LIMOUX, who can't see a rule without breaking it. His Chloé★ made from Merlot and Cabernet, without any of the 'Mediterranea varieties obligatory in Limoux; it mixes the flavours of BORDEAUX with a b of southern warmth. Also red and white Grande Cuvée★ and good fizz★

DEUTZ *Champagne AC, Champagne, France* This small company has bee owned by ROEDERER since 1993 and considerable effort and investmer have turned a good producer into an excellent one. The non-vintag Brut★★ is now regularly one of the best in CHAMPAGNE, often boasting cedary scent, while the top wines are the classic Blanc de Blancs★★, th weightier Cuvée William Deutz★★ and the de luxe vintage blanc d blancs Amour de Deutz★★. Deutz has licensed Pernod Ricard in Ne Zealand to use its brand on their sparkling wine. Best years: (2006) 05 0 02 **00 99 98 96 95 90 89 88**.

DÉZALEY *Lavaux, Vaud, Switzerland* The top wine commune in the VAUI making surprisingly powerful, mineral wines from the Chasselas grape Best producers: Louis Bovard★, La Chenalettaz, Conne, Dubois★, Pinget★ J & P Testuz★.

D F J VINHOS *Portugal* In the early 1990s, UK wine shippers D & F bega working with one of Portugal's most innovative winemakers, José Neiva this relationship evolved into D F J Vinhos, and Neiva is now sole owne The large range includes off-dry Pink Elephant rosé, Segada red an white from LISBOA and Pedras do Monte from PENINSULA DE SETÚBAL. At th top end are the Grand'Arte reds, including fruity, peppery Trincadeira and beefy Alicante Bouschet★, the DFJ range (Alvarinho Chardonnay★, Tinta Roriz-Merlot, Touriga Nacional-Touri Franca★) and prestige wines from the DOURO (Escada★), ALENQUI (Francos Reserva) and LISBOA (Consensus).

DIAMOND CREEK *Napa Valley AVA, California, USA* Small Diamon Mountain estate specializing in Cabernet: Volcanic Hill★★★, Red Roc Terrace★★, Gravelly Meadow★★. Traditionally huge, tannic wines tha when tasted young, I swear won't ever come round. Yet there's usually sweet inner core of fruit that envelops the tannin over 10–15 years; recer releases show far less tannin, and wonderful perfume and balance even i their youth. Best years: 2006 05 04 03 02 01 **00 99 98 97 96 95 94 92 91 9**

SCHLOSSGUT DIEL *Burg Layen, Nahe, Germany* Armin Diel is now one o the leading producers of classic-style Rieslings. Spätlese and Auslese from Dorsheim's top sites (Burgberg, Goldloch, Pittermännchen) are regular ★★. Good Sekt too. Best years: (2009) 08 07 **06 05 04 03 02 01 00**.

DISTELL *Stellenbosch, South Africa* South Africa's largest wine company; som of the allied wineries – such as Neethlingshof★, Stellenzicht★ an Durbanville Hills★ – are performing well. The Fleur du Cap★ range showing exciting improvement across the board. Two wineries in PAARI Nederburg and Plaisir de Merle★, are run separately. Nederburg Ingenuity range is stirring interest: the White★ is a harmonious blend o 8 varieties; the Red a vibrant mix of Sangiovese and Barbera wit Nebbiolo. Botrytized Edelkeur★ is sold only through an annual auction

CH. DOISY-DAËNE★★ *Sauternes AC, 2ème Cru Classé, Bordeaux, Franc* Owned by enology professor Denis Dubourdieu (see Ch. REYNON), consistently good property in BARSAC (although it uses the SAUTERNES AC fo its wines) and unusual in that the sweet wine is made exclusively from Sémillon. It ages well for 10 years or more. The extra-rich Extravagant★★★ is produced in exceptional years. Doisy-Daëne Sec★

a good, perfumed, barrel-fermented dry white. Drink young. Best years: (sweet) 2007 06 05 **04 03 02 01 99 98 97 96 95 90 89**.

.H. DOISY-VÉDRINES★★ *Sauternes AC, 2ème Cru Classé, Bordeaux, France* Next door to DOISY-DAËNE (and also selling wines under the SAUTERNES AC), Doisy-Védrines is a richly botrytized wine, fatter and more syrupy than most BARSAC. Best years: (sweet) 2007 05 **04 03 02 01 99 98 97 96 95 90 89 88 86**.

OLCETTO One of Italy's most charming grapes, producing, for the most part, purple wines bursting with fruit. Virtually exclusive to PIEDMONT and LIGURIA, it boasts 11 DOCs and 1 DOCG (Dogliani) in Piemonte, with styles ranging from intense and rich in Alba, Ovada and Diano d'Alba, to lighter and more perfumed in Acqui and Asti. The most serious wines are from Dogliani and Alba. Usually best drunk within 1–2 years, traditionally vinified wines can last 10 years or more. Best producers: (Alba) Alario★★, ALTARE★★, Boglietti★★, Bongiovanni★★, Bricco Maiolica★★, Bricco Rosso★, Brovia★★, Elvio Cogno★★, Aldo CONTERNO★, Conterno-Fantino★★, B Marcarini★, Bartolo MASCARELLO★, Giuseppe MASCARELLO★★, Paitin★, Pelissero★★, PRUNOTTO★, RATTI★, Albino Rocca★★, SANDRONE★★, Vajra★★, Vietti★, Gianni Voerzio★, Roberto VOERZIO★; (Dogliani) M & E Abbona★, Chionetti★★, Luigi Einaudi★★, Pecchenino★★, San Fereolo★★, San Romano★.

ÔLE *Valais, Switzerland* Red wine from the VALAIS made from at least 51% Pinot Noir, the rest being Gamay. Dôle is generally a light wine – the deeper, richer (100% Pinot Noir) styles may call themselves Pinot Noir. Most should be drunk young and lightly chilled. Best producers: G Clavien, Faye, Jean-René Germanier, A Mathier, Provins, G Raymond.

OMAINE CARNEROS *Carneros AVA, California, USA* Very successful TAITTINGER-owned sparkling wine house. The vintage Brut might match Taittinger's fizz from Champagne, if it were made a little drier. Far classier are vintage Le Rêve★★ (100% Chardonnay) and attractive Pinot Noirs★★. The winery also makes a small amount of a White Pinot Noir.

OMAINE CHANDON *Yarra Valley, Victoria, Australia* MOËT & CHANDON's Aussie offshoot makes fine Pinot Noir-Chardonnay fizz: non-vintage Brut and Cuvée Riche, vintage Brut★★, Rosé★★, Blanc de Blancs★, Blanc de Noirs★, ZD★★ (Zero Dosage), YARRA VALLEY Brut★★ and a Tasmanian Cuvée★★; plus sparkling red Pinot-Shiraz★. Table wines, often of ★★ quality, under the Green Point label with Reserve Shiraz★★ standing out and Chardonnay increasingly impressive. The Green Point name is also used on fizz for export markets.

OMAINE CHANDON *Napa Valley AVA, California, USA* California's first French-owned (MOËT & CHANDON) sparkling wine producer majors on reasonable price, but doesn't match the quality of Moët's subsidiaries in Australia or Argentina. Reserve bottlings can be rich and creamy. Étoile★ is an aged de luxe wine, also made as a flavourful Rosé★.

OMAINE DROUHIN OREGON *Willamette Valley AVA, Oregon, USA* Burgundy wine merchant Robert DROUHIN bought 40ha (100 acres) in OREGON in 1987, with plans to make fine Pinot Noir on New World land, with an Old World philosophy. The regular Pinot Noir★ is lean but attractive, and the de luxe Pinot Noir Laurène★★ is supple and voluptuous. Pinot Noir Louise★★ is a selection of the finest barrels in the winery. Also very good Chardonnay Arthur★★. Best years: (Pinot Noir) 2008 07 06 **05 04 03 02 01 00 99 98**.

DOMAINE SERENE Willamette Valley AVA, Oregon, USA Ken and Gra
Evenstad purchased 17ha (42 acres) of land in the WILLAMETTE VALLEY
1989, naming the property after their daughter, Serene. Devoted
Pinot Noir and Chardonnay, they have established a fine reputation. T
full-bodied Pinot Noir Evenstad Reserve★★ is aged in French oak a
has striking black cherry and currant flavours. Single-vineyard Pir
Noirs are a focus of the winery (Mark Bradford Vineyard★★, Jerusale
Hill Vineyard★). The Chardonnay Clos du Soleil★★, made from Dij
clones, has a rich apple and hazelnut character. **Best years:** (Pinot No
2008 07 06 **05 04 03 02 01 00 99.**

DOMECQ Jerez y Manzanilla DO, Spain Bought by Pernod Ricard in 20(
who sold the sherry company to OSBORNE, who continue to use the bra
for Amontillado 51-1a, Oloroso Sibarita and Pedro Ximénez Venerab
Former Domecq brands Fino La Ina, Amontillado Botaina, Oloroso R
Viejo and Pedro Ximénez Viña 25 – and the soleras from which the
wines come – have been sold to rival LUSTAU.

DOMINIO DEL PLATA Mendoza, Argentina Superstar winemaker Susa
Balbo and top viticulturalist Pedro Marchevsky craft exquisite wines in t
shadow of the Andes. The emphasis is firmly on Malbec and Caberr
Sauvignon. Top wine Nosotros★ is a blockbuster not typical of t
estate, but Susana Balbo Malbec★★ is elegant and delicious. Brioso★
a BORDEAUX-style blend, is structured and pure and the BenMar
Malbec★ and Cabernet Sauvignon★ are very good. The Crios rang
which includes a beautiful Torrontés★, is exceptional value for mone

DOMINUS★★ Napa Valley AVA, California, USA Owned by Christian MOUE
director of Bordeaux superstar PETRUS. Wines are based on Cabern
Sauvignon, with leavenings of Merlot and Cabernet Franc. Early releas
were excessively tannic, but recent wines are mellow and delicious. B
years: (2007) 06 05 04 03 **02 01 00 99 97 96 95 94 91 90.**

DOÑA PAULA Mendoza, Argentina A winery at
the vanguard of modern Argentine wine. The
talented head winemaker and viticulturalist,
Edy del Popolo, believes in wines with a sense
of place and real purity of flavour. The Estate
Malbec★★ is plush and thrilling with beautiful
violet-edged fruit. Single-vineyard expressions
are equally exciting. Look out for the
concentrated, fresh, honeyed apricots of Naked
Pulp Viognier★★ or the pure blueberry and

black cherry flavours of Alluvia Cabernet Franc★★. Also sharp, fre
Los Cardos Sauvignon Blanc★. The top wine, Selección de Bode
Malbec★★, has really begun to hit form.

DONAULAND See WAGRAM.

DÖNNHOFF Oberhausen, Nahe, Germany Helmut Dönnhoff is the qui
winemaking genius of the NAHE, conjuring from a string of top sites son
of the most mineral dry and naturally sweet Rieslings in the worl
The very best are the subtle, long-lived wines from the Niederhäus
Hermannshöhle★★★ and Oberhäuser Brücke★★★ vineyard
Eiswein★★★ is equally exciting. **Best years:** (Hermannshöhle Riesli
Spätlese) (2009) 08 07 06 **05 04 03 02 01 00 99 98.**

DOURO DOC Douro, Portugal As prices soar for the best wines, decidi
whether to use top grapes for unfortified Douro wine or PORT has becon
much harder for Douro producers. Quality can be superb when the lus

scented fruit is not smothered by new oak. Reds may improve for 10 years or more. Whites from higher-altitude vineyards have improved, but best drunk young. Best producers: (reds) ALIANCA (Quinta dos Quatro Ventos★★), Maria Doroteia Serôdio Borges (Fojo★★), Casal de Loivos★★, Chryseia★★★, Quinta do CÔTTO, Quinta do CRASTO★★, FERREIRA★ (Barca Velha★★★, Quinta da Leda★★), Quinta da Gaivosa★, Quinta de Macedos★, Muxagat, NIEPOORT★★, Quinta do NOVAL★★, Quinta do Passadouro (Reserva★★), Pintas★★, Poeira★★, Quinta do Portal★, RAMOS PINTO★, Quinta de Roriz★, Quinta de la ROSA★, Quinta do Vale Dona Maria★★, Quinta do Vale Meao★★★, Quinta do Vale da Raposa★, Quinta do Vallado★, Quinta de VESÚVIO★★, Xisto★. Best years: (reds) (2009) (08) **07 05 04 03 01 00 97 95**.

OW Port DOC, Douro, Portugal The grapes for Dow's Vintage PORT★★★ come mostly from the Quinta do Bomfim, also the name of the excellent single quinta★★. Dow ports are relatively dry compared with those of GRAHAM and WARRE (the 2 other major brands belonging to the Symington family). There are also good Crusted★ and some excellent aged tawnies★★. Quinta Senhora da Ribeira★ has made impressive ports since 1998, released 'en primeur'. Best years: (Vintage) 2007 **03 00 97 94 91 85 83 80 77 70 66 63 60 55 45**; (Bomfim) **2005 99 98 95 92 87 86 84**; (Senhora da Ribeira) **2006 05 04 99 98**.

JOSEPH DROUHIN Beaune, Burgundy, France Beaune-based merchant with substantial holdings in CHABLIS as well as DOMAINE DROUHIN OREGON. Flagship CÔTE D'OR whites include BEAUNE Clos des Mouches★★ and MONTRACHET Marquis de Laguiche★★★. Finer still are the graceful perfumed reds such as CHAMBOLLE-MUSIGNY Premier Cru★★ and Grands Crus Grands-ÉCHÉZEAUX★★★, MUSIGNY★★★, etc. Good-value cheaper wines too. Best years: (top reds) (2009) 08 07 05 **02 99 96 95**.

PIERRE-JACQUES DRUET Bourgueil AC, Loire Valley, France A passionate producer with an esoteric approach. Druet's BOURGUEILS les Cent Boisselées★, Grand Mont★★ and Vaumoreau★★ are subtly different, spicy expressions of Cabernet Franc that attain wonderful purity with age – keep for at least 3–5 years. Also small quantities of CHINON★★. Best years: (top cuvées) (2009) 08 07 06 **05 04 03 02 01 00 99 97 96 90 89**.

DRY CREEK VALLEY AVA Sonoma, California, USA Best known for Sauvignon Blanc, Zinfandel and Cabernet Sauvignon, this valley runs parallel west of ALEXANDER VALLEY AVA, and similarly becomes hotter moving northwards. Best producers: DRY CREEK VINEYARD★, Duxoup★, FERRARI-CARANO★, GALLO (Zinfandel★, Cabernet Sauvignon★), Lambert Bridge★, Michel-Schlumberger★, Nalle★★, Pezzi King★, Preston★, Quivira★, Rafanelli (Zinfandel★★), RIDGE (Lytton Springs★★). Best years: (reds) 2006 05 03 **02 01 00**.

DRY CREEK VINEYARD Dry Creek Valley AVA, California, USA An early advocate of Fumé Blanc★, Dry Creek remains faithful to the brisk racy style. Fumé Blanc DCV3★ (sometimes ★★) is from the original (1972) Dry Creek Valley vineyard and displays subtle notes of fig and herb. A drink-young Chardonnay (Reserve★) is attractive, but the stars here are a superb Dry Chenin Blanc★★, red Meritage★, Merlot★ and Old Vine Zinfandel★★. Best years: (Old Vine Zin) 2006 05 **03 02 01 00**.

DRY RIVER Martinborough, North Island, New Zealand Low yields and an uncompromising attitude to quality at this tiny winery have created some of the country's top Gewurztraminer★★★, Pinot Gris★★★, powerful, long-lived Craighall Riesling★★★, sleek Chardonnay★★ and intense, succulent yet mineral Pinot Noir★★★. Excellent Syrah★★ is made in tiny

quantities. Now owned by a wealthy American, but founder Ne
McCallum continues as chief winemaker. Best years: (Craighall Rieslin,
2009 **08 06 03 01 00**; (Pinot Noir) (2009) **08 07 06 03 01 00**.

GEORGES DUBOEUF *Beaujolais, Burgundy, France* Duboeuf is responsib
for more than 10% of the wine produced in BEAUJOLAIS, although he is n
longer considered by many to be among the region's most excitir
producers. Given the size of his operation, the quality of the wines
reasonable. Duboeuf also makes wine from the MÂCONNAIS, the souther
RHÔNE VALLEY and the LANGUEDOC. His BEAUJOLAIS NOUVEAU is usual
reliable, but his top wines are those he bottles for independent grower
particularly Jean Descombes★ in MORGON, Dom. des Quatre Vents★ an
la Madone★ in FLEURIE and Dom. de la Tour du Bief★ in MOULIN-À-VEN

DUCKHORN *Napa Valley AVA, California, USA* Best known for its very chunk
tannic Merlot★ – now, thankfully, softer and riper. The Cabern
Sauvignon★ and Sauvignon Blanc provide easier drinking. Paraduxx is
Zinfandel-Cabernet blend; Decoy is the budget line. The company
Pinot Noir project is Goldeneye★ in ANDERSON VALLEY. Best years: (Merlo
2006 **05 03 02 01 99 98 97 96**.

CH. DUCRU-BEAUCAILLOU★★★ *St-Julien AC, 2ème Cru Classé, Haut-Médo*
Bordeaux, France Traditionally the epitome of ST-JULIEN, mixing charm an
austerity, fruit and firm tannins. Vintages from the mid-1980s to 199
were flawed; back on form since 95, more luscious since 03. Second win
la Croix de Beaucaillou. Best years: 2008 07 06 05 **04 03 02 01 00 99 98 96 9!**

DUJAC *Morey-St-Denis, Côte de Nuits, Burgundy, France* Owner Jacques Seysse
estate is based in MOREY-ST-DENIS, with some choice vineyards elsewhere i
the CÔTE DE NUITS. The wines are all perfumed and elegant, including
small quantity of white Morey-St-Denis★, but the outstanding bottling
are the Grands Crus – ÉCHÉZEAUX★★★, CLOS DE LA ROCHE★★★, BONNE
MARES★★★ and CLOS ST-DENIS★★★, to which CHAMBERTIN and ROMANÉE-S
VIVANT have been added since 2005. All need to age for a decade or mor
Son Jeremy makes *négociant* cuvées under the label Dujac Fils et Pèr
Best years: (Grands Crus) (2009) 08 07 06 05 03 02 **01 00 99 98 96 95 90 8**

DUNHAM CELLARS *Columbia Valley AVA, Washington State, USA* Family
owned winery in a rustic, remodelled airplane hangar near the Wal
Walla airport. The wines here are powerful and extracted, includin
Cabernet Sauvignon★★, Syrah★, a limited-release Lewis Vineya
Syrah Reserve★★, Trutina★ (a BORDEAUX-style blend), Three Legge
Red (named after one of the winery dogs) and 'Shirley Ma
Chardonnay. Best years: (reds) (2008) 07 06 05 **04 03 02**.

DUNN VINEYARDS *Howell Mountain AVA, California, USA* Austere, concer
trated, hauntingly perfumed, long-lived Cabernet Sauvignon★★★ fro
HOWELL MOUNTAIN; NAPA VALLEY Cabernets★★ are less powerful but st
scented. Thankfully Randy Dunn has resisted the move toward hig
alcohol, and his wines' ability to age beautifully is evidence of thi
Best years: 2005 03 01 **00 99 97 96 95 94 93 92 91 90 88 87 86 85 84 8**

DURBANVILLE WO *South Africa* Tucked into the folds of the Tygerbe
Hills, Durbanville borders Cape Town's northern suburbs. Cool breez
from both the Atlantic Ocean and False Bay suit Sauvignon Blanc: win
are vivid, often with an invigorating minerality. Semillon also does we
Merlot shows promise both as a varietal wine and blended with Cabern
Sauvignon, though the latter sometimes struggles to ripen. Be
producers: De Grendel, Diemersdal, Durbanville Hills★, Meerendal, Nitida

DURIF See PETITE SIRAH.

EAN DURUP *Chablis, Burgundy, France* The largest vineyard owner in CHABLIS, Jean Durup is a great believer in unoaked Chablis, which tends to be clean without any great complexity. Best are the Premiers Crus Fourchaume★ and Montée de Tonnerre★★. Wines also appear under Ch. de Maligny and l'Eglantière labels. **Best years:** (2009) 08 **07 06 05**.

DUTTON GOLDFIELD *Russian River Valley AVA, California, USA* Racy, elegant and deeply flavoured Chardonnays★, Pinot Noirs★★, Zinfandels★★, and a superb cool-climate Syrah★★ from long-time cool-climate winemaker Dan Goldfield. Most of the fruit, grown by Steve Dutton, is from RUSSIAN RIVER. The superb Freestone Hill Pinot Noir★★★ is from one of the coldest parts of SONOMA COUNTY. Goldfield also makes wine from fruit grown in even-cooler Marin County. Most wines take years to reach their peak. **Best years:** (2007) 06 **05 04 01** 99.

JOHN DUVAL *Barossa Valley, South Australia* John Duval was the winemaker for Penfolds GRANGE from 1986 to 2002. He started his family label in 2003, specializing in Shiraz and Shiraz blends sourced from old-vine BAROSSA fruit. Plexus★★ is a plush, vibrant, deeply flavoured and approachable Shiraz-Grenache-Mourvèdre blend; Entity Shiraz★★★ a seamless varietal that combines elegance, finesse and approachability with concentration of flavour and power; ultra-concentrated Eligo Shiraz★★ is made from the best parcels from the vintage. He also consults in WASHINGTON STATE, Chile and elsewhere in Australia and is increasingly recognized as one of Australia's finest winemakers.

DUVAL-LEROY *Champagne AC, Champagne, France* Run by Carol Duval-Leroy since 1991, this is one of the largest but least well-known family-owned producers in CHAMPAGNE, with 170ha (420 acres) of vineyards. While its entry-level non-vintage styles are unremarkable, its vintage★ wines, prestige cuvée Femme★★ and wines under the Authentis★★ label are well worth seeking out. **Best years:** 2004 03 02 **99 96 95**.

ÉCHÉZEAUX AC *Grand Cru, Côte de Nuits, Burgundy, France* The Grands Crus of Échézeaux and the smaller and more prestigious Grands-Échézeaux are sandwiched between the world-famous CLOS DE VOUGEOT and VOSNE-ROMANÉE. Look for subtlety, intricacy, delicacy from Échézeaux and a little more weight, deepening over the years to a gamy, chocolaty richness, from the 'Grands' version. **Best producers:** R Arnoux★★, BOUCHARD PÈRE ET FILS★★, Cacheux-Sirugue★★★, DROUHIN★★, DUJAC★★★, Eugénie★★ (formerly Engel), GRIVOT★★★, A-F GROS★★★, Jayer-Gilles★★, Mugneret-Gibourg★★★, Perdrix★, Dom. de la ROMANÉE-CONTI★★★, E Rouget★★★. **Best years:** (2009) 08 07 06 05 03 02 **01** 99 **98 97 96 95 93 90**.

DOM. DE L'ECU *Muscadet Sèvre-et-Maine, Loire Valley, France* One of the finest producers in MUSCADET, especially the top cuvées from different soil types: Gneiss, Orthogneiss★ and fuller-bodied, minerally Granite★★. Guy Bossard's biodynamically run estate also produces GROS PLANT DU PAYS NANTAIS white, a velvety red vin de pays Cabernet blend and a refreshing sparkler, Ludwig Hahn. **Best years:** (Granite) **2008 07 06 05 04 03 02 01 00**.

EDEN VALLEY See BAROSSA, pages 72–3.

CH. L'ÉGLISE-CLINET★★★ *Pomerol AC, Bordeaux, France* A tiny 5.5ha (13-acre) domaine in the heart of POMEROL, with a very old vineyard – one of the reasons for the depth and elegance of the wines. The other is the winemaking ability of owner Denis Durantou. The wine is expensive and in limited supply. It can be enjoyed young, though the best vintages should be cellared for 10 years or more. Second wine: La Petite Église. **Best years:** 2008 07 06 05 **04 03 02 01 00** 99 98 96 95 90 89.

ELGIN WO *South Africa* This high-lying ward within the Overberg distric is being targeted by some of the Cape's leading winemakers. Summe cloud helps to keep temperatures reasonable, creating good condition for pure-fruited Sauvignon Blanc, Chardonnay, Riesling and Pinot Noi Best producers: Paul CLUVER★★, Neil ELLIS★★, Iona★, Oak Valley★, THELEMA★

DOM. ELIAN DA ROS *Côtes du Marmandais AC, South-West France* Elian i making waves throughout France with his eclectic wines. His models ar in ALSACE and BURGUNDY, and his love of the LOIRE shows in his use c Cabernet Franc. Top wines are Chante Coucou★ and Clos Baquey★★ these wines need aging. Best years: (2009) (08) 06 **05 04 02 01**.

ELK COVE *Willamette Valley AVA, Oregon, USA* Back in 1974, Elk Cove was on of the pioneers of the WILLAMETTE VALLEY. Today the Campbell famil produces Pinot Gris★, Riesling and a Riesling-based dessert wine calle Ultima. Basic Pinot Noir★★ frequently matches the more expensiv single-vineyard Pinot Noirs (Roosevelt, Windhill★, La Bohème★). Bes years: (Pinot Noir) 2008 07 06 **05 04 03 02**.

NEIL ELLIS *Stellenbosch WO, South Africa* Winemaker and *négocian* renowned for powerful, invigorating Groenekloof Sauvignon Blanc★★ and striking STELLENBOSCH reds (blackcurranty Cabernet Sauvignon★★ supple Cabernet-Merlot★). An ageworthy single-vineyard Syrah★ an Cabernet★ (both from Jonkershoek Valley fruit), and a subtly deliciou Chardonnay★★ from cool ELGIN, confirm his versatility. Best years (Cabernet) 2007 **06 05 04 03 01 00**; (whites) 2009 **08 07 06 05 04 03 02 01**

ELQUI *Chile* Home to the grapes that make Pisco (grape brandy) an Chile's northernmost wine region, close to the Atacama desert, wit steep, arid valleys, cold winds and exceptional clarity of light (some of th world's finest space observatories are located in Elqui), and high-altitud vineyards, mainly planted to Cabernet Sauvignon. However, it is Syrah in an elegant, fragrant style, that excels in this cool, sunny climate, alon with crisp Sauvignon Blanc and fresh Chardonnay. Best producer FALERNIA★ (Syrah★★), Mayu★, SAN PEDRO★.

ERNIE ELS *Stellenbosch WO, South Africa* Jean Engelbrecht's joint ventur with his golfing friend Ernie Els has resulted in a dark, serious BORDEAUX blend under the Ernie Els★★ label. Engelbrecht Els★ forges Shiraz wit Bordeaux varieties in a dense, rich, international style. The Guardia Peak range offers quality blends and good-value varietal wines Engelbrecht also makes outstanding Cirrus Syrah★★ in partnership wit SILVER OAK of California. Best years: (Ernie Els) 2007 **06 05 04 03 02 01 00**

ELTVILLE *Rheingau, Germany* Large town, making some of the RHEINGAU' most Rieslings. Best producers: Hessische Staatsweingüter (Kloste Eberbach), Koegler, Langwerth von Simmern★. Best years: (2009) 08 07 06 0! **04 02 01**.

EMILIA-ROMAGNA *Italy* One region, dominated by the Po valley, but ir vinous terms two very different entities. Emilia specializes in frothing wine like Lambrusco while Romagna is all Sangiovese and Trebbiano, including some top wines. See also COLLI PIACENTINI, ROMAGNA.

EMILIANA ORGÁNICO *Colchagua, Chile* Venture from the Guilisast family, main shareholders at CONCHA Y TORO, with leading winemake Alvaro Espinoza contributing his biodynamic and organic approach to viticulture. Adobe is good entry-level range; Novas★★ range i significantly better; and red blend Coyam★★ (sometimes ★★★) is one o

Chile's most fascinating wines. Gê★★, a 'Super Coyam', is a dense, powerful long-distance runner. Best years: 2009 08 07 06 **05 04 03 02 01**.

MRICH-SCHÖNLEBER *Monzingen, Nahe, Germany* Although Monzingen is not the most prestigious of NAHE villages, Werner Schönleber has steadily brought his 16ha (40-acre) property into the front ranks. His vigorous, spicy Rieslings are consistently ★ to ★★ and his Eisweins are ★★★. Best years: (2009) 08 07 06 **05 04 03 02 01 00**.

NATE *Somontano DO, Aragón, Spain* Barrel-fermented Chardonnay★ is rich, buttery and toasty, Gewürztraminer★ is exotic and convincing. International grape varieties also feature in the red Crianza, Reserva★ (100% Cabernet Sauvignon), Reserva Especial★★ (Cabernet-Merlot) and blockbuster Merlot-Merlot and Syrah-Shiraz. Best years: (reds) 2007 06 **05 04 03 01 00 99 98**.

NTRE-DEUX-MERS AC *Bordeaux, France*
This large AC between the rivers Garonne and Dordogne increasingly represents some of the freshest, snappiest dry white wine in France. In general, drink the latest vintage, though better wines will last a year or two. Most of Bordeaux's basic red wine under the Bordeaux AC comes from here too. Sweet wines are sold as PREMIÈRES CÔTES DE BORDEAUX, St-Macaire, LOUPIAC and STE-CROIX-DU-MONT. Best producers: BONNET★, Castenet Greffier, de Fontenille★, Landereau★, Marjosse★, Nardique la Gravière★, Ste-Marie★, Tour de Mirambeau★, Toutigeac★, Turcaud★.

CHÂTEAU
BONNET
ENTRE-DEUX-MERS
MIS EN BOUTEILLE AU CHÂTEAU

SAUVIGNON BLANC
SÉMILLON · MUSCADELLE

ANDRÉ LURTON

OM. D'EOLE *Coteaux d'Aix-en-Provence AC, Provence, France* Top wines from this organic estate are rosé Cuvée Caprice★ and Cuvée Léa★★, a 50:50 blend of Syrah and Grenache. Best years: 2008 07 06 **05 03 01** 00.

RBACH *Rheingau, Germany* Erbach's famous Marcobrunn vineyard is one of the top spots for Riesling along the Rhine. The village wines are elegant while those from Marcobrunn more powerful. Best producers: Jakob Jung★, Knyphausen, Langwerth von Simmern★★, SCHLOSS REINHARTSHAUSEN★★, Schloss Schönborn★★. Best years: (2009) 08 07 06 **05 04 03 02 01**.

RDEN *Mosel, Germany* Middle MOSEL village with the superb Prälat and Treppchen vineyards. Wines are rich and succulent with a strong mineral character. Best producers: Christoffel★★, Erbes, Dr Hermann, Dr LOOSEN★★★, Mönchhof★, Pauly-Bergweiler★, Dr Weins-Prüm★. Best years: (2009) 08 07 06 **05 04 03 02 01**.

RRÁZURIZ *Aconcagua, Chile* One of Chile's oldest family-run wineries (founded in 1870); rapidly modernizing under dynamic Eduardo Chadwick. Its portfolio includes SEÑA and Arboleda – originally joint ventures with MONDAVI, now 100% Errázuriz, and much improved as a result. The classic label is Don Maximiano Founder's Reserve★★ (sometimes ★★★), a Cabernet Sauvignon-based red from ACONCAGUA, also the source of La Cumbre Shiraz★, rich, perfumed Kai Carmenère★ and dense red The Blend★. Single-vineyard Cabernet Sauvignon Viñedo Chadwick★★★ comes from Puente Alto, a classic area of MAIPO. Also very good 'Wild Ferment' Chardonnay★★ and Pinot Noir★★ from CASABLANCA. New cool-climate coastal Aconcagua vineyards are exciting, especially for Sauvignon★★. Best years: (reds) (2009) 08 07 06 **05 04 03 02 01**.

CH. D'ESCLANS *Côtes de Provence AC, Provence, France* Sacha Lichine h
created what is claimed to be the 'most expensive rosé in the worl
Garrus★, an explosive, wood-aged blend of old-vine Grenache ar
Rolle. For lesser mortals, there are Les Clans★, the château wine and th
sweeter Whispering Angel★. First vintage was 2006.

ESPORÃO *Reguengos DOC, Alentejo, Portugal* Huge estate in the heart of th
ALENTEJO, where Australian David Baverstock makes a broad range
wines. Principal labels are Esporão (red★★ and white★ Reservas), Vinh
da Defesa★, Monte Velho and Alandra. Also some delightful varieta
Trincadeira★, Aragonês, Touriga Nacional★, Syrah★, Alican
Bouschet★ and Verdelho★. Best years: (reds) (2008) 07 **05 04 01 00**.

EST! EST!! EST!!! DI MONTEFIASCONE DOC *Lazio, Italy* Trebbianc
based white whose quality is distinctly inferior to the renown it ha
earned in myth. Best producers: Bigi (Graffiti), FALESCO (Poggio dei Gelsi★
Mazziotti (Canuleio★).

CH. DES ESTANILLES *Faugères AC, Languedoc, France* Michel Louison so
the property to financier Julien Seydoux in 2009; there is no reason fe
him not to maintain Louison's standards. The best site is the Clos d
Fou★★, with its very steep schistous slope planted with Syrah. Grand
Cuvée★★ includes a little Mourvèdre and Grenache. Also a wood
fermented and aged rosé, plus characterful white★. Best years: (red
(2009) 08 07 06 **05 04 02 01**.

ESTREMADURA See LISBOA.

L'ÉTOILE AC *Jura, France* A tiny area within the CÔTES DU JURA that has i
own AC for whites, mainly Chardonnay and Savagnin, and for *vin jaur*
and *vin de paille*. Best producers: Ch. de l'Étoile★, Geneletti★
Montbourgeau★★, P Vandelle★. Best years: (2008) 07 **06 05 04 02**.

CH. L'ÉVANGILE★★ *Pomerol AC, Bordeaux, France* A neighbour to PETRL
and CHEVAL BLANC, this estate has been wholly owned and managed by th
Rothschilds of LAFITE-ROTHSCHILD since 1999. The wine is quintessenti
POMEROL – rich, fat and exotic. Recent vintages have been very goo
(sometimes ★★★), but expect further improvement as the Rothschil
effect intensifies. Second wine: Blason de l'Évangile. Best years: 2008 0
06 05 **04 03 02 01 00 99 98 95 90 89**.

FABRE MONTMAYOU *Mendoza and Patagonia, Argentina* Owner, Frenchma
Hervé Joyaux Fabre, was one of the original foreign investors i
Argentina, back in the early 1990s. In an old area of MENDOZA calle
Luján de Cuyo, his estate is famous for Malbec, especially the dens
damson and plum Grand Vin★★. More recent investment in vineyarc
and a winery in PATAGONIA have added breadth to the portfolio wit
attractive wines under the Phebus★ label (also in Mendoza). Look out to
for the Viñalba label for fruit-driven expressions of Malbec in particula

FAIRVIEW *Paarl WO, South Africa* Owner Charles Back believes Sout
Africa's strength, especially in warmer areas, lies with Rhône varieties
These are expressed in the ever-expanding 'Goats' range: Goat-Roti★
Goats do Roam, Goats do Roam in Villages etc. Geddit
Complementing these is Bored Doe, a classic BORDEAUX-style blend. Th
French authorities are not amused but fans on both sides of the Atlanti
can't get enough. Fine Shiraz★★ (Eenzaamheid★★, The Beacon★★
Jakkalsfontein★★), Pinotage★ (Primo★★), Pegleg Carignan★, Merlot★
and Cabernet Sauvignon★. Good whites include Oom Pagε
Semillon★★, Viognier★ and outstanding sweet wine La Beryl★★★. Bac
also owns SPICE ROUTE. Best years: (Shiraz) 2008 07 06 05 04 03 02 01 00

JOSEPH FAIVELEY *Nuits-St-Georges, Côte de Nuits, Burgundy, France* There's been a revolution in this famous house since Erwan Faiveley took the helm in 2005. Gone are the dry-as-dust tannic reds, replaced by vibrant fruit and a great sense of *terroir* from such famous vineyards as CORTON★★★, CHAMBERTIN-Clos-de-Bèze★★★ and Mazis-Chambertin★★ as well as a range of less expensive wines from MERCUREY★, among others. Recent expansion into the CÔTE DE BEAUNE in PULIGNY★★ – with the remarkable acquisition of more than 1ha (2.5 acres) of Grand Cru – and MEURSAULT★. Best years: (top reds) (2009) 08 07 06 05 **99 90**; (whites) (2009) 08 07 **06 05**.

ALERNIA *Elqui, Chile* Established in 1998 when Italian immigrants Aldo Olivier and his brother-in-law Giorgio Flessati forsook Piedmont for the stunning ELQUI valley and swiftly made a name for themselves with Alta Tierra Reserva Syrah★★ from vines at 2000m (6500ft).

FALERNO DEL MASSICO DOC *Campania, Italy* Falernian was one of the ancient Romans' star wines. Today's DOC, with white Falanghina and reds from either Aglianico and Piedirosso or from Primitivo, has so far promised more than it has delivered. Best producers: Michele Moio★, Villa Matilde★ (Vigna Camarato★★). Best years: (reds) (2009) (08) 07 06 **05 04** 03 01 00.

FALESCO *Lazio, Italy* Property of the Cotarella brothers: Renzo is ANTINORI's technical director (responsible for SOLAIA, TIGNANELLO, etc.); Riccardo is a high-profile consultant enologist, working all over Italy from Piedmont to Sicily. Located at Montefiascone, their Poggio dei Gelsi★ is considered the best of the EST! EST!! EST!!! wines, but they are better known for their Merlot Montiano★, the essence of smooth if somewhat soulless modernity. Best years: (Montiano) (2009) (08) 07 06 **04 03 01 00 99**.

CH. FALFAS★ *Côtes de Bourg AC, Bordeaux, France* Biodynamic estate making concentrated, structured wine that needs 4–5 years to soften. Le Chevalier★ is an old-vines cuvée. Best years: 2008 **06 05** 04 03 02 01 00.

CH. DE FARGUES★★ *Sauternes AC, Bordeaux, France* Property run by the Lur-Saluces family, who until 1999 also owned Ch. d'YQUEM. The quality of this fine, rich wine is more a tribute to their commitment than to the inherent quality of the vineyard. Best years: 2007 06 05 **04 03 02 01 99 98 97 96 95 90 89 88 86**.

BY FARR *Geelong, Victoria, Australia* Having established BANNOCKBURN as one of Australia's best boutique wineries, Gary Farr is now making wine with his son, Nick, from his 4.8ha (12-acre) family vineyard. Farr is a traditionalist at heart who is making wines of rare quality. The Viognier★ is heady, complex and alluring; the Chardonnay★ austere yet tangy and elegant; the Pinot Noir★★★ ethereal and deliciously varietal; the Shiraz★★ meaty, minerally, dry and firm. Nick Farr makes more moderately priced wines under the Farr Rising label: classy, textural Chardonnay; delicate, silky smooth, dry Saignée (a Pinot rosé); and two silky yet weighty Pinot Noirs from GEELONG★ and MORNINGTON.

FAUGÈRES AC *Languedoc, France* The schistous hills north of Béziers in the Hérault produce red wines whose ripe, plummy flavour marks them out from other LANGUEDOC reds. Best producers: Abbaye Sylva Plana★, Alézon, Jean-Michel ALQUIER★, Léon Barral★, Chenaie★, ESTANILLES★, Faugères co-op, Haut Lignières, HECHT & BANNIER★, la Liquière★, Ollier-Taillefer (Castel Fossibus★), Saint-Antonin. Best years: (2009) 08 07 06 **05 04 03 01**.

FAUSTINO *Rioja DOCa, País Vasco and Rioja, and Cava DO, Spain* Family-owned and technically very well equipped, this RIOJA company makes fair Reserva V and Gran Reserva I red Riojas, as well as a more modern, oak-aged

153

red, Faustino de Autor, and fruit-driven Faustino de Crianza. But the could try harder. New top-end Faustino 9 Mil★ is ambitious and convincing. Best years: (reds) 2005 **04 03 01 99 98 96 95 94 92 91 90.**

FEILER-ARTINGER *Rust, Neusiedlersee, Burgenland, Austria* Kurt Feiler makes sumptuous Ausbruch dessert wines★★; the finest are labelled Essenz★★★. Also dry whites★ and reds: Solitaire★★ is a suave red blend of Merlot with Blaufränkisch and Cabernet Sauvignon. Best years: (sweet whites) (2009) 08 07 06 **05 04 02 01 99 98**; (Solitaire) (2008) 07 06 **05 04 03 02 0**

LIVIO FELLUGA *Colli Orientali del Friuli DOC, Friuli-Venezia Giulia, Italy* A younger generation has continued the great work of Livio Felluga at this large Friuli estate. Merlot-Cabernet blend Vertigo★★, raspberryish straight Merlot Riserva Sossó★★, Pinot Grigio★, Picolit Riserva★★ and Friulano★ are all class acts. Shàrjs★ combines Chardonnay with

Ribolla and oak, but there's more to stimulate the palate in Terre Alte★★, an aromatic blend of Friulano, Pinot Bianco and Sauvignon. Best years: (whites) (2009) (08) 07 **06 04 02 01 00.**

FATTORIA DI FELSINA *Chianti Classico DOCG, Tuscany, Italy* Full, chunky CHIANTI CLASSICO★★ wines which improve with several years' bottle age. Quality is good to outstanding; most notable are the single-vineyard Riserva Rancia★★★ and (under the regional IGT Toscana) Sangiovese Fontalloro★★★. Also good Cabernet Maestro Raro★ and Chardonnay Sistri★ . Best years: (Fontalloro) (2009) (08) 07 06 **04 03 01 00 99 97 95**

FELTON ROAD *Central Otago, South Island, New Zealand* Runaway success with vineyards in the old goldfields of Bannockburn. Intensely fruity seductive Pinot Noir★★ is surpassed by very limited quantities of concentrated, complex Block 3 Pinot Noir★★★ and Block 5★★★. Intense and spicy Calvert★★★ and fleshy, scented Cornish Point Pinot Noir★★ are from separate vineyards. Three classy Rieslings (all ★★) range from dry to sweet. Mineral, citrus unoaked Elms Chardonnay★★ can be one of New Zealand's best; barrel-fermented Chardonnay★★ is funky and delicious while limited edition Block 2★★★ is sensational. Best years: (Pinot Noir) (2009) 08 07 06 05 03 02 01.

FENDANT *Valais, Switzerland* Chasselas wine from the steep slopes of the VALAIS. Good Fendant should be slightly *spritzig*, with a nutty character, but many are thin and virtually characterless. Drink very young. Best producers: Chappaz, Jean-René Germanier, A Mathier, Simon Maye, D Mercier.

FERNGROVE *Great Southern, Western Australia* Ambitious winery founded in 1998, based in Frankland River and now with a cellar door in MARGARET RIVER. The quality potential in Frankland River is unquestioned, being sunny yet cool. Lack of water is a limiting factor, but that also means yields are naturally limited and flavours intensified – although I've noticed a slight coarsening of flavours recently. Cossack Riesling★ and Diamond Chardonnay★ are good but used to have more verve. Sauvignon-Semillon is tangy, King Malbec★★ is scented and lush and Cabernet-Merlot★ rich and eucalyptusy. The flagship Stirlings Shiraz-Cabernet blend★ is pretty good, though I'd like less oak.

FERRARI *Trento DOC, Trentino, Italy* Founded in 1902, the firm is a leader for sparkling wine. Consistent, classy wines include Ferrari Brut★, Maximum Brut★, Perlé★, Rosé★ and vintage Giulio Ferrari Riserva del Fondatore★★, aged 8 years on its lees and an Italian classic.

ERRARI-CARANO *Dry Creek Valley AVA, California, USA* Full-bodied Chardonnay: the regular bottling★ has apple-spice fruit, while the Reserve★ is deeply flavoured with more obvious oak. Fumé Blanc★ is also good. Red wines include Trésor★★ (a BORDEAUX blend), Siena★★ (based on Sangiovese), Syrah★, Merlot★ and Zinfandel★, with a new line of premium reds called PreVail. I'm a bit concerned about alcohol levels, which have been creeping upward recently. Best years: (reds) 2006 05 **03 02** 01 **00 99** 97 96 95.

ERREIRA *Port DOC and Douro DOC, Douro, Portugal* Old PORT house owned by SOGRAPE. Ferreira is best known for excellent tawny ports: creamy, nutty Quinta do Porto 10-year-old★ and Duque de Braganza 20-year-old★★. The Vintage★★ is increasingly good. Ferreira's unfortified wine operation, known as Casa Ferreirinha, produces Portugal's most sought-after red, Barca Velha★★★ (sometimes); made from DOURO grape varieties (mainly Tinta Roriz), it is produced only in the finest years – just 15 vintages since 1953. Marginally less good years are now sold as Casa Ferreirinha Reserva★ (previously Reserva Especial). Quinta da Leda reds★★ are also fine. Best years: (Vintage) 2007 **03 00** 97 95 94 91 85 83 82 78 77 70 66 63; (Barca Velha) 2000 99 95 91 85 83 82 81 78.

CH. FERRIÈRE★★ *Margaux AC, 3ème Cru Classé, Haut-Médoc, Bordeaux, France* Ferrière was bought by the Merlaut family, owners of Ch. CHASSE-SPLEEN, in 1992 but is now owned and managed by Claire Villars. The ripe, rich and perfumed wines are among the best in MARGAUX AC. Best years: 2008 07 06 05 **04 03 02** 01 00 99 98 96.

ETZER VINEYARDS *Mendocino County, California, USA* Important winery that I feel could push the quality level higher. Locals swear by the quality of the special cellar door releases, but we never see these in the outside world. Basic wines are good, with tasty Gewürztraminer, Riesling and Syrah★. Bargain-priced Valley Oaks line is decent value. Also a leader in organic viticulture with slowly improving Bonterra range from organically grown grapes: Chardonnay, Viognier★, Merlot, Roussanne★, Zinfandel★, Cabernet Sauvignon and Sangiovese. Best years: (reds) 2007 06 05 **03 02** 01 99 98 97 96.

IANO Exciting, distinctive, low-yielding southern Italian white grape variety. Best producers: (Molise) Di Majo Norante; (Fiano di Avellino DOC in CAMPANIA) Colli di Lapio★, Feudi di San Gregorio★★, MASTROBERARDINO★, Terredora di Paolo★, Vadiaperti★; (non-DOC) L Maffini (Kràtos★★); (Sicily) PLANETA (Cometa★★), Settesoli (Inycon★); (Australia) Coriole, Fox Gordon, Oliver's Taranga.

CH. DE FIEUZAL *Pessac-Léognan AC, Cru Classé de Graves, Bordeaux, France* Under new ownership since 2001; the objective is to recapture the form of the 1980s when Fieuzal was the most exotic and irresistible of all PESSAC-LÉOGNANs. With help from the owner of ANGÉLUS, it's beginning to work. The red★ is juicy and drinkable almost immediately, but ages well. The white★, a gorgeous, perfumed (and ageworthy) wine, is the star performer. Second wine (red and white): l'Abeille de Fieuzal. Best years: (reds) 2008 07 06 **01 00** 98 96 95 90 89 88; (whites) 2008 07 **06** 05 02 01 00 99 98 96.

CH. FIGEAC★★ *St-Émilion Grand Cru AC, 1er Grand Cru Classé, Bordeaux, France* Leading property whose wine traditionally has a delightful fragrance and gentleness of texture. It has an unusually high percentage (70%) of

155

Cabernets Franc and Sauvignon, making it more structured than othe ST-ÉMILIONS. Somewhat erratic in the late 1980s, but since 1996 far mo: like the lovely Figeac of old: consistent in style and quality. Second win la Grange Neuve de Figeac. Best years: 2008 07 06 05 **04 03 02 01 00 99 9 96 95 90 89.**

FINGER LAKES AVA *New York State, USA* Cool region in central NEW YOR STATE, where some winemakers are establishing a regional style for d: (and sweet) Riesling. Chardonnay and sparkling wines also star, wit Pinot Noir and Cabernet Franc the best reds. Wineries around Senec and Cayuga lakes can now use those smaller designations on their label Best producers: ANTHONY ROAD★, Casa Larga (Ice Wine), Chateau Lafayet Reneau★, FOX RUN★, Dr Konstantin FRANK★, Heron Hill, LAMOREAU LANDING★, Red Newt, Swedish Hill, Wagner, Hermann J WIEMER★.

FITOU AC *Languedoc, France* One of the success stories of the 1980 Quality subsequently slumped, but with the innovative MONT TAUC co-op taking the lead, Fitou is once again an excellent place to seek ou dark, herb-scented reds. Best producers: Abelanet, Bertrand-Bergé★★ Lerys★, Milles Vignes, MONT TAUCH co-op★, Nouvelles★, Rochelière, Rollan Roudène★. Best years: (2009) 08 07 06 **05 04 03 01 00.**

FIXIN AC *Côte de Nuits, Burgundy, France* Although it's next door to GEVRE CHAMBERTIN, Fixin rarely produces anything really magical. The wines ar often sold as CÔTE DE NUITS-VILLAGES. Best producers: Charlopin★, Coillo Galeyrand★, Pierre Gelin★, Alain Guyard★, Joliet/Clos de la Perrière★★ Best years: (reds) (2009) 08 **07 06 05 03 02 99.**

FLEURIE AC *Beaujolais, Burgundy, France* The best-known BEAUJOLAIS Cru Fleurie reveals the happy, carefree flavours of the Gamay grape at its bes plus heady perfumes and a delightful juicy fruit. But demand has mear that many wines are overpriced and dull. Best producers: de Beauregard★ Berrod★, P-M Chermette★/Vissoux, M Chignard★, Clos de la Roilette★ Coquard★ DUBOEUF (la Madone★, Quatre Vents★), la Madone/Despres★ Y Métras★, Métrat★, A & M Morel★, Point du Jour★. Best years: **2009 08 07**

CH. LA FLEUR-PÉTRUS★★ *Pomerol AC, Bordeaux, France* Like the better known PETRUS and TROTANOY, this is owned by the dynamic MOUEIX family Unlike its stablemates, it is situated entirely on gravel soil and tends t produce tighter wines with less immediate fruit but considerable eleganc and cellar potential. Among POMEROL's top dozen properties. Best year: 2008 06 05 **04 03 02 01 00 99 98 96 95 94 90 89.**

FLORA SPRINGS *Napa Valley AVA, California, USA* Best known for red wine such as Merlot★★, Cabernet Sauvignon★★ and a BORDEAUX blend calle Trilogy★★. Barrel-fermented Chardonnay★★ tops the whites, an Soliloquy★, a barrel-fermented Sauvignon Blanc, has attractive melo fruit. The winery also works with Italian varietals; a weighty Pino Grigio★ and a lightly spiced Sangiovese★ are consistent successes. Bes years: (Trilogy) 2006 05 04 03 **02 01 00 99 97 96 95.**

FLOWERS *Sonoma Coast AVA, California, USA* Small producer whose estat vineyard, Camp Meeting Ridge, a few miles from the Pacific, yield wines of great intensity. Camp Meeting Ridge Pinot Noir★★★ an Chardonnay★★★ are usually made with native yeasts and offe beautifully restrained, subtly balanced aromas and flavours. Wines mad from purchased fruit with a SONOMA COAST designation are ★★; Andree: Gale★★ are excellent full-flavoured barrel selections. Best year: (Chardonnay) 2007 06 **05 04 03 01 00**; (Pinot Noir) 2007 06 **05 04 03 0 00 99.**

ENUTE AMBROGIO & GIOVANNI FOLONARI *Tuscany, Italy* A few years ago the Folonari family, owners of the giant RUFFINO, split asunder and this father and son team went their own way. Their properties/brands include Cabreo (Sangiovese-Cabernet Il Borgo, Chardonnay La Pietra) and Nozzole (powerful, long-lived Cabernet Il Pareto★★) in CHIANTI CLASSICO, plus VINO NOBILE estate Gracciano-Svetoni, Campo del Mare in BOLGHERI and BRUNELLO producer La Fuga.

ONSECA *Port DOC, Douro, Portugal* Owned by the same group as TAYLOR (Fladgate Partnership), Fonseca makes ports in a rich, densely plummy style. Vintage★★★ is magnificent, the aged tawnies★★ superb. Guimaraens★★ is the 'off-vintage' wine, Crusted★ and Late Bottled Vintage★ are among the best examples of their styles, as is Bin No. 27★ of a premium ruby port. Quinta do Panascal★ is the single-quinta vintage. Best years: (Vintage) 2007 03 **00 97 94 92 85 83 77 75 70 66 63 55**.

OSÉ MARIA DA FONSECA *Península de Setúbal, Portugal* Long-established company making a huge range of wines, from fizzy Lancers Rosé to serious reds. Best include Vinya★ (Syrah-Aragonez), Domingos Soares Franco Private Collection★, and Garrafeiras with codenames like RA★★ and TE★★. Optimum★★ is top of the range. Periquita is the mainstay, with Clássico★ made only in the best years. Also SETÚBAL made mainly from the Moscatel grape: 5-year-old★ and 20-year-old★★. Older vintage-dated Setúbals are rare but superb.

OM. FONT DE MICHELLE *Châteauneuf-du-Pape AC, Rhône Valley, France* CHÂTEAUNEUF-DU-PAPE reds★★, in particular Cuvée Étienne Gonnet★★, with richness and southern herb fragrance – and good value for money. Fresh, accomplished whites★★. Best years: (Étienne Gonnet red) 2009 07 06 **05 04 03 01 00 99 98 97 95 90 89**.

FONTANAFREDDA *Barolo DOCG, Piedmont, Italy* Large property, formerly the hunting lodge of the King of Italy. As well as BAROLO Serralunga d'Alba★, it produces several single-vineyard Barolos★ (La Delizia★★), a range of PIEDMONT varietals, 4 million bottles of ASTI and a good dry sparkler, Contessa Rosa. Best years: (Barolo) (2009) (08) (07) 06 **04 03 01 00 99 97**.

CASTELLO DI FONTERUTOLI *Chianti Classico DOCG, Tuscany, Italy* This estate has belonged to the Mazzei family since the 15th century. The focus is on CHIANTI CLASSICO Riserva★, along with excellent Siepi★★★ (Sangiovese-Merlot). Belguardo★ is a more recent venture in the MAREMMA, with IGT and MORELLINO DI SCANSANO wines.

FONTODI *Chianti Classico DOCG, Tuscany, Italy* The Manetti family has built this superbly sited estate into one of the most admired in CHIANTI CLASSICO, with fine *normale*★★ and Riserva Vigna del Sorbo★★. Flaccianello della Pieve★★★, from a single vineyard of old vines, has served as a shining example of an excellent 100% Sangiovese. Pinot Nero and Syrah★ are made under the Case Via label. Best years: (Flaccianello) (2009) (08) 07 06 **04 03 01 00 99 97 95 93 90 88 85**.

FORADORI *Teroldego Rotaliano DOC, Trentino, Italy* Producer of dark, spicy, berry-fruited wines, including a regular TEROLDEGO ROTALIANO★ and barrique-aged Granato★★. Elisabetta Foradori's interest in Syrah is producing excellent results, both in the varietal Ailanpa★★ and the smoky, black-cherry lushness of Cabernet-Syrah blend Karanar★. Best years: (Granato) (2009) (08) 07 06 **04 03 01 00 99 97**.

FORST *Pfalz, Germany* Village with outstanding vineyard sites, including the Ungeheuer or 'Monster'; wines from the Monster can indeed be quite savage, with a marvellous mineral intensity and richness. Equally good

157

are the Kirchenstück, Jesuitengarten, Freundstück and Pechstein. Be**st** producers: BASSERMANN-JORDAN★★, von BUHL★★, BÜRKLIN-WOLF★★, MOSBACHER★★, E Müller, Spindler, WOLF★★. Best years: (2009) 08 07 **06 05 0**4 **03 02 01 99.**

O FOURNIER *Argentina, Chile, Spain* Exciting Tempranillo and Malbec fro**m** old vines in the La Consulta area of MENDOZA's Uco Valley. Alfa Crux★ (a Tempranillo-Malbec-Merlot blend) is top of the line, while Alfa Cru**x** Malbec★★ is an excellent, juicy expression of Argentina's flagship re**d** grape. Also very good Syrah★. B Crux★ is the lighter, but deliciou**s** second label. O Fournier also has a venture in RIBERA DEL DUERO, Spai**n** with O Fournier★★ and Alfa Spiga★ cuvées. A new venture in Chile **is** based in MAULE and SAN ANTONIO; excellent Centauri Sauvignon Blanc★ from the Leyda Valley and Centauri★★ red blend of old-vine Carignan**,** Cabernet and Merlot.

FOX CREEK *McLaren Vale, South Australia* Impressive, opulent, superrip**e** MCLAREN VALE reds. Reserve Shiraz★★ and Reserve Caberne**t** Sauvignon★★ have wowed the critics; JSM (Shiraz-Cabernets)★★ **is** rich and succulent; Merlot★★ is a little lighter but still concentrated an**d** powerful. Vixen sparkling Shiraz★ is also lip-smacking stuff.

FOX RUN *Finger Lakes AVA, New York State, USA* A leader in Dry Riesling★. Fox Run has teamed up with Red Newt and ANTHONY ROAD wineries t**o** produce Tierce, a co-operative effort to define a regional style for Riesling**.** Fox Run also features an elegant Reserve Chardonnay★, spicy, attractiv**e** Pinot Noir and Cabernet Franc, and a complex, fruit-forward red Meritag**e.**

FRAMINGHAM *Marlborough, South Island, New Zealand* Small winery owne**d** by SOGRAPE. Much of Framingham's success is thanks to the thoughtfu**l** and uncompromising approach of English winemaker Dr Andre**w** Hedley. Best wines are made from aromatic grape varieties, particularl**y** Select Riesling★★, off-dry Classic★ and Dry★★ Rieslings. Pure, spic**y** Gewürztraminer★★ and sleek, ethereal Pinot Gris★★ are among Ne**w** Zealand's best. Best years: (Riesling) **2009 07 06 05.**

FRANCIACORTA DOCG *Lombardy, Italy* CHAMPAGNE-method fizz mad**e** from Pinot and Chardonnay grapes. Still whites from Pinot Bianco an**d** Chardonnay and reds from Cabernet, Barbera, Nebbiolo and Merlot ar**e** all DOC with the appellation Terre di Franciacorta or Curtefranca. Bes**t** producers: BELLAVISTA★★, Fratelli Berlucchi★, Guido Berlucchi★, CA' DE**L** BOSCO★★, Castellino★, Cavalleri★, La Ferghettina★, Enrico Gatti★, Monte Rossa★, Il Mosnel★, Ricci Curbastro★, San Cristoforo★, Uberti★, Villa★.

FRANCISCAN *Napa Valley AVA, California, USA* Consistently good wines a**t** fair prices: the Cuvée Sauvage Chardonnay★★ is a blockbusting, savour**y** mouthful, and the Cabernet Sauvignon-based meritage Magnificat★ **is** very attractive. Part of huge Constellation.

DR KONSTANTIN FRANK *Finger Lakes AVA, New York State, USA* The goo**d** doctor was a pioneer of *vinifera* grapes in the FINGER LAKES region in th**e** 1960s. Now under the direction of his grandson Fred, the winer**y** continues to spotlight the area's talent with Riesling★ and Rkatsiteli, a**n** obscure Georgian grape. There's also some nice Chateau Frank fizz.

FRANKEN *Germany* 6060ha (15,000-acre) wine region specializing in dry wines – recognizable by their squat Bocksbeutel bottles (familiar because of the Portuguese wine Mateus Rosé). Silvaner is the traditional variety, although Müller-Thurgau now predominates. The most famous vineyards are on slopes around WÜRZBURG, RANDERSACKER, IPHOFEN and Escherndorf.

FRANSCHHOEK WO *South Africa* Huguenot refugees settled in this picturesque valley, encircled by breathtaking mountain peaks, in the 17th century. Many wineries and other landmarks still bear French names. The valley is recognized for its whites – Semillon is a local speciality (a few vines are over 100 years old) – though reds are establishing a reputation. Best producers: Graham BECK★, BOEKENHOUTSKLOOF★★, Cabrière Estate, CAPE CHAMONIX★★, La Motte★, La Petite Ferme, L'Ormarins, Solms-Delta★, Stony Brook. Best years: (reds) 2007 **06 05 04 03 02 01 00**.

FRASCATI DOC *Lazio, Italy* Once one of Italy's most famous whites, Rome's quaffing wine. It may be made from Trebbiano or Malvasia or any blend thereof; the better examples have a higher proportion of Malvasia. There's much mediocre stuff, but good Frascati is worth seeking out for its gentle, dry creaminess. Other light, dry Frascati-like wines come from neighbouring DOCs in the hills of the Castelli Romani and Colli Albani, including Marino, Montecompatri, Velletri and Zagarolo. But when it's a contest between vineyard space and real estate in the Roman suburbs, guess which wins. Best producers: Casale Marchese★, Castel de Paolis★, Colli di Catone★, Piero Costantini/Villa Simone★, Fontana Candida★, Zandotti★.

FREESTONE VINEYARD *Sonoma Coast AVA, California, USA* The Napa Valley's Joseph PHELPS wanted better sources of Chardonnay and Pinot Noir so he planted 40ha (100 acres) in 3 parcels at Freestone in the coldest region of SONOMA COUNTY, out toward Bodega Bay on the coast. The first releases were in 2006 and the lushness of the Chardonnay★★ and the rich yet scented fruit of the Pinot Noir★ immediately marked Freestone out as a top SONOMA COAST producer. Good second label Fogdog★ and top Chardonnay Ovation★★.

FREIXENET *Cava DO, Cataluña, Spain* The second-biggest Spanish sparkling wine company (after CODORNÍU) makes the famous Cordon Negro Brut CAVA in a vast network of cellars in Sant Sadurní d'Anoia. Freixenet also owns a number of other Cava brands (including Castellblanch and Segura Viudas) as well as PENEDÈS winery René Barbier and a stake in PRIORAT's Viticultors del Priorat (Morlanda). International interests in Champagne, California, Australia, Argentina and Bordeaux.

FRESCOBALDI *Tuscany, Italy* Ancient Florentine company selling large quantities of inexpensive blended CHIANTI, but from its own vineyards (some 1000ha/2470 acres in Tuscany) it produces good to very good wines at Castello di Nipozzano (CHIANTI RUFINA Nipozzano Riserva★★, Montesodi★★ and my favourite, the BORDEAUX-blend Mormoreto★★), Castello di Pomino★ (Benefizio Chardonnay★) and Castelgiocondo (BRUNELLO DI MONTALCINO★★), where Sangiovese for Brunello and Merlot for the 'Super-Tuscan' Luce are grown. Frescobaldi owns several other estates in Tuscany including, since 2005, a majority stake in the famous Bolgheri estate, ORNELLAIA. It also owns the historic Attems estate in COLLIO. Best years: (premium reds) (2009) (08) (07) **06 04 03 01 00 99 97 95**.

FRIULANO Friulano (formerly Tocai Friulano) is a north-east Italian grape producing dry, nutty, oily whites of great character in COLLIO and COLLI ORIENTALI. Friuli producers have now, under pressure from the

Hungarians, removed the name Tocai. Best producers: Borgo del Tiglio★, L FELLUGA★, JERMANN★, Edi Keber★, Miani★★, Princic★, Ronco del Gelso★★ Russiz Superiore★★, SCHIOPETTO★★, Le Vigne di Zamò★★, Villa Russiz★.

FRIULI GRAVE DOC *Friuli-Venezia Giulia, Italy* DOC in western Friuli covering 19 wine types. Good affordable Merlot, Refosco, Chardonnay, Pinot Grigio, Traminer and Tocai. Best producers: Borgo Magredo★, D Lenardo★, Le Fredis★, Orgnani★, Pighin★, Pittaro★, Plozner★, Pradio★ Russolo★, Scarbolo, Vigneti Le Monde★, Villa Chiopris★, Vistorta★. Best years (whites) (2009) (08) **07 06 04 02**.

FRIULI ISONZO DOC *Friuli-Venezia Giulia, Italy* Classy southern neighbour of COLLIO with wines of outstanding value. The DOC covers 20 styles including Merlot, Chardonnay, Pinot Grigio and Sauvignon. The bes from neighbouring Carso DOC are also good. Best producers: (Isonzo Borgo San Daniele★, Colmello di Grotta★, Sergio & Mauro Drius★★, Li Neris★★, Masùt da Rive★, Pierpaolo Pecorari★★, Giovanni Puiatti★, Ronco del Gelso★★, Vie di Romans★★; (Carso) Castelvecchio Edi Kante★★. Best years: (whites) (2009) (08) **07 06 04 03 02**.

FRIULI-VENEZIA GIULIA *Italy* North-east Italian region bordering Austria and Slovenia. The hilly DOC zones of COLLIO and COLLI ORIENTALI produce some of Italy's finest whites from Chardonnay, Pinot Bianco, Pinot Grigio, Sauvignon and Friulano (Tocai), and excellent reds mainly from Cabernet, Merlot and Refosco. Good-value wines from the DOCs of Friuli Aquileia, FRIULI ISONZO, Friuli Latisana and FRIULI GRAVE, in the rolling hills and plains

FROMM *Marlborough, South Island, New Zealand* Small winery where low-yielding vines and intensively managed vineyards are the secret behind a string of winning white wines, including fine Burgundian-style Clayvin Vineyard Chardonnay★★, German-style Riesling★★ and Riesling Auslese★. Despite its success with whites, Fromm is perhaps best known for intense, long-lived reds, including Clayvin Vineyard Pinot Noir★★★, Fromm Vineyard Pinot Noir★★ and a powerful, peppery Syrah★★. Best years: (Pinot Noir) (2009) **06 05 04 03 02 01**.

FRONSAC AC *Bordeaux, France* Small area west of POMEROL making good-value Merlot-based wines. The top producers have taken note of the feeding frenzy in neighbouring Pomerol and sharpened up their act accordingly, with finely structured wines, occasionally perfumed, and better with at least 5 years' age. Best producers: Carles (Haut-Carles★) Dalem★, la Dauphine★, Fontenil★, la Grave, Magondeau Beau-Site, Mayne-Vieil (Cuvée Aliénor★), Moulin Haut-Laroque★, Richelieu★, la Rivière★ (Aria★), la Rousselle★, Tour du Moulin, les Trois Croix★, la Vieille Cure★ Villars★. Best years: (2009) 08 06 **05 03 01 00 98 96 95 90**.

FRONTON AC *South-West France* From north of Toulouse, some of the most distinctive reds – silky, with hints of violets and licorice – of South-West France. Négrette is the chief grape, but some producers add bite at the cost of character by blending in Cabernet and other grapes. Best producers: Baudare★, Bellevue-la-Forêt, Boujac, Cahuzac★, Caze★, Joliet, Laurou, PLAISANCE★, le Roc★. Best years: 2009 **08 06 05**.

FUMÉ BLANC See SAUVIGNON BLANC, pages 280–1.

RUDOLF FÜRST *Bürgstadt, Franken, Germany* Paul Fürst's dry Rieslings★★ are unusually elegant for a region where white wines can be earthy, while his Burgundian-style Spätburgunder (Pinot Noir) reds★★ and barrel-fermented Weissburgunder (Pinot Blanc) whites★★ are some of the best in Germany. Sensual, intellectual wines with excellent aging potential. Best years: (dry Riesling) (2009) 08 07 **06 05 04 03 02**; (reds) (2009) 08 07 06 **05 04 03 02**.

ʲAN-NOËL GAGNARD *Chassagne-Montrachet, Côte de Beaune, Burgundy, France* Run since 1989 by Gagnard's daughter Caroline Lestimé, who consistently makes some of the best wines of CHASSAGNE-MONTRACHET, particularly Premiers Crus Caillerets★★★ and Morgeot★★. Top wine is rich, toasty BÂTARD-MONTRACHET★★★. All whites are capable of extended cellaring. Reds★ are good, but not in the same class. Best years: (whites) (2009) 08 07 06 05 **04 02 01 00 99**.

ʲAILLAC AC *South-West France* The whites, mainly from Mauzac and Len de l'El, range from dry to ultra-sweet. Reds and rosés are from local grapes too – Braucol, Duras – and sometimes Syrah. Some reds are matured in wood and need some aging. Sparkling Gaillac undergoes only one fermentation and has no added yeasts or sugar; less alcohol, too. Best producers: CAUSSE MARINES★★, Escausses★, Labarthe★, Mas Pignou, Palvié★★, Pialentou, PLAGEOLES★★, la RAMAYE★★, ROTIER★. Best years: (reds) (2009) **06 05 04**; (sweet whites) (2009) **07 06 05**.

ʲAJA *Barbaresco DOCG, Piedmont, Italy* Angelo Gaja was instrumental in bringing about the transformation of PIEDMONT from an old-fashioned region that Italians swore made the finest red wine in the world yet the rest of the world disdained, to an area buzzing with excitement. He introduced international standards and charged staggeringly high prices, thus giving other Piedmont growers the chance to get a decent return for their labours. Into this fiercely conservative area, full of fascinating grape varieties but proudest of the native Nebbiolo, he introduced French grapes like Cabernet Sauvignon (Darmagi★★), Sauvignon Blanc (Alteni di Brassica★) and Chardonnay (Gaia & Rey★★). He has also renounced the Barbaresco and Barolo DOCGs for his best wines! Gaja's traditional strength has been in single-vineyard wines from the BARBARESCO region: his Sorì San Lorenzo★★★, Sorì Tildìn★★★ and Costa Russi★★★, now sold under the LANGHE Nebbiolo DOC, which permits 15% of other grapes in the blend, are often cited as Barbaresco's best of the modern style, although they tend to be more 'Gaja' than 'Barbaresco'. Only one 100% Nebbiolo bottling of Barbaresco DOCG★★★ is now made. His outstanding Sperss★★ and Conteisa★★★ (from BAROLO) are also sold as Langhe Nebbiolo. Gaja has also invested in BRUNELLO DI MONTALCINO (Pieve Santa Restituta) and BOLGHERI (Ca' Marcanda). Best years: (Barbaresco) (2009) (08) (07) 06 **04 03 01 00 99 98 97 96 95 93 90 89 88 85 82 79 78 71 64 61**.

ʲALICIA *Spain* Up in Spain's hilly, verdant north-west, Galicia is renowned ʲor its Albariño whites. There are 5 DOs: RÍAS BAIXAS can make excellent, ʲragrant Albariño, with modern equipment and serious winemaking; Ribeiro ʲO has also invested heavily in new equipment, and better local white grapes ʲuch as Treixadura are now being used; it's a similar story with the Godello ʲrape in the mountainous Valdeorras DO, where producers such as the young ʲafael Palacios, from the ubiquitous Rioja-based family, are reaching new ʲeights for ageworthy, individual whites. Some increasingly ambitious reds ʲrom the Mencía grape are also made there and in the Ribeira Sacra DO. ʲonterrei DO is technically backward but shows some potential with its ʲative white grape, Doña Blanca. Most wines are best drunk young.

GALLO *Central Valley, California, USA* Gallo, the world's second-largest win
company – and for generations a byword for cheap, drab wines – ha
made a massive effort to change its reputation since the mid-1990s. Th
began with the release of Sonoma Estate Chardonnay and Caberne
Sauvignon. The emphasis is still on Sonoma Chardonnay and Caberne
Sauvignon, with Zinfandel and Cabernet Sauvignon from DRY CREE
VALLEY and ALEXANDER VALLEY. New SONOMA COAST vineyards are in a ver
cool area south of Santa Rosa; stylish single-vineyard Two Roc
Chardonnay. Vineyards in RUSSIAN RIVER VALLEY and the Sonoma Coas
have been planted to Pinot Noir and Pinot Gris (some of it to make th
premium MacMurray wines). Even so, Gallo continues to produc
oceans of ordinary wine. Turning Leaf and Sierra Valley aren't going t
turn many heads, but the company has taken Rancho Zabaco upscale an
added a parallel brand, Dancing Bull, in which Sauvignon Blanc★ an
Zinfandel★ are budding stars. In 2002, Gallo acquired historic Louis M
Martini in NAPA VALLEY, adding the famed Monte Rosso vineyard to it
holdings, and then bought Mirassou, Barefoot Cellars (a fast-growin
brand), William Hill and CENTRAL COAST's Bridlewood.

GAMAY The only grape allowed for red BEAUJOLAIS. In general Gamay wine i
rather rough-edged and quite high in raspy acidity, but in Beaujolais, s
long as the yield is not too high, it can achieve a wonderful, juicy-frui
gluggability, almost unmatched in the world of wine. Elsewhere i
France, it is successful in the Ardèche and the Loire and less so in th
Mâconnais. In Switzerland it is blended with Pinot Noir to create DÔ
and Goron. There are occasional plantings in Canada, Brazil, Nev
Zealand, Australia, South Africa and Italy.

GANTENBEIN *Fläsch, Graubunden, Switzerland* Since 1982 Daniel Gantenbei
has focused on producing intense and powerful versions of th
Burgundian varieties, and has won a fine reputation above all for hi
Pinot Noir★★, as well as Chardonnay and Riesling★. Best years: (Pino
Noir) (2009) (08) 07 06 05 **04 03 02**.

GARD, VIN DE PAYS DU *Languedoc, France* Mainly reds and rosés from th
western side of the RHÔNE delta. Most red is light, spicy and attractive
Some fresh young rosés and whites have been improved by moder
winemaking. Best producers: des Aveylans★, Cantarelles, Coste Plane
Grande Cassagne★, Guiot★, Mas des Bressades★.

GARNACHA BLANCA See GRENACHE BLANC.

GARNACHA TINTA See GRENACHE NOIR.

GATTINARA DOCG *Piedmont, Italy* Nebbiolo-based red from north
central PIEDMONT which consistently disappoints Barolo-lovers, having a
earthier, less porty-sweet character than its famous rival. Best producer
Antoniolo★, Anzivino, Nervi★, Travaglini★.

DOM. GAUBY *Côtes du Roussillon-Villages AC, Roussillon,*
France Gérard Gauby can make marvellously
concentrated and balanced wines. Highlights
include powerful CÔTES DU ROUSSILLON-VILLAGES
Vieilles Vignes★★, white and red les
Calcinaires★★ and Muntada★★ as well as a
gorgeously seductive white vin de pays Coume
Gineste★. Best years: (reds) (2009) 08 07 06 05 04
03 02 01 00.

DOMAINE
GAUBY
2003

Les Calcinaires

Côtes du Roussillon Villages
RED ROUSSILLON WINE

GAVI DOCG *Piedmont, Italy* This fashionable and rapidly improving Cortese-based, steely, lemony white can age up to 5 years, providing it starts life with enough fruit. Mainly still, occasionally sparkling. **Best producers:** Battistina★, Bergaglio★, Broglia★, La Chiara★, Chiarlo★, FONTANAFREDDA, La Giustiniana★★, Pio Cesare, San Pietro★, La Scolca★, Tassarolo★, Villa Sparina★.

CH. GAZIN★★ *Pomerol AC, Bordeaux, France* One of the largest châteaux in POMEROL, situated next to the legendary PETRUS. The wine, traditionally a succulent, sweet-textured Pomerol, seemed to lose its way in the 1980s but has now got much of its character back under owner Nicolas de Bailliencourt. **Best years:** 2008 07 06 05 **04 03 02 01 00 99 98 96 95 90 89**.

GEELONG *Victoria, Australia* Cool-climate, maritime-influenced region revived in the 1960s after destruction by phylloxera in the 19th century. Can be brilliant; potentially a match for the YARRA VALLEY. Impressive Pinot Noir, Chardonnay, Riesling, Sauvignon and Shiraz. **Best producers:** Austin's★, BANNOCKBURN★, By FARR★★, Lethbridge★, Scotchmans Hill★.

GEROVASSILIOU *Macedonia AO, Greece* Bordeaux-trained Evángelos Gerovassiliou has 40ha (100 acres) of vineyards and a modern winery in Epanomi in northern Greece. High-quality fruit results in Syrah-dominated Gerovassiliou red★ and some fresh, modern whites, including Viognier★, barrel-fermented Chardonnay, Fumé, and the Gerovassiliou★ white, a most original Assyrtiko-Malagousia blend.

GEVREY-CHAMBERTIN AC *Côte de Nuits, Burgundy, France* A new generation of growers has restored the reputation of Gevrey as a source of well-coloured, firmly structured, powerful, perfumed wines that become rich and gamy with age. Village wines should be kept for at least 5 years, Premiers Crus and the 9 Grands Crus for 10 years or more, especially CHAMBERTIN and Clos-de-Bèze. The Premier Cru Clos St-Jacques is worthy of promotion to Grand Cru. **Best producers:** D Bachelet★★, Louis Boillot★, A Burguet★★, B CLAIR★★, P Damoy★★, DROUHIN★, C Dugat★★★, B Dugat-Py★★, S Esmonin★★, FAIVELEY★★, Fourrier★★, Geantet-Pansiot★★, JADOT★★, Denis MORTET★★★, Rossignol-Trapet★★, J Roty★★, ROUSSEAU★★★, Sérafin★★, J & J-L Trapet★★, C Tremblay. **Best years:** (2009) 08 **07** 06 05 **03 02** 01 99 98 96 95 93 90.

GEWÜRZTRAMINER *Gewürz* means spice, and the wine certainly can be spicy and exotically perfumed, as well as being typically low in acidity. It is thought to have originated in the village of Tramin, in Italy's ALTO ADIGE, and the name Traminer is used by many producers. It makes an appearance in many wine-producing countries; quality is mixed and styles vary enormously, from the fresh, light, florally perfumed wines produced in Alto Adige to the rich, luscious, late-harvest ALSACE Vendange Tardive. Best in France's Alsace and also good in Austria's Styria (STEIERMARK), southern Germany, Chile and New Zealand. Improving off a tiny base in South Africa.

GEYSER PEAK *Alexander Valley AVA, Sonoma County, California, USA* Australian winemaker Daryl Groom (now gone) set the tone here. Typical are the fruity SONOMA COUNTY Cabernet★ and Merlot★ – ripe, juicy and delicious upon release. The Reserve Alexandre Meritage★★, a BORDEAUX-style blend, is made for aging, and the Reserve Shiraz★★ has a cult following. Block Collection features limited production, single-vineyard wines. There's also a highly popular Sauvignon Blanc★ (Block Collection★★). **Best years:** (Alexandre) 2005 **02 01 00** 99 98 97 94 91.

GIACONDA *Beechworth, Victoria, Australia* In spite of (or perhaps because of) Giaconda's tiny production, Rick Kinzbrunner is one of Australia's most influential winemakers. Following on from his success, BEECHWORTH has become one of the country's most exciting viticultural regions. His tightly structured, minerally, savoury Chardonnay★★★ is one of Australia's best – as are both the serious and beautiful Pinot Noir★★★ (a Beechworth-YARRA blend) and the deep, gamy, HERMITAGE-style Warner Vineyard Shiraz★★★. The Cabernet★ is ripe, deep and complex. The Aeolia Roussanne and Nantua Les Deux Chardonnay-Roussanne are complex and textural. Look for the new estate vineyard Shiraz and joint venture wines with CHAPOUTIER from the Nantua Vineyard. Best years: (Chardonnay) 2008 07 06 05 **04 02 01 00 99 98 96 93 92**.

BRUNO GIACOSA *Barbaresco DOCG, Piedmont, Italy* One of the great winemakers of the LANGHE hills, indeed of Italy, still basically traditionalist, though he has reduced maturation time for his BARBARESCOS and BAROLOS to a maximum of 4 years. Superb Barbarescos Asili★★★, Santo Stefano★★★ and Rabajà★★★, and Barolos including Rocche de Falletto★★★ and Falletto★★. Excellent BARBERA D'ALBA★, Dolcetto d'Alba★, ROERO Arneis★, MOSCATO D'ASTI★★ and sparkling Extra Brut★★. Giacosa suffered a stroke in 2006 but he is back in business, having sold his 2006s in bulk, even though others consider 06 a great year.

GIGONDAS AC *Rhône Valley, France* Gigondas red wines are mainly Grenache, plus Syrah. They offer big, southern flavours and good value; most drink well with 5 years' age, but will happily age for much longer. Best producers: P Amadieu★★, la Bouïssière★★, Brusset★★, Cassan★★, Cayron★, Clos des Cazaux★★, Clos du Joncuas★, Cros de la Mûre★★, DELAS★, Espiers★★, Font-Sane★, la Fourmone★, les Goubert★, Gour de Chaulé★, Grand Bourjassot, Grapillon d'Or★★, JABOULET, Longue-Toque★, Montvac★★, Moulin de la Gardette★★, les Pallières★★, Perrin & Fils★, Pesquier★, Piaugier★, Raspail-Ay★★, Redortier★, Roubine★, St-Cosme★★, ST-GAYAN★, Santa Duc★★, Tardieu-Laurent★★, la Tourade★, Tourelles★★, Trignon★. Best years: 2009 08 **07 06 05 04 03 01 00 99 98 95 90**.

CH. GILETTE★★ *Sauternes AC, Bordeaux, France* These astonishing wines are stored in concrete vats as opposed to the more normal wooden barrels. This virtually precludes any oxygen contact, and it is oxygen that ages wine. Consequently, when released at up to 20 years old, they are bursting with life and lusciousness. Best years: **1988 86 85 83 82 81 79 78 76 75 70 67 61 59 55 53 49**.

GIPPSLAND *Victoria, Australia* Diverse wineries along the southern VICTORIA coast, all tiny but with massive potential. Results are erratic, occasionally brilliant. Nicholson River's exotic, hedonistic Chardonnay sometimes hits ★★, Shiraz can be ★★★. Bass Phillip Pinot Noirs, especially Reserve★★ and Premium★★, are among the best in Australia, with a cult following. McAlister★ is a tasty red BORDEAUX blend. Best producers: Bass Phillip★★★, William Downie★, McAlister★, Nicholson River★★.

VINCENT GIRARDIN *Santenay, Côte de Beaune, Burgundy, France* A grower in SANTENAY who developed a thriving *négociant* business in MEURSAULT, but is now concentrating on a significantly enhanced domaine, specializing in whites from CHASSAGNE (Cailleret★★) and PULIGNY★★. Good reds too: Santenay Gravières★★. Best years: (whites) (2009) 08 07 **06 05 04 02**.

GISBORNE *North Island, New Zealand* Gisborne, with its hot, humid climate and fertile soils, delivers both quality and quantity. Christened (by local growers) 'The Chardonnay Capital of New Zealand', although the focus is rapidly shifting to Pinot Gris, while Gewürztraminer and Chenin Blanc are also a success. Good reds, however, are hard to find. **Best producers:** MILLTON★★, MONTANA, Vinoptima★★. **Best years:** (Chardonnay) (2009) **07 05 04**.

GIVRY AC *Côte Chalonnaise, Burgundy, France* Important CÔTE CHALONNAISE village. The reds have an intensity of fruit and ability to age that are unusual in the region. There are some attractive, fairly full, nutty whites, too. **Best producers:** Bourgeon★, Chofflet-Valdenaire★, B CLAIR★, Clos Salomon★, Joblot★★, F Lumpp★★, Ragot★, Sarrazin★. **Best years:** (reds) (2009) 08 **07 05 03 02 99**; (whites) (2009) **08 07 06 05**.

GLAETZER *Barossa Valley, South Australia* Colin Glaetzer has been one of the BAROSSA VALLEY's most enthusiastic and successful winemakers for decades. He made his reputation working for other people, and now he and his son Ben make tip-top Barossa wines for the family label. There is fleshy Wallace Shiraz-Grenache★, rich, superripe Bishop Shiraz★★ (from 30–60-year-old vines), the amazingly opulent, succulent and velvety Amon-Ra Shiraz★★ and Anaperenna★★ (formerly Godolphin), a deep, dense Shiraz-Cabernet blend. Ben also makes reds and whites for the Heartland label using fruit from vineyards in Langhorne Creek and LIMESTONE COAST, but recent releases have lost their initial zip. **Best years:** (Bishop Shiraz) (2008) 06 **05 04 02 01 99 98 96**.

GLEN CARLOU *Paarl WO, South Africa* Started by the Finlaysons in the 1980s and now owned by Donald HESS. Elegant standard Chardonnay★ and restrained single-vineyard Quartz Stone Chardonnay★★ lead the whites. Reds, with rather more New World panache, feature sweet-textured Pinot Noir★; deep, dry Syrah★; Grand Classique★, a red BORDEAUX blend with excellent aging potential; and concentrated Gravel Quarry Cabernet★. **Best years:** (Chardonnay) 2009 **08 07 06 05 04 03 02**.

CH. GLORIA★ *St-Julien AC, Haut-Médoc, Bordeaux, France* An interesting property, created out of tiny plots of Classed Growth land scattered all round ST-JULIEN. Generally very soft and sweet-centred, the wine nonetheless ages well. Same owner as Ch. ST-PIERRE. Second wine: Peymartin. **Best years:** 2008 **07** 06 05 **04 03 01 00 99 98 95 90**.

GONZÁLEZ BYASS *Jerez y Manzanilla DO, Andalucía, Spain* Tio Pepe★ fino is the world's biggest-selling sherry. The old sherries are superb: intense, dry Amontillado del Duque★★★; rich, complex sweet Oloroso Matusalem★★ and Palo Cortado Apóstoles★★; treacly Noé Pedro Ximénez★★★. One step down is the Alfonso Dry Oloroso★. The firm pioneered the rediscovery of single-vintage (non-solera) dry olorosos★★ and palos cortados★★.

GOSSET *Champagne AC, Champagne, France* Gosset, the oldest wine producer in CHAMPAGNE, based in the Grand Cru of Aÿ, makes fairly austere wines that need extra aging to show at their best. The top wine, Celebris★★, is a class act, also produced in rosé★★ and Blanc de Blancs★★ styles. **Best years:** (2003) (02) 00 99 **98 96 95 90**.

HENRI GOUGES *Nuits-St-Georges, Côte de Nuits, Burgundy, France* The original Henri Gouges was mayor of NUITS-ST-GEORGES in the 1930s and was instrumental in classifying the large number of Premiers Crus in his appellation. Today, the domaine is back on form, producing impressive, meaty, long-lived reds (Les St Georges★★★, Clos des Porrets★★, Les Vaucrains★★) as well as excellent white Nuits-St-Georges Premier Cru La Perrière★★. **Best years:** (2009) 08 07 06 05 **02 01** 99 **98** 96 90.

GRAACH *Mosel, Germany* Important Middle MOSEL wine village with 4 vineyard sites, the most famous being Domprobst (also the best) and Himmelreich. A third, the Josephshöfer, is wholly owned by the von KESSELSTATT estate. The wines have an attractive fullness to balance their steely acidity, and great aging potential. Best producers: Kees-Kieren★, von KESSELSTATT, Markus MOLITOR★★, J J PRUM★★, S A PRUM★, Max Ferd RICHTER★★ Willi SCHAEFER★★★, SELBACH-OSTER★★, Dr Weins-Prüm★. Best years: (2009) 08 07 **06 05 04 03 02 01 00 99 98 97**.

GRACIANO Rare, low-yielding but excellent Spanish grape, traditional in RIOJA, NAVARRA and Extremadura. It makes dense, highly structured, fragrant reds, and its high acidity adds life when blended with low-acid Tempranillo. In Portugal it is called Tinta Miúda. Also grown by BROWN BROTHERS and others in Australia.

GRAHAM *Port DOC, Douro, Portugal* Part of the Symington empire, making rich, florally scented Vintage Port★★★, sweeter than DOW's and WARRE's but with the backbone to age. In non-declared years makes a fine vintage wine called Malvedos★★. Six Grapes★ is one of the best premium rubies, and Crusted★★ and 10-year-old★ and 20-year-old★★ tawnies are consistently good. Best years: (Vintage) 2007 **03 00 97 94 91 85 83 80 77 75 70 66 63 60**; (Malvedos) 2005 01 99 98 **95 92 90**.

ALAIN GRAILLOT *Crozes-Hermitage AC, Rhône Valley, France* Excellent family estate producing concentrated, rich, fruity reds. The top wine is CROZES-HERMITAGE la Guiraude★★, but the regular Crozes-Hermitage★★ is wonderful too, and great for early drinking, as are the ST-JOSEPH★★ and a fragrant white Crozes-Hermitage★. Keep top reds for at least 5 years. Son Max has promising Dom. des Lises estate and Equis brand (also CORNAS, ST-JOSEPH). Best years: (la Guiraude) 2009 **07 06 05 04 03 01 00 99 95**.

GRAMPIANS AND PYRENEES *Victoria, Australia* Two adjacent cool-climate regions in central western VICTORIA, producing some of Australia's most characterful Shiraz, distinguished Riesling, subtle Pinot Gris and savoury Chardonnay. Best producers: BEST'S★, Blue Pyrenees, Dalwhinnie★★, MOUNT LANGI GHIRAN★★, Redbank★, SEPPELT★★, The Story★★, Summerfield★ Taltarni★. Best years: (Shiraz) 2009 07 06 05 04 03 **02 01 99 98 97 96 94 91 90**.

CH. GRAND-PUY-DUCASSE★ *Pauillac AC, 5ème Cru Classé, Haut-Médoc, Bordeaux, France* After great improvement in the 1980s, form dipped in the early 90s but recovered again after 95. Approachable after 5 years, but the best vintages can improve for considerably longer. Second wine: Artigues-Arnaud. Best years: 2008 07 06 05 **04 03 02 00 96 95 90 89**.

CH. GRAND-PUY-LACOSTE★ *Pauillac AC, 5ème Cru Classé, Haut-Médoc, Bordeaux, France* Classic PAUILLAC, with lots of blackcurrant and cigar-box perfume. It begins fairly dense, but as the wine develops, the flavours mingle with the sweetness of new oak to become one of Pauillac's most memorable taste sensations. Second wine: Lacoste-Borie. Best years: 2008 07 06 05 **04 03 02 01 00 99 98 96 95 94 90 89 88 86 85**.

GRANDS-ÉCHÉZEAUX AC See ÉCHÉZEAUX AC.

GRANGE★★★ *Barossa Valley, South Australia* In 1950, Max Schubert, chief winemaker at PENFOLDS, visited Europe and came back determined to make a wine that could match the great BORDEAUX reds. Undeterred by lack of Cabernet Sauvignon grapes and French oak barrels, he set to work with BAROSSA Shiraz and barrels made from the more pungent American oak. Initially ignored and misunderstood, Schubert eventually achieved global recognition for his wine, a stupendously complex, thrillingly rich red that only begins to reveal its magnificence after 10 years in bottle – but is even better after 20. Best years: (2008) (06) 05 04 02 01 99 98 **96 94 92 91 90 88 86 84 83 76 71 66 62 53**.

DOM. DE LA GRANGE DES PÈRES *Vin de Pays de l'Hérault, Languedoc, France* With only 500 cases produced each year, demand is high for the meticulously crafted unfiltered red★★, a blend of Syrah, Mourvèdre and Cabernet Sauvignon. The white★★, based on Roussanne, with Marsanne and Chardonnay, is produced in even smaller quantities. Best years: (red) 2008 07 06 05 04 03 **02 01 00 99 98**.

GRANGEHURST *Stellenbosch WO, South Africa* Boutique winery known for modern Pinotage★, Cabernet-Merlot★★ with Bordeaux-ish appeal and Nikela★, a blend of all three varieties with Shiraz and owner/winemaker Jeremy Walker's answer to the Cape blend. More recent additions to the range include two Cabernets (Reserve★) and Shiraz-Cabernet Reserve★. Best years: (Cabernet-Merlot) **2004 03 02 01 00 99 98**.

GRANS-FASSIAN *Leiwen, Mosel, Germany* LEIWEN owed its reputation initially to Gerhard Grans. Both sweet and dry Rieslings have gained in sophistication over the years: Spätlese★★ and Auslese★★ from TRITTENHEIMer Apotheke are particularly impressive. Eiswein is ★★★ in good vintages. Best years: (2009) 08 07 06 **05 04 03 02 01 99**.

ALFRED GRATIEN *Champagne AC, Champagne, France* This small company makes some of my favourite CHAMPAGNE. Its wines are made in wooden casks, which is very rare nowadays. The non-vintage★★ blend is usually 4 years old when sold, rather than the normal 3 years, and can age further. The vintage★★★ is deliciously ripe and toasty when released but can age for another 10 years. The prestige cuvée, Cuvée Paradis★★, is non-vintage. Best years: 1999 98 **97 96 95 91 90 89 88 85 83**.

GRAVES **AC** *Bordeaux, France* The Graves region covers the area south of the city of Bordeaux to Langon, but the villages in the northern half broke away in 1987 to form the PESSAC-LEOGNAN AC. In the southern Graves, a new wave of winemaking has produced plenty of clean, bone-dry white wines with lots of snappy freshness, as well as more complex

PRODUCE OF FRANCE

CLOS FLORIDENE

GRAVES

2008

DENIS & FLORENCE DUBOURDIEU
MIS EN BOUTEILLE A LA PROPRIÉTÉ

soft, nutty barrel-aged whites, and some juicy, quick-drinking reds. Sweet white wines take the Graves Supérieures AC; the best make a decent substitute for the more expensive SAUTERNES. Best producers: Archambeau★, Ardennes★, Brondelle★, Chantegrive★, Clos Floridène★★, Crabitey★, l'Hospital, Léhoul★, Magence, Magneau★, Rahoul, Respide (Callipyge★), Respide-Médeville★, St-Robert (cuvée Poncet Deville★), Seuil, Venus, Vieux-Ch.-Gaubert★, Villa Bel-Air★; (sweet) Brondelle, Léhoul. Best years: (reds) (2009) 08 05 04 01 00 98 96 95; (dry whites) (2009) 08 07 06 05 04 02 01 00 98.

GRAVNER *Friuli-Venezia Giulia, Italy* Josko Gravner, FRIULI's most zealous winemaker, sets styles with his wood-aged, oxidative whites which people either love or hate. Along with high-priced Chardonnay★★, Sauvignon★★ and Ribolla Gialla★, he combines several white varieties in Breg★★. Reds are Rosso Gravner★ (predominantly Merlot) and Rujno★★ (Merlot-Cabernet Sauvignon).

GREAT SOUTHERN *Western Australia* A vast, cool-climate regio encompassing the sub-regions of Frankland River, Denmark, Mour Barker, Albany and Porongurup. Frankland River is particularl successful with Riesling, Shiraz and Cabernet; Denmark wit Chardonnay and Pinot Noir; Mount Barker with Riesling and Shira Albany with Pinot Noir; Porongurup with Riesling. Plantings hav boomed in recent years, especially in Frankland River. Best producer Alkoomi, Castle Rock★, CHERUBINO★★, FERNGROVE★, Forest Hill★★ Frankland Estate★, Gilberts★, Goundrey★★, HAREWOOD★★, HOUGHTON★★ HOWARD PARK★★, PLANTAGENET★★, West Cape Howe★, Wignalls★.

GRECHETTO Italian grape centred on UMBRIA, the main component o ORVIETO DOC, also making tasty, anise-tinged dry white varietal Occasionally used in VIN SANTO in TUSCANY. Best producers: Antonell Barberani-Vallesanta★, Caprai★, FALESCO★, Palazzone, Castello della SALA.

PATRICIA GREEN CELLARS *Willamette Valley, Oregon, USA* Patty Gree and Jim Anderson's goal is to produce wines that reflect the specifi *terroirs* of the Willamette Valley. As many as 15 or 16 different bottling of Pinot Noir are produced each vintage from vineyards in Ribbo Ridge, the Dundee Hills, the Chehalem Mountains and the Eola Hills highlights include Croft Vineyard★★, Eason Vineyard★, Balcomb Vineyard★, Notorious★★ and Pinot Noir Reserve★. Fine Sauvigno Blanc★ and a CHABLIS-like Chardonnay are worth seeking out. Best year (Pinot Noir) (2008) 07 **06 04 02**.

GRENACHE BLANC A common white grape in the south of France, bu without many admirers. Except me, that is, because I love the pear scented wine flecked with anise that a good producer can achieve. Low yield examples take surprisingly well to oak. Generally best within a yea of the vintage, although the odd old-vine example can age impressivel Grown as Garnacha Blanca in Spain, where it's now producing som stunning examples in PRIORAT. A few old vines are contributing to som interesting wines in South Africa.

GRENACHE NOIR Among the world's most widely planted red grapes the bulk of it in Spain, where it is called Garnacha Tinta. It is a hot climate grape and in France it reaches its peak in the southern RHÔNE especially in CHÂTEAUNEUF-DU-PAPE, where it combines great alcoholi strength with rich yet refined raspberry fruit and a perfume hot from th herb-strewn hills. It is generally given more tannin, acid and structure b blending with Syrah, Mourvèdre, Cinsaut or other southern Frenc grapes. With Cinsaut, it can make wonderful rosé in TAVEL, LIRAC an CÔTES DE PROVENCE, as well as in NAVARRA in Spain. It makes lovely juic reds and pinks in Aragón's CALATAYUD, CAMPO DE BORJA and CARIÑENA, an forms the backbone of the impressive reds of PRIORAT; in RIOJA it add weight to the Tempranillo. It is also the basis for the *vins doux naturels* o BANYULS and MAURY in southern France. Also grown in CALIFORNIA an SOUTH AUSTRALIA, where it is finally being accorded respect as imaginativ winemakers realize there is a great resource of century-old vines capabl of making wild and massively enjoyable reds, either alone or with Syra and/or Mourvèdre. More is being planted in South Africa, where it is popular component in Rhône-style wines. See also CANNONAU.

GRGICH HILLS ESTATE *Rutherford AVA, California, USA* Mike Grgich makes classic NAPA VALLEY and CARNEROS Chardonnay★★, which can age for at least a decade, as well as ripe, rich Cabernet★, plummy Merlot★ and a huge, old-style Zinfandel★. Best years: (Chardonnay) 2007 06 **05 04 03 02 01 00**.

GRIOTTE-CHAMBERTIN AC See CHAMBERTIN AC.

JEAN GRIVOT *Vosne-Romanée, Côte de Nuits, Burgundy, France* Étienne Grivot settled into a successful stride from 1995 and has raised his game from 2004 with increasingly ripe yet always fine and complex wines from a host of VOSNE-ROMANÉE Premiers Crus (Beaumonts★★★) as well as brilliant CLOS DE VOUGEOT★★★ and RICHEBOURG★★★. Best years: (2009) 08 07 **06** 05 04 03 02 **01** 99 98 96 95.

GROS *Côte de Nuits, Burgundy, France* Brilliant CÔTE DE NUITS wines from various members of the family, especially Anne Gros, Michel Gros, Gros Frère et Soeur and Anne-Françoise Gros. Look out for CLOS DE VOUGEOT★★★, ÉCHÉZEAUX★★★ and RICHEBOURG★★★ as well as good-value HAUTES-CÔTES DE NUITS★. Best years: (2009) 08 07 06 05 **03 02** 99 98 96 95 90.

GROS PLANT DU PAYS NANTAIS VDQS *Loire Valley, France* Gros Plant (or Folle Blanche) can be searingly acidic, but the wine is well suited to the seafood guzzled in the region. Look for a *sur lie* bottling and drink the youngest available. Best producers: Brochet, les Coins, l'ECU, la Grange, Saupin.

GROSSET *Clare Valley, South Australia* Jeffrey Grosset is a perfectionist, crafting tiny quantities of hand-made wines. A Riesling specialist, he sources single-vineyard Watervale★★★ and Polish Hill★★★ from his own properties; both are supremely good and age well. Cabernet blend Gaia★★ is smooth and seamless. Also outstanding ADELAIDE HILLS wines: Piccadilly Chardonnay★★★, very fine Pinot Noir★★ and one of Australia's finest, tautest Semillon-Sauvignon★★. Best years: (Riesling) 2009 06 **05** 04 03 02 **01 00** 99 98 97 96 94 93 92 90.

CH. GRUAUD-LAROSE★ *St-Julien AC, 2ème Cru Classé, Haut-Médoc, Bordeaux, France* One of the largest ST-JULIEN estates. Until the 1970s these wines were classic, cedary St-Juliens; since the early 80s, the wines have been darker, richer and coated with new oak, yet inclined to exhibit an unnerving feral quality. Recent vintages have mostly combined considerable power with finesse, despite disappointments in 02 and 03. Consistency hasn't yet been achieved. Second wine: Sarget de Gruaud-Larose. Best years: 2008 07 06 05 **04 01 00** 99 98 96 95 90 89 88.

GRÜNER VELTLINER Austrian grape, also grown in the Czech Republic, Slovakia and Hungary. It is at its best in Austria's KAMPTAL, KREMSTAL and the WACHAU, where the soil and cool climate bring out all the lentilly, white-peppery aromas. Styles vary from light and tart to savoury, mouthfilling yet appetizing wines equalling the best in Europe.

GUELBENZU *Spain* The Guelbenzu name and many of the family's vineyards in NAVARRA and ARAGÓN were bought in October 2009 by a Navarra financial group with a portfolio of other wineries across northern Spain. They will continue to produce Azul★ (Tempranillo-Cabernet-Merlot), Cabernet Sauvignon-based Evo★ and occasional Lautus★; the wines are non-DO and are labelled as Vinos de la Tierra Ribera del Queiles. The Guelbenzu family have launched a new, smaller operation called Bodega del Jardín. Best years: (Evo) 2006 05 **04 03 01**.

GUIGAL *Côte-Rôtie AC, Rhône Valley, France* Marcel Guigal is the mos
internationally famous name in the RHÔNE, producing wines from his ow
big spread of vineyards in CÔTE-RÔTIE under the Ch. d'Ampuis★★ label a
well as Dom. de Bonserine★ (La Garde★★) and the Guigal range fror
some domaine and some purchased grapes. Côte-Rôtie Brune et Blond
is ★★ since 1998. La Mouline, La Turque and La Landonne all rate ★★
in most critics' opinions. Well, I have definitely had profound wines fror
La Landonne and La Mouline, and to my surprise and delight th
considerable new oak aging had not dimmed the Côte-Rôtie beauty an
fragrance. However, Guigal is uniquely talented; lesser producers usin
this amount of new oak rarely manage to save the balance of the wine
CONDRIEU★★ (la Doriane★★★) is wonderfully fragrant. Red and whi
HERMITAGE★★ are also good, ST-JOSEPH★★ improving, as are the top-valu
red, white and rosé CÔTES DU RHÔNE★, chunky GIGONDAS★ and bright, fu
TAVEL rosé. Best years: (top reds) 2009 07 06 05 04 **03** 01 00 99 98 97 95 94 9
90 89 88 85 83 82 78.

CH. GUIRAUD★★ *Sauternes AC, 1er Cru Classé, Bordeaux, France* Since th
1980s this SAUTERNES estate has returned to the top-quality fold. Hig
price reflects the fact that only the best grapes are selected an
fermentation takes place in 100% new oak barrels. New ownership fror
2006. Keep best vintages for 10 years or more. Second wine: Le Dauphi
de Guiraud. Also dry white G de Guiraud. Best years: 2007 06 05 **04** 03 0
01 99 98 97 96 95 90 89 88.

GUNDERLOCH *Nackenheim, Rheinhessen, Germany* Fritz and Agne
Hasselbach's estate has become one of Germany's best. Sensational
concentrated and luscious Beerenauslese★★ and Trocker
beerenauslese★★★ dessert Rieslings are expensive for RHEINHESSEN, bu
worth it. Dry and off-dry Rieslings, at least ★, however, are good value
Late-harvest Spätlese and Auslese are ★★ year in, year out. Best year
(2009) 08 07 **06** 05 04 03 02 01 00 99 98.

GUNDLACH-BUNDSCHU *Sonoma Valley AVA, California, USA* Family-owne
winery, founded in 1858. From the Rhinefarm estate vineyards com
outstanding juicy, fruity Cabernet Sauvignon★★, rich yet tight
structured Merlot★★, Zinfandel★ and Pinot Noir★. Whites includ
Chardonnay★, attractive Riesling and dramatic dry Gewürztraminer★★
The Bundschu family also operates the boutique winery Bartholome
Park, which specializes in Cabernet blends.

FRITZ HAAG *Brauneberg, Mosel, Germany* MOSEL grower with vineyards in th
BRAUNEBERGer Juffer and Juffer Sonnenuhr. Pure, elegant Rieslings at leas
★★ quality, Auslese and above often reaching ★★★. Best years: (2009) 0
07 06 **05** 04 03 02 01 99 98 97.

REINHOLD HAART *Piesport, Mosel, Germany* Theo Haart produces sensa
tional Rieslings – with blackcurrant, peach and citrus aromas – from th
great Piesporter Goldtröpfchen vineyard. Ausleses are often ★★★
Wines from his vineyards in Wintrich can be bargains. Best years: (200
08 07 06 **05** 04 03 02 01 99 98 97.

HAMILTON RUSSELL VINEYARDS *Hemel en Aarde Valley WO, South Afri*
This WALKER BAY property celebrates 30 vintages of Pinot Noir in 201
Pinot Noir★★ is broad-shouldered and delicately scented, whi
Chardonnay★★ returns to its minerally and exciting self after sho
2007. Ashbourne and Southern Right are separate operation
Ashbourne★ is an intriguing Pinotage, Sandstone★ a Sauvignon Blan
based blend with subtle complexity, while Southern Right Sauvigno

Blanc★ is zingy and easy-drinking. **Best years:** (Pinot Noir) (2009) 08 **07 06 05 04 03 02 01 00**; (Chardonnay) 2009 08 **07 06 05 04 03 02 01 00**.

ANDLEY *Mendocino County, California, USA* Outstanding producer of sparkling wines, including one of California's best Brut Rosés★. Aromatic Gewürztraminer★★ and Riesling★★ are among the state's finest. Two bottlings of Chardonnay, from the DRY CREEK VALLEY★ and ANDERSON VALLEY★, are worth seeking out. The Anderson Valley estate Pinot Noirs (regular★, Reserve★★) are in a lighter, more subtle style. Syrah★ is excellent. **Best years:** (Pinot Noir Reserve) (2005) 04 **03 01 00 99**.

ANGING ROCK *Macedon Ranges, Victoria, Australia* Highly individual, gutsy sparkling wine Macedon Cuvée XII★★ (stunning late-disgorged Cuvée★★) stands out at John and Ann (née TYRRELL) Ellis's ultra-cool-climate vineyard high in the Macedon Ranges. Tangy estate-grown 'The Jim Jim' Sauvignon Blanc★★ is mouthwatering stuff, while HEATHCOTE Shiraz★★ is the best red.

ARAS DE PIRQUE *Maipo, Chile* Located in Pirque, a sub-region of MAIPO in the foothills of the Andes, this winery started production in 2002 and soon became an important player. Elegance★★, a dense and spicy Cabernet Sauvignon, leads the portfolio; Character★★, another Cabernet, is equally impressive, and more approachable. Savoury Cabernet-Carmenère blend Albis is a joint venture with Italy's ANTINORI.

ARDYS *McLaren Vale, South Australia* Despite the takeover of BRL Hardy by American giant Constellation, wines under the Hardys flagship label so far still taste reassuringly Australian. Varietals (especially Shiraz and Grenache) under the Nottage Hill label are among Australia's more reliable gluggers. Top of the tree are the Eileen Hardy Shiraz★★★ and Thomas Hardy Cabernet★★★, both dense reds for hedonists. Eileen Hardy Chardonnay★★ is more elegant, tightly structured and focused than it used to be. **Best years:** (Eileen Hardy Shiraz) (2008) (06) 05 04 03 02 **01 00 98 97 96 95 93**.

AREWOOD *Great Southern, Western Australia* James Kellie made a name for himself producing white wine for HOWARD PARK before his family purchased and revived one of Denmark's finest vineyards, Harewood Estate. His portfolio now shows evidence of Kellie's skill and knowledge of the GREAT SOUTHERN, especially with powerful Cabernet Sauvignon★, gutsy yet silky smooth Frankland River Shiraz★, intense, zesty Riesling★★, tangy Sauvignon-Semillon and elegant single-vineyard Denmark Chardonnay★★.

ARLAN ESTATE *Oakville AVA, California, USA* Estate in the western hills of OAKVILLE, whose BORDEAUX blend has become one of California's most sought-after reds. Full-bodied and robustly tannic, Harlan Estate★★★ offers layers of ripe black fruits and heaps of new French oak. Dense but thrilling upon release, the wine is built to develop for 10 years.

ARTENBERG ESTATE *Stellenbosch WO, South Africa* Shiraz is the prime performer at this Bottelary Hills winery. Regular Shiraz★ is fleshy and accessible, while The Stork★ and single-vineyard Gravel Hill★★ reflect the soils they grow in. Merlot★ and Cabernet also perform well, but The Mackenzie Cabernet-Merlot blend★ tops both. Whites include a pair of Chardonnays (standard, and refined, complex The Eleanor★) and an off-dry, limy Riesling★. **Best years:** (premium reds) 2007 **06 05 04 03 02 01 00**.

HARTFORD FAMILY *Russian River Valley AVA, California, USA* Chardonnays a
Pinot Noirs from RUSSIAN RIVER and SONOMA COAST bear the Hartford Cou
label; most have textbook cool-climate intensity and acidity. Pinot Noi
include massive Arrendell Vineyard★★★, Land's Edge★★★, F
Dance★★★, Far Coast★★, Seascape★★; Chardonnays include Fo
Hearts★, Stone Côte★, Seascape★★. Hartford label old-vine Zinfande
include Russian River Valley★, Fanucchi-Wood Road★★ a
Highwire★. Owned by Jackson Family Wines.

HARTWELL *Stags Leap District AVA, Napa Valley, California, USA* Wine collect
Bob Hartwell has been producing a gloriously fruity and elega
Cabernet Sauvignon★★ from his small vineyard in the STAGS LEAP DISTRI
since 1993. Recently, an equally supple Merlot★★ and lower-pric
Misté Hill Cabernet Sauvignon★. Best years: (Cabernet Sauvignon) 2005
02 **01 00 99 98 97 96 94**.

HATTENHEIM *Rheingau, Germany* RHEINGAU village with 13 vineyard site
including a share of the famous Marcobrunn vineyard. Best produce
Barth★, Lang, Langwerth von Simmern★, Ress, SCHLOSS REINHARTSHAUSEN★
Schloss Schönborn★★. Best years: (2009) 08 07 **06 05 04 03 02 01**.

CH. HAUT-BAGES-LIBÉRAL★ *Pauillac AC, 5ème Cru Classé, Haut-Méd*
Bordeaux, France Little-known PAUILLAC property that has quietly bee
gathering plaudits for some years now: loads of unbridled delicious fru
a positively hedonistic style – and its lack of renown keeps the price ju
about reasonable. The wines will age well, especially the latest vintage
Best years: 2008 07 06 05 **04 03 02 01 00 99 98 96 95 90 89**.

CH. HAUT-BAILLY★ *Pessac-Léognan AC, Cru Classé de Graves, Bordeaux, Fran*
Traditionally one of the softest and most charming of the PESSAC-LÉOGNA
Classed Growths, and on good form during the 1990s. New ownership
from 1998 initially produced erratic returns, some wines being too toug
some being almost milky soft, some being delicious, but there's been
good run since 2004. Drinkable early, but ages well. Second wine:
Parde-de-Haut-Bailly. Best years: 2008 07 06 05 **04 02 01 00 98 96 95 9
89 88 86**.

CH. HAUT-BATAILLEY★ *Pauillac AC, 5ème Cru Classé, Haut-Médoc, Bordea*
France This estate has produced too many wines that are ligh
attractively spicy, but rarely memorable. Owner François-Xavier Borie
GRAND-PUY-LACOSTE is changing this and from 2004 the wines have show
improvement, becoming distinctly more substantial. Best years: 2008 07
05 **04 03 02 01 00 98 96 95**.

CH. HAUT-BRION *Pessac-Léognan AC, 1er Cru Classé, Graves, Fran*
This property's excellent gravel-based vineyard is now part of Bordeaux
suburbs. The red wine★★★ is one of Bordeaux's most subtle, with
magical ability to age. There is a small amount of white★★★ which, at i
best, is memorably rich yet marvellously dry, blossoming over 5–10 yea
Second wine: (red) le Clarence de Haut-Brion (from 2007); previous
Bahans-Haut-Brion. Best years: (red) 2008 07 06 05 **04 03 02 01 00 99
97 96 95 90 89 88**; (white) 2008 07 **06 05 04 03 02 01 00 98 96 95**.

CH. HAUT-MARBUZET★★ *St-Estèphe AC, Haut-Médoc, Bordeaux, Fran*
Impressive ST-ESTÈPHE wine worthy of classification with great, ric
mouthfilling blasts of flavour and lots of new oak. Best years: 2008 06
04 03 02 01 00 99 98 96 95 90 89 88.

HAUT-MÉDOC AC *Bordeaux, France* The finest gravelly soil is here in t
southern half of the MEDOC peninsula; this AC covers all the dece
vineyard land not included in the 6 village ACs (MARGAUX, MOULIS, LISTRA

ST-JULIEN, PAUILLAC and ST-ESTÈPHE). Wines vary in quality and style. Best producers: d'Agassac★, Belgrave★, Belle-Vue★, Bernadotte★, Cambon la Pelouse★, Camensac, CANTEMERLE★, Charmail★, Cissac★, Citran★, Coufran, la LAGUNE★, Lanessan★, Malescasse★, Maucamps★, Peyrabon★, Sénéjac★, SOCIANDO-MALLET★★, la Tour-Carnet★, Tour-du-Haut-Moulin★, Villegeorge. Best years: (2009) 08 06 **05 04 03 02 01 00** 96 95 90 89 88 86 85.

AUTES-CÔTES DE BEAUNE AC See BOURGOGNE-HAUTES-CÔTES DE BEAUNE AC.
AUTES-CÔTES DE NUITS AC See BOURGOGNE-HAUTES-CÔTES DE NUITS AC.

AWKES BAY *North Island, New Zealand* New Zealand's second largest and ne of its most prestigious wine regions. Plenty of sunshine, moderately edictable weather during ripening and a complex array of soils make it ideal r a range of wine styles. Traditionally known for Cabernet Sauvignon and, rticularly, Merlot, it has recently produced some superb Syrahs. Whites can very good too, especially Chardonnay. Free-draining Gimblett Gravels is e outstanding area, followed by the Red Metal Triangle (formerly the gatarawa Triangle). Best producers: Alpha Domus★, Bilancia★, CHURCH ROAD★, earview★, COOPERS CREEK★, CRAGGY RANGE★★, Esk Valley★★★, Matariki★, ATUA VALLEY★, Mission, MORTON ESTATE★, Newton Forrest★ (Cornerstone★★★), GATARAWA★, Parituta★, C J PASK★, Sacred Hill★★, Stonecroft★, Te Awa★, MATA★★, TRINITY HILL★★, Unison★★, Vidal★★, VILLA MARIA★★. Best years: emium reds) (2009) 08 **07** 06 04 02.

EATHCOTE *Central Victoria, Australia* This wine region's unique feature is the deep russet Cambrian soil, formed more than 600 million years ago, which is found on the best sites and is proving ideal for Shiraz. BROWN BROTHERS and TYRRELL'S (Rufus Stone★★ is outstanding) have extensive new plantings. Best producers: BROWN BROTHERS★, Greenstone, Heathcote Estate★★, Heathcote Winery★★, Jasper Hill★★★, Red Edge★, Sanguine★★, Shelmerdine, TYRRELL'S★, Wild Duck Creek★. Best years: (Shiraz) 2009 08 06 05 04 03 **02 01 00** 97 96 95 94 91 90.

ECHT & BANNIER *Languedoc, France* An exciting partnership of two Dijon wine marketing graduates, Gregory Hecht and François Bannier. They are selecting and aging some rich, finely crafted wines from FAUGÈRES★, ST-CHINIAN★, MINERVOIS★ and CÔTES DU ROUSSILLON-VILLAGES★.

EDGES FAMILY ESTATE *Columbia Valley AVA, Washington State, USA* Top wines here are Cabernet-Merlot blends using fruit from prime Red Mountain AVA vineyards: Three Vineyards★ is powerful and ageworthy, with bold tannins but plenty of cassis fruit; Red Mountain Reserve★ shows more polish and elegance. Red CMS★ (Cabernet-Merlot-Syrah) and crisp white CMS (Chardonnay-Marsanne-Sauvignon) form the bulk of the production. Best years: (top reds) (2008) 07 06 05 **04 03 02**.

R HEGER *Ihringen, Baden, Germany* Joachim Heger specializes in powerful, dry Weissburgunder (Pinot Blanc)★ and Spätburgunder (Pinot Noir)★, with Riesling a sideline in this warm climate. Winklerberg Grauburgunder★★ is serious stuff, while his ancient Yellow Muscat vines deliver powerful dry wines★ and rare but fabulous TBAs★★. Wines from rented vineyards are sold under the Weinhaus Joachim Heger label. Best years: (white) (2009) 08 07 **05 04 03 02 01**.

HARLES HEIDSIECK *Champagne AC, Champagne, France* Charles Heidsieck, owned by Rémy Cointreau, is the most consistently fine of all the major houses, with vintage★★★ Champagne declared only in the very best

years. The non-vintage★★ is regularly of vintage quality; these age we
for at least 5 years. Best years: 2000 **96 95 90 89 88 85 82.**

HEITZ CELLAR *Napa Valley AVA, California, USA* Star attraction here is t
Martha's Vineyard Cabernet Sauvignon★★. Many believe that ear
bottlings of Martha's Vineyard are among the best wines ever produce
in CALIFORNIA. After 1992, phylloxera forced replanting; although bottli
only resumed in 1996, the 1997 vintage was exceptional and set the tot
for the modern era. Heitz also produces Trailside Vineyard Cabernet
Bella Oaks Vineyard Cabernet★ and a NAPA Cabernet★ that takes time
understand but can be good. Dry Grignolino Rosé is an attractive picn
curiosity. Best years: (Martha's Vineyard) 2005 04 03 02 **97 96 92 91 86 8**

HENRIOT *Champagne AC, Champagne, France* In 1994 Joseph Henriot boug
back the name of his old-established family company. Henri
CHAMPAGNES have a limpid clarity, and no Pinot Meunier is used. T
range includes non-vintage Brut Souverain★, Blanc Souverain★ ar
Rosé Brut★; vintage Brut★★ and Rosé; and de luxe Cuvée de
Enchanteleurs★★. Best years: **2000 98 96 95 90 89 88 85.**

HENRIQUES & HENRIQUES *Madeira DOC, Madeira, Portugal* The wines
look for are the 10-year-old★★ and 15-year-old★★ versions of t
classic varieties. Vibrant Sercial and Verdelho, and rich Malmsey ar
Bual are all fine examples of their styles. Henriques & Henriques also h
vintage Madeiras★★★ of extraordinary quality.

HENRY OF PELHAM *Niagara Peninsula VQA, Ontario, Canada* A pioneer
vinifera wines in the Niagara Peninsula. Best are Riesling Icewine
Speck Family Reserve Riesling★, Chardonnay★ and Cabernet-Merlo

HENSCHKE *Eden Valley, South Australia* Fifth-generation winemaker Stephe
Henschke and his viticulturist wife Prue make some of Australia
grandest reds from old vines: HILL OF GRACE★★★ is stunning. Mou
Edelstone Shiraz★★★, Tappa Pass Shiraz★★, Cyril Hensch
Cabernet★★, Johann's Garden Grenache★, and Shiraz blends Henry
Seven★ and Keyneton Estate★ are also top wines. The whites have lift
in recent years, led by the seductive, perfumed Julius Riesling★★ ar
toasty yet fruity Louis Semillon★★. ADELAIDE HILLS plantings at Lenswo
yield waxy, toasty Croft Chardonnay★, scented Giles Pinot Noir★★ ar
impressive Abbotts Prayer Merlot-Cabernet★★. Best years: (Mou
Edelstone) (2008) (07) 06 05 04 02 **01 99 96 94 92 91 90 88 86.**

HÉRAULT, VIN DE PAYS DE L' *Languedoc, France* A huge region, coverir
the entire Hérault *département*. Red wines predominate, based c
Carignan, Grenache and Cinsaut, and most of the wine is sold in bul
But things are changing. There are lots of hilly vineyards with gre
potential, and MAS DE DAUMAS GASSAC followed by GRANGE DES PÈRES ar
Gérard Depardieu's Référence are making waves internationally. Whit
are improving, too. The better-known OC is often used in preference
Hérault. Best producers: Capion★, GRANGE DES PÈRES★★, Marfée, M
Conscience, MAS DE DAUMAS GASSAC★, Poujol.

HERMITAGE AC *Rhône Valley, France* Great Hermitage, from a steep, oft
granite, vineyard above the town of Tain l'Hermitage in the norther
RHÔNE, is revered throughout the world as a rare, rich red wine
expensive, memorable and classic. Not all Hermitage achieves such a
exciting blend of flavours, but the best growers, with mature red Syra
vines, can create superbly original wine, needing 5–10 years' aging eve
in a light year and a minimum of 15 years in a ripe vintage. Whi
Hermitage, from Marsanne and Roussanne, is less famous but the bes

wonderfully rich wines, made by traditionalists, can outlive the reds, sometimes lasting as long as 40 years. Best producers: A Belle★, CHAPOUTIER★★, J-L CHAVE★★★, Y Chave★, Colombier★, COLOMBO★, DELAS★★, B Faurie★★, Fayolle Fils & Fille★, Ferraton★, GUIGAL★★, Paul JABOULET, Nicolas-Perrin, Remizières★, J-M Sorrel★, M Sorrel★★, TAIN co-op★, Tardieu-Laurent★★, les Vins de Vienne★★. Best years: (reds) 2009 07 06 05 04 **03 01 00 99 98 97 96 95 94 91 90 89 88 85 83 78**.

HE HESS COLLECTION *Mount Veeder AVA, California, USA* Known for powerful MOUNT VEEDER Cabernet Sauvignon★ – but after a change in winemaking direction, recent vintages lack polish and balance; Mount Veeder Mountain Cuvée★ is better. Hess Estate Cabernet★ is good value. Chardonnay★ is ripe with tropical fruit and balanced oak. Vineyard-designated NAPA Chardonnay★ and Cabernet★ can be good. Budget label: Hess Select. Best years: (Cabernet) 2005 03 **01 00 99 98 97 96 95 94 91 90**.

ESSISCHE BERGSTRASSE *Germany* A small (436ha/1080-acre), warm gion near Darmstadt. Lovely Eiswein★★ is made by the Staatsweingut. mon-Bürkle★ is reliable too. Riesling is still the most prized grape.

EYMANN-LÖWENSTEIN *Winningen, Mosel, Germany* A leading estate in WINNINGEN in the Lower MOSEL. Its dry Rieslings are unusually full-bodied for the region; those from the Röttgen and Uhlen sites often reach ★★. Also powerful Auslese★★. Best years: (2009) 08 07 **06 05 04 03 02**.

IDALGO *Jerez y Manzanilla DO, Andalucia, Spain* Hidalgo's Manzanilla La Gitana★★ is deservedly one of the best-selling manzanillas in Spain. Hidalgo is family-owned, and only uses grapes from its own vineyards. Brands include Amontillado Napoleon★★, Jerez Cortado Wellington★★ and rich but dry Oloroso Viejo★★.

ILL OF GRACE★★★ *Eden Valley, South Australia* A stunning wine with dark, exotic flavours made by HENSCHKE from a single plot of Shiraz. The Hill of Grace vineyard was first planted in the 1860s, and the old vines produce a powerful, structured wine with superb ripe fruit, chocolate, coffee, earth, leather and the rest. Can be cellared for 20 years or more. Best years: (2008) (07) (06) (05) 04 02 01 **99 98 97 96 95 94 93 92 91 90 88 86**.

ILLTOP *Neszmély, Hungary* Under chief winemaker Akos Kamocsay, this winery provides fresh, bright wines, especially white, at friendly prices. Indigenous varieties such as Irsai Olivér and Cserszegi Füszeres line up with Gewürztraminer, Sauvignon Blanc★, Pinot Gris and Chardonnay. Hilltop also produces a good but controversial TOKAJI.

ILLTOPS *New South Wales, Australia* Promising high-altitude cherry-growing region with a small but fast-growing area of vineyards around the town of Young. Good potential for reds from Cabernet Sauvignon and Shiraz, plus bright, tangy Riesling. Best producers: Chalkers Crossing★★, Freeman, Grove Estate, MCWILLIAM's/Barwang★, Moppity, Woodonga Hill.

RANZ HIRTZBERGER *Wachau, Niederösterreich, Austria* Highly consistent quality for many years. The finest wines are the concentrated, elegant Smaragd Rieslings from Singerriedel★★★ and Hochrain★★. The best Grüner Veltliner comes from Honivogl★★★. Best years: (Riesling Smaragd) (2009) 08 07 **06 05 04 03 02 01 00 99 98**.

OCHHEIM *Rheingau, Germany* Village best known for having given the English the word 'Hock' for Rhine wine, but it has good individual vineyard sites, especially Domdechaney, Hölle (hell!) and Kirchenstück.

Best producers: Joachim Flick, Franz KUNSTLER★★, W J Schäfer, Werner
Best years: (2009) 08 07 **06 05 04 03 02 01 99**.

HORTON VINEYARDS *Virginia, USA* Horton's Viognier★ establishe
VIRGINIA's potential as a wine region and ignited a rush of wineri
wanting to make the next CONDRIEU. Innovations include a sparklir
Viognier and varietals such as Tannat and Petit Manseng. The Cabern
Franc★ is consistently among the best red wines of the eastern US.

DOM. DE L'HORTUS *Pic St-Loup, Coteaux du Languedoc AC, Languedoc, Fran*
One of PIC ST-LOUP's pioneering estates. Bergerie de l'Hortus★, a read
to-drink unoaked Syrah-Mourvèdre-Grenache blend, has delightf
flavours of herbs, plums and cherries. Big brother Grande Cuvée★
needs time for the fruit and oak to come into harmony. The whi
Grande Cuvée★ is a Chardonnay-Viognier-Roussanne blend. Best year
(Grande Cuvée red) (2009) 08 07 06 **05 04 03 01 00**.

HOSPICES DE BEAUNE *Côte de Beaune, Burgundy, France* Scene of
theatrical auction on the third Sunday in November each year, no
under the auspices of Christie's, the Hospices is an historic foundatic
which sells the wine of the new vintage from its holdings in the CÔTE D'C
to finance its charitable works. Pricing reflects charitable status rath
than common sense, but the auction trend is regarded as an indicator
which way the market is heading. Much depends on the Hospice
winemaking, which has been variable, as well as on the maturation an
bottling which are in the hands of the purchaser of each lot.

CH. L'HOSPITALET *La Clape, Coteaux du Languedoc AC, Languedoc, Fran*
With his purchase of this domaine, Gérard Bertrand entered the b
time in the Languedoc. Best wines are red and white La CLAPE★ and re
and white Vin de Pays d'OC, Cigalus★★. He also has vineyards i
MINERVOIS, CORBIÈRES and LIMOUX. Best years: (2009) 08 07 06 **05 04 03 0**

HOUGHTON *Swan District, Western Australia* WESTERN AUSTRALIA's bigge
winery, owned by Constellation, sources fruit from its own outstandir
vineyards (unbelievably, many of these are currently for sale) and fro
growers in premium regions. The budget-priced 'Stripe' range include
the flavoursome White Classic★ (formerly White Burgundy, or HWB i
the EU), good Sauvignon Blanc-Semillon★, Chardonnay and Cabern
Excellent 'experimental' The Bandit wines: Sauvignon-Pinot Gri
Chardonnay-Viognier and Shiraz-Tempranillo. Moondah Bro
Cabernet Sauvignon★★ and Shiraz★★ are a leap up in quality and eve
better value. The regional range has been rebadged as Wisdom: a GRE
SOUTHERN Riesling★★; Shiraz★★ from Frankland River; a MARGARET RIV
Cabernet★★; and some of the best wines yet seen from the emergir
PEMBERTON region – sublime funky Chardonnay★★, pure, taut Sauvigno
Blanc★★. Opulent, dense yet elegant Gladstones Cabernet★★★ fro
Margaret River and powerful, lush Jack Mann Cabernet Sauvignon★★
from Frankland River have also contributed to Houghton's burgeonir
profile. Look for their latest premium release CW Ferguson Caberne
Malbec. Best years: (Jack Mann) (2009) (08) (07) 05 **04 01 99 98 96 95 9**

HOWARD PARK *Margaret River, Western Australia* Howard Park has i
headquarters, a winery and the Leston vineyard in MARGARET RIVER: in th
GREAT SOUTHERN there is a winery at Denmark and the 41ha (100-acr
Mount Barrow vineyard in Porongurup planted in 2005. The class
Cabernet Sauvignon★★★ (now known as the Abercrombie) has leapt u
a notch in recent vintages. Also impressive are the occasional Be
Barrels Merlot★★, intense, floral Riesling★★ and supremely clas

Chardonnay★★. Highlights of the regional range are the tasty Scotsdale Shiraz★ and elegant Leston Cabernet★★. The more affordable MadFish label is good for Riesling★, Shiraz, Sauvignon-Semillon★ and unwooded Chardonnay★. Exquisite Chardonnay★★, Pinot Noir★★ and Shiraz★, as well as tiny quantities of Burgundies (yes, French Burgundies) under the super-premium Marchand & Burch label. Best years: (Cabernet) (2007) 05 04 **03 02** 01 99 96 94 92 91 90 88 86; (Riesling) 2008 **06 05 04 03** 02 01 97 95 92 91 89.

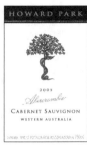

OWELL MOUNTAIN AVA Napa Valley, California, USA NAPA's north-eastern corner is noted for powerhouse Cabernet Sauvignon and Zinfandel as well as exotic, full-flavoured Merlot. **Best producers:** BERINGER (Merlot★★), Cakebread, DUNN★★★, La Jota★★, Ladera★★, Liparita★, O'Shaughnessy★, PINE RIDGE (Cabernet Sauvignon★), Viader★★, White Cottage★★. **Best years:** (reds) 2005 03 **02** 01 00 99 98 97 96 95 94 91 90.

UADONG WINERY Shandong Province, China The first producer of varietal and vintage wines in China, Huadong has received massive foreign investment as well as state support. Money, however, can't change the climate, and the summer rainy season causes problems. Even so, Riesling and Chardonnay (under the Tsingtao label) are not at all bad and Cabernet Sauvignon and Chardonnay in special 'feng shui' bottles are pretty tasty.

UBER Malterdingen, Baden, Germany For two decades the reticent Bernhard Huber has been crafting full-bodied Chardonnay★★ and Pinot Noir★★. Over-oaked in the past, they are now more fleshy and balanced. Charming Muskateller★ too. **Best years:** (2009) 08 07 **06 05** 04.

UET Vouvray AC, Loire Valley, France Complex, traditional VOUVRAY that can age for decades. Biodynamic methods are bringing into even sharper focus the individual traits of its 3 excellent sites – le Haut-Lieu, Clos du Bourg and le Mont. These yield dry★★, medium-dry★★★ or sweet★★★ and Pétillant★★ or Mousseux★★ sparkling wines, depending on the vintage. Sublime Première Trie Moelleux are site specific. Cuvée Constance *liquoreux*, made in exceptional years, is a blend of parcels. **Best years:** (sec, demi-sec) 2008 **07** 06; (moelleux) (2009) 05 04 **03** 02 **01** 00 99 98 97 96 95 90 89.

UGEL Alsace AC, Alsace, France Best wines are sweet ALSACE Vendange Tardive★★ and Sélection de Grains Nobles★★★. Big-volume Tradition wines can be dull, but Jubilee wines are often ★★. Patriarch Jean Hugel died in 2009. Will this herald a change in style? **Best years:** (Vendange Tardive Riesling) (2009) 08 07 **05 03** 01 00 98 97 96 95 90 89 88.

UNTER VALLEY New South Wales, Australia NEW SOUTH WALES' oldest wine zone overcomes a tricky climate to make fascinating, ageworthy Semillon and rich, buttery Chardonnay. Shiraz is the mainstay for reds, aging well but often developing a leathery overtone; Cabernet is occasionally successful. Premium region is the Lower Hunter Valley; the Upper Hunter has few wineries but extensive vineyards. **Best producers:** Allandale★, Audrey Wilkinson, BROKENWOOD★★, Capercaillie, De Iuliis★, Hope★, Lake's Folly★, Margan Family, Mount Pleasant★★/ MCWILLIAM'S, MEEREA PARK★★, Oakvale, THOMAS★★, TOWER, Tulloch, Keith Tulloch★, TYRRELL'S★★★. **Best years:** (Shiraz) 2007 06 04 03 02 **00 99 98** 97 96 94 91.

HUNTER'S *Marlborough, South Island, New Zealand* One of MARLBOROUGH
stars, with fine, if austere, Sauvignon★, savoury Burgundia
Chardonnay★, vibrant Riesling★ and sophisticated Pinot Noir★. Als
attractive Miru Miru fizz★. Best years: (Chardonnay) **2009 07 06 05 03**.

CH. DU HUREAU *Saumur-Champigny AC, Loire Valley, France* Philippe Vata
barely uses oak; his SAUMUR-CHAMPIGNY are particularly lifted and silk
The basic red★ is deliciously bright and fruity; special cuvé
Lisagathe★★ and Fevettes★★ need a bit of time. Jasmine-scented whi
SAUMUR★ is exceptional in top years. Decent fizz and occasional swe
Coteaux de Saumur. Best years: (top reds) (2009) 08 **06 05 04 03 02 99 9**

INNISKILLIN *Niagara Peninsula VQA, Ontario, Canada* One of Canada's leadir
wineries, with good Pinot Noir★ and Cabernet Franc, well-round
Chardonnay★ and rich Vidal Icewine★★, Cabernet Franc Icewine
Riesling Icewine★ and Sparkling Vidal Icewine★. Another Inniskill
winery is in the OKANAGAN VALLEY in British Columbia. Best years: (Vic
Icewine) 2008 **07 05 04 03 02 00 99**.

IPHOFEN *Franken, Germany* Important wine town in FRANKEN for d
Riesling and Silvaner. Both are powerful, with a pronounced earthines
Best producers: JULIUSSPITAL★, Johann Ruck★, Hans Wirsching★, Zehntkeller
Best years: (2009) 08 07 **06 05 04 03 02 01 00 99**.

IRANCY AC *Burgundy, France* This northern outpost of vineyards, ju
south-west of CHABLIS, is an unlikely champion of the clear, pure flavou
of the Pinot Noir grape. But red Irancy can be delicate and ligh
touched by the ripeness of plums and strawberries, and can age we
Best years: (2009) 08 **07** 06 05 03.

IRON HORSE VINEYARDS *Sonoma County, California, USA* A pioneer of t
Green Valley AVA, part of the RUSSIAN RIVER VALLEY. Outstandi
sparkling wines with vintage Brut★★ and Blanc de Blancs★★ delicio
on release but highly suitable for aging. The Brut LD★★★ (La
Disgorged) is a heavenly mouthful – yeasty and complex. Weddi
Cuvée★ Blanc de Noirs and Brut Rosé★ have been joined by Ult
Brut★ and Joy!★★, which is aged for 10–15 years before releas
Still wines include a lovely Pinot Noir★★, stunningly fresh, crisp Ru
Clone Chardonnay★★, a seductive Viognier★★ and a delightful Pin
Noir Rosé★.

IROULÉGUY AC *South-West France* The only Basque wines made
France. Tannat, usually blended with Cabernet Franc, gives fascinatir
robust reds that are softer than MADIRAN. Whites are mainly fro
Petit Courbu. Best producers: Ameztia★, ARRETXEA★★, Brana★, Ilarria
Irouléguy co-op (Mignaberry★), Mourguy. Best years: (reds) (2009) (08) **06**
04 01.

ISOLE E OLENA *Chianti Classico DOCG, Tuscany, Italy* Paolo De Marchi h
long been one of the pacesetters in CHIANTI CLASSICO. His Chia
Classico★★, characterized by clean, elegant and spicily perfumed fru
excels in every vintage. The powerful Cepparello★★★, made fro
100% Sangiovese, is the top wine. Excellent Syrah★★, Cabern
Sauvignon★★★, Chardonnay★★ and VIN SANTO★★★. Best yea
(Cepparello) (2009) (08) 07 06 **04 03 01 99** 98 97 95 90 88.

CH. D'ISSAN★ *Margaux AC, 3ème Cru Classé, Haut-Médoc, Bordeaux, Fran*
This lovely moated property disappointed me far too often in the dista
past, but pulled its socks up in the 1990s. When successful, the wine c
be one of the most delicate and scented in the MARGAUX AC. Best yea
2008 07 06 05 **04 03 02 01 00 99** 98 96 95 90 89.

VINEYARDS *Sonoma County, California, USA* Established as a sparkling wine house by Judy Jordan and still affiliated with JORDAN. With new winemaker George Bursick (formerly at FERRARI-CARANO) the J★ fizz is an attractive mouthful. J also makes a series of top-notch RUSSIAN RIVER Pinot Noirs★★ including excellent vineyard designates, as well as a small amount of tasty Pinotage★.

AUL JABOULET AÎNÉ *Rhône Valley, France* During the 1970s, Jaboulet led the way in raising the world's awareness of the great quality of RHÔNE wines. Although many of the wines are still good, they have risen in price and are no longer the star in any appellation. Best wines are top red HERMITAGE La Chapelle (this was a ★★★ wine in its heyday) and whites La Chapelle★ and Chevalier de Stérimberg★. CROZES-HERMITAGE Dom. de Thalabert is of adequate quality. Attractive CORNAS Dom. de St-Pierre★, reliable CÔTES DU RHÔNE Parallèle 45, good-value VENTOUX★ and sweet, perfumed MUSCAT DE BEAUMES-DE-VENISE★★. In 2006, Jaboulet was bought by Swiss financier Jean-Jacques Frey, owner of Ch. la LAGUNE. Best years: (La Chapelle) 2009 07 **06** 05 **04** 03 01 99 98 97 96 95 94 91 90 89 88 78.

ACKSON ESTATE *Marlborough, South Island, New Zealand* An established grapegrower with vineyards in MARLBOROUGH's most prestigious district. Sauvignon Blanc has regrettably changed from tangy to sweaty since 2007 (please go back to the old style), but barrel-fermented Grey Ghost Sauvignon Blanc★★ can improve with a little age; restrained Chardonnay and powerful Vintage Widow Pinot Noir★. Best years: (Pinot Noir) **2008** 06 05 04 03.

ACKSON-TRIGGS *Okanagan Valley VQA, British Columbia, Canada* Top-flight reds (Cabernet Sauvignon-Shiraz★★, Shiraz★) and Riesling Icewine★ in the Grand Reserve range. Also the single-vineyard Sun Rock Shiraz★. There's another Jackson-Triggs estate in NIAGARA PENINSULA. Osoyoos Larose★★ is an excellent BORDEAUX blend made for a joint-venture partnership between Canadian giant Vincor and French group Taillan.

ACOB'S CREEK *Barossa Valley, South Australia* Australia's leading export brand, selling more than 7 million cases a year, is owned by Pernod Ricard. The company has rebranded some of the wines formerly sold under the Orlando label: Jacob's Creek Steingarten Riesling★★★ from Eden Valley, Jacob's Creek St Hugo Cabernet Sauvignon★ from COONAWARRA and rich Jacob's Creek Centenary Hill Shiraz★★ from the BAROSSA. Flagship reds remain Orlando Jacaranda Ridge Cabernet★ from Coonawarra and Orlando Lawson's Shiraz★★ from PADTHAWAY. New super-premiums, Jacob's Creek Johann Shiraz-Cabernet and Reeves Point Chardonnay★★, are worth a look. Jacob's Creek Reserve and Limited Release★★ wines are very good. Basic Jacob's Creek wines are probably the best of the global Aussie brands, with Riesling★ and Grenache-Shiraz★ particularly good. Also tasty new Blanc de Blancs fizz. Best years: (St Hugo) (2009) 08 05 **04** 03 02 01 00 99 98 96 94 91 90 88 86.

ACQUESSON *Champagne AC, Champagne, France* Top-class small producer of classic vintage Brut★★. Its non-vintage is an austerely-styled one-off that changes each year to produce the best possible blend. Cuvée No. 734★★ (the seventh version made), based on the 2006 harvest, was released in March 2010. Superb single-vineyard, single-cru and single grape variety Champagnes from Avize Champ Caïn (Chardonnay)★★, Ay Vauzelle Terme (Pinot Noir)★★ and Dizy Corne Bautray (Chardonnay)★★ and a saignée pink fizz, Dizy Terres Rouges Rosé★★. Best years: (2002) **00** 97 96 **95** 93 90 89 88 85.

JEREZ Y MANZANILLA DO/SHERRY

Andalucía, Spain

The Spanish now own the name outright. At least in t'
EU, and soon in Australia, South Africa and Califorr
following the signing of new treaties, the only wines th
can be sold as sherry come from the triangle of vineya
land between the Andalusian towns of Jerez de
Frontera (inland), and Sanlúcar de Barrameda and Puerto de Sar
María (by the sea).

The best sherries can be spectacular. Three main factors contribute
the high-quality potential of wines from this region: the chalky-spon
albariza soil where the best vines grow, the Palomino Fino grape
unexciting for table wines but potentially great once transformed by t'
sherry-making processes – and a natural yeast called flor. All sherry mu
be a minimum of 3 years old, but fine sherries age in barrel for mu
longer. Sherries must be blended through a solera system. About a thi
of the wine from the oldest barrels is bottled, and the barrels topped
with slightly younger wine from another set of barrels and so on, for
minimum of 3 sets of barrels. The idea is that the younger wine takes
the character of older wine, as well as keeping the blend refreshed.

MAIN SHERRY STYLES

Fino and manzanilla Fino sherries derive their extraordinary, tang
pungent flavours from flor. Young, newly fermented wines destined i
these styles of sherry are deliberately fortified very sparingly to ju
15–15.5% alcohol before being put in barrels for their minimum of
years' maturation. The thin, soft, oatmeal-coloured mush of flor grow
on the surface of the wines, protecting them from the air (and there
keeping them pale) and giving them a characteristic sharp, pungent tan
The addition of younger wine each year feeds the flor, maintaining
even layer. Manzanillas are fino-style wines that have matured in t'
cooler seaside conditions of Sanlúcar de Barrameda, where the flor grow
thickest and the fine, salty tang is most accentuated.

Amontillado True amontillados are fino sherries that have continued
age after the flor has died (after about 5 years) and so finish their agi
period in contact with air. These should all be bone dry. Medium-swe
amontillados are concoctions in which the dry sherry is sweetened wi
mistela, a blend of grape juice and alcohol.

Oloroso This type of sherry is strongly fortified after fermentation
deter the growth of flor. Olorosos therefore mature in barrel in conta
with the air, which gradually darkens them while they remain dry, b
develop rich, intense, nutty and raisiny flavours.

Other styles Manzanilla pasada is aged manzanilla, with greater dep
and nuttiness. Palo cortado is an unusual, deliciously nutty, dry sty
somewhere in between amontillado and oloroso. Sweet oloroso crea
and pale creams are almost without exception enriched solely for t'
export market. Sweet varietal wines are made from sun-dried Ped
Ximénez or Moscatel.

See also individual producers.

BEST PRODUCERS AND WINES

Argüeso (Manzanilla San León, Manzanilla Fina Medallas).

BARBADILLO (Manzanilla Eva, Manzanilla En Rama, Manzanilla Solear, Amontillado Príncipe, Amontillado de Sanlúcar, Oloroso Seco Cuco, Palo Cortado Obispo Gascón).

Delgado Zuleta (Manzanilla Pasada La Goya).

DOMECQ (Amontillado 51-1A, Oloroso Sibarita, Pedro Ximénez Venerable).

El Maestro Sierra.

Equipo Navazos (La Bota de…)

Fernando de Castilla.

Garvey (Palo Cortado, Amontillado Tio Guillermo, Pedro Ximénez Gran Orden).

GONZÁLEZ BYASS (Tio Pepe Fino, Amontillado del Duque, Matusalem Oloroso Muy Viejo, Apóstoles Palo Cortado Muy Viejo, Noé Pedro Ximénez, Vintage Oloroso).

HIDALGO (Manzanilla La Gitana, Manzanilla Pasada Pastrana, Jerez Cortado Wellington, Amontillado Napoleon, Oloroso Viejo).

La Ina Fino.

LUSTAU (Almacenista single-producer wines, East India Solera, Puerto Fino).

OSBORNE (Amontillado Coquinero, Fino Quinta, Oloroso Bailén, Oloroso Solera India, Pedro Ximénez).

Sánchez Romate (Pedro Ximénez Cardenal Cisneros).

Tradición.

VALDESPINO (Amontillado Coliseo, Amontillado Tio Diego, Palo Cortado Cardenal, Fino Inocente, Oloroso Don Gonzalo, Pedro Ximénez Niños).

Williams & Humbert (Alegría Manzanilla).

LOUIS JADOT *Beaune, Côte de Beaune, Burgundy, France*   Ambitious merchant which has been expanding southward, especially in MOULIN-À-VENT (Château des Jacques★) and POUILLY-FUISSÉ (Jeandeau, Ferret★★). Top domaine whites from the CÔTE D'OR include PULIGNY-MONTRACHET Folatières★★ and CHEVALIER-MONTRACHET les Demoiselles★★★, while the reds range from attractive BEAUNE Premiers Crus★★ through to sumptuous GEVREY-CHAMBERTIN Clos St-Jacques★★ and CLOS ST-DENIS★★. Best years: (top reds) (2009) 08 07 06 05 **03 02 99 90**; (whites) (2009) 08 **07 06 05 04 02**.

JAMET★★★ *Côte-Rôtie AC, Rhône Valley, France*   A domaine in top form; Jean-Paul and Jean-Luc Jamet are two of the most talented growers of CÔTE-RÔTIE, with excellent vineyards on vertiginous slopes above the Rhône. The full-bodied wines, led by the marvellous Côte Brune★★★, age well for a decade or more. Long-lived CÔTES DU RHÔNE★★ and Syrah vin de pays★★. Best years: 2009 07 **06** 05 **04 03** 01 **00 99 98 97 96 95** 91 90 89 8?

JANUIK *Columbia Valley AVA, Washington State, USA*   Former head winemaker at CHATEAU STE MICHELLE, Mike Januik's experience and knowledge of Washington's vineyards allow him to source fruit from exceptional sites. His Chardonnays (Elerding★ and Cold Creek★★) are among the top in the state. Lewis Vineyard Syrah★★ is rich, earthy and bold, and Cabernet Sauvignons (Champoux Vineyard★★, Ciel du Cheval★★) are chocolaty, complex and ageworthy. Best years: (reds) (2008) 07 06 05 **04 03 02**.

JARDIN See JORDAN, South Africa.

JASNIÈRES AC *Loire Valley, France*   Tiny AC north of Tours. Reputation for long-lived, bone-dry whites from Chenin Blanc, though new movers and shakers here and in neighbouring appellation Coteaux du Loir (which additionally makes delicate Pineau d'Aunis and Gamay reds) are picking Chenin riper. Sweet wine may be made in good years. Best producers: Bellivière★★, le Briseau★, J Gigou★★, Les Maisons Rouges★, J P Robinot★. Best years: (2009) 08 07 **05 04 03 02 01 99 97**.

JEREZ Y MANZANILLA DO/SHERRY See pages 180–1.

JERMANN *Friuli-Venezia Giulia, Italy*   Silvio Jermann produces non-DOC Chardonnay★, Sauvignon Blanc★, Pinot Bianco★ and Pinot Grigio★. Long-lived Vintage Tunina★★ is based on Sauvignon-Chardonnay with Ribolla, Malvasia and Picolit; Capo Martino★ is also a blend of local varieties; Vinnae★ is based on Ribolla. Barrel-fermented Chardonnay★ is labelled, rather ungrammatically, 'Were dreams, now it is just wine'.

JOHANNISBERG *Rheingau, Germany*   Probably the best known of all the Rhine wine villages, with 10 vineyard sites, including the famous Schloss Johannisberg. Best producers: Prinz von Hessen★, Johannishof★★, SCHLOSS JOHANNISBERG★, Trenz. Best years: (2009) 08 07 **06 05 04 03 02 01**.

KARL H JOHNER *Bischoffingen, Baden, Germany*   Johner specializes in new oak-aged wines. The vividly fruity Pinot Noir★ and Pinot Blanc★ are excellent, the Chardonnay SJ★★ is one of Germany's best Chardonnays and the rich, silky Pinot Noir SJ★★ can be one of Germany's finest reds. Best years: (Pinot Noir SJ) (2008) 07 **06 05 04 03 02**.

JORDAN *Alexander Valley AVA, Sonoma County, California, USA*   Ripe, fruity Cabernet Sauvignon★ with a cedar character rare in California. The winery has recently moved toward greater use of mountain-grown Cabernet. Chardonnay★ from RUSSIAN RIVER VALLEY fruit is nicely balanced. Best years: (Cabernet) 2006 05 04 03 02 **01 00 97 96 95** 94 91 86.

JORDAN *Stellenbosch WO, South Africa*   Meticulously groomed hillside vineyards, with a variety of aspects and soils. Chardonnays (regular★★ with creamy/limy complexity; Nine Yards★★, dense, nutty, but balanced) are

delicious peppery Chenin★★ head a strong white range. Syrah★★, Cabernet Sauvignon★, Merlot★ and BORDEAUX-blend Cobblers Hill★★ are understated but beautifully balanced for aging. Sophia★ is a rich Bordeaux-blend red. Sold under the Jardin label in the USA. Best years: (Chardonnay) 2009 **08 07 06 05 04 03 02 01**; (Cobblers Hill) 2007 **06 05 04 03 02 01 00**.

ONI JOST *Bacharach, Mittelrhein, Germany* Peter Jost was the grower who put the MITTELRHEIN on the map. From the Bacharacher Hahn site come some delicious, racy Rieslings★; Auslese★★ adds creaminess without losing that pine-needle scent. Best years: (2009) 08 07 **06 05 04 03 02 01**.

ULIÉNAS AC *Beaujolais, Burgundy, France* Juliénas is attractive, 'serious' BEAUJOLAIS which can be big and tannic enough to develop in bottle. Best producers: Coquard★, DUBOEUF (Ch. des Capitans★), D Desvignes★, Ch. de Juliénas★, J-P Margerand★, Pelletier★, N Potel★★, B Santé★, M Tête★. Best years: **2009 08 07**.

ULIUSSPITAL *Würzburg, Franken, Germany* A 16th-century charitable foundation, with 170ha (420 acres) of vineyards, known for its dry wines – especially from IPHOFEN and WÜRZBURG. Look out for the Würzburger Stein wines, sappy Müller-Thurgau, grapefruity Silvaners★★ and petrolly Rieslings★★. Best years: (2009) 08 07 **06 05 04 03 02**.

UMILLA DO *Murcia and Castilla-La Mancha, Spain* Jumilla's reputation is for brutal alcoholic reds, but dense, serious yet balanced reds from Monastrell (Mourvèdre) show the region's potential. Very few whites. Best producers: Carchelo, Casa Castillo★★, Casa de la Ermita, Juan Gil★, Luzón★, El Nido★★. Best years: (2008) 07 **06 05 04 03 01 00**.

URA See ARBOIS, CHÂTEAU-CHALON, CÔTES DU JURA, CRÉMANT DU JURA, L'ÉTOILE.

URANÇON AC *South-West France* The sweet white wine made from late-harvested grapes can be heavenly, with floral, spicy, apricot-quince flavours. The lemony dry wine, Jurançon Sec, can be just as ageworthy. Best producers: Bellegarde★, Bordenave★, Bru-Baché★, Castera★, CAUHAPE★★, Clos Guirouilh★, Clos Lapeyre★★, Clos Thou★, CLOS UROULAT★, Larrédya★, Souch★★. Best years: (sweet) **2007 05 04 01 00 97**.

KAISERSTUHL *Baden, Germany* A 4000ha (10,000-acre) volcanic stump rising to 600m (2000ft) and overlooking the Rhine plain. Pinot varieties excel. Best producers: BERCHER★★, Gleichenstein★, Dr HEGER★★, Karl H JOHNER★★, Franz Keller★, Koch, Salwey★, Schneider★★. Best years: (dry whites) (2009) 08 07 **06 05 04 02 01**.

KAMPTAL *Niederösterreich, Austria* 4000ha (10,000-acre) wine region centred on the town of Langenlois, making some impressive dry Riesling and Grüner Veltliner. Best producers: BRÜNDLMAYER★★★, Ehn★★, Eichinger★, Hiedler★, Hirsch★, Jurtschitsch★, Fred Loimer★★, Schloss Gobelsburg★★, Topf. Best years: (2009) 08 07 **06 05 04 03 02 01**.

KANONKOP *Stellenbosch WO, South Africa* Winemaker Abrie Beeslaar creates traditional, long-lived red wines – now, thanks to virus-free vine material, often with brighter fruit. Pinotage and Kanonkop are synonymous; the newest member of the range, the black label Pinotage★★ is made in miniscule quantities from one of the oldest blocks still extant in South Africa, planted in 1953. The standard Pinotage★★, now from younger vines, lacks for nothing in quality or style. Muscular, savoury BORDEAUX-blend Paul Sauer★★ really does mature for 10 years or more. A straight Cabernet Sauvignon★ adds to this enviable red wine reputation. Best years: (Paul Sauer) 2006 **05 04 03 02 01 00 99 98 97 95**.

KARTHÄUSERHOF *Trier, Mosel, Germany* Top Ruwer estate which has gone
from strength to strength under Christoph Tyrell and winemaker
Ludwig Breiling. Rieslings combine aromatic extravagance with racy
brilliance. Most wines are now ★★, some Auslese and Eiswein ★★★.
Best years: (2009) 08 07 06 **05 04 03 02 01** 99 97.

KATNOOK ESTATE *Coonawarra, South Australia* Chardonnay★★ has
consistently been the best of the fairly expensive whites, though
Riesling★ and Sauvignon★★ are very tasty, too. Well-structured
Cabernet Sauvignon★ and treacly Shiraz★ lead the reds, with Odyssey
Cabernet Sauvignon★★ and Prodigy Shiraz★★ mixing power with
indulgence. Now owned by Spanish giant Freixenet. Best years: (Odyssey)
(2008) (06) 05 04 03 02 **01 00** 99 98 97 96 94 92 91.

KÉKFRANKOS See BLAUFRANKISCH.

KELLER *Flörsheim-Dalsheim, Rheinhessen, Germany* Klaus Keller and son Klaus-
Peter are the leading winemakers in the hill country of RHEINHESSEN, away
from the Rhine riverbank. They produce a range of varietal dry wines and
naturally sweet Rieslings, as well as extra-special dry Rieslings★★ from
three single vineyards. Astonishing TBA★★★ from Riesling and
Rieslaner. Best years: (2009) 08 07 **06 05 04 03 02 01** 99.

KENDALL-JACKSON *Sonoma County, California, USA* Jess Jackson founded
KJ in bucolic Lake County in 1982 after buying a vineyard there; now
based in SONOMA COUNTY, with operations throughout the state, and
producing about 4 million cases. Since the 2004 vintage, KJ's volume
leader, the Vintner's Reserve Chardonnay (2 million cases) is made
entirely from estate-grown fruit. Higher levels of quality are found in the
Grand Reserve reds and whites, the vineyard-based Highland Estates★
series and the top-of-the-range Stature★★ (red meritage).

KENWOOD *Sonoma Valley AVA, California, USA* This
winery has always represented very good quality
at reasonable prices. The Sauvignon Blanc★
has floral and melon flavours with a slightly
earthy finish. Long-lived Artist Series
Cabernet Sauvignon★★ is the flagship, Jack
London Zinfandel★★ is impressive, and
RUSSIAN VALLEY Pinot Noir★ is superb value.
Best years: (Zinfandel) 2006 05 04 **03 02 01 00** 99
98 97 96 95 94.

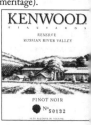

VON KESSELSTATT *Trier, Mosel, Germany* Good traditional Rieslings (★ to
★★) from some top sites at GRAACH (Josephshöfer) and PIESPORT in the
MOSEL, Scharzhofberg in the Saar and Kasel in the Ruwer. Best years:
(2009) 08 07 **06 05 04 03 02**.

KIEDRICH *Rheingau, Germany* Top vineyard here is the Gräfenberg, giving
long-lived, mineral Rieslings. Other good sites are Sandgrub and
Wasseros. Best producers: Prinz von Hessen, Knyphausen, WEIL★★. Best years:
(2009) 08 07 **06 05 04 02 01** 99.

KING ESTATE *Oregon, USA* Over 400ha (1000 acres) are certified organic
at the King Estate vineyard in Lorane, far south of the more popular
WILLAMETTE VALLEY. A tremendous amount of time and money has been
invested in this property, and the results are beginning to pay off. The
Pinot Gris★ is first-rate. The Pinot Noirs have taken time to perfect but
today The Signature Collection Pinot Noir★ is a powerful currant- and
cassis-flavoured wine, and the Domaine Collection★ is a fine example of
Oregon Pinot Noir. Best years: (reds) 2008 07 06 **05 04**.

:H. KIRWAN★ *Margaux AC, 3ème Cru Classé, Haut-Médoc, Bordeaux, France* This MARGAUX estate has shown considerable improvement since the mid-1990s. Investment in the cellars, more attention to the vineyards and the advice of consultant Michel Rolland (until 2007) have produced wines of greater depth and power but less perfume. Now working on bringing the elegance back. Second wine: Les Charmes de Kirwan. Best years: 2008 07 06 05 **04 03 01 00 99 98 96 95.**

:ISTLER *Sonoma Valley AVA, California, USA* One of California's trail-blazing Chardonnay producers, with wines from individual vineyards: Kistler Vineyard, Durell Vineyard and Dutton Ranch can be ★★★; McCrea Vineyard and ultra-cool-climate Camp Meeting Ridge Vineyard ★★. All possess great complexity with good aging potential. Also a number of single-vineyard Pinot Noirs★★ that go from good to very good. Best years: (Kistler Vineyard Chardonnay) 2006 **05 04 03 02 01 00 99 98 97.**

:LEIN CONSTANTIA *Constantia WO, South Africa* Showpiece estate fast regaining stature. The area's aptitude for white wines is reflected in crisp, nicely weighted Sauvignon Blanc★ (occasional vibrant Perdeblokke★★), good Chardonnay, excellent barrel-fermented white blend Madame Marlbrook★★, attractive dry Riesling and Vin de Constance★★ (recent vintages ★★★), a thrilling Muscat dessert wine based on the 18th-century Constantia. In reds, Marlbrook, a Cabernet-led BORDEAUX-style blend, is showing the benefit of clean, brighter fruit. Best years: (Vin de Constance) 2006 **05 04 02 01 00 99 98 97 96 95 94 93 92 91.**

:NAPPSTEIN *Clare Valley, South Australia* Knappstein has been revitalized under Lion Nathan's ownership. There are 3 outstanding single-vineyard wines from mature vines: Ackland Riesling★★★, Enterprise Cabernet★★ and Yertabulti Shiraz★★. The regular Riesling★★ is reliably good and Three★ intriguingly combines Gewürztraminer with Riesling and Pinot Gris. The Enterprise Brewery (established 1878) has been re-opened with refreshing results. Best years: (Enterprise Cabernet Sauvignon) (2009) (08) 06 05 04 03 02 **01 00 99 98.**

:MMERICH KNOLL *Unterloiben, Wachau, Niederösterreich, Austria* Since the late 1970s, some of the greatest Austrian dry white wines. The rich, complex Riesling and Grüner Veltliner are packed with fruit and invariably ★★ quality, with versions from both the Loibenberg and Schütt sites ★★★. They repay keeping for 5 years or more. Best years: (Riesling Smaragd) (2009) 08 07 **06 05 04 03 02 01 00 99 98.**

:OEHLER-RUPRECHT *Kallstadt, Pfalz, Germany* Powerful, concentrated dry Rieslings★★★ from the Kallstadter Saumagen site, oak-aged botrytized Elysium★ and Burgundian-style Spätburgunder (Pinot Noir)★. Best years: (Saumagen Riesling) (2009) 08 07 06 **05 04 03 02 01 00 99.**

:OOYONG *Mornington Peninsula, Victoria, Australia* Owned by the Gjergja family, who also have nearby Port Phillip Estate, and driven by the winemaking talents of Sandro Mosele. From 1995, 30ha (74 acres) at Kooyong were planted to Pinot Noir (the Haven★★★, Ferrous★★ and Meres★ Vineyards) and Chardonnay (the Faultline★★ and Farrago★★ Vineyards). Entry-level Clonale Chardonnay★ and Massale Pinot Noir★ show varietal character at bargain prices, while the Kooyong Estate Chardonnay★★ is structured, complex and restrained and the Estate Pinot Noir★★ needs time to show its seductive best.

ALOIS KRACHER *Illmitz, Burgenland, Austria* Unquestionably Austria's greatest sweet winemaker until his untimely death in 2007. Son Gerhard is following in his footsteps. Nouvelle Vague wines are aged in new barriques while Zwischen den Seen wines are aged in steel tanks. The Grande Cuvée and TBAs from Scheurebe, Welschriesling and Chardonnay are all ★★★. Best years: (whites) (2009) 08 07 **06 05 04 02 0**0 **00 99 96.**

KREMSTAL *Niederösterreich, Austria* 2600ha (6420-acre) wine region around Krems, producing some of Austria's best whites. From 2007 the DAC appellation can be used for dry Riesling and Grüner Veltliner. Best producers: Malat★★, Mantlerhof★, Sepp Moser, NIGL★★, NIKOLAIHOF★★, Franz Proidl★, Salomon★★, Stadt Krems★. Best years: (2009) 08 07 **06 05 04 02 01**

KRUG *Champagne AC, Champagne, France* Serious CHAMPAGNE house, making seriously expensive wines. The non-vintage Grande Cuvée★★ used to knock spots off most other de luxe brands in its rich, rather over-the-top traditional style. Since LVMH took control the style seems to have changed dramatically: it's fresher, leaner, more modern – good, but that's not why I buy Krug. Also an impressive vintage★★, a rosé★★ and ethereal, outrageously expensive, single-vineyard Clos du Mesnil★★★ Blanc de Blancs. Best years: 1998 96 **95 90 89** 88 85 82 81 79.

KRUTZLER *Deutsch-Schützen, Südburgenland, Austria* Perwolff★★, one of Austria's finest red wines, is a generously oaked blend of Blaufränkisch and Cabernet Sauvignon. The Blaufränkisch Reserve★ is almost as fine. Best years: (2008) 07 06 **05 04 03 02 01 00.**

PETER JAKOB KÜHN *Oestrich, Rheingau, Germany* A brilliant grower and winemaker, Kühn frequently makes headlines with his substantial dry Rieslings and thrilling nobly sweet wines, all usually ★★. Best years: (2009) 08 07 **06 05 04 03 02 01**.

KUMEU/HUAPAI *Auckland, North Island, New Zealand* A small but significant viticultural area north-west of Auckland. The 11 wineries profit from their proximity to New Zealand's largest city, but most make little or no wine from grapes grown in their home region. Best producers: COOPERS CREEK★, KUMEU RIVER★★, MATUA VALLEY★, West Brook. Best years: (Chardonnay) (2009) **07 05**.

KUMEU RIVER *Kumeu, Auckland, North Island, New Zealand* This family winery has been transformed by New Zealand's first Master of Wine, Michael Brajkovich, with adventurous, high-quality wines: a big, complex Chardonnay★★★ and three single-vineyard Chardonnays – Maté's★★★ Coddington★★ and Hunting Hill★★ – complex oak-aged Pinot Gris★ and a MARLBOROUGH Sauvignon Blanc. Only Pinot Noir disappoints so far. Best years: (Chardonnay) **2007** 06 05.

KUNDE ESTATE *Sonoma Valley, California, USA* The Kunde family have grown wine grapes in SONOMA COUNTY for more than 100 years; in 1990 they started producing wines, with spectacular results. Impressive Chardonnay★ (Reserve★★). The Century Vines Zinfandel★★ gets rave reviews, as do the peppery Syrah★★, the zesty Magnolia Lane Sauvignon Blanc★★ and the explosively fruity Viognier★★. Winemaker Tim Bell is also making a wide range of excellent smaller-production wines from Semillon, Gewurztraminer, Barbera, Primitivo, and more. Best years: (Zinfandel) 2007 **06 05 02 01 00**.

FRANZ KÜNSTLER *Hochheim, Rheingau, Germany* Gunter Künstler makes some of the best dry Rieslings in the RHEINGAU – powerful, mineral wines★★, with the Hölle wines often ★★★. Sweet wine quality has been erratic lately, but the best are fantastic. Powerful, earthy and pricey Pinot Noir. Best years: (2009) 08 07 **06 05 04 03 02 01**.

KWV *Paarl WO, South Africa* This industry giant produces a huge range of South African spirits as well as wine. The flagship Cathedral Cellar range features bright-fruited, well-oaked Cabernet-based Triptych★, rich bold Cabernet Sauvignon★ and modern-style Pinotage. Among whites, barrel-fermented Chardonnay shows pleasing fruit/oak balance, and Sauvignon★ is tangy. Produced in best years only, and in very limited quantities, single-vineyard Perold is an ultra-ripe international-style Shiraz lavishly adorned with new American oak. PORT-style and Muscadel fortifieds remain superb value.

VIÑA LA ROSA *Cachapoal, Rapel, Chile* One of Chile's oldest wineries, founded in 1824 by the Ossa family, and recently rejuvenated. The La Palma unoaked Chardonnay and Merlot are good easy drinkers. La Cornellana is a label for estate-grown wines. The La Capitana★ and Don Reca★ labels are a step up in quality and terrific value. New 'icon' Ossa Sixth Generation★★ proves La Rosa can also produce world-class reds.

CH. LABÉGORCE-ZÉDÉ★ *Margaux AC, Haut-Médoc, Bordeaux, France* Cherished and improved by Luc Thienpont of POMEROL until 2005. 2008 marks the last vintage of this château; in 2009 it was amalgamated with neighbouring Ch. Labégorce (owner since 2005) to form one estate – as was originally the case until the late 18th century. The wine isn't that perfumed, but is well poised between concentration and finesse. Age for 5 years or more. Second wine: Domaine Zédé. Best years: (2008) 06 05 **04 03 01 00 99 98 96 95 90 89**.

LADOIX AC *Côte de Beaune, Burgundy, France* Most northerly village in the CÔTE DE BEAUNE. The village includes some of the Grand Cru CORTON, and the lesser vineyards may be sold as Ladoix-Côte de Beaune or CÔTE DE BEAUNE-VILLAGES. Reasonably priced reds, quite light in colour and a little lean in style, from several good growers. Best producers: (reds) Cachat-Ocquidant★, Chevalier★, E Cornu★, M Mallard★; (whites) R & R Jacob★, S Loichet★. Best years: (reds) (2009) 08 **07** 05 **03** 02 99.

MICHEL LAFARGE *Volnay, Côte de Beaune, Burgundy, France* The doyen of VOLNAY; son Frédéric is now in charge. These are not easy wines to understand, and I've been disappointed as often as I've been thrilled. Some outstanding red wines, notably Volnay Clos des Chênes★★, Volnay Clos du Château des Ducs★★ (a monopole) and less fashionable BEAUNE Grèves★★. BOURGOGNE Rouge★ is good value. Top wines may seem a little lean at first, but are expected to blossom after 10 years or more aging. Best years: (top reds) (2009) 08 07 06 05 03 02 99 **98 97 96 95 91 90**.

CH. LAFAURIE-PEYRAGUEY★★ *Sauternes AC, 1er Cru Classé, Bordeaux, France* One of the most improved SAUTERNES properties of the 1980s and now frequently one of the best Sauternes of all: sumptuous and rich when young, and marvellously deep and satisfying with age. Best years: 2007 06 05 **04** 03 02 01 99 98 97 96 95 90 89 88 86 85 83.

CH. LAFFITTE-TESTON *Madiran AC, Pacherenc du Vic-Bilh AC, South-West France* Jean-Marc Laffitte makes some of the most characterful but also approachable MADIRAN in this sometimes fearsome appellation; his Vieilles Vignes★★ is one of the best. His dry cuvée Ericka★★ and the sweet Rêve d'Automne★★ are regularly among the top PACHERENCS. Best years: (reds) (2009) 08 06 **05** 04 02 01; (sweet whites) **2007** 06 05 04 03.

CH. LAFITE-ROTHSCHILD★★★ *Pauillac AC, 1er Cru Classé, Haut-Médoc, Bordeaux, France* Already famous in the early 19th century, this property was bought by the Rothschild banking family in 1868 and they still own it today. This PAUILLAC First Growth is frequently cited as the epitome of elegance, indulgence and expense. Since the late 1990s vintages have been superb, with added depth and body to match the wine's traditional finesse. Second wine: les Carruades de Lafite-Rothschild. Best years: 2008 07 06 05 04 03 **02 01 00** 99 98 97 96 95 94 90 89 88 86 85 82.

CH. LAFLEUR★★★ *Pomerol AC, Bordeaux, France* Using some of POMEROL's most traditional winemaking, this tiny estate can seriously rival the great PETRUS for texture, flavour and aroma. But a high percentage (50%) of Cabernet Franc makes this a more elegant wine. Second wine: Pensées de Lafleur. Best years: 2008 07 06 05 04 03 **02 01 00 99 98 96 95 90 89 88**.

LAFON *Meursault, Côte de Beaune, Burgundy, France* One of Burgundy's current superstars, with prices to match. Early exponent of biodynamics for brilliant MEURSAULT (Clos de la Barre★★, Charmes★★★, Perrières★★★) le MONTRACHET★★★ and exciting long-lived reds from VOLNAY (Santenots-du-Milieu★★★). Also MÂCON★ (Clos du Four★, Clos de la Crochette★). Best years: (whites) (2009) 08 07 06 05 03 **02 99 98 96** 90; (reds) (2009) 08 07 06 05 03 **02 99 98 96 90**.

CH. LAFON-ROCHET★ *St-Estèphe AC, 4ème Cru Classé, Haut-Médoc, Bordeaux, France* Good-value, affordable Classed Growth claret. Recent vintages have seen an increase of Merlot in the blend, making the wine less austere. Delicious and blackcurranty after 10 years. Best years: 2008 06 05 **04 03 02 01 00 99 98 96 95 94 90 89**.

ALOIS LAGEDER *Alto Adige DOC, Trentino-Alto Adige, Italy* Among the leading independents in ALTO ADIGE, making good, medium-priced varietals and pricey estate and single-vineyard wines such as Löwengang Cabernet★ and Chardonnay★★★, Sauvignon Lehen★★, Cabernet Cor Römigberg★, Pinot Noir Krafuss★, Pinot Bianco Haberle★ and Pinot Grigio Benefizium Porer★. Also owns the historic Casòn Hirschprunn estate: white Contest★★ is based on Pinot Grigio and Chardonnay, with Marsanne and Roussanne; the red Casòn★★ is Merlot-Cabernet based.

CH. LAGRANGE★★ *St-Julien AC, 3ème Cru Classé, Haut-Médoc, Bordeaux, France* Since the Japanese company SUNTORY purchased this large estate in 1983 it has become a single-minded wine of good fruit, meticulous winemaking and fine quality, an occasional surfeit of tannin being the only cautionary note. Dry white les Arums de Lagrange since 1997. Second wine: les Fiefs de Lagrange. Best years: 2008 06 05 04 **03 02 01 00** 98 96 95 90 89 88.

LAGREIN Black grape of ALTO ADIGE, producing deep-coloured, brambly, chocolaty reds and full-bodied, attractively scented rosés. Best producers: Colterenzio co-op (Cornell★), Glögglhof, Gries co-op★, Hofstätter★, LAGEDER★, Laimburg★, Muri-Gries★, J Niedermayr, I Niedriest★, Plattner-Waldgries★, Hans Rottensteiner★, Terlano co-op★★, Thurnhof★★, TIEFENBRUNNER★★, Zemmer★.

CH. LA LAGUNE★ *Haut-Médoc AC, 3ème Cru Classé, Haut-Médoc, Bordeaux, France* The closest MÉDOC Classed Growth to Bordeaux city. The soils are sandy-gravel and the wines round and elegant in style. Took a dip in the late 1990s but new investment from 2000 has improved things without adding any real personality. Second wine: Moulin de la Lagune. Best years: 2008 06 05 **04 03 02 00** 98 96 95 90 89.

LALANDE-DE-POMEROL AC *Bordeaux, France* To the north of its more famous neighbour POMEROL, this AC produces ripe, plummy wines with an unmistakable mineral edge that are very attractive to drink at 3–4 years old, but age reasonably well too. Even though they lack the concentration of top Pomerols, the wines are not particularly cheap. Best producers: Annereaux★, Bertineau St-Vincent★, La Croix des Moines★, la Croix-St-André★, les Cruzelles★, la Fleur de Boüard★★, Garraud★, Grand Ormeau★, Haut-Chaigneau, les Hauts Conseillants, Jean de Gué★, Laborderie-Mondésir★, Perron (La Fleur★), Sergant, la Sergue★, Siaurac★, Tournefeuille★, Viaud. Best years: (2009) 08 **06 05 04 03 02 00 98 96 95 90 89**.

AMBRUSCO *Emilia-Romagna, Italy* 'Lambrusco' refers to a family of black grape varieties, grown in 3 DOC zones on the plains of EMILIA and 1 in LOMBARDY. Today the cheap and cheerful stuff of the 1980s is all but forgotten, but there is genuine quality Lambrusco (especially Lambrusco di Sorbara and Grasparossa di Castelvetro), frothing dry or off-dry, ideal as a partner with the rich local foods based on cheese and pork products. Best producers: Barbieri, Barbolini, F Bellei★, Casali, Cavicchioli★, Chiarli, Vittorio Graziano★, Oreste Lini, Stefano Spezia, Venturini Baldini.

AMOREAUX LANDING *Finger Lakes AVA, New York State, USA* One of the most versatile and consistently good wineries in the FINGER LAKES. Its Chardonnay Reserve★ is a regular medal winner, and the Pinot Noir★ is arguably the region's best. Merlot★ and Cabernet Franc★ are also attractive, as are Dry Riesling★ and good, quaffable fizz.

ANDMARK *Sonoma County, California, USA* This producer concentrates on Chardonnay and Pinot Noir. Chardonnays include Overlook★★ and the oakier Damaris Reserve★★ and Lorenzo★★. Tropical-fruited Courtyard Chardonnay★ is lower-priced. Pinot Noir from Kastania Vineyard★★ (SONOMA COAST) is beautifully focused.

ANGHE DOC *Piedmont, Italy* Important DOC covering blends (Rosso, Bianco) and varietals from the Langhe hills around Alba, the 'varietals' crucially allowing 15% grapes other than that announced on the label, thus allowing people like Angelo GAJA to sell as Langhe what he used to sell as Barbaresco and Barolo. Best producers: (reds) ALTARE★★, Boglietti (Buio★★), Bongiovanni (Falletto★★), CERETTO★★, Chiarlo★, Cigliuti★★, CLERICO★★, Aldo CONTERNO★★, Conterno-Fantino (Monprà★★), Luigi Einaudi★, GAJA★★★, A Ghisolfi★★, Marchesi di Gresy (Virtus★★), F Nada (Seifile★★), Parusso (Bricco Rovella★★), Rocche dei Manzoni (Quatr Nas★), Vajra★, Gianni Voerzio (Serrapiu★★), Roberto VOERZIO★★. Best years: (reds) (2009) (08) 07 06 **04 03 01 00 99**.

CH. LANGOA-BARTON★★ *St-Julien AC, 3ème Cru Classé, Haut-Médoc, Bordeaux, France* Owned by the Barton family since 1821, Langoa-Barton is usually less scented and elegant, though often richer than its ST-JULIEN stablemate LÉOVILLE-BARTON, but it is still extremely impressive and excellent value. Drink after 7 or 8 years, although it may improve for 15–20. Second wine: Réserve de Léoville-Barton (a blend from the young vines of both Barton properties). Best years: 2008 07 06 05 **04 03 02 01 00 99 98 96 95 90 89 88 86 85**.

ANGUEDOC-ROUSSILLON *France* This vast area of southern France, running from Nîmes to the Spanish border and covering the *départements* of the GARD, HÉRAULT, Aude and Pyrénées-Orientales, is still a source of undistinguished cheap wine, but is also one of France's most exciting wine regions. The transformation is the result of better grape varieties, modern winemaking and ambitious producers, from the heights of GRANGE DES PÈRES to very good local co-ops. The best wines are the reds, particularly those from CORBIÈRES, MINERVOIS, COTEAUX DU LANGUEDOC and PIC ST-LOUP, and some

new-wave Cabernets, Merlots and Syrahs, as well as the more tradition
vins doux naturels, such as BANYULS, MAURY and MUSCAT DE RIVESALTES; but we a
now seeing exciting whites as well, particularly as new plantings
Chardonnay, Marsanne, Roussanne, Viognier, Vermentino (Rolle) an
Sauvignon Blanc mature. An all-embracing appellation, called simpl
Languedoc AC, was agreed in 2007 and covers all of Coteaux du Languedoc
plus Corbières, Minervois and the ROUSSILLON appellations. For the momen
producers of Coteaux du Languedoc can choose between Coteaux d
Languedoc or the new appellation. See also BLANQUETTE DE LIMOUX, CABARDÈ
COLLIOURE, CÔTES DU ROUSSILLON, CÔTES CATALANES, CÔTES DE THONGUE, FAUGÈRE
FITOU, LIMOUX, MUSCAT DE FRONTIGNAN, MUSCAT DE ST-JEAN-DE-MINERVOIS, OC
RIVESALTES, ST-CHINIAN.

LANSON *Champagne AC, Champagne, France* Non-vintage Lanson Blac
Label★ is reliably tasty and, like the rosé★ and vintage★★ wine
especially de luxe Noble Cuvée★★, improves greatly with aging. In 2006
Lanson (and associated brands Besserat de Bellefon, Gauthier, Mass
and Alfred Rothschild) was bought by Boizel Chanoine Champagne
where Bruno PAILLARD is the majority shareholder. Best years: **1999 98 9
96 95 93 90 89 88 85 83 82.**

DOM. LAROCHE *Chablis, Burgundy, France* Significant CHABLIS domaine wit
associated *négociant*, plus interests in Languedoc, Chile and Sout
Africa, merged in 2009 with larger Jeanjean operation, retainin
minority share. Should not change wine styles noticeably.

CH. LASCOMBES★ *Margaux AC, 2ème Cru Classé, Haut-Médoc, Bordeaux, Franc*
One of the great underachievers in the MARGAUX AC and little wort
drinking in the 1980s and 90s, but new American ownership and invest
ment and the advice of consultant enologist Michel Rolland have begu
to make a difference – and the 2004 is the best effort for a generation
Best years: 2007 06 05 **04 03** 01 **00** 96 95.

LAS MORAS *San Juan, Argentina* Highly successful winery in SAN JUAN
producing consistently attractive wines at all price levels. Famed for it
Three Valleys Gran Shiraz★, powerful, spicy, laden with blackberry an
licorice flavours with a lovely floral edge. Mora Negra★, an aromati
blend of Malbec and Bonarda, is also classy stuff.

CH. LATOUR★★★ *Pauillac AC, 1er Cru Classé, Haut-Médoc, Bordeaux, Franc*
Latour's reputation is based on powerful, long-lasting classic wines
Strangely, in the early 1980s there was an attempt to make lighter, mor
fashionable wines, with mixed results. The late 80s saw a return to classi
Latour, much to my relief. Its reputation for making fine wine in les
successful vintages is well deserved. After 30 years in British hands i
returned to French ownership in 1993. Spanking new cellars from 2004
Second wine: les Forts de Latour. Best years: **2008** 07 06 05 04 03 **02** 01 0
99 98 97 96 95 94 90 89 88 86.

LOUIS LATOUR *Beaune, Burgundy, France* Merchant almost as well know
for his COTEAUX DE L'ARDÈCHE Chardonnays as for his Burgundies. Latour'
white Burgundies are much better than the reds, although the re
CORTON-Grancey★★ can be very good. Latour's oaky CORTON
CHARLEMAGNE★★, from his own vineyard, is his top wine, but there i
also good CHEVALIER-MONTRACHET★★, BÂTARD-MONTRACHET★★ and l
MONTRACHET★★. Even so, as these are the greatest white vineyards i
Burgundy, there really should be more top performances; there are som
signs of a resurgence. Best years: (top whites) (2009) 08 07 **06 05 02 00.**

CH. LATOUR-MARTILLAC *Pessac-Léognan AC, Cru Classé de Graves, Bordeaux, France* The vineyard here is strictly organic, and has many ancient vines. The deep, dark, well-structured reds★ improved considerably in the 1990s. Whites★ are thoroughly modern and of good quality. Good value as well. Best years: (reds) 2008 06 05 **04 03 02 01 00** 98 96 95 90; (whites) **2008** 07 06 05 04 02 01 00 99.

CH. LATOUR-À-POMEROL★ *Pomerol AC, Bordeaux, France* Directed by Christian MOUEIX of PETRUS fame, this property makes luscious wines with loads of gorgeous fruit and enough tannin to age well. Best years: 2008 07 06 05 **04 03 02 01 00** 99 98 95 90 89.

LATRICIÈRES-CHAMBERTIN AC See CHAMBERTIN AC.

LAUREL GLEN *Sonoma Mountain AVA, California, USA* Owner/winemaker Patrick Campbell makes only Cabernet★★ at his mountaintop winery. The top wine, Laurel Glen★★, is rich with deep fruit flavours, aging after 6–10 years to a perfumed, complex BORDEAUX style. Counterpoint★ is a label for wine that

does not make it into the top-level Cabernet. Terra Rosa (Malbec) is from established vineyards in MENDOZA, Argentina. Zinfandel-based Reds, from Lodi-grown fruit, is great value. Best years: 2006 05 **02 01** 99 98 97 96 95 94 91 90.

LAURENT-PERRIER *Champagne AC, Champagne, France* Large, family-owned CHAMPAGNE house, offering flavour and quality at reasonable prices. Non-vintage★ is light and savoury; the vintage★ is very good, and the top wine, Grand Siècle★★ (sometimes★★★) can be among the finest Champagnes of all. Non-vintage rosé★ is good, vintage Alexandra Rosé★★★ is excellent. Best years: (2002) 00 **99 97 96 95** 90 88 85 82.

L'AVENIR *Stellenbosch WO, South Africa* Now part of the Advini group, the new company formed by the merger of LAROCHE and Jeanjean. All remains as before in the cellar. Chenin Blanc and Pinotage remain the focus. Three Pinotages, from cheerfully fruity, via well-oaked to ageworthy Grand Vin Pinotage★★, are echoed by a stylish trio of Chenin Blancs (Icon range★★, Platinum★). Promising Chardonnay★, Cabernet★ and BORDEAUX-blend Stellenbosch Classic★. Best years: (Pinotage) 2008 **07 06 05 04 03 02 01 00**.

CH. LAVILLE-HAUT-BRION★★★ *Pessac-Léognan AC, Cru Classé de Graves, Bordeaux, France* One of the finest white PESSAC-LÉOGNANs, with a price tag to match. Fermented in barrel, it needs 10 years or more to reach its savoury but luscious peak. Best years: 2008 07 06 **05 04 03 02 01 00** 96 95 94 93 90 89.

DOMAINE COSTA LAZARIDI *Drama, Greece* State-of-the-art, Bordeaux-inspired winery making good use of indigenous and international varieties. Fresh gooseberry Amethystos white★ (Sauvignon Blanc, Sémillon and Assyrtiko); a fascinatingly intense Viognier★ with a stunning, oily, peach kernel finish; tasty Château Julia Chardonnay★; and fine Amethystos Cava★, an oak-aged Cabernet from very low yields.

LAZIO *Italy* The nation's political centre is not famous for wine, being able to boast not much more than glugging whites based on Trebbiano and Malvasia, such as EST! EST!! EST!!! DI MONTEFIASCONE and FRASCATI. The region's most interesting wines are reds based on Cesanese, an up and coming variety.

Best producers: Casale del Giglio★, Castel de Paolis (Quattro Mori★★), Cervete co-op (Tertium★), FALESCO (Montiano★), Giuliani Marcella★, Paola di Mauro (Vig del Vassallo★★), l'Olivella★, Pietra Pinta★, Trappolini★, Villa Santa★.

LEASINGHAM *Clare Valley, South Australia* Now a Constellation label. T winery has been closed and most of the vineyards have been sold off; t 70ha (173-acre) Provis vineyard has been retained. For the time being, least, Riesling★★ and Sparkling Shiraz★★ can be among CLARE VALLE best; Bin 56 Cabernet-Malbec★ and Bin 61 Shiraz★ are powerful, mi price reds; Classic Clare Shiraz★★ and Cabernet★ are high-alcoho heavily oaked, heavily priced blockbusters. The budget-priced Magn range represents good value.

L'ECOLE No 41 *Walla Walla Valley AVA, Washington State, USA* Velvety ar deeply flavoured Seven Hills Vineyard Merlot★, good Cabern Sauvignon★ and lush Syrah★★; a BORDEAUX blend called Apogee★ from the Pepper Bridge vineyard in WALLA WALLA is dark and challengin The best wines are the barrel-fermented Semillons: a nutty COLUMB VALLEY★★ version and exciting single-vineyard Fries Vineyard★★ ar Luminesce Seven Hills Vineyard★★. The Chardonnay★ is pleasant ar minerally. Best years: (top reds) (2009) (08) 07 06 05 **04 03 02.**

LEEUWIN ESTATE *Margaret River, Western Australia* MARGARET RIVER perennial high flier, with pricey, supremely balanced Art Seri Chardonnay★★★ that gets Burgundy lovers drooling. Art Series Cabern Sauvignon★★ (sometimes ★★★) exhibits superb blackcurrant and ced balance. Art Series Riesling★★ is complex and fine, and Shiraz★★ is no exceptional. Prelude (Chardonnay★★) and Siblings (Sauvignon Blan Semillon) give Leeuwin pleasure at lower prices. Best years: (Art Seri Chardonnay) (2009) (08) 07 06 **05 04 02 01 00 99 98 97 96 95.**

DOM. LEFLAIVE *Puligny-Montrachet, Côte de Beaune, Burgundy, France* Famou white Burgundy producer with extensive holdings in some of the greate vineyards of PULIGNY-MONTRACHET (les Pucelles★★★), Chevalie MONTRACHET★★★, BÂTARD-MONTRACHET★★★ and a tiny slice of MONTRACHET★★★. Anne-Claude Leflaive has taken the family domain right back to the top using biodynamic methods. These extraordinari fine wines can age for 20 years and are understandably expensive. Mor reasonably priced Mâcon-Verzé. Best years: (2009) 08 07 **06 05 03 02 0 00 99.**

OLIVIER LEFLAIVE *Puligny-Montrachet, Côte de Beaune, Burgundy, Franc* *Négociant* Olivier Leflaive specializes in crisp, modern white wines fro the CÔTE D'OR and the CÔTE CHALONNAISE, mostly for early drinking. Less ACs – ST-ROMAIN★, MONTAGNY★, ST-AUBIN★, RULLY★ – offer good valu but the rich, oaky BÂTARD-MONTRACHET★★★ is the star turn. Best year (top whites) (2009) 08 **07 06 05.**

PETER LEHMANN *Barossa Valley, South Australia* BAROSSA doyen Lehman buys grapes from many local growers and owns the superb Stonewe vineyard, which contributes its fruit and name to his great Shiraz★★★ The 1885 Shiraz★★★ from the Ebenezer vineyard is another stunne Juicy, fruit-packed reds include Grenache-Shiraz★, Ment (Cabernet)★★ and Eight Songs Shiraz★★. The talking point of the pa few years has been the consistently sublime quality of the top Pete Lehmann whites: impeccably balanced Wigan Eden Valle Riesling★★★ and rich, pure, zesty, unwooded Margaret Semillon★★ from Barossa Valley old vines. Also lemony Semillon★★ and Chenin★

and dry, long-lived Eden Valley Riesling★★. Bought by California-based Donald HESS in 2003. Befuddling array of budget lines – but the quality is holding up so far. Best years: (Stonewell Shiraz) (2009) (08) 06 05 04 03 **02 01 99 98 96 94 93 90 89**.

JOSEF LEITZ *Rüdesheim, Rheingau, Germany* Some of the RHEINGAU's best dry and off-dry Rieslings come from this RÜDESHEIM grower, especially from the Berg Rottland★★ and Berg Schlossberg★★ sites, whose recent vintages go from strength to strength. Best years: (2009) 08 07 **06 05 04 03 02 01 99**.

LEIWEN *Mosel, Germany* In the 1990s this unspectacular village became a hotbed of the MOSEL Riesling revolution, as a number of estates made the most of the village's unrealized potential. Still a source of excellent, reasonably priced Rieslings. Best producers: GRANS-FASSIAN★★, Carl Loewen★★, Josef Rosch★, St Urbans-Hof★★, Heinz Schmitt. Best years: (2009) 08 07 06 05 **04 03 02 01**.

LEMBERGER See BLAUFRANKISCH.

LENZ WINERY *Long Island, New York State, USA* A leading LONG ISLAND winery focused on BORDEAUX varietal reds exclusively from estate fruit. The Estate Merlot★★ is elegant and powerful with soft, balanced tannins; dry Gewürztraminer★ is spicy and tasty; Chardonnay★ is mostly good. Sparkling wines are limited in quantity though not in quality.

LEONETTI CELLAR *Walla Walla Valley AVA, Washington State, USA* The first winery in WALLA WALLA VALLEY opened in 1977. Today it produces highly sought-after, rich and velvety Cabernet Sauvignon★★ and Merlot★★ aged in a combination of French and American oak. A dense and powerful Reserve★★★ uses the best barrels. Sangiovese★★ has very fine texture and lots of new wood. The focus is on vineyard management and most of the fruit is now estate grown. Best years: (2008) 07 06 05 **04 03 02**.

CH. LÉOVILLE-BARTON★★★ *St-Julien AC, 2ème Cru Classé, Haut-Médoc, Bordeaux, France* Made by Anthony Barton, whose family has run this ST-JULIEN property since 1826, this fine claret is a traditionalist's delight. Dark, dry and tannic, and not overly oaked, the wines are often underestimated, but over 10–20 years they achieve a lean yet sensitively proportioned beauty rarely equalled in Bordeaux. Moreover, they are not overpriced. Second wine: Réserve de Léoville-Barton. Best years: 2008 07 06 05 **04 03 02 01 00 99 98 96 95 94 93 90 89 88 86**.

CH. LÉOVILLE-LAS-CASES★★★ *St-Julien AC, 2ème Cru Classé, Haut-Médoc, Bordeaux, France* The largest of the three Léoville properties, making wines of startlingly deep, dark concentration. I now find them so dense and thick in texture that it is difficult to identify them as ST-JULIEN. Second wine: Clos du Marquis. Best years: 2008 07 06 05 04 03 **02 01 00 99 98 96 95 94 93 90 89 88 86 85**.

CH. LÉOVILLE-POYFERRÉ★★ *St-Julien AC, 2ème Cru Classé, Haut-Médoc, Bordeaux, France* Since the 1986 vintage Didier Cuvelier has gradually increased the richness of the wine without wavering from its reserved and elegant style. A string of excellent wines in the 90s and 00s frequently show more classic ST-JULIEN style than those of neighbour LEOVILLE-LAS-CASES. Second wine: Moulin-Riche. Best years: 2008 07 06 05 04 **03 02 01 00 99 98 96 95 90 89 86**.

DOM. LEROY *Vosne-Romanée, Côte de Nuits, Burgundy, France* In 1988 Lalou Bize-Leroy bought the former Dom. Noëllat in VOSNE-ROMANEE, renaming it Domaine Leroy. It should not be confused with her *négociant* house, Maison Leroy, which contains stocks of great mature vintages, or

her personal estate, Dom. d'Auvenay. Here she produces fiendishI
expensive, though fabulously concentrated, wines with biodynam
methods and almost ludicrously low yields from top vineyards such a
CHAMBERTIN★★★, CLOS DE VOUGEOT★★★, MUSIGNY★★★, RICHEBOURG★★
and ROMANÉE-ST-VIVANT★★★. Best years: (top reds) (2009) 08 07 06 05 **03 0**
01 00 99 98 96 90 89.

LEYDA See SAN ANTONIO.

LIGER-BELAIR *Côte de Nuits, Burgundy, France* Vicomte Louis-Michel Liger
Belair makes stylish, perfumed wines at the family estate in VOSN
ROMANÉE, including the monopoly of la ROMANÉE★★★ itself, while h
cousin Thibault Liger-Belair makes rich, plump wines from his NUITS-S
GEORGES base, including Premier Cru les St-Georges★★ and Grand
Crus RICHEBOURG★★ and CLOS DE VOUGEOT★★. Best years: (Vicomte) (2009
08 07 06 05 03 **02 01**; (Thibault) (2009) 08 07 06 05 **04 03 02**.

LIGURIA *Italy* Thin coastal strip of north-west Italy, running from th
French border at Ventimiglia to the Tuscan border. Best grape: Vermentin
(try Lambraschi★). Best wines, mostly drunk by natives or tourists, are th
Cinqueterre, Colli di Luna, Riviera Ligure di Ponente and Rossese c
Dolceacqua DOCs.

LIMARÍ *Chile* During the past decade this valley – 400km (250 miles) nort
of Santiago – has shown that its cold ocean influence, long sunshine hou
and chalky/clay soils can produce world-class wines. Chardonnay and Syra
are the top performers, both expressing fresh, vibrant flavours and subtle ye
clear minerality, with the best Chardonnays coming from Quebrada Seca sub
region. There are also some salty Sauvignons from the coastal region. Bes
producers: DE MARTINO, Maycas del Limarí★/CONCHA Y TORO, TABALÍ★ (Syrah★★
Tamaya. Best years: **2009 08 07**.

LIMESTONE COAST *South Australia* Zone for south-east of South Austral
including COONAWARRA, PADTHAWAY, Mount Benson and Wrattonbully
Plantings near Mount Gambier, Bordertown and Robe may seek offici
recognition in the future. New vineyards in this far-flung area hav
Coonawarra-like terra rossa soil with great potential. The Foster's Win
Group, YALUMBA, Constellation and Pernod Ricard are all involved, as we
as private estates.

LIMOUX AC *Languedoc, France* The first AC in the LANGUEDOC to allo
Chardonnay and Chenin Blanc, which must be vinified in oa
Production is dominated by the SIEUR D'ARQUES co-op. Red Limoux A
(from 2004) is made from Merlot and Cabernet with local varieties. Be
producers: d'ANTUGNAC★, Bégude★, Rives-Blanques★, SIEUR D'ARQUES★. Se
also BLANQUETTE DE LIMOUX, CRÉMANT DE LIMOUX.

LINDEMANS *Murray Darling, Victoria, Australia* Large, historic company, pa
of the Foster's Wine Group. Underperforming for some years – indee
Lindemans is now a 'global' brand, sourcing wines from wherever the
choose – but the Bin range, especially Bin 65 Chardonnay, and th
Cawarra wines, show encouraging signs of starting to put quality fir
again. Traditionally strong in COONAWARRA, where the best wines are th
minerally St George Cabernet★★, spicy Limestone Ridge Shira
Cabernet★★ and red BORDEAUX-blend Pyrus★★. Good Reserve-lab
reds from the LIMESTONE COAST. Best years: (Coonawarra reds) 2009 08 06 0
04 01 99 98 96 94 91 90.

INDEN VINEYARDS *Virginia, USA* For nearly three decades, Jim Law has quietly farmed a hillside vineyard called Hardscrabble about an hour's drive west of Washington DC. He crafts European-styled wines of impressive concentration and finesse. While he does bottle single-varietal wines, Law prefers blending his reds to give the fullest expression of the land. Best are the Hardscrabble, Red blend of BORDEAUX varieties and Hardscrabble Chardonnay★.

IRAC AC *Rhône Valley, France* Underrated AC between TAVEL and CHÂTEAUNEUF-DU-PAPE. Reds have the spicy red fruit of Châteauneuf without quite the intensity and are helped by Mourvèdre. They age over 8–10 years but are good, if stony, young. Refreshing rosé has lovely strawberry fruit; whites can be good and have the body to match full flavours. Best producers: Amido★, Aquéria, Beaumont★, Boucarut★, Bouchassy★, Clos de Sixte★, Corne-Loup, Duseigneur, la Genestière★, Alain Jaume★, Joncier★, Lafond-Roc-Épine★★, Lorentine★, Maby★, Mont-Redon★, la Mordorée★★, Pélaquié★, Roger Sabon★★, St-Roch★, Ségriès, Tavel co-op★. Best years: **2009 07 06 05 04 03**.

ISBOA *Portugal* This used to be labelled Estremadura, and is Portugal's most productive region, occupying the western coastal strip, with an increasing number of clean, characterful wines. The leading area is ALENQUER DOC and there are eight other DOC regions; however, much of the region's best wine is simply labelled as Vinho Regional Lisboa. Spicy, perfumed reds are often based on Castelão, but Aragonez (Tempranillo), Cabernet Sauvignon, Syrah and Touriga Nacional contribute to top examples, which can benefit from 4 or 5 years' aging. Top producers also make fresh, aromatic whites. Best producers: Quinta de Chocapalha★, Quinta da Cortezia★, D F J VINHOS, Quinta dos Loridos (Merlot★), Quinta do Monte d'Oiro★★, Companhia Agricola do Sanguinhal, Casa SANTOS LIMA★. See also BUCELAS. Best years: (reds) (2008) **07 05 04 03 01 00**.

ISTRAC-MÉDOC AC *Haut-Médoc, Bordeaux, France* Set back from the Gironde and away from the best HAUT-MÉDOC gravel ridges, Listrac wines can be good but never thrilling, and are marked by solid fruit, a slightly coarse tannin and an earthy flavour. More Merlot is now being used to soften the style. Best producers: Cap Léon Veyrin, CLARKE★, Ducluzeau, Fonréaud, Fourcas-Dupré★, Fourcas-Hosten, Fourcas-Loubaney, Grand Listrac co-op, Mayne-Lalande★, Saransot-Dupré. Best years: **(2009) 08 06 05 03 01 00 96 95 90**.

LANO ESTACADO *Texas High Plains, Texas, USA* Texas' largest premium winery, in the High Plains AVA in the western part of the state. Llano produces a wide array of wines at consistent quality and reasonable prices. One of the best is an exotically perfumed white blend called Viviana★.

OIRE VALLEY *France* The Loire river cuts right through the heart of France. The middle reaches are the home of world-famous SANCERRE and POUILLY-FUMÉ. The region of TOURAINE makes good Sauvignon Blanc and Gamay, while at VOUVRAY and MONTLOUIS-SUR-LOIRE the Chenin Blanc makes some pretty good fizz and scintillatingly fresh, minerally still whites, ranging from sweet to very dry. The Loire's best reds are made in SAUMUR-CHAMPIGNY, CHINON, ST-NICOLAS-DE-BOURGUEIL and BOURGUEIL, mainly from Cabernet Franc, with ANJOU-VILLAGES improving fast. Anjou is famous for rosé, but the best wines are white Chenin Blanc, either sweet from the Layon Valley or dry

from SAVENNIÈRES and ANJOU where a new generation of producers are makin
richer, barrel-fermented and aged wines. Near the mouth of the river aroun
Nantes is MUSCADET. See also BONNEZEAUX, CABERNET D'ANJOU, CHEVERNY, CÔT
ROANNAISE, COTEAUX DE L'AUBANCE, COTEAUX DU LAYON, CRÉMANT DE LOIRE, GRO
PLANT DU PAYS NANTAIS, JASNIÈRES, MENETOU-SALON, POUILLY-SUR-LOIRE, QUARTS D
CHAUME, QUINCY, REUILLY, ROSE DE LOIRE, SAUMUR, SAUMUR MOUSSEUX, VAL DE LOIR

LOMBARDY *Italy* Lombardy, whose capital is Milan, is a larger consume
than producer, though OLTREPÒ PAVESE does produce a lot of grapes, many
them used in Italy's *spumante* industry. There are some interesting wines fron
Oltrepò; also from VALTELLINA, Volcalepio and Garda's LUGANA. FRANCIACORT
makes top quality sparklers.

LONG ISLAND *New York State, USA* Long Island encompasses 3 AVAs: th
Hamptons; North Fork; and the broader Long Island AVA. People hav
likened growing conditions to BORDEAUX, and the long growing seaso
combined with a maritime influence, does produce similarities. Certainl
Merlot and Cabernet Franc are the best reds, with Chardonnay the be
white. **Best producers:** BEDELL★, CHANNING DAUGHTERS★, LENZ★, Macar
Martha Clara, Palmer★, Paumanok★, Pellegrini★, Pindar, Raphael, Shinn Estat
WÖLFFER★. **Best years:** (reds) (2009) (08) 07 06 **02 01 00.**

LONG SHADOWS VINTNERS *Columbia Valley AVA, Washington State, US*
This is a series of small partnerships, led by Allen Shoup, encompassin
a coterie of wineries in the heart of the COLUMBIA VALLEY AVA. It include
Pedestal★★ with Michel Rolland, Feather★★ with Randy DUNN, Poet'
Leap★ with Armin Diel of Schlossgut DIEL, Saggi★ with Ambrogio an
Giovanni FOLONARI, Sequel★★ with John DUVAL, and Chester-Kidder
with Allen Shoup and Gilles Nicault, the head winemaker for the group
Best years: (reds) (2008) 07 06 **05 04.**

DR LOOSEN *Bernkastel, Mosel, Germany*
Loosen's estate has portions of some of
the MOSEL's most famous vineyards:
Treppchen and Prälat in ERDEN,
Würzgarten in ÜRZIG, Sonnenuhr in
WEHLEN, Himmelreich in GRAACH and
Lay in BERNKASTEL. Most of the wines
achieve ★★, and Spätlese and Auslese
from Wehlen, Ürzig and Erden

frequently ★★★. The basic Riesling is excellent, year in year out. A join
venture with CHATEAU STE MICHELLE in Washington revolutionized Rieslin
production in that state. **Best years:** (2009) 08 07 **06 05** 04 03 02 01 99 9
97. See also J L WOLF.

LÓPEZ DE HEREDIA *Rioja DOCa, Rioja, Spain* Family-owned RIOJA compan
still aging wines in old oak casks. Younger red wines are called Viñ
Cubillo★, and mature wines Viña Tondonia★ and Viña Bosconia★
Gran Reserva red and white wines are a notch above, sometimes ★★
(especially whites). Good, oaky whites, including Viña Gravonia★. Bes
years: (Viña Tondonia) 2000 99 **98 96 95** 94 93 91 87 86 85.

LOUPIAC AC *Bordeaux, France* A sweet wine area across the Garonne rive
from BARSAC. The wines are attractively sweet without being gooey
Drink young in general, though the best can age. **Best producers:** Clo
Jean★, Cros★, Loupiac-Gaudiet, Mémoires★, Noble★, Ricaud, les Roques★
Best years: (2009) **07 05** 03 02 01 99 98 97 96.

CH. LA LOUVIÈRE *Pessac-Léognan AC, Bordeaux, France* The star of PESSAC-LÉOGNAN's non-classified estates, its reputation almost entirely due to owner André Lurton. Well-structured reds★ and fresh, Sauvignon-based whites★★ are excellent value. Best years: (reds) 2008 06 05 **04 02 01 00** 99 98 96 95; (whites) 2008 07 06 05 04 03 02 01 00 99.

LUBÉRON AC *Rhône Valley, France* Production is dominated by the co-ops east of Avignon along the Durance Valley; their light wines drink young. Domaine wines have more body. Whites are often oaked. Best producers: Bonnieux co-op, Ch. la Canorgue, la Citadelle★, Fontenille★, Ch. de l'Isolette★, Ch. St-Estève de Néri★, la Tour-d'Aigues co-op, Ch. des Tourettes, Val Joanis, la Verrerie. Best years: **2009** 07.

STEFANO LUBIANA *Tasmania, Australia* One of the stars of the Tasmanian wine scene. Vintage★, non-vintage★ and Prestige★ (10 years on lees) sparkling wines rank with the best in Australia. Chardonnay★ is restrained and elegant, Sauvignon Blanc shows greengage and passionfruit characters, while the Pinot Noir★ has weight, concentration and a velvety texture. Entry level 'Primavera' Pinot is pretty tasty.

LUGANA DOC *Lombardy, Italy* Dry white (occasionally sparkling) from the Trebbiano di Lugana grape (aka Verdicchio) grown on the southern shores of Lake Garda. Well-structured wines from the better producers can develop excitingly over a few years. Best producers: Ca' dei Frati★★, Ottella★, Provenza★, Visconti★, Zenato★, Zeni.

LUIS FELIPE EDWARDS *Colchagua, Chile* Progressive family-owned winery that combines commercial winemaking with innovation and investment in new vineyard locations. The latest development is the 'Hilltop' project, a series of vineyards at between 500 and 900m (1600 –3000ft) above the Colchagua Valley floor – mostly Cabernet, Syrah and Carmenère, but also Mourvèdre and Grenache. 150ha (370 acres) have been planted in the Leyda Valley. Top wines are the Gran Reserva★ reds and Cabernet-dominant Doña Bernarda★.

LUNGAROTTI *Torgiano DOC, Umbria, Italy* Leading, nearly sole, producer of the fine, black-cherry-flavoured Torgiano DOC. The Torgiano Riserva (Vigna Monticchio★★) is DOCG. Also makes red San Giorgio★ (Cabernet-Sangiovese) and Chardonnay Palazzi.

LUSSAC-ST-ÉMILION AC *Bordeaux, France* Much of the wine from this AC, which tastes like a lighter ST-ÉMILION, is made by the first-rate local co-op and should be drunk within 4 years of the vintage; certain properties are worth seeking out. Best producers: Barbe-Blanche★, Bel-Air, Bellevue, Courlat★, la Grenière, Lussac★, Lyonnat★, Mayne Blanc, des Rochers★. Best years: **(2009)** 08 05 03 01 00 98 96 95.

EMILIO LUSTAU *Jerez y Manzanilla DO, Andalucia, Spain* Specializes in supplying 'own-label' wines to supermarkets. Quality is generally good, and there are some real stars at the top, especially the Almacenista range★★: very individual sherries from small, private producers.

CH. LYNCH-BAGES *Pauillac AC, 5ème Cru Classé, Haut-Médoc, Bordeaux, France* I am a great fan of Lynch-Bages red★★★ – with its almost succulent richness, its gentle texture and its starburst of flavours, all butter, blackcurrants and mint – and it is now one of PAUILLAC's most popular wines. Sadly, it's no longer underpriced but it's still worth the money. Impressive at 5 years, beautiful at 10 and irresistible at 20. Second wine: Echo de Lynch-Bages (since 2008); previously Haut-Bages-Averous. Also a small amount of white wine, Blanc de Lynch-Bages★. Best years: (reds) 2008 07 06 05 04 **03 02 01 00** 99 98 96 95 94 90 89 88 86.

LYNMAR *Russian River Valley AVA, California, USA* Small producer of super Chardonnay★★ and Pinot Noir★★, using largely estate-grown fru from its Quail Hill Vineyard. The gracious, supple Pinots age well, an winemaker Hugh Chappelle also makes a peppery, cold-climate Syrah as well as an elegant Pinot Noir rosé★.

FRÉDÉRIC MABILEAU *St-Nicolas-de-Bourgueil AC, Loire Valley, France* Although established only in 1991, meticulous attention to detail and a gentl handling regime yield ST-NICOLAS-DE-BOURGUEIL (Les Rouillères★, Le Coutures★★, Éclipse★★) and BOURGUEIL (Racines★) of startling fru purity and finesse. A white SAUMUR★★ and ANJOU Blanc (maiden vintage 2007 and 2009) attest to Frédéric's passion for Chenin Blanc. ANJO Cabernet Sauvignon also new in 2007. Certified organic with effect fro 2009. Best years: (top reds) (2009) 08 **07 06 05 04 03 02 01 00.**

LE MACCHIOLE *Bolgheri, Tuscany, Italy* One of the leading quality estates the new Tuscany. Mainstay is Paleo Rosso★★, a pure Cabernet Fran Best known wine is the Merlot Messorio★★, while Scrio★★ is one of th best Syrahs in Italy. Best years: (2009) (08) 07 06 **04 03 01 00 99.**

MÂCON AC *Mâconnais, Burgundy, France* The basic Mâcon AC, but mo whites in the region are labelled under the superior MÂCON-VILLAGES A The wines are rarely exciting. Mâcon Blanc, especially, is a rathe expensive basic quaffer. Drink young. Mâcon Supérieur has sensibly bee discontinued. Best producers: Bertillonnes, Bruyère, DUBOEUF, LAFON★.

MÂCON-VILLAGES AC *Mâconnais, Burgundy, France* There is a sea modestly priced and often modest wines under this appellation, whic covers 26 villages. Co-ops still dominate production, but these days handful of growers make more exciting wines from individually name villages such as Mâcon-Lugny and Mâcon la Roche Vineuse. Be villages: Bussières, Chaintré, Chardonnay, Charnay, Clessé, Cruzille Davayé, Igé, Lugny, Prissé, la Roche Vineuse, Uchizy, Verzy. Be producers: D & M Barraud★★, A Bonhomme★★, Bret Brothers★★, Deu Roches★, la Greffière★★, Guillot-Broux★★, LAFON★, J-J Litaud★, Jea Manciat★, O Merlin★★, R Michel★, Rijckaert★, Robert-Denogent★★ Saumaize-Michelin★, Valette★, VERGET★★, J-J Vincent★. Best years: (2009) 0 **07 06.** See also VIRÉ-CLESSÉ.

MACULAN *Breganze DOC, Veneto, Italy* Fausto Maculan makes an impressiv range under the Breganze DOC, led by Cabernet-Merlot blen Fratta★★ and Cabernet Palazzotto★, along with excellent reds★★ an whites★★ from the Ferrata vineyards. Even more impressive are swe Torcolato★★ and outstanding Acininobili★★★, made mainly fro botrytized Vespaiolo grapes.

MADEIRA DOC *Madeira, Portugal* The holiday island of Madeira seems a unlikely place to find a serious wine. However, Madeiras are very seriou wines indeed and the best can survive to a great age. Modern Madeir was shaped by the oïdium epidemic of the 1850s, which wiped out th vineyards, and phylloxera, which struck in the 1870s. Replantation wa with hybrid, non-*vinifera* vines greatly inferior to the 'noble' an traditional Malvasia (or Malmsey), Boal (or Bual), Verdelho and Sercia varieties. There are incentives to replant the hybrids with Europea varieties, but progress is slow, and most of the replantations are of the re Tinta Negra. The typically burnt, tangy taste of inexpensive Madeir comes from *estufagem*, heating in huge vats, but modern controls giv better flavours than used to be possible. The best wines are aged naturall in the subtropical warmth. All except dry wines are fortified early on an may be sweetened with fortified grape juice before bottling. Basic 3-year-old Madeira is made mainly from Tinta Negra, whereas higher-quality 10-year-old, 15-year-old and vintage wines (from a single year, aged in cask for at least 20 years) tend to be made from 1 of the 4 'noble' grapes. Colheita is an early-bottled vintage Madeira, which can be released after 5 years in wood (7 years for Sercial). Best producers: Barbeito, Barros e Souza, H M Borges, HENRIQUES & HENRIQUES, Vinhos Justino Henriques, MADEIRA WINE COMPANY, Pereira d'Oliveira.

MADEIRA WINE COMPANY *Madeira DOC, Madeira, Portugal* This company ships more than half of all Madeira exported in bottle. Among the brand names are Blandy's, Cossart Gordon, Leacock and Miles. Now controlled by the Symington family from the mainland. Big improvements have taken place in 5-, 10- and 15-year-old wines, including a tasty 5-year-old (a blend of Malvasia and Bual) called Alvada★. The vintage wines★★★ are superb. Specially blended 'early release' colheita wines are tasty and complete.

MADIRAN AC *South-West France* The gentle hills of Vic-Bilh, north of Pau, have seen a steady revival of the Madiran AC. Several of the best producers use new oak and micro-oxygenation, or *microbullage* – bubbling tiny amounts of oxygen into the wine, either during fermentation or during barrel aging – which helps to soften the rather aggressive wine, based on the tannic Tannat grape. If you're lucky, you'll taste damsons and bitter chocolate. Best producers: AYDIE★★, Barréjat★, Clos Baste★, BERTHOUMIEU★★, Bouscassé★★, Capmartin★★, CHAPELLE LENCLOS★★, du Crampilh★, Labranche-Laffont★★, LAFFITTE-TESTON★★, MONTUS★★, PLAIMONT, Viella★. Best years: (2009) 08 **06 05 04 02 01**.

CH. MAGDELAINE★ *St-Émilion Grand Cru AC, 1er Grand Cru Classé, Bordeaux, France* Dark, rich, aggressive wines, yet with a load of luscious fruit and oaky spice. In lighter years the wine has a gushing, easy, tender fruit and can be enjoyed at 5–10 years. Owned by the quality-conscious company of MOUEIX. Best years: 2008 06 05 **04 03 01 00 99 98 96 95 90 89**.

MAIPO *Chile* Historic heart of the Chilean wine industry and increasingly encroached upon by Chile's capital, Santiago. Cabernet is king and many premium-priced reds come from here. Good Chardonnay from vineyards close to the Andes. Best producers: ALMAVIVA★★★, Antiyal★★, CARMEN★★, CONCHA Y TORO★★, COUSIÑO MACUL★, DE MARTINO★★, ERRÁZURIZ★★ (Viñedo Chadwick★★★), HARAS DE PIRQUE★★, PÉREZ CRUZ★, SANTA RITA★, UNDURRAGA.

MAJELLA *Coonawarra, South Australia* The Lynn family are long-term grapegrowers turned successful winemakers. A trademark lush, sweet vanillin oakiness to the reds is always balanced by dense, opulent fruit. The profound Malleea★★★ (Cabernet-Shiraz) is the flagship, while the Cabernet Sauvignon★★★ (a succulent, fleshy cassis bomb) and Shiraz★★ are almost as good and very reasonably priced; the Musician★★ (Cabernet-Shiraz) is rich but deliciously drinkable.

MÁLAGA DO *Andalucía, Spain* Málaga is a curious blend of sweet wine, alcohol and juices; production is dwindling. The best are intensely nutty, raisiny and caramelly. A 'sister' appellation, Sierras de Málaga, includes non-fortified wines. Best producers: Cortijo Los Aguilares★, Gomara★, López Hermanos★★, Jorge Ordóñez★★, Telmo RODRIGUEZ★, Friedrich Schatz★.

CH. MALARTIC-LAGRAVIÈRE★★ *Pessac-Léognan AC, Cru Classé de Graves, Bordeaux, France* A change of ownership in 1997 and massive investment in the vineyard and cellars have seen a considerable improvement here since the 98 vintage. The tiny amount of white★★ is made from a majority of Sauvignon Blanc (80%) and usually softens after 3–4 years into a lovely nutty wine. Best years: (reds) 2008 07 06 05 04 03 02 01 00 99 98 96; (whites) **2008 07 06 05 04 03 02 01 99**.

MALBEC A red grape, rich in tannin and flavour, from South-West France. The major ingredient in CAHORS wines, where it is known as Auxerrois, it is also planted in the LOIRE, where it is called Côt. However, it is also successful in Chile and especially in Argentina, where it produces lush, textured, ripe, perfumed, damsony reds. In California and New Zealand it sometimes appears in BORDEAUX-style blends. In South Africa and Australia it is used both in blends and for varietal wines.

CH. MALESCOT ST-EXUPÉRY★ *Margaux AC, 3ème Cru Classé, Haut-Médoc, Bordeaux, France* Once one of the most scented, exotic reds in Bordeaux, a model of perfumed MARGAUX. In the 1980s Malescot lost its reputation and some vintages were pale, dilute and uninspired, but since 1995 it has begun to rediscover that cassis and violet perfume and return to its former glory. Can reach ★★, for example in 2004. Best years: 2008 07 06 05 **04 03 02 01 00 99 98 96 95 90**.

HERDADE DA MALHADINHA NOVA *Alentejo DOC, Portugal* 2003 arrival on the ALENTEJO wine scene, owned by the Soares family (who also have an Algarve wine-shop chain). Ultra-modern winery and wines, making Monte da Peceguinha red, white and rosé, and top wines, Malhadinha Tinto★★, Malhadinha Branco★ and Marias da Malhadinha★★.

MALVASIA This grape, of Greek origin via the port of Venice, is widely planted in Italy and is found in many guises, both white and red. In Friuli and over the border in Croatia it is known as the Malvasia Istriana and produces light, mildly fragrant wines of some charm, while in TUSCANY, UMBRIA and the rest of central Italy it is widely used to make innocuous dry and sweet whites. On the islands, Malvasia is used in rich, dry or sweet wines in Bosa and Cagliari (in SARDINIA) and in Lipari off the coast of SICILY to make really tasty, apricotty sweet wines. As a black grape, Malvasia Nera is blended with Negroamaro in PUGLIA and occasionally with Sangiovese in CHIANTI. Variants of Malvasia grow in Spain's Canary Islands and mainland Portugal. On the island of MADEIRA it produces sweet fortified wine, usually known by its English name, Malmsey.

LA MANCHA DO *Castilla-La Mancha, Spain* Spain's vast central plateau is Europe's biggest delimited wine area. Since 1995, DO regulations have allowed for irrigation and the planting of new, higher-quality grape varieties, including Macabeo (Viura), Verdejo, Chardonnay, Cabernet Sauvignon, Petit Verdot, Merlot and Syrah – and also banned new plantings of the simple white Airén grape. Whites are rarely exciting but nowadays are often fresh and attractive (see AIRÉN). Reds can be light and fruity, or richer. Best producers: Ayuso, Campos Reales★, Vinícola de Castilla (Castillo de Alhambra, Señorío de Guadianeja), Finca Antigua★, Fontana★, Muñoz (Blas Muñoz★), Rodriguez & Berger (Santa Elena), Torres Filoso (Arboles de Castillejo), Casa de la Viña.

MANCHUELA DO *Castilla-La Mancha, Spain* Higher, hillier, cooler than its huge neighbour La MANCHA. The international recognition gained since 2000 by Finca Sandoval has helped a small band of private producers and quality-conscious co-ops get a foothold in foreign markets. **Best producers:** Altolandón★, Cien y Pico★, Finca Sandoval★★, Monegrillo, Ponce★, San Antonio Abad, Vega Tolosa, Vitis Natura, Vitivinos.

DOM. ALBERT MANN *Alsace AC, Alsace, France* Powerful, flavoursome and ageworthy wines from a range of Grand Cru vineyards, including intense, mineral Rieslings from Furstentum★★ and Schlossberg★★ and rich Furstentum Gewurztraminer★★. Impressive range of Pinot Gris culminates in some astonishingly concentrated Sélections de Grains Nobles★★★. Basic wines are increasingly stylish. **Best years:** (Sélection de Grains Nobles Gewurztraminer) 2007 **05 01 00 98 97 94 89.**

MAN O'WAR *Waiheke Island, Auckland, North Island, New Zealand* Wealthy businessman John Spencer is the largest vineyard (and land) owner on WAIHEKE ISLAND; almost 90 small pockets of vines are spread over his 1800ha (4500-acre) estate. After a slow start they're now making some cracking wines, including an heroic Valhalla Chardonnay★ and even more powerful Ironclad Cabernet★, plus strong, spicy Dreadnought Syrah★★. **Best years:** (reds) (2009) 08 **07.**

MARANGES AC *Côte de Beaune, Burgundy, France* AC right at the southern tip of the CÔTE DE BEAUNE. Slightly tough red wines of medium depth which are mainly sold as CÔTE DE BEAUNE-VILLAGES. Less than 5% of production is white. **Best producers:** M Charleux★, Chevrot★, Contat-Grangé★, DROUHIN. **Best years:** (reds) (2009) 08 **07 05 03 02 99.**

MARCASSIN *Sonoma County, California, USA* Helen Turley focuses on cool-climate Chardonnay and Pinot Noir. Incredible depth and restrained power are the hallmarks here. Tiny quantities of single-vineyard Chardonnays (Alexander Mountain Upper Barn, Three Sisters Vineyard, Marcassin Vineyard) and Pinot Noirs (Marcassin Vineyard, Three Sisters Vineyard, Blue Slide Vineyard) are very difficult to obtain but can rank ★★★ with those who manage to get a mouthful. **Best years:** (2005) **04 03 02 01 00 99 98.**

MARCHE *Italy* Adriatic region producing increasingly good reds from Montepulciano and Sangiovese, led by ROSSO CONERO and ROSSO PICENO; also from the curiously aromatic, indigenous Lacrima di Morro d'Alba. Good international varietals such as Cabernet, Chardonnay and Merlot under the Marche IGT or Esino DOC are becoming more common, as well as blends with the native grapes. Best of the reds are Boccadigabbia's Akronte★★ (Cabernet), Oasi degli Angeli's Kurni★★ (Montepulciano), Monte Schiavo's Adeodato★★ (Montepulciano), Umani Ronchi's Pelago★★ (Montepulciano-Cabernet-Merlot), La Monacesca's Camerte★★ (Sangiovese-Merlot) and le Terrazze's Chaos★★ (Montepulciano-Merlot-Syrah). However, the truly original wines here are the whites from VERDICCHIO DEI CASTELLI DI JESI.

MARCILLAC AC *South-West France* Curranty, dry red wines (and a little rosé), largely made from a local grape, Mansois. The reds are rustic but full of fruit and should be drunk at 2–5 years old. **Best producers:** Costes, Cros/Philippe Teulier★, Marcillac-Vallon co-op, Jean-Luc Matha★, Mioula★.

MAREMMA *Tuscany, Italy* The name given to the Tuscan Tyrrhenian coast, notably the southern part. DOCs include (south to north): Capalbio, Parrina, Bianco di Pitigliano, MORELLINO DI SCANSANO, Montecucco,

Monteregio di Massa Marittima, Val de Cornia, BOLGHERI. IG'
Maremma Toscana covers the province of Grosseto. In these clime
compared with inland, Sangiovese comes softer and jammier, th
BORDEAUX grapes thrive and vintages count for much less.

MARGARET RIVER *Western Australia* Planted on the advice of agronomis
John Gladstones from the late 1960s, this coastal region quickl
established its name as a leading area for Cabernet, with marvellousl
deep, BORDEAUX-like structured reds. Now Chardonnay, concentrate
and opulent, vies with Cabernet for top spot, but there is also fine grass
Semillon, often blended with citrus-zest Sauvignon. Increasingly popula
Shiraz provides the occasional gem, but there's too much dull stuff. Be
producers: Amberley★, Arlewood, Ashbrook★, Brookland Valley★★, CAF
MENTELLE★★, Chapman Grove, Clairault★, CULLEN★★★, Devil's Lair★★
Edwards, Evans & Tate★★, Fermoy Estate★, Fraser Gallop, Gralyn★, HOWAR
PARK★★, Juniper Estate, LEEUWIN ESTATE★★★, Lenton Brae★, McHenr
Hohnen★, MOSS WOOD★★, PIERRO★★, SANDALFORD★, Stella Bella★★, VASS
FELIX★★, VOYAGER ESTATE★★, Watershed, Windance, Woodlands★★
Woodside Valley★, Xanadu★. Best years: (Cabernet-based reds) 2009 08 07 0
04 03 01 00 99 98 96 95.

MARGAUX AC *Haut-Médoc, Bordeaux, France* AC centred on the village c
Margaux. Gravel banks dotted through the vineyards mean the wines a
rarely heavy and should have a divine perfume after 7–12 years. Be
producers: (Classed Growths) Boyd-Cantenac★, BRANE-CANTENAC★★
Cantenac Brown, Dauzac★, FERRIÈRE★★, Giscours★, ISSAN★, KIRWAN★
LASCOMBES, MALESCOT ST-EXUPÉRY★, MARGAUX★★★, PALMER★★, PRIEURI
LICHINE★, RAUZAN-SEGLA★★, Tertre★; (others) ANGLUDET★, Eyrins★,
Gurgue★, LABÉGORCE-ZÉDÉ★, Monbrison★, SIRAN★. Best years: (2009) 08 06 0
04 03 02 01 00 99 96 95.

CH. MARGAUX★★★ *Margaux AC, 1er Cru Classé, Haut-Médoc, Bordeaux, Franc*
Frequently the greatest wine in the MÉDOC. Has produced almost flawles
wines since 1978, and inspired winemaker Paul Pontallier continues t
produce the best from this great *terroir*. Also some delicious white
Pavillon Blanc★★, from Sauvignon Blanc, but it must be the mo
expensive BORDEAUX AC wine by a mile. Second wine: Pavillon Rouge★★
Best years: (reds) 2008 07 06 05 04 **03 02 01 00 99 98 96 95 90 89 88 86 8**
(whites) **2008 07 06 05 04 02 01 00 99 98 96 95**.

MARIAH *Mendocino Ridge AVA, Mendocino County, California, USA* Boutiqu
winery producing Zinfandel from a vineyard at 600m (2000f
overlooking the Pacific Ocean. The wines have cherry fruit and natural
high acidity. Mariah Vineyard Zinfandel★★ is the flagship; Po
Ranch★ is lighter but elegant. A tiny amount of fruit-forward Syrah★
also made. Best years: (Zinfandel) 2006 05 **02 01 00**.

MARIMAR ESTATE See Marimar TORRES.

MARLBOROUGH *South Island, New Zealand* This wine region has enjoye
such spectacular success that it is difficult to imagine that the first commerci
vines were planted as recently as 1973. Marlborough is now home to mo
than half the country's vines. Its 2 main vineyard areas are Wairau Valley an
AWATERE VALLEY, and its long, cool and relatively dry ripening season, co
nights and free-draining stony soils are the major assets. Its snappy, aromat
Sauvignon Blanc first brought the region fame worldwide. Fine-flavoure
Chardonnay, steely Riesling, elegant CHAMPAGNE-method fizz and lusciou
botrytized wines are other successes. Pinot Noir is now establishing a stror

regional identity. Best producers: ASTROLABE★★, Cape Campbell★, CLOUDY BAY★★, The Crossings★, Dog Point★★, Forrest★★, Foxes Island★, FRAMINGHAM★, FROMM★★, HUNTER'S★, JACKSON ESTATE, Lawson's Dry Hills★, Mahi★, MONTANA★, MORTON ESTATE★, Mount Riley★, Nautilus★, SAINT CLAIR★★, SERESIN★, Stoneleigh★, VILLA MARIA★★, WITHER HILLS★. Best years: (Chardonnay) **2009** 07 06 05; (Pinot Noir) **2007** 06 05 04 03; (Sauvignon Blanc) **2009** 07 06 05. See also AWATERE VALLEY.

MARQUÉS DE CÁCERES *Rioja DOCa, Rioja, Spain* Go-ahead RIOJA winery making crisp, aromatic, modern whites★ and rosés★, and fleshy, fruity reds (Reservas★) with the emphasis on aging in bottle, not barrel. There is also a luxury red, Gaudium★. Best years: (reds) (2007) 06 05 **04 03 01** 99 98 96 95 94 92 91 90 89.

MARQUÉS DE GRIÑÓN *Castilla-La Mancha, Spain* From his estate at Malpica, near Toledo, now with its own Dominio de Valdepusa DO, Carlos Falcó (the eponymous Marqués) produces some impressive if super-ripe wines: the basic Caliza, Dominio de Valdepusa Cabernet Sauvignon★, Petit Verdot★, Syrah★ and Eméritus★, a blend of the 3 varieties. Graciano★★, stunning since 2005, is now the estate's top wine. Best years: (Eméritus) 2005 04 03 02 01 00 99 98.

MARQUÉS DE MURRIETA *Rioja DOCa, Rioja, Spain* This RIOJA bodega faithfully preserves the traditional style of long aging, but typical time in barrel has been reduced by a third. The ornately labelled Castillo Ygay Gran Reserva★★ is less forbidding than in the past. There's a more international-styled, oaky cuvée, Dalmau★★. Whites are dauntingly oaky but age brilliantly, reds are packed with savoury mulberry fruit. Best years: (reds) (2006) 05 04 **03 01 00** 99 96 95 94 92 91 89 87 85.

MARQUÉS DE RISCAL *Rioja DOCa, País Vasco and Rueda DO, Castilla y León, Spain* A producer which has restored its reputation for classic pungent RIOJA reds (Reserva★, Gran Reserva★★). Expensive Barón de Chirel★★, with significant Cabernet contents recreating the winery's tradition, is made only in selected years. Attractively aromatic RUEDA whites★. Best years: (Barón de Chirel) 2001 99 96 95 94.

MARSALA DOC *Sicily, Italy* Fortified wines, once as esteemed as sherry or Madeira. A taste of an old Vergine (unsweetened) Marsala, fine and complex, will show why. Today most is sweetened. Purists say this mars its delicate nuances, but DOC regulations allow for sweetening Fine and Superiore versions. Best producers: DE BARTOLI★★, Florio (Baglio Florio★, Terre Arse★), Pellegrino (Soleras★, Riserva 1962★).

MARSANNAY AC *Côte de Nuits, Burgundy, France* Village almost in Dijon, best known for its pleasant but quite austere rosé. Reds are much better: light, but frequently one of Burgundy's more fragrant wines. Whites mostly dull. Best producers: Audoin★, P Charlopin★★, B CLAIR★★, Geantet-Pansiot★★, JADOT★, MÉO-CAMUZET★, D MORTET★★, Pataille★★, J & J-L Trapet★. Best years: (reds) (2009) 08 **07** 06 05.

MARSANNE Undervalued white grape yielding rich, nutty, wines in the northern Rhône (notably HERMITAGE, CROZES-HERMITAGE, ST-JOSEPH and ST-PÉRAY), often with the more scented, lively Roussanne. Generally drink young, except the Hermitage, which can mature for decades. Also used in southern Rhône, PIC ST-LOUP and other LANGUEDOC wines, and performs well in Australia, especially at Mitchelton and TAHBILK. As Ermitage, it produces some good wines in Swiss VALAIS.

MARTINBOROUGH/WAIRARAPA North Island, New Zealand   A cool, d
climate, free-draining soil and a passion for quality are this region's greate
assets. Mild autumn weather promotes intense flavours balanced by goo
acidity: top Pinot Noir and complex Chardonnay, intense Cabernet blends i
favourable years, full Sauvignon Blanc and honeyed Riesling. **Best producer**
(Martinborough) ATA RANGI★★★, CRAGGY RANGE★, DRY RIVER★★★
Escarpment★★, Kusuda★★, MARTINBOROUGH VINEYARD★★, Murdoch James★, N
Waka★, PALLISER ESTATE★★; (Wairarapa) Johner★, Matahiwi★, Schubert★. Be
years: (Pinot Noir) (2009) **08 07 06 03 01 00.**

MARTINBOROUGH VINEYARD Martinborough, North Island, New Zealar
Famous for Pinot Noir★★ but also makes impressive Chardonnay★
spicy Riesling★, creamy Pinot Gris★ and luscious botrytized styles★
when vintage conditions allow. Good vineyard sites and sensitiv
winemaking have produced a string of very elegant wines. **Best year**
(Pinot Noir) (2009) **08 07 06 03 01 00.**

MARTÍNEZ BUJANDA Rioja DOCa, País Vasco, Spain   This family-owned firm
known for producing some of the best modern RIOJA, was split in two i
2007: Carlos and Pilar Martínez-Bujanda retain the Finca Valpiedra an
Finca Antigua estates and the Cosecheros y Criadores wine compan
while Jesús Martínez-Bujanda keeps the Valdemar winery in Rioja. Th
2006 vintage saw a commendable modernization of style for Valpiedr
young-vines red Cantos★ is soft and lush, Reserva★★ is scented an
refined. Whites and rosés are young and crisp.

MARYLAND USA   Maryland's Boordy Vineyards was the pioneer in Frenc
hybrid varieties, but the state fell behind its neighbour VIRGINIA in growth an
quality, despite sharing a similar moderate climate and benefits of the Blu
Ridge Mountains. However, things have improved dramatically since the tur
of the century as new wineries have implemented rigorous vineyard standard
Best producers: Black Ankle, Boordy, Elk Run, Sugarloaf Mountain.

MARZEMINO This red grape of northern Italy's TRENTINO province make
deep-coloured, plummy and zesty reds that are best drunk within 3–
years. **Best producers: Battistotti★, La Cadalora★, Cavit★, Concilio Vini★, D**
Tarczal★, Isera co-op★, Letrari★, Mezzacorona, Eugenio Rosi★, Simoncelli★
Spagnolli★, De Tarczal★, Vallarom★, Vallis Agri★.

DOM. DU MAS BLANC Banyuls AC, Roussillon, France   Run by the Parc
family, this estate makes great traditional BANYULS, specializing in th
rimage (early-bottled vintage) style (La Coume★★). Also Banyuls Hoi
d'Age from a solera laid down in 1955, plus a range of Jean-Michel Parc
COLLIOURES★★. **Best years: (2009) 08 07 06 05 04 03 01 00 98.**

MAS BRUGUIÈRE Pic St-Loup, Coteaux du Languedoc AC, Languedoc, France   Th
PIC ST-LOUP red L' Arbouse★ has rich, spicy Syrah character, while L
Grenadière★★ develops buckets of black fruit and spice after 3 year
Super-cuvée Le Septième★★ (seventh generation) blends Mourvèdr
with some Syrah. Calcadiz is an easy-drinking red; aromatic, fruit
refreshing white Les Mûriers★ is based on Roussanne. **Best years: (red**
(2009) 08 07 06 05 04 03 01.

MAS LA CHEVALIÈRE Vin de Pays d'Oc, Languedoc, France   State-of-the-a
winery created by Chablis producer LAROCHE in the early 1990
Innovative wines include La Croix Chevalière★, a blend of Merlo

Syrah and Grenache, and Mas la Chevalière Rouge★, from the estate vineyard. Best years: (2009) 08 07 06 **05 04 03 01**.

MAS DE DAUMAS GASSAC *Vin de Pays de l'Hérault, Languedoc, France*

Aimé Guibert has proved for over 20 years that the HERAULT, normally associated with cheap table wine, can produce fine, ageworthy reds. The tannic yet rich Cabernet Sauvignon-based red★, more concentrated Cuvée Emile Peynaud★★ and the lush, scented white★ (Viognier, Chardonnay, Petit Manseng and Chenin) are impressive, if expensive. Sweet Vin de Laurence★★ is a triumph. Best years: (reds) (2009) 08 07 06 **05 04 03 02 01 00**.

MAS DOIX *Priorat DOCa, Cataluña, Spain* The Doix and Llagostera families own some extraordinary old Garnacha and Cariñena vineyards, which provide the grapes for some equally impressive wines. Doix Vinyes Velles★★★ is probably the first of the new generation PRIORATs to reach the heights of the pioneers such as CLOS ERASMUS, CLOS MOGADOR and Alvaro PALACIOS' L'Ermita. Best years: 2006 05 04 03 **02 01**.

BARTOLO MASCARELLO *Barolo DOCG, Piedmont, Italy* Bartolo Mascarello died in 2005; his daughter Maria Teresa has run the winery since the early 1990s. Proudly traditional, the BAROLO★★★ remains a blend of vineyards in the traditional manner. The Dolcetto★ and Barbera★ can need a little time to soften. Best years: (Barolo) (2009) (08) (07) 06 **04 03 01 00 99 98 97 96 95 90 89 88 86 85**.

GIUSEPPE MASCARELLO *Barolo DOCG, Piedmont, Italy* The old house of Giuseppe Mascarello (now run by grandson Mauro) is renowned for dense, vibrant Dolcetto d'Alba (Bricco★★) and intense Barbera (Codana★★), but the pride of the house is BAROLO from the superb south-west-facing Monprivato★★★ vineyard in Castiglione Falletto. A little is now produced as a Riserva, Cà d'Morissio★★★, in top years. Small amounts are also made from the Bricco, Santo Stefano di Perno and Villero vineyards. Best years: (Monprivato) (2009) (08) (07) 06 **04 03 01 00 99 98 97 96 95 93 91 90 89 88 85 82 78**.

MASI *Veneto, Italy* Family firm, one of the driving forces in VALPOLICELLA. Brolo di Campofiorin★ (effectively if not legally a *ripasso* Valpolicella) is worth looking out for, as is AMARONE (Mazzano★★ and Campolongo di Torbe★★). Valpolicella's Corvina grape is also used in red blend Toar★; Osar★ is made from a local grape, Oseleta, rediscovered by Masi. The wines of Serègo Alighieri★ are also produced by Masi. Best years: (Amarone) (2009) (08) 07 06 **04 03 01 00 97**.

MASTROBERARDINO *Campania, Italy* For many years this family firm flew the flag almost alone for CAMPANIA in southern Italy, though it has now been joined by numerous others. Best known for red TAURASI★★ and white Greco di Tufo★ and Fiano di Avellino★. Best years: (Taurasi Radici) (2009) (08) (07) 06 05 **04 03 01** 99 97 96 95 90 89 88 85 68.

MATANZAS CREEK *Bennett Valley AVA, Sonoma County, California, USA* Sauvignon Blanc★ is taken seriously here, and it shows in a complex, zesty wine; Chardonnay★★ is rich and toasty but not overblown. Merlot★★ has silky, mouthfilling richness. Journey Chardonnay★★ and Merlot★★ are opulent but pricey. Among the experiments here includes one in which Chardonnay is being aged in acacia wood barrels. Owned by Jackson Family Wines. **Best years:** (Chardonnay) 2006 05 04 **03 02 01 00**; (Merlot) 2005 04 03 02 **01 00 99 97 96 95**.

MATETIC VINEYARDS *San Antonio, Chile* Matetic has been making high quality organic wines from SAN ANTONIO – especially under the EQ label – since it burst on to the scene in 2001. Exceptional, concentrated and scented Syrah★★ is the star, but there's also a fleshy Pinot Noir★, juicy Sauvignon Blanc★ and refreshing Coastal Sauvignon★.

MATUA VALLEY *Auckland, North Island, New Zealand* This once exciting and innovative winery has become more commercial since becoming part of the giant Foster's Group. Top wines are still good, with whites more consistent than reds: sensuous, scented Ararimu Chardonnay★★; lush strongly varietal Gewürztraminer★; tangy MARLBOROUGH Sauvignon Blanc★; fine Merlot★; and Ararimu★ red blend. Second label: Shingle Peak. **Best years:** (Ararimu red) (2008) **07 04 03 02 00**.

CH. MAUCAILLOU★ *Moulis AC, Haut-Médoc, Bordeaux, France* Maucaillou shows that you don't have to be a Classed Growth to make high-quality claret. Expertly made by the Dourthe family, it is soft but classically flavoured. It is accessible early on but ages well for 10–12 years. **Best years:** 2008 06 05 04 03 02 00 98 96 95 90.

MAULE *Chile* The most southerly sub-region of Chile's CENTRAL VALLEY, with wet winters and a large day/night temperature difference. Nearly 30% of Chile's vines are planted here, with nearly 10,000ha (25,000 acres) of Cabernet Sauvignon. Merlot does well on the cool clay soils and there is some tasty Carmenère and Syrah. Whites are mostly Chardonnay and Sauvignon Blanc. A new community of producers has recently been redefining Maule's identity, especially using old-vine Carignan in the Cauquenes sub-region. Miguel TORRES has developed an exciting sub-region called Empedrado, which promises styles reminiscent of PRIORAT, and there's a general feeling that Maule's old 'bulk' mentality is giving way to a quality focus. **Best producers:** J Bouchon, CONCHA Y TORO★, DE MARTINO★★, O FOURNIER★★, Gillmore★★, La Reserva de Caliboro★★, Odfjell★, Palo Alto, VALDIVIESO★.

MAURO *Castilla y León, Spain* After making a name for himself as VEGA SICILIA's winemaker for 30 years, Mariano García propelled his family's estate to the forefront in Spain and abroad. Wines include Crianza★★, Vendimia Seleccionada★★ and Terreus★★★. **Best years:** (2007) 06 05 **04 03 02 01 00** 99 98 97 96 95 94.

MAURY AC *Roussillon, France* A *vin doux naturel*, mainly from Grenache Noir. This strong, sweetish wine can be made in either a young, fresh style (vintage) or the locally revered old *rancio* style. **Best producers:** la Coume du Roy★, Mas Amiel★★, Maury co-op★, Maurydoré★, la Pléiade★.

MAXIMIN GRÜNHAUS *Grünhaus, Mosel-Saar-Ruwer, Germany* One of Germany's great wine estates, with 2 top vineyards, Abtsberg and Herrenberg, both of monastic origin. Dr Carl von Schubert makes chiefly dry and medium-dry wines of great subtlety. In good vintages the top wines are ★★★ and are among the most long-lived white wines in the world. **Best years:** (2009) 08 07 06 **05 04 03 01 00** 99 97 95 94 93 92 90.

MAZIS-CHAMBERTIN, MAZOYÈRES-CHAMBERTIN See CHAMBERTIN AC.

McLAREN VALE *South Australia* Sunny maritime region south of Adelaide, producing superb full-bodied wines from Shiraz, Grenache and Cabernet. Traditionally whites have been overshadowed, but Fiano, Savagnin, Marsanne, Roussanne, Verdelho and Viognier are now making their mark, along with chubby Chardonnay. More than 60 small wineries, plus big boys Constellation and the Foster's Wine Group. Best producers: Cascabel, CHAPEL HILL★★, CLARENDON HILLS★★, Coriole★, D'ARENBERG★★, FOX CREEK★★, Gemtree, HARDYS★★, Kangarilla Road★, Maxwell★, Geoff MERRILL★, Mitolo, Oliver's Taranga★, S C PANNELL★★, Paxton, Penny's Hill, Pirramimma, PRIMO ESTATE★★, RockBare, Scarpantoni, Shingleback, Tatachilla★, WIRRA WIRRA★★, Woodstock.

cWILLIAM'S *Riverina, New South Wales, Australia* Large family winery, whose Hanwood brand is a joint venture with California's GALLO, delivering good flavours at a fair price. Best are the Mount Pleasant wines from the HUNTER VALLEY: classic bottle-aged Semillons (Elizabeth★★★, Lovedale★★★), buttery Chardonnays★ and special-vineyard Shirazes – Old Paddock & Old Hill★★, Maurice O'Shea (★★★ in the best years) and Rosehill★. Classy sweet Semillon★★ and Liqueur Muscat★★ from RIVERINA, and good table wines from HILLTOPS Barwang★ vineyard. McWilliam's own Lillydale in the YARRA (sublime Chardonnay★★), BRAND's in COONAWARRA, and in 2008 bought the good-quality Evans & Tate label following the collapse of the MARGARET RIVER-based company. Best years: (Elizabeth Semillon) (2009) (08) (07) (06) 05 04 03 **02 01 00** 99 98 97 96 95 94 87 86 84 83.

ÉDOC AC *Bordeaux, France* The Médoc peninsula north of Bordeaux on the left bank of the Gironde river produces a good fistful of the world's most famous reds. These are all situated in the HAUT-MÉDOC, the southern, more gravelly half of the area. The Médoc AC, for reds only, covers the northern part. Merlot dominates in these flat clay vineyards and the wines can be attractive in warm years: earthily dry but juicy. Best at 3–5 years old. Best producers: Bournac★, Escurac★, Goulée★, les Grands Chênes★, Greysac★, L'Inclassable★, Loudenne★, Lousteauneuf★, les Ormes-Sorbet★, Patache d'Aux, POTENSAC★★, Preuillac, Ramafort★, Rollan de By★ (Haut Condissas★), la Tour de By★, la Tour Haut-Caussan★, Tour St-Bonnet★, Vieux-Robin★. Best years: **(2009) 08 06 05 04 03 01 00 96 95**.

EEREA PARK *Hunter Valley, New South Wales Australia* Brothers Rhys and Garth Eather specialize in single-vineyard, old-vine HUNTER VALLEY Semillon and Shiraz; they are helping breathe new life into the region with classy, pristine, ageworthy wines. Hell Hole Semillon★ is vibrant, lemony and restrained when young; gently toasty, minerally and delicious with age. Alexander Munro Shiraz★ shows seamless integration of fruit, oak and tannins, and pure brambly flavours.

EERLUST *Stellenbosch WO, South Africa* Under cellarmaster Chris Williams this venerable estate's celebrated reds show greater freshness and harmony: Cabernet★★ is supple yet vibrant, Merlot★ plush and finely textured, together with Cabernet Franc in Rubicon★, one of the Cape's first BORDEAUX blends, achieving harmony and complexity. A silky Pinot Noir completes the range. Sole white in this focused, classic range is an elegant, fresh Chardonnay★. Best years: (Rubicon) (2006) 05 **04 03 01 00** 99 98 97; (Chardonnay) (2009) 08 **07 06 05 04 03 01**.

LPHONSE MELLOT *Sancerre AC, Loire Valley, France* Biodynamic producer with an equal focus on white and red SANCERRE, made with obsessive attention to detail by Alphonse 'Junior', the 19th generation of the family. Other than unoaked white cuvée La Moussière★, wines come exclusively from old vines and show a fine balance of fruit and oak. New cuvée Satellite★★ is from 60-year-old vines. White Edmond★★ and red and white Génération XIX★★ are outstanding and reward keeping. Also

makes aromatic, fruity Chardonnay and Pinot Noir★ vins de pays Le
Pénitents. Best years: (Edmond white) 2008 **07 06 05 04 03 02 01**.

CHARLES MELTON *Barossa Valley, South Australia* One of the leading light
in the renaissance of hand-crafted Shiraz, Grenache and Mourvèdre i
the BAROSSA. Fruity Grenache rosé Rose of Virginia★★ is arguabl
Australia's best; RHÔNE-blend Nine Popes★★, heady, sumptuou
Grenache★★, smoky Shiraz★★ and Sparkling Red★★ have all attaine
cult status. Cabernet Sauvignon is variable, but ★★ at best. Two single
site Shiraz: fleshy, blackberry-pastille Grains of Paradise★★ from th
Barossa Valley, and fragrant, elegant, brambly Voices of Angels★★ fror
the Eden Valley. Best years: (Nine Popes) (2009) 05 04 **03 02 01 99 98 9**
95 94 91 90.

MENDOCINO COUNTY *California, USA* The northernmost county of th
North Coast AVA. It includes cool-climate ANDERSON VALLEY, exceller
for sparkling wines and a little Pinot Noir; and the warmer Redwoo
Valley AVA, with good Zinfandel and Cabernet. Coro is a stylis
Zinfandel-based blend made by numerous Mendocino wineries. Bes
producers: Brutocao★, Claudia Springs★, FETZER, Goldeneye★, Graziand
HANDLEY★★, Husch, Lazy Creek★, Littorai★, McDowell Valley★
NAVARRO★★★, Pax★, ROEDERER ESTATE★★, Saracina★, SCHARFFENBERGE
CELLARS★★. Best years: (reds) 2006 05 04 **03 01 00 99 97 96 95 94 93 91 90**

MENDOCINO RIDGE AVA *California, USA* One of the most unusual AVA
in California. Mendocino Ridge starts at an altitude of 365m (1200ft) o
the timber-covered mountaintops of western MENDOCINO COUNT
Because of the topography, the AVA is non-contiguous: rising above th
fog, the vineyards are commonly referred to as 'islands in the sky
Currently only 30ha (75 acres) are planted, primarily with Zinfande
Best producers: Edmeades★, Greenwood Ridge★, MARIAH★, STEELE★★.

MENDOZA *Argentina* The most important wine province in Argentina
accounting for around 80% of the country's wine. Situated in the easter
foothills of the Andes, Mendoza's bone-dry climate produces powerfu
high-alcohol reds.The region is complex and vast. Altitude is the key, th
higher the vineyards the higher the quality, so the Uco Valley, har
against the Andes, has the freshest whites and the raciest reds. Ancier
areas to the south and west of Mendoza city, including Vistalba, Agrelo
Perdriel and Las Compuertas, are famed for profound, intens
structured reds. Best producers: ACHAVAL FERRER★★★, Bressia★, CATENA★★
Clos de Chacras★, COBOS★★, Cuvelier Los Andes★★, DOMINIO DEL PLATA★★
DOÑA PAULA★★, FABRE MONTMAYOU★, Finca Sophenia, O FOURNIER★★
Lurton★, Mendel★★, NORTON★, PASCUAL TOSO★, Pulenta★, TERRAZAS DE LC
ANDES★★, TRAPICHE★★, ZUCCARDI★.

MENETOU-SALON AC *Loire Valley, France* Attractive, chalky-clea
Sauvignon whites and cherry-fresh Pinot Noir reds and rosés from wes
of SANCERRE. Badly hit by hail in 2009. Best producers: R Champaul
Chatenoy★, Chavet★, J-P Gilbert★, N Girard, P Jacolin, J Mellot, H Pellé★
J-M Roger★, J Teiller★, Tour St-Martin★.

MÉO-CAMUZET *Vosne-Romanée, Côte de Nuits, Burgundy, France* Super-qualit
estate. New oak barrels and luscious, rich fruit combine in superb wine
which age well. CLOS DE VOUGEOT★★★, RICHEBOURG★★★ and CORTON★
are the grandest wines, along with the VOSNE-ROMANÉE Premiers Crus (au
Brulées★★, Cros Parantoux★★★, les Chaumes★★). Fine NUITS-ST
GEORGES aux Boudots★★ and aux Murgers★★, and also some less expens
ive *négociant* wines. Best years: (2009) 08 07 06 05 **03 02 01 00 99 96 95 9**

ERCUREY AC *Côte Chalonnaise, Burgundy, France* The red from this village is usually pleasant and strawberry-flavoured, sometimes rustic, and can take some aging. There is not much white, but I like its buttery, even spicy, taste. Best at 3–4 years old. Best producers: (reds) FAIVELEY★, Hasard★, E Juillot★, M Juillot★, Lorenzon★★, F Raquillet★★, RODET★, de Suremain★★, de Villaine★★; (whites) FAIVELEY (Clos Rochette★), M Juillot★, O LEFLAIVE★, Ch. de Chamirey★. Best years: (reds) (2009) **08 07 05 03 02**.

ERLOT See pages 210–11.

EOFF MERRILL *McLaren Vale, South Australia* High-profile winemaker with a long track record. He doesn't like overripened fruit, so there's a nicely bottle-aged Reserve Cabernet★ in a light, early-picked, slightly eccentric style, Reserve Shiraz★ (Henley★★) and Chardonnay★ (Reserve★★). Also a moreish unoaked, yet ageworthy, Bush Vine Grenache★.

ERRYVALE *Napa Valley AVA, California, USA* A Chardonnay powerhouse (Silhouette★★, CARNEROS★★, Starmont★★), but reds are not far behind, with BORDEAUX-blend Profile★★ and juicy NAPA VALLEY Merlot★★. Best years: (Chardonnay) (2008) 07 06 **05 04 03 02 01 00 99**.

EURSAULT AC *Côte de Beaune, Burgundy, France* The biggest and most popular white wine village in the CÔTE D'OR. There are no Grands Crus, but a whole cluster of Premiers Crus, of which Perrières, Charmes and Genevrières stand out. The general standard is better than in neighbouring PULIGNY. The golden wine is lovely to drink young but ought to age for 5–8 years. Virtually no Meursault red is now made. Best producers: M Ampeau★★, M BOUZEREAU★★, V Bouzereau★, Boyer-Martenot★, Coche-Bizouard★★, COCHE-DURY★★★, Deux MONTILLE★, DROUHIN★, A Ente★★, J-P Fichet★★, Henri Germain★, V GIRARDIN★, Grux★, JADOT★★, P Javillier★★, François Jobard★★, Rémi Jobard★★, LAFON★★★, Latour-Labille★, Matrot★★, Mikulski★, Pierre Morey★★, G Roulot★★★. Best years: (2009) 08 07 **06 05 04 02 00 99**.

H. MEYNEY★ *St-Estèphe AC, Haut-Médoc, Bordeaux, France* One of the most reliable ST-ESTÈPHEs, producing broad-flavoured wine with dark, plummy fruit. Second wine: Prieur de Meyney. Best years: 2008 06 05 **04 03 02 01 00 99 98 96 95 94 90 89**.

ETER MICHAEL WINERY *Sonoma County, California, USA* British-born Sir Peter Michael has turned a country retreat into an impressive winery known for its small-batch wines. Les Pavots★★ is the estate red BORDEAUX blend (L'Espirit des Pavots★★ is also good). Top Chardonnays include Mon Plaisir★★, Cuvée Indigène★, Ma Belle-Fille★★ and La Carrière★. Also Le Caprice Pinot Noir★. Best years: (Les Pavots) 2006 05 04 03 02 **01 00 99 97 96 95 94 91 90**.

IILLTON *Gisborne, North Island, New Zealand* Organic vineyard using biodynamic methods, whose top wines include the powerful Clos de Ste Anne Chardonnay★, lush Riverpoint Viognier★, Opou Vineyard Riesling★ and complex barrel-fermented Chenin Blanc★★. Chardonnays and Rieslings both age well. Surprising, and deliciously savoury Syrah★★ and good, gentle Pinot Noir★. Excellent Clos Samuel sweet Viognier★★. Best years: (whites) **2009 07 05 04**.

INER FAMILY VINEYARDS *Oakville AVA, California, USA* Dave Miner has 32ha (80 acres) planted on a ranch 300m (1000ft) above the OAKVILLE valley floor. Highlights include yeasty, full-bodied Chardonnay★ (Oakville Ranch★★, Wild Yeast★★) as well as intense Merlot★★ and Cabernet Sauvignon★★ that demand a decade of aging. Also a stylish Viognier★★ and a striking Rosé★ from purchased fruit.

MERLOT

Red wine without tears. That's the reason Merlot has vaulte from being merely Bordeaux's red wine support act, we behind Cabernet Sauvignon in terms of class, to being the r wine drinker's darling, planted like fury all over the world. It able to claim some seriousness and pedigree, but – crucially can make wine of a fat, juicy character mercifully low in tannic bitternes which can be glugged with gay abandon almost as soon as the juice ha squirted from the press. Yet this doesn't mean that Merlot is the jell baby of red wine grapes. Far from it. Some of Bordeaux's greatest win are based on it.

WINE STYLES

Bordeaux Merlot The great wines of Pomerol and St-Émilion, on th right bank of the Dordogne, are largely based on Merlot and the best these – for example, Château Pétrus, which is almost 100% Merlot – ca mature for 20–30 years. In fact, there is more Merlot than Cabern Sauvignon planted throughout Bordeaux, and I doubt if there is a singl red wine property that does not have some growing, because the varie ripens early, can cope with cool conditions and is able to bear a heav crop of fruit. In a cool, damp area like Bordeaux, Cabernet Sauvigno cannot always ripen, so the soft, mellow character of Merlot is fundamental component of the blend even in the best, Caberne dominated, Médoc estates, imparting a supple richness an approachability to the wines. Up-and-coming areas like Blaye and Côt de Castillon depend on it.

Other European regions The south of France has briskly adopted th variety, producing easy-drinking, fruit-driven wines, but in the ho Languedoc the grape often ripens too fast to express its full personalit and can seem a little simple, even raw-edged, unless handled well. Ital has long used very high-crop Merlot to produce simple, light quaffers i the north, particularly in the Veneto, though today Friuli and Alto Adig make fuller styles. There are some very impressive examples too fro Tuscany and as far south as Sicily. The Swiss canton of Ticino is ofte unjustly overlooked for its intensely fruity, oak-aged versions. Easter Europe has the potential to provide fertile pastures for Merlot and so fa the most convincing, albeit simple, styles have come from Hungary an Bulgaria: the younger examples are almost invariably better than the ol Spain has developed decent Merlot credentials since the mid-1990s, bu has few sites cool enough for the variety.

New World Youth is also important in the New World, nowhere mor so than in Chile. Chilean Merlot, mostly blended with Carmenère, ha leapt to the front of the pack of New World examples with gorgeou garnet-red wines of unbelievable crunchy fruit richness that cry out to b drunk virtually in their infancy. California Merlots often have mor serious pretensions, but the nature of the grape is such that its soft, juic quality still shines through. Cooler sites in Washington State hav produced some impressive wines, and the east coast of the US has goo examples from places such as Long Island. With some French inpu South Africa is starting to get Merlot right, and in New Zealand th warm, dry conditions of Hawkes Bay and Waiheke Island are producin classic styles. Only Australia seems to find Merlot problematic, but the are some fine exceptions from cooler areas, including some surprisingl good fizzes – red fizzes, that is!

BEST PRODUCERS

France
Bordeaux (St-Émilion) ANGELUS, AUSONE, BEAU-SEJOUR BECOT, Clos Fourtet, la Mondotte, TERTRE-ROTEBOEUF, TROPLONG-MONDOT, VALANDRAUD; *(Pomerol)* le BON PASTEUR, Certan-de-May, Clinet, la CONSEILLANTE, l'EGLISE-CLINET, l'EVANGILE, la FLEUR-PETRUS, GAZIN, LATOUR-A-POMEROL, PETIT-VILLAGE, PETRUS, le PIN, TROTANOY.

Other European Merlots
Italy (Friuli) Livio FELLUGA; *(Tuscany)* Castello di AMA (l'Apparita), Castelgiocondo (Lamaione), Le MACCHIOLE, ORNELLAIA (Masseto), Petrolo, San Giusto a Rentennano, TUA RITA; *(Lazio)* FALESCO; *(Sicily)* PLANETA.

Spain (Navarra) Nekeas; *(Penedès)* Can Ràfols dels Caus; *(Somontano)* ENATE; *(Vino de la Tierra de Castilla)* Pago del Ama.

Switzerland Gialdi (Sassi Grossi), Daniel Huber, Stucky, Tamborini, Christian Zündel.

New World Merlots
USA (California) ARROWOOD, BERINGER, CHATEAU ST JEAN, MATANZAS CREEK, MERRYVALE, NEWTON, Pahlmeyer, SHAFER; *(Washington)* ANDREW WILL, LEONETTI, LONG SHADOWS (Pedestal), WOODWARD CANYON; *(New York)* BEDELL, LENZ.

Australia BRAND'S, CLARENDON HILLS, COLDSTREAM HILLS, Elderton, Irvine, PARKER COONAWARRA ESTATE, TAPANAPPA, Tatachilla, YALUMBA (Heggies).

New Zealand CRAGGY RANGE, Esk Valley, Sacred Hill (Broken Stone), TRINITY HILL, VILLA MARIA.

South Africa Bein, STEENBERG, THELEMA, VEENWOUDEN, VERGELEGEN.

Chile CARMEN, CASA LAPOSTOLLE (Cuvée Alexandre), CASABLANCA (Nimbus Estate), CONCHA Y TORO, CONO SUR (20 Barrels), Gillmore.

211

MINERVOIS AC *Languedoc, France* Attractive, mostly red wines from nort
east of Carcassonne, made mainly from Syrah, Carignan and Grenac
The local co-ops produce good, juicy, quaffing wine at reasonable pric
but the best wines are made by the estates: full of ripe, red fruit and pir
dust perfume, for drinking young. It can age, especially if a little new o
has been used. A village denomination, La Livinière, covering 6 super
communes whose wines can be particularly scented and fine, can
appended to the Minervois label. **Best producers:** (reds) Aires Hautes
Ch. Bonhomme★, Borie de Maurel★, CLOS CENTEILLES★★, Pierre Cros
Fabas★, la Grave, HECHT & BANNIER★, Maris★, Oupia, Oustal Blanc★, Pri
Palatum, Pujol, Senat★★, Ste-Eulalie★, TOUR BOISEE★, Villerambert-Julien
Best years: (2009) 08 07 06 **05 04 03 02 01**.

CH. LA MISSION-HAUT-BRION★★★ *Pessac-Léognan AC, Cru Classé de Grav*
Bordeaux, France 2008 was the year I finally accepted the true brilliance
La Mission. In the past I had often found the wine long on power b
short on grace, but the owners laid on a vertical tasting reaching way ba
into the 1920s and the general quality level was majestic, with t
vintages since 1990 actually outshining the admittedly beautiful earl
wines. Muscularity and richness combined with depth and fragrance
quite a challenge, but La Mission meets it triumphantly. **Best years:** 20
07 06 05 04 **03 02 01** 00 **98 96 95 94 90 89 88 85**.

MISSION HILL *Okanagan Valley VQA, British Columbia, Canada* The winery h
expanded its operations and hired consultant Michel Rolland to he
Kiwi winemaker John Simes craft some of the most noteworthy wir
from the OKANAGAN VALLEY. Excellent Chardonnay★★, Pinot Blanc★ a
Sauvignon-Semillon★ are joined by Merlot★, Cabernet Sauvignc
Pinot Noir and Shiraz★, and a red BORDEAUX-style blend, Oculus★★.

MITCHELL *Clare Valley, South Australia* Jane and Andrew Mitchell turn o
some of CLARE VALLEY's most ageworthy Watervale Riesling★★ and
classy barrel-fermented Semillon★★. Grenache-Sangioves
Mourvedre★ is an unwooded, heady fruit bomb. Peppertree Shiraz★
and Sevenhill Cabernet Sauvignon★ are plump, chocolaty and satisfyir
Aged release McNicol Riesling★ and Shiraz★★ show the cellari
potential of Clare's best.

MITTELRHEIN *Germany* Small 460ha (1135-acre), northerly wine regic
Two-thirds of the wine here is Riesling, but the vineyard area is shrinking
the sites are steep and difficult to work. The best growers (like Toni JOST
Müller★, Ratzenberger★ and Weingart★★), clustered around Bacharach a
Boppard, make wines of a striking mineral tang and dry, fruity intensity. B
years: (2009) 08 07 06 **05 04 02**.

MOËT & CHANDON *Champagne AC, Champagne, France* Moët & Chand
dominates the CHAMPAGNE market (more than 25 million bottles a yea
and has become a major producer of sparkling wine in Californ
Argentina, Brazil and Australia too. Non-vintage has started to exhil
distressing unreliability, and some recent releases have really not be
acceptable. There has been a change of winemaker and hopefully this w
put the vintage release at least back on track. Interestingly, the vinta
rosé★★ can show a rare Pinot Noir floral fragrance. Dom Pérignon★★
is the de luxe cuvée. It can be one of the greatest Champagnes of all, b
you've got to age it for a number of years after release or you're wasti
your money. **Best years: 2003** (02) **00 99 98 96 95 90 88 86 85 82**.

ARKUS MOLITOR *Bernkastel-Wehlen, Mosel, Germany* Dynamic estate with fine vineyards throughout Middle MOSEL. Brilliant Riesling Auslesen, often ★★★, and probably the best Spätburgunder (Pinot Noir)★ from the Mosel. Best years: (2009) 08 07 **06** 05 04 03 02 01 **99**.

ONBAZILLAC AC *South-West France* BERGERAC's best-known sweet wine. An increasing number of estates are making wines of a richness to rival some SAUTERNES, with the ability to age 10 years and more. Best producers: l'ANCIENNE CURE★★, Bélingard (Blanche de Bosredon★), le Fagé, Grande Maison★★, Haut-Bernasse, Haut-Montlong (Grande Cuvée), les Hauts de Caillevel★★, Pécoula, La Rayre, Theulet★, TIRECUL LA GRAVIÈRE★★, VERDOTS★★. Best years: **2007** 06 05 04 03 00.

H. MONBOUSQUET★ *St-Émilion Grand Cru AC, Grand Cru Classé, Bordeaux, France* Gérard Perse, owner of Ch. PAVIE, has transformed this struggling estate into one of ST-ÉMILION's 'super-crus'. The reward was promotion to Grand Cru Classé in 2006. Rich, voluptuous and very expensive, the wine is drinkable from 3–4 years but will age longer. Also a plush white Monbousquet★ (BORDEAUX AC). Best years: 2008 **07** 06 **05** 04 03 02 01 00 99 98 96 95.

OBERT MONDAVI *Napa Valley, California, USA* A Californian institution, best known for open and fruity regular Cabernet Sauvignon★ and Reserve Cabernet★★ with enormous depth and power. A regular★ and a Reserve★★ Pinot Noir are velvety smooth and supple wines with style, perfume and balance. For many years the Mondavi signature white was Fumé Blanc (Sauvignon Blanc), but in recent years Chardonnay★ (Reserve★★) has overtaken it. The Robert Mondavi Winery is now part of Constellation's Icon Estates portfolio; Mondavi's lower-priced 'lifestyle' lines, Private Selection and Woodbridge (from Lodi in the CENTRAL VALLEY), are promoted separately. Recent vintages of Cabernet Sauvignon seem to have become far weightier than any that ever appeared under the late Bob Mondavi's stewardship. Best years: (Cabernet Sauvignon Reserve) 2005 04 03 **02 01** 00 99 98 97 96 95 94.

ONSANTO *Chianti Classico DOCG, Tuscany, Italy* Fabrizio Bianchi, with his daughter Laura, makes a range of Sangiovese-based wines topped by the CHIANTI CLASSICO Riserva Il Poggio★★★, a complex and attention-demanding single-vineyard cru which until recently would have been considered too 'traditional' for its discreet austerity and need of bottle age. 100% Sangiovese IGT 'Fabrizio Bianchi'★★ is almost as fine. Best years: (2009) (08) 07 06 04 **01** 99 97 88 82 77.

ONT TAUCH *Fitou AC, Languedoc-Roussillon, France* A big, quality-conscious co-op producing a large range of wines, from good gutsy FITOU★ and CORBIÈRES to rich MUSCAT DE RIVESALTES★ and light but gluggable vin de pays. Top wines: Les Quatre★, Les Douze★. Best years: (Les Douze) (2009) 08 07 06 05 03 01 00.

ONTAGNE-ST-ÉMILION AC *Bordeaux, France* A ST-ÉMILION satellite with rather good red wines. The wines are normally ready to drink in 4 years but age quite well in their slightly earthy way. Best producers: Beauséjour★, Calon★, La Couronne, Croix Beauséjour★, Faizeau★, Gachon★, Haut Bonneau, Maison Blanche, Montaiguillon★, Rocher Corbin★, Roudier, Teyssier, Vieux-Ch.-St-André★. Best years: **(2009)** 08 05 03 01 00 98 96 95.

ONTAGNY AC *Côte Chalonnaise, Burgundy, France* Wines from this CÔTE CHALONNAISE village can be rather lean, but are greatly improved now that some producers are aging their wines for a few months in new oak. Generally best with 2–3 years' bottle age. Best producers:

S Aladame★★, BOUCHARD PÈRE ET FILS★, la BUXYNOISE★, Davenay
FAIVELEY, Louis LATOUR★, O LEFLAIVE★, A Roy★, J Vachet★. Best years: (200
08 07.

MONTALCINO See BRUNELLO DI MONTALCINO DOCG.

MONTANA *Auckland, Gisborne, Hawkes Bay and Marlborough, New Zeala*
Owned since 2005 by French giant Pernod Ricard, which produces
estimated 40% of New Zealand's wine. Montana's MARLBOROU
Sauvignon Blanc★ and GISBORNE Chardonnay★ are in a considerable w
to thank for putting New Zealand on the international wine map. Esta
bottlings of whites are generally good, while Gisborne Ormo
Chardonnay★★ is usually excellent. Montana is now one of the worl
biggest producers of Pinot Noir★, and each vintage the quality improv
and the price stays fair. Consistent Lindauer fizz and, with the help
the Champagne house DEUTZ, austere yet full-bodied Deutz Presti
Cuvée NV Brut★★. As well as Corbans, Pernod Ricard also acquir
Stoneleigh, with top-selling Marlborough Sauvignon Blanc★ a
Riesling★ and tasty Rapaura Series★. Extensive plantings in Waipa
are now bearing exciting results under the Camshorn label. See al
CHURCH ROAD.

MONTECARLO DOC *Tuscany, Italy* Distinctive reds (Sangiovese wi
Syrah) and whites (Trebbiano with Sémillon and Pinot Grigio) from t
province of Lucca. Also non-DOC Cabernet, Merlot, Pinot Bianc
Roussanne and Vermentino. Best producers: Buonamico★, Carmignani
Montechiari★, La Torre★, Wandanna★. Best years: (reds) (2009) (08) 07 06
03 01 00.

MONTEFALCO DOC *Umbria, Italy* Good Sangiovese-based Montefal
Rosso is outclassed by dense, massive Sagrantino di Montefalco DOC
(dry) and glorious sweet red Sagrantino Passito from dried grapes. Be
producers: Adanti★, Antonelli★, Caprai★★ (25 Anni★★★), Colpetrone★
Best years: (Sagrantino) (2009) (08) (07) 06 04 03 01 00 99 98 97.

MONTEPULCIANO Grape grown mostly in eastern Italy (unconnect
with TUSCANY's Sangiovese-based wine VINO NOBILE DI MONTEPULCIANO).
ABRUZZO, can produce deep-coloured, fleshy, brambly, spicy wines wi
moderate tannin and acidity, which also helps to keep the rosé win
(called Cerasuolo) fresh. Besides Montepulciano d'Abruzzo DOC, it
used in ROSSO CONERO and ROSSO PICENO in the MARCHE and also in UMBR
Molise and PUGLIA. Best producers: (Montepulciano d'Abruzzo) Cata
Madonna★, Contesa★★, Cornacchia★, Filomusi Guelfi★, Illuminati
La Valentina★, Marramiero★★, Masciarelli★★, Montori★, Umani Ronchi
Valentini★★★. Best years: (2009) (07) 06 04 01 99.

MONTEREY COUNTY *California, USA* Large CENTRAL COAST county south
San Francisco in the Salinas Valley boasting a mix of small estates ar
vast plantations (one even has a drag strip in the middle of it). The mo
important AVAs are Monterey, Arroyo Seco, Chalone, Carmel Vall
and Santa Lucia Highlands. Best grapes are Chardonnay, Riesling ar
Pinot Blanc, with some good Cabernet Sauvignon and Merlot in Carm
Valley and superb Pinot Noir in the Santa Lucia Highlands in the co
middle of the county. Best producers: Belle Glos★★, Bernardus★
Capiaux★, Chalone★, Estancia★, Jekel★, Joullian★★, Mer Soleil★, Morgan★
Roar, TALBOTT★★, Testarossa★, Ventana★★. Best years: (reds) 2006 05 04
01 00 99 97 96 95 94 91 90.

MONTES *Colchagua, Chile* One of Chile's pioneering wineries in the modern era, notable for innovative development of top-quality vineyard land on the steep Apalta slopes of COLCHAGUA and the virgin country of Marchíhüe out toward the Pacific. Sauvignon Blanc★ (Leyda★★) and

Chardonnay★ (Alpha★★) are good and fruit-led; all the reds are more austere and need bottle age. In the past 5 years, top-of-the-line Cabernet-based Montes Alpha M★★ has been consistently good. The most impressive reds, however, are Montes Alpha Syrah★★, Montes Folly★★ and a vibrant, scented Carmenère called Purple Angel★★. Montes Alpha Pinot Noir shows ripe flavours and extensive use of oak.

MONTEVERTINE *Tuscany, Italy* Based in the heart of CHIANTI CLASSICO, Montevertine is famous for its non-DOC wines, particularly Le Pergole Torte★★★. This was the first of the so-called 'Super-Tuscans' made solely with Sangiovese, and it remains one of the best. A little Canaiolo is included in the excellent Montevertine Riserva★★. Best years: (Le Pergole Torte) (2009) (08) 07 06 **04 03 01** 00 **99 97 95 93 90 88 85**.

MONTHELIE AC *Côte de Beaune, Burgundy, France* Attractive, mainly red wine village lying halfway along the CÔTE DE BEAUNE behind MEURSAULT and VOLNAY. The wines generally have a lovely cherry fruit and make pleasant drinking at a good price. Best producers: BOUCHARD PÈRE ET FILS, COCHE-DURY★, Darviot-Perrin★, P Garaudet★, R Jobard★, LAFON★★, O LEFLAIVE★, G Roulot★★, de Suremain★. Best years: (reds) (2009) 08 **07 06 05 03**.

MONTILLA-MORILES DO *Andalucía, Spain* Sherry-style wines that used to be sold almost entirely as lower-priced sherry substitutes. However, the wines *can* be superb, particularly the top dry amontillado, oloroso and rich Pedro Ximénez styles. Best producers: Alvear★★, Aragón, Gracia Hermanos, Pérez Barquero★★, Toro Albalá★★.

DOM. DE MONTILLE *Côte de Beaune, Burgundy, France* Brought to fame by *Mondovino* star Hubert de Montille, and now run by son Étienne. Consistent producer of stylish reds that demand aging, from VOLNAY (especially Mitans★★, Champans★★, Taillepieds★★★) and POMMARD (Pezerolles★★, Rugiens★★). Also top PULIGNY Le Cailleret★★★. Very expensive. From 2005 outstanding VOSNE-ROMANÉE Malconsorts★★★. Étienne and his sister have also started a *négociant* business, Deux Montille★. Best years: (2009) 08 07 05 **03 02 99 96 90 88**.

MONTLOUIS-SUR-LOIRE AC *Loire Valley, France* On the opposite bank of the Loire to VOUVRAY, Montlouis makes similar styles (dry, medium, sweet and CHAMPAGNE-style fizz) that are typically more accessible with exuberant fruit. New blood is injecting a healthy dose of ambition. Mousseux, the green, appley fizz, is best drunk young. Still wines need 5–10 years, particularly the sweet Moelleux. Best producers: L Chatenay★, F CHIDAINE★★, Delétang★, L & B Jousset, Levasseur-Alex Mathur★, des Liards★/Berger, F Saumon★, Taille aux Loups★★/BLOT. Best years: (sec) 2008 **07 06**; (moelleux) (2009) **05 04 03 02 01 99 97 96**.

MONTRACHET AC *Côte de Beaune, Burgundy, France* This world-famous Grand Cru straddles the boundary between the villages of CHASSAGNE-MONTRACHET and PULIGNY-MONTRACHET. Wines have a unique combination of concentration, finesse and perfume; white Burgundy at its most

sublime. Chevalier-Montrachet, immediately above it on the slop
yields slightly leaner wine that is less explosive in its youth, but goc
examples become ever more fascinating with age. Best producer
BOUCHARD★★★, M Colin★★★, DROUHIN (Laguiche)★★★, LAFON★★★, Lou
LATOUR★★, Dom. LEFLAIVE★★★, LEROY★★★, RAMONET★★★, Dom. de
ROMANÉE-CONTI★★★, SAUZET★★, Thénard★★. Best years: (2009) 08 07 06 0
04 03 **02 00 99 97 95 92 90 89**.

MONTRAVEL AC *South-West France* Mostly dry white wines from th
western end of the BERGERAC region. Medium-sweet whites from Côtes d
Montravel AC and ultra-sweet Haut-Montravel AC. Ambitious re
Montravel is made from a minimum 50% Merlot, although most red
from the area are sold as Bergerac or Côtes de Bergerac. Best producer
du Bloy★, Jonc Blanc★, Laulerie, Libarde, Mallevieille, Masburel★, Moul
Caresse★, Pique-Sègue, Puy-Servain★★, le Raz. Best years: (sweet) 2007 06 0
04 03 00; (red) (2009) 06 **05 04 02**.

CH. MONTROSE★★ *St-Estèphe AC, 2ème Cru Classé, Haut-Médoc, Bordeau
France* A leading ST-ESTÈPHE property, once famous for its dark, broodin
wine that would take around 30 years to reach its prime. In the late 197(
and early 80s the wines became lighter, but Montrose has now returne
to a powerful style, though softer than before. Recent vintages have bee
extremely good. Sold in 2006; plenty of investment but still classic i
style. Second wine: la Dame de Montrose. Best years: 2008 07 06 05 04 0
01 00 99 98 96 95.

CH. MONTUS *Madiran AC, South-West France* Alain Brumont pioneere
MADIRAN's revival, using 100% Tannat, deft public relations and hig
investment. All the AC wines are aged in new oak. He has 2 propertie
Montus (Prestige★★) and Bouscassé (Vieilles Vignes★★). Both als
make enjoyable dry PACHERENC DU VIC-BILH★ and fine Moelleux★★ i
varying degrees of sweetness. Best years: (red) (2009) 06 **05 04 01 00**; (whit
2007 06 05 04.

MORELLINO DI SCANSANO DOCG *Tuscany, Italy* Morellino is the loca
name for the Sangiovese grape in the south-west of TUSCANY. The wine
which used to be agreeable gluggers, are becoming more serious unde
DOCG, not necessarily to their advantage. Best producers: E Banti★
Belguardo★/FONTERUTOLI, Lohsa★/POLIZIANO, Cecchi★, Il Macereto★
Mantellassi★, Morellino di Scansano co-op★, Moris Farms★, Podere 414★
Poggio Argentaria★, Le Pupille★★. Best years: (2009) (08) 07 06 04 03 0(
00 99.

MOREY-ST-DENIS AC *Côte de Nuits, Burgundy, France* Morey has 5 Grand
Crus (CLOS DES LAMBRAYS, CLOS DE LA ROCHE, CLOS ST-DENIS, CLOS DE TART an
a share of BONNES-MARES) as well as some very good Premiers Crus. Basi
village wine is sometimes unexciting, but from a quality grower the win
has good fruit and acquires an attractive depth as it ages. A tiny amoun
of startling nutty white wine is also made. Best producers: Pierre Amiot★
Arlaud★★, Dom. des Beaumont★, CLAIR★★, David Clark, DUJAC★★★
A Jeanniard★★, Dom. des Lambrays★★, H Lignier★★★, Lignier-Michelot★★
H Perrot-Minot★★, Ponsot★★, ROUMIER★★, ROUSSEAU★★, Sérafin★★
Taupenot-Merme★★. Best years: (2009) 08 07 06 05 03 02 01 00 99 98 96 95 9(

MORGENHOF *Stellenbosch WO, South Africa* A 300-year-old Cape farm
grandly restored and run with French flair by owner Anne Cointreau
The range spans Cap Classique sparkling to PORT styles. Best are a well
oaked, muscular Chenin Blanc★, structured Merlot and the dark
berried, supple Morgenhof Estate★, a BORDEAUX-style blend.

MORGON AC *Beaujolais, Burgundy, France* The longest-lasting of BEAUJOLAIS Crus, wines that – at their best – have the structure to age and delightful cherry fruit; look out for named sub-zones like Côte de Py and Javernières, which are considered to be the source of many of the best Morgons. There are, however, many more Morgons, made in a commercial style for early drinking, which are nothing more than a pleasant, fruity – and pricey – drink. **Best producers:** N Aucoeur★, D Desvignes★, L-C Desvignes★, DUBOEUF (Jean Descombes★), J Foillard★★, M Jonchet★, M Lapierre★★. **Best years: 2009 08 07.**

MORNINGTON PENINSULA *Victoria, Australia* Exciting cool-climate maritime region dotted with small vineyards. Chardonnay runs the gamut from honeyed to leafy, but increasing numbers are oatmealy and scented; Pinot Noir can be very stylish in warm years, especially from vineyards in the mild Moorooduc area. **Best producers:** Crittenden★, Dexter, Eldridge, Hurley★, KOOYONG★★, Main Ridge★★, Montalto, Moorooduc★★, Paradigm Hill, PARINGA ESTATE★★, Port Phillip Estate★, Scorpo, STONIER★★, Ten Minutes by Tractor★★, T'Gallant★, Tuck's Ridge, Willow Creek, Yabby Lake★★. **Best years:** (Pinot Noir) 2009 08 07 06 **05 04 03 02 01 00 99 98 97 95 94.**

MORRIS *Rutherglen, Victoria, Australia* Historic winery with an outstanding fortified wine portfolio. David Morris is the custodian of a store of aged fortifieds that have been with his family since 1859. He continues to make old favourites like Liqueur Muscat★★ and Tokay★★ (Old Premium★★★), 'ports', 'sherries' and robust table wines to very high quality levels.

DENIS MORTET *Gevrey-Chambertin, Côte de Nuits, Burgundy, France* Before his untimely death in 2006, Denis Mortet had built a brilliant reputation for his GEVREY-CHAMBERTIN (various cuvées, all ★★★) and tiny amounts of CHAMBERTIN★★★. Early vintages are deep coloured and powerful; recent years show increased finesse, a trend being continued by son Arnaud. **Best years:** (2009) 08 07 06 05 **03 02 01 96 95 93.**

MORTON ESTATE *Marlborough, Hawkes Bay, Bay of Plenty, Auckland, New Zealand* Founded in 1983 by Morton Brown, who built a distinctive Cape-style winery in Katikati. Now owned by John Coney, it is one of the country's larger wineries, making wine from all major regions. Top-of-the-line Black Label wines can be very good and include a full-bodied Chardonnay★★ and Merlot-Cabernet★ from HAWKES BAY plus a stylish MARLBOROUGH Sauvignon Blanc★ and a rich, complex, vintage-dated sparkling wine. White Label wines offer excellent value, particularly Chardonnay and Pinot Gris★. **Best years:** (Chardonnay) **2009 07 06 04.**

GEORG MOSBACHER *Forst, Pfalz, Germany* This small estate makes dry white and dessert wines in the village of FORST. Best of all are the dry Rieslings★★ from the Forster Ungeheuer site, which are among the lushest in Germany. Delicious young, but worth cellaring for a few years. **Best years:** (2009) 08 07 **06 05 04 02 01 99.**

MOSCATO D'ASTI DOCG *Piedmont, Italy* Utterly beguiling, delicately scented, gently bubbling wine, made from Moscato Bianco grapes grown in the hills between Acqui Terme, Asti and Alba in north-west Italy. The DOCG is the same as for ASTI, but only select grapes go into this wine, which is frizzante (semi-sparkling) rather than fully sparkling. Drink while they're bubbling with youthful fragrance. **Best producers:** Araldica/Alasia★, ASCHERI★, Bava★, Bera★★, Braida★, Cascina Castlèt★, La Caudrina★★, Michele Chiarlo, Giuseppe Contratto★, Coppo★, Cascina Fonda★,

Forteto della Luja★, Bruno GIACOSA★★, Icardi★, Marenco★, Beppe Marino★, La Morandina★, Marco Negri★, Perrone★, Cascina Pian d'Or★, Saracco★★, Scagliola★, La Spinetta★★, I Vignaioli di Santo Stefano★, Gianni Voerzio★.

MOSCATO PASSITO DI PANTELLERIA DOC *Sicily, Italy* Powerful dessert wine made from the Muscat of Alexandria, or Zibibbo, grape. Pantelleria is a small island south-west of SICILY, closer to Africa than it is to Italy. The grapes are picked in mid-August and laid out in the hot sun to shrivel for a couple of weeks. They are then crushed and fermented to give an amber-coloured, intensely flavoured sweet Muscat. The wines are best drunk within 5–7 years of the vintage. Best producers: Benanti★, D'Ancona★, DE BARTOLI★★, Donnafugata (Ben Ryé★), Murana★, Nuova Agricoltura co-op★, Pellegrino.

MOSEL *Germany* A collection of vineyard areas on the Mosel and its tributaries, the Saar and the Ruwer, amounting to 9000ha (22,230 acres). The Mosel river rises in the French Vosges before forming the border between Germany and Luxembourg. In its first German incarnation in the Upper Mosel the light, tart Elbling grape holds sway, but with the Middle Mosel begins a series of villages responsible for some of the world's very best Riesling wines: LEIWEN, TRITTENHEIM, PIESPORT, BRAUNEBERG, BERNKASTEL, GRAACH, WEHLEN, ÜRZIG and ERDEN. The wines have tremendous slatiness and an ability to blend the greenness of citrus leaves and fruits with the golden warmth of honey. Great wines are rarer between Erden and Koblenz, although WINNINGEN is an island of excellence. The Saar can produce wonderful, piercing wines in villages such as Serrig, Ayl, OCKFEN and Wiltingen. Ruwer wines are slightly softer; the estates of MAXIMIN GRÜNHAUS and KARTHÄUSERHOF are on every list of the best in Germany. Since 2007 only the name 'Mosel' is permitted on labels in place of the region's former name Mosel-Saar-Ruwer.

MOSHIN VINEYARDS *Russian River Valley, California, USA* Retired mathematics professor Rick Moshin spent 4½ years building his RUSSIAN RIVER winery and today, five years after its construction, has developed a strong, almost cultish, following for his brilliant Pinot Noirs★★ and a handful of other wines (Zinfandel★, Petite Sirah★, Merlot★) made in small quantities. Best years: 2007 06 05 04 03 02 01.

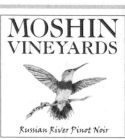

MOSHIN VINEYARDS

Russian River Pinot Noir

MOSS WOOD *Margaret River, Western Australia* Seminal MARGARET RIVER winery at the top of its form. From its home vineyard come heavenly scented Cabernet★★★ needing 5 years to blossom, classy Chardonnay★★, pale, fragrant Pinot Noir★ and crisp, fruity but ageworthy Semillon★★. Range is expanding with excellent Ribbon Vale★★ wines (from a nearby single vineyard owned by Moss Wood), very good Amy's Cabernet★ and a MORNINGTON PENINSULA Pinot, added from 2008 to allow the winemakers to work with a cool-climate expression of the variety. Best years: (Cabernet) (2009) (08) 07 05 04 03 02 01 00 99 98 96 95 94 91 90 85.

J P MOUEIX *Bordeaux, France* As well as owning PETRUS, la FLEUR-PETRUS, BELAIR-MONANGE, MAGDELAINE, TROTANOY, Hosanna and other properties, the Moueix family runs a thriving merchant business specializing in the wines of the Right Bank, particularly POMEROL and ST-ÉMILION. Quality is generally high.

MOULIN-À-VENT AC *Beaujolais, Burgundy, France* Potentially the greatest of the BEAUJOLAIS Crus, taking its name from an ancient windmill that stands above Romanèche-Thorins. The granitic soil yields a majestic wine that with time transforms into a rich Burgundian style more characteristic of the Pinot Noir than the Gamay. Best producers: Champagnon★, DUBOEUF (Tour du Bief★), H Fessy, Ch. des Jacques★/JADOT, O Merlin★, Richard Rottiers (Climat Champ de Cour★), B Santé★. Best years: **2009 08 07**.

MOULIS AC *Haut-Médoc, Bordeaux, France* Small AC within the HAUT-MÉDOC. Much of the wine is excellent – delicious at 5–6 years old, though good examples can age 10–20 years – and not overpriced. Best producers: Anthonic, Biston-Brillette★, Branas-Grand-Poujeaux, Brillette, CHASSE-SPLEEN★, Duplessis, Gressier-Grand-Poujeaux★, MAUCAILLOU★, Moulin-à-Vent, POUJEAUX★. Best years: (2009) 08 **06 05 03 02 01 00 96 95 90 89**.

MOUNT HORROCKS *Clare Valley, South Australia* Stephanie Toole has transformed this label into one of the CLARE VALLEY's best, with taut, minerally, limy Riesling★★★ from a single vineyard in Watervale; waxy, cedary Semillon★★; complex, savoury Shiraz★; and one of Australia's most delicious stickies (dessert wine), the Cordon Cut Riesling★★★, which shows varietal character with a satisfying lush texture.

MOUNT LANGI GHIRAN *Grampians, Victoria, Australia* This winery made its reputation with remarkable dark plum, chocolate and pepper Shiraz★★ (now often ★★★). Delightful Riesling★, honeyed Pinot Gris★ and melony unwooded Chardonnay★. Joanna★★ Cabernet is dark and intriguing. Less expensive Cliff Edge★ and Billi Billi★. Best years: (Shiraz) (2009) (08) (07) 06 05 **04 03 99 98 97 96 95 94 93**.

MOUNT MARY *Yarra Valley, Victoria, Australia* Classic YARRA VALLEY property, producing controversial cult wines. It uses only estate-grown BORDEAUX grapes, with dry white Triolet★★ blended from Sauvignon, Semillon and Muscadelle, and Quintet★★ (★★★ for keen Francophiles), from Cabernet Sauvignon and Franc, Merlot, Malbec and Petit Verdot, that ages beautifully. The Pinot Noir★★ is almost as good. Best years: (Quintet) (2008) 07 06 05 03 **02 01 00 99 98 97 96 95 94 93 92 91 90 88 86**.

MOUNT VEEDER AVA *Napa Valley, California, USA* Small AVA in south-west NAPA, with Cabernet Sauvignon and Zinfandel in an impressive, rough-hewn style. Best producers: Chateau Potelle★, Robert Craig★★, HESS COLLECTION★, Lokoya★★, Mayacamas Vineyards★, Mount Veeder Winery★.

MOURVÈDRE The variety originated in Spain, where it is called Monastrell. It dominates the JUMILLA DO and also Alicante, Bullas and Yecla. It needs lots of sunshine to ripen, which is why it performs well on the Mediterranean coast at BANDOL. It is increasingly important as a source of body and tarry, pine-needle flavour in the wines of CHÂTEAUNEUF-DU-PAPE and parts of LANGUEDOC-ROUSSILLON. It is making quite a reputation in Australia and California, where it is sometimes known as Mataro, and is also starting to make its presence felt in South Africa.

MOUTON-CADET *Bordeaux AC, Bordeaux, France* The most widely sold red BORDEAUX in the world was created by Baron Philippe de Rothschild in the 1930s. Blended from the entire Bordeaux region, the wine is undistinguished – and never cheap. A new label and somewhat fruitier style were introduced in 2004. Also a white, rosé, MÉDOC and GRAVES.

CH. MOUTON-ROTHSCHILD★★★ *Pauillac AC, 1er Cru Classé, Haut-Médoc,*
Bordeaux, France Baron Philippe de Rothschild died in 1988, having
raised Mouton from a run-down Second Growth to its promotion to
First Growth in 1973, and a reputation as one of the greatest wines in the
world. It can still be the most magnificently opulent of the great MEDOC
reds, but inexcusable inconsistency frequently makes me want to
downgrade it. Recent vintages (since 2004) seem back on top form.
When young, it is rich and indulgent on the palate, aging after 15–20
years to a complex bouquet of blackcurrant and cigar box. There is also a
white wine, Aile d'Argent. Second wine: Le Petit-Mouton. **Best years:**
(red) 2008 07 06 05 04 **03 02 01 00 99 98 97 96 95 90 89 88 86 85**.

MUDGEE *New South Wales, Australia* Small region neighbouring HUNTER
VALLEY, with a higher altitude and marginally cooler temperatures.
Proximity to the famous Hunter meant its wines were long overlooked,
or, indeed, trucked to the Hunter when needed. Major new plantings are
giving it a fresh lease of life and producers are beginning to make the best
use of very good fruit. **Best producers:** Abercorn, Farmer's Daughter, Logan,
Lowe Family, Miramar, Oatley★.

MUGA *Rioja DOCa, Rioja, Spain* Traditional family winery making high-
quality, rich red RIOJA★ (Gran Reserva Prado Enea★★). It is the only
bodega in Rioja where every step of red winemaking is still carried out in
oak containers. The modern Torre Muga Reserva★ marks a major stylistic
change. Top cuvée is Aro★★. Whites★★ are excellent and rosés★ are
good. **Best years:** (Torre Muga Reserva) 2005 04 **03 01 99 98 96 95**.

J-F MUGNIER *Chambolle-Musigny, Côte de Nuits, Burgundy, France* Since giving up
his other career as an airline pilot in 1998, Frédéric Mugnier has
produced a series of beautifully crafted, lightly extracted wines at the
Château de Chambolle-Musigny, especially from les Amoureuses★★
and Grand Cru MUSIGNY★★★. In 2004 the 9ha (23-acre) NUITS-ST-GEORGES
Clos de la Maréchale★★ vineyard came back under his control; first
vintages are very stylish and a small section has been grafted over
to white wine production. **Best years:** (2009) 08 07 06 05 **04 02 01 00 99 98
96 93 90 89**.

MULDERBOSCH *Stellenbosch WO, South Africa* At the helm since the
inaugural 1991 vintage, winemaker Mike Dobrovic has moved on.
Hopefully, consistency will remain a hallmark of this white-dominated
range. Sleek, gooseberry-infused Sauvignon Blanc★★ is deservedly a cult
wine. Purity and intensity mark out the Chardonnays (regular★ and
barrel-fermented★★) and oak-brushed Chenin Blanc★ (previously
labelled Steen op Hout). The handful of reds includes Faithful Hound, a
Cabernet-Merlot blend, BORDEAUX-like but easy-drinking. **Best years:**
(barrel-fermented Chardonnay) (2008) **07 06 05 04 03 02 01**.

MÜLLER-CATOIR *Neustadt-Haardt, Pfalz, Germany* This PFALZ producer
makes wine of a piercing fruit flavour and powerful structure rarely
surpassed in Germany, including Riesling, Scheurebe, Rieslaner,
Gewürztraminer, Muskateller and Pinot Noir – all ★★. BA and TBA are
invariably ★★★. **Best years:** (2009) 08 07 **06 05 04 03 02 01 99 98**.

EGON MÜLLER-SCHARZHOF *Scharzhofberg, Mosel, Germany* Some of the
world's greatest – and most expensive – sweet Rieslings are this
perfectionist estate's Auslese, Beerenauslese, Trockenbeerenauslese and
Eiswein: all usually rating ★★★. Regular Kabinett and Spätlese wines are
pricey but classic. **Best years:** (2009) 08 07 06 05 **04 03 02 01 99 97 95 93 90**.

MÜLLER-THURGAU The workhorse grape of Germany, with around 13% of the country's vineyards. When yields are low it produces pleasant floral wines, but this is rare since modern clones are all super-productive. It is occasionally better in England – and a few good examples, with a slightly green edge to the grapy flavour, come from Switzerland (here known as Riesling-Sylvaner), Luxembourg (as Rivaner) and Italy's TRENTINO and ALTO ADIGE, which latter boasts one of Europe's highest vineyards in TIEFENBRUNNER's Feldmarschall at 1000m (3280ft).

G H MUMM *Champagne AC, Champagne, France* Mumm's top-selling non-vintage brand, Cordon Rouge, disappointing in the 1990s, improved when Dominique Demarville took over as winemaker in 1998, but he left in 2006 to join VEUVE CLICQUOT. His efforts at improving quality were confirmed by the 2005 release of Mumm Grand Cru★ and elegant de luxe Cuvée R Lalou★★. Improvements seem to have stayed on track under Pernod Ricard's ownership. Best years: (2002) **99 98 96 95 90 89 88 85 82**.

MUMM NAPA *Napa Valley AVA, California, USA* The California offshoot of Champagne house MUMM has always made good bubbly, and after a slight dip is now back on form. Brut Prestige★ is a fair drink; Brut Rosé★ is better than most pink Champagnes. Elegant vintage-dated Blanc de Blancs★★ and flagship DVX★★. Part of Pernod Ricard.

RENÉ MURÉ *Alsace AC, Alsace, France* The pride and joy of this domaine's fine vineyards is the Clos St-Landelin, a parcel within the Grand Cru Vorbourg. The Clos is the source of lush, concentrated wines, with particularly fine Riesling★★ and Pinot Gris★★. Since 2005, most Muré wines have been getting drier, and are all the better for it. The Muscat Vendange Tardive★★ is rare and remarkable, as is the opulent old-vine Sylvaner Cuvée Oscar★. The Vendange Tardive★★ and Sélection de Grains Nobles★★★ wines are among the best in Alsace. Best years: (Clos St-Landelin Riesling) (2009) 08 07 06 **05 04 02 01 00 97 96 95**.

ANDREW MURRAY VINEYARDS *Santa Barbara County, California, USA* Working with RHÔNE varieties, winemaker Andrew Murray has created an impressive array of wines. Rich, aromatic Viognier★ and Roussanne★★ whites, as well as several Syrahs (Roasted Slope★★, Hillside Reserve★★). Espérance★ is a spicy blend patterned after a serious CÔTES DU RHÔNE. Best years: (Syrah) 2005 **04 03 02 01 00 99 98 97**.

MUSCADET AC *Loire Valley, France* AC for the region around Nantes in north-west France, best drunk young and fresh as an apéritif or with the local seafood. Wines from 3 better-quality zones (Muscadet Coteaux de la Loire, Muscadet Côtes de Grand-Lieu and Muscadet Sèvre-et-Maine) are typically labelled *sur lie*. They must be matured on the lees for a maximum of 12 months and show greater depth of flavour and more fruit. Ironically, ageworthy top cuvées from specific vineyards or soils (granite, gneiss, schist) are usually aged *sur lie* for well over 12 months so cannot use this term on the label. Best producers: Bidière, Bonhomme★, Bonnet-Huteau★, Chéreau-Carré★, Choblet/Herbauges★, Bruno Cormerais★, Michel David★, Dorices★, Douillard, l'ECU★, Gadais★, Jacques Guindon★, les Hautes Noëlles★/Serge Bâtard, l'Hyvernière, Landrons★, Luneau-Papin★, Metaireau★, de la Pépière, RAGOTIERE★, Sauvion★, la Touche★. Best years: (sur lie) **2008 07 05**.

MUSCAT See pages 222–3.

MUSCAT

It's strange, but there's hardly a wine grape in the world which makes wine that actually tastes of the grape itself. Yet there's one variety which is so joyously, exultantly grapy that it more than makes up for all the others – the Muscat, generally thought to be the original wine vine. In fact there seem to be about 200 different branches of the Muscat family worldwide, but the noblest of these and the one that always makes the most exciting wine is called Muscat Blanc à Petits Grains (the Muscat with the small berries). These berries can be crunchily green, golden yellow, pink or even brown – as a result Muscat has a large number of synonyms. The wines they make may be pale and dry, rich and golden, subtly aromatic or as dark and sweet as treacle.

WINE STYLES

France Muscat is grown from the far north-east right down to the Spanish border, yet is rarely accorded great respect in France. This is a pity, because the dry, light, hauntingly grapy Muscats of Alsace are some of France's most delicately beautiful wines. It pops up sporadically in the Rhône Valley, especially in the sparkling wine enclave of Die. Mixed with Clairette, the Clairette de Die Tradition is a fragrant grapy fizz that deserves to be better known. Muscat de Beaumes-de-Venise is a delicious manifestation of the grape, this time fortified, musky and sweet. Its success has encouraged the traditional fortified winemakers of Languedoc-Roussillon to make fresher, more perfumed wines as well as unfortified late-harvest wines and, especially around Rivesaltes, dry vins de pays.

Italy Various types of Muscat are grown in Italy. In the north-west, especially Piedmont, Moscato Bianco/Moscato di Canelli makes the fragrantly sweet sparklers called Asti or (less bubbly) Moscato d'Asti; the same grape makes Tuscany's Moscadello di Montalcino. Orange Muscat (Moscato Giallo/Goldmuskateller) is used in the north-east for making passito-style dessert (or occasionally dry) wines, while Muscat of Alexandria prevails in the south, especially in relation to the great passitos of Pantelleria. Italy also has red varieties: Moscato Nero for rare sweet wines in Lazio, Lombardy and Piedmont; Moscato Rosa/Rosenmuskateller for delicately sweet wines in Trentino-Alto Adige and Friuli-Venezia Giulia.

Other regions Elsewhere in Europe, Muscat is a component of some Tokajis in Hungary, Crimea has shown how good it can be in the Massandra fortified wines, and the rich golden Muscats of Samos and Patras are among Greece's finest wines. As Muskateller in Austria and Germany it makes primarily dry, subtly aromatic wines. In Spain, Moscatel de Valencia is sweet, light and sensational value, Moscatel de Grano Menudo is on the resurgence in Navarra and Castilla-La Mancha and it has also been introduced in Mallorca. Portugal's Moscatel de Setúbal is also wonderfully rich and complex. California grows Muscat, often calling it Muscat Canelli, but South Africa and Australia make better use of it. With darker berries, and called Brown Muscat in Australia and Muscadel in South Africa, it makes some of the world's sweetest and most luscious fortified wines, especially in the north-east Victoria regions of Rutherglen and Glenrowan in Australia.

BEST PRODUCERS

Sparkling Muscat
France (Clairette de Die) Achard-Vincent, Clairette de Die co-op, Jean-Claude Raspail.

Italy (Asti) G Contratto, Gancia; *(Moscato d'Asti)* Bera, Braida, Caudrina, Saracco, La Spinetta, Gianni Voerzio.

Dry Muscat
Austria (Muskateller) Gross, Lackner-Tinnacher, POLZ, TEMENT.

France (Alsace) J-M Bernhard, Paul Buecher, Dirler-Cadé, Kientzler, Kuentz-Bas, Ostertag, Rolly Gassmann, SCHOFFIT, Bruno Sorg, TRIMBACH, WEINBACH, ZIND-HUMBRECHT.

Germany (Muskateller) BERCHER, Dr HEGER, HUBER, MÜLLER-CATOIR, REBHOLZ.

Spain (Alicante) Bocopa co-op; *(Málaga)* Jorge Ordóñez; *(Penedès)* TORRES (Viña Esmeralda).

Italy (Goldmuskateller) LAGEDER.

Sweet Muscat
Australia (Liqueur Muscat) All Saints, Baileys of Glenrowan, BROWN BROTHERS, Buller, Campbells, CHAMBERS, John Kosovich, MCWILLIAM'S, MORRIS, Pfeiffer, Seppeltsfield, Stanton & Killeen, Talijancich, YALUMBA.

France (Alsace) Ernest Burn, René MURÉ, Rolly Gassmann, SCHOFFIT; *(Beaumes-de-Venise)* Bernardins, Durban, Paul JABOULET, Pigeade; *(Frontignan)* la Peyrade; *(Lunel)* Lacoste; *(Rivesaltes)* CAZES, Jau.

Greece SAMOS co-op.

Italy (Goldmuskateller) Viticoltori Caldaro, Thurnhof; *(Moscato Passito di Pantelleria)* DE BARTOLI, Murana.

Portugal (Moscatel de Setúbal) BACALHÔA, J M da FONSECA.

South Africa KLEIN CONSTANTIA.

Spain (Navarra) Camilo Castilla, CHIVITE; *(Valencia)* Gandía; *(Alicante)* Gutiérrez de la Vega, Enrique Mendoza, Primitivo Quiles; *(Jumilla)* Silvano García; *(Sierras de Málaga)* Jorge Ordóñez, Telmo RODRIGUEZ.

223

MUSCAT OF ALEXANDRIA This grape rarely shines in its own right bu performs a useful job worldwide, adding sultry perfume and fleshy fru to what would otherwise be dull, neutral white wines. It is common fc sweet and fortified wines throughout the Mediterranean basin (in Sicil it is called Zibibbo) and in South Africa (where it is also known a Hanepoot), as well as being a fruity, perfumed bulk producer there and i Australia, where it is known as Gordo Blanco or Lexia.

MUSCAT DE BEAUMES-DE-VENISE AC *Rhône Valley, France* Deliciou Muscat *vin doux naturel* from the southern Rhône. It has a fruity acidit and a bright fresh feel, and is best drunk young – as an aperitif or desse wine – to get all that lovely grapy perfume and bright fruit at its peal Becomes very rich and concentrated when aged. Best producer Beaumalric★, Beaumes-de-Venise co-op, Bernardins★★, DELAS★, Durban★★ Fenouillet★, JABOULET★★, Pigeade★★, Vidal-Fleury★.

MUSCAT BLANC À PETITS GRAINS See MUSCAT, pages 222–3.

MUSCAT DE FRONTIGNAN AC *Languedoc, France* Muscat *vin dou naturel* on the Mediterranean coast. Quite impressive but can be a b cloying. Muscat de Mireval AC, a little further inland, can have a touc more acid freshness and quite an alcoholic kick. Also Muscat de Lune further east. Best producers: (Frontignan) Mas Rouge, la Peyrade★, Ston (Lunel) Mas de Bellevue★; (Mireval) la Capelle★, Mas des Pigeonniers, Moulina

MUSCAT DE LUNEL, MUSCAT DE MIREVAL See MUSCAT DE FRONTIGNAN

MUSCAT DE RIVESALTES AC *Roussillon, France* Made from Muscat Blan à Petits Grains and Muscat of Alexandria, the wine can be very goo from go-ahead producers who keep the aromatic skins in the juice fc longer periods to gain extra perfume and fruit. Most delicious whe young. Best producers: Baixas co-op (Dom. Brial★, Ch. les Pins★), CASENOVE★, CAZES★★, Chênes★, Corneilla, Fontanel★, Força Réal★, l'Heritie Jau★, Laporte★, MONT TAUCH★, de Nouvelles★, Piquemal★, des Vents.

MUSCAT DE ST-JEAN-DE-MINERVOIS AC *Languedoc, France* AC in th remote Minervois hills for fortified Muscat. Less cloying, more tangerin and floral than some Muscats from the plains. Best producers: Barroubie CLOS BAGATELLE, Clos du Gravillas, Combebelle, Vignerons de Septimanie.

MUSIGNY AC *Grand Cru, Côte de Nuits, Burgundy, France* One of a handful c truly great Grands Crus, combining power with an exceptional depth c fruit and lacy elegance – an iron fist in a velvet glove. Best producer DROUHIN★★★, JADOT★★★, Dom. LEROY★★★, J-F MUGNIER★★★, J Prieur★★ ROUMIER★★★, VOGÜÉ★★★, VOUGERAIE★★★. Best years: (2009) 08 07 06 05 C 02 01 00 99 98 96 95 93 90 89 88.

NAHE *Germany* 4155ha (10,260-acre) wine region named after the Rive Nahe, which rises below Birkenfeld and joins the Rhine by BINGEN, opposi RÜDESHEIM in the RHEINGAU. The Rieslings from this geologically comple region are often among Germany's best. The finest vineyards are those c Niederhausen and SCHLOSSBÖCKELHEIM, situated in the dramatic, rocky Upp Nahe Valley, and at Dorsheim and Münster in the lower Nahe.

CH. NAIRAC★ *Barsac AC, 2ème Cru Classé, Bordeaux, France* An establishe name in BARSAC which, by dint of enormous effort, produces a sweet win sometimes on a par with the First Growths. The influence of aging i new oak casks, adding spice and even a little tannin, means this can aç for 10–15 years. Best years: 2007 05 04 03 02 01 99 98 97 96 95.

NAPA VALLEY AVA *California, USA* An AVA so inclusive that it is almost completely irrelevant. It includes vineyards that are outside the Napa River drainage system – such as Pope Valley and Chiles Valley. A number of sub-AVAs have been and are in the process of being created. There are a significant number that, over a generation or so, have proved that their wines do have a particular personality; among them, I'd include CARNEROS, STAGS LEAP, HOWELL MOUNTAIN, Diamond Mountain, SPRING MOUNTAIN, OAKVILLE and RUTHERFORD. See also pages 226–7.

NAVARRA DO *Navarra, Spain* This buzzing region has increasing numbers of vineyards planted to Cabernet Sauvignon, Merlot and Chardonnay in addition to Tempranillo, Garnacha and Moscatel (Muscat). This translates into a wealth of juicy reds, barrel-fermented whites and modern sweet Muscats, but quality is still fairly haphazard. Best producers: Artazuri, Azul y Garanza★, Camino del Villar★, Camilo Castilla (Capricho de Goya Muscat★★), CHIVITE★ (Pago de Arínzano estate★★), Iñaki Núñez★★, Inurrieta★, Lezaun★, Magaña★, Castillo de Monjardin★, Nekeas co-op★, Ochoa, Palacio de la Vega, Príncipe de Viana, Quaderna Via, Señorío de Otazu, Señorío de Sarria. Best years: (reds) **2006 05 04 03 01**.

NAVARRO VINEYARDS *Anderson Valley AVA, California, USA* Small, family-owned producer of sensational Gewürztraminer★★★, Pinot Gris★★, Riesling★★, Dry Muscat★★ and late-harvest Riesling★★★, perfectly balanced Pinot Noir★★ and a dozen other stellar wines.

NEBBIOLO The grape variety responsible for the majestic wines of BAROLO and BARBARESCO, rarely successful outside north-west Italy. Its name may derive from the Italian for fog, *nebbia*, because it ripens late when the hills are shrouded in autumn mists. It needs a thick skin to withstand this fog, so often gives very tannic wines that need years to soften. When grown in the limestone soils of the Langhe hills around Alba, Nebbiolo produces wines that are only moderately deep in colour but have a wonderful array of perfumes and an ability to develop great complexity with age. Barolo is usually considered the best and longest-lived of the Nebbiolo wines; the best Barolos now reach a plateau within 10 years and then subtly mature for decades. Barbaresco also varies widely in style between the traditional and the new. The variety is also used for NEBBIOLO D'ALBA and ROERO, and for barrique-aged blends, often with Barbera and/or Cabernet, sold under the LANGHE DOC. Nebbiolo is also the principal grape for reds of Carema on the VALLE D'AOSTA border as well as of northern PIEDMONT's GATTINARA and Ghemme, where it is called Spanna. In LOMBARDY it is known as Chiavennasca and is used in the Valtellina DOC and VALTELLINA SUPERIORE DOCG wines. Outside Italy, rare good examples are made in Australia (S C PANNELL is outstanding. Fermoy Estate, Longview and Pizzini are very good), California and South Africa.

NEBBIOLO D'ALBA DOC *Piedmont, Italy* Red wine from Nebbiolo grown around Alba, but excluding the BAROLO and BARBARESCO zones. Vineyards in the LANGHE and ROERO hills are noted for sandy soils that produce a fragrant, fruity style for early drinking, though some growers make wines that improve for 5 years or more. Best producers: Alario★, Bricco Maiolica★★, Burlotto★, CERETTO, Cascina Chicco★, Correggia★★, Bruno GIACOSA★, Giuseppe MASCARELLO★, Pio Cesare★, PRUNOTTO★, RATTI★, SANDRONE★, Vietti★. Best years: (2009) (08) 07 **06 04 03 01 00 99**.

NAPA VALLEY

California, USA

From the earliest days of California wine, and throug all its ups and downs, the Napa Valley has been th standard-bearer for the whole industry and the drivin force behind quality and progress. The magical Nap name – derived from an Indian word for plenty – applie to the fertile valley itself, the county in which it is found and the AVA fo the overall area, but the region is so viticulturally diverse that th appellation is virtually meaningless.

The valley was first settled by immigrants in the 1830s, and by the la 19th century Napa, and in particular the area around the communities o Rutherford and Oakville, had gained a reputation for exciting Cabern Sauvignon. Despite the long, dark years of Prohibition, this reputatio survived and when the US interest in wine revived during the 1970 Napa was ready to lead the charge.

GRAPE VARIETIES

Most of the classic French grapes are grown and recent replantings hav done much to match varieties to the most suitable locations. Cabern Sauvignon is planted in profusion and Napa's strongest reputation is fo varietal Cabernet and Bordeaux-style (or meritage) blends, mostl Cabernet-Merlot. Pinot Noir and Chardonnay, for both still an sparkling wines, do best in the south, from Yountville down to Carnero Zinfandel is grown mostly at the north end of the valley. Syrah an Sangiovese are relatively new here.

SUB-REGIONS

The most significant vine-growing area is the valley floor running fro Calistoga in the north down to Carneros, below which the Napa Rive flows out into San Pablo Bay. It has been said that there are more so types in Napa than in the whole of France, but much of the soil in th valley is heavy, clayish, over-fertile, difficult to drain and really not fit make great wine. Some of the best vineyards are tucked into th mountain slopes at the valley sides or in selected spots at higher altitude

There is as much as a 10°C temperature difference between torri Calistoga and Carneros at the mouth of the valley, cooled by Pacific fo and a benchmark for US Pinot Noir and cool-climate Chardonna About 20 major sub-areas have been identified along the valley floor an in the mountains, although there is much debate over how many have real claim to individuality. Rutherford, Oakville and Yountville in th mid-valley produce Cabernet redolent of dust, dried sage and ultra-rip blackcurrants. Softer flavours come from Stags Leap to the east. Th higher-altitude vineyards of Diamond Mountain, Spring Mountain an Mount Veeder along the Mayacamas mountain range to the we produce deep Cabernets, while Howell Mountain in the north-east ha stunning Zinfandel and Merlot.

See also CARNEROS AVA, HOWELL MOUNTAIN AVA, MOUNT VEEDER AVA, NAPA VALLE' AVA, OAKVILLE AVA, RUTHERFORD AVA, SPRING MOUNTAIN AVA, STAGS LEAP DISTRIC' AVA; and individual producers.

BEST YEARS

BEST PRODUCERS

Cabernet Sauvignon and meritage blends
Abreu, Altamura, Anderson's Conn Valley, ARAUJO, Barnett (Rattlesnake Hill), Beaulieu, BERINGER, Bryant Family, Burgess Cellars, Cafaro, Cain, Cakebread, CAYMUS, CHATEAU MONTELENA, Chateau Potelle (VGS), CHIMNEY ROCK, Cliff Lede, Clos Pegase, CLOS DU VAL, Colgin, Conn Creek (Anthology), Corison, Cosentino, Robert Craig, DALLA VALLE, Darioush, Del Dotto, DIAMOND CREEK, DOMINUS, DUNN, Elyse, Far Niente, FLORA SPRINGS, Forman, Freemark Abbey, Frog's Leap, Grace Family, Groth, HARLAN ESTATE, HARTWELL, HEITZ, Honig, Jarvis, Leo Joseph, Ladera, La Jota, Lang & Reed, Lewis Cellars, Livingston Moffett, Lokoya, Long Meadow Ranch, Long Vineyards, Markham, Mayacamas Vineyards, MERRYVALE, Peter MICHAEL, MINER, MONDAVI, Monticello, Mount Veeder Winery, NEWTON, OPUS ONE, O'Shaughnessy, Pahlmeyer, Palladian, Paradigm, Robert Pecota, Peju (HB Vineyard), PHELPS, PINE RIDGE, Plumpjack, Pride, Quintessa, Raymond, Rubicon/COPPOLA, Rudd Estate, Saddleback, St Clement, ST SUPÉRY, SCREAMING EAGLE, Seavey, SHAFER, SILVER OAK, SILVERADO, SPOTTSWOODE, Staglin Family, STAG'S LEAP WINE CELLARS, Swanson, The Terraces, Turnbull, Viader, Villa Mt Eden, Vine Cliff, Vineyard 29, Von Strasser, Whitehall Lane, ZD.

227

NELSON *South Island, New Zealand* A range of mountains separates Nelso from MARLBOROUGH at the northern end of South Island. Nelson is made up a series of small hills and valleys with a wide range of mesoclimates. Pin Noir, Chardonnay, Riesling and Sauvignon Blanc do well. **Best producer** Brightwater★, Greenhough★★, Himmelsfeld, Kina Beach, NEUDORF★★, Rim Grove★, Seifried★, Waimea. **Best years: (whites) 2009 07 06 05 04**.

NERO D'AVOLA The name of SICILY's great red grape derives from the tow of Avola near Siracusa, although it is now planted all over the island. I deep colour, high sugars and acidity make it useful for blendin, especially with the lower-acid Nerello Mascalese, but also with Caberne Merlot and Syrah. On its own, and from the right soils, it can be brillian with a soft, ripe, spicy black fruit character. Examples range from simp quaffers to many of Sicily's top reds.

NEUCHÂTEL *Switzerland* Swiss canton with high-altitude vineyard mainly Chasselas whites and Pinot Noir reds and rosé. **Best producer** Ch. d'Auvernier, Chambleau, Châtenay-Bouvier, Grillette.

NEUDORF *Nelson, South Island, New Zealand* Owners Tim and Judy Fin produce some of New Zealand's most stylish and sought-after wine including gorgeous, creamily textured Chardonnay★★, rich but scente Pinot Noir★★, Sauvignon Blanc★★, Riesling★★ and Pinot Gris★. Be years: (Chardonnay) (2009) **08 06 05 04 03**; (Pinot) (2009) **07 06 05 03 0**.

NEW SOUTH WALES *Australia* Australia's most populous state responsible for about 25% of the country's grape production. The large centres of production are the irrigated areas of RIVERINA, and Murray Darlin Swan Hill and Perricoota on the Murray River, where better viticultural an winemaking practices and lower yields have led to significant quality. Small premium-quality regions include the old-established HUNTER VALLEY, Cowr higher-altitude MUDGEE and, especially, ORANGE and HILLTOPS. CANBERRA is a area of tiny vineyards and great potential at chilly altitudes, as is Tumbarumb at the base of the Snowy Mountains.

NEW YORK STATE *USA* Wine grapes were first planted on Manhatta Island in the mid-17th century, but it wasn't until the early 1950s that serious wine industry began to develop in the state as *vinifera* grapes we planted to replace natives such as *Vitis labrusca*. Weather condition particularly in the north, can be challenging, but improved vineyard practic have made a good vintage possible in most recent years. The most importa region is the FINGER LAKES in the north of the state, which is enjoying a surge consumer interest in Riesling. The boom that had LONG ISLAND vintne atwitter at the turn of the century seems to have fizzled, though top produce still make serious BORDEAUX-styled reds and good Chardonnay. The Hudso River Region has a couple of good producers and a few upstarts are producir noteworthy wines amid the ocean of plonk along the shores of Lake Erie.

NEWTON *Napa Valley AVA, California, USA* Spectacular winery and stee vineyards high above St Helena, owned by French luxury giant LVMH Cabernet Sauvignon★★, Merlot★★ and Claret★ are some of Californi, most pleasurable examples. Even better is the challenging, intellectua single-vineyard Cabernet Sauvignon-based The Puzzle★★★. Newtc pioneered the unfiltered Chardonnay★★ style but the cheaper Red Lab

Chardonnay★ is also very attractive. The reds age remarkably well and end up tasting surprisingly like top BORDEAUX. Best years: (Cabernet Sauvignon) 2005 03 02 01 **00 99 97 96 95 94 91 90**.

GATARAWA *Hawkes Bay, North Island, New Zealand* Viticulture here is organic, with Chardonnay★, botrytized Riesling and Cabernet-Merlot under the premium Alwyn Reserve label. The Glazebrook range includes attractive Chardonnay★ and Cabernet-Merlot★, both of which are best drunk within 5 years. Best years: (reds) (2009) **08 07 06 04**.

NIAGARA PENINSULA *Ontario, Canada* Sandwiched between lakes Erie and Ontario, the Niagara Peninsula benefits from regular winds off Lake Ontario, buffeted by the Niagara escarpment. Icewine, from Riesling and Vidal, is the showstopper, with growing international acclaim. Chardonnay leads the dry whites, with Pinot Noir, Merlot and Cabernet Franc showing most promise among the reds. Best producers: Cave Spring★, Château des Charmes★, Le CLOS JORDANNE★, Flat Rock Cellars, HENRY OF PELHAM★, Hidden Bench★★, INNISKILLIN★, Southbrook★, Stratus★★, Tawse★★, THIRTY BENCH★. Best years: (Icewine) **2008 07 05 04 03 02 00 99 98**.

NIEPOORT *Port DOC and Douro DOC, Douro, Portugal* Remarkable small wine and PORT producer of Dutch origin. Outstanding Vintage ports★★★, old tawnies★★★ and colheitas★★★. Unfiltered LBVs★★ are among the best in their class – intense and complex. The Vintage port second label is called Secundum★★. Niepoort also produces fine red, white and rosé DOURO Redoma★★; red Vertente★★, Batuta★★★ and Charme★★ are already established among Portugal's leading reds. Best years: (Vintage) 2007 05 03 **00 97 94 92 91 87 85 82 80 77 70 66 63**.

NIERSTEIN *Rheinhessen, Germany* Confusingly, both a small town and a large Bereich which includes the infamous Grosslage Gutes Domtal. The town boasts 23 vineyard sites and the top ones (Pettenthal, Brudersberg, Hipping, Oelberg and Orbel) are some of the best in the Rhine Valley. Best producers: GUNDERLOCH★★, Heyl zu Herrnsheim★, Kühling-Gillot★, St Antony★, Schneider★, Strub. Best years: (2009) 08 07 **06 05 04 02 01**.

NIGL *Senftenberg, Kremstal, Austria* Consistently fine and crystalline Riesling and Grüner Veltliner from this organic estate. Top vineyard is called Piri★ but each year Martin Nigl releases his best wines under the Privat★★ label. Best years: (2009) 08 07 **06 05 04 02 01**.

NIKOLAIHOF *Wachau, Niederösterreich, Austria* The Saahs family makes some of the best wines in the WACHAU as well as in nearby Krems-Stein in KREMSTAL, including steely, intense Rieslings from the famous Steiner Hund vineyard, always ★★. A biodynamic estate. Best years: (2009) 08 07 **06 05 04 02 01**.

DOM. DE NIZAS *Languedoc, France* Owned by John Goelet, also owner of NAPA-based CLOS DU VAL. Nizas makes an intense, red Réserve★, a blend of Petit Verdot, Cabernet Sauvignon and Syrah; a spicy COTEAUX DU LANGUEDOC; and an old-vine Carignan★. Entry-level red Le Mas is Cabernet Sauvignon-Syrah-based and white is Sauvignon with Viognier and a drop of Rolle (Vermentino). Best years: (Réserve) (2009) 08 07 06 **05 04**.

NOBILO *Kumeu/Huapai, Auckland, North Island, New Zealand* Wines range from medium-dry White Cloud to premium varietals. Tangy though restrained Sauvignon Blanc and a vibrant Chardonnay★ are the top wines from MARLBOROUGH. Nobilo (part of Constellation) owns Selaks in AUCKLAND and Drylands in Marlborough; intense Drylands Marlborough Sauvignon Blanc★, Chardonnay★ and Riesling★. Best years: (Chardonnay) **2009 07 06 05**.

NOEMÍA *Patagonia, Argentina* The partnership between Noemi Cinzan (owner of Argiano in Tuscany) and famed winemaker Hans Vinding Diers discovered these precious few hectares of near-derelict, ancie Malbec vineyards. A period of intensive care and conversion t biodynamic practices has transformed the winery into arguably the world top Malbec producer. Noemía★★★ is elegant, complex and ageworthy and expensive. Second wine, J Alberto★★, is exceptional and its siblin A Lisa★, is glorious on release. Best years (Noemía): 2007 06 **04** 02.

NORTON *Mendoza, Argentina* Austrian-owned winery where reds impres more than whites. Enjoyable everyday wines under the Norton Reserv label. Norton Privada★★, a lush, chocolaty blend of Malbec, Cabern and Merlot has been consistently fine over many years and good value fo money. Newer wines such as Finca Perdriel★, a dense blend of old-vin fruit, and the icon wine, Gernot Langhes★, from low-yielding vineyard are ones to keep your eye on. Torrontés★ is best of the whites.

QUINTA DO NOVAL *Port DOC and Douro DOC, Douro, Portugal* Owned by AXA-Millésimes, this property is the source of extraordinary Quinta do Noval Nacional★★★, made from ungrafted vines – virtually unobtainable except at auction. Other Noval ports (including Quinta do Noval Vintage★★★ and Silval★★) are excellent too. Also fine colheitas★★ and stunning 40-year-old

tawny★★★. Also DOURO red, Quinta do Noval Tinto★★. Best year (Nacional) 2007 03 00 **97 94 87** 85 70 66 63 62 60 31; (Vintage) 2007 04 0 00 **97 95 94 91 87 85 70 66 63 60 31.**

NUITS-ST-GEORGES AC *Côte de Nuits, Burgundy, France* This large AC one of the few relatively reliable 'village' names in Burgundy. Although has no Grands Crus, many of its Premiers Crus (it has 38!) are extreme good. The red can be rather slow to open out, often needing at least years, but it ages to a delicious, chocolaty, deep figs-and-prune frui Minuscule amounts of white are made by GOUGES★, l'Arlot, Chevillo and RION. Best producers: l'Arlot★, R Arnoux★★, S CATHIAR J Chauvenet★★, R Chevillon★★, J-J Confuron★★, FAIVELEY★★, H GOUGES★ GRIVOT★★, Jayer-Gilles★★, Lechenaut★, T LIGER-BELAIR★★, MEO-CAMUZET★ A Michelot★, Mugneret★★, J-F MUGNIER★★, POTEL★★, RION★★. Best year (reds) (2009) 08 07 06 05 **03 02** 01 99 98 96 95 90.

NYETIMBER *West Sussex, England* England's flagship sparkling win producer. The wines – Classic Cuvée★★ and 100% Chardonnay Blar de Blancs★★ – usually have good balance and great length; th Nyetimber style is long-aged with tasty brioche flavours on the nose, an crisp acidity. A new winemaking team took over in 2007. New plantin have taken the area under vine from 16ha (40 acres) to 142ha (350 acres and a new 1 million bottle winery is planned. Since their reputation h been based on well-aged sparklers, let's hope they don't try to expand to fast. Best years: **2005 03 02 98.**

OAKRIDGE *Yarra Valley, Victoria, Australia* Outstanding boutique winer admirably showcasing the YARRA's strengths. Run by David Bicknell, on of Australia's most exciting winemaking talents. The 864 range includ complex, oatmealy Chardonnay★★, lush, structured Cabern Merlot★★ and ultra-concentrated yet seamless Shiraz★★. The mediun priced Oakridge range (especially Chardonnay★ and Pinot Noir) and budget-priced Over the Shoulder range represent excellent value.

OAKVILLE AVA *Napa Valley, California, USA* This region is cooler than RUTHERFORD, which lies immediately to the north. Planted primarily to Cabernet Sauvignon, the area contains some of NAPA's best vineyards, both on the valley floor (MONDAVI, OPUS ONE, SCREAMING EAGLE) and hillsides (HARLAN ESTATE, DALLA VALLE), producing wines that display lush, ripe black fruits and firm tannins. Best years: (Cabernet Sauvignon) 2006 05 **04 03 02 01 00 99 95 94 91 90**.

OC, VIN DE PAYS D' *Languedoc-Roussillon, France* Important vin de pays covering LANGUEDOC-ROUSSILLON. Overproduction and consequent underripeness have not helped its reputation, but an increasing number of fine reds and whites show what can be done. Best producers: l'Aigle★, Clovallon (Viognier★), Condamine Bertrand, Croix de St-Jean, J-L DENOIS★, l'HOSPITALET, J & F Lurton★, MAS LA CHEVALIÈRE, Ormesson★, Pech-Céleyran (Viognier★), Quatre Sous★, SKALLI-FORTANT, VAL D'ORBIEU (top reds★).

OCKFEN *Mosel* Village with one famous individual vineyard site, the Bockstein. The wines can be superb in a sunny year, never losing their cold steely streak but packing in delightful full-flavoured fruit as well. Best producers: St Urbans-Hof★★, Dr Heinz Wagner★, ZILLIKEN★★. Best years: (2008) 07 06 05 **04 03 02** 01 99 97.

OKANAGAN VALLEY *British Columbia, Canada* The most important wine-producing region of British Columbia and first home of Canada's rich, honeyed Icewine. The Okanagan Lake helps temper the bitterly cold nights but October frosts can be a problem. Chardonnay, Pinot Blanc, Pinot Gris and Pinot Noir are the top performers. South of the lake, Cabernet, Merlot and even Shiraz are now being grown successfully. Best producers: Blue Mountain★, Burrowing Owl★, CedarCreek★, INNISKILLIN, JACKSON-TRIGGS★, Joie Farm★, MISSION HILL★★, Quails' Gate★, Road 13★★, Sandhill, SUMAC RIDGE★. Best years: (reds) 2008 **06 05 04 03 02**.

OLTREPÒ PAVESE DOC *Lombardy, Italy* Italy's main source of Pinot Nero, used mainly for sparkling wines that may be called Classese when made by the CHAMPAGNE method. Still reds from Barbera, Bonarda and Pinot Nero and whites from the Pinots, Riesling and Chardonnay can be impressive, although there's much mediocre Pinot Grigio. Best producers: Cà di Frara★, Le Fracce★, Frecciarossa★, Castello di Luzzano/Fugazza, Mazzolino★, Monsupello★, Montelio★, Vercesi del Castellazzo★, Bruno Verdi★. Best years: (reds) (2009) 08 07 **06 04 03** 01.

WILLI OPITZ *Neusiedlersee, Burgenland, Austria* The eccentric and publicity-conscious Willi Opitz produces a remarkable, unusual range of dessert wines from his 12ha (30-acre) vineyard, including red Eiswein. The best are ★★, but dry wines are average.

OPUS ONE★★ *Oakville AVA, California, USA* BORDEAUX-blend wine, a joint venture initially between Robert MONDAVI and Baron Philippe de Rothschild of MOUTON-ROTHSCHILD, now between Constellation and Baroness Philippine de Rothschild. Most Opus bottlings have been in the ★★ range, some achieving ★★★, in a beautifully cedary, minty manner whose balance and elegance can be a delight in modern-day NAPA. Best years: 2005 **04 03 02 01** 99 98 97 96 95 94 93 92 91 90 86 85.

ORANGE *New South Wales, Australia* Uniquely in Australia, the Orange region is defined by altitude: its grapes must be grown more than 600m (1900ft) above sea level. Orange is a relatively small, wonderfully picturesque region, established in the early 1980s. Although it is planted to 60% red

231

grapes, the finest wines to date have been the whites, with Sauvignon Blanc, Chardonnay and Riesling most impressive. Pinot Noir has made the most exciting reds, although Cabernet Sauvignon, Shiraz and blends from carefully chosen sites have enormous potential. Best producers: Angullong, Bloodwood, Cumulus, Logan, Printhie, Philip SHAW★, Word of Mouth.

DOM. ORATOIRE ST-MARTIN *Côtes du Rhône AC, Rhône Valley, France* Top class estate, good value too. Careful fruit selection in a mature, high sloped vineyard is the secret of Frédéric and François Alary's intense CAIRANNE reds and whites. Haut-Coustias white★ has peach and exotic fruit aromas, while the red★★ is a luscious mouthful of raspberries, herbs and spice. Top red Cuvée Prestige★★ is deep and intense with dark, spicy fruit. Best years: (Cuvée Prestige) 2009 **07 06 05 04 03 01**.

OREGON *USA* Oregon shot to international stardom in the early 1980s following some perhaps overly generous praise of its Pinot Noir, but it is only with the release of a succession of fine recent vintages (2007 being an unfortunate exception) and some soul-searching by the winemakers about what style they should be pursuing that we can now begin to accept that some of the hype was deserved. Consistency is still a problem, however, with surprisingly warm weather now offering challenges along with the traditional ones of overcast skies and unwelcome rain. Chardonnay can be quite good in an austere, understated style. The rising star is Pinot Gris, which can be delicious, with surprising complexity. Pinot Blanc and Riesling are also gaining momentum. The WILLAMETTE VALLEY is considered the best growing region, although the more BORDEAUX-like climate of the Umpqua and Rogue Valleys can produce good Cabernet Sauvignon and Merlot. Best producers: (Rogue, Umpqua) ABACELA★, Bridgeview, Foris★, Henry Estate, Valley View.

TENUTA DELL'ORNELLAIA *Bolgheri, Tuscany, Italy* This beautiful property was developed by Lodovico ANTINORI, brother of Piero. Now owned by FRESCOBALDI-controlled Tenute di Toscana. Ornellaia★★, a Cabernet-Merlot blend, doesn't quite have the class of neighbouring SASSICAIA, but it is more lush. Also superb Merlot, Masseto★★★, and second wine Le Serre Nuove di Ornellaia★. Best years: (Ornellaia) (2009) (08) (07) 06 05 04 **03 01 00 99 98 97 96 95**.

ORTENAU *Baden, Germany* A chain of steep granitic hills between Baden-Baden and Offenburg, which produce the most elegant (generally dry) Rieslings in BADEN, along with fragrant, medium-bodied Spätburgunder (Pinot Noir) reds. Best producers: Franckenstein★, Laible★★, Nägelsförst★, Schloss Neuweier★★, Wolff Metternich★.

ORVIETO DOC *Umbria, Italy* Traditionally a lightly sweet white wine made from a blend of grapes including Procanico (Trebbiano) and Umbria's native Grechetto, basic Orvieto is today usually dry and ordinary. In the superior Classico zone, however, the potential for richer, more complex wines exists, especially in the Superiore category. There are also some very good botrytis-affected examples. Best producers: (dry) Barberani-Vallesanta (Superiore Castagnolo★★), La Carraia★, Decugnano dei Barbi★, Palazzone (Superiore Campo del Guardiano★★), Castello della SALA★, Salviano★, Conte Vaselli★, Le Velette★; (sweet) Barberani-Vallesanta (Calcaia★★), Decugnano dei Barbi★, Palazzone (Muffa Nobilis★★), Castello della SALA★.

OSBORNE *Jerez y Manzanilla DO, Andalucía, Spain* The biggest drinks company in Spain, Osborne does most of its business in brandy and other spirits. Its sherry arm in Puerto de Santa María specializes in the light Fino

Quinta★. Amontillado Coquinero★, rich, intense Bailén Oloroso★★ and Solera India Oloroso★★ are very good indeed. It has also created a large red wine estate at Malpica de Tajo in CASTILLA-LA MANCHA.

PAARL WO *South Africa* This district accounts for just under 17% of all South Africa's vineyards. A great diversity of soil and climate favour everything from Cap Classique sparkling wines to sherry styles, but the fact that Paarl was famous for sherry tells you that it's fairly hot, and it is now big reds that are setting the quality pace, especially Shiraz. Its white RHÔNE counterpart, Viognier, solo and in white blends, is also performing well. FRANSCHHOEK, Simonsberg-Paarl, Voor Paardeberg and Wellington are wards within the Paarl district. Best producers: (Paarl) Boschendal, DISTELL (Nederburg), FAIRVIEW★★, Val de Vie, VEENWOUDEN★★, Vilafonté★; (Simonsberg-Paarl), DISTELL (Plaisir de Merle★), GLEN CARLOU★, Rupert & Rothschild★; (Voor Paardeberg) Scali★; (Wellington) Diemersfontein★, Mont du Toit★. Best years: (premium reds) 2008 07 **06 05 04 03 02 01**.

PACHERENC DU VIC-BILH AC *South-West France* MADIRAN's white wines, ranging from dry to sweet late-harvest styles Best producers: AYDIE★, Barréjat, BERTHOUMIEU★, Brumont (Bouscassé★, MONTUS★), Capmartin★, du Crampilh★, Damiens, Labranche-Laffont★, LAFFITTE-TESTON★★, PLAIMONT★. Best years: (sweet) (2008) **07 06 05 04**.

PACIFIC RIM VINEYARDS *Washington State, USA* Randall Grahm, whose BONNY DOON wines are a Californian legend, headed to WASHINGTON STATE 'to craft the best Riesling in America'. The single-vineyard wines are exceptional examples of New World Riesling: the Wallula Vineyard★ bottlings (one being biodynamic) are both expressive of their *terroir*; the Dauenhauer is from Oregon's WILLAMETTE VALLEY; the Solstice Vineyard★★ is the jewel. Best years: (2009) (08) **07**.

PADTHAWAY *South Australia* This wine region has always been the alter ego of nearby COONAWARRA, growing whites to complement Coonawarra's reds; Chardonnay has been particularly successful. Nowadays there are some excellent reds, especially from Henry's Drive; Orlando's premium Lawson's Shiraz★★ is 100% Padthaway; even GRANGE has included Padthaway grapes. For many years HARDYS' Eileen Hardy Shiraz★★★ included Padthaway fruit, though it is now 100% MCLAREN VALE. Best producers: Browns of Padthaway, Henry's Drive★★, LINDEMANS★, Orlando/JACOB'S CREEK★, Padthaway Estate, SEPPELT, Stonehaven★.

BRUNO PAILLARD *Champagne AC, Champagne, France* Bruno Paillard is one of the very few individuals to have created a new CHAMPAGNE house in the 20th century. Paillard still does the blending himself. Non-vintage Première Cuvée★ is lemony and crisp; Réserve Privée★ is a blanc de blancs; vintage Brut★★ is a serious wine. De luxe cuvée Nec Plus Ultra★★ is a barrel-fermented blend of Grands Crus made in top vintages. Best years: **1999 96 95 90 89 88**.

ALVARO PALACIOS *Priorat DOCa, Cataluña, Spain* The young Alvaro Palacios was already a veteran with Bordeaux and Napa experience when he launched his boutique winery in PRIORAT, in the rough hills of southern CATALUÑA in the late 1980s. He is now one of the driving forces of the area's rebirth. His red wines (super-expensive, highly concentrated L'Ermita★★★, Finca Dofí★★ and affordable Les Terrasses★) from old Garnacha vines and a dollop of Cabernet Sauvignon, Merlot, Cariñena and Syrah have won a cult following. Best years: (2007) 06 05 04 **03 01 00 99 98 97 96 95 94**.

PALETTE AC *Provence, France* Tiny AC just east of Aix-en-Provence. Even though the local market pays high prices, I find the reds and rosés rather tough and charmless. However, Ch. Simone manages to achieve a white wine of some flavour from mostly basic southern French grapes (Furmint is also planted at Simone). Best producers: Crémade, Ch. Simone★.

PALLISER ESTATE *Martinborough, North Island, New Zealand* State-of-the-art winery producing some of New Zealand's best Sauvignon Blanc★★ outside MARLBOROUGH, as well as Riesling★, delightful Chardonnay★★ and Pinot Gris★, and impressive, rich-textured Pinot Noir★★. Exciting botrytized dessert wines in favourable vintages. Méthode★ fizz is good too. Pencarrow is the very tasty second label. Best years: (Pinot Noir) (2009) 08 **07 06 03**.

CH. PALMER★★ *Margaux AC, 3ème Cru Classé, Haut-Médoc, Bordeaux, France* This estate was named after a British major-general who fought in the Napoleonic Wars, and is one of the leading properties in MARGAUX AC. The wine is wonderfully perfumed, with irresistible plump fruit (lots of Merlot). The very best vintages can age for 30 years or more. Second wine: Alter Ego★ (frequently an excellent, scented red). Best years: 2008 07 06 05 04 **03 02 01 00 99 98 96 95 90 89 88 86 85**.

S C PANNELL *McLaren Vale, South Australia* Steve Pannell enjoyed corporate success as BRL HARDYS' chief red winemaker. Now, without vineyards or a winery, he specializes in producing MCLAREN VALE Shiraz and Grenache and he has had equally rapid-fire success with ADELAIDE HILLS Sauvignon★. Textural and lavishly concentrated Shiraz-Grenache★★ and complex Shiraz★★ show more restraint and elegance than is common in the region, while Nebbiolo★★ (from Adelaide Hills) is some of the best you'll find outside BAROLO.

CH. PAPE-CLÉMENT *Pessac-Léognan AC, Cru Classé de Graves, Bordeaux, France* The expensive red wine★★ has not always been as consistent as it should be – but things settled down into a high-quality groove during the 1990s. In style it is mid-way between the refinement of HAUT-BRION and the firmness of la MISSION-HAUT-BRION. More elegance and seduction since 2001. Also a small amount of fine, aromatic white wine★★. Second wine: (red) Clémentin. Best years: (reds) 2008 07 06 05 **04 03 02 01 00 99 98 96 95 90 89**; (white) **2008 07 06 05 04 03 02 01 00 99**.

PARELLADA This Catalan exclusivity is the lightest of the trio of white grapes that go to make CAVA wines in north-eastern Spain. It also makes still wines, light, fresh and gently floral, with good acidity. Drink it as young as possible, while it still has the benefit of freshness.

PARINGA ESTATE *Mornington Peninsula, Victoria, Australia* Teacher-turned-winemaker Lindsay McCall planted his well-protected, steep, north-facing, suntrap site at Red Hill South in 1985. His attention to detail in the vineyard and flair in the winery has brought him enormous success with his Pinot Noirs (entry level Peninsula label, Estate★ and Reserve★★) the best of which are ethereal with silky smooth texture, depth, power and finesse. Also multi-layered, intense, cool-climate Shiraz★★.

PARKER COONAWARRA ESTATE *Coonawarra, South Australia* Established by John Parker, who built the estate into one of the region's finest boutiques. Following his death, it was bought by the Rathbone family who own Yering Station, MOUNT LANGI GHIRAN and Xanadu, and is performing better than ever. The top label, cheekily named First

Growth★★ in imitation of illustrious BORDEAUX reds, is regularly one of COONAWARRA's most impressively balanced reds. It is released only in better years. Second-label Terra Rossa Cabernet Sauvignon★ is lighter and leafier. The Merlot★★ is among the best in Australia. Best years: (First Growth) (2008) 06 05 04 01 **99 98 96 93 91 90**.

PASCUAL TOSO *Mendoza, Argentina* Consultant winemaker Californian Paul Hobbs (who also owns the boutique COBOS winery), has turned Toso from an also-ran into a champion in just a few years. Malbec is the star here. The rich Reserve Malbec★ sets the house style. Inky deep Finca Pedregal★★ is magical and the top cuvée, Magdalena Toso★★, is powerful, dense and very long lived.

C J PASK *Hawkes Bay, North Island, New Zealand* Chris Pask made the first wine in the now-famous Gimblett Gravels area of HAWKES BAY. Flagship Declaration label includes an intensely oaky Syrah★, rich Merlot and a powerful Cabernet-Merlot-Malbec blend. Mid-range wines under the Gimblett Road label. Best years: (reds) (2009) **08 07 06 04 02**.

PASO ROBLES AVA *California, USA* A large AVA at the northern end of SAN LUIS OBISPO COUNTY. Cabernet Sauvignon and Zinfandel perform well in this warm region, and Syrah is gaining an important foothold, but too many producers are chasing OTT alcohol levels. The Perrin family from Ch. de BEAUCASTEL selected this AVA to plant RHÔNE varieties for their California project, Tablas

Creek, whose whites so far outshine their mid-weight reds. Best producers: Adelaida★, Eberle★, Eos★, Justin★, J Lohr★, Peachy Canyon★, Rabbit Ridge, Tablas Creek★, Wild Horse★.

PATAGONIA *Argentina* 750km (465 miles) south of MENDOZA lie the two wine-producing regions of northern Patagonia: Río Negro, with a 100-year history of wine production, and its neighbour to the west, the brand new Neuquén, the world's only genuine 21st century wine region. Extreme day/night temperature differences and relentless southerlies are common to both, leading to deeply coloured, intense and healthy wines. Racy Pinot Noirs, graphite-edged Malbecs, pure, round Merlot and sublime sparkling wines are the order of the day. Best producers: (Río Negro) Humberto Canale, Chacra★★, FABRE MONTMAYOU★, NOEMÍA★★; (Neuquén) NQN★, Familia Schroeder★.

LUÍS PATO *Beira Litoral, Portugal* Leading 'modernist' in BAIRRADA, passionately convinced of the Baga grape's ability to make great reds on chalky-clay soil. He labels his wines as BEIRAS after arguing with Bairrada's bosses. Wines such as the Vinhas Velhas★, Vinha Barrosa★★, Vinha Pan★★ and the flagship Quinta do Ribeirinho Pé Franco★★ (from ungrafted vines) rank among Portugal's finest modern reds: some can reach ★★★ with age. Good white, Vinha Formal★, is 100% Bical. Also good fizz. Daughter Filipa makes delightful reds and whites under Lokal★★ and Ensaios FP★ labels. Best years: (reds) (2009) (08) **05 04 03 01 00 97 96 95 92**.

PAUILLAC AC *Haut-Médoc, Bordeaux, France* The deep gravel banks around the town of Pauillac in the HAUT-MÉDOC are the heartland of Cabernet Sauvignon. For many wine lovers, the king of red wine grapes finds its ultimate expression in the 3 Pauillac First Growths (LATOUR, LAFITE-ROTHSCHILD and MOUTON-ROTHSCHILD). The large AC also contains 15 other

Classed Growths. The uniting characteristic of Pauillac wines is their intense blackcurrant fruit flavour and heady cedar and pencil-shavings perfume. These are the longest-lived of BORDEAUX's great red wines. Best producers: Armailhac★, BATAILLEY★, Bellegrave, Clerc-Milon★, Duhart-Milon★ Fonbadet, GRAND-PUY-DUCASSE★, GRAND-PUY-LACOSTE★★, HAUT-BAGES-LIBERAL★ HAUT-BATAILLEY★, LAFITE-ROTHSCHILD★★★, LATOUR★★★, LYNCH-BAGES★★★ Lynch-Moussas, MOUTON-ROTHSCHILD★★★, Pibran★, PICHON-LONGUEVILLE★★★ PICHON-LONGUEVILLE-LALANDE★★★, PONTET-CANET★★. Best years: (2009) 08 06 05 04 **03** 02 01 00 96 95 90 89 88 86.

CH. PAVIE★★ *St-Émilion Grand Cru AC, 1er Grand Cru Classé, Bordeaux, France*
The style of the wine may be controversial – dense, rich, succulent – and it has as many enemies as friends, but there's no doubting the progress made at Pavie since Gérard Perse acquired the property in 1998. The price has also soared. Pavie-Decesse★ and MONBOUSQUET★ are part of the same stable. Best years: 2008 07 06 05 04 **03** 02 01 00 99 98 90 89 88.

CH. PAVIE-MACQUIN★★ *St-Émilion Grand Cru AC, 1er Grand Cru Classé, Bordeaux, France* This has become one of the stars of the ST-ÉMILION GRAND CRU since the 1990s, with promotion to Premier Grand Cru Classé in 2006. Rich, firm and reserved, the wines need 7–8 years and will age longer. Best years: 2008 07 06 05 04 **03** 02 01 00 99 98 96 95.

DOM. DU PECH *Buzet AC, South-West France* Magali Tissot and Ludovic Bonnelle are exemplars of the biodynamic movement, dispensing with all artificial aids and 'improvements'. They make what are undoubtedly the best and most characterful of the wines of this appellation (Domaine du Pech★★, Badinerie du Pech★★), even though in doing so they raise the eyebrows of the traditionalist authorities. Best years: (2009) **06** 05 04.

PÉCHARMANT AC *South-West France* Improving red wines from small AC north-east of BERGERAC. The wines are full-bodied, deriving their firmness from the iron in the sub-soil. Good vintages easily last 10 years and match a good HAUT-MEDOC. Best producers: Chemins d'Orient★, Clos les Côtes★, Costes★, d'Elle, Grand Jaure, Haut-Pécharmant★, Terre Vieille★ Tiregand★. Best years: (2009) (08) **05** 04 01 00.

PECORINO Relatively recently rescued from near-extinction, this is ABRUZZO's finest white grape variety, capable (also in Le MARCHE) of making dry sappy whites of considerable complexity. Best producers: Cataldi Madonna★, Citra★, Contesa★★, La Valentina★★, Marramiero★, Montori★, Pasetti★, San Lorenzo★, Terra d'Aligi★, Tiberio★★.

PEGASUS BAY *Canterbury, South Island, New Zealand* Matthew Donaldson and Lynette Hudson make lush, mouthfilling Chardonnay★★, an almost chewy Pinot Noir★★ and its even richer big sister Prima Donna Pinot Noir★★, powerful, idiosyncratic Sauvignon Blanc-Semillon★★, all kinds of very stylish Riesling★★ and an occasional heavenly Gewurztraminer★★★. These are some of the most original wines in New Zealand, and all will age well. Best years: (Pinot Noir) (2009) **08 03** 02 01.

PEMBERTON *Western Australia* Exciting emergent cool-climate region, deep in the Karri forests of the south-west, which has long divided opinion about which varieties will most suit the region. At this stage, the whites have done best, especially taut, tangy Sauvignon Blanc and thrilling, minerally Chardonnay. There are occasional superb examples of Riesling, Viognier, Semillon and Marsanne as well as Western Australia's only distinguished sparkling wine. Best of the reds so far is

Pinot Noir, with Shiraz rewarding patience in its best (warmest) vintages, and occasional BORDEAUX blends. HOUGHTON leads the way – thanks to the outstanding fruit from the vineyard they purchased in 1992 – with their Wisdom range. Best producers: Bellarmine★, Fonty's Pool, HOUGHTON★★, Lillian, Pemberley★★, Picardy★, Salitage.

PENEDÈS *Cataluña, Spain* The booming CAVA industry is based in Penedès, and the majority of the still wines are white, made from the Cava trio of Parellada, Macabeo and Xarel-lo, clean and fresh when young, but never exciting. Better whites are made from Chardonnay. The reds are variable, the best made from Cabernet Sauvignon and/or Tempranillo and Merlot. Best producers: Albet i Noya★, Can Feixes★, Can Ràfols dels Caus★★, Cavas Hill, Jean León★, Marques de Monistrol, Masía Bach★, Albert Milà i Mallofré, Puig i Roca★, Sot Lefriec★, TORRES★, Vallformosa, Jané Ventura★.

PENFOLDS *Barossa Valley, South Australia* While it was part of the giant Southcorp group, Penfolds proved that quality can go hand in hand with quantity, but for a long time its performance as part of the Foster's Wine Group has been uneven, particularly at the lower end. It still makes the country's most famous red wine, GRANGE★★★, and other superb reds such as RWT Shiraz★★★, Magill Estate★★, St Henri★, Bin 707 Cabernet★★, Bin 389 Cabernet-Shiraz★, Bin 28 Kalimna★ and Bin 128 Coonawarra Shiraz. Its Cellar Reserve wines are difficult to find but outstanding, and occasional releases of Special Bin reds are among Australia's best. However, further down the range they need to reverse a dispiriting blandness which entered into previously reliable wines like Koonunga Hill and Rawson's Retreat when Penfolds became part of the brewing group. Whites are led by expensive but excellent Yattarna Chardonnay★★★, stunningly good Reserve Bin Chardonnay★★★ and impressive cool-climate Bin 311 Chardonnay★★; there's also citrus Eden Valley Riesling★ and decent Rawson's Retreat Riesling. Thomas Hyland Cabernet, Shiraz and Chardonnay are pretty good. Best years: (top reds) 2009 08 06 05 **04 02 98 96 94 91 90**.

PENÍNSULA DE SETÚBAL *Portugal* Warm, maritime area south of Lisbon. Vinho Regional with some decent whites and good reds; the best reds are from old Castelão vines, often under the Palmela DOC. SETÚBAL produces sweet fortified wine. Best producers: (reds) ALIANÇA (Palmela Particular★), BACALHÔA VINHOS DE PORTUGAL★★, Herdade da Comporta, D F J VINHOS★, Ermelinda Freitas★, José Maria da FONSECA★★, Pegões co-op★, Pegos Claros★, Soberanas. Best years: 2008 07 **05 04 03 01 00 99 97 96 95**.

PENLEY ESTATE *Coonawarra, South Australia* Kym Tolley, a member of the PENFOLD family, launched Penley Estate in 1991. From 1997 Cabernet Sauvignon★★★ has been outstanding. Chardonnay and Hyland Shiraz can reach ★★; Gryphon Merlot★ and fizz★ are good, too. Best years: (Cabernet Reserve) (2009) (08) 07 06 05 **04 02 00 99 98 96 94 93 92 91**.

PENNSYLVANIA *USA* Pennsylvania has seen its wine industry blossom over the last two decades, to more than 120 wineries today; it now ranks seventh in US wine grape production. The state boasts the two highest elevation vineyards in the US east of the Rocky Mountains. Native and French hybrid grapes are common, with *vinifera* making inroads. Best producers: Allegro, CHADDSFORD, Presque Isle, Stargazers.

PEPPER BRIDGE WINERY *Walla Walla Valley AVA, Washington State, US*
This estate's vineyards, Pepper Bridge and Seven Hills, are two o
WASHINGTON STATE's best. The Cabernet Sauvignon★ is powerful an
requires aging to show its potential; Merlot★ is a muscular version of th
variety; BORDEAUX-style blend Reserve★★ is produced in very smal
amounts. Best years: (2008) 07 06 05.

PÉREZ CRUZ *Maipo, Chile* Modern winery in the Alto Maipo, with 150h
(370 acres) of red vines in a unique microclimate close to the Ande
foothills. Noted for its minty Cabernet Sauvignon★, Cot★ (Malbec)
Syrah★ and Liguai★★ (Syrah-Cabernet Sauvignon-Carmenère).

PERNAND-VERGELESSES AC *Côte de Beaune, Burgundy, France* The little
known village of Pernand-Vergelesses contains a decent chunk of th
great Corton hill, including much of the best white CORTON-CHARLEMAGN
Grand Cru vineyard. The red wines sold under the village name are ver
attractive when young, with a nice raspberry pastille fruit and a sligh
earthiness, and will age for 6–10 years. Best vineyard: Île de Vergelesse
As no one ever links poor old Pernand with the heady heights of Corton
Charlemagne, the whites sold under the village name can be a bargair
The wines can be a bit lean and dry to start with but fatten up beautifull
after 2–4 years in bottle. Best producers: (reds) CHANDON DE BRIAILLES★★
C Cornu★, Denis Père et Fils★, Dubreuil-Fontaine★, Laleure-Piot★; (whites
CHANDON DE BRIAILLES★, Dubreuil-Fontaine★, Germain/Ch. de Chorey
A Guyon, JADOT, J-M Pavelot★, Rapet★, Rollin★. Best years: (reds) (2009) 0
07 05 03 02 99; (whites) (2009) 08 07 06 05.

ANDRÉ PERRET *Condrieu AC, Rhône Valley, France* A top CONDRIEU growe
with 2 standout cuvées: Clos Chanson★★ is mineral and full
Chéry★★★, made with some later-picked Viognier, is gloriously musky
floral and rich. Impressive white and red ST-JOSEPH, notably Le
Grisières★★ from old Syrah vines. Very good vin de pays Syrah an
Marsanne. Best years: (Condrieu Chéry) 2009 08 07 06 05 04.

JOSEPH PERRIER *Champagne AC, Champagne, France* The NV★ an
vintage★★ Blanc de Blancs are classy and the NV Cuvée Royale★ i
biscuity and creamy. Prestige Cuvée Josephine★★ has length an
complexity, but the much cheaper Cuvée Royale Vintage★★ is the bes
deal. Best years: 2002 99 98 96 95 90 89 88 85 82.

PERRIER-JOUËT *Champagne AC, Champagne, France* Perrier-Jouët has ha
three owners in the past 10 years (it's now owned by Pernod Ricard)
This doesn't help consistency, but Perrier-Jouët had fallen so low durin
the 1990s that any change would be beneficial. Certainly the NV is now
a decent drink once more, the Blason Rosé★ is charming and the de lux
vintage cuvée Belle Époque★ (known as Fleur de Champagne in the US
reasonably classy. Best years: 2002 99 98 96 95 90 89 85 82.

PESQUERA *Ribera del Duero DO, Castilla y León, Spain* Tinto Pesquera reds
richly coloured, firm, fragrant and plummy-tobaccoey, have long bee
among Spain's best. They are 100% Tempranillo and sold as Crianza
and Reserva★. Gran Reserva★★ and Janus★★ are made in the bes
years. The firm founded by Alejandro Fernández in 1972 owns anothe
RIBERA DEL DUERO estate, Condado de Haza★ (Alenza★★), plus ventures i
Zamora (Dehesa La Granja★) and La MANCHA (Vínculo). Best years
(Pesquera Crianza) 2007 06 05 04 01 99 96 95 94 93 92 91 90 89.

PESSAC-LÉOGNAN AC *Bordeaux, France* AC created in 1987 for th
northern (and best) part of the GRAVES region and including all the Grave
Classed Growths. The supremely gravelly soil tends to favour red wine

over the rest of the Graves. Now, thanks to cool fermentation and the use of new oak barrels, this is also one of the most exciting areas of France for top-class white wines. **Best producers: (reds) Carbonnieux★, les Carmes Haut-Brion★, Dom. de CHEVALIER★★, Couhins-Lurton★★, FIEUZAL★, HAUT-BAILLY★, HAUT-BRION★★★, Larrivet-Haut-Brion★, LATOUR-MARTILLAC★, la LOUVIÈRE★, MALARTIC-LAGRAVIÈRE★, la MISSION-HAUT-BRION★★★, PAPE-CLEMENT★★, SMITH-HAUT-LAFITTE★★; (whites) Brown★, Carbonnieux★, Dom. de CHEVALIER★★★, Couhins-Lurton★, FIEUZAL★, HAUT-BRION★★★, LATOUR-MARTILLAC★, LAVILLE-HAUT-BRION★★, la LOUVIÈRE★★, MALARTIC-LAGRAVIÈRE★★, PAPE-CLEMENT★★, Rochemorin★, SMITH-HAUT-LAFITTE★★. Best years: (reds) (2009) 08 06 05 04 02 01 00 99 98 96 95; (whites) (2009) 08 07 06 05 04 02 01 00 99 98.**

ETALUMA *Adelaide Hills, South Australia* A public company founded by Brian Croser, probably Australia's most influential winemaker (see TAPANAPPA). Now owned by brewer Lion Nathan. CHAMPAGNE-style Croser★ is stylish and fruitier than before. COONAWARRA★ (Cabernet-Merlot) and Chardonnay★ are consistently good and Hanlin Hill Riesling★★★ from the CLARE VALLEY is at the fuller end of the spectrum and matures superbly. **Best years: (Coonawarra) (2009) (08) (07) 06 05 04 03 02 01 00 99 97 94 91 90 88.**

PETIT VERDOT A rich, tannic variety, grown mainly in Bordeaux's HAUT-MÉDOC to add depth, colour and violet fragrance to top wines. Late ripening and erratic yield limit its popularity, but warmer-climate plantings in Australia, California, South Africa, Chile, Argentina, Spain and Italy are giving exciting results, often from including only a few per cent in blends.

CH. PETIT-VILLAGE★ *Pomerol AC, Bordeaux, France* This POMEROL used to be rather dry and dense, but has considerably softened up in recent vintages. New cellar and even better quality from 2006. Generally worth aging for 8–10 years. **Best years: 2008 07 06 05 04 03 02 01 00 99 98 95 90 89 88.**

PETITE ARVINE A Swiss grape variety from the VALAIS, Petite Arvine has a bouquet of peach and apricot, and develops a spicy, honeyed character. Dry, medium or sweet, the wines have good aging potential – thank goodness: I've still got one from 1969. **Best producers: Chappaz★, R Favre, A Mathier, Maye, Dom. du Mont d'Or★, Rouvinez★, Varone.**

PETITE SIRAH Once used primarily as a blending grape in California, this variety is identical to the obscure Rhône blender Durif. Some 500 or more California wineries now make a varietal Petite Sirah. At its best, it is deep, tannic and long-lived, but can be monstrously huge and unfriendly. Australian, Mexican and Israeli examples are softer though still hefty, and can occasionally develop a floral scent and blackberry fruit. **Best producers: (California) FETZER, Foppiano, Girard, Granite Springs, Lava Cap, RAVENSWOOD★, RIDGE★, Rosenblum, Stags' Leap Winery★★, TURLEY★★; (Australia) Campbells, DE BORTOLI, Nugan Estate, Rutherglen Estates★, Stanton & Killeen, WESTEND★; (Mexico) L A CETTO★.**

CH. PÉTRUS★★★ *Pomerol AC, Bordeaux, France*   The powerful, concentrate
wine (one of the most expensive red wines in the world) is the result of
the caring genius of Pétrus' owners, the MOUEIX family, who have
maximized the potential of the vineyard of almost solid clay, although
the impressive average age of the vines has been much reduced by recent
replantings. Drinkable for its astonishingly rich, dizzying blend of fruit
and spice flavours after a decade, but top years will age for much longer,
developing exotic scents of tobacco and chocolate and truffles. Best years:
2008 07 06 05 04 03 **02** 01 **00 99 98 96 95 90 89 88 86 85**.

DOM. PEYRE ROSE *Coteaux du Languedoc AC, Languedoc, France*   Organic
viticulture, ultra-low yields, lengthy aging, but total absence of oak are
hallmarks of Marlène Soria's wines. Syrah is the dominant grape in both
the raisin- and plum-scented Clos des Cistes★ and the dense, velvety
Clos Syrah Léone★★. Best years: (reds) (2008) 07 06 05 04 **03** 02 98.

CH. DE PEZ★ *St-Estèphe AC, Haut-Médoc, Bordeaux, France*   One of ST-ESTÈPHE
leading non-Classed Growths, de Pez makes mouthfilling, satisfying
claret with sturdy fruit. Slow to evolve, good vintages often need 10 years
or more. Owned by Champagne house ROEDERER. Best years: 2008 07 06 0
04 03 02 01 00 99 98 96 95 90 89.

PFALZ *Germany*   This immense wine region, with 23,460ha (58,000 acres),
makes a lot of mediocre wine, but the quality estates can match the best that
Germany has to offer. The Mittelhaardt can produce profound full-bodied
Riesling, especially round the villages of BAD DÜRKHEIM, WACHENHEIM, FORST and
Deidesheim, though Freinsheim, Kallstadt, Ungstein, Gimmeldingen and
Haardt also produce fine Riesling as well as Scheurebe, Rieslaner and Pinot
Gris. In the Südliche Weinstrasse the warm climate makes the area ideal for
Spät-, Weiss- and Grauburgunder (aka Pinots Noir, Blanc and Gris), as well
as Gewürztraminer, Scheurebe, Muscat and red Dornfelder, the last often
dark and tannic, sometimes with oak influence.

JOSEPH PHELPS *Napa Valley AVA, California, USA*   Joseph Phelps' BORDEAUX
blend Insignia★★ is usually one of California's top reds, strongly fruit
driven with a lively spicy background. Phelps' pure Cabernets include
Napa Valley★ and huge Backus Vineyard★★, beautifully balanced wit
solid ripe fruit. The Napa Merlot★ is ripe and elegant, with layers of fruit
Phelps was the first California winery to successfully major on RHÔNE
varietals, and makes an intense Viognier★ and complex Syrah★. See also
FREESTONE. Best years: (Insignia) 2005 04 03 02 **01 00 99 96 95 94 93 91 85**

PHILIPPONNAT *Champagne AC, Champagne, France*   Quality across the
whole range has improved over the past 5 years. The non-vintage★ is
now one of the best in Champagne, while single-vineyard Clos de
Goisses★★★, from an extremely steep, south-facing vineyard, is some of
the purist, ripest and longest-lasting wine in the whole of Champagne.
Best years: 2002 00 **99 98 96 95 90**.

CH. DE PIBARNON *Bandol AC, Provence, France*   Blessed with excellently
located vineyards, Pibarnon is one of BANDOL's leading properties. The
reds★★, extremely attractive when young, develop a truffly, wild herb
character with age. Average white and a ripe, strawberryish rosé. Best
years: (reds) 2008 07 06 **05** 03 01 00 99 98.

PIC ST-LOUP *Coteaux du Languedoc AC, Languedoc, France*   This appellation
north of Montpellier, is one of the coolest growing zones in the Midi
and, along with la CLAPE, produces some of the best reds in the

Languedoc. Syrah is the dominant variety, along with Grenache and Mourvèdre. Whites from Marsanne, Roussanne and Rolle are showing promise. **Best producers:** Cazeneuve★, CLOS MARIE★, Ermitage du Pic St-Loup, l'Euzière★, l'HORTUS★, Lancyre★, Lascaux★, Lavabre★, MAS BRUGUIERE★, Mas de Mortiès★, Valflaunès. **Best years:** (reds) (2009) 08 07 06 **05 04 03 01**.

RANZ X PICHLER *Wachau, Niederösterreich, Austria* One of Austria's most famous producers of dry wines. Grüner Veltliner and Riesling 'M'★★★ (for monumental) and Riesling Unendlich★★★ (endless) – alcoholically potent but balanced – are amazing. 'FX', as he is known, is gradually handing the reins to his son Lucas. **Best years:** (Riesling/Grüner Veltliner Smaragd) (2009) 08 07 06 **05 04 03 02 01 00**.

UDI PICHLER *Wachau, Niederösterreich, Austria* Pichler has progressed from being one of the WACHAU's most reliable producers to a secure place in the top tier. Riesling Achleiten and Grüner Veltliner Kollmütz and Hochrain are regularly ★★. **Best years:** (2009) 08 07 06 **05 04 02**.

H. PICHON-LONGUEVILLE★★★ *Pauillac AC, 2ème Cru Classé, Haut-Médoc, Bordeaux, France* Despite its superb vineyards, Pichon-Longueville (called Pichon-Baron until 1988) wines were 'also-rans' for a long time. In 1987 the property was bought by AXA and Jean-Michel Cazes of LYNCH-BAGES took over the management. The improvement was immediate and thrilling. Cazes has now left, but most recent vintages have been of First Growth standard, with firm tannic structure and rich dark fruit. Cellar for at least 10 years, although it is likely to keep for 30. Second wine: les Tourelles de Pichon Longueville. **Best years:** 2008 07 06 05 04 03 **02 01 00 99 98 96 95 90 89 88 86**.

H. PICHON-LONGUEVILLE-LALANDE★★★ *Pauillac AC, 2ème Cru Classé, Haut-Médoc, Bordeaux, France* The inspirational figure of May de Lencquesaing forged the modern reputation of this property. It's now (since 2007) controlled by Champagne house ROEDERER but with the same winemaking and management team. Divinely scented and lush at 6–7 years, the wines usually stay gorgeous for 20 at least. Recent years have been excellent. Second wine: Réserve de la Comtesse. **Best years:** 2008 07 06 05 04 **03 02 01 00 99 98 96 95 90 89 88 86 85**.

IEDMONT *Italy* The most important Italian region for the tradition of uality wines. In the north, there is Carema, Ghemme and GATTINARA. To the ›uth, in the LANGHE hills, there's BAROLO and BARBARESCO, both masterful ‹amples of the Nebbiolo grape, and other wines from Dolcetto and Barbera rapes. In the Monferrato hills, in the provinces of Asti and Alessandria, ıe Barbera, Moscato and Cortese grapes hold sway. The broad DOCs of anghe and Monferrato and the regionwide Piemonte appellation are esigned to classify all wines of quality from a great range of grape ırieties. See also ASTI, GAVI, MOSCATO D'ASTI, NEBBIOLO D'ALBA, ROERO.

IEROPAN *Veneto, Italy* Exceptionally good SOAVE Classico★ and, from 2 single vineyards, Soave Classico crus Calvarino★★ and La Rocca★★. Excellent RECIOTO DI SOAVE Le Colombare★★ and opulent Passito della Rocca★★, a barrique-aged blend of Sauvignon, Riesling Italico (Welschriesling) and Trebbiano di Soave. Single-vineyard Soaves can improve for 5 years or more, as can the Recioto and other sweet styles.

H. PIERRE-BISE *Coteaux du Layon AC, Loire Valley, France* Claude Papin has a professorial grasp of *terroir*. His COTEAUX DU LAYON vineyard is divided into over 20 mini parcels based on factors like soil depth, topography and

wind and sun exposure that help him analyse optimum ripeness. And t
results are sublime: rich, yet pure-fruited and precise Coteaux
Layon★★★ and QUARTS DE CHAUME★★★ with a mineral undertow. Ve
good dry ANJOU BLANC★, SAVENNIÈRES★ and ANJOU-VILLAGES★★. Best yea
(sweet) (2009) 07 05 03 02 **01 00 97 96 95 90 89**.

PIERRO *Margaret River, Western Australia*   Mike Peterkin doesn't make th
much Pierro Chardonnay★★★, yet it is a masterpiece of elegance a
complexity. The Semillon-Sauvignon LTC★★ is full with just a hint
leafiness, while the Pinot Noir★ approaches ★★ as the vines matu
Dark, dense Cabernet Sauvignon-Merlot★ is the serious, BORDEAUX-li
member of the family. The Fire Gully range is from a vineyard next do
to MOSS WOOD and is consistently good. Best years: (Chardonnay) (2009)
07 06 **05 04 03 02 01 00**.

PIESPORT *Mosel, Germany*   Generic Piesporter Michelsberg wines, so
sweet and forgettable, have nothing to do with the excellent Rieslin
from the top Goldtröpfchen site. With their intense peach a
blackcurrant aromas they are unique among MOSEL wines. Best produce
GRANS-FASSIAN★★, J Haart★, Reinhold HAART★★, Kurt Hain★, v
KESSELSTATT★, Lehnert-Veit, St Urbans-Hof★★. Best years: (2009) 08 07 06
04 02 01 00 99 98.

CH. LE PIN★★★ *Pomerol AC, Bordeaux, France*   Now one of the most expensi
wines in the world. The first vintage was 1979 and the wines, which a
concentrated but elegant, sumptuous yet refined, are produced fro
100% Merlot. The tiny 2ha (5-acre) vineyard lies close to those
TROTANOY and VIEUX-CH.-CERTAN. Best years: 2008 07 06 05 04 **02 01 00**
98 96 95 94 90 89 88 86 85.

PINE RIDGE *Stags Leap District AVA, California, USA*   Wines come from sever
NAPA AVAs, but its flagship Cabernet remains the supple, plummy STA
LEAP DISTRICT★★. Andrus Reserve★★, a BORDEAUX blend, has mo
richness and power, while the HOWELL MOUNTAIN Cabernet★ offers inten
fruit and structure for long aging. CARNEROS Merlot★ is spicy and cher
fruited, and Carneros Chardonnay★ looks good. Best years: (Stags Le
Cabernet) 2005 03 **02 01 00 99 97 96 95 94 91**.

DOMINIO DE PINGUS *Ribera del Duero DO, Castilla y León, Spain*   Pet
Sisseck's tiny vineyards and winery have attracted worldwide attentic
since 1995 due to the extraordinary depth and character of the cult wi
they produce, Pingus★★★. Second wine Flor de Pingus★★ is also supe
Best years: (Pingus) (2007) 06 05 04 **03 01 00 99 96 95**.

PINOT BIANCO See PINOT BLANC.

PINOT BLANC Wines have a clear, yeasty, appley taste, and good exampl
can age to a delicious honeyed fullness. In ALSACE it is taking over t
'workhorse' role from Sylvaner and Chasselas and is the mainstay of mo
CRÉMANT D'ALSACE. Important in northern Italy as Pinot Bianco a
especially in ALTO ADIGE where it reaches elevated levels of purit
complexity and longevity. Taken seriously in southern Germany ar
Austria (as Weissburgunder), producing imposing wines with ripe pe
and peach fruit and a distinct nutty character. Also successful
Hungary, Slovakia, Slovenia and the Czech Republic and promising
California (notably from Robert Sinskey), Oregon's WILLAMETTE VALL
and British Columbia, Canada.

PINOT GRIGIO See PINOT GRIS.

PINOT GRIS At its finest in ALSACE; with lowish acidity and a deep colour the grape produces fat, rich dry wines that somehow mature wonderfully. It is very occasionally used in BURGUNDY (as Pinot Beurot) to add fatness to a wine. Italian Pinot Grigio, often boring, occasionally delicious, is currently so popular worldwide that New World producers are tending to use the Italian name in preference to the French version. Also successful in Austria and Germany as Ruländer or Grauburgunder, and as Malvoisie in the Swiss VALAIS. There are good Romanian and Czech examples, as well as spirited ones in Hungary (as Szürkebarát). In a crisp style, it can be successful in Oregon and is showing promise in California, Virginia and OKANAGAN VALLEY in Canada. Now very fashionable in New Zealand and cooler regions of Australia.

PINOT MEUNIER An important ingredient in CHAMPAGNE, along with Pinot Noir and Chardonnay. Occasionally found in the LOIRE, and also grown in Germany under the name of Schwarzriesling.

PINOT NERO See PINOT NOIR.

PINOT NOIR See pages 244–5.

PINOTAGE A Pinot Noir x Cinsaut cross, conceived in South Africa in 1925 and covering 6% of the country's vineyards. DeWaal's Top of the Hill is the oldest, planted in 1950 and still bearing. Highly versatile; classic versions are full-bodied and well-oaked with ripe plum, spice and maybe some mineral, redcurrant, banana or marshmallow flavours. New Zealand and California have interesting examples. Graziano in MENDOCINO and J VINEYARDS in RUSSIAN RIVER VALLEY make stylish versions. Best producers: (South Africa) Ashbourne★, Graham BECK★, BEYERSKLOOF★★, DeWaal★ (Top of the Hill★★), Diemersfontein★, FAIRVIEW★ (Primo★★), GRANGEHURST★, Kaapzicht★, KANONKOP★★, Laibach★, L'AVENIR★★, SIMONSIG★ (Redhill★★), Tukulu; (New Zealand) Muddy Water★, Te Awa★.

PIPER-HEIDSIECK *Champagne AC, Champagne, France* They've put a big effort into restoring Piper's reputation: non-vintage★ is now gentle and biscuity, and the vintage★★ is showing real class. They've also launched a plethora of new cuvées: Sublime (demi-sec), Divin (blanc de blancs), Rosé Sauvage and Rare★★, a de luxe blend available in 1999, 98, 88 and 79 vintages. Best years: (2004) (02) **00 96 95 90 89 85 82**.

PISANO *Canelones, Uruguay* Family-owned winery with some of Uruguay's truest expressions of the Tannat grape: RPF is a good example and pure, dense Axis Mundi is from old vines. The more sophisticated Arretxea★ blends Tannat with Cabernet and Merlot. Best years: (reds) **2005 04 02**.

ROBERT PLAGEOLES *Gaillac AC, South-West France* Both traditionalists and modernizers, Robert and Bernard Plageoles have revived 14 ancient Gaillac grape varieties, including Prunelard, Verdanel and the rare Ondenc, which goes into their lusciously sweet Vin d'Autan★★★. Dry wines include Mauzac★, Ondenc★ and bone-dry Mauzac Nature★ fizz.

PRODUCTEURS PLAIMONT *Madiran AC, St-Mont AC and Vin de Pays des Côtes de Gascogne, South-West France* This Gascon grouping is the largest, most reliable and most successful co-op in the South-West. The whites★, full of crisp fruit, are reasonably priced and are best drunk young. The reds, especially Ch. de Sabazan★, are very good too. Also good MADIRAN and sweet PACHERENC DU VIC-BILH★.

PINOT NOIR

There's this myth about Pinot Noir that I think I'd better lay to rest. It goes something like this. Pinot Noir is an incredibly tricky grape to grow and an even more difficult grape to vinify in fact Pinot Noir is such a difficult customer that the only place that regularly achieves magical results is the thin stretch of land known as the Côte d'Or, between Dijon and Chagny in France where mesoclimate, soil conditions and 2000 years of experience weave an inimitable web of pleasure.

This just isn't so. The thin-skinned, early-ripening Pinot Noir is undoubtedly more difficult to grow than other great varieties like Cabernet or Chardonnay, but that doesn't mean that it's impossible to grow elsewhere – you just have to work at it with more sensitivity and seek out the right growing conditions. And although great red Burgundy is a hauntingly beautiful wine, it is not the only brilliant interpretation of this remarkable grape variety. The glorious thing about places like New Zealand, California, Oregon, Chile, Australia and Germany is that we are seeing an ever-increasing number of wines that are thrillingly different from anything produced in Burgundy, yet with flavours that are unique to Pinot Noir.

WINE STYLES

France All France's great Pinot Noir wines come from Burgundy's Côte d'Or. Rarely deep in colour, they should nonetheless possess a wonderful fruit quality when young – raspberry, strawberry, cherry or plum – that becomes more scented and exotic with age, the plums turning to figs and pine, and the richness of chocolate mingling perilously with truffles and well-hung game. Strange, challenging hedonistic. France's other Pinots – in north and south Burgundy, the Loire Valley, Jura, Savoie, Alsace and now occasionally in the south of France – are lighter and milder, and in Champagne its pale, thin wine is used to make sparkling wine.

Other European regions Since the 1990s, helped by good vintages, German winemakers have made considerable efforts to produce serious Pinot Noir (generally called Spätburgunder). Switzerland, where it is also called Blauburgunder, and Italy (as Pinot Nero) both have fair success, especially in Alto Adige. Austria and Spain have a couple of good examples. Romania, the Czech Republic and Hungary produce significant amounts of Pinot Noir, though of generally low quality.

New World Light, fragrant wines have given Oregon the reputation for being 'another Burgundy'; but I get more excited about the sensual wines of the cool, fog-affected areas of California: the ripe, stylish Russian River Valley examples; the exotically scented wines of Carneros, Anderson Valley and Sonoma Coast; the startlingly original offerings from Santa Barbara County (notably Santa Rita Hills) and Santa Lucia Highlands on east-facing slopes of western Monterey County.

New Zealand produces wines of thrilling fruit and individuality, most notably from Martinborough, Canterbury's Waipara district and Central Otago, with its wild thyme-flavoured wines. In the cooler regions of Australia – including Yarra Valley, Mornington Peninsula, Adelaide Hills, Geelong, north-east Victoria and Tasmania – producers are beginning to find their way with the variety. New Burgundian clones and increased confidence among winemakers bode well in South Africa. Chile's San Antonio/Leyda and Bío Bío areas are beginning to shine.

BEST PRODUCERS

France (Burgundy) d'ANGERVILLE, l'Arlot, Comte Armand, D Bachelet, G Barthod, J-M Boillot, BOUCHARD, CATHIARD, CHANDON DE BRIAILLES, R Chevillon, CLAIR, J-J Confuron, DROUHIN, C Dugat, B Dugat-Py, DUJAC, FAIVELEY, GIRARDIN, GOUGES, GRIVOT, Anne GROS, JADOT, LAFARGE, LAFON, Dom. LEROY, H Lignier, MÉO-CAMUZET, de MONTILLE, MORTET, J-F MUGNIER, Ponsot, POTEL, RION, Dom. de la ROMANÉE-CONTI, E Rouget, ROUMIER, ROUSSEAU, Sérafin, TOLLOT-BEAUT, de VOGÜÉ; *(Alsace)* J-B ADAM.

Germany Becker, BERCHER, FÜRST, HUBER, JOHNER, KELLER, Kesseler, Meyer-Näkel, MOLITOR, REBHOLZ, Stodden.

Switzerland Adank, GANTENBEIN, Adrian Mathier.

Italy CA' DEL BOSCO, Franz Haas, Haderburg, Hofstätter, Nals-Margreid.

New World Pinot Noirs
USA (California) ACACIA, AU BON CLIMAT, Byron, CALERA, Clos Pepe, DEHLINGER, DE LOACH, DUTTON GOLDFIELD, Merry Edwards, Gary Farrell, FLOWERS, HARTFORD FAMILY, KISTLER, Kosta Browne, La Crema, LANDMARK, Littorai, LYNMAR, MARCASSIN, Morgan, Papapietro Perry, Patz & Hall, RASMUSSEN, ROCHIOLI, SAINTSBURY, SANFORD, Sea Smoke, Siduri, Joseph SWAN, Talley, WILLIAMS SELYEM; *(Oregon)* ARGYLE, BEAUX FRERES, DOMAINE DROUHIN, DOMAINE SERENE, Ken WRIGHT.

Australia Ashton Hills, BANNOCKBURN, Bass Phillip, BAY OF FIRES, Bindi, Bream Creek, Castle Rock, COLDSTREAM HILLS, Curly Flat, DE BORTOLI, Diamond Valley, By FARR, Freycinet, Gembrook Hill, GIACONDA, Giant Steps, Hurley, KOOYONG, Paradigm Hill, Stefano LUBIANA, Moorooduc, OAKRIDGE, PARINGA, STONIER, Tamar Ridge, TARRA-WARRA, Ten Minutes by Tractor, Tomboy Hill, Yabby Lake.

New Zealand ATA RANGI, Carrick, CRAGGY RANGE, DRY RIVER, Escarpment, FELTON ROAD, Foxes Island, FROMM, Greenhough (Hope Vineyard), MARTINBOROUGH VINEYARD, NEUDORF, PALLISER ESTATE, PEGASUS BAY, Peregrine, QUARTZ REEF, VAVASOUR, WITHER HILLS.

South Africa BOUCHARD FINLAYSON, Paul CLUVER, HAMILTON RUSSELL.

Chile AGUSTINOS, ANAKENA, CASAS DEL BOSQUE, CONO SUR (20 Barrels, Ocio), Viña Leyda, Porta.

245

CH. PLAISANCE *Fronton AC, South-West France*   Perhaps the best and best-
known of the FRONTON growers, Marc Pénavayre makes a range of 4 reds
including a Rouge Tradition★ and a lightly oaked cuvée Thibaut★★
Best years: (2009) **08 06 05**.

PLANETA *Sicily, Italy*   Rapidly expanding, dynamic estate. Chardonnay★★ i
one of the best in southern Italy; Cabernet Sauvignon Burdese★★ and
Merlot★★ are among Italy's most impressive; and rich, peppery Santa
Cecilia★★ (Nero d'Avola) has star quality. The white Cometa★★ is a
fascinating Sicilian version of FIANO. Gluggable Cerasuolo di Vittoria★
and La Segreta red★ and white★ blends are marvellously fruity.

PLANTAGENET *Great Southern, Western Australia*   Influential winery in the
GREAT SOUTHERN region. The spicy Shiraz★★ is among the best producer
in Western Australia; limy Riesling★★ and classy Cabernet Sauvignon★
also impress. Omrah is the good second label, made from bought-i
grapes: Sauvignon Blanc★, Chardonnay★ and Pinot Noir★ stand out
Best years: (Shiraz) (2009) 08 07 05 04 03 **02 01 99 98 97 95 93**.

IL POGGIONE *Brunello di Montalcino DOCG, Tuscany, Italy*   Extensive property
(more than 100ha/250 acres) which sets the standard for traditional-style
BRUNELLO DI MONTALCINO★★ (Riserva★★★) at a reasonable price. Also fine
ROSSO DI MONTALCINO★ and Cabernet-Sangiovese blend San Leopoldo★
Best years: (2009) (08) (07) (06) 04 **03 01 99 98 97 95 90 88 85**.

POL ROGER *Champagne AC, Champagne, France*   Non-vintage Brut Réserve★
(formerly known as White Foil) is biscuity and dependable rather than
thrilling. The new ultra-dry wine is called Pure. Pol Roger also produce
a vintage★★, a vintage rosé★★ and a vintage Chardonnay★★. Its top
Champagne, the Pinot-dominated Cuvée Sir Winston Churchill★★, is a
deliciously refined drink. All vintage wines will improve with at least
5 years' keeping. Best years: (2002) **00 99 98 96 95 90 89 88 85 82**.

POLIZIANO *Vino Nobile di Montepulciano DOCG, Tuscany, Italy*   A leading light in
Montepulciano. VINO NOBILE★★ is smoother if more international than
average, especially the Riserva Asinone★★. Le Stanze★★ (Cabernet
Sauvignon-Merlot) has been outstanding in recent vintages – the fruit in
part coming from owner Federico Carletti's other estate, Lohsa, in
MORELLINO DI SCANSANO. Best years: (Vino Nobile) (2009) (08) 07 06 **04 03 0**
99 98 97.

POLZ *Steiermark, Austria*   Consistent producer of aromatic dry white wines
few wines fail to reach ★, and Weissburgunder (Pinot Blanc), Morillon
(Chardonnay), Muskateller and Sauvignon Blanc frequently deserve ★★
for their combination of intensity and elegance. Steierische Klassi
indicates wines vinified without oak. Best years: (2009) 08 07 **06 05 04 02**

POMEROL AC *Bordeaux, France*   This AC includes some of the world's mos
sought-after red wines. Pomerol's unique quality lies in its deep cla
(though gravel also plays a part in some vineyards) in which the Merlo
grape flourishes. The result is seductively rich, almost creamy wine with
wonderful mouthfilling fruit flavours: often plummy, but with
blackcurrants, raisins and chocolate, too, and mint to freshen it up. Bes
producers: Beauregard★, Bonalgue, le BON PASTEUR★★, Certan-de-May★
Clinet★★, Clos l'Église★★, Clos René, la CONSEILLANTE★★, l'ÉGLISE-CLINET★★★
l'ÉVANGILE★, Feytit-Clinet★, la FLEUR-PETRUS★★, GAZIN★★, Hosanna★★
LAFLEUR★★★, LATOUR-À-POMEROL★, Montviel, Nénin★, PETIT-VILLAGE★
PÉTRUS★★★, Le PIN★★★, Rouget, TROTANOY★★, VIEUX-CHÂTEAU-CERTAN★★
Best years: (2009) 08 07 06 05 **04 01 00 98 96 95 94 90 89 88 86 85**.

POMINO DOC See CHIANTI RUFINA.

OMMARD AC *Côte de Beaune, Burgundy, France* The first village south of Beaune. At their best, the wines should have full, round, beefy flavours. Can age well, often for 10 years or more. There are no Grands Crus but les Rugiens Bas and les Épenots (both Premiers Crus) are the best sites. **Best producers:** Aleth-Girardin★, Comte Armand★★, J-M Boillot★★, Courcel★★, Dancer★, M Gaunoux★, V GIRARDIN★★, Huber-Verdereau★★, LAFARGE★★, Lejeune★, de MONTILLE★★, J & A Parent★, Ch. de Pommard★, Pothier-Rieusset★. **Best years:** (2009) 08 07 06 05 03 **02 99 98 96 95 90**.

OMMERY *Champagne AC, Champagne, France* High-quality CHAMPAGNE house now owned by Vranken, who in recent years have launched 10 – yes 10 – non-vintage cuvées! I can't keep up. Along with Brut Royal and Apanage★, the range now includes Summertime blanc de blancs, Wintertime blanc de noirs and Springtime, a Pinot Noir-dominated rosé. Austere vintage Brut★ is delicious with maturity, and the prestige cuvée Louise, both white★★ and rosé★★, can be the epitome of discreet, perfumed elegance. **Best years:** (2002) 00 **99 98 96 95 92 90 89 88 85 82**.

ONDALOWIE *Bendigo, Victoria, Australia* Dominic and Krystina Morris are dynamic producers making a name for their red wines, including top Shiraz★, Shiraz-Viognier★ and dramatic, opulent Tempranillo★★.

H. PONTET-CANET★★ *Pauillac AC, 5ème Cru Classé, Haut-Médoc, Bordeaux, France* This property's vineyards are near those of MOUTON-ROTHSCHILD and are run organically. Since 2000 the wine has been on fine form: typically big, chewy, intense PAUILLAC that develops a beautiful blackcurrant fruit. It's one of the wines of the vintage in 2004 and 2005 – and that's saying something. One of the best value of the Classed Growths. **Best years:** 2008 07 06 05 04 **03 02 01 00 99 98 96 95 90 89 86 85**.

ONZI VINEYARDS *Willamette Valley AVA, Oregon, USA* The dream became reality in 1974, when Dick and Nancy Ponzi sold their first wine from a vineyard they bought in the late 1960s. The second generation is taking the business to new heights: winemaker Luisa Ponzi is crafting exceptionally fine Pinot Gris★★, Pinot Blanc★ and Chardonnay★ – juicy whites for early drinking. The Pinot Noirs★ are developing in complexity and profile. **Best years:** (reds) 2008 07 **06 04**.

ORT See pages 248–9.

NICOLAS POTEL *Burgundy, France* All change from 2009 as the eponymous Nicolas has left the company; he now trades as domaine and *négociant* under Dom. de Bellene label. Sound reds, especially VOLNAY★★, and good whites. **Best years:** (Nicolas Potel label reds) 2007 **06** 05 **03** 02.

CH. POTENSAC★★ *Médoc AC, Bordeaux, France* Owned and run by the Delon family, of LÉOVILLE-LAS-CASES, Potensac's fabulous success is based on a rich, sturdy personality, consistency and value for money. The wine can be drunk at 4–5 years, but fine vintages will improve for at least 10 years. **Best years:** 2008 07 06 **05 04** 03 02 01 00 99 98 96 95.

OUILLY-FUISSÉ AC *Mâconnais, Burgundy, France* The sexiest name in the MÂCONNAIS sometimes lives up to its billing for heady white Burgundy. But there is quite a difference in style from producers who vinify their wines simply in stainless steel to those who age them for up to 18 months in oak. The AC covers 5 villages: the richest wines come from Fuissé, the most mineral from Vergisson. **Best producers:** D & M Barraud★★, Beauregard, Bret Brothers★★, Cordier★★, Corsin★★, C & T Drouin★, J-A Ferret★★, Ch. Fuissé★★, Guffens-Heynen (VERGET)★★, R Lassarat★★, R Luquet★, O Merlin★★, Robert-Denogent★★, Ch. des Rontets★★, Saumaize-Michelin★★, Valette★★. **Best years:** (2008) 07 **06** 05 04 02 00 99.

PORT DOC

Douro, Portugal

The Douro region in northern Portugal, where the grapes for port are grown, is wild and beautiful, and classified as a World Heritage Site. Steep hills covered in vineyard terraces plunge dramatically down to the Douro river. Grapes are one of the few crops that will grow in the inhospitable climate, which gets progressively drier the further inland you travel. But not all the Douro's grapes qualify to be made into port. A quota is established every year, and the rest are made into increasingly good unfortified Douro wines.

Red port grapes include Touriga Franca, Tinta Roriz, Touriga Nacional, Tinta Barroca, Tinta Cão and Tinta Amarela. Grapes for white port include Côdega, Gouveio, Malvasia Fina, Rabigato and Viosinho. Grapes for both are partially fermented, and then *aguardente* (grape spirit) is added – fortifying the wine, stopping the fermentation and leaving sweet, unfermented grape sugar in the finished port.

PORT STYLES

Vintage Finest of the ports matured in bottle, made from grapes from the best vineyards. Vintage port is not 'declared' every year (usually there are 3 or 4 declarations per decade), and only during the second calendar year in cask if the shipper thinks the standard is high enough. It is bottled after 2 years, and may be consumed soon afterwards, as is not uncommon in the USA; at this stage it packs quite a punch. The British custom of aging for 20 years or more can yield exceptional mellowness. Vintage port throws a thick sediment, so requires decanting.

Single quinta (Vintage) A single-quinta port comes from an individual estate; many shippers sell a vintage port under a quinta name in years which are not declared as a vintage. It is quite possible for these 'off vintage' ports to equal or even surpass the vintage wines from the same house.

Aged tawny Matured in cask for 10, 20, 30 or even 40 years before bottling, older tawnies have delicious nut and fig flavours. The age is stated on the label.

Colheita Tawny from a single vintage, matured in cask for at least 7 years – potentially the finest of the aged tawnies.

Late Bottled (Vintage) (LBV) Port matured for 4–6 years in vat, then usually filtered to avoid sediment forming in the bottle. Traditional unfiltered LBV has much more flavour and requires decanting; it can generally be aged for another 5 years or more.

Crusted This is a blend of good ports from 2–3 vintages, bottled without filtration after 3–4 years in cask. A deposit (crust) forms in the bottle and the wine should be decanted. A gentler, junior type of 'vintage' flavour.

Reserve (most can be categorized as Premium Ruby) has an average of 3–5 years' age. A handful represent good value.

Ruby The youngest red port with only 1–3 years' age. Ruby port should be bursting with young, almost peppery, fruit, and there has been an improvement in quality of late, except at the cheapest level.

Tawny Cheap tawny is either an emaciated ruby, or a blend of ruby and white port, and is usually best avoided.

White Only the best taste dry and nutty from wood-aging; most are coarse and alcoholic, best with tonic water and a slice of lemon.

BEST YEARS

2007 05 **03 00 97 94 92 91
87 85 83 80 77 70 66 63 60
55 48 47 45 35 34 31 27 12
08 04 1900**

BEST PRODUCERS

Vintage BURMESTER, CHURCHILL, COCKBURN, CROFT, DOW, FERREIRA, FONSECA, GRAHAM, NIEPOORT, Quinta do NOVAL, RAMOS PINTO, SMITH WOODHOUSE, TAYLOR, WARRE.

Single quinta (Vintage) CHURCHILL (Quinta da Gricha), COCKBURN (Quinta dos Canais), Quinta do CRASTO, CROFT (Quinta da Roêda), DOW (Quinta do Bomfim, Quinta Senhora da Ribeira), FONSECA (Guimaraens), GRAHAM (Malvedos), Quinta do Passadouro, Pintas, Quinta de la ROSA, TAYLOR (Quinta de Terra Feita, Quinta de Vargellas), Quinta do Vale Dona Maria, Quinta do Vale Meão, Quinta do Vallado, Quinta do VESUVIO, WARRE (Quinta da Cavadinha).

Aged tawny Barros, BURMESTER, COCKBURN, DOW, FERREIRA, FONSECA, GRAHAM, Krohn, NIEPOORT, NOVAL, RAMOS PINTO, SANDEMAN, TAYLOR, WARRE.

Colheita Andresen, Barros, BURMESTER, Cálem, Feist, Kopke, Krohn, Messias, NIEPOORT, NOVAL.

Traditional Late Bottled Vintage Andresen, CHURCHILL, Quinta do CRASTO, FONSECA, Quinta do Infantado, NIEPOORT, NOVAL, Poças, RAMOS PINTO, Quinta de la ROSA, SMITH WOODHOUSE, WARRE.

Crusted CHURCHILL, DOW, FONSECA, GRAHAM.

Reserve Ruby COCKBURN, FERREIRA, FONSECA, GRAHAM, Quinta de la ROSA, SANDEMAN, SMITH WOODHOUSE, TAYLOR, WARRE.

White CHURCHILL, NIEPOORT.

POUILLY-FUMÉ AC *Loire Valley, France* Fumé means 'smoked' in French and a good Pouilly-Fumé has a pungent smell often likened to gunflint – as if you'd know. The grape is Sauvignon Blanc, and the extra smokiness comes from a flinty soil called silex. With a few notable exceptions, lacks something of the energy and ambition of SANCERRE. Best producers: F Blanchet★, Henri BOURGEOIS★, A Cailbourdin★, J-C Chatelain★, Didier DAGUENEAU★★, Serge Daguenau★, A Dezat★, A & E Figeat★, Fouaissière★, Ladoucette★, Landrat-Guyollot★, Masson-Blondelet★, M Redde★, H Seguin, Tinel-Blondelet★, Ch. de Tracy★. Best years: (2009) 08 **07 06 05 02**.

POUILLY-LOCHÉ AC See POUILLY-VINZELLES AC.

POUILLY-SUR-LOIRE AC *Loire Valley, France* Light appley wines from the tiny plantings (40ha/100 acres) of the Chasselas grape around Pouilly-sur-Loire, the town which gave its name to POUILLY-FUMÉ (which has 1200ha/2965 acres under vine). Drink as young as possible. Best producers: Serge Daguenau★, Landrat-Guyollot★.

POUILLY-VINZELLES AC *Mâconnais, Burgundy, France* Small AC which, with its neighbour Pouilly-Loché, lies somewhat in the shadow of POUILLY-FUISSÉ. Most wines come through the co-operative, but there are some good domaines. Best producers: Cave des Grands Crus Blancs, la Soufrandière★★, Tripoz★, Valette★. Best years: (2009) **08 07 06 05.**

CH. POUJEAUX★ *Moulis AC, Haut-Médoc, Bordeaux, France* Frequently Poujeaux is the epitome of MOULIS – beautifully balanced, gentle ripe fruit jostled by stony dryness – but just lacking that something extra to propel it to a higher plane. Attractive at 5–6 years old, good vintages can easily last for 10–20 years. Since 2007 same ownership as Clos Fourtet in ST-ÉMILION. Best years: 2008 07 06 05 **04 03 02 01 00 99 98 96 95 90 86.**

PRAGER *Wachau, Niederösterreich, Austria* Toni Bodenstein is one of the pioneers of the WACHAU, producing top dry Rieslings from the Achleiten and Klaus vineyards★★★ and excellent Grüner Veltliners from Achleiten★★. Best years: (Riesling/Grüner Veltliner Smaragd) (2009) 08 07 06 **05 04 03 02 01 00 99 98.**

PREMIÈRES CÔTES DE BLAYE AC *Bordeaux, France* A much improved AC on the right bank of the Gironde. The fresh, Merlot-based reds are ready at 2–3 years but will age for more. Top red wines can be labelled under the quality-driven Blaye AC from 2000. Part of Côtes de Bordeaux AC from 2008. Best producers: (reds) Bel-Air la Royère★, Confiance★, Gigault (Cuvée Viva★), les Grands Maréchaux, Haut-Bertinerie★, Haut-Colombier★, Haut-Grelot, Haut-Sociando, les Jonqueyres★, Mondésir-Gazin★, Montfollet★, Roland la Garde★, Segonzac★, Tourtes★; (whites) Haut-Bertinerie★, Charron (Acacia★), Cave des Hauts de Gironde (Chapelle de Tutiac★), Tourtes (Prestige★). Best years: (2009) **08 05 04 03 01 00 98.**

PREMIÈRES CÔTES DE BORDEAUX AC *Bordeaux, France* Hilly region overlooking GRAVES and SAUTERNES across the Garonne. For a long time the AC was best known for its sweet wines, particularly from CADILLAC, LOUPIAC and STE-CROIX-DU-MONT, but the juicy reds and rosés have now forged ahead. Usually delicious at 2–3 years old, but should last for 5–6 years. Part of Côtes de Bordeaux AC from 2008. Best producers: (reds) Bauduc★, Carignan★, Chelivette, Clos Ste-Anne, Grand-Mouëys★, Lamothe-de-Haux★, Lezongars★, Mont-Pérat★, Plaisance★, Puy-Bardens★, REYNON★, Ste-Marie (Alios★), Suau★. Best years: (reds) (2009) **08 05 00 98 96 95.**

CH. PRIEURÉ-LICHINE★ *Margaux AC, 4ème Cru Classé, Haut-Médoc, Bordeaux, France* Underachieving property that saw several false dawns before being sold in 1999. Right Bank specialist Stéphane Derenoncourt (PAVIE-

MACQUIN★★, CANON-LA-GAFFELIERE★★) is now the consultant winemaker, and the wines have more fruit, finesse and perfume, especially the 2004. Best years: 2008 07 06 **04 03 01 00 99 98 96 95**.

▶**RIEURÉ DE ST-JEAN DE BÉBIAN** *Coteaux du Languedoc AC, Languedoc, France* One of the pioneering estates in the Midi, producing an intense, spicy, generous red★★, second wine La Chapelle de Bébian and a barrel-fermented white★. Sold in 2009 to Russian investors, but winemaking team remains the same. Best years: (reds) (2009) 08 07 06 **05 04 02 01 00**.

▶**RIMITIVO DI MANDURIA DOC** *Puglia, Italy* The most important appellation for PUGLIA's Primitivo grape, which has been enjoying a renaissance since it was found to be almost identical to California's Zinfandel. The best wines combine outstanding ripeness and concentration with a knockout alcohol level. Good Primitivo is also sold as IGT Primitivo del Tarantino and Gioia del Colle DOC. Best producers: Felline★★, Pervini★, Giovanni Soloperto. Best years: (2009) 08 07 **06 05 04 03**.

▶**RIMO ESTATE** *McLaren Vale, South Australia* Joe Grilli continues to be one of Australia's most thoughtful and innovative winemakers. For his premium label, Joseph, Grilli adapts the Italian AMARONE method for Moda Cabernet-Merlot★★ (★★★ with 10 years' age) and makes a dense, eye-popping, complex Joseph Red fizz★★. He also does a sensuous Botrytis Riesling La Magia★★, surprising dry white La Biondina Colombard★, cherry-ripe Il Briccone★ (Shiraz-Sangiovese), bright, velvety Merlesco (Merlot) and fine, powerful Nebbiolo★. Best years: (Moda Cabernet-Merlot) (2007) 06 05 04 **02 01 00 99** 98 97 96 95 94 93 91.

▶**RINCE EDWARD COUNTY** *Ontario, Canada* A newly designated viticultural area jutting into Lake Ontario, east of Toronto. Deep limestone makes the region ideal for Pinot Noir and Chardonnay and a dozen wineries have opened since 2000. Best producers: Closson Chase, Norman Hardie, Huff Estates, Long Dog, Rosehall Run.

▶**RIORAT DOCa** *Cataluña, Spain* A hilly, isolated district with very low-yielding vineyards planted on precipitous slopes of deep slate soil. Old-style fortified *rancio* wines used to attract little attention. Then in the 1980s a group of young winemakers revolutionized the area, bringing in state-of-the-art winemaking methods and grape varieties such as Cabernet Sauvignon to back up the native Garnacha and Cariñena. Their rare, expensive wines have taken the world by storm. Ready at 5 years old, the best will last much, much longer. Best producers: Bodegas B G (Gueta-

Lupia★), Capafons-Ossó★, Cims de Porrera★★, CLOS ERASMUS★★★, CLOS MOGADOR★★★, Combier-Fischer-Gérin★★ (Trio Infernal 2/3★★★), La Conreria d'Scala Dei★, Costers del Siurana (Clos de l'Obac★), J M Fuentes (Gran Clos★★), Ithaca★, Mas Alta★★, MAS DOIX★★★, Mas d'en Gil (Clos Fontà★), Mas Martinet (Clos Martinet★), Merum, Alvaro PALACIOS★★★, Pasanau Germans (Finca la Planeta★), Rotllan Torra★, Scala Dei★, Terroir al Limit/SADIE FAMILY★★ (Les Tosses★★★), TORRES★, VALL LLACH★★. Best years: (reds) (2008) 07 05 **04 03 01 00 99** 98 96 95 94 93.

▶**PROSECCO DOC/DOCG** *Veneto and Friuli-Venezia Giulia, Italy* Following years of mis-use and abuse, the laws relating to this north-eastern Italian grape variety, and the slightly off-dry *spumante* or *frizzante* (occasionally still) wines derived from it, have been substantially revised. The grape has

been renamed Glera. The DOCG applies only to the wines of th
historic Conegliano and Valdobbiadene zones, and to the sub-zone o
Valdobbiadene called Cartizze, usually considered the best. Bes
producers: Adami★, Bisol★, Carpene Malvolti★, Le Colture★, Nino Franco★
La Riva dei Frati★, Ruggeri★, Zardetto★.

PROVENCE *France* Provence is home to France's oldest vineyards but th
region has been better known for its beaches and arts festivals than for i
wines. However, it seems even Provence is caught up in the revolutio
sweeping through the vineyards of southern France. The area has 5 small AC
(BANDOL, les BAUX-DE-PROVENCE, BELLET, CASSIS and PALETTE), but most of the win
comes from the much larger areas of the CÔTES DE PROVENCE (and three ne
sub-appellations: Ste-Victoire, La Londe and Fréjus), COTEAUX VAROIS
Coteaux de Pierrevert and COTEAUX D'AIX-EN-PROVENCE. Vin de Pays de
BOUCHES-DU-RHÔNE and Vin des Pays des Alpilles are also becomin
increasingly important. Reds can be good, ranging from less interesting lea
examples to full-bodied rich wines. Rosés are getting fresher in flavour an
creamier in texture, though not less expensive. Whites have a way to go bu
top producers are making good wines from Rolle.

J J PRÜM *Bernkastel, Mosel, Germany* Estate making some of Germany's bes
Riesling in sites like the Sonnenuhr★★★ in WEHLEN, Himmelreich★★ i
GRAACH and Lay★★ and Badstube★★ in BERNKASTEL. Slow to develop bu
they all have great aging potential. Best years: (2009) 08 07 06 05 **04 03 02 0**
99 98 97 96 95 94 93 90.

S A PRÜM *Wehlen, Mosel, Germany* There are a confusing number of Prüm
in the MOSEL – the best known is J J PRÜM, but S A Prüm comes a decen
second. The most interesting wines are Riesling from WEHLENer Sonnenuhr
especially Auslese★★; there's also good wine from sites in BERNKASTEL★
ÜRZIG★ and GRAACH★. Best years: (2009) 08 07 06 **05 04 03 02 01 99**.

PRUNOTTO *Barolo DOCG, Piedmont, Italy* One of the great BAROLO producers
now ably run by Albiera, Piero ANTINORI's eldest daughter. Highlight
include Barolo Bussia★★★ and Cannubi★★, BARBERA D'ALBA Pian
Romualdo★★, BARBERA D'ASTI Costamiòle★★, BARBARESCO Bric Turot★★
and NEBBIOLO D'ALBA Occhetti★. Also good MOSCATO D'ASTI★, Barbera
d'Asti Fiulot★ and ROERO Arneis★. Best years: (Barolo) (2009) (08) (07) 06
04 03 01 00 99 98 97 95 90 89 88 85.

PUGLIA *Italy* This southern region is a prolific source of blending wines
but exciting progress has been made with native varieties: red Uva di Troia in
CASTEL DEL MONTE; white Greco for characterful Gravina, revived b
Botromagno; and Verdeca and Bianco d'Alessano for Locorotondo. The red
Primitivo, led by examples from producers under the RACEMI umbrella, make
a big impact (whether under the PRIMITIVO DI MANDURIA DOC or more genera
IGTs). But it is the Negroamaro grape grown on traditional bush-trained o
alberello vines in the Salento peninsula that provides the best wines, whether
red or rosé. Outstanding examples include Vallone's Graticciaia★★,
Candido's Duca d'Aragona★★, Masseria Monaci's le Braci★★ and Taurino's
Patriglione★★. Brindisi and SALICE SALENTINO are good-value, reliable DOCs.

PUISSEGUIN-ST-ÉMILION AC *Bordeaux, France* Small ST-ÉMILION satellite.
The wines are generally fairly solid but with an attractive chunky fruit,
for drinking at 3–5 years. Best producers: Bel-Air, Branda, Durand-

Laplagne★, Fongaban, Guibeau-la-Fourvieille, Laurets, la Mauriane★, Producteurs Réunis, Soleil★. Best years: **(2009) 08 05 03 01 00 98 96 95**.

ULIGNY-MONTRACHET AC *Côte de Beaune, Burgundy, France* Puligny is one of the finest white wine villages in the world and adds the name of its greatest Grand Cru, le MONTRACHET, to its own. There are 3 other Grands Crus (BÂTARD-MONTRACHET, Bienvenues-BÂTARD-MONTRACHET and Chevalier-MONTRACHET) and 11 Premiers Crus. The flatter vineyards use the Puligny-Montrachet AC. Good vintages really need 5 years' aging, while Premiers Crus and Grands Crus may need 10 years and can last for 20 or more. A few barrels of red wine are made. Best producers: J-M Boillot★★, CARILLON★★★, Chavy★, Deux MONTILLE★, DROUHIN★★, A Ente★★, B Ente★, FAIVELEY★★, JADOT★★, Larue★★, LATOUR★, Dom. LEFLAIVE★★★, O LEFLAIVE★, P Pernot★★, Ch. de Puligny-Montrachet★★, RAMONET★★, SAUZET★★. Best years: (2008) 07 **06** 05 **04** 02 00 99.

YRENEES See GRAMPIANS AND PYRENEES.

QUARTS DE CHAUME AC *Loire Valley, France* The Chenin Blanc grape finds one of its most rewarding mesoclimates here. Quarts de Chaume is a 40ha (100-acre) AC within the larger COTEAUX DU LAYON AC overlooking the Loire; steep, sheltered, schistous slopes favour optimal ripening and noble rot. The result is intense, sweet wines with a mineral backbone, which can last for longer than almost any in the world – although many can be drunk after 5 years. Best producers: BAUMARD★★★, Bellerive★★, Bergerie★★, Laffourcade★, PIERRE-BISE★★★, Plaisance★, Joseph Renou★★, Suronde★★, la Varière★. Best years: **(2009) 07 06 05 03 02 01 99 97 96 95 90 89**.

QUARTZ REEF *Central Otago, South Island, New Zealand* Austrian-born winemaker/owner Rudi Bauer is one of the region's leading lights in winemaking innovation. Best known for its powerful, serious Pinot Noir★★ and sleek bottle-fermented sparkling wine★ (vintage★★). Intensely-flavoured, minerally, almost chewy Pinot Gris★ is one of their lesser known stars. Best years: (Pinot Noir) **(2009) 08 07 06 05**.

QUEENSLAND *Australia* The Queensland wine industry – closely linked to tourism – is expanding fast. About 60 wineries perch on rocky hills in the main region, the Granite Belt, near the NEW SOUTH WALES border. New areas south Burnett (north-west of Brisbane), Darling Downs (around the town of Toowoomba) and Mount Tamborine in the Gold Coast hinterland are showing promise. Best producers: Barambah, BOIREANN★, Robert Channon★, Clovely Estate, Heritage, Jimbour Station, Lucas Estate, Preston Peak★, Pyramids Road, Robinsons Family, Sirromet, Summit Estate, Witches Falls.

QUERCIABELLA *Chianti Classico DOCG, Tuscany, Italy* Modern Chianti producer with a gorgeously scented, rich-fruited CHIANTI CLASSICO★★. But it has made an even greater splash with its Burgundy-like white Batàr★★ (Pinot Bianco-Chardonnay) and tobaccoey, spicy Camartina★★★ (Sangiovese-Cabernet). Mongrana★, a juicy, smooth-but-serious blend of Sangiovese, Merlot and Cabernet Sauvignon, is from a new estate in MAREMMA. Best years: (Camartina) (2009) (08) 07 06 **04** 03 01 99 97 95 90 88.

QUILCEDA CREEK *Washington State, USA* One of America's top Cabernet Sauvignons★★★, a wine with intense concentration and exceptional character. It benefits from cellaring for 7–10 years. Supple, rich Merlot★★★ is produced in small quantities. A less expensive Columbia Valley Red★★ offers a tantalizing glimpse of the winemaking style. Best years: (2008) (07) 06 05 04 03 **02** 01 99 97.

QUINCY AC *Loire Valley, France* Appealingly aggressive gooseberry-flavoured
dry white wine from Sauvignon Blanc vineyards west of Bourges. Can
age for a year or two. Best producers: Ballandors★, H BOURGEOIS★, Mardon★,
J C Roux★, J Rouzé, Silices de Quincy★, Tremblay, Trotereau★.

QUINTARELLI *Valpolicella DOC, Veneto, Italy* Giuseppe Quintarelli is the
great traditional winemaker of VALPOLICELLA. His philosophy is one of
growing the very best grapes and letting nature do the rest. His Classico
Superiore★★ is left in cask for about 4 years and his famed AMARONE★★
and RECIOTO★★ for up to 7 years before release. Alzero★★ is a spectacular
Amarone-style wine made from Cabernets Franc and Sauvignon. Best
years: (Amarone) (2009) (08) (07) 06 04 **03 01 99 97 95 93 90 88 85 83**.

QUPÉ *Santa Maria Valley AVA, California, USA* Owner/winemaker Bob Lindquist
is focused on cooler-climate Syrahs with a peppery aroma and makes
savoury, tasty Bien Nacido Syrah★. His Reserve Chardonnay★ and Bien
Nacido Cuvée★ (a Viognier-Chardonnay blend) have beguiling apple
fruit and perfume. A leading exponent of red and white RHÔNE-style
wines, including Viognier★, Marsanne★ and Roussanne★★. Best years:
(Syrah) 2007 06 05 04 03 **02 01 00 99 98 97 96 95 94 91 90**.

RACEMI *Puglia, Italy* Premium venture run by Gregory Perrucci, scion of a
long-established family of bulk shippers of basic Puglian wines. Modern-
style reds, mainly from Primitivo and Negroamaro, under various
producers' names: Felline (Vigna del Feudo★★), Pervini (PRIMITIVO DI
MANDURIA Archidamo★★), Masseria Pepe (Dunico★★). Best years: (red)
(2009) 08 **07 06 05 04 03 01**.

CH. DE LA RAGOTIÈRE *Muscadet Sèvre-et-Maine, Loire Valley, France* The
Couillaud brothers claim to have salvaged the reputation of Muscadet in
US restaurants with M★★, an old-vines wine matured *sur lie* for almost
3 years. The standard Muscadet★ is elegant and built to last, too; light
ones come from the Couillauds' other property, Ch. la Morinière. In the
pays Chardonnay★ is a speciality and experimental varieties appear under
the Collection Privée label, including Sauvignon Gris★, Viognier and
late-harvest Petit Manseng. Best years: (M) (2009) **06 01 99 97**.

RAÏMAT *Costers del Segre DO, Cataluña, Spain* Owned by CODORNÍU, this large,
irrigated estate makes pleasant and refreshingly balanced wines from
Tempranillo, Cabernet Sauvignon (Mas Castell vineyard★) and
Chardonnay. Lively 100% Chardonnay CAVA and upscale red blend
4 Varietales. Best years: (reds) **2006 05 04 03 01 00 99 98**.

DOM. DE LA RAMAYE *Gaillac AC, South-West France* High-quality wines:
whites, mostly from Mauzac, include Les Cavaillés Bas★★, sweet
Sous-Bois de Rayssac★★ and, in great years, Quintessence★★★. Reds
include La Combe d'Avès★★, a Duras-Braucol blend, and Prunelard-
based Le Grand Tertre★★. Best years: (2009) (08) **06 05 04 01**.

RAMEY WINE CELLARS *Sonoma County, California, USA* David Ramey is one
of the state's most creative winemakers (as well as a consultant for many
other wineries) and his primarily CARNEROS and RUSSIAN RIVER-based
Chardonnays★★ (Hyde★★, Ritchie★★), NAPA-based Cabernet
Sauvignons★ and SONOMA-based Syrahs★★ are among the most sought-
after in the state. Best years: 2007 **06 05 01**.

RAMONET *Chassagne-Montrachet, Côte de Beaune, Burgundy, France* The
Ramonets (Noël and Claude) produce some of the most complex of all
white Burgundies from 3 Grands Crus (BÂTARD-MONTRACHET★★★,
Bienvenues-BÂTARD-MONTRACHET★★★ and le MONTRACHET★★★) and
Premiers Crus including Ruchottes★★★, Caillerets★★★, Boudriotte★★

Vergers★★, Morgeot★★ and Chaumées★★★. If you want to spare your wallet try the ST-AUBIN★★ or the CHASSAGNE-MONTRACHET white★★ or red★★. Best years: (whites) (2009) 08 07 **06** 05 **04 02 00** 99.

JOÃO PORTUGAL RAMOS *Alentejo, Portugal* João Portugal Ramos has built his ALENTEJO and TEJO (Falua) empire from nothing. Smoky, peppery Trincadeira★★, spicy Aragonês (Tempranillo)★, powerful Syrah★ and intensely dark-fruited red blend Vila Santa★★. Good Marquês de Borba★ reds and whites, and a brilliant red Reserva★★. Tagus Creek is juicy and affordable. Best years: (2008) **05 04 01 00 99 97**.

RAMOS PINTO *Douro DOC and Port DOC, Douro, Portugal* Innovative PORT company owned by ROEDERER, making complex, full-bodied Late Bottled Vintage★ and aged tawnies (10-year-old Quinta de Ervamoira★★ and 20-year-old Quinta do Bom Retiro★★★). Vintage ports★★ are rich and early maturing. DOURO reds Duas Quintas (Reserva★, Reserva Especial★) and white Bons Ares★ are reliable. Best years: (Vintage) 2007 04 **03 00 97 95 94** 83.

CASTELLO DEI RAMPOLLA *Chianti Classico DOCG, Tuscany, Italy* Outstanding if French-influenced CHIANTI CLASSICO★★. Sammarco, sometimes ★★★, is mostly Cabernet with some Sangiovese; Vigna d'Alceo★★★ adds Petit Verdot to Cabernet Sauvignon. Best years: (Sammarco) (2009) (08) 07 06 **04 03 01 00 99 98 97** 95; (Vigna d'Alceo) (2009) (08) 07 06 **04 03 01 00 99 98 97**.

RANDERSACKER *Franken, Germany* Important wine village just outside the city of WÜRZBURG, producing excellent dry Rieslings, dry Silvaners, spicy Traminer and piercingly intense Rieslaner. Best producers: Bürgerspital, JULIUSSPITAL★, Schmitt's Kinder★, Störrlein★. Best years: (2009) 08 07 **06** 05 **04 03 02**.

RAPEL *Chile* One of Chile's most exciting red wine regions, the cradle of Chilean Carmenère, Rapel covers both the Cachapoal Valley in the north and the COLCHAGUA Valley in the south. Best producers: Altaïr★★/SAN PEDRO, ANAKENA★, CASA LAPOSTOLLE★★, CASA SILVA★, CONCHA Y TORO★★, CONO SUR★, EMILIANA★★, Gracia★, LA ROSA★, Los Vascos, Misiones de Rengo★, MONTES★★, MontGras, Neyen★★, VENTISQUERO★, Viu Manent★.

KENT RASMUSSEN *Carneros AVA, California, USA* Delicious, oatmealy Chardonnay★★ capable of considerable aging and a fascinating juicy and also long-lasting Pinot Noir★★ are made by ultra-traditional methods. Ramsay is the second label, for Pinot Noir★, Cabernet Sauvignon and Merlot. Best years: (Pinot Noir) 2006 05 **02** 01 00 99 98 95 94 91 90.

RASTEAU *Rhône Valley, France* The single-village AC is for fortified Grenache red or white wine and a reviving *rancio* version which is left in barrel for 2 or more years. However, much of the best wine from Rasteau is robust and spicy dry red, sold as CÔTES DU RHÔNE-VILLAGES. Best producers: E Balme, Beaurenard★, Cave des Vignerons, Escaravailles, Gourt de Mautens★★, Grand Nicolet, Perrin★, Rabasse-Charavin, ST-GAYAN, Santa Duc★, la Soumade★, du Trapadis★. Best years: (reds) 2009 **07 06 05 04 03**.

RENATO RATTI *Barolo DOCG, Piedmont, Italy* The late Renato Ratti was a leading modernist in the Alba area with BAROLO and BARBARESCO of better balance, colour and richness and softer in tannins than the traditional models. Today his son Pietro and nephew Massimo Martinelli produce sound Barolo Marcenasco★ and crus Conca★★ and Rocche★★ from the Marcenasco vineyards at La Morra, as well as good BARBERA D'ALBA Torriglione★, Dolcetto d'Alba Colombè★, NEBBIOLO D'ALBA Ochetti★ and Monferrato DOC Villa Pattono★, a Barbera-Cabernet-Merlot blend.

RAUENTHAL *Rheingau, Germany* Only a few producers live up to the reputation earned by this RHEINGAU village's great Baiken and Gehrn sites for intense, spicy Rieslings. **Best producers: Georg BREUER★★, Eser, Langwerth von Simmern★, Staatsweingut★.** Best years: (2009) 08 07 **06 05 04 03 02 01**

CH. RAUZAN-SÉGLA★★ *Margaux AC, 2ème Cru Classé, Haut-Médoc, Bordeaux, France* A dynamic change in winemaking in 1982 and the purchase of the property by Chanel in 1994 propelled Rauzan-Ségla up the quality ladder. Now the wines have a rich blackcurrant fruit, round, mellow texture, powerful woody spice and good concentration. Second wine Ségla. **Best years: 2008 07 06 05 04 03 02 01 00 98 96 95 90 89 88 86 85**

JEAN-MARIE RAVENEAU *Chablis, Burgundy, France* Beautifully nuanced CHABLIS from 3 Grands Crus (Blanchot★★★, les Clos★★★, Valmur★★★) and 4 Premiers Crus (Montée de Tonnerre★★★, Vaillons★★, Butteaux★★★, Chapelot★★), using a combination of old oak and stainless-steel fermentation. The wines can age for a decade or more. **Best years: (top crus) (2009)** 08 07 **06 05 02 00 99 95 90**

RAVENSWOOD *Sonoma Valley AVA, California, USA* Zinfandel expert Joe Peterson established Ravenswood in 1976. Constellation bought the winery in 2001, but Peterson remains in charge. Early 21st-century offerings were disappointing – especially large-volume Vintners Blend – but this has now picked up, and the old-vine Zinfandels (Lodi★) are tasty and characterful. Single-vineyard wines can be ★★. Super-premium Icon★★ is now a blend of Carignane, Petite Sirah, Zinfandel and other grapes from ancient (pre-Prohibition) vines.

CH. RAYAS *Châteauneuf-du-Pape, Rhône Valley, France* Emmanuel Reynaud, nephew of the eccentric Jacques Reynaud, runs this estate in his late uncle's inimitable rule-breaking style, producing exotically fragrant rich reds★★★ and whites★★★ that age incredibly well. Methods are traditional, prices are high, but recent vintages are on top form – at its best Rayas is thrilling. The red is made entirely from low-yielding Grenache vines, while the white is a blend of Clairette, Grenache Blanc and (so rumour has it) Chardonnay. Second-label Pignan

can also be impressive. CÔTES DU RHÔNE Ch. de Fonsalette★★ is usually wonderful. Also good VACQUEYRAS Ch. des Tours★. **Best years: (Châteauneuf-du-Pape) 2009 08 07 06 05 04 03 01 99 98 96 95 94 91 90 88 86; (whites) 2009 08 07 06 05 04 03 01 00 99 98 97 96 95 94 91 90 89**

REBHOLZ *Siebeldingen, Pfalz, Germany* This estate produces crystalline Riesling★★, Weissburgunder★★ (Pinot Blanc) and Grauburgunder★ (Pinot Gris), with vibrant fruit aromas. Top of the range are intensely mineral dry Riesling★★★ from the Kastanienbusch and Sonnenschein vineyards, and extravagantly aromatic dry Muskateller★★. The sparkling wine★★, from barrel-fermented Pinot varieties, is among Germany's most elegant. Also Germany's finest Chardonnay★★ and serious Spätburgunder★★ (Pinot Noir) reds. **Best years: (whites) (2009) 08 07 06 05 04 03 02 01 99; (reds) (2009) (08) 07 06 05 04 03 02.**

RECIOTO DELLA VALPOLICELLA DOC *Veneto, Italy* The great sweet wine of VALPOLICELLA, made from grapes picked earlier than usual and left to dry on straw mats until February or even March. The wines are deep in colour, with a rich, bitter-sweet cherryish fruit. Top wines age well for 10 years, but most are best drunk young. As with Valpolicella, the Classico tag is important, if not essential. Best producers: Accordini★, ALLEGRINI★★, Bolla (Spumante★), Brigaldara★, BUSSOLA★★★, Michele Castellani★★, DAL FORNO★★★, MASI★, QUINTARELLI★★, Le Ragose★, Le Salette★, Serègo Alighieri★★, Speri★, Tedeschi★, Tommasi★, Villa Monteleone★★, VIVIANI★★. Best years: (2009) (08) **06 05 04 03 01 00**.

ECIOTO DI SOAVE DOCG *Veneto, Italy* Sweet white wine made in the SOAVE zone from dried grapes, like RECIOTO DELLA VALPOLICELLA. Garganega grapes give wonderfully delicate yet intense wines that age well for up to a decade. One of the best, ANSELMI's I Capitelli, is now sold as IGT Veneto. Best producers: ANSELMI★★, La Cappuccina★★, Cà Rugate★, Coffele★★, Gini★★, PIEROPAN★★, Pra★, Bruno Sartori★, Tamellini★★. Best years: (2009) (08) **06 04 03 01 00 98 97**.

ÉGNIÉ AC *Beaujolais, Burgundy, France* In good years this BEAUJOLAIS Cru is light, aromatic and enjoyable along the style of CHIROUBLES, but can be thin in lesser years. Best producers: J-M Burgaud★, Coquard★, DUBOEUF (des Buyats★), Bulliats★, Gilles Roux/de la Plaigne★. Best years: **2009 08**.

OM. LA RÉMÉJEANNE *Côtes du Rhône AC, Rhône Valley, France* First-class property making a range of strikingly individual, punchy wines. CÔTES DU RHÔNE-VILLAGES les Genévriers★★ has the weight and texture of good CHÂTEAUNEUF-DU-PAPE, while CÔTES DU RHÔNE les Eglantiers★★ is superb. Both need at least 3–5 years' aging. Also good Côtes du Rhône les Chèvrefeuilles★ and les Arbousiers★ (red and white). Best years: (les Eglantiers) 2009 **07 06 05 04 03**.

EMELLURI *Rioja DOCa, País Vasco, Spain* Organic RIOJA estate producing red wines with far more fruit than usual and good concentration for aging – the best are ★★. There is also a delicate, barrel-fermented white★★. Best years: (Reserva) 2005 **04 03 02 01 99 98 96 95 94 91 89**.

ETSINA *Greece* Resinated white (and rosé) wine common all over Greece, although both production and sales are falling. Poor Retsina is diabolical but the best are deliciously oily and piny. Drink young – and cold.

EUILLY AC *Loire Valley, France* Dry but attractive Sauvignon from west of SANCERRE. Some pale Pinot Noir red and Pinot Gris rosé. Best producers: H Beurdin★, G Bigonneau, D Jamain★, C Lafond, A Mabillot, J-M Sorbe, J Vincent.

H. REYNON *Premières Côtes de Bordeaux AC, Bordeaux, France* Property of enology professor Denis Dubourdieu. The dry whites, particularly the fruity, minerally Sauvignon Blanc★, are delightful and the red★ has come on tremendously since 1997. In the same stable is the lovely white GRAVES Clos Floridène★★, which is vinified at Reynon. Best years: (reds) 2008 **07 06 05 04 03 01 00**; (whites) **2008 07 06 05 04 02 01**.

HEINGAU *Germany* 3125ha (7720-acre) wine region on a south-facing retch of the Rhine flanking the city of Wiesbaden, planted mostly with esling and some Spätburgunder (Pinot Noir). At their best, the Rieslings e racy and slow-maturing. Famous names are no longer a guarantee of top ality, as a new generation of winemakers is producing many of the best wines. e also ELTVILLE, ERBACH, HATTENHEIM, HOCHHEIM, JOHANNISBERG, KIEDRICH, UENTHAL, RÜDESHEIM, WINKEL. Best years: (2009) 08 07 **06 05 04 03 02 01**.

HEINHESSEN *Germany* 26,440ha (65,300-acre) wine region with a mber of famous top-quality estates, especially at Bodenheim, Nackenheim, ERSTEIN and Oppenheim. BINGEN, to the north-west, also has a fine vineyard

area along the left bank of the Rhine. Further away from the river a handf
of growers, such as KELLER and WITTMANN, also make superlative wines. Rieslir
accounts for only 14% of the vineyard area; Weissburgunder (Pinot Blanc)
the rising star. Best years: (2009) 08 07 **05 04 03 02 01 99**.

RHÔNE VALLEY *France* The Rhône starts out as a river in Switzerland
ambling through Lake Geneva before hurtling westward into France. In th
area south of Lyon, between Vienne and Avignon, the valley becomes one
France's great wine regions. In the northern part precipitous granite slope
overhang the river and the small amount of wine produced has remarkab
individuality and great finesse. The Syrah grape reigns here in CÔTE-RÔTIE an
on the great hill of HERMITAGE. ST-JOSEPH, CROZES-HERMITAGE and CORNAS als
make excellent reds, while the white Viognier grape yields perfumed, musk
wine at CONDRIEU and the tiny CHÂTEAU-GRILLET. In the southern part the stee
slopes give way to hot, wide, alluvial plains, with hills both in the west an
east. Most of these vineyards are either CÔTES DU RHONE or CÔTES DU RHÔN
VILLAGES, reds, whites and rosés, but there are also specific ACs, the best know
being CHÂTEAUNEUF-DU-PAPE, GIGONDAS and the luscious, golden dessert win
MUSCAT DE BEAUMES-DE-VENISE. See also BEAUMES-DE-VENISE, CAIRANNE, CLAIRETTE [
DIE, COSTIÈRES DE NÎMES, COTEAUX DE L'ARDÈCHE, COTEAUX DU TRICASTIN, LIRA
LUBÉRON, RASTEAU, ST-PÉRAY, TAVEL, VACQUEYRAS, VENTOUX, VINSOBRES.

RÍAS BAIXAS DO *Galicia, Spain* The best of GALICIA's DOs. The mag
ingredient is the Albariño grape, making dry, fruity whites with
glorious fragrance and citrus tang. In general drink young, but there a
now ageworthy whites and fragrant, Atlantic-cooled reds from nativ
grape varieties. Best producers: Agro de Bazán★★, Castro Martín, Mart
Códax★, Condes de Albarei★, Quinta de Couselo, Fillaboa★, Forjas d
Salnés (reds ★), Adegas Galegas★, Lagar de Besada★, Lagar de Fornelos★, l
Val★, Gerardo Méndez (Do Ferreiro Cepas Vellas★★), Viña Nora★, Pabl
Padín, Palacio de Fefiñanes★★, Pazo de Barrantes★, Pazo de Señoras★
Pazos de Lusco★★, Santiago Ruiz★, Terras Gauda★★, Valmiñor★.

RIBATEJO See TEJO.

RIBERA DEL DUERO DO *Castilla y León, Spain* The dark, mouthfilling re
in this DO, from Tinto Fino (Tempranillo), sometimes with a litt
Cabernet Sauvignon and more rarely Merlot, are generally natural
richer and more concentrated than those of RIOJA. But excessive expansio
of vineyards, increase in yields and excessive use of oak may threaten i
supremacy. Best producers: AALTO★★, Alión★★, Arroyo, Arzuaga
Astraies★, Dominio de Atauta★★, Balbás★, Hijos de Antonio Barceló, Brieg
Felix Callejo, Cillar de Silos★, Convento San Francisco★, Hermanos Cuadrad
García, O FOURNIER★, Hacienda Monasterio★★, Matarromera
Montecastro★★, Emilio Moro★★, Pago de los Capellanes★★, Pago
Carraovejas★★, Parxet, Pedrosa/Pérez Pascuas, Peñafiel, PESQUERA★
PINGUS★★★, Protos★, Rodero★, Telmo RODRIGUEZ★, Hermanos Sastre★
Tarsus★, Valdubón, Valduero★, Valtravieso, VEGA SICILIA★★★, Alonso d
Yerro★★. Best years: 2007 05 **04 03 01 00 99 96 95 94 91 90 89 86 85**.

BARONE RICASOLI *Chianti Classico DOCG, Tuscany, Italy* The estate whe
modern CHIANTI was perfected by Baron Bettino Ricasoli in the mid-19
century. The flagship is Chianti Classico Castello di Brolio★★, name
after the magnificent medieval castle of that name. Riserva Guicciarda★
good value. Casalferro★★ is a Sangiovese-Merlot blend. Best year
(Casalferro) (2009) (08) 07 **06 04 03 01 00**.

DOM. RICHEAUME *Côtes de Provence AC, Provence, France* German-owned property, run on organic principles and producing impressively deep-coloured reds★; Les Terrasses★★ is from Syrah aged in new wood. Best years: (Terrasses) 2008 07 06 **05 04 03**.

RICHEBOURG AC *Grand Cru, Côte de Nuits, Burgundy, France* Rich, fleshy wine from the northern end of VOSNE-ROMANÉE. Most domaine-bottlings are exceptional. Best producers: GRIVOT★★★, Anne GROS★★★, A-F GROS★★★, Hudelot-Noëllat★★, Dom. LEROY★★★, T LIGER-BELAIR★★, MÉO-CAMUZET★★★, Dom. de la ROMANÉE-CONTI★★★. Best years: (2009) 08 07 06 05 03 02 **01 00** 99 98 97 96 95 93 91 90.

MAX FERD RICHTER *Mülheim, Mosel, Germany* Racy Rieslings from some of the best sites in the MOSEL, including WEHLENer Sonnenuhr★★, BRAUNEBERGer Juffer★★ and GRAACHer Domprobst★. Richter's Mülheimer Helenenkloster vineyard produces a magical Eiswein★★★ virtually every year unless wild boar eat the crop. Best years: (2009) 08 07 06 **05 04 03 02 01 99 98.**

RIDGE VINEYARDS *Santa Cruz Mountains AVA, California, USA* Trailblazing winery which produces some of California's most pleasing and original wines, with a particular emphasis on old vine fruit. Paul Draper's Zinfandels★★★, made with grapes from various sources, have great intensity and age wonderfully. Other reds, led by cool-climate Cabernet-based Monte Bello★★★, show impressive personality and require years, if not decades, to come around. Geyserville★★ is a fascinating blend of Zinfandel with old-vine Carignan, Syrah and Petite Sirah which is good young but better old. There's fine Chardonnay★★, too. Best years: (Monte Bello) 2006 05 03 02 01 **00** 99 98 97 95 94 93 92 91 90 87 85 84.

RIDGEVIEW *West Sussex, England* Specialist sparkling wine producer using classic CHAMPAGNE varieties to make an excellent – and continually improving – range of wines. Cavendish★★ and Bloomsbury★★ are traditional 3-variety blends; Knightsbridge★ is a blanc de noirs; Grosvenor★ is a blanc de blancs; and Fitzrovia★★ is a Chardonnay-Pinot Noir rosé. New vineyards coming onstream in the next couple of years will add considerable capacity. Best years: **2007 06 05.**

RIECINE *Chianti Classico DOCG, Tuscany, Italy* Small estate in Gaiole making exquisite wines. Yields are low, so there is a great intensity of fruit and a superb definition of spiced cherry flavours. English winemaker Sean O'Callaghan continues to fashion ever better CHIANTI CLASSICO★★, Riserva★★★ and barrique-aged La Gioia★★★. Best years: (La Gioia) (2008) (07) 06 **04 03** 01 99 98 97 95.

RIESLANER One of the few German grape crossings of real merit, Rieslaner resembles Riesling, but with greater breadth and even higher acidity. This makes it an ideal sweet wine grape, as MÜLLER-CATOIR (Pfalz), KELLER (Rheinhessen) and some Franken growers have demonstrated.

RIESLING See pages 260–1.

RIESLING ITALICO See WELSCHRIESLING.

CH. RIEUSSEC★★★ *Sauternes AC, 1er Cru Classé, Bordeaux, France* Apart from the peerless Ch. d'YQUEM, Rieussec is often the richest, most succulent wine of SAUTERNES. Cellar for at least 10 years. Dry white 'R' is nothing special. Second wine: Carmes de Rieussec. Owned by LAFITE-ROTHSCHILD. Best years: 2007 06 05 **04 03 02** 01 99 98 97 96 95 90 89 88.

RIESLING

If you have tasted wines with names like Laski Riesling, Olasz Riesling, Welschriesling, Gray Riesling, Riesling Italico, Cape Riesling and the like and found them bland or unappetizing – do not blame the Riesling grape. These wines have filched Riesling's name, but have nothing whatsoever to do with the great grape itself.

Riesling is Germany's finest contribution to the world of wine – and herein lies the second problem. German wines fell to such a low level of general esteem through the proliferation of wines like Liebfraumilch during the 1980s that Riesling was dragged down with them.

So what is true Riesling? It is a very ancient German grape, probably the descendant of wild vines growing in the Rhine Valley. It certainly performs best in the cool vineyard regions of Germany's Rhine, Nahe and Mosel Valleys, and in Alsace and Austria. It also does well in Ontario in Canada, New Zealand and both warm and cool parts of Australia. Ironically, the Riesling revival is being led more by Australia than Germany. It is widely planted in Washington State, less so in northern Italy, and there's a tiny amount in South Africa and in Chile.

Young Rieslings often show a delightful floral perfume, sometimes blended with the crispness of green apples, often lime, peach, nectarine or apricot, sometimes even raisin, honey or spice depending upon the ripeness of the grapes. As the wines age, the lime often intensifies, and flavour perhaps of slate, perhaps of petrol/kerosene intrudes. In general, Rieslings may be drunk young, but top dry wines can improve for many years, and the truly sweet German styles can age for generations.

WINE STYLES

Germany These wines have a marvellous perfume and an ability to hold on to a piercing acidity, even at high ripeness levels, so long as the ripening period has been warm and gradual rather than broiling and rushed. German Rieslings can be bone dry, through to medium and lusciously sweet. Styles range from crisp elegant Mosels to riper, fuller wines from the Rheingau and Nahe, with rounder, fatter examples from the Pfalz and Baden regions in the south. The very sweet Trockenbeerenauslese (TBA) Rieslings are made from grapes affected by noble rot; for Eiswein (icewine), also intensely sweet, the grapes are picked and pressed while frozen.

Other regions In the valleys of the Danube in Austria, Riesling gives stunning dry wines that combine richness with elegance, but the most fragrant wines, apart from German examples, come from France's Alsace. The mountain vineyards of northern Italy and the cool vineyards of the Czech Republic, Slovakia and Switzerland can show a floral sharp style. Australia is the southern hemisphere's world-class producer, with cool areas of South Australia, Victoria and Western Australia all offering superb – and different – examples typified by a citrus, mineral scent, and often challenging austerity. New Zealand's style is floral, fresh and frequently attractively off-dry, but with enough acidity to age. South Africa's best examples are sweet, but some dry versions are appearing. Chile is growing some delicate, fragrant examples. The USA has fragrant dry Rieslings from New York, mostly off-dry from the Pacific Northwest and slightly sweet styles from California. Drier Rieslings are becoming more common. Michigan and Ohio also have excellent potential. Canada produces bone-dry Riesling to ultra-sweet Icewine.

BEST PRODUCERS

Germany
Dry BASSERMANN-JORDAN, Georg BREUER, BÜRKLIN-WOLF, Christmann, HEYMANN-LÖWENSTEIN, KELLER, KOEHLER-RUPRECHT, KÜNSTLER, J LEITZ, REBHOLZ, SAUER, WITTMANN.

Non-dry DIEL, DÖNNHOFF, GUNDERLOCH, HAAG, HAART, HEYMANN-LÖWENSTEIN, KARTHÄUSERHOF, von KESSELSTATT, KÜHN, KÜNSTLER, Dr LOOSEN, MAXIMIN GRÜNHAUS, MOLITOR, MÜLLER-CATOIR, Egon MÜLLER-SCHARZHOF, J J PRÜM, St Urbans-Hof, Willi SCHAEFER, SCHÄFER-FRÖHLICH, SELBACH-OSTER, WEIL, ZILLIKEN.

Austria
Dry Alzinger, BRÜNDLMAYER, Hiedler, HIRTZBERGER, J Högl, KNOLL, Loimer, Malat, NIGL, NIKOLAIHOF, F X PICHLER, Rudi PICHLER, PRAGER, Schloss Gobelsburg, Schmelz.

France
(Alsace) Dry J-B ADAM, P BLANCK, A Boxler, DEISS, Dirler-Cadé, HUGEL, Josmeyer, Kientzler, Kreydenweiss, A MANN, MURÉ, Ostertag, SCHOFFIT, TRIMBACH, WEINBACH, ZIND-HUMBRECHT.

Non-dry Léon Beyer, DEISS, HUGEL, Ostertag, TRIMBACH, WEINBACH, ZIND-HUMBRECHT.

Australia
Tim ADAMS, Jim BARRY, Bloodwood, Leo Buring (Leonay), Larry CHERUBINO, Crabtree, Eden Road, Forest Hill, Frankland Estate, Freycinet, Frogmore Creek, GROSSET, Heggies, HENSCHKE, HOUGHTON, HOWARD PARK, JACOB'S CREEK (Steingarten), Kilikanoon, KNAPPSTEIN, KT & the Falcon, Peter LEHMANN, Mesh, MOUNT HORROCKS, O'Leary Walker, Paulett, PETALUMA (Hanlin Hill), Pewsey Vale, Pipers Brook, SEPPELT (Drumborg), SKILLOGALEE.

New Zealand
CLOUDY BAY, DRY RIVER, FELTON ROAD, Foxes Island, FRAMINGHAM, FROMM, Mt Difficulty, Mount Edward, NEUDORF, PEGASUS BAY, VILLA MARIA.

South Africa
Sweet Paul CLUVER, Fleur du Cap, Neethlingshof.

USA
(Washington) CHATEAU STE MICHELLE (Eroica), LONG SHADOWS (Poet's Leap); *(New York)* ANTHONY ROAD, FOX RUN, Dr Konstantin FRANK, Hermann J WIEMER.

RIOJA DOCa *Rioja, Navarra, País Vasco and Castilla y León, Spain* Rioja, in northern Spain, is not all oaky, creamy white wines and elegant, barrel-aged reds, combining oak flavours with wild strawberry and prune fruit. Over half Rioja's red wine is sold young, never having seen the inside of a barrel, and as such is one of Spain's best glugging reds; the white is increasingly tasty and fresh. Wine quality, as could be expected from such a large region with more than 400 producers, is inconsistent but a growing gang of ambitious new producers is taking quality seriously. **Best producers** (reds) Alavesas, ALLENDE★★, Altanza, Altos de Lanzaga★/Telmo RODRIGUEZ ARTADI★★★, Baron de Ley★, Bodegas Bilbaínas, CAMPILLO★, CAMPO VIEJO CONTINO★★, CVNE★★, FAUSTINO, Viña Ijalba, Lan (Culmen★), LÓPEZ DE HEREDIA★★, MARQUES DE CÁCERES★, MARQUES DE MURRIETA★★, MARQUES DE RISCAL★★, Marqués de Vargas★★, MARTÍNEZ BUJANDA★, Abel Mendoza★★, Montecillo★, MUGA★, Ostatu, Viñedos de Páganos★★, Palacios Remondo★ REMELLURI★★, Fernando Remírez de Ganuza★★, La RIOJA ALTA★★, RIOJANAS★, Roda★★, ROMEO★, Sierra Cantabria★★, Señorío de San Vicente★★, Tobía, Valdemar★, Valpiedra★, Ysios; (whites) ALLENDE★★, CAMPO VIEJO, CONTINO★, CVNE★, LÓPEZ DE HEREDIA★★, MARQUES DE CÁCERES★, MARQUES DE MURRIETA★, REMELLURI★★, RIOJANAS★, Valdemar★. **Best years** (reds) 2007 05 **04 01 00** 96 95 94 91 89 87 85.

LA RIOJA *Argentina* Important region in Argentina. Not a source of fine wine, but producers here are astute and specialize in excellent quality value-for-money wines. La Rioja is also home to the largest FairTrade winery in South America. **Best Producers:** Chañarmuyo, La Riojana co-op (FairTrade), San Huberto, Valle de la Puerta.

LA RIOJA ALTA *Rioja DOCa, Rioja, Spain* One of the best of the older RIOJA producers, making mainly Reservas and Gran Reservas. Its only Crianza, Viña Alberdi, fulfils the minimum age requirements for a Reserva anyway. Viña Arana★ and Viña Ardanza★★ Reservas age splendidly, and Gran Reservas 904★★ and 890★★ are among the very best of traditional Rioja. Barón de Oña★ and Áster★ are high-quality, modern, single-estate wines. **Best years:** (Gran Reserva 890) **1995 94** 89 87 85 82 81.

BODEGAS RIOJANAS *Rioja DOCa, Rioja, Spain* Quality winery producing Reservas and Gran Reservas in 2 styles – elegant Viña Albina★ and richer Monte Real★★ – plus refined Gran Albina★ and now a more modern Monte Real Crianza. White Monte Real Blanco Crianza is one of RIOJA's best. The whites and Reservas can be kept for 5 years after release, Gran Reservas for 10 or more. **Best years:** (Monte Real Gran Reserva) 2001 **98 96 95** 94 91 89 87 85.

RION *Nuits-St-Georges, Côte de Nuits, Burgundy, France* Patrice Rion was winemaker at Dom. Daniel Rion from 1979 to 2000, making consistently fine but often austere reds such as VOSNE-ROMANEE les Beaux-Monts and les Chaumes, ECHEZEAUX and CLOS DE VOUGEOT. His own label brings rich, concentrated BOURGOGNE Rouge★★, CHAMBOLLE-MUSIGNY les Cras★★ and NUITS-ST-GEORGES Clos des Argillières★★ from his own vines plus a small *négociant* range. **Best years:** (top reds) (2009) 08 07 **06** 05 03 02.

RIVERINA *New South Wales, Australia* Centred on the town of Griffith and irrigated by the waters of the Murrumbidgee River, the Riverina is an important source of reliable quaffing wines. Many of Australia's best-known brands, though not mentioning the Riverina on the label, are based on wines from here. There is potential for quality, and locally based companies such as DE BORTOLI (Deen, Montage, Sacred Hill), Berton, Casella (YELLOWTAIL, Yendah), MCWILLIAM'S (Hanwood, Inheritance),

Nugan Estate★ (Cookoothama, Talinga Park) and WESTEND★ (Richland) have lifted quality at budget prices. Remarkable sweet wines, led by Noble One Botrytis Semillon★★★ from De Bortoli; others from Cookoothama★, Lillypilly, McWilliam's★, Westend (Golden Mist★).

RIVERLAND *Australia* This important irrigated region, responsible for about 12% of the national grape crush, lies along the Murray River in SOUTH AUSTRALIA near the border with VICTORIA. A great deal goes to cheap quaffers but an increased awareness of quality has seen inferior varieties replaced and yields lowered. Here and there, wines of real character are emerging, including some remarkable reds from the Petit Verdot grape. But Australia's prolonged drought and oversupply of grapes for commercial blends may see some vineyards being abandoned in the near future. Best producers: Angove, Banrock Station, Kingston Estate, Renmano, YALUMBA (Oxford Landing).

RIVESALTES AC *Roussillon, France* *Vin doux naturel* from a large area around the town of Rivesaltes. These greatly underrated fortified wines are some of southern France's best and can be made from various grapes, mainly white Muscat (when it is called MUSCAT DE RIVESALTES) and Grenache Noir, Gris and Blanc. A *rancio* style ages beautifully. Best producers: Baixas coop, la CASENOVE★, CAZES★★, Chênes★, Fontanel★, Força Réal★, GAUBY★, Joliette★, Laporte, Nouvelles★, Rivesaltes co-op, Sarda-Malet★.

ROBERTSON WO *South Africa* Hot, dry inland area with lime-rich soils, uncommon in the Cape, that are ideal for vines. Chenin Blanc and Colombard remain the major white varieties, though just over a quarter of all South Africa's Chardonnay also grows here, for both still and sparkling styles. Sauvignon can also be good. Muscadel (Muscat Blanc à Petits Grains) yields a benchmark fortified wine, usually unoaked and released young. A red revolution is under way: Shiraz, Merlot and Cabernet have made an excellent start. Best producers: Graham BECK★, Bon Courage, De Wetshof, Quando, Robertson Winery, SPRINGFIELD ESTATE★, Van Loveren, Weltevrede, Zandvliet.

ROC DE CAMBES★★ *Côtes de Bourg AC, Bordeaux, France* François Mitjavile of TERTRE-RÔTEBOEUF has applied diligence and genius to this property since he acquired it in 1988. Full and succulent, with ripe dark fruit, this wine takes the CÔTES DE BOURG appellation to new heights. Best years: 2008 07 06 05 **04 03 02 01 00** 99 98 97 96 95.

DOM. DES ROCHES NEUVES *Saumur-Champigny AC, Loire Valley, France* A shift to biodynamic methods and more hands-off winemaking (especially less new oak) has elevated very good wines to a higher level. Fresh, pure and mineral, top cuvées Insolite SAUMUR★★ (Chenin Blanc) and Marginale SAUMUR-CHAMPIGNY★★ (Cabernet Franc) are excellent expressions of fruit and *terroir*; generic Saumur-Champigny and Terres Chaudes★ are good value; Franc de Pieds is from young, ungrafted vines and Bulles de Roche is a finely fruity sparkler. Best years: (Marginale) 2008 **06 05 04 03 02 01 00 99 97**.

ROCHIOLI *Russian River Valley AVA, California, USA* Well-known grape growers, the Rochioli family are equally good at winemaking, offering silky, black cherry Pinot Noir★★ and a richer, dramatic West Block Reserve Pinot★★. Also a good Sauvignon Blanc and a range of cult Chardonnays★★. Best years: (Pinot Noir) 2007 06 05 04 **03 02 01 00**.

ROCKFORD *Barossa Valley, South Australia* Wonderfully nostalgic wines from Robert O'Callaghan, a great respecter of the old vines so plentiful in the BAROSSA, who delights in using antique machinery to create wines of

irresistible drinkability. Masterful Basket Press Shiraz★★, Riesling★★
Moppa Springs★ (Grenache-Shiraz-Mourvèdre), Rifle Rang
Cabernet★★ and Australia's best sparkling Black Shiraz★★★. Best ye
(Basket Press Shiraz) (2009) (08) 06 05 04 **03 02 01 99 98 96 95 92 91 9**

ANTONIN RODET *Mercurey, Côte Chalonnaise, Burgundy, France* This merchan
was sold in 2009 to BOISSET empire after losing its way since the departur
of the Devillard family. Also responsible for Ch. de RULLY★.

TELMO RODRÍGUEZ *Spain* The former winemaker for REMELLURI has forme
a team of enologists and viticulturists that is active throughout Spain:
forms joint ventures with local growers and manages the winemakin
process. The results are often spectacular. Top wines: Molino Real★ (Sierr
de MÁLAGA), Matallana★ (RIBERA DEL DUERO), Altos de Lanzaga★ (RIOJA), Dehes
Gago Pago La Jara★★ (TORO), Viña 105 (Cigales), Basa★ (RUEDA).

LOUIS ROEDERER *Champagne AC, Champagne, France* Renowned firm makin
some of the best, full-flavoured CHAMPAGNE around. As well as th
excellent non-vintage★★ and pale vintage rosé★★, it also makes a big
exciting vintage★★, delicious vintage Blanc de Blancs★★ and the famou
Roederer Cristal★★★ and Cristal Rosé★★★, de luxe cuvées which ar
nearly always magnificent. Both the vintage and Cristal can usually b
aged for 10 years or more; the non-vintage benefits from a bit of aging
too. Best years: (2006) (05) 04 03 02 **00 99 97** 96 **95 90 89 88 85**.

ROEDERER ESTATE *Anderson Valley AVA, California, USA* Offshoot of Loui
ROEDERER, whose wines show how suitable the ANDERSON VALLEY is for fizz
The Brut★★ (sold in the UK as Quartet) is austere but impressive, an
it will age beautifully; the top bottling, L'Ermitage★★★, is stunning
Also lovely rosé★★. Best years: (L'Ermitage) 2002 00 99 97 96 **94 92 91**.

ROERO DOCG *Piedmont, Italy* The Roero hills lie across the Tanaro rive
from the LANGHE hills, home of BAROLO and BARBARESCO. Long noted as
source of supple, fruity Nebbiolo-based red wines to drink in 2–5 year
Roero has recently been turning out Nebbiolos of Barolo-like intensit
from producers such as Correggia and Malvirà. Best producers: (reds
G Almondo★, Ca' Rossa★, Cascina Chicco★, Correggia★★, Deltetto★★
Funtanin★, F Gallino★, Malvirà★★, Monchiero Carbone★, Angelo Negro★
Porello★. Best years: (reds) (2009) (08) 07 06 **04 03 01 00 99**. See also ARNEI

ROMAGNA *Emilia-Romagna, Italy* Romagna's white wines are from Trebbian
(ineffably dull), Pagadebit (dry and sweet) and Albana (Albana di Romagn
DOCG, dry or sweet). The best of the Sangiovese-based reds can rival goo
CHIANTI CLASSICO. Best producers: (Sangiovese) La Berta★, Castelluccio★★
L Conti★, Drei Donà-La Palazza★★, G Madonia★, San Patrignano co-op/Terre d
Cedro★ (Avi★★), Tre Monti★, Zerbina★★.

LA ROMANÉE AC★★★ *Grand Cru, Côte de Nuits, Burgundy, France* Tin
Grand Cru of the very highest quality, owned and now made by Vicomt
LIGER-BELAIR; up to 2002 it was distributed by BOUCHARD PÈRE ET FILS. Bes
years: (2009) 08 07 06 05 03 **02 99 98**.

LA ROMANÉE-CONTI AC★★★ *Grand Cru, Côte de Nuits, Burgundy, Franc*
For many extremely wealthy wine lovers this is the pinnacle of re
Burgundy. It is an incredibly complex wine with great structure and pur
clearly defined fruit flavour, but you've got to age it 15 years to see wha
all the fuss is about. The vineyard, wholly owned by Dom. de la ROMANÉ
CONTI, covers only 1.8ha (4½ acres). Best years: (2009) 08 07 06 05 03 02 0
00 99 **98 97** 96 95 **93 90 89 88 85 78**.

DOM. DE LA ROMANÉE-CONTI *Vosne-Romanée, Côte de Nuits, Burgundy, France*
This famous domaine owns a string of Grands Crus in VOSNE-ROMANÉE (la TÂCHE★★★, RICHEBOURG★★★, ROMANÉE-CONTI★★★, ROMANÉE-ST-VIVANT★★★, ÉCHÉZEAUX★★★ and Grands-Échézeaux★★★) as well as a small parcel of le MONTRACHET★★★. The wines are ludicrously expensive but can be sublime – full of fruit when young, but capable of aging for 15 years or more to a marriage made in the heaven and hell of richness and decay. Best years: (reds) (2009) (08) 07 06 05 03 02 01 **00 99 98 97 96 95 93 90 89 85 78**.

ROMANÉE-ST-VIVANT AC *Grand Cru, Côte de Nuits, Burgundy, France* The largest of VOSNE-ROMANÉE's 6 Grands Crus. At 10–15 years old the wines should reveal the keenly balanced brilliance of which the vineyard is capable, but a surly, rough edge sometimes gets in the way. Best producers: l'Arlot★★, R Arnoux★★★, S CATHIARD★★★, J-J Confuron★★★, DROUHIN★★★, Hudelot-Noëllat★★, JADOT★★★, Dom. LEROY★★★, Dom. de la ROMANÉE-CONTI★★★. Best years: (2009) 08 07 06 05 03 02 **01 00 99 98 96 95 93 90**.

CH. ROMANIN *Les Baux-de-Provence AC, Provence, France* Biodynamically run vineyard owned by Jean-Louis Charmolüe, former owner of Ch. MONTROSE in Bordeaux. Top wine is Le Coeur de Romanin★★ from Syrah, Mourvèdre, Cabernet Sauvignon and Grenache – the same mix as for the delightfully textured Château Romanin★★. La Chapelle de Romanin★ is a third, rich and tasty label. Best years: (Le Coeur) 2008 07 06 05 **04 03 01 00**.

BENJAMIN ROMEO *Rioja DOCa, La Rioja, Spain* ARTADI's former winemaker launched his own estate with a collection of tiny old vineyards, and immediately caused a sensation with his superripe, dense, powerful wines, Contador★★, La Viña de Andrés Romeo★★ and La Cueva del Contador★★; also tasty Macizo★ white from CATALUÑA. Best years: (2008) 06 05 04 **03 02 01 00**.

QUINTA DOS ROQUES *Dão DOC, Beira Alta, Portugal* One of DÃO's finest producers, the wines of 2 estates with quite different characters are made here. Quinta dos Roques red★ is ripe and supple, while Quinta das Maias★ is a smoky, peppery red. The top wines are the Roques Reserva★★, made from old vines and aged in 100% new oak, and Touriga Nacional★★. Both estates also have a decent dry white, especially Roques Encruzado★. Best years: 2009 08 **05 04 03 01 00 97 96**.

QUINTA DE LA ROSA *Douro DOC and Port DOC, Douro, Portugal* The Bergqvist family have transformed this property into a small but serious producer of both PORT and unfortified DOURO★ (Reserva★★) wines. The Vintage Port★★ is excellent, as is unfiltered LBV★★; Finest Reserve and Tonel No. 12, a 10-year-old tawny★, are also good. Best years: (Vintage) 2007 05 04 **03 00 97 96 95 94 92 91**.

ROSÉ DE LOIRE AC *Loire Valley, France* Dry rosé from ANJOU, SAUMUR and TOURAINE. It can be a lovely drink, full of red berry fruits, but drink as young as possible, chilled. It's far superior to Rosé d'Anjou AC, which is usually sweetish without much flavour. Best producers: Hautes Ouches, F MABILEAU, Passavant, St-Arnoud, Trottières.

ROSÉ DES RICEYS AC *Champagne, France* Still, dark pink wine made from Pinot Noir grapes in the southern part of the CHAMPAGNE region. Best producers: Alexandre Bonnet★, Devaux★, Guy de Forez, Morel.

ROSEMOUNT ESTATE *Hunter Valley, New South Wales, Australia* Winery buying and growing grapes in several regions to produce some of Australia's most popular wines, but many seem sweeter and flatter than before and any sense of 'estate' has virtually disappeared. The flagship Roxburgh Chardonnay★ has undergone a dramatic and not entirely successful style change. Best of the other whites is Orange Vineyard Chardonnay★. Top-level Show Reserve reds are a bit stodgy, as is dense Balmoral Syrah, but GSM★ (Grenache-Syrah-Mourvèdre) can be good. Really needs to rediscover its roots. Part of the Foster's Wine Group. Best years: (Balmoral Syrah) 2008 06 05 04 02 01 **00 98 97 96 94 92 91 90**.

ROSSO CONERO DOC *Marche, Italy* Red wines from the Adriatic coast, made solely or principally from Montepulciano. The best are classed Conero DOCG and have a wonderfully spicy richness. Best producers: Fazi Battaglia★, Garofoli★ (Grosso Agontano★★), Lanari★ (Fibbio★★), Leopardi Dittajuti★, Malacari★, Mecella (Rubelliano★), Monte Schiavo (Adeodato★★), Moroder★ (Dorico★★), Le Terrazze★ (Sassi Neri★★, Visions of J★★), Umani Ronchi★ (Cúmaro★★). Best years: (2009) (08) 07 06 **04 03 01 00**.

ROSSO DI MONTALCINO DOC *Tuscany, Italy* The little brother of BRUNELLO DI MONTALCINO generally spends much less time aging in wood, enabling the wines to retain a wonderful exuberance of flavour. Best producers: Agostina Pieri★★, Altesino★, Argiano★, Gianni Brunelli★, Camigliano★, Caparzo★, Casanova di Neri★★, Ciacci Piccolomini d'Aragona★★, Col d'Orcia★, Collemattoni★, COSTANTI★★, Fuligni★, Gorelli-Due Portine★, M Lambardi★★, Lisini★, Siro Pacenti★★, Poggio Antico★, Poggio Salvi★, il POGGIONE★, Salicutti★★, San Filippo-Fanti★, Talenti★, Valdicava★. Best years: (2009) 08 **07 06 05 04 03**.

ROSSO DI MONTEPULCIANO DOC *Tuscany, Italy* Some VINO NOBILE producers use this DOC in order to improve selection for the main wine; the best deliver delightfully plummy, chocolaty flavours. Not to be confused with Montepulciano d'ABRUZZO. Best producers: La Braccesca★/ ANTINORI, La Ciarliana★, Contucci★, Dei★, Del Cerro★, Il Faggeto★, Fassati★, Nottola★, POLIZIANO★, Salcheto★★, Valdipiatta★, Villa Sant'Anna★. Best years: (2009) 08 **07 06 04 03 01**.

ROSSO PICENO DOC *Marche, Italy* Often considered a poor relative of ROSSO CONERO, but it can be rich and seductive when the full complement (70%) of Montepulciano is used, and also when it comes from the more restricted Superiore zone. Best producers: Boccadigabbia★ (Villamagna★★), Le Caniette★, Laurentina★, Monte Schiavo★, Saladini Pilastri★, Velenosi★. Best years: (2009) 08 **07 06 04 03**.

RENÉ ROSTAING *Côte-Rôtie AC, Rhône Valley, France* Modern, lightly oaked, enormously fine wines with deep colour and softly elegant fruit flavours, from some of the best sites in CÔTE-RÔTIE: classic Côte-Rôtie★, Côte Blonde★★★ and la Landonne★★. There's a very good CONDRIEU★★ too. Best years: (top crus) 2009 07 06 05 **04 03 01 00** 99 98 95 94 91 90 88.

DOM. ROTIER *Gaillac AC, South-West France* This estate makes wines using local and more classic grapes. Red Renaissance★, with flavours of wild thyme, blends Duras, Braucol, Syrah and Cabernet Sauvignon. There are both dry and sweet★★ versions of white Renaissance, based on local grape Len de l'El. Best years: (2009) 08 **06 05 04**.

GEORGES ROUMIER *Chambolle-Musigny, Côte de Nuits, Burgundy, France* Christophe Roumier is one of Burgundy's top winemakers, devoting as much attention to his vineyards as to cellar technique, believing in severe pruning, low yields and stringent grape selection. Roumier rarely uses more than one-third new oak. His best wine is often BONNES-MARES★★★; other Grands Crus include MUSIGNY★★★, Ruchottes-Chambertin★★ and CORTON-CHARLEMAGNE★★. Best value are usually the village CHAMBOLLE★★ and an exclusively owned Premier Cru in MOREY-ST-DENIS, Clos de la Bussière★★. Best years: (reds) (2009) 08 07 06 05 **03 02 01** 00 99 98 96 95 90.

ROUSSANNE The RHÔNE VALLEY's best white grape, frequently blended with Marsanne. Roussanne is the more aromatic and elegant of the two, less prone to oxidation and with better acidity, but growers usually prefer Marsanne due to its higher yields and greater body. Now being planted in the Midi. There are some interesting examples in SAVOIE (where it is called Bergeron) and Australia. While much of the Roussanne first planted in California has been identified as Viognier, there are a few true plantings that produce fascinating, complex wines.

ARMAND ROUSSEAU *Gevrey-Chambertin, Côte de Nuits, Burgundy, France* Highly respected CHAMBERTIN estate, with vineyards in Chambertin★★★, Clos-de-Bèze★★★, Mazis-Chambertin★★ and Charmes-Chambertin★★ as well as GEVREY-CHAMBERTIN Clos St-Jacques★★★ and CLOS DE LA ROCHE★★★ in MOREY-ST-DENIS. The long-lived wines are outstandingly harmonious, elegant, yet rich. Best years: (2009) 08 07 06 05 03 **02** 99 96 **93 91** 90 89 88.

ROUSSETTE DE SAVOIE AC *Savoie, France* Separate SAVOIE AC for dry or off-dry, floral and mineral whites made from the Altesse grape variety. Best producers: Dupasquier★★, E Jacquin★, Lupin★, Prieuré Saint Christophe★★, Saint-Germain. Best years: 2008 **07 06** 05.

ROUSSILLON *France* The snow-covered peaks of the Pyrenees form a spectacular backdrop to the ancient region of Roussillon, now the Pyrénées-Orientales *département*. The vineyards produce a wide range of fairly priced wines, mainly red, from the ripe, raisin-rich *vins doux naturels* to light, fruity-fresh vins de pays. Once dominated by co-operatives, there are now some really exciting wines, both white and red, appellation and vin de pays, being made, especially by individual estates. See also BANYULS, COLLIOURE, CÔTES DU ROUSSILLON, CÔTES DU ROUSSILLON-VILLAGES, MAURY, MUSCAT DE RIVESALTES, RIVESALTES.

RUBICON ESTATE See Francis Ford COPPOLA.

RUCHOTTES-CHAMBERTIN AC See CHAMBERTIN AC.

RÜDESHEIM *Rheingau, Germany* Village producing silky, aromatic wines from steep terraced vineyards high above the Rhine (Berg Schlossberg, Berg Rottland, Berg Roseneck and Bischofsberg). Best producers: Georg BREUER★★★, Johannishof★, Kesseler★★, Josef LEITZ★★, Ress, Schloss Schönborn★, WEGELER★. Best years: (2009) 08 07 06 **05 04 03 02 01** 99 98.

RUEDA DO *Castilla y León, Spain* The RIOJA firm of MARQUES DE RISCAL launched the reputation of this white wine region in the 1970s, first by rescuing the almost extinct Verdejo grape, then by introducing Sauvignon Blanc. Fresh young whites have been joined by barrel-fermented wines aiming for a longer life, particularly at Castilla La Vieja, Ossian and Belondrade y Lurton. Best producers: Alvarez y Diez★, Antaño (Viña Mocén★), Belondrade y Lurton★, Castelo de Medina★, Bodegas de Crianza Castilla La Vieja★, Cerrosol (Doña Beatriz), Viña Garedo★, José Pariente★, Hermanos Lurton, MARQUES DE RISCAL★, Viñedos de Nieva★, Ossian★, Palacio de Bornos★, Javier Sanz★, Vinos Sanz★, Viña Sila★ (Naia, Naiades), Sitios de Bodega★, Angel Rodríguez Vidal (Martinsancho★).

RUFFINO *Tuscany, Italy* Huge operation, partly owned by American giant Constellation; production is still controlled by a branch of the FOLONARI family, and is increasingly orientated toward quality. Top wines include La Solatia★ (Chardonnay); Modus★ (Sangiovese-Cabernet-Merlot); Nero del Tondo★ (Pinot Noir); and Romitorio di Santedame★ (Colorino and Merlot). Ruffino also owns VINO NOBILE estate Lodola Nuova, BRUNELLO Il Greppone Mazzi and Borgo Conventi in COLLIO.

RUINART *Champagne AC, Champagne, France* Ruinart has a surprisingly low profile given the quality of its wines. Non-vintage★ is very good, and better value than the Blanc de Blancs★, but the top wines here are the supremely classy Dom Ruinart Blanc de Blancs★★ and the Dom Ruinart Rosé★★. Best years: (2004) 02 **00 98 96 95 90 88 85 83 82**.

RULLY AC *Côte Chalonnaise, Burgundy, France* Best known for white wines, often oak-aged. Reds are light, with a fleeting strawberry and cherry perfume. Most wines are reasonably priced. Best producers: (whites) d'Allaines★, J-C Brelière★, M Briday★, DROUHIN★, Dureuil-Janthial★, Duvernay, FAIVELEY★, V GIRARDIN★, Hasard★, H & P Jacqueson★★, JADOT★, O LEFLAIVE★, RODET★, Villaine★; (reds) Dureuil-Janthial★, la Folie, H & P Jacqueson★. Best years: (whites) (2009) **08 07**; (reds) (2009) **08 07**.

RUSSIAN RIVER VALLEY AVA *Sonoma County, California, USA* Beginning south of Healdsburg this valley cools as it meanders toward the Pacific. Green Valley, a sub-AVA, is home to IRON HORSE, DUTTON GOLDFIELD and Marimar TORRES. Along with SONOMA COAST and CARNEROS it is the leading producer of high-quality Pinot Noir and Chardonnay in north coast California. Best producers: ALYSIAN, DE LOACH★, DEHLINGER★★, DUTTON GOLDFIELD★★, Merry Edwards★★, Gary Farrell★★, HARTFORD★★, IRON HORSE★★, Kosta Browne★, LYNMAR★★, MOSHIN★, Papapietro Perry★, RAMEY★★, ROCHIOLI★★, SONOMA-CUTRER★, Rodney Strong★, Joseph SWAN★, Marimar TORRES★★, WILLIAMS SELYEM★★. Best years: (Pinot Noir) (2007) 06 05 04 **03 02 01 00**.

LYNMAR ESTATE
Russian River Valley

RUST EN VREDE *Stellenbosch WO, South Africa* After a recent springclean, owner Jean Engelbrecht believed the time was right for some new additions to this red-only property. Single Vineyard Syrah★ and 1694 Classification★ (the year the property was granted), a Cabernet-Shiraz blend, make a big, bold statement in build as well as heavyweight packaging. Rust en Vrede★ is a Cabernet-Shiraz-Merlot blend reflecting the farm's *terroir*; Shiraz★, Merlot and Cabernet all benefit from young, virus-free vines, showing fine, soft tannins and fresh fruit. Best years: (Rust en Vrede estate wine) 2006 **05 04 03 02 01**.

RUSTENBERG *Stellenbosch WO, South Africa* Top-notch wines led by single vineyard Peter Barlow★★, a big but classically structured Cabernet, and bold Five Soldiers★★ (Chardonnay). There's also a complex, layered BORDEAUX-style blend John X Merriman★★, while RHÔNE-style wines are represented by a lean but scented Roussanne and intricate, refined Syrah★★. Straw Wine is an occasional heavenly 'sticky'. A delightful, heady Viognier★★ and increasingly complex savoury Shiraz★ are the pick of the value Brampton range. Best years: (Peter Barlow) (2007) 06 05 **04 03 01**; (Five Soldiers) 2008 **07 06 05 04 03 02 01**.

RUTHERFORD AVA *Napa Valley, California, USA* This viticultural area in mid-NAPA VALLEY has inspired hours of argument over whether it has a distinct identity. Thankfully, producers have largely stopped pursuing ultra-ripeness and it *is* now possible to see a true Rutherford character. The heart of the area, the Rutherford Bench, does seem to be a prime Cabernet Sauvignon zone, and many traditional Napa Cabernets come from here and exhibit the 'Rutherford dust' flavour. **Best producers: Beaulieu (Private Reserve★), Cakebread, CAYMUS★★, FLORA SPRINGS★★, Freemark Abbey★ (Bosché★★), Frog's Leap★, Hall★, PINE RIDGE★, Quintessa★, Rubicon/COPPOLA★★, ST SUPÉRY★, Sequoia Grove★, Staglin★★. Best years:** (Cabernet) 2006 05 **04 03 02 01 00 99 95 94 93 91 90**.

RUTHERGLEN *Victoria, Australia* This region in north-east VICTORIA is the home of heroic reds from Shiraz, Cabernet and Durif (Petite Sirah), and luscious, world-beating fortifieds from Muscat and Tokay (Muscadelle). Good sherry- and PORT-style wines. **Best producers:** (fortifieds) All Saints★, Buller★★, Campbells★★, CHAMBERS★★, MORRIS★★, Stanton & Killeen★★.

SAALE-UNSTRUT *Germany* Vines can only flourish in the folds of the river valleys in this bleak expanse of the former East Germany near Leipzig. This far north, it is only just possible to ripen most grape varieties, yet global warming is having an effect, and 80 different varieties are now grown here, 15 of which are of some importance: Riesling, Müller-Thurgau, Silvaner and Weissburgunder (Pinot Blanc) are the current favourites. Only 685ha (1690 acres), mostly on limestone slopes, with a very dry, fragrant style being the most successful. **Best producers:** Gussek, Lützkendorf★, Pawis★.

SACHSEN *Germany* 462ha (1140-acre) wine region centred on the cities of Meissen and Dresden along the Elbe Valley. At more than 50°N, grapes don't ripen easily, and as recently as 1996 frosts of -28°C virtually destroyed the year's harvest; global warming is easing conditions, and some lovely, delicate dry Rieslings are beginning to appear, along with good Müller-Thurgau, Gewürztraminer, Silvaner and Weissburgunder (Pinot Blanc). **Best producers:** Schloss Proschwitz★, Schwartz, Klaus Zimmerling★.

THE SADIE FAMILY *Swartland WO, South Africa* Eben Sadie takes a non-interventionist approach in his vineyards, with biodynamics playing an increasing role. He crafts minute quantities of a red and a white wine: both benefit from aging. Columella★★★, Syrah with a little Mourvèdre, combines richness and power and is clearly influenced by Eben's project in Spain, Terroir al Limit in PRIORAT. Palladius★★, a Viognier-based dry white, is a generously textured wine whose flavours evolve endlessly in the glass. Sequillo, a slightly larger Swartland venture, produces a mineral-fresh Syrah-based red★★ and elegant barrel-fermented Chenin-based white★★. **Best years:** (Columella) 2007 06 **05 04 03 02 01**.

ST-AMOUR AC *Beaujolais, Burgundy, France* The most northerly BEAUJOLAIS cru, much in demand through the romantic connotation of its name. The granitic vineyards produce wines with great intensity of colour that may be initially harsh, needing a few months to soften. **Best producers:** des Billards★, Coquard★, DUBOEUF★ (des Sablons★), des Duc★. **Best years: 2009 08 07**.

ST-AUBIN AC *Côte de Beaune, Burgundy, France* These days almost as good a source of white Burgundy (though in a less rich style) as its MONTRACHET neighbours, PULIGNY and CHASSAGNE, and much more affordable. En Remilly and Murgers Dents de Chien stand out as vineyards, along with Frionnes for pretty, perfumed Pinot Noir. **Best producers:** J-C Bachelet★★, F & D Clair★★, M Colin★★, Deux MONTILLE★, DROUHIN★, JADOT★, H Lamy★★,

Lamy-Pillot★, Larue★, O LEFLAIVE★, B Morey★, RAMONET★★. Best year (reds) (2009) 08 **07 06 05 03 02**; (whites) (2009) 08 **07 06 05 04 02**.

ST-BRIS AC *Burgundy, France* Appellation near CHABLIS for Sauvignon Blan wines are less interesting than a decade ago. Drink young. **Best produce** Clotilde Davenne, J-H Goisot.

ST-CHINIAN AC *Languedoc, France* Large AC of hill villages, coverin strong, spicy red wines with more personality and fruit than run-of-th mill HÉRAULT. Best producers: Berloup co-op, BORIE LA VITARÈLE★, CANE VALETTE★, Cazal-Viel★, CLOS BAGATELLE★, la Dournie, HECHT & BANNIER Jougla★, Mas Champart★, Maurel Fonsalade★, Moulin de Ciffre, Moulinié Navarre, Rimbert★, Roquebrun co-op, Tabatau (Lo Tabataire★). Best year (2009) 08 07 06 **05 04 03 01 00**.

SAINT CLAIR *Marlborough, South Island, New Zealand* Important player with variety of Sauvignon bottlings, some of which have been getting a b sweaty for me of late. Even so, Wairau Reserve can be★★, as can single vineyard Pioneer Block labels (my favourite is the tangy Sawcut★★ Excellent Reserve Chardonnay★★, tasty Riesling★ and Gewürztraminer Vicar's Choice is impressive entry-level label. Various Pinot Noirs (Doctor's Creek★★) and serious, chocolaty Rapaura Reserve Merlot★ lead the reds. Best years: (Sauvignon Blanc) **2009 07 06 04**.

ST-ÉMILION AC *Bordeaux, France* The scenic Roman hill town of S Émilion is the centre of Bordeaux's most historic wine region. The fine vineyards are on the plateau and *côtes*, or steep slopes, around the tow although an area to the west, called the *graves*, contains 2 famou properties, CHEVAL BLANC and FIGEAC. It is a region of smallholdings, wit over 1000 properties, and consequently the co-operative plays a important part. The dominant early-ripening Merlot grape gives win with a 'come hither' softness and sweetness rare in red BORDEAU. St-Émilion AC is the basic generic AC, with 4 'satellites' (LUSSA MONTAGNE, PUISSEGUIN, ST-GEORGES) allowed to annex their name to it. Th best producers, including the Classed Growths, are found in the mo tightly controlled ST-ÉMILION GRAND CRU AC category but there a anomalies, e.g. La Mondotte★★. Best years: **(2009) 08 05 01 00 98 96 9!**

ST-ÉMILION GRAND CRU AC *Bordeaux, France* ST-ÉMILION's top-quali AC, which includes the estates classified as Grand Cru Classé an Premier Grand Cru Classé (below). The classification is revise approximately every 10 years; after a legal battle the 1996 revision wa reinstated with the 2006 promotions added. There are currently 5 Grands Crus Classés. This AC also includes many of the new wave o limited edition *vins de garage*. Best producers: (Grands Crus Classé l'ARROSEE★, Balestard-la-Tonnelle★, Bellevue★, CANON-LA-GAFFELIÈRE★★, Clo de l'Oratoire★★, la Dominique★, Fleur Cardinale★, Grand Mayne★★, Gran Pontet★, Larcis-Ducasse★★, Larmande★, MONBOUSQUET★, Pavie-Decesse★, Tour Figeac★; (others) Bellevue★, Faugères★, Fombrauge★, la Gomerie★ Gracia★, Moulin St-Georges★, Quinault l'Enclos★, Rol Valentin★, TERTRE RÔTEBOEUF★★, Teyssier, VALANDRAUD★★. Best years: (2009) 08 **05 03 01 0 98 96 95 90 89**.

ST-ÉMILION PREMIER GRAND CRU CLASSÉ *Bordeaux, France* The St Émilion élite level, divided into 2 categories – 'A' and 'B' – with only th much more expensive CHEVAL BLANC and AUSONE in category 'A'. There a 13 'B' châteaux, with PAVIE-MACQUIN and TROPLONG MONDOT added from the 2006 Classification. Best producers: ANGELUS★★★, AUSONE★★★, BEAU SÉJOUR BÉCOT★★, Beauséjour★, BELAIR-MONANGE★★, CANON★★, CHEVA

BLANC★★★, Clos Fourtet★, FIGEAC★★, la Gaffelière★, MAGDELAINE★, PAVIE★★, PAVIE-MACQUIN★★, TROPLONG MONDOT★★, Trottevieille★. Best years: (2009) 08 06 05 **04** 03 02 01 **00** 98 96 95 90 89 88.

ST-ESTÈPHE AC *Haut-Médoc, Bordeaux, France* Large AC north of PAUILLAC with 5 Classed Growths. St-Estèphe wines have high tannin levels, but given time (10–20 years) those sought-after flavours of blackcurrant and cedarwood do peek out. More Merlot has been planted to soften the wines and make them more accessible at an earlier age. As summers are drier and hotter, these wines are coming into their own. Best producers: CALON-SÉGUR★★, COS D'ESTOURNEL★★★, Cos Labory★, HAUT-MARBUZET★★, LAFON-ROCHET★, Lilian-Ladouys★, Marbuzet★, MEYNEY★, MONTROSE★★, les Ormes-de-Pez★, PEZ★, Phélan Ségur★. Best years: (2009) 08 06 05 04 **03** 02 01 00 96 95 90 89 88 86.

DOM. ST-GAYAN *Gigondas AC, Rhône Valley, France* The Meffre family rely on very old vines, making and maturing their wines in vat and large barrels, which lend power to the chunky, long-lived GIGONDAS★ (★★ in top years). Other reds, such as RASTEAU, are good value. Best years: (Gigondas) 2009 07 06 **05** 04 03 01 00 **99** 98 97 95 90.

ST-GEORGES-ST-ÉMILION AC *Bordeaux, France* The smallest satellite of ST-ÉMILION, with lovely, soft wines that can nevertheless age for 6–10 years. Best producers: Calon, Macquin St-Georges★, St-André Corbin★, Ch. St-Georges★, Tour-du-Pas-St-Georges★, Vieux-Montaiguillon★. Best years: **(2009)** 08 05 03 01 00 98 96 95.

ST HALLETT *Barossa Valley, South Australia* Following a merger with MCLAREN VALE's Tatachilla, the wineries were snapped up by brewer Lion Nathan. The excellent quaffer Gamekeeper's Reserve Shiraz-Grenache has been joined by a delicious easy-drinking Gamekeeper's Shiraz. These and the EDEN VALLEY Riesling★ are performing pretty well; venerable Old Block Shiraz★★ is regaining top form and the excellent Shiraz siblings Blackwell★ and Faith★ are deep and tasty. Best years: (Old Block) (2009) (08) 06 04 **03** 02 98 96 94 93 91 90.

ST INNOCENT WINERY *Willamette Valley AVA, Oregon, USA* St Innocent produces a number of *terroir*-driven single-vineyard Pinot Noirs (Justice Vineyard Pinot Noir★★, Zenith Vineyard Pinot Noir★) as well as a blended Villages Cuvée★. White wines include two stylish Chardonnays (Anden Vineyard★, Freedom Hill Vineyard), Pinot Gris (Vitae Springs★, Freedom Hill) and crisp, apple-scented Pinot Blanc. Best years: (Pinot Noir) (2008) 06 **05** 04 02.

ST-JOSEPH AC *Rhône Valley, France* Long AC, up and down the opposite bank of the Rhône to HERMITAGE. Made from Syrah, the reds have mouthfilling fruit with irresistible blackcurrant richness. Brilliant at 1–2 years, they can last for at least 10. The white wines are usually pleasant and flowery to drink young, although an increasing number can age. Best producers: (reds) Boissonnet, CHAPOUTIER★★, J-L CHAVE★★, Chêne★, L Chèze★, Courbis★, COURSODON★★, CUILLERON★★, DELAS★, E & J Durand★★, Faury★, P Gaillard★★, Gonon★★, GRAILLOT★, B Gripa★, GUIGAL★★, Paul JABOULET, P Jamet, P Marthouret, Monier★, Monteillet★★, Paret★, A PERRET★★, C Pichon★, Richard (Nuelles★), TAIN co-op★, Tardieu-Laurent★★, Vallet★, G Vernay★, F Villard★★; (whites) CHAPOUTIER (Granits★★), Chêne★★, L Chèze★, Courbis★ (Royes★★), CUILLERON★★, DELAS★, Ferraton★, P Finon, G Flacher, P Gaillard★★, Gonon★★, B Gripa★, GUIGAL, Monteillet★, A PERRET★, Villard★★. Best years: (reds) 2009 07 06 05 03 01 00 99 98 95; (whites) 2009 08 07 06 05 04 03 00.

ST-JULIEN AC *Haut-Médoc, Bordeaux, France*
For many, St-Julien produces perfect claret, with an ideal balance between opulence and austerity and between the brashness of youth and the genius of maturity. It is the smallest of the principal HAUT-MEDOC ACs but almost all is first-rate vineyard land and quality is high. Best producers: BEYCHEVELLE★,

CHÂTEAU BEYCHEVELLE
GRAND VIN 2003
— SAINT-JULIEN —

BRANAIRE-DUCRU★★, DUCRU-BEAUCAILLOU★★★, GLORIA★, GRUAUD-LAROSE★★, LAGRANGE★★, LANGOA-BARTON★★, LÉOVILLE-BARTON★★★, LÉOVILLE-LAS-CASES★★★, LÉOVILLE-POYFERRE★★, ST-PIERRE★★, TALBOT★. Best years: 2007 06 05 04 **03** 02 01 00 99 98 96 95 94 90 89 88 86.

ST-MONT AC *South-West France* A good, recently promoted, former VDQS noted principally for a large range of whites, though there are red and rosé wines too. Best producer: Producteurs PLAIMONT★.

ST-NICOLAS-DE-BOURGUEIL AC *Loire Valley, France* An enclave within the larger BOURGUEIL AC, and similarly producing light wines from vineyards toward the river, sturdier bottles from up the hill. Almost all the wine is red and with the same piercing red fruit flavours of Bourgueil and much better after 7–10 years, especially in warm vintages. Best producers: Y Amirault/Pavillon du Grand Clos★★, Clos des Quarterons★, T Amirault, la Cotelleraie/G Vallée★★, L & M Cognard-Taluau★, F MABILEAU★★, J Taluau★. Best years: (2009) 08 **06** 05 04 03 02 01 97 96.

ST-PÉRAY AC *Rhône Valley, France* Small appellation opposite Valence. Underrated white wines, mainly Marsanne, are fragrant and mineral on the finish. Also some rather hefty traditional-method fizz. Best producers: S Chaboud★, CHAPOUTIER★, CLAPE★, COLOMBO★, B Gripa★★, J Lemenicier★, TAIN co-op★, Tardieu-Laurent★, J-L Thiers★, Tunnel★, Vins de Vienne, A Voge★ (Fleur de Crussol★★). Best years: **2009** 08 07 06 05 04 03 01.

CH. ST-PIERRE★★ *St-Julien AC, 4ème Cru Classé, Haut-Médoc, France* Small ST-JULIEN property making wines that have become a byword for ripe, lush fruit wrapped round with the spice of new oak. Drinkable early, but top vintages can improve for 20 years. Best years: 2008 06 05 **04 03** 02 01 00 99 98 96 95 94 90 89 85.

ST-ROMAIN AC *Côte de Beaune, Burgundy, France* Red wines with a firm, bitter-sweet cherrystone fruit and flinty-dry whites. Usually good value by Burgundian standards, but take a few years to open out. Best producers: (whites) Bazenet★, H & G Buisson, Chassorney★★, A Gras★★, O LEFLAIVE★, VERGET★★; (reds) A Gras★. Best years: (whites) (2009) 08 **07** 06 05 04 02; (reds) (2009) 08 **07** 06 05.

ST SUPÉRY *Napa Valley, California, USA* This French-owned property in RUTHERFORD gets most of its fruit from its Dollarhide Ranch in Pope Valley to the east. Tangy Sauvignon Blanc★★, Merlot★ and ripe, juicy Cabernet Sauvignon★★, as well as an excellent white Meritage blend called Virtú★★, with a substantial amount of Semillon, and Cabernet-based red Élu★★. Best years: 2007 **06** 05 03 02 01.

ST-VÉRAN AC *Mâconnais, Burgundy, France* Often thought of as a POUILLY-FUISSÉ understudy, this is gentle, fairly fruity, normally unoaked Mâconnais Chardonnay. Overall quality is good. Drink young. Best producers: D & M Barraud★, Cordier★, Corsin★★, Croix Senaillet, Deux Roches★, DUBOEUF★, Gerbeaux★, R Lassarat★, O Merlin★, Poncetys★, Saumaize-Michelin★, VERGET★, J-J Vincent★. Best years: (2009) **08** 07.

STE-CROIX-DU-MONT AC *Bordeaux, France* Best of the 3 sweet wine ACs that gaze jealously at SAUTERNES and BARSAC across the Garonne river (the others are CADILLAC and LOUPIAC). The wine is mildly sweet rather than splendidly rich. Top wines can age for at least a decade. Best producers: Crabitan-Bellevue★, Loubens★, Lousteau-Vieil, Mailles, Mont, Pavillon★, la Rame★. Best years: (2009) 07 05 03 02 01 99 98 97 96 95.

SAINTSBURY *Carneros AVA, California, USA* Deeply committed CARNEROS winery. Its Pinot Noirs★★ are brilliant examples of the perfume and fruit quality of Carneros; vineyard-designated Pinots, led by the exquisite Brown Ranch★★★, are deeper and oakier, while Garnet★ is a delicious lighter style. The Chardonnays★★ are also impressive, best after 2–3 years. Best years: (Pinot Noir) (2007) 06 05 04 03 02 01 00 99 98 97 96 95.

CASTELLO DELLA SALA *Orvieto DOC, Umbria, Italy* Belongs to the ANTINORI family, making good ORVIETO★ and outstanding oak-aged Cervaro★★★ (Chardonnay and a little Grechetto). Also Pinot Nero★ and sweet Muffato della Sala★★.

DUCA DI SALAPARUTA *Sicily, Italy* Corvo is the brand name for Sicilian wines made by this firm. Red and white Corvo are pretty basic, but there are superior whites, Colomba Platino★ and Bianca di Valguarnera★, and 2 fine reds, Terre d'Agala★ and Duca Enrico★★.

SALICE SALENTINO DOC *Puglia, Italy* One of the better DOCs in the Salento peninsula, using Negroamaro tempered with a dash of perfumed Malvasia Nera for ripe, chocolaty wines that acquire hints of roast chestnuts and prunes with age. Drink after 3–4 years, although they may last as long again. The DOCs of Alezio, Brindisi, Copertino, Leverano, Squinzano and others, plus various IGTs, are similar. Best producers: Candido★, Casale Bevagna★, Leone De Castris★, Due Palme★, Taurino★, Vallone★★, Conti Zecca. Best years: (reds) (2009) (08) 06 04 03 01 00.

SALTA *Argentina* The vineyards of Salta province, 700km (435 miles) north of MENDOZA, are concentrated along the Calchaquí Valley. The most important location is Cafayate, at about 1750m (5750ft), where most of the traditional producers are located, Colomé, a little further up the valley, has been producing wine for nearly 200 years and its new vineyards, at over 3000m (10,000ft) are the highest in the world. High altitude, sandy soils and almost no rain produce wines of intense colour and high alcohol content, with scented white Torrontés and lush inky Malbec. Best producers: (Cafayate) Domingo Hermanos, El Porvenir de los Andes, Felix Lavaque, Michel Torino; (Colomé) COLOMÉ★.

SAMOS *Greece* The island of Samos has a centuries-old reputation for rich, sweet, Muscat-based wines. The Samos co-op's wines include deep gold, honeyed Samos Nectar★★, made from sun-dried grapes; apricotty Palaio★, aged for up to 20 years; and seductively complex Samos Anthemis★, fortified and cask-aged for up to 5 years.

SAN ANTONIO *Chile* A region of many parts, the most prominent of which has so far been the sub-region of Leyda. Water shortage is a problem. Closeness to the Pacific Ocean and the icy Humboldt Current decides whether you are best at snappy Sauvignon Blanc and fragrant Pinot Noir (Lo Abarca, Leyda), or scented, juice-laden Syrah (Rosario). There are half a dozen estates here, but big companies like CONCHA Y TORO, CONO SUR, MontGras, SANTA RITA and MONTES are also making exciting wine from the region's fruit. Best producers: CASA MARÍN★★, Chocalàn★, O FOURNIER★, Garcés Silva/Amayna★, Viña Leyda★★, LUIS FELIPE EDWARDS, MATETIC★, MONTES.

SAN JUAN *Argentina* The second largest wine-producing region in Argentina, lying 2 hours north of MENDOZA. Three transverse valleys – Pedernal, Tulum and the Zonda, make up the lunar landscape. It's hot and dry here, think BAROSSA VALLEY, but with less rain, so it's no surprise to see varieties like Shiraz and Viognier performing well here. Best producers: Callia, Graffigna, LAS MORAS★, Xumek.

SAN LEONARDO *Trentino, Italy* Marchese Carlo Guerrieri Gonzaga, a former winemaker at SASSICAIA, has established his Cabernet-Merlot blend San Leonardo★★★ as the northern equivalent of the famous Tuscan. Villa Gresti★★ is an almost equally impressive Merlot. Best years: (2009) (08) 07 06 **04 03 01 00 99 97 96 95**.

SAN LUIS OBISPO COUNTY *California, USA* CENTRAL COAST county best known for Chardonnay, Pinot Noir, a bit of old-vine Zinfandel, Syrah and Cabernet Sauvignon. There are 5 AVAs: Edna Valley, PASO ROBLES, SANTA MARIA VALLEY (shared with SANTA BARBARA COUNTY), Arroyo Grande Valley and York Mountain. Best producers: ALBAN★★, Claiborne & Churchill★, Eberle★, Edna Valley★★, Justin★, Laetitia, J Lohr (Hilltop Cabernet Sauvignon★★), Meridian★, Norman★, Saucelito Canyon★, Savannah-Chanelle★, Talley★★, Tolosa Estate, Wild Horse★. Best years: (reds) 2005 04 **03 02 01 00 99 98 97 95 94**.

SAN PEDRO TARAPACÁ *Curicó, Chile* The group runs 11 wineries among its subsidiaries, including 2 in Argentina (Tamarí and Finca la Celia). Most prominent among the Chilean operations are the quality-focused Viña Leyda in SAN ANTONIO and TABALÍ in LIMARÍ. After a shaky start, Cachapoal-based Altaïr★★ found its stride in the excellent 2005 vintage. San Pedro remains the dominant player: its Castillo de Molina Reservas★★ are outstanding and Cabo de Hornos Cabernet Sauvignon★ is a true Chilean classic. Look out for exciting new reds from MAULE and ELQUI and outstanding single-vineyard wines under the 1865★★ label.

SANCERRE AC *Loire Valley, France* White Sancerre can provide the perfect expression of the bright green tang of the Sauvignon grape, and from a good grower can be deliciously refreshing – as can the rare Pinot Noir rosé – but the very best also age well. Some growers produce a richer style using new oak. Pinot Noir reds from top producers are now a serious proposition. The wines are more consistent than those of neighbouring POUILLY. Prices reflect the appellation's popularity. Best producers: F & J Bailly-Reverdy★, G Boulay★★, H BOURGEOIS★★, H Brochard★, R Champault★, F Cotat★★, F Crochet★, L Crochet★, Delaporte★, A Dezat★, Gitton★, V Grall, P Jolivet★, Serge Laloue★, Martin★, A MELLOT★★, J Mellot★, Mollet-Maudry★, H Natter★, V Pinard★★, J Reverdy★, P & N Reverdy★, C Riffault★, J-M Roger★, Thomas-Labaille★★, VACHERON★★, André Vatan★. Best years: (2009) **08 07 06 05 02**.

SANDALFORD *Swan Valley, Western Australia* One of WESTERN AUSTRALIA's original wineries (founded in 1840) and a pioneer of the MARGARET RIVER, where Sandalford planted a large vineyard in 1972. However, it generally underperformed until the arrival of winemaker Paul Boulden in 2001. There are 4 ranges: flagship Prendiville, Estate and Margaret River, as well as Element which offers quality at fair prices. Whites – Sauvignon Blanc-Semillon, Verdelho★ and Chardonnay★ – are impressive, and the reds are even better: dark, classically ripe, fleshy Shiraz★★, Cabernet Sauvignon★★★, complex, lush Prendiville Cabernet★★★ and seductive Prendiville Shiraz★★. Best years: (Cabernet Sauvignon) (2009) 08 07 05 **04 03 02 01 00 99**.

ANDEMAN *Port DOC, Douro, Portugal, and Jerez y Manzanilla DO, Spain* The PORT operation is now owned by SOGRAPE and run by George Sandeman (7th-generation descendant of the founder). Excellent aged tawnies: 20-year-old★ and 30-year-old★★. Vintage ports are more patchy. Vau Vintage★ is good second label, for early drinking. In 2004 Sogrape sold its Jerez assets to Garvey, which now makes the Sandeman sherry brands as a sub-contractor. Best years: (Vintage) 2007 **03 00 97 94 66 63 55**.

UCIANO SANDRONE *Barolo DOCG, Piedmont, Italy* Luciano Sandrone has become one of PIEDMONT's leading wine stylists, renowned for his BAROLO Cannubi Boschis★★★ and Le Vigne★★★, as well as BARBERA D'ALBA★★ and Dolcetto d'Alba★★, which rank with the best.

ANFORD *Santa Rita Hills AVA, California, USA* Richard Sanford planted the great Sanford & Benedict vineyard in the Santa Ynez Valley in 1971, thus establishing SANTA BARBARA as a potentially top-quality vineyard region. He subsequently planted an estate vineyard west of Highway 101 in the SANTA RITA HILLS, an area that has burst on to the Pinot Noir scene with some spectacular wines (sharply focused, dark-fruited Pinot Noir★★, Chardonnay★★). Richard Sanford left in 2005 to found high-quality Alma Rosa label. Best years: (Pinot Noir) 2007 06 05 **04 02 01 00 99**.

OM. LE SANG DES CAILLOUX *Vacqueyras AC, Rhône Valley, France* Top VACQUEYRAS estate with big, peppery, authentic reds led by the old-vines Grenache-Syrah Cuvée de Lopy★★ that bursts with fruit and vigour over 10 or more years. Doucinello★ and Azalaïs★ reds are more restrained, but still full. Best years: 2009 **07 06 05 04 03 01 00 99 98**.

ANGIOVESE Sangiovese, the most widely planted grape variety in Italy, reaches its greatest heights in central TUSCANY, especially in Montalcino, whose BRUNELLO must be 100% varietal. This grape has produced a wide range of sub-varieties, plus a growing number of 'improved' clones, which makes generalization difficult. Much care is being taken in the current wave of replanting, whether in CHIANTI CLASSICO, Brunello di Montalcino, VINO NOBILE DI MONTEPULCIANO or elsewhere. Styles range from pale, lively and cherryish through vivacious, mid-range Chiantis to excellent Riservas and top Tuscan blends. Some fine examples are also produced in ROMAGNA. California producers including Robert Pepi, Vino Noceto and SEGHESIO are having a go at taming the grape, without much success, though it seems to do quite well in the SIERRA FOOTHILLS. Australia has good examples from King Valley in VICTORIA (Gary Crittenden, Pizzini, Greenstone), MCLAREN VALE (Coriole), BAROSSA (amazingly Kalimna, source of GRANGE, has some) and MUDGEE (Oatley make a very snappy rosé). Also grown in Argentina, Chile, South Africa and New York.

ANTA BARBARA COUNTY *California, USA* CENTRAL COAST county, north-west of Los Angeles, known for Chardonnay, Riesling, Pinot Noir and Syrah. Main AVAs are SANTA RITA HILLS, Santa Ynez Valley and most of SANTA MARIA VALLEY (the remainder is in SAN LUIS OBISPO COUNTY), all top areas for Pinot Noir. Best producers: AU BON CLIMAT★★, Babcock, Beckmen★★, Brander★, Brewer-Clifton★★, Foxen★★, Hitching Post★★, Lane Tanner★★, Longoria★, Melville★, Andrew MURRAY★★, Ojai★★, Fess Parker★, QUPE★, SANFORD★★, Zaca Mesa★. Best years: (Pinot Noir) 2007 06 **05 04 03 02 01 00**.

ANTA CRUZ MOUNTAINS AVA *California, USA* A sub-region of the CENTRAL COAST AVA. Notable for long-lived Chardonnays and Cabernet Sauvignons, including the stunning Monte Bello from RIDGE. Also small amounts of robust Pinot Noir. Best producers: BONNY DOON★★, Davi‖ Bruce★★, Clos La Chance★, Thomas Fogarty★, Kathryn Kennedy★★, Mour‖ Eden Vineyards★★, RIDGE★★★, Santa Cruz Mountain Vineyard★.

SANTA MARIA VALLEY AVA *Santa Barbara County and San Luis Obispo Count*
California, USA Cool Santa Maria Valley is coming on strong as ‖ producer of Chardonnay, Pinot Noir and Syrah. Look for wines mad‖ from grapes grown in Bien Nacido and Sierra Madre vineyards by sever‖ small wineries. Best producers: AU BON CLIMAT★★, Belle Glos★★, Byron★★ Cambria, Foxen★★, Lane Tanner (Pinot Noir★★), Longoria★, QUPE★★.

SANTA RITA *Maipo, Chile* Long-established MAIPO giant. Red blends suc‖ as superb Triple C★★ (Cabernet Franc-Cabernet Sauvignon-Carmenèr‖ show real flair. Floresta whites (Leyda Sauvignon Blanc★★) and re‖ (Apalta Cabernet Sauvignon★★) are tremendous. Cabernet-based Cas‖ Real★ is expensive and old fashioned, but some people love it.

SANTA RITA HILLS AVA *Santa Barbara*
County, California, USA This small AVA lies at the western edge of the Santa Ynez Hills in SANTA BARBARA COUNTY. Fog and wind from the Pacific keep temperatures reasonably cool. Pinot Noir is the primary grape (along with small amounts of Syrah and Chardonnay) and the wines have deeper colour, greater varietal intensity and

CLOS PEPE ESTATE

STA. RITA HILLS
PINOT NOIR
2007

higher acidity than others in the region but they have pretty hig‖ alcohols, too. Best producers: Babcock, Brewer-Clifton★★, Clos Pepe★★ Fiddlehead★★, Foley★★, Lafond★, Melville★, SANFORD★★, Sea Smoke★★.

SANTENAY AC *Côte de Beaune, Burgundy, France* Red Santenay wines ofte‖ promise good ripe flavour, though they don't always deliver it, but a‖ worth aging for 4–6 years in the hope that the wine will open out. Mar‖ of the best wines, both red and white, come from les Gravières Premi‖ Cru on the border with CHASSAGNE-MONTRACHET. Best producers: (red‖ R Belland★, Chevrot★, F & D Clair★, M Colin★, J Girardin★, V GIRARDIN★★ Monnot★, Morey★★, L Muzard★★, J-M Vincent★★; (whites) V GIRARDIN★ Jaffelin, René Lequin-Colin★. Best years: (reds) (2008) 07 05 **03 02 99**.

CASA SANTOS LIMA *Alenquer DOC, Lisboa, Portugal* A beautiful estate wi‖ a wide range: fruity, tasty Espiga reds and whites; spicy red★ and cream‖ perfumed white Palha Canas; red and white Quinta das Setencostas★ Also Touriz★ (from DOURO varieties), varietal Touriga Nacional★ Touriga Franca★, Trincadeira★, Tinta Roriz★ and peachy, herb‖ Chardonnay★.

CAVES SÃO JOÃO *Beira Litoral, Portugal* A pioneer of cool-fermente‖ white BAIRRADA, and makes rich, oaky Cabernet Sauvignon from its ow‖ vines. Rich, complex traditional reds and whites include outstandir‖ Frei João★ (Reserva★★) from Bairrada and Porta dos Cavaleiros★ from DÃO – they demand at least 10 years' age to show their quality.

SARDINIA *Italy* Grapes of Spanish origin, like the white Vermentino ar‖ Torbato and the red Monica, Cannonau and Carignano, domina‖ production on this huge, hilly Mediterranean island, but they vie with‖ Malvasia of Greek origin and natives like Nuragus and Vernaccia. The cool‖ northern part (Gallura) favours whites, especially Vermentino, while t‖ southern and eastern parts are best suited to reds from Cannonau ar‖

Monica, with Carignano dominating in the south-west. The wines used to be powerful, alcoholic monsters, but the current trend is for a lighter, modern, more international style. Foremost among those in pursuit of quality are RGIOLAS, Capichera, Cantina Gallura, Còntini, Alberto Loi, Santadi and SELLA K MOSCA. See also CARIGNANO DEL SULCIS.

ASSICAIA DOC★★★ *Tuscany, Italy* Legendary Cabernet Sauvignon-Cabernet Franc blend. Vines were planted in 1944 to satisfy the Marchese Mario Incisa della Rocchetta's thirst for fine red Bordeaux, which was in short supply during the war. The wine remained purely for family consumption until nephew Piero ANTINORI and winemaker Giacomo Tachis persuaded the Marchese to refine production practices and to release several thousand bottles from the 1968 vintage. Since then, under Mario's son Niccolò, Sassicaia's fame has increased as it proved itself to be one of the world's great Cabernets, combining a blackcurrant power of blistering intensity with a heavenly scent of cigars. Since 1995 it has its own DOC within the BOLGHERI appellation. Best years: (2009) (08) (07) 06 04 **03 01 99 98 97 95 90 88 85 68**.

HORST SAUER *Escherndorf, Franken, Germany* Horst Sauer shot to stardom in the late 1990s. His dry Rieslings★★ and Silvaners★ are unusually juicy and fresh for a region renowned for blunt, earthy wines. His late-harvest wines are unchallenged in the region and frequently ★★★; they will easily live a decade, sometimes much more. Best years: (dry Riesling, Silvaner) (2009) 08 07 **06 05 04 03 02**.

SAUMUR AC *Loire Valley, France* Dry white wines, mainly from Chenin Blanc, with up to 20% Chardonnay; the best combine bright fruit with a mineral seam. The reds are lighter than those of SAUMUR-CHAMPIGNY and Saumur Puy-Notre-Dame, recently awarded its own AC. Also dry to off-dry Cabernet rosé, and sweet Coteaux de Saumur in good years. Best producers: Château-Gaillard★, Clos Rougeard★★, Collier★, Filliatreau★, Fosse-Seche, HUREAU★, Langlois-Château★, R-N Legrand★, F MABILEAU★★, Mélaric★, la Paleine★, ROCHES NEUVES★★, St-Just★, Saumur co-op, Tour Grise★, VILLENEUVE★★, Yvonne★★. Best years: (whites) 2009 **08 07 06 05 04 03**.

SAUMUR-CHAMPIGNY AC *Loire Valley, France* Saumur's best red wine. Cabernet Franc is the main grape and, on Saumur's soft limestone soils, produces among the Loire's most seductively perfumed, silky Cabernet Franc. Delicious young, it can age for 6–10 years, top cuvées even longer. Best producers: Clos Cristal★, Clos Rougeard★★, de la Cune, B Dubois★, Filliatreau★, HUREAU★★, R-N Legrand★, Nerleux★/Régis Neau, la Perruche★, Retiveau-Rétif★, ROCHES NEUVES★★, A Sanzay★, Saumur co-op, St-Vincent★/Patrick Vadé, VILLENEUVE★★, Yvonne★. Best years: (2009) 08 **06 05 04 03 02 01**.

SAUMUR MOUSSEUX AC *Loire Valley, France* Reasonable CHAMPAGNE-method sparkling wines, mainly from Chenin Blanc. Adding Chardonnay and Cabernet Franc makes the wine softer and more interesting. Usually non-vintage. Small quantities of rosé are also made. Best producers: Bouvet-Ladubay★, Gratien & Meyer★, Grenelle★, la Paleine★, la Perruche★, Saumur co-op, Veuve Amiot.

SAUTERNES AC *Bordeaux, France* The name Sauternes is synonymous with the best sweet wines in the world. Sauternes and BARSAC both lie on the banks of the little river Ciron and are 2 of the very few areas in France where noble rot occurs naturally. Production of these intense, sweet, luscious wines from botrytized grapes is a risk-laden and extremely

expensive affair, and the wines are never going to be cheap. From goo
producers the wines are worth their high price – as well as 14% alcoho
they have a richness full of flavours of pineapples, peaches, syrup an
spice. Good vintages should be aged for 5–10 years and often last twic
as long. Best producers: Bastor-Lamontagne★, Clos Haut-Peyraguey★★, Cl
Barréjats★, DOISY-DAENE★★, DOISY-VÉDRINES★★, FARGUES★★, GILETTE★★
GUIRAUD★★, Haut-Bergeron★, les Justices★, LAFAURIE-PEYRAGUEY★★
Lamothe-Guignard★, Malle★, Rabaud-Promis★, Raymond-Lafon★★, Rayne
Vigneau★, RIEUSSEC★★★, Sigalas Rabaud★★, SUDUIRAUT★★, la TOU
BLANCHE★★, YQUEM★★★. Best years: (2009) 07 05 **03 02 01 99 98 97 96 9**
90 89 88 86 83.

SAUVIGNON BLANC See pages 280–1.

SAUZET *Puligny-Montrachet, Côte de Beaune, Burgundy, France* A producer with
♀ reputation for classic, rich, full-flavoured white Burgundies, but recentl
showing more classical restraint. Prime sites in PULIGNY-MONTRACHET★ an
CHASSAGNE-MONTRACHET★ (Premiers Crus usually ★★), as well as sma
parcels of BÂTARD-MONTRACHET★★★ and Bienvenues-BÂTARD
MONTRACHET★★★. Best years: (2009) 08 07 **06** 05 04 02.

SAVENNIÈRES AC *Loire Valley, France* Wines from Chenin Blanc, produce
♀ on steep vineyards south of Anjou. Usually steely and dry, although som
richer wines are being produced by a new generation using new oak an
malolactic fermentation. The top wines usually need at least 8 years t
mature, and can age for longer. Two vineyards have their own ACs: l
Coulée de Serrant and Roche aux Moines. Best producers: BAUMARD★★
Bergerie, CLOS DE LA COULÉE-DE-SERRANT★★, Closel★★, Épiré★★, Dom. F L★
Gué d'Orger/L Mahe, Damien Laureau★, aux Moines★, Eric Morgat★, PIERR
BISE★, Taillandier★. Best years: (2008) 07 06 **05** 04 03 02 01 99 97 96 95.

SAVIGNY-LÈS-BEAUNE AC *Côte de Beaune, Burgundy, France* Large villag
🍷 with reds dominating; usually dry and lean, they need 4–6 years to ope
out. Top Premiers Crus, such as Lavières, Peuillets and La Dominode
are more substantial. The white wines show a bit of dry, nutty class afte
2–3 years. The wines are generally reasonably priced. Best producers:
Bize★, Camus-Bruchon★★, Champy★, CHANDON DE BRIAILLES★, B CLAIR★
M Écard★★, J J Girard★, Guyon★, L Jacob★★, Dom. LEROY★★, C Maréchal★
J-M Pavelot★★, TOLLOT-BEAUT★★. Best years: (reds) (2009) 08 07 05 **03 02 99**

SAVOIE *France* Savoie's high Alpine vineyards produce fresh, snappy whit
wines from the local Jacquère grape (to drink young), Chasselas and the mor
interesting Altesse (see ROUSSETTE DE SAVOIE) and Bergeron grapes (ak
Roussanne, grown only in Chignin). There are attractive light reds and rosé
too, from Gamay or Pinot and, in hot years, some positively Rhône-like red
from the Mondeuse grape, which DNA testing recently confirmed as relate
to Syrah. The 18 best villages can add their own name to the label; thes
include Apremont, Abymes, Chignin and Arbin, near Chambéry, an
Jongieux near Aix-les-Bains, along with Crépy and Ripaille growing Chassela
near Lac Léman (Geneva). Seyssel has its own AC for sparkling and dr
whites. Best producers: Belluard★, Berlioz★, Berthollier★, Dupasquier★, l'Idyll
E Jacquin★, Magnin★, J Masson★, Prieuré St-Christophe★★, A & M Quenard★
J-P & J-F Quenard, P & A Quénard★, Ch. de Ripaille★, Saint-Germain, Trosset★

SAXENBURG *Stellenbosch WO, South Africa* In-demand red wines, led b
🍷 dense, burly Private Collection Shiraz★★ and an even richer, bigge
Shiraz Select★★, plus excellent Cabernet★★ and Merlot★. Privat

Collection Sauvignon Blanc★★ and Chardonnay★ head the white range. Drink whites young; reds will improve for 5–8 years. Best years: (premium reds) 2007 06 **05** 04 03 02 01 **00**.

WILLI SCHAEFER *Graach, Mosel, Germany* Classic MOSEL wines: Riesling Spätlese and Auslese from the GRAACHER Domprobst vineyard have a balance of piercing acidity and lavish fruit that is every bit as dramatic as Domprobst's precipitous slope. Extremely long-lived, they're frequently ★★★, as is the sensational Beerenauslese Schaefer produces in good vintages. Even his QbA wines are ★. Best years: (Riesling Spätlese, Auslese) (2009) 08 07 06 **05** 04 03 02 01 99 98 97.

SCHÄFER-FRÖHLICH *Bockenau, Nahe, Germany* From vineyards in SCHLOSSBOCKELHEIM and the more obscure Bockenau, Tim Fröhlich has since 2003 been producing racy dry Rieslings★★ and sumptuous nobly sweet wines★★★. Best years: (2009) 08 07 06 **05** 04 03.

SCHARFFENBERGER CELLARS *Anderson Valley AVA, California, USA* The quality trailblazer in the chilly ANDERSON VALLEY, now owned by top-performing neighbour ROEDERER. Non-vintage Brut★★, with lovely toasty depth, exuberant Rosé★★ and excellent vintage Blanc de Blancs★★.

SCHEUREBE Silvaner x Riesling crossing found in Germany's PFALZ and RHEINHESSEN. In Austria it is sometimes labelled Sämling 88. At its best in Trockenbeerenauslese and Eiswein. When ripe, it has a marvellous flavour of honey, exotic fruits and the pinkest of pink grapefruit.

SCHILCHER Rosé and sparkling wine from the Blauer Wildbacher grape, a speciality of the West STEIERMARK in Austria. Its very high acidity means you either love it or detest it. Best producer: Strohmeier.

SCHIOPETTO *Friuli-Venezia Giulia, Italy* The late Mario Schiopetto pioneered the development of scented varietals and high-quality, intensely concentrated white wines from COLLIO. Outstanding are Friulano★★, Pinot Bianco★★ and Sauvignon★★, plus white blends Blanc des Rosis and Mario Schiopetto Bianco.

SCHLOSS JOHANNISBERG *Johannisberg, Rheingau, Germany* This noble and historic 35ha (86-acre) estate has not always lived up to its reputation. A new director has maintained estate traditions, but refined and greatly approved the winemaking. TBA★★★ has long been outstanding (and costly), but drier styles of Riesling★★ are now vigorous and spicy. Best years: (2009) 08 07 06 **05** 04.

SCHLOSS LIESER *Lieser, Mosel, Germany* Since Thomas Haag (son of Wilhelm, of the Fritz HAAG estate) took over the winemaking in 1992 (and then bought the property in 97), this small estate has shot to the top. MOSEL Rieslings★★ marry richness with great elegance. Best years: (2009) 08 07 06 **05** 04 03 02 01.

SCHLOSS REINHARTSHAUSEN *Erbach, Rheingau, Germany* Estate formerly owned by the Hohenzollern family, rulers of Prussia. Top sites include the great ERBACHER Marcobrunn. Much improved under new management since 2003. Good Rieslings★★ in all styles and Sekt★. Best years: (2009) 08 07 06 **05** 04 03 02 01 99.

SCHLOSS SAARSTEIN *Serrig, Mosel, Germany* Fine Saar estate with austere Riesling Trocken; Kabinett★, Spätlese★ and Auslese★★ are better balanced, keeping the startling acidity but coating it with fruit, often with the aromas of slightly unripe white peaches. Occasional spectacular Eiswein★★★. Best years: (2009) 08 07 06 **05** 04 03 02 01 99.

SAUVIGNON BLANC

Of all the world's grapes, the Sauvignon Blanc is leader of the 'love it or loathe it' pack. It veers from being wildly fashionable to totally out of favour depending upon where it is grown and which country's wine writers are talking, but you, the consumers, love it – and so do I. Sauvignon is always at its best when full rein is allowed to its very particular talents, because this grape does give intense, sometimes shocking flavours, and doesn't take kindly to being put into a straitjacket. Periodically, producers lose confidence in its fantastic, brash, tangy personality and try to calm it down. Don't do it. Let it run free – it's that lip-smacking, in-yer-face nettles and lime zest and passionfruit attack that drinkers love. There's no more thirst-quenching wine than a snappy, crunchy young Sauvignon Blanc. Let's celebrate it.

WINE STYLES

Sancerre-style Sauvignon Although it had long been used as a blending grape in Bordeaux, where its characteristic green tang injected a bit of life into the blander, waxier Sémillon, Sauvignon first became trendy as the grape used for Sancerre, a bone-dry Loire white whose green gooseberry fruit and slightly smoky perfume inspired the winemakers of other countries to try to emulate, then often surpass, the original model.

The range of styles Sauvignon produces is as wide as, if less subtly nuanced than, those of Chardonnay. It is highly successful when picked slightly underripe, fermented cool in stainless steel, and bottled early. This is the New Zealand model and they in turn adapted and improved upon the Sancerre model from France. New Zealand is now regarded as the top Sauvignon country, and many new producers in places like Australia, South Africa, southern France, Hungary, Spain and Chile are emulating this powerful mix of passionfruit, gooseberry and lime. South African and Chilean examples, from the coolest coastal regions, with tangy fruit and mineral depth, are beginning to challenge New Zealand for quality.

Using oak Sauvignon also lends itself to fermentation in barrel and aging in new oak, though less happily than does Chardonnay. This is the model of the Graves region of Bordeaux, although generally here Sémillon would be blended in with Sauvignon to good effect.

New Zealand again excels at this style, and there are good examples from California (often known as Fumé Blanc), Australia and northern Italy. The mix, usually led by Sémillon, is becoming a classy speciality of South Africa's coastal regions. In Austria, producers in southern Styria (Steiermark) make powerful, aromatic versions, sometimes with a touch of oak. In all these regions, the acidity that is Sauvignon's great strength should remain, with a nectarine fruit and a spicy, biscuity softness from the oak. These oaky styles are best drunk either within about a year, or after aging for 5 years or so, and can produce remarkable, strongly individual flavours that you'll either love or loathe.

Sweet wines Sauvignon is also a crucial ingredient in the great sweet wines of Sauternes and Barsac from Bordeaux, though it is less susceptible than its partner Sémillon to the sweetness-enhancing 'noble rot' fungus, botrytis.

Sweet wines from the USA, South Africa, Australia and New Zealand range from the interesting to the outstanding – but the characteristic green tang of the Sauvignon should be found even at ultra-sweet levels.

France
Pouilly-Fumé J-C Chatelain, Didier DAGUENEAU, Ladoucette, Masson-Blondelet, de Tracy; *Sancerre* H BOURGEOIS, F Cotat, L Crochet, A MELLOT, V Pinard, J-M Roger, VACHERON; *Pessac-Léognan* Dom. de CHEVALIER, Couhins-Lurton, FIEUZAL, HAUT-BRION, MALARTIC-LAGRAVIERE, SMITH-HAUT-LAFITTE.

Other European Sauvignons
Austria Gross, Lackner-Tinnacher, POLZ, E Sabathi, Sattlerhof, TEMENT.

Italy Colterenzio co-op, Peter Dipoli, GRAVNER, Edi Kante, LAGEDER, Castello di Montepò/Jacopo BIONDI-SANTI, SCHIOPETTO, Vie di Romans, Villa Russiz.

Spain (*Rueda*) Alvarez y Diez (Mantel Blanco), Castelo de Medina, MARQUES DE RISCAL, Palacio de Bornos, Javier Sanz, Vinos Sanz, Sitios de Bodega; (*Penedès*) TORRES (Fransola).

New Zealand
ASTROLABE, Cape Campbell, Clifford Bay, CLOUDY BAY, Crossings, Forrest Estate, JACKSON ESTATE, Lawson's Dry Hills, NEUDORF, PALLISER, PEGASUS BAY, SAINT CLAIR, SERESIN, VAVASOUR, VILLA MARIA.

Australia
Angullong, BANNOCKBURN, Bird in Hand, Brookland Valley, Larry CHERUBINO, DE BORTOLI (Yarra Valley), Edwards, Hamelin Bay, HANGING ROCK, HOUGHTON (Wisdom), Karribindi, KATNOOK ESTATE, Lenton Brae, Logan, Nepenthe, S C PANNELL, Printhie, Philip SHAW, SHAW & SMITH, Stella Bella, Tamar Ridge, Geoff WEAVER, Word of Mouth.

USA
California Abreu, ARAUJO, Brander, DRY CREEK (DCV3), FLORA SPRINGS (Soliloquy), Honig, KENWOOD, KUNDE, Mason, MATANZAS CREEK, Murphy-Goode, Quivira, ST SUPÉRY, Saracina, SPOTTSWOODE, Voss.

Chile
CASA MARÍN, CASAS DEL BOSQUE, CONCHA Y TORO (Terrunyo), CONO SUR (20 Barrels), Viña Leyda, MONTES (Leyda), SANTA RITA (Floresta), UNDURRAGA (T.H.).

South Africa
CAPE POINT VINEYARDS, Constantia Glen, Neil ELLIS, Flagstone, Fleur du Cap, Fryer's Cove, MULDERBOSCH, Oak Valley, SPRINGFIELD ESTATE, STEENBERG, THELEMA, VERGELEGEN.

SCHLOSS VOLLRADS *Oestrich-Winkel, Rheingau, Germany* Quality at thi
historic estate has improved greatly this century, with some brillian
Eiswein★★ and TBA★★. Best years: (2009) 08 07 **05 04 02**.

SCHLOSSBÖCKELHEIM *Nahe, Germany* This village's top sites are the
Felsenberg and Kupfergrube, but good wines also come from Mühlberg
and Königsfels. Best producers: Dr Crusius★, DÖNNHOFF★★★
Gutsverwaltung Niederhausen-Schlossböckelheim★, SCHÄFER-FRÖHLICH★★
Best years: (2009) 08 07 **06 05 04 03 02 01**.

SCHNAITMANN *Württemberg, Germany* A rising star, with varietal red an
white wines of equal excitement. Rainer Schnaitmann trained in Nev
Zealand, and his Sauvignon Blanc★ is one of Germany's best. Fine
Spätburgunder★ too. Best years: (2009) 08 07 **06 05 04 03**.

DOM. SCHOFFIT *Alsace AC, Alsace, France* One of the two main owners o
the outstanding Rangen Grand Cru vineyard, also making a range o
deliciously fruity non-cru wines. Top-of-the-tree Clos St-Théobalc
wines from Rangen are often ★★★ and will improve for at least 5–6 years
after release, Rieslings for even longer. The Cuvée Alexandre range is
essentially declassified ALSACE Vendange Tardive. Best years: (Clos St
Théobald Riesling) (2009) 08 07 **05 04 02 01 00 99 98 97 96 95**.

SCHRAMSBERG *Napa Valley AVA, California, USA* The first California winer
to make really excellent CHAMPAGNE-style sparklers from the classic
grapes. Though all releases do not achieve the same heights, these wines
can be among California's best, and as good as fine Champagne. The
Crémant★ is an attractive slightly sweetish sparkler, the Blanc de
Noirs★★ and the Blanc de Blancs★ are more classic. Bold, powerfu
J Schram★★ is rich and flavoursome and increasingly good. Top of the
line is the Reserve Brut★★. Vintage-dated wines can be drunk with up tc
10 years' age and can achieve ★★★ quality. A rosé sparkler★ is superb
summer quaffer. The J Davies Cabernet Sauvignon★★, from Diamonc
Mountain, is named in honour of the late founder, Jack Davies.

SCREAMING EAGLE *Oakville AVA, California, USA* Real estate agent Jear
Phillips first produced a Cabernet Sauvignon from her OAKVILLE valley
floor vineyard in 1992. Made in very limited quantities, Screaming
Eagle★★★ is one of California's most sought-after Cabernets each
vintage, a huge, brooding wine that displays all the lush fruit of Oakville
Sold in 2006; the new owners propose to change as little as possible.

SEGHESIO *Sonoma County, California, USA* Having grown grapes in SONOMA
COUNTY for a century, the Seghesio family is today known for its own
Zinfandel. All bottlings, from Sonoma County★★ to the single-vineyard
San Lorenzo★★ and Cortina★★, display textbook black fruit and
peppery spice. Sangiovese★ from 1910 vines is one of the best in the
state. Also look for fascinating Aglianico★ and crisp Italian whites such
as Pinot Grigio★ and Arneis★.

SELBACH-OSTER *Zeltingen, Mosel, Germany* Johannes Selbach is one of the
MOSEL's new generation of stars, producing pure, elegant Riesling★★ from
the Zeltinger Sonnenuhr site. Also fine wine from WEHLEN, GRAACH and
BERNKASTEL. Best years: (2009) 08 07 **06 05 04 03 02 01 00 99**.

SELLA & MOSCA *Sardinia, Italy* As well as rich, port-like Anghelu Ruju★
made from semi-dried Cannonau grapes, this much-modernized old firm
today part of the Campari group, produces good dry whites, Terre
Bianche★ (Torbato) and La Cala★ (Vermentino), and oak-aged reds
Marchese di Villamarina★ (Cabernet) and Tanca Farrà★ (Cannonau-
Cabernet). Best years: (Marchese di Villamarina) (2008) (07) 06 05 **04 01 00 97**.

SELVAPIANA *Chianti Rufina DOCG, Tuscany, Italy* This estate has always produced excellent CHIANTI RUFINA. But since 1990 it has vaulted into the top rank of Tuscan estates, particularly with single-vineyard crus Fornace★★ and Bucerchiale Riserva★★★. Very good VIN SANTO★★. Best years: (Bucerchiale) (2009) (08) (07) 06 **04 01 99 98 95 93 91 90 88 85**.

SÉMILLON Found mainly in South-West France, especially in the sweet wines of SAUTERNES, BARSAC, MONBAZILLAC and Saussignac, because it is prone to noble rot (*Botrytis cinerea*). Also blended for its waxy texture with Sauvignon Blanc to make dry wine – almost all the great PESSAC-LEOGNAN Classed Growths are based on this blend. Performs well in Australia (aged Semillon from the HUNTER, BAROSSA and CLARE VALLEY can be wonderful) on its own or as a blender with Chardonnay (the accent over the é is dropped on New World labels). Sémillon is also blended with Sauvignon in Australia, New Zealand, California (including ST SUPÉRY's Virtu★) and Washington State. In cooler regions of South Africa it is producing some outstanding results, often barrel-fermented, and, increasingly, in flagship blends with Sauvignon.

SEÑA★★ *Aconcagua, Chile* The quality of this ripe, dense Cabernet-based super-blend has leapt since the Chadwick family of ERRÁZURIZ took total control in 2005. Best years: 2009 07 **05**.

SEPPELT *Grampians, Victoria, Australia* In one of 2008's most controversial moves, Foster's sold Seppeltsfield (the BAROSSA base of Seppelt and its entire fortified resources) to a group centring on the CLARE VALLEY producer, Kilikanoon. From its GRAMPIANS base, Seppelt continues to excel with its flagship St Peters Shiraz★★, the definitive Show Sparkling Shiraz★★★ and the Original Sparkling Shiraz★. The sparkling whites appear to be suffering from a lack of focus. Drumborg Riesling★ and Drumborg Pinot Gris from the super-cool Henty region of south-western VICTORIA stand out, and there are some excellent budget-priced table wines in the Victorian range.

SERESIN *Marlborough, South Island, New Zealand* Film producer Michael Seresin's winery has made a big impact on the MARLBOROUGH scene with its range of stylish organic wines. Intense Sauvignon Blanc★★ is full of youthful exuberance. Creamy Chardonnay★★, succulent Pinot Gris★ and several labels of rich, oaky Pinot Noir★, the best of which will age for up to 7 years. Best years: (Pinot Noir) **2009 07 06**.

SETÚBAL DOC *Portugal* Fortified wine from the Setúbal Peninsula south of Lisbon, called 'Moscatel de Setúbal' when made from at least 85% Moscatel, and 'Setúbal' when it's not. Best producers: BACALHÔA VINHOS DE PORTUGAL★★, José Maria da FONSECA★★.

SEYVAL BLANC Hybrid grape whose disease resistance and ability to continue ripening in a damp autumn make it a useful variety in England, Quebec, NEW YORK STATE and other areas in the eastern US. Gives clean, sappy, grapefruit-edged wines that with age can sometimes give a very passable imitation of bone-dry CHABLIS.

SHAFER *Stags Leap District AVA, California, USA* One of the best NAPA wineries, run by the erudite and thoughtful Doug Shafer, and making unusually fruity One Point Five Cabernet★★ and stunning, focused Reserve-style Hillside Select★★★ that ages to a cedary beauty over a generation.

Merlot★★ is also exciting. Relentless★ is made from estate-grown Syrah. Red Shoulder Ranch Chardonnay★★★ is classic full-bodied but scented CARNEROS style. Best years: (Hillside Select) (2005) 04 03 **02 01 00 99 98 97 96 95 94 93 91 90 84**.

SHARPHAM *Devon, England* Beautiful vineyard on a bend in the river Dart with a stylish range of still and sparkling wines, including white Bacchus★ and Madeleine Angevine-based Estate Selection, and red Beenleigh (Cabernet Sauvignon-Merlot). Best years: (still) **2007**.

PHILIP SHAW *Orange, New South Wales, Australia* Philip Shaw is one of Australia's winemaking giants, a restless, energetic mover and shaker who is now a major influence on the ORANGE region. He was at the winemaking helm guiding the rise of ROSEMOUNT in the 1990s, and moved to Orange to build a family wine business around the picturesque Koomooloo vineyard which he had planted in 1989. The Philip Shaw No 19 Sauvignon Blanc★ is pristine, tight and zesty; the No 11 Chardonnay★ powerful, rich and minerally; and the No 5 Cabernet Sauvignon★ fleshy, weighty and elegant.

SHAW & SMITH *Adelaide Hills, South Australia* This winery has been influential in determining the styles that other Australian wineries have adopted. Cousins Martin Shaw and Michael Hill Smith are now able to source much of their fruit from their M3 and Balhannah vineyards and the wines are showing the benefit of this. Tangy Sauvignon Blanc★★ has been a runaway success since its first vintage in 1989; increasingly brilliant single-vineyard M3 Chardonnay★★★; and impressive, fleshy, cool-climate Shiraz★★. Delightful Riesling★ and Pinot Noir★ (expect these to be ★★ soon). Best years: (M3 Chardonnay) 2009 **08 07 06 05 04 03 02**.

SHERRY See JEREZ Y MANZANILLA DO, pages 180–1.

SHIRAZ See SYRAH, pages 296–7.

SICILY *Italy* The Mediterranean's largest island is a historically prolific producer of good wine, with sweet Malvasias from the Eolian islands and Zibibbos (see MOSCATO PASSITO DI PANTELLERIA) joining the fortified brews from MARSALA and elegant table wines from the Nerello (black) and Carricante (white) varieties in the north-east (Etna and Messina's Faro), not to mention the powerful Nero d'Avolas and delicate Frappatos of the south-east. Things went somewhat pear-shaped in the early part of the 20th century, but well before the dawn of the 21st there had begun a flurry of activity which has seen Sicily re-assert the enological diversity that was ever her birthright. Nero d'Avola has spread all over the island, varietally or blended now with Frappato, now with Syrah. Marsala, not so long ago a laughing stock, is beginning to command respect again (see DE BARTOLI), and the high slopes of Etna are for the first time since the 19th century bringing forth the bottles that have had them compared with fine Burgundy. Co-ops like Settesoli – with attractive budget label Inycon and top-end

Mandrarossa (often ★★) – are doing a tremendous job on the large-scale commercial front, and modern-thinking wineries, using both native and international grapes, are mushrooming. Best producers: Abbazia Santa Anastasia★★, Avide★, Benanti★★, Il Cantante★★, Ceuso★★, COS★, Cottanera★★, Cusumano★, Donnafugata★★, Firriato★, Florio★, Gulfi★★, Morgante★★, Palari★★★, PLANETA★★, Duca di SALAPARUTA★, TASCA D'ALMERITA★★.

SIERRA FOOTHILLS AVA *California, USA* The key word here is foothills, since valley floor locations 130km (80 miles) east of San Francisco tend to be warmer and less likely to produce fine wine. Some of the state's oldest Zinfandel is here. The region also does well with Italian varieties like Sangiovese and Barbera, and some old-vine Petite Sirahs are superb, long-lived brutes. **Best producers: Granite Springs★, Latcham, Lava Cap★, Perry Creek★, Sobon Estate, Twisted Oak★, Vino Noceto.**

SIEUR D'ARQUES, LES VIGNERONS DU *Limoux AC, Languedoc, France* This modern co-op makes around 80% of the still and sparkling wines of LIMOUX. The BLANQUETTE DE LIMOUX★ and CREMANT DE LIMOUX★ are reliable, but the real excitement comes with the Toques et Clochers Chardonnays★. The co-op also makes a range of vins de pays. A scandal concerning the supply of dubious Pinot Noir to GALLO in California for its Red Bicyclette brand hasn't exactly enhanced their reputation.

SILVER OAK CELLARS *Napa Valley, California, USA* Only Cabernet Sauvignon is made here, with bottlings from ALEXANDER VALLEY★★ and NAPA VALLEY★★ grapes. Forward, generous, fruity wines, impossible not to enjoy young, yet with great staying power. **Best years: (Napa Valley) (2006) 05 04 03 02 01 00 99 97 96 95 94 93 92 91 90 86.**

SILVERADO VINEYARDS *Stags Leap District AVA, California, USA* The estate Cabernet Sauvignon★ has intense fruit and is drinkable fairly young; Limited Reserve★★ (not made every year) has more depth and is capable of aging; Solo★★, from STAGS LEAP DISTRICT, displays the cherry fruit and supple tannins of this AVA. Also a fruity Merlot★, refreshing Sauvignon Blanc★ and Chardonnay★ with soft, inviting fruit and a silky finish. **Best years: (Limited Reserve) 2005 02 01 99 95 94 91 90.**

SIMI *Alexander Valley AVA, California, USA* Historic winery owned by Constellation. The ALEXANDER VALLEY Cabernet Sauvignon★, Chardonnay★ and Sauvignon Blanc★ attain good quality levels. **Best years: (reds) 2006 05 01 99 97 95 94 91 90.**

SIMONSIG *Stellenbosch WO, South Africa* Family-run property with broad range of styles. Most consistent are the reds: regular Shiraz and lavishly oaked Merindol Syrah; a delicious unwooded Pinotage★★ and well-oaked old-vine Redhill Pinotage★★; the svelte BORDEAUX-blend Tiara★; and dense, powerful Frans Malan Reserve★, a Cape blend of Pinotage, Cabernet Sauvignon and Merlot. Whites are sound, if less exciting. Cap Classique sparklers, Kaapse Vonkel and Cuvée Royale, are biscuity and creamy. **Best years: (premium reds) (2008) 07 06 05 04 03 02 01 00.**

CH. SIRAN★ *Margaux AC, Haut-Médoc, Bordeaux, France* Owned by the same family since 1848, this estate produces consistently good claret – increasingly characterful, approachable young, but with enough structure to last for as long as 20 years. Second wine: S de Siran. **Best years: 2008 07 06 05 04 03 02 01 00 99 98 96 95 90 89 86.**

SKALLI-FORTANT DE FRANCE *Languedoc-Roussillon, France* The influential Robert Skalli was a pioneer of varietal wines in the Midi. Modern winemaking and the planting of international grape varieties were the keys to success. The Fortant de France brand includes a range of single-variety Vins de Pays d'OC: Grenache and Chardonnay are among the best. Also estates in CORSICA, CHATEAUNEUF-DU-PAPE and CALIFORNIA.

SKILLOGALEE *Clare Valley, South Australia* Good range from some of CLARE VALLEY's coolest vineyards: a stony Riesling★ typical of the region and an attractive lemony Gewürztraminer★. Reds include full, fresh Shiraz★★ and minty Cabernet Sauvignon★★. Also a rich, raisiny Liqueur Muscat★★.

CH. SMITH-HAUT-LAFITTE *Pessac-Léognan AC, Cru Classé de Graves, Bordeaux, France* A change of ownership in 1990 heralded a decade of hard graft, resulting in massively improved quality. The reds, traditionally lean, now have much more fruit and perfume and can approach ★★. The white is a shining example of modern white Bordeaux and at best is ★★★. Second wine (red and white): Les Hauts de Smith. Best years: (reds) 2008 07 06 05 04 03 02 01 00 99 98 96 95; (whites) **2008** 07 06 05 04 02 01 00 99 98 96.

SMITH WOODHOUSE *Port DOC, Portugal* Underrated but consistently satisfying PORT from this shipper in the Symington group. Good Vintage★★ and single-quinta Madalena★. Late Bottled Vintage★ is the rich and characterful, figgy, unfiltered type. Best years: (Vintage) 2007 **03** 00 97 94 92 91 85 83 80 77 70 63; (Madalena) **2001** 99 96 95.

SOAVE DOC *Veneto, Italy* In the hilly Soave Classico zone near Verona, the Garganega and Trebbiano di Soave (aka Verdicchio) grapes can produce ripe, nutty, scented wines. The blend may include 30% Chardonnay or Pinot Bianco, but while there are good examples of this style they tend to lack the personality of those made without resort to French grapes. Soave Superiore has been DOCG for some years, but the top private producers continue to ignore it in protest at the anomalous rules governing the denomination and top wines nearly all remain Soave Classico DOC. Best producers: Bertani★, Ca' Rugate★, La Cappuccina★, Coffele★★, Fattori★, Gini★★, Inama★, MASI★, Cecilia Beretta★, PIEROPAN★★, Portinari★, Prà★, Suavia★, Tamellini★. See also ANSELMI, RECIOTO DI SOAVE.

CH. SOCIANDO-MALLET★★ *Haut-Médoc AC, Haut-Médoc, Bordeaux, France* It wasn't classified in 1855, but every single vintage nowadays outshines many properties that were. The wines massively repay 10–20 years' aging, but exhibit classic Bordeaux flavours from as early as 5 years old. Best years: 2008 06 05 04 **03** 02 01 00 98 96 95 90 89 88 86 85.

SOGRAPE *Portugal* This Portuguese giant revolutionized quality in some of Portugal's most reactionary wine regions. Mateus Rosé is still the company's golden egg, but Sogrape makes good to very good VINHO VERDE (Quinta de Azevedo★★), DOURO (Reserva Tinto★) and ALENTEJO (Vinha do Monte, Herdade do Peso★). A high-tech winery in DÃO produces Duque de Viseu★ and the Quinta dos Carvalhais range, with promising varietal Encruzado★ (white) and Touriga Nacional (red); Reserva★★ and Único★★★ reds are further steps up. Callabriga★ reds from Douro, Alentejo and Dão are based on Aragonez (Tempranillo), blended with local varieties. Subsidiaries FERREIRA, SANDEMAN and Offley provide top-flight ports. Also owns Finca Flichman in Argentina and FRAMINGHAM in New Zealand.

SOLAIA★★ *Tuscany, Italy* One of ANTINORI's 'Super-Tuscans', sourced, like TIGNANELLO, from the Santa Cristina vineyard. Solaia is a blend of Cabernet Sauvignon, Sangiovese and Cabernet Franc. Intense, with rich fruit and a classic structure, it is not produced in every vintage. Best years: (2009) (08) 07 06 04 **03** 01 99 98 97 95 94 93 91 90 88 86 85.

SOMONTANO DO *Aragón, Spain* Erratic but eternally promising region in the Pyrenean foothills, with a mixture of international and local grapes. Chardonnay and Gewürztraminer are successful whites. Rosés are generally fresh and flavourful while reds, particularly from the native Parraleta and Moristel or old-vine Garnacha, can be quite impressive. Best producers: Otto Bestué, Blecua★★, ENATE★★, Fábregas, Irius★, Lalanne★, Laus★, Pirineos★, VIÑAS DEL VERO★ (Secastilla★★). Best years: (reds) 2007 05 04 03 01 99 98 97 96.

ONOMA COAST AVA *California, USA* A huge appellation, defined on its western boundary by the Pacific Ocean, that attempts to bring together the coolest regions of SONOMA COUNTY. It encompasses the Sonoma part of CARNEROS and overlaps parts of SONOMA VALLEY and RUSSIAN RIVER. The heart of the appellation are vineyards on the high coastal ridge only a few miles from the Pacific. Intense Chardonnays and Pinot Noirs are the focus. Best producers: Capiaux★, COBB★★, DUTTON GOLDFIELD★★, FLOWERS★★, FREESTONE★★, HARTFORD FAMILY★★, KISTLER★★, Kosta Browne★, Littorai★★, MARCASSIN★★, Patz & Hall★, W H Smith★★, Sonoma Coast Vineyards★★ (Balistreri Vineyard★★★).

ONOMA COUNTY *California, USA* Sonoma's vine-growing area is big and sprawling – some 25,500ha (63,000 acres) – with dozens of soil types and mesoclimates, from the fairly warm SONOMA VALLEY and ALEXANDER VALLEY regions to the cool Green Valley, lower RUSSIAN RIVER VALLEY and SONOMA COAST. The best wines are from Chardonnay, Sauvignon Blanc, Cabernet Sauvignon, Pinot Noir and Zinfandel. Often the equal of rival NAPA in quality and originality of flavours. See also CARNEROS, DRY CREEK VALLEY, SONOMA COAST.

ONOMA-CUTRER *Russian River Valley AVA, Sonoma County, California, USA* Rich, oaky, popular, but often overhyped Chardonnays. Single-vineyard Les Pierres★★ is the most complex and richest; Cutrer★★ can also have a complexity worth waiting for; Founders Reserve★★ is made in very limited quantities; Russian River Ranches★ is much improved in recent releases. Pinot Noir★ is tasty stuff. Best years: 2007 06 05 04 03 02 01 00.

ONOMA VALLEY AVA *California, USA* The oldest wine region north of San Francisco, Sonoma Valley is on the western side of the Mayacamas Mountains, which separate it from NAPA VALLEY. Best varieties are Chardonnay and Zinfandel, with Cabernet and Merlot from hillside sites also good. Best producers: ARROWOOD★★, CHATEAU ST JEAN★, B R Cohn, Fisher★, GUNDLACH-BUNDSCHU★★, KENWOOD★, KUNDE★★, LANDMARK★★, LAUREL GLEN★★, MATANZAS CREEK★★, Moon Mountain★★, RAVENSWOOD★, St Francis★, Sebastiani★. Best years: (Zinfandel) 2005 04 03 01 00 99 98 97 96 95 94.

DOM. SORIN *Bandol AC, Provence, France* As well as red and rosé BANDOL★, Luc Sorin makes various CÔTES DE PROVENCE wines: white Cuvée Tradition★ is a mouthwatering oak-aged blend of Rolle and Sémillon; Terra Amata★ is crisp pink grapefruit- and cranberry-flavoured rosé. Best years: (red Bandol) 2008 07 06 05 03 01.

SOTER VINEYARDS *Willamette Valley AVA, Oregon, USA* A sage and a scientist, Tony Soter worked in the NAPA VALLEY and founded Etude Wines in 1982. When he sold the business, he followed his passion for Pinot Noir and moved to Oregon, planting his first Pinot Noir in 2002. The Mineral Springs Pinot Noir★★ is outstanding, with *terroir*-driven flavours showing from a very young site; Beacon Hill Pinot Noir★ has appealing ripe cherry character; North Valley Pinot Noir★ is the basic cuvée. Also small amounts of sparkling wine★★. Best years: 2008 07 06.

SOUTH AUSTRALIA Australia's biggest grape-growing state, with some 70,000ha (173,000 acres) of vineyards and almost half the country's total production. Covers many climates and most wine styles, from bulk wines to the very best. Established regions are ADELAIDE HILLS, Adelaide Plains, CLARE, BAROSSA and Eden Valleys, MCLAREN VALE, Langhorne Creek, COONAWARRA, PADTHAWAY and RIVERLAND. Newer regions creating excitement include Mount Benson and Wrattonbully, both in the LIMESTONE COAST zone.

...hough Champagne is still the benchmark for top-class sparkling ...nes all over the world, the Champagne houses themselves have taken ...the message to California, Australia and New Zealand via wineries they've established in these regions. However, Champagne-method fizz doesn't necessarily have to feature the traditional Champagne grape varieties (Chardonnay, Pinot Noir and Pinot Meunier), and this allows a host of other places to join the party. Describing a wine as Champagne method is strictly speaking no longer allowed (only original Champagne from France is officially sanctioned to do this), but the use of a phrase like Traditional Method should not distract from the fact that these wines are still painstakingly produced using the complex system of secondary fermentation in the bottle itself.

STYLES OF SPARKLING WINE

France French fizz ranges from the sublime to the near-ridiculous. The best examples have great finesse and include appley Crémant d'Alsace, produced from Pinot Blanc and Pinot Gris, sometimes with a little Chardonnay too; often inexpensive yet eminently drinkable Crémant de Bourgogne, based mainly on Chardonnay; and some stylish examples from the Loire Valley, notably in Saumur, Montlouis-sur-Loire and Vouvray. Clairette de Die Tradition is deliciously grapey, while Blanquette and Crémant de Limoux are good dry sparklers. Limoux and Gaillac also make a little *ancestrale* fizz – sweeter and sometimes cloudy.

Rest of Europe Franciacorta DOCG is a success story for Italy. Most *metodo classico* sparkling wine is confined to the north, where ripening conditions are closer to those of Champagne, but a few good examples do pop up in unexpected places – Sicily, for instance. Asti, Lambrusco and Prosecco are not usually Champagne-method wines. In Spain, the Cava wines of Cataluña offer an affordable style for everyday drinking. German Sekt comes in two basic styles: one made from Riesling grapes, the other using Champagne varieties. England is proving naturally suited to growing grapes for sparkling wine.

Australia and New Zealand Australia has a wide range of styles, though there is little overt varietal definition. Blends are still being produced using fruit from many areas, but regional characters are starting to emerge. Chilly Tasmania is the star performer, making some top fizz from local grapes. Red sparklers, notably those made from Shiraz, are an irresistible Australian curiosity with an alcoholic kick. Cool-climate New Zealand is now producing some world-class examples difficult to tell from good Champagne; as in Australia, some have Champagne connections.

USA In California, some magnificent examples are produced – the best ones using grapes from Carneros or the Anderson Valley. Quality has been transformed by the efforts of French Champagne houses. Oregon is also a contender in the sparkling stakes.

South Africa Cap Classique is the local name for the Champagne method. The best are very good and those from the limy soils of Robertson are starting to show particularly well, but too many brands seem to lack the desire to excel. Consistency is a problem; also, high demand means many are released too young.

BEST PRODUCERS

Australia *white* BAY OF FIRES (Arras), BROWN BROTHERS, Cope-Williams, DOMAINE CHANDON (Green Point), Freycinet (Radenti), HANGING ROCK, Stefano LUBIANA, PETALUMA (Croser), Pipers Brook (Kreglinger), Taltarni (Clover Hill), Tamar Ridge, YALUMBA (Jansz), Yarrabank, Yellowglen (Perle); *red* Peter LEHMANN (Black Queen), Charles MELTON, PRIMO ESTATE, ROCKFORD, SEPPELT.

Austria BRÜNDLMAYER, Schlumberger.

France *Alsace* Ostertag, TURCKHEIM co-op; *Burgundy* Bailly co-op, Louis Bouillot, Lugny co-op, Albert Sounit; *Die* J-C Raspail; *Limoux* SIEUR D'ARQUES; *St-Péray* Chaboud, J-L Thiers; *Crémant de Loire* Langlois-Château; *Saumur* Bouvet-Ladubay, Gratien & Meyer; *Vouvray* CLOS NAUDIN, HUET.

Germany *Nahe* DIEL; *Pfalz* REBHOLZ; *Rheingau* Barth, BREUER, Solter, WEGELER; *Rheinhessen* Raumland.

Italy *Franciacorta* BELLAVISTA, CA'DEL BOSCO; *Trento* FERRARI; *Sicily* TASCA D'ALMERITA.

New Zealand CLOUDY BAY (Pelorus), DEUTZ, HUNTER'S, No. 1 Family Estate, PALLISER, QUARTZ REEF.

Portugal ALIANCA, Loridos/BACALHÔA, Vértice (Super Reserva).

South Africa Ambeloui, Graham BECK, Bon Courage, High Constantia, STEENBERG, Twee Jonge Gezellen, VILLIERA.

Spain *Cava* Can Ràfols dels Caus, CODORNÍU, Colet, FREIXENET, Gramona, Parxet, Recaredo, Signat, Agustí Torelló.

UK Balfour, BREAKY BOTTOM, CAMEL VALLEY, CHAPEL DOWN, DENBIES, NYETIMBER, RIDGEVIEW.

USA *California* DOMAINE CARNEROS, DOMAINE CHANDON, Gloria Ferrer, HANDLEY, IRON HORSE, J VINEYARDS, Laetitia, MUMM NAPA, ROEDERER ESTATE, SCHARFFENBERGER CELLARS, SCHRAMSBERG; *Oregon* ARGYLE.

289

SOUTH-WEST FRANCE South-West France has many lesser-known and rapidly improving ACs and vins de pays, over 10 *départements* from the Massif Central to the Pyrenees. Bordeaux grapes (Cabernet Sauvignon, Merlot and Cabernet Franc for reds; Sauvignon Blanc, Sémillon and Muscadelle for whites) are used in BERGERAC, CÔTES DE DURAS, CÔTES DU MARMANDAIS and BUZET but further away from Bordeaux you will find interesting local varieties such as Tannat (in MADIRAN), Gros and Petit Manseng (in Gascony and JURANÇON) and Mauzac (in GAILLAC). See also BERGERAC, CAHORS, COTEAUX DU QUERCY, CÔTES DE GASCOGNE, FRONTON, IROULÉGUY, MARCILLAC, MONBAZILLAC, MONTRAVEL, PACHERENC DU VIC-BILH, PECHARMANT, SAINT-MONT, TURSAN.

SPÄTBURGUNDER See PINOT NOIR.

SPICE ROUTE WINE COMPANY *Swartland WO, South Africa* Owned by Charles Back of FAIRVIEW. Ripe, well-oaked Flagship Syrah★★ and polished, Shiraz-based Malabar★★ now head the pack. Whites showing promise include rich, barrel-fermented Chenin Blanc★, fresh, flavoursome Viognier and pure yet restrained Sauvignon Blanc★ from Darling. Best years: (premium reds) 2007 06 05 04 03 02 01.

SPOTTSWOODE *Napa Valley AVA, California, USA* Replanted in the mid-1990s, this beautifully situated 16ha (40-acre) vineyard west of St Helena has not missed a beat since the winery opened in 1982. Deep, blackberry- and cherry-fruited Cabernet Sauvignon★★★ is wonderful to drink early, but is best at 5–10 years. Sauvignon Blanc★★ (blended with a little Semillon and barrel fermented) is a sophisticated treat. Best years: (Cabernet) 2006 05 04 03 02 01 00 99 98 97 96 95 94 91.

SPRING MOUNTAIN AVA *Napa Valley, California, USA* Divided by the Mayacamas Mountains road that winds west, this rugged, forested area has some odd exposures that make superb Cabernet Sauvignons and even Chardonnays, as well as Sauvignon Blanc and Riesling. The wines do not always follow the standard vintage patterns: in some supposedly 'off' vintages, the wines made here are better than the rest of NAPA VALLEY. Best producers: Barnett, Pride, Smith-Madrone★, Spring Mountain Vineyard★.

SPRINGFIELD ESTATE *Robertson WO, South Africa* Abrie Bruwer's approach is strictly hands-off in his efforts to capture his vineyard's *terroir*. Méthode Ancienne Chardonnay★ is barrel fermented with vineyard yeasts and bottled without fining or filtration. Not every vintage makes it! Cabernet Sauvignon is also made as Méthode Ancienne★. The unwooded Wild Yeast Chardonnay★ and flinty, lively Life from Stone Sauvignon Blanc★ are also notably expressive. Work of Time★ is a Cabernet Franc-Merlot-based blend. Best years: (Sauvignon Blanc) 2009 08 07 06.

STAGS LEAP DISTRICT AVA *Napa County, California, USA* One of California's best-defined appellations. Located in south-eastern NAPA VALLEY, it is cooler than OAKVILLE or RUTHERFORD to the north, and the red wines have a recognizably mellow, balanced character. A little Sauvignon Blanc and Chardonnay are grown, but the true stars are Cabernet Sauvignon and Merlot. Best producers: CHIMNEY ROCK★★, Cliff Lede★, CLOS DU VAL★★, HARTWELL★★, PINE RIDGE★★, SHAFER★★★, SILVERADO★★, Robert Sinskey★★, STAG'S LEAP WINE CELLARS★★, Stags' Leap Winery★.

STAG'S LEAP WINE CELLARS *Stags Leap District AVA, California, USA* Cabernet Sauvignon★★ can be stunning, particularly the SLV★★★ from estate vineyards and the Fay★★; the Cask 23 Cabernet Sauvignon★★ can be very good, but is overhyped. After a dip in quality, recent vintages are back on form. A lot of work has gone into the Chardonnay★ (Arcadia

Vineyard★★) and the style is one of NAPA's most successful. Sauvignon Blanc★ (Rancho Chimiles★★) is intensely flavoured, with brisk acidity. Founder Warren Winiarski sold the property (excepting Arcadia Vineyard) in 2007 to CHATEAU STE MICHELLE and ANTINORI of Italy. Best years: (Cabernet) 2005 04 03 02 **01 00 99 98 97 96 95 94 91 90 86**.

TANLAKE PARK *Berkshire, England* This 10ha (25-acre) vineyard has, over the past 25 years, produced many stunning wines. The range includes several varietal whites and fragrant Regatta blend; Ruscombe red and occasional barrel-aged Pinot Noir; sparkling Heritage Brut (from Seyval Blanc and other grapes) and Stanlake Brut★ (Pinot Noir-Chardonnay). Best years: (still) **2008 07**.

TEELE *Lake County, California, USA* Owner/winemaker Jed Steele is a master blender. He sources grapes from all over California and Washington and shapes them into exciting wines, usually featuring vivid fruit with supple mouthfeel. He also offers single-vineyard wines and has, in current release, 4–6 Chardonnays, most ★★. His Zinfandels★★ and Pinot Noirs★★ (CARNEROS, SANTA MARIA VALLEY) are usually very good. Shooting Star label provides remarkable value in a ready-to-drink style.

TEENBERG *Constantia WO, South Africa* The oldest farm in CONSTANTIA produces some of South Africa's best and most consistent Sauvignon Blanc: smoky, flinty Reserve★★ is brilliantly tangy, but it also ages well; straight Sauvignon★★ is pure upfront fruit. Barrel-fermented Semillon★★ (occasionally pushing ★★★) matches them in quality, while Magna Carta★★, the Sauvignon Blanc-Semillon blend, will be complex and thrilling after a few years' aging. Reds include minty and nuanced Merlot★★; Catharina★★, a blend based on Cabernet and Merlot; and exciting, smoky Shiraz★★. Fast-improving Steenberg Brut 1682★ Cap Classique fizz is elegant and biscuity. Best years: (whites) 2009 **08 07 06 05 04 03 02 01**.

STEIERMARK *Austria* 4400ha (10,850-acre) region (Styria in English) in outh-east Austria is divided into 3 areas: Süd-Oststeiermark, Südsteiermark the most important) and Weststeiermark. Technically it is the warmest of he Austrian wine regions, but the best vineyards are on cool, high-altitude lopes. The tastiest wines are Morillon (Chardonnay, often unoaked), Sauvignon Blanc and Gelber Muskateller (Muscat). Best producers: Gross★★, Lackner-Tinnacher★, POLZ★★, E Sabathi★, Sattlerhof★, Walter Skoff, TEMENT★★, Winkler-Hermaden★, Wohlmuth★.

STELLENBOSCH WO *South Africa* District with the greatest concentration of wineries in the Cape; the vineyards straddle valley floors and stretch up the mountain slopes. Climates, soils and wine styles are diverse; smaller units of origin – wards – are now being demarcated to more accurately reflect this diversity. The renowned reds are matched by some excellent Sauvignon Blanc and Chardonnay, as well as modern Chenin Blanc and Semillon. Best producers: BEYERSKLOOF★, De Toren★, DE TRAFFORD★★, DeWaal★, Dornier★, Neil ELLIS★★, Ernie ELS★★, Ken Forrester★, The Foundry★★, GRANGEHURST★★, HARTENBERG★, JORDAN★★, Kaapzicht★, KANONKOP★★, Kleine Zalze★, Laibach★, L'AVENIR★, Le Riche★★, MEERLUST★, Meinert★, MORGENHOF★, Morgenster★, MULDERBOSCH★, Neethlingshof★, Quoin Rock★, RUST EN VREDE★, RUSTENBERG★★, SAXENBURG★★, SIMONSIG★, Stellenzicht★, Sterhuis★, THELEMA★★, Tokara★★, VERGELEGEN★★, VILLIERA★, WARWICK★, Waterford★★, Waterkloof (Circumstance★).

SWEET WINES OF THE WORLD

I'm not talking about cheap sugar-water wines here; these are normally made from highly cropped grapes, and simply have sugar or grape juice added to a dry wine to create sweetness. I'm talking about the great sweet wines, which tend to cost a good deal, and only use the intense sweetness of their own grapes to give you a lush, rich, heady taste experience. But it's not at all easy to grow grapes with enough sweetness. There are several ways to gain sweetness, but the classic way is through something called 'noble rot' or botrytis.

MAIN SWEET WINE STYLES

Botrytis Traditionally there were only a very few areas of the world where good summers would ripen the grape, and then as autumn set in a mixture of warm sunshine and fog or mists would cause the grapes to rot. Obviously rot will usually destroy crops – but there is a type of fungal infection called 'noble rot' that actually concentrates the sugars and acid in the grapes, so that the juice becomes more and more like a ridiculously sweet syrup. These grapes are then harvested late in the season, often berry by berry. They're so sweet that they have an enormous potential alcohol (alcohol is created by the transformation of sugar into alcohol by yeast action), but yeasts can only operate up to 15–16% alcohol, at which point they die. Any remaining sugar stays in the wine as sweetness.

The areas of the world where conditions for noble rot appear fairly regularly are led by Bordeaux. Sauternes and Barsac are famous for luscious syrupy wines with intense flavours of peach and pineapple, barley sugar spices and beeswax honey. Nearby parts of South-West France make similar though usually lighter wines. The main grape varieties are Sémillon and Sauvignon. Sauternes in particular has been taken as the model for ambitious winemakers around the world.

The Loire Valley is France's other main sweet wine area; it can get noble rot in its Chenin Blanc vines, particularly in Quarts de Chaume, Bonnezeaux, Coteaux du Layon and Vouvray. Tokaji in Hungary also gets regular botrytis infection.

The other European area with a great sweet wine tradition is Germany, where the Riesling grape manages to combine high acidity with stratospheric sugar levels when conditions are right. These will normally be labelled Beerenauslese or Trockenbeerenauslese. Austria makes similar, though weightier styles.

Semillon, Sauvignon and Riesling grapes are used in parts of Australia, New Zealand and the USA to make sweet wines when conditions allow.

Eiswein This is a German and, occasionally, Austrian rarity, made from frozen Riesling grapes picked in the depth of winter, which manages a thrilling marriage of fierce acidity and unctuous sweetness. Canada has made a speciality of icewine made from Riesling or Vidal grapes.

Muscat The Mediterranean countries, Australia and South Africa have a variety of sweet Muscat wines, many of them fortified wines.

Late harvest Throughout the world, many fairly sweet wines are made from late-harvested (therefore very ripe) but not botrytis-infected grapes.

Recioto A speciality of Veneto, Italy, made from dried grapes.

See also BARSAC, BANYULS, BORDEAUX WHITE WINES, COTEAUX DU LAYON, MADEIRA, MARSALA, MAURY, MONBAZILLAC, MUSCAT, PORT, RECIOTO DELLA VALPOLICELLA, RECIOTO DI SOAVE, SHERRY, SAUTERNES, TOKAJI, VIN SANTO, VOUVRAY; and individual producers.

Château Suduiraut
PREMIER CRU CLASSÉ EN 1855

SAUTERNES

2007

BEST PRODUCERS

France *Alsace* HUGEL, WEINBACH, ZIND-HUMBRECHT; *Bordeaux* CLIMENS, Clos Haut-Peyraguey, COUTET, DOISY-DAENE, DOISY-VEDRINES, FARGUES, GILETTE, GUIRAUD, LAFAURIE-PEYRAGUEY, NAIRAC, Raymond-Lafon, RIEUSSEC, Sigalas-Rabaud, SUDUIRAUT, la TOUR BLANCHE, YQUEM; *Loire* Bablut, BAUMARD, F CHIDAINE, CLOS NAUDIN, Fesles, HUET, Montgilet/V Lebreton, Ogereau, PIERRE-BISE, Taille aux Loups/BLOT, la Varière; *South West* (Monbazillac) l'ANCIENNE CURE, Grande Maison, TIRECUL LA GRAVIÈRE, VERDOTS; (Saussignac) Clos d'Yvigne; (Jurançon) CAUHAPE, Clos Lapeyre, CLOS UROULAT, Souch; (Pacherenc du Vic-Bilh) AYDIE, LAFFITTE-TESTON.

Italy ANSELMI, AVIGNONESI (Vin Santo), Dri (Ramandolo), MACULAN (Torcolato), PIEROPAN.

Germany DÖNNHOFF, EMRICH-SCHÖNLEBER, GUNDERLOCH, KELLER, KÜHN, DR LOOSEN, MÜLLER-SCHARZHOF, J J PRÜM, Horst SAUER, Willi SCHAEFER, SCHLOSS JOHANNISBERG, Robert WEIL.

Austria FEILER-ARTINGER, KRACHER, Nittnaus, Tschida.

Hungary *Tokaji* Disznókö, Chateau Megyer, Chateau Pajzos, Royal Tokaji, Szepsy, Tokaj Kereskedöház.

Australia BROWN BROTHERS (Noble Riesling), Cookoothama, DE BORTOLI (Noble One), MCWILLIAM'S (Morning Light), MOUNT HORROCKS (Cordon Cut Riesling), PRIMO ESTATE (La Magia), Tamar Ridge (Botrytis Riesling), WESTEND (Golden Mist).

New Zealand FELTON ROAD, FRAMINGHAM, PEGASUS BAY.

USA ANTHONY ROAD, BERINGER (Nightingale), Casa Larga (Ice Wine), Far Niente (Dolce), NAVARRO (Cluster Select Late Harvest Riesling).

Canada INNISKILLIN, JACKSON-TRIGGS.

STONIER *Mornington Peninsula, Victoria, Australia* The peninsula's bigges
winery and one of its best, though Lion Nathan, via PETALUMA, now has
controlling interest. KBS Vineyard★★ and Reserve Chardonnay★★ an
Windmill Vineyard★★ and Reserve Pinot Noir★★ are usuall
outstanding, and there are fine standard bottlings in warm vintages.

STONY HILL *Napa Valley AVA, California USA* Founded by Fred and Eleano
McCrea in 1953, the first winery in NAPA VALLEY after Prohibition, thi
tiny rock-strewn hillside produces sublime, ageworthy Chardonnays★★
dry Rieslings★ and Gewurztraminers. The McCreas' son Peter and hi
wife Willinda now operate the property with long-time winemaker Mik
Chelini. Followers swear that the Chardonnays improve for decades.

STONYRIDGE *Waiheke Island, Auckland, North Island, New Zealand* The leadin
winery on WAIHEKE ISLAND, Stonyridge specializes in reds. The top labe
Larose★★★, is a remarkably BORDEAUX-like red of real intensit
Pilgrim★★ is a sexy, sultry CHÂTEAUNEUF-DU-PAPE lookalike. Best year
(Larose) (2009) 08 **07 05 02**.

CH. SUDUIRAUT★★ *Sauternes AC, 1er Cru Classé, Bordeaux, France* Togethe
with RIEUSSEC, Suduiraut is regarded as a close runner-up to d'YQUEI
Although the wines are delicious at only a few years old, the richness an
excitement increase enormously after a decade or so. Seemed to b
under-performing in the 1980s and mid-90s but now owned by AX
(see PICHON-LONGUEVILLE) and back on irresistible song. Best years: 2007 0
05 04 03 02 01 **99 98 97** 96 95 90 89 86 82.

SUMAC RIDGE *Okanagan Valley VQA, British Columbia, Canada* Exceller
Sauvignon Blanc★ and Gewürztraminer Reserve★, fine Pinot Blanc an
one of Canada's best CHAMPAGNE-method fizzes, Steller's Jay Brut★. To
reds include Cabernet Sauvignon, Cabernet Franc, Merlot, Pinot No
and Meritage★. Owned by Constellation Brands.

SUNTORY *Japan* Red Tomi and sweet white Noble d'Or (made fro
botrytized grapes) are top brands for wine made exclusively from grape
grown in Japan. Classic varieties – Cabernets Sauvignon and Fran
Chardonnay, Sémillon and Sauvignon – are also having success.

SWAN DISTRICT *Western Australia* The original WESTERN AUSTRALIA win
region, spread along the fertile silty flats of Perth's Swan River. It used
specialize in fortified wines, but SOUTH AUSTRALIA and north-east VICTOR
do them better. New-wave whites and reds are fresh and generou
without being that memorable. Best producers: Paul Conti, Faber★, Heafc
Glen, HOUGHTON★, John Kosovich, Lamont★, Oakover, Pinelli, SANDALFORD
Sittella, Upper Reach.

JOSEPH SWAN VINEYARDS *Russian River Valley AVA, California, USA* Th
late Joseph Swan made legendary Zinfandel in the 1970s and was one
the first to age Zinfandel★★ in French oak. In the 1980s he turned t
Pinot Noir★ which is made in a rather old fashioned but satisfying wa
Also some old-style Syrah. Best years: (Zinfandel) 2005 **02 01 99 98 97 9
95**.

SYNCLINE WINE CELLARS *Columbia Valley AVA, Washington State, USA* Th
focus here is on Rhône-style wines. The COLUMBIA VALLEY Syrah★ show
lots of game and mineral flavours; single-vineyard McKinley Sprin
Syrah★ has intriguing coffee bean aromas; Mourvèdre★ is full of eartl
flavours. Viognier★ is crisp and refreshing, Roussanne★ has pear an
stone fruit elements, and a bright and zesty Rosé★★ has a hauntir
similarity to a BANDOL rosé. Best years: (2008) 07 **06 05**.

SYRAH See pages 296–7.

LA TÂCHE AC★★★ *Grand Cru, Côte de Nuits, Burgundy, France* Along with la ROMANÉE and la ROMANÉE-CONTI, the greatest of the great VOSNE-ROMANÉE Grands Crus, owned by Dom. de la ROMANÉE-CONTI. The wine provides layer on layer of flavours; keep it for 10 years or you'll only experience a fraction of the pleasure you paid big money for. Best years: (2009) 08 07 06 05 03 02 01 **00** 99 98 **97** 96 **95 93 90 89 88**.

VIÑA TABALÍ *Limarí, Chile* Winery set up in the up-and-coming LIMARÍ valley in 1993 by one of Chile's wealthiest industrialists, Guillermo Luksic, along with the (now) SAN PEDRO TARAPACÁ wine group; Tabalí also owns the excellent Viña Leyda. Best wines are the Reserva Especial Syrah★★ and Chardonnay★★. New Caliza vineyard close to the ocean is producing some tangy Sauvignon Blanc★.

TAHBILK *Goulburn Valley, Central Victoria, Australia* Wonderfully old-fashioned family company making traditionally big, gumleafy/minty reds, matured largely in old wood. 1860 Vines Shiraz★★ and the Reserve reds – now Eric Stevens Purbrick Shiraz and Eric Stevens Purbrick Cabernet – are full of character, even if they need years of cellaring. White Marsanne★★ is rich and perfumed, as is a floral-scented Viognier★. Best years: (Eric Stevens Purbrick Shiraz) (2009) (08) (06) 05 04 03 02 01 **00 99 98 97 96 94**.

CAVE DE TAIN *Hermitage, Rhône Valley, France* Large, progressive co-op offering good-value wines from the northern Rhône. Greatly improved quality, even at the lower levels. Impressive CROZES-HERMITAGE les Hauts du Fief★, fine CORNAS★ and both red and white ST-JOSEPH★ and HERMITAGE★. Topping the range are an old-vine red Hermitage Gambert de Loche★★ and a deliciously rich Vin de Paille★★ from Marsanne. Also still and sparkling ST-PÉRAY★. Best years: (top reds) 2009 07 **06** 05 04 03 01 00 99 98 97 95.

TAITTINGER *Champagne AC, Champagne, France* The top wine, Comtes de Champagne Blanc de Blancs★★★, can be memorable for its creamy, foaming pleasures; the Comtes de Champagne rosé★★ is elegant and oozing class. Prélude is an attractive, fuller-bodied non-vintage style made from 4 Grands Crus and aged for 4 years before release. Non-vintage Les Folies de la Marquetterie is from a steeply sloping single vineyard. Best years: 2004 03 **02 00 99 98** 96 **95 90 89 88 85 82**.

CH. TALBOT★ *St-Julien AC, 4ème Cru Classé, Haut-Médoc, Bordeaux, France* Chunky, soft-centred but sturdy, capable of aging well for 10–20 years and increasingly good this century. This isn't classic, cedary St-Julien but is consistently full-bodied and well priced. Also a tasty white wine, Caillou Blanc de Talbot★. Second wine: Connétable de Talbot. Best years: 2008 07 06 05 **04 03 02 01 00** 99 98 96 95 90 89 88 86 85.

TALBOTT *Monterey County, California, USA* Estate known for its Chardonnays from vineyards in MONTEREY COUNTY: Sleepy Hollow Vineyard★★ (from the Santa Lucia Highlands), Cuvée Cynthia★★ and Diamond T Estate★★ are all packed with ripe tropical fruit and ample oak. Kali Hart Chardonnay★ gives a taste of the style on a budget. Also Chardonnay and Pinot Noir under the Logan label.

TAPANAPPA *Adelaide Hills, South Australia* The partnership of the families of Brian Croser (formerly of PETALUMA), Arnould d'Hautefeuille (BOLLINGER) and Jean-Michel Cazes (LYNCH-BAGES) explores the notion of *terroir*. Sublime Chardonnay from the Tiers Vineyard★★★ in the ADELAIDE HILLS; one of the country's most elegant Cabernet-Shiraz blends from the mature Whalebone Vineyard★★ at Wrattonbully; and Pinot Noir from the Foggy Hill Vineyard★★ on the Southern Fleurieu Peninsula.

SYRAH/SHIRAZ

 Syrah's popularity is rising fast and it now produces world-class wines in France, in Australia – where as Shiraz it produces some of the New World's most remarkable reds – and in California and possibly South Africa, Argentina and Chile, too. And wherever it appears it trumpets a proud and wilful personality based on loads of flavour and unmistakable originality.

When the late-ripening Syrah grape is grown in the coolest, most marginal areas for full ripening, such as Côte-Rôtie, it produces very classy, elegant wines. Syrah's heartland – Hermitage and Côte-Rôtie in the northern Rhône Valley – comprises a mere 365ha (900 acres) of steeply terraced, often granite, vineyards, producing barely enough wine to spread the word to new drinkers. This may be one reason for its relatively slow uptake by growers in other countries, who simply had no idea as to what kind of flavour the Syrah grape produced, so didn't copy it. But the situation is rapidly changing and Syrah's popularity in both the warm and the reasonably cool wine regions of the world becomes more evident with every vintage.

WINE STYLES

French Syrah The flavours of Syrah are most individual, but with modern vineyard practices and winemaking techniques they are far less daunting than they used to be. Traditional Syrah had a savage, almost coarse, throaty roar of a flavour. And from the very low-yielding Hermitage vineyards, it sometimes took decades for the flavours to come together. But improved winemaking and a mix of scented new clones with the haughty old vines have revealed Syrah with a majestic depth of fruit – blackberry and damson, loganberry and plum – some quite strong tannin, occasionally bacon smoke and potato skins, but also a warm creamy aftertaste, and a promise of chocolate and occasionally a scent of violets. These characteristics have made Syrah popular throughout southern France as an 'improving' variety for its traditional red wines.

Australian Shiraz Australia's most widely planted red variety has become, in many respects, its premium varietal. Shiraz gives spectacularly good results when taken seriously – especially in the Barossa, Clare, Eden Valley and McLaren Vale regions of South Australia. An increasingly diverse range of high-quality examples is also coming from Victoria's high country and cool-climate vineyards, more traditional examples from New South Wales' Hunter Valley, and exciting, more restrained styles from Western Australia, Victoria's Yarra Valley and South Australia's Adelaide Hills, as well as patches of Canberra and Queensland. Just about everywhere, really. Flavours are rich, intense, thick sweet fruit coated with chocolate, and seasoned with leather, herbs and spice, or fragrant, floral and flowing with damson and blackberry fruit.

Other regions In California and Washington State producers are turning out superb Rhône-style blends as well as varietal Syrahs modelled closely on Côte-Rôtie or Hermitage, although California producers struggle to persuade wine lovers to buy them. In South Africa Syrah ranks fourth in vineyard area and, as in Chile, more exciting varietal wines and blends appear every vintage. New Zealand's offerings are thrillingly different. Italy, Spain, Portugal, Switzerland and Argentina are beginning to shine, and even North Africa is having a go.

WINE OF CHILE

FALERNIA

ELQUI VALLEY

Syrah

2006
RESERVA

BEST PRODUCERS

France
Rhône ALLEMAND, F Balthazar,
G Barge, A Belle, CHAPOUTIER,
J-L CHAVE, Y Chave, Chêne, CLAPE,
Clusel-Roch, COLOMBO, Courbis,
COURSODON, CUILLERON, E Darnaud,
DELAS, Duclaux, E & J Durand, B
Faurie, Fayolle, Gaillard, J-M Gérin,
Gonon, GRAILLOT, Gripa, GUIGAL,
JAMET, P Jasmin, S Ogier, V Paris,
ROSTAING, M Sorrel, Tardieu-Laurent,
F Villard; *Languedoc* Jean-Michel
ALQUIER, ESTANILLES, GAUBY, PEYRE ROSE.

Other European Syrah
Italy (*Piedmont*) Bertelli; (*Tuscany*)
D'ALESSANDRO, FONTODI, Fossi, ISOLE E
OLENA, Le MACCHIOLE, Poggio al Sole;
(*Sicily*) Cottanera, PLANETA.
Portugal CORTES DE CIMA (Incógnito),
Lagoalva da Cima, Quinta do Monte
d'Oiro. *Spain* Albet i Noya, Castaño,
Casa Castillo, Finca Sandoval,
Enrique Mendoza, Pago del Ama.

New World Syrah/Shiraz
Australia Tim ADAMS, BAROSSA VALLEY
ESTATE, Jim BARRY, BEST'S, Rolf Binder,
BROKENWOOD, Grant BURGE,
CLARENDON HILLS, CLONAKILLA,
Craiglee, Dalwhinnie, D'ARENBERG,
DE BORTOLI, Dutschke, John DUVAL,
FOX CREEK, GLAETZER, HARDYS (Eileen
Hardy), Henry's Drive, HENSCHKE,
Hewitson, HOWARD PARK (Scotsdale),
Jasper Hill, Peter LEHMANN, MAJELLA,
Charles MELTON, MOUNT LANGI
GHIRAN, S C PANNELL, PENFOLDS,
PLANTAGENET, PONDALOWIE,
ROCKFORD, SEPPELT (St Peters), SHAW
& SMITH, TORBRECK, Turkey Flat,
TYRRELL'S, WENDOUREE, The Willows,
WIRRA WIRRA (RSW), YALUMBA, Yering
Station (Reserve), Zema.

New Zealand Bilancia, CRAGGY
RANGE, DRY RIVER, Esk Valley, FROMM,
MAN O'WAR, Passage Rock,
Stonecroft, Te Awa, TE MATA, TRINITY
HILL, Vidal, VILLA MARIA.

South Africa BOEKENHOUTSKLOOF,
DE TRAFFORD, Eagles' Nest, FAIRVIEW,
The Foundry, HARTENBERG, SADIE
FAMILY, SAXENBURG, SPICE ROUTE,
STEENBERG, Stellenzicht.

USA (*California*) ALBAN, ARAUJO,
BONNY DOON, Cline, DEHLINGER,
DUTTON GOLDFIELD, Havens, Jade
Mountain, Lewis, LYNMAR, Andrew
MURRAY, Pax, QUPE, RAMEY, Swanson,
Sean Thackrey, Tor, Truchard.

Chile FALERNIA, Kingston, Loma Larga,
Maycas del Limarí/CONCHA Y TORO,
MATETIC, MONTES, PÉREZ CRUZ, TABALÍ.

297

DOM. DU TARIQUET *Vin de Pays des Côtes de Gascogne, South-West France* O
their 900ha (2,200-acre) property the Grassa family, innovative CÔTES D
GASCOGNE★ producers, have transformed Gascony's thin raw whites int
some of France's snappiest, fruitiest dry wines (Côté★ is a Sauvignon
Chardonnay blend). Also oak-aged★ and late-harvest★ styles.

TARRAWARRA *Yarra Valley, Victoria, Australia* Founder Marc Besen wanted t
make a MONTRACHET, and hang the expense. It's a long haul, but th
winemakers are doing well, with all fruit now sourced from estat
vineyards. Reserve Chardonnay★★ is deep and multi-faceted, and Reserv
Pinot Noir★★ has almost CÔTE DE NUITS flavour and concentration. Unde
the Estate label there is an easy-drinking Chardonnay, a Marsanne
Roussanne-Viognier blend and a delicious Pinot Noir. Best years: (Pino
Noir) (2008) 06 05 **04 03 02 01** 99 98 97 96 94 92.

TASCA D'ALMERITA *Sicily, Italy* This estate in the highlands of centra
SICILY makes some of southern Italy's best wines. Native grape varietie
give excellent Rosso del Conte★★ (based on Nero d'Avola) and whit
Nozze d'Oro★ (based on Inzolia), but there are also Chardonnay★★ an
Cabernet Sauvignon★★ of extraordinary intensity and elegance
Almerita Brut★ (Chardonnay) is a fine CHAMPAGNE-method sparkle
Relatively simple Regaleali Bianco and Rosato are good value.

TASMANIA *Australia* Tasmania may be a minor state viticulturally, wit
only 1200ha (2965 acres) of vines, but the island has a diverse range o
mesoclimates and sub-regions. The generally cool climate has alway
attracted seekers of greatness in Pinot Noir and Chardonnay, and good resul
are becoming more consistent. Riesling, Gewürztraminer and Pinot Gr
perform well, but the real star is fabulous premium fizz. Best producer
Apsley Gorge, BAY OF FIRES★★, Bream Creek, Domaine A, Freycinet★★, Frogmor
Creek★, Heemskerk★, Stefano LUBIANA★★, Moorilla★, Pipers Brook★, Piri
Pressing Matters, Providence, Stoney Rise, Tamar Ridge★. Best years: (Pinot Noir
2007 06 05 **03 02 01 00** 99 98 97 95 94.

TAURASI DOCG *Campania, Italy* MASTROBERARDINO created Taurasi's reputa
tion; now the great potential of the Aglianico grape is being exploited b
others, both within this DOCG and elsewhere in CAMPANIA. Drink a
5–10 years. Best producers: A Caggiano★★, Feudi di San Gregorio★★
MASTROBERARDINO★★, S Molettieri★, Struzziero, Terredora di Paolo★. Bes
years: (2009) (08) 07 06 **04 03 01 00** 98 97.

TAVEL AC *Rhône Valley, France* Rosé from north-west of Avignon, in tw
styles: aromatic-aperitif or chunky and alcoholic. The latter style is bes
with food. Best producers: Aquéria★, Genestière★, GUIGAL, Lafond Roc
Épine★, Maby★, de Manissy, Montézargues★★, la Mordorée★★, Moulin-la
Viguerie, Rocalière, Vignerons de Tavel, Trinquevedel★.

TAYLOR *Port DOC, Douro, Portugal* The aristocrat of the PORT industry, ove
300 years old and still going strong. Now part of the Fladga
Partnership, along with FONSECA and CROFT. Its Vintage★★ (sold a
Taylor Fladgate in the USA) is superb; Quinta de Vargellas★ is a
elegant, cedary, single-quinta vintage port made in the best of the 'off
vintages'. Quinta de Terra Feita★★, the other main component c
Taylor's Vintage, is also often released as a single-quinta. Taylor's 20
year-old★★ is a very fine aged tawny. First Estate is a successful premiu
ruby. Best years: (Vintage) 2007 **03 00** 97 94 92 85 83 80 77 75 70 66 63 6
55 48 45 27; (Vargellas) 2005 04 **01** 99 98 96 95 91 88 87 86 82 78 67 64 6

TEJO *Portugal* Portugal's second-largest wine region straddles the river Tagus (Tejo). Hotter and drier than LISBOA to the west, vineyards in the fertile flood plain are being uprooted in favour of less vigorous soils away from the river. The Ribatejo DOC includes 6 sub-regions. Vinho Regional wines are labelled Tejo. Best producers: (reds) Quinta da Alorna, Quinta do Alqueve, Casa Cadaval★, Quinta do Casal Branco (Falcoaria★), D F J VINHOS★, Caves Dom Teodosio, Quinta do Falcão, Falua/J P RAMOS (Reserva★), Quinta da Lagoalva de Cima★, Companhia das Lezírias, Quinta da Ribeirinha (Vale de Lobos), Val d'Algares.

TE MATA *Hawkes Bay, North Island, New Zealand* HAWKES BAY's glamour winery, best known for its reds, Coleraine★★ and Awatea★★, both based on Cabernet Sauvignon with varying proportions of Merlot and Cabernet Franc. Also toasty Elston Chardonnay★★. Exceptional vintages of all 3 wines might be aged for 5–10 years. Scented, peppery, elegant Bullnose Syrah★★, trailblazing Woodthorpe Viognier★, gorgeous, crunchy Gamay★★ and delicious Cape Crest Sauvignon Blanc★★. Best years: (Coleraine) (2009) 08 **07** 06 04 02 00.

TEMENT *Südsteiermark, Austria* Austria's best Sauvignon Blanc★★ (single-site Zieregg★★★) and Morillon (Chardonnay)★★. Both varieties are fermented and aged in oak, giving power, depth and subtle oak character. The Gelber Muskatellers are unusually racy – perfect aperitif wines. Red Arachon★★ is a joint venture with F X PICHLER and Szemes in BURGENLAND. Best years: (Morillon, Zieregg) (2009) 08 07 **06** 05 04 02.

TEMPRANILLO Spain's best native red grape can make wonderful wine with wild strawberry and spicy, tobaccoey flavours. It is important in RIOJA, PENEDÉS (as Ull de Llebre), RIBERA DEL DUERO (as Tinto Fino or Tinta del País), LA MANCHA and VALDEPEÑAS (as Cencibel), TORO (as Tinta de Toro), NAVARRA, SOMONTANO and UTIEL-REQUENA. In Portugal it is found in the ALENTEJO (as Aragonez) and in the DOURO, DÃO and LISBOA (as Tinta Roriz). Wines can be deliciously fruity for drinking young, but Tempranillo also matures well, and its flavours blend happily with oak. It is now being taken more seriously in Argentina, and new plantings have been made in California, Oregon (ABACELA), Washington (CAYUSE), Australia (Tim ADAMS, Gemtree, Nepenthe, PONDALOWIE, Sanguine), New Zealand (TRINITY HILL) and South Africa.

TEROLDEGO ROTALIANO DOC *Trentino-Alto Adige, Italy* Teroldego is a TRENTINO grape variety, producing mainly deep-coloured, leafy, blackberry-flavoured wine from gravel soils of the Rotaliano plain. Best producers: Barone de Cles★, M Donati★, Dorigati★, Endrizzi★, FORADORI★★, Conti Martini★, Mezzacorona (Riserva★), Cantina Rotaliana★, A & R Zeni★. Best years: (2009) (08) 07 **06** 04 03 01 00 99 97.

TERRAS DO SADO see PENÍNSULA DE SETÚBAL.

TERRAZAS DE LOS ANDES *Mendoza, Argentina* Offshoot of the LVMH empire, and a terrific source of reds from high-altitude vineyards around Luján de Cuyo in MENDOZA. Top reds are Afincado, Malbec★★ and Cabernet Sauvignon★★ (heading for ★★★). A joint venture with CHEVAL BLANC of ST-ÉMILION has yielded Cheval des Andes★★★, a stunning Cabernet Sauvignon-Malbec blend.

CASTELLO DEL TERRICCIO *Tuscany, Italy* Estate in the Pisan hills. Changes in philosophy seem to have deprived top red Lupicaia★ (Cabernet-Merlot) and less pricey Tassinaia★ (Sangiovese-Cabernet-

Merlot) of much of their exciting, scented, potentially ★★★ personality. White wines are Rondinaia (Chardonnay)★★ and Con Vento (Sauvignon Blanc)★. Best years: (Lupicaia) (2008) 06 **04 03 01 00 98 97**.

TERTRE-RÔTEBOEUF★★ *St-Émilion Grand Cru AC, Bordeaux, France* ST-ÉMILION's most exceptional unclassified estate. The richly seductive, Merlot-based wines sell at the same price as the Premiers Grands Crus Classés – and so they should. Same ownership as the outstanding ROC DE CAMBES. Best years: 2008 07 06 05 **04 03 02 01 00 99 98 96 95 90 89 88**.

TEXAS *USA* Texas has enjoyed the tremendous wine industry growth that has hit the USA this decade, with the number of wineries soaring to 181. The state has 8 AVAs, with the Texas High Plains the most significant. Mediterranean grapes such as Grenache, Tempranillo, Syrah and Sangiovese have risen in favour over the traditional Cabernets and Chardonnay. Thunderstorms are capable of destroying entire crops in minutes. Best producers: Becker, Fall Creek, Flat Creek, Haak, LLANO ESTACADO★, McPherson★, Messina Hof.

THELEMA *Stellenbosch WO, South Africa* With maturing vineyards in ELGIN, as well as on the home farm, now undergoing conversion to organics, output has increased in recent years. Thanks to Gyles Webb's meticulous attention to detail, consistency has not been compromised. A pair of Cabernet Sauvignons – blackcurranty regular★★ and self-descriptive The Mint★★ – ripe fleshy Merlot★ (Reserve★★), spicy, accessible Shiraz★, barrel-fermented Chardonnay★★, vibrant Sauvignon Blanc★★ and citrus Riesling★ are among the leaders. Also exciting Elgin Sauvignon★. Best years: (Cabernet Sauvignon) (2008) 07 **06 05 04 03 01 00 99 98 97**; (Chardonnay) 2009 **08 07 06 05 04 03 02 01**.

THERMENREGION *Niederösterreich, Austria* Warm, 2500ha (6175-acre) region, south of Vienna, taking its name from the spa towns of Baden and Bad Vöslau. Gumpoldskirchen, near Vienna, has rich and sometimes sweet white wines from local varieties. The red wine area around Baden produces improving Pinot Noir and Cabernet. Best producers: Alphart, Biegler, Fischer★, Johanneshof★, Piriwe, Schellmann, Stadlmann★, Zierer. Best years: (reds) (2008) 07 06 **05 04 03**.

THIRTY BENCH *Niagara Peninsula VQA, Ontario, Canada* Thirty Bench is known for its excellent Rieslings★★, very good BORDEAUX-style red blends★ and a fine barrel-fermented Chardonnay★.

THOMAS *Hunter Valley, New South Wales, Australia* Andrew Thomas produces exemplary Semillon and Shiraz. Braemore Vineyard Semillon★★ is a traditional, ageworthy HUNTER white, while the OC Semillon★ is a delicious early-drinking style. Kiss Vineyard Shiraz★★, from old vines, is ripe, powerful, complex and velvety.

THREE CHOIRS *Gloucestershire, England* Martin Fowke makes a large range of wines from 30ha (74 acres) of vines, plus bought-in grapes. Bacchus★ and Sieggerebe★ varietals are fragrant and delightful, reds are some of England's best, plus sparkling Classic Cuvée★ (Seyval Blanc-Pinot Noir). Occasional Late Harvest dessert wine. Best years: (still) **2009 08 07**.

TICINO *Switzerland* Italian-speaking Swiss canton. Eighty per cent of production here is Merlot, usually soft and gluggable, but sometimes more serious with some oak barrel-aging. Best producers: Brivio, Delea★, Gialdi, Huber★, Werner Stucky★, Tamborini★, Terreni alla Maggia★, Valsangiacomo, Christian Zündel★.

TIEFENBRUNNER *Alto Adige DOC, Trentino-Alto Adige, Italy* Herbert Tiefenbrunner began his career at this castle (Schloss Turmhof) as a teenager in 1943. In his 80s, he still helps son Christof in the winery, producing 20-plus wine styles, mostly under the ALTO ADIGE DOC. The focus is on purity of fruit and varietal character, mainly among whites such as Chardonnay Linticlarus★★ and Müller-Thurgau Feldmarschall★★ which, at 1000m (3280ft), is too high to qualify as DOC under Italy's relentlessly silly laws. Best years: (Feldmarschall) (2009) 08 **07** 06 04 03 01 **00 99 98 97**.

TIGNANELLO★★ *Tuscany, Italy* In the early 1970s, Piero ANTINORI employed the almost unheard-of practice of aging in small French oak barrels and used Cabernet Sauvignon (20%) in the blend with Sangiovese. The quality was superb, and Tignanello's success sparked off the 'Super-Tuscan' movement. Top vintages are truly great; lesser years are of good CHIANTI CLASSICO quality. Best years: (2009) (08) 07 06 **04** 03 01 **00 99 98 97 95 93 90 88 85**.

TINTA RORIZ See TEMPRANILLO.

CH. TIRECUL LA GRAVIÈRE *Monbazillac AC, South-West France* Generally considered the best (and certainly the most expensive) of MONBAZILLAC wines, and usually rated in the company of top SAUTERNES. The Bilancinis grow a high proportion of Muscadelle and enjoy unusually regular benefit from botrytization. The top wine, Cuvée Madame★★★, is a wine of world class. Best years 2007 **05 04 03 01 00**.

TOCAI FRIULANO See FRIULANO.

TOKAJI *Hungary* Hungary's classic, liquorous wine of historic reputation, with its unique, sweet-and-sour, sherry-like tang, comes from 28 villages on the Hungarian–Slovak border. Mists from the Bodrog river ensure that noble rot on the Furmint, Hárslevelü and Muscotaly (Muscat Ottonel) grapes is a fairly common occurrence. Degrees of sweetness are measured in *puttonyos*. Discussions continue about traditional oxidized styles versus fresher modern versions. Best producers: Disznókö★★, Château Megyer★★, Oremus★, Château Pajzos★★, Royal Tokaji Wine Co★★, Istvan Szepsy★★, Tokaj Kereskedöház★. Best years: **2004 03 00 99 97 93**.

TOLLOT-BEAUT *Chorey-lès-Beaune, Burgundy, France* Good reds with lots of fruit and a pronounced new oak character, though I've recently noted a more extractive style in one or two of them. The village-level CHOREY-LÈS-BEAUNE★★, ALOXE-CORTON★★ and SAVIGNY-LÈS-BEAUNE★★ are all excellent, as is the top BEAUNE Premier Cru Clos du Roi★★. Whites are more variable, but at best delicious. Best years: (reds) (2009) 08 07 06 05 **03 02 99**.

TORBRECK *Barossa Valley, South Australia* Dave Powell specializes in opulent, well-structured reds from 60–120-year-old Shiraz, Grenache and Mataro (Mourvèdre) vines. Made in minute quantities, the flagship RunRig★★★, single-vineyard Descendant★★ and Factor★★ are all richly concentrated, powerful, complex Shiraz. The Steading★ and Juveniles★ are Grenache-Mataro-Shiraz blends (the latter unoaked), while the Woodcutter's Semillon and Shiraz are lightly oaked, mouth-filling quaffers.

TORO DO *Castilla y León, Spain* Mainly red wines, which are robust, full of colour and tannin, and pretty high in alcohol. The main grape, Tinta de Toro, is a variant of Tempranillo, and there is some Garnacha. In the late 1990s, the arrival of some of Spain's top wineries gave the sleepy area a major boost, as did the 2008 sale of Numanthia-Termes to France's ritzy LVMH group. Best producers: Viña Bajoz, Campo Eliseo★★, Fariña★, Frutos Villar (Muruve★), Garanza, Matarredonda, Maurodos★★, Monte La Reina,

Numanthia-Termes★★, Pintia★★/VEGA SICILIA, Quinta de la Quietud★ Sobreño, Telmo RODRIGUEZ★★, Teso La Monja★, Toresanas/Bodegas de Crianza Castilla la Vieja★, Vega Saúco, Villaester.

TORRES *Penedès DO, Cataluña, Spain* Large family winery led by visionary Miguel Torres, making good to excellent wines with local grapes and international varieties. Viña Sol★ is a delightful, citrony quaffer, Viña Esmeralda★ (Muscat Blanc à Petits Grains and Gewürztraminer) is grapy and spicy, Fransola★★ (Sauvignon Blanc with some Parellada) is barrel-fermented yet leafy, and Milmanda★ is a delicate, expressive Chardonnay. Successful reds are soft, oaky and blackcurranty Gran Coronas★ (Tempranillo-Cabernet), fine, relatively rich though increasingly international Mas La Plana★★ (Cabernet Sauvignon), floral, perfumed Mas Borràs (Pinot Noir) and raisiny Atrium★ (Merlot). The top reds – Grans Muralles★★, a blend of Catalan grapes, and Reserva Real★★, a BORDEAUX-style blend – are fascinating, if expensive, and improve with every vintage. The new PRIORAT winery is producing a distinguished red, Perpetual★. The family also owns outstanding wineries in RIBERA DEL DUERO (Celeste), RIOJA (Ibéricos), Chile and California. Best years: (Mas La Plana) 2005 04 **03 01** 00 99 98 97 96 95 94.

MARIMAR TORRES ESTATE *Sonoma County, California, USA* The sister of Spanish winemaker Miguel TORRES has established her own winery in the cool Green Valley region of RUSSIAN RIVER VALLEY, only a few miles from the Pacific Ocean. She specializes in Chardonnay and Pinot Noir, the best of which are from the Don Miguel Vineyard: the Chardonnay★★ is big and intense, initially quite oaky, but able to age gracefully to fascinating maturity at 10 years old. Acero★★ is a minerally unoaked version. Recent vintages of full-flavoured Pinot Noir★★ are the best yet. Best years: (Pinot Noir) 2006 **05** 03 02 01.

MIGUEL TORRES *Curicó, Chile* TORRES' Chilean operation, which began in the early 1970s, is now producing its best ever wines: snappy Sauvignon Blanc★, grassy, fruity Santa Digna rosé★, weighty, blackcurranty Manso de Velasco Cabernet★★, exciting, sonorous old-Carignan-based Cordillera★★ and Conde de Superunda★★, a tremendous, dense blend based on Cabernet and Tempranillo. Best years: (Manso de Velasco) 2006 05 04 **03** 02 01 00 99.

CH. LA TOUR BLANCHE★★ *Sauternes AC, 1er Cru Classé, Bordeaux, France* This estate regained top form in the 1980s with the introduction of new oak barrels for fermentation, lower yields and greater selection. Full-bodied, rich and aromatic, it now ranks with the best of the Classed Growths. Second wine: Les Charmilles de la Tour Blanche. Best years: 2007 06 05 **04** 03 02 01 99 98 97 96 95 90 89 88 86.

CH. TOUR BOISÉE *Minervois AC, Languedoc, France* Top wines here are the red Jardin Secret★, Cuvée Marie-Claude★, aged for 12 months in barrel, the fruity Cuvée Marielle et Frédérique, and the white Cuvée Marie-Claude★, with a hint of Muscat Blanc à Petits Grains for added aroma. Best years: (red) (2009) 08 07 06 **05** 04 03 02.

CH. TOUR DES GENDRES *Bergerac AC, South-West France* Luc de Conti's BERGERACS are made with as much sophistication as the better Crus Classés of BORDEAUX. Generously fruity Moulin des Dames★ and the more serious la Gloire de Mon Père★★ reds are mostly Cabernet Sauvignon. Full, fruity and elegant Moulin des Dames★★ white is a blend of Sémillon, Sauvignon Blanc and Muscadelle. Best years: (reds) (2009) (08) **06** 05 04 01 00.

TOURAINE AC *Loire Valley, France* General AC in the central LOIRE; largely everyday wines to drink young, though its tradition for wines that could do with some aging is being restored by an ambitious minority, many of whose wines are labelled Vin de Pays du VAL DE LOIRE or even Vin de France. Most reds are from Gamay and, in hot years, can be juicy, rustic-fruited wines. There is a fair amount of red from Cabernets Sauvignon and Franc too, and some good Côt (Malbec). Best whites are Sauvignon Blanc, which can be a good substitute for SANCERRE at half the price, and the rare Romorantin; decent Chenin and Chardonnay. White and rosé sparkling wines are made by the traditional method but rarely have the distinction of the best VOUVRAY and CRÉMANT DE LOIRE. Best producers: Brulée, Clos de la Briderie★/Girault, La Chapinière, F CHIDAINE★, Clos Roche Blanche★, Corbillières★, J Delaunay★, Robert Denis★, A Fouassier, de la Garrelière★, L & B Jousset, J-C Mandard, Marcadet★, H Marionnet/la Charmoise★, J-F Merieux★, Michaud★, A & B Minchin, Octavie★, Pré Baron★, J Preys★, Ricard★, Sauvète. Best years: (reds) (2009) 08 **06 05 04 03 02**.

TOURIGA NACIONAL High-quality red Portuguese grape, rich in aroma and fruit. It contributes deep colour and tannin to PORT, and is rapidly increasing in importance for table wines throughout the country. Small but important plantings in South Africa enhance some of the impressive port styles emerging across the country.

TOWER ESTATE *Hunter Valley, New South Wales, Australia* This syndicate, founded by the late, great Len Evans, focuses on sourcing top-notch grapes from their ideal regions. So, there is powerful, stylish COONAWARRA Cabernet★★, top-flight BAROSSA Shiraz★★, fine floral CLARE Riesling★★, fruity ADELAIDE HILLS Sauvignon Blanc★ and classic Semillon★★, Shiraz★ and Chardonnay★ from the HUNTER VALLEY.

TRAPICHE *Mendoza, Argentina* The fine wine arm of Peñaflor, Argentina's biggest wine producer, where chief winemaker Daniel Pi has triumphantly turned quality around since taking over in 2002. Medalla Cabernet Sauvignon★★ is dense and satisfying, Malbec-Merlot blend Iscay★ is solid and rich, and the annual trio of single-vineyard Malbecs★★★ are stunning expressions of how good the grape can be. Origen label for fresh, attractive reds and whites.

TRÁS-OS-MONTES *Portugal* Impoverished north-eastern province, producing pretty rustic stuff. The Vinho Regional is Transmontano. Best producers: Quinta do Sobreiró de Cima, Casa de Valle Pradinhos.

TREBBIANO The most widely planted white Italian grape variety. As Trebbiano Toscano, it is the base for EST! EST!! EST!!! and any number of other neutral, dry whites, as well as much VIN SANTO. But there are other grapes masquerading under the Trebbiano name that aren't anything like as neutral. The most notable are the Trebbianos from SOAVE, LUGANA and ABRUZZO – grapes capable of full-bodied, fragrant wines. Called Ugni Blanc in France, where it is primarily used for distilling, as it should be.

TRENTINO *Italy* Wines from this northern Italian region rarely have the verve or perfume of ALTO ADIGE examples, but can make up for this with riper, softer flavours, where vineyard yields have been kept in check. The Trentino DOC covers 20 different styles of wine, including whites Pinot Bianco and Grigio, Chardonnay, Moscato Giallo, Müller-Thurgau and Nosiola, and reds Lagrein, Marzemino and Cabernet. Trento Classico is a DOC for CHAMPAGNE-method fizz. Best producers: N Balter★, N Bolognani★, La Cadalora★, Castel Noarna★, Cavit co-op, Cesconi★★, De Tarczal★, Dorigati, FERRARI★★, Graziano Fontana★, FORADORI★★, Letrari★, Longariva★, Conti Martini★, Masi Cantanghel★★, Maso Furli★, Maso Roveri★, Mezzacorona, Pojer & Sandri★, Pravis★, SAN LEONARDO★★★, Simoncelli★, E Spagnolli★, Vallarom★, La Vis co-op. See also TEROLDEGO ROTALIANO.

DOM. DE TRÉVALLON *Provence, France* Iconoclastic Eloi Dürrbach makes brilliant reds★★ (at best ★★★) – a tradition-busting blend of Cabernet Sauvignon and Syrah, mixing herbal wildness with a sweetness of blackberry, blackcurrant and black, black plums – and a tiny quantity of white★★★. Both are labelled Vin de Pays des BOUCHES-DU-RHÔNE. The reds age well, but are intriguingly drinkable in their youth. Best years: (reds) (2009) (08) (07) 06 05 04 **03 01 00 99 98**.

TRIMBACH *Alsace AC, Alsace, France* An excellent grower/merchant whose trademark is beautifully structured, emphatically dry, subtly perfumed elegance. Top wines are Gewurztraminer Cuvée des Seigneurs de Ribeaupierre★★, Riesling Cuvée Frédéric Émile★★ and Riesling Clos Ste-Hune★★★. Also very good Vendange Tardive★★ and Sélection de Grains Nobles★★. Trimbach basics are a bit pricey, but enjoyable in their austere manner. Best years: (Clos Ste-Hune) (2009) 08 07 05 **04 03 02 01 00 99 98 97 96 95 93 92 90**.

TRINITY HILL *Hawkes Bay, North Island, New Zealand* Passionate owner/ winemaker John Hancock produces many top wines from the Gimblett Gravels area, including flagship Homage Syrah★★★, co-fermented with a small amount of Viognier, an irresistibly soft yet peppery Syrah★★, an impressively proportioned Merlot★★, gutsy long-lived Cabernet Sauvignon-Merlot★, powerful The Gimblett★★, plus a big and complex Chardonnay★★. Trinity also makes a good job of less mainstream styles such as Montepulciano★, Tempranillo★, Arneis and Viognier★★. Also sweet Noble Viognier★★. Best years: (reds) (2009) 08 **07 06 04 02 00**.

TRITTENHEIM *Mosel, Germany* Important village with some excellent vineyard sites, notably the Apotheke (pharmacy) and Leiterchen (little ladder). The wines are sleek, with crisp acidity and plenty of fruit. Best producers: Clüsserath-Eifel, Clüsserath-Weiler★, GRANS-FASSIAN★★, Josef Rosch★. Best years: (2009) 08 07 **06 05 04 02 01**.

CH. TROPLONG-MONDOT★★ *St-Émilion Grand Cru AC, 1er Grand Cru Classé, Bordeaux, France* Owner Christine Valette has been producing quality wines at this property since the mid-1980s. Her reward – elevation to Premier Grand Cru Classé in 2006. The wines are powerfully structured and mouthfillingly textured for long aging. Best years: 2008 07 06 05 **04 03 02 01 00 99 98 96 95 90 89**.

CH. TROTANOY★★ *Pomerol AC, Bordeaux, France* This POMEROL estate (like PÉTRUS and LATOUR-À-POMEROL) has benefited from the brilliant touch of the MOUEIX family. Back on form after a dip in the mid-80s (due to lots of replanting). Best years: 2008 07 06 05 04 **03 02 01 00 98 96 95 90 89**.

TUA RITA *Tuscany, Italy* Since the early 1990s, this estate in the MAREMMA has established itself at the top of the Italian Merlot tree with Redigaffi★★★; Cabernet-Merlot blend Giusto di Notri★★ is almost as renowned. Best years: (2009) (08) 07 06 **05 04 03** 01 00 99 98 97 96 95.

CAVE DE TURCKHEIM *Alsace AC, Alsace, France* Important co-op with good basics in all varieties. The Reserve tier of all wines merits ★, while Brand★, Hengst★★ and Ollwiller★ bottlings are rich and concentrated. Reds, rosés and CRÉMANT D'ALSACE★ are consistent. Best years: (Grand Cru Gewurztraminer) (2009) **07 05 04 02** 01 00 99 98 97 95.

TURLEY *Napa Valley AVA, California, USA* Larry Turley's ultra-ripe Zinfandels★★, from a number of old vineyards, are either praised for their profound power and depth or damned for their tannic, high-alcohol, PORT-like nature. Petite Sirah★★ is similarly built. Best years: (Zins) (2008) 07 06 **05 04 03 02 01 00**.

TURSAN VDQS *South-West France* These wines are made on the edge of les Landes, the pine-forested area south of Bordeaux. The white is made, unusually, from the Baroque grape; it is clean, crisp and refreshing. Reds are Tannat-based with increasing proportions of the Cabernets. All for drinking young. Best producers: Baron de Bachen★, Dulucq★, Tursan co-op.

TUSCANY *Italy* Tuscany's rolling hills, clad with vines, olive trees and cypresses, have produced wine since at least Etruscan times. Today, its many DOC/DOCGs are based on the red Sangiovese grape and are led by CHIANTI CLASSICO, BRUNELLO DI MONTALCINO and VINO NOBILE DI MONTEPULCIANO, as well as famous Super-Tuscans like ORNELLAIA and TIGNANELLO. The term 'Super-Tuscan' was coined in the 1980s by journalists, who applied it to wines which, despite their superior quality and use of expensive equipment in the winery, did not satisfy the restrictive local DOC regulations (usually Chianti) and therefore had to be labelled Vino da Tavola. In the 1990s the wine laws changed and the majority of Super-Tuscans are now sold under the regionwide IGT Toscana. White wines, despite sweet VIN SANTO, and the occasional excellent Chardonnay and Sauvignon, do not figure highly. See also BOLGHERI, CARMIGNANO, MAREMMA, MONTECARLO, MORELLINO DI SCANSANO, ROSSO DI MONT-ALCINO, ROSSO DI MONTEPULCIANO, SASSICAIA, SOLAIA, VERNACCIA DI SAN GIMIGNANO.

TYRRELL'S *Hunter Valley, New South Wales, Australia* Top-notch family-owned company with prime HUNTER vineyards celebrated its 150th anniversary in 2008. It is expanding into COONAWARRA, MCLAREN VALE and HEATHCOTE, with impressive results. Comprehensive range, from good-value quaffers (Old Winery★, Lost Block★) to excellent Vat 47 Chardonnay★★★ and Vat 8 Shiraz★. Semillon is the speciality, with 4 single-vineyard wines (all ★★) – Lost Block, Stevens, Belford and the rare HVD – and, best of all, the superb Vat 1★★★. Best years: (Vat I Semillon) (2009) (08) (2007) 05 **04 03 02** 01 00 99 98 97 96 95 94 93 92 91 90 89 87 86 77 76 75; (Vat 47 Chardonnay) (2009) 08 07 06 05 **04 03 02** 01 00 99 98 97 96 95.

UGNI BLANC See TREBBIANO.

UMATHUM *Frauenkirchen, Neusiedlersee, Burgenland, Austria* Resisting the trend in Austria toward heavily oaked blockbuster reds, Josef Umathum emphasizes finesse and sheer drinkability. The single-vineyard Ried Hallebühl★★ is usually his top wine, but the St Laurent Vom Stein★ and the Zweigelt-dominated Haideboden★ sometimes match it in quality. Best years: (reds) (2008) 07 06 **04 03** 01.

UMBRIA *Italy* Wine production in this region is dominated by ORVIETO, accounting for almost 70% of DOC wines. However, some of the most characterful wines are reds from Torgiano and MONTEFALCO. Latest interest centres on international-style reds made by the ubiquitous Riccardo Cotarella at estates such as Pieve del Vescovo (Lucciaio★★), La Carraia (Fobiano★★), Lamborghini (Campoleone★★) and La Palazzola (Rubino★★).

UNDURRAGA *Maipo, Chile* A long-established family winery that seemed stuck in old ways, making unexciting offerings. But new management in 2008 has brought radical change and an injection of quality. Wines in the T.H.★ (Terroir Hunter) and Sibaris ranges are transforming the reputation of the winery, aided by the consultancy of Alvaro Espinoza. There has been considerable investment in sparkling wine production.

ÜRZIG *Mosel, Germany* Middle MOSEL village with the famous red slate Würzgarten (spice garden) vineyard tumbling spectacularly down to the river and producing marvellously spicy and long-lived Riesling. Best producers: J J Christoffel★★, Jos. Christoffel★★, Erbes★, Dr LOOSEN★★★, Molitor★★, Mönchhof★, Pauly-Bergweiler★, S A PRÜM, Dr Weins-Prüm. Best years: (2009) 08 07 **06 05 04 03 02 01 99**.

UTIEL-REQUENA DO *Valencia, Spain* Renowned for its rosés, mostly from the Bobal grape. Reds, with Tempranillo often complementing Bobal, are on the up. The groundbreaking Mustiguillo★★ winery now has its own appellation, Vinos de la Tierra Terrerazo. Best producers: Coviñas, Gandía, Murviedro, Palmera (L'Angelet★), Torre Oria, Dominio de la Vega.

DOM. VACHERON *Sancerre AC, Loire Valley, France* Unusually for a SANCERRE domaine, Vacheron, now biodynamic, is more reputed for its Pinot Noir reds than for its whites, but the whole range is currently on top form. Intense and expensive Belle Dame★★ red and Les Romains★★ white lead the way. The basic Sancerres – a cherryish red★ and a grapefruity white★ – have reserves of complexity that set them above the crowd. Best years: (Belle Dame) (2009) (07) **06 05 04 03 02 01 00 99**.

VACQUEYRAS AC *Rhône Valley, France* Red wines, mainly Grenache, account for 95% of production; they have a warm, spicy bouquet and a rich deep flavour that seems infused with the herbs and pine dust of the south and its plateau vineyards. Lovely to drink at 2–3 years, though good wines will age for 10 years. Best producers: Amouriers★, Burle, la Charbonnière★, Clos de Caveau, Clos des Cazaux★★, Couroulu★★, DELAS★, Font de Papier★, la Fourmone★, la Garrigue★, JABOULET★, Alain Jaume, Monardière★, Montirius★, Montmirail★, Montvac★, Ondines, Perrin & Fils, SANG DES CAILLOUX★★, Tardieu-Laurent★, la Tourade★, Ch. des Tours★. Best years: 2009 **07 06 05 04 03 01 99 98**.

VAL DE LOIRE, VIN DE PAYS DU *Loire Valley, France* Replaces Vin de Pays du Jardin de la France with effect from the 2007 vintage. It covers all 14 designated wine-producing regions of the LOIRE VALLEY – over 7,300ha (18,000 acres), accounting for around 500,000hl of wine. Key whites are Sauvignon Blanc, Chardonnay and Chenin Blanc, with some Grolleau Gris, Melon de Bourgogne, Folle Blanche and Pinot Blanc. The focus for reds is Gamay, Cabernets Franc and Sauvignon, with some Pinot Noir. It is increasingly a refuge for ambitious producers whose wines punch well above the weight of their appellation, especially in TOURAINE. Best producers: Ampelidae, M Angeli/Sansonnière★★, C Battais, S Bernaudeau, l'ECU★, Ch. Gaillard, la Garrelière, La Grange aux Belles, Henry Marionnet★, Alphonse MELLOT★, J-F Merieau★, RAGOTIÈRE★★, Ricard, Robinot★.

VAL D'ORBIEU, LES VIGNERONS DU *Languedoc-Roussillon, France* One of France's largest wine-exporting companies, selling more than 20 million cases a year. Membership includes several top co-ops (Cucugnan, Cuxac, Montredon, Ribaute) and individual producers (Dom. de Fontsainte, Ch. la VOULTE-GASPARETS). Its upmarket blended wines (Cuvée Chouette★, Chorus★, Elysices★, la Cuvée Mythique★) are a mix of traditional Mediterranean varieties with Cabernet or Merlot.

VALAIS *Switzerland* Swiss canton flanking the Rhône. Between Martigny and Sierre the valley turns north-east, creating an Alpine suntrap, and this short stretch of terraced vineyard land provides many of Switzerland's most individual wines from Fendant, Johannisberger (Silvaner), Pinot Noir and Gamay, and several stunning examples from Syrah, Chardonnay, Ermitage (Marsanne) and Petite Arvine. **Best producers:** Bonvin★, Chappaz★, Cina★, G Clavien★, Cottagnoud★, Dorsaz★, Jean-René Germanier★, Adrian Mathier★, S Maye★, Mercier★, Dom. du Mont d'Or★, Provins, Rouvinez★, M Zufferey★.

CH. VALANDRAUD★★ *St-Émilion Grand Cru AC, Bordeaux, France* The precursor of the 'garage wine' sensation in ST-ÉMILION, a big, rich, extracted wine from low yields, from grapes mainly grown in different parcels around St-Émilion. The core of the wine has been a top-quality limestone-based property and we can now see an impressive, consistent Valandraud style developing. Also a white Blanc de Valandraud from 2003. **Best years:** 2008 07 06 05 04 **03 02** 01 00 99 98 96 95.

VALDEPEÑAS DO *Castilla-La Mancha, Spain* Valdepeñas offers some of Spain's best inexpensive oak-aged reds, but there is an increasing number of unoaked, fruit-forward reds as well. In fact, there are more whites than reds, at least some of them modern, fresh and fruity. **Best producers:** Miguel Calatayud, Los Llanos, Luís Megía, Real, Félix Solís, Casa de la Viña.

VALDESPINO *Jerez y Manzanilla DO, Andalucía, Spain* New owner Grupo Estévez (Marqués del Real Tesoro, Tío Mateo) is probably the quality leader in Jerez today, and the exemplary character of Valdespino's sherries appears unaffected by the change of ownership. Fino Inocente★★ (can be ★★★), Palo Cortado Cardenal★★★, Pedro Ximénez Niños★★★ and dry Amontillado Coliseo★★★ are stunning examples of sherry's different styles.

VALDIVIESO *Curicó, Chile* Important winery, finally getting back on track after a few lean years. Varietals are attractive and direct, Reserves from cooler regions a definite step up, and Single Vineyard Chardonnay★ and Malbec★ are quite impressive. Multi-varietal, multi-vintage blend Caballo Loco★★ (mad horse) is always fascinating and unpredictable, and Eclat★★, based on old Carignan, is chewy and rich.

VALENCIA *Spain* The best-known wines from Valencia DO are the inexpensive, sweet, grapy Moscatels. Simple, fruity whites, reds and rosés are also good. Alicante DO to the south produces a little-known treasure, the Fondillón dry or semi-dry fortified wine, as well as a cluster of wines made by a few quality-conscious modern wineries. Monastrell (Mourvèdre) is the main red grape variety. **Best producers:** (Valencia) J Belda, Rafael Cambra★, Heretat de Cesilia★, Cherubino Valsangiacomo (Marqués de Caro), Enguera, Gandía, Los Pinos★, Murviedro, Celler del Roure★; (Alicante) Bernabé Navarro★, Bocopa★, Gutiérrez de la Vega (Casta Diva Muscat★★), Laderas de Pinoso★, Enrique Mendoza★★, Salvador Poveda★, Primitivo Quiles★. See also UTIEL-REQUENA.

VALL LLACH *Priorat DOCa, Spain* This tiny winery, owned by Catalan folk singer Lluís Llach, has joined the ranks of the best PRIORAT producers with its powerful reds★★ dominated by old-vine Cariñena. Best years: (2006) 05 04 03 **01 00 99 98**.

VALLE D'AOSTA *Italy* Tiny Alpine valley sandwiched between PIEDMONT and the French Alps in northern Italy. The regional DOC covers 17 wine styles, referring either to a specific grape variety (like Gamay or Pinot Nero) or to a delimited region like Donnaz, a northern extension of Piedmont's Carema, producing a light red from steeply sloping Nebbiolo vineyards. Perhaps the finest wine from this valley is the sweet Chambave Moscato. Best producers: R Anselmet★, C Charrère/Les Crêtes★, La Crotta di Vegneron★, Grosjean, Institut Agricole Regional★, Onze Communes co-op, Ezio Voyat★.

VALLE CENTRAL See CENTRAL VALLEY, Chile.

VALPOLICELLA DOC *Veneto, Italy* Styles range from a light, cherryish red to dense, burly AMARONE and rich, PORT-like RECIOTO. Most of the better examples are Valpolicella Classico Superiore from the hills north-west of Verona and are made predominantly from Corvina and Corvinone grapes, plus Rondinella. The most concentrated, ageworthy examples are made either from a particular vineyard, or by refermenting the wine on the skins and lees of the Amarone, a style called *ripasso*, or by using a portion of dried grapes. Best producers: Accordini★, ALLEGRINI★★★, Bertani★, Brigaldara★, Brunelli★, BUSSOLA★★★, Michele Castellani★, Cecilia Beretta★, Valentina Cubi★, DAL FORNO★★★, Guerrieri-Rizzardi★, MASI★, Mazzi★, QUINTARELLI★★★, Le Ragose★, Le Salette★, Serègo Alighieri★, Speri★, Tedeschi★, Villa Monteleone★, VIVIANI★★, Zenato★, Zeni★. Best years: (Valpolicella Superiore) (2008) **06 04 03 01 00 97 95 93 90**.

VALTELLINA SUPERIORE DOCG *Lombardy, Italy* Red wine produced on the precipitous slopes of northern LOMBARDY. There is a basic light Valtellina DOC red, made from at least 90% Nebbiolo (here called Chiavennasca), but the best wines are Valtellina Superiore DOCG under sub-zonal names like Grumello, Inferno, Sassella and Valgella. From top vintages the wines are attractively perfumed and approachable. Sfursat or Sforzato is a dense, high-alcohol AMARONE-like red (up to 14.5%) made from semi-dried grapes. Best producers: La Castellina★, Enologica Valtellinese★, Fay★, Nino Negri★, Nera★, Rainoldi★, Conti Sertoli Salis★, Triacca★. Best years: (2009) (08) 07 06 **04 03 01 99 98 97**.

VAN VOLXEM *Wiltingen, Mosel, Germany* Roman Niewodniczanski bought this estate, with its great old vineyards in Scharzhofberg and Wiltinger Gottesfuss, in 2000. His style, off-dry and opulent, is atypical and controversial, but often ★★. Best years: (2009) 08 07 **06 05 04 03**.

CH. VANNIÈRES *Bandol AC, Provence, France* Leading BANDOL estate, owned by the Boisseaux family since the 1950s. In recent years, wood has replaced cement tanks, wines are bottled unfiltered, and the percentage of Mourvèdre has gone from 50 to 95. Besides red Bandol★★, Vannières produces CÔTES DE PROVENCE and vin de pays. Best years: 2008 07 06 05 **04 01 00 98**.

VASSE FELIX *Margaret River, Western Australia* MARGARET RIVER's first vineyard and winery turned 40 in 2007. New vineyards have been purchased in Wilyabrup (mainly for Cabernet) and Karridale (for whites) and the winery is clearly focused on what Margaret River does best: Cabernet, Chardonnay and Semillon-Sauvignon. Even 20-year-old Shiraz vines are being ripped up. The flagship Heytesbury Chardonnay★★ is tighter, leaner and finer than before, while the powerful Cabernet-blend red Heytesbury★★ shows greater elegance. There's a decadently rich Cabernet Sauvignon★ and oak-led Shiraz★, and the regular Chardonnay★ is pleasurable drinking for a modest price. **Best years:** (Heytesbury red) (2009) (08) 07 05 04 **01 99 97 96 95**.

VAUD *Switzerland* The Vaud's main vineyards border Lake Geneva (Lac Léman), with 5 sub-regions: la Côte, Lavaux, CHABLAIS, Côtes de l'Orbe-Bonvillars, Vully. Fresh light white wines are made from Chasselas; at DÉZALEY it gains depth. Reds from Gamay and Pinot Noir. **Best producers:** Henri Badoux, Louis Bovard★, Conne, Dubois, Obrist, J & P Testuz★.

VAVASOUR *Marlborough, South Island, New Zealand* First winery in Marlborough's AWATERE VALLEY, now enjoying spectacular success. One of New Zealand's best Chardonnays★★, a fine, lush Pinot Noir★★ and palate-tingling, oak-tinged Sauvignon Blanc★★. Second-label Dashwood is also top stuff, particularly the tangy Sauvignon Blanc★★. **Best years:** (Sauvignon Blanc) **2009 07 06**.

VEENWOUDEN *Paarl WO, South Africa* Reds based on BORDEAUX varieties remain the focus of attention: sumptuous, well-oaked Merlot★★ and firm and silky-fruited Veenwouden Classic★★, more recently with better freshness and structure. Also an expressive, supple-tannined Syrah★. A tiny quantity of fine Chardonnay★ is made. **Best years:** (Merlot, Classic) 2006 **04 03 02 00 99**.

VEGA SICILIA *Ribera del Duero DO, Castilla y León, Spain* Among Spain's most expensive wines, rich, fragrant, complex and very slow to mature, and by no means always easy to appreciate. This estate was the first in Spain to introduce French varieties, and almost a quarter of the vines are now Cabernet Sauvignon, two-thirds are Tempranillo and the rest Malbec and Merlot. Vega Sicilia Unico★★★ – the top wine – is aged in wood for 5 or 6 years. Second wine: Valbuena★★. A subsidiary winery produces the more modern Alión★, and the new Pintia★★ winery makes some of the most distinctive wines in TORO. **Best years:** (Unico) 1999 96 **95 94 91 90 89 87 86 85 83 82 81 80 79 76 75 74 70 68**.

VELICH *Neusiedlersee, Burgenland, Austria* Heinz Velich makes Austria's most mineral and sophisticated Chardonnay★★ from old vines in the Tiglat vineyard. Also spectacular ★★ and ★★★ dessert wines. **Best years:** (Tiglat Chardonnay) (2009) 08 **07 06 05 04**; (sweet) (2009) 08 07 **06 05 04 02 01**.

VENETO *Italy* Veneto is among the most prolific production zones in Italy, taking in as it does the Veronese denominations of VALPOLICELLA, BARDOLINO and SOAVE as well as DOCs from Garda (e.g. BIANCO DI CUSTOZA) in the west to Piave on the border with FRIULI GRAVE. Pretty well every wine style is covered somewhere in Veneto: still and sparkling, light to full reds, dry to sweet whites, from native grapes and international grapes. With its port of Venice and crossroads-cities like Verona linking it with points south and north, Veneto has become the most cosmopolitan of regions, though it retains more than its share of local peculiarities such as the dried-grape method of producing so-called *vini da meditazione*. See also AMARONE, RECIOTO DELLA VALPOLICELLA, RECIOTO DI SOAVE and PROSECCO.

VIÑA VENTISQUERO *Maipo, Chile* State-of-the-art, ecologically friendly winery started in the late 1990s. Flagship wine in the Ventisquero range is the Grey Syrah. Also a range under the Yali brand. Pangea★★, from the Apalta region of COLCHAGUA, is a joint venture wine with the Australian John Duval (who made Penfolds GRANGE famous).

VENTOUX AC *Rhône Valley, France* Vineyards around the southern and western slopes of Mt Ventoux. When well made, the red wines have lovely juicy fruit, or in the case of JABOULET and Pesquié, some real stuffing. Good, fresh rosés. Best producers: Anges★, Bedoin co-op, Brusset, Cascavel★, Cave Courtoise★, La Croix des Pins★, Fenouillet, Ferme St-Pierre, Font-Sane, Grand Jacquet, Paul JABOULET★, Cave de Lumières★, la Martinelle★, le Murmurium, Pesquié★, Unang, Valcombe★, Vidal-Fleury, la Vieille Ferme. Best years: (reds) **2009 07**.

VERDICCHIO DEI CASTELLI DI JESI, VERDICCHIO DI MATELICA DOC *Marche, Italy* Verdicchio, grown in the hills near the Adriatic around Jesi and in the Apennine foothills enclave of Matelica, has blossomed into central Italy's most promising white variety. When fresh and fruity, Verdicchio (aka Trebbiano di LUGANA or Trebbiano di SOAVE) is the ideal wine with fish, but some Verdicchio can age into a white of surprising depth of flavour. A few producers, notably Garofoli with Serra Fiorese★★, age it in oak, but even without wood it can develop an almost Burgundy-like complexity. A little is made sparkling. Best producers: (Jesi) Brunori★, Bucci★★, Colonnara★, Coroncino★★, Fazi Battaglia★, Garofoli★, Mancinelli★, Monte Schiavo★★, Santa Barbara★, Sartarelli★★, Tavignano★, Terre Cortesi Moncaro★, Umani Ronchi★, Fratelli Zaccagnini★; (Matelica) Belisario★, Bisci★, Mecella★, La Monacesca★★.

VIGNOBLE DES VERDOTS *Bergerac AC and Monbazillac AC, South-West France* David Fourtout's BERGERACS are some of the best, from the everyday, good-value Clos des Verdots★ range to Château les Tours des Verdots★ (barrique-aged), to the top of the tree Verdots★★ and Le Vin★. Outstanding MONBAZILLAC★★. Best years: (reds) (2009) (08) **06 05 04 01 00**.

VERGELEGEN *Stellenbosch WO, South Africa* This historic farm's Sauvignon Blancs are considered benchmarks: the regular bottling★★ is aggressive and racy, streaked with tropical fruit: the single-vineyard Reserve★★ is flinty, dry and fascinating. Topping both is barrel-fermented white Vergelegen★★, a Semillon-Sauvignon blend that ages superbly for at least 8 years. There is also a ripe-textured, stylish Chardonnay Reserve★★. Of the reds, Vergelegen★★★, a BORDEAUX blend, shows classic mineral intensity, and Merlot★★ and Cabernet Sauvignon★★ are often among South Africa's best. Single-vineyard Cabernet Sauvignon-based 'V'★★ is an attention-grabbing individual. Best years: (premium reds) (2007) 06 05 **04 03 02 01 00 99**.

VERGET *Mâconnais, Burgundy, France* *Négociant* house run by Jean-Marie Guffens-Heynen, with outstanding Premiers Crus and Grands Crus from the CÔTE D'OR, notably CHASSAGNE-MONTRACHET★★ and BÂTARD-MONTRACHET★★. Guffens-Heynen also has his own domaine, with excellent MÂCON-VILLAGES★★ and POUILLY-FUISSÉ★★. But beware, the wines are made in a very individualistic style. Best years: (2009) 08 **07 06 05**.

VERITAS See Rolf BINDER.

VERMENTINO The best dry white wines of SARDINIA generally come from the Vermentino grape. The best examples – full-bodied and flavoursome – tend to be from the north-east of the island, where the Vermentino di

310

Gallura DOCG zone is located. Vermentino di Sardegna DOC is lighter and less interesting. Vermentino is also grown in coastal areas of LIGURIA and TUSCANY, though here it generally lacks the complexity of Gallura. It is believed to be the same as Rolle, found in many blends in PROVENCE, but increasingly single varietal in the best white wines. Best producers: (Sardinia) ARGIOLAS★, Capichera★★, Cherchi★, Contini★, Gallura co-op★, Giogantinu★, Piero Mancini★, Pedra Majore★, Mura★, Santadi co-op★, SELLA & MOSCA★, Vermentino co-op★; (Provence) La Courtade★, Sarrins★.

VERNACCIA DI SAN GIMIGNANO DOCG *Tuscany, Italy* TUSCANY is not renowned for its whites, the most famous being this dry, variable and generally underwhelming wine made from the Vernaccia grape grown in the hills around the towered, tourist-infested town of San Gimignano. Up to 10% other grapes, e.g. Chardonnay, are allowed in the blend. There is a San Gimignano DOC for the zone's reds, though the best are sold as IGT Toscana. Best producers: Cà del Vispo★, Le Calcinaie★, Casale-Falchini★, V Cesani★, La Lastra (Riserva★), Melini (Le Grillaie★), Montenidoli★, G Panizzi★, Il Paradiso★, Pietrafitta★, La Rampa di Fugnano★, Guicciardini Strozzi★, Teruzzi & Puthod (Terre di Tufi★★), Casa alle Vacche★, Vagnoni★.

QUINTA DO VESÚVIO★★ *Port DOC, Douro, Portugal* A consistently top vintage PORT (and, now, DOURO wine★★) from the Symington stable that appears only when the high quality can be maintained. Best with at least 10 years' age. Best years: (Vintage) 2007 06 05 04 **03 01 00** 99 97 96 95 94 **92 91 90**.

VEUVE CLICQUOT *Champagne AC, Champagne, France* Owned by the LVMH luxury goods group, these CHAMPAGNES can still live up to the high standards set by the original Widow Clicquot at the beginning of the 19th century, although many are released too young. The non-vintage is full, toasty and satisfyingly weighty, or lean and raw, depending on your luck; the vintage★ used to be reliably impressive, but recent releases have shown none of the traditional Clicquot class. Look out for Veuve Clicquot Rare Vintage★★, recent releases of top older vintages. The de luxe Grande Dame★★★ is both powerful and elegant. Grande Dame Rosé★★★ is exquisite. Best years: 2002 **00 99 98** 96 **95 90 89** 88 85 82.

VICTORIA *Australia* Despite its relatively small area, Victoria has arguably more land suited to quality grape-growing than any other state in Australia, with climates ranging from hot Murray Darling and Swan Hill on the Murray River to cool MORNINGTON PENINSULA and GIPPSLAND in the south. The range of flavours is similarly wide and exciting. With more than 500 wineries, Victoria leads the boutique winery boom, particularly in Mornington Peninsula. See also BEECHWORTH, BENDIGO, CENTRAL VICTORIA, GEELONG, GRAMPIANS AND PYRENEES, HEATHCOTE, RUTHERGLEN, YARRA VALLEY.

VIEUX-CHÂTEAU-CERTAN★★ *Pomerol AC, Bordeaux, France* Slow-developing, tannic red with up to 30% Cabernet Franc and 10% Cabernet Sauvignon in the blend, which after 15–20 years finally resembles more a fragrant, refined MÉDOC than a hearty POMEROL. Best years: 2008 07 06 05 04 **02 01 00** 99 98 96 95 90 89 88 86 85.

DOM. DU VIEUX TÉLÉGRAPHE *Châteauneuf-du-Pape AC, Rhône Valley, France* The vines are some of the oldest in CHÂTEAUNEUF and the Grenache-based red★★★ is among the best, most complex wines of the RHÔNE VALLEY, and lives for 20 years. There is a small amount of white★★, which is rich and heavenly when very young; also ages well. Good second wine Télégramme. Also owns improving la Roquette★ in Châteauneuf and very fine les Pallières★★ in GIGONDAS. Best years: (reds) 2009 08 07 06 05 04 03 01 00 99 98 97 96 95 90 89 88.

VILLA MARIA *Auckland and Marlborough, New Zealand* Founder George Fistonich also owns Esk Valley and Vidal (both in HAWKES BAY). Villa Maria Reserve Merlot-Cabernet★★★, Reserve Merlot★★, Esk Valley The Terraces★★★ and Vidal Merlot-Cabernet★★ are superb. Syrahs are among New Zealand's best: Esk Valley and Villa Maria Reserve both ★★★, Vidal★★. Reserve Chardonnay from Vidal★★ and Villa Maria★★ are suave and serious. The Villa Maria range includes various MARLBOROUGH Sauvignon Blancs, with Clifford Bay Reserve★★, Wairau Reserve★★ and Taylors Pass★★ outstanding. Also from Marlborough, impressive Pinot Noir Reserve★★, Seddon Pinot Gris★, Reserve Riesling★ and stunning botrytized Noble Riesling★★★. Best years (Hawkes Bay reds) (2009) 08 **07** 06 04 02.

CH. DE VILLENEUVE *Saumur-Champigny AC, Loire Valley, France* The secret of this property's success lies in low yields, picked when properly ripe. First-class SAUMUR-CHAMPIGNY★, with concentrated, mineral Vieilles Vignes★★ and le Grand Clos★★. Ageworthy barrel-fermented Saumur Les Cormiers★★ develops Burgundian complexity. Best years: (2009) 08 06 05 04 03 02 01 97 96.

VILLIERA *Stellenbosch WO, South Africa* The speciality is Cap Classique sparklers (Monro Brut★, additive-free Brut Natural Chardonnay★). Still whites include Sauvignon Blanc (Bush Vine★), a consistent Riesling and 2 delicious Chenin Blancs★ with different degrees of oaking. Monro, a structured Merlot-led BORDEAUX blend, is best among the reds. Fired Earth★ is a tasty Late Bottled PORT style. Also 'mentor' to neighbouring M'hudi project (Pinotage★, Sauvignon Blanc★).

VIN SANTO *Tuscany, Italy* The 'holy wine' of TUSCANY can be one of the world's great sweet wines – but the term has been wantonly abused (happily the *liquoroso* version, made by adding alcohol to partially fermented must, is no longer recognized as a legitimate style). Made from grapes either hung from rafters or laid on mats to dry, the wines fermented and aged in small barrels (*caratelli*), for between 3 and 10 years should be nutty, oxidized, full of the flavours of dried apricots and crystallized orange peel, concentrated and long. Also made in UMBRIA, and in TRENTINO as Vino Santo using the Nosiola grape. Occasional rare red version. Best producers: Castello di AMA★, AVIGNONESI★★★, Fattoria di Basciano★★, Bindella★★, Cacchiano★, Capezzana★★, Fattoria del Cerro★★ Corzano e Paterno★★, FONTODI★★, ISOLE E OLENA★★★, Romeo★★, San Felice★★, San Gervasio★★, San Giusto a Rentennano★★★, SELVAPIANA★★★, Villa Sant'Anna★★, Villa di Vetrice★, VOLPAIA★.

VIÑAS DEL VERO *Somontano DO, Aragón, Spain* Minerally unoaked Chardonnay and its toasty barrel-fermented counterpart★ are joined by more original whites such as Clarión★, a blend of Chardonnay Gewürztraminer and Macabeo. Top reds are Secastilla★★ (old-vine Garnacha with some Syrah), Gran Vos★ (Merlot-Cabernet-Pinot Noir) and the red blend made by its subsidiary Blecua★★.

VINHO VERDE DOC *Minho and Douro Litoral, Portugal* 'Vinho Verde' can be red or white – 'green' only in the sense of being young. The whites are the most widely seen outside Portugal and range from sulphured and acidic to aromatic, flowery and fruity. Some that fall outside the DOC regulations are sold as Vinho Regional Minho (Quinta do CÔTTO's Paço de Teixeiró). Best producers: Quinta de Alderiz, Quinta do Ameal★, Quinta da Aveleda, Quinta de Azevedo★★/SOGRAPE, Quinta da Baguinha★, Encostas dos Castelos, Quinta de Gomariz, Monção co-op (Deu la Deu Alvarinho★, Muralhas de Monção), Muros de Melgaço★, Quintas de Melgaço, Palácio de Brejoeira, Casa de Sezim★, Quinta de Simães, Quinta de Soalheiro★★, Quinta do Tamariz★.

VINO NOBILE DI MONTEPULCIANO DOCG *Tuscany, Italy* The 'noble wine' from the hills around the town of Montepulciano is made from the Sangiovese grape, known locally as Prugnolo Gentile, with the help of a little Canaiolo and Mammolo (and increasingly, Merlot). At its best, it combines the power and structure of BRUNELLO DI MONTALCINO with the finesse and complexity found in top CHIANTI. Unfortunately, the best was a rare beast until relatively recently; improvement since the 1990s has been impressive. The introduction of what is essentially a second wine, ROSSO DI MONTEPULCIANO, has certainly helped. Best producers: AVIGNONESI★★, Bindella★, BOSCARELLI★★, La Braccesca★★/ANTINORI, Le Casalte★, La Ciarliana★, Contucci★★, Dei★★, Del Cerro★★, Fassati★★, Gracciano★, Il Macchione★, Nottola★★, Palazzo Vecchio★★, POLIZIANO★★, Redi★, Romeo★, Salcheto★★, Trerose★ (Simposio★★), Valdipiatta★. Best years: (2009) (08) 07 06 **04 03 01 00 99 97**.

VINSOBRES AC *Rhône Valley, France* Southern RHÔNE village whose hallmark is clear fruit. A good, fresh area for Syrah, which goes into the blend with Grenache. Best producers: Chaume-Arnaud★, Constant-Duquesnoy, Coriançon★, Deurre★, Gramenon, Jaume★, Moulin★, Perrin & Fils★, Rouanne, la Vinsobraise co-op. Best years: (reds) 2009 **07 06 05 04 03**.

VIOGNIER Traditionally grown only in the northern RHÔNE VALLEY, most famously for the rare and expensive wines of CONDRIEU, Viognier is traditionally a poor yielder, prone to disease and difficult to vinify. The wine can be delicious: pear-fleshy, apricotty with a soft, almost waxy texture, usually a fragrance of spring flowers and sometimes a taste like crème fraîche. New, higher-yielding clones are now being grown in LANGUEDOC-ROUSSILLON, Ardèche and the southern Rhône as well as in Spain, Switzerland, Italy, Austria, the USA, Argentina, Chile, Australia, New Zealand and South Africa. Traditionally used in CÔTE-RÔTIE to co-ferment with Syrah (Shiraz); this practice is now becoming popular in other parts of the world. It is also increasingly being used as a blender with other, more neutral, white varieties to add perfume, texture and fruit, and often dominates proceedings.

VIRÉ-CLESSÉ AC *Mâconnais, Burgundy, France* Appellation created in 1998 out of 2 of the best MÂCON-VILLAGES. Originally, the rules outlawed wines with residual sugar, thus excluding Jean Thévenet's extraordinary cuvées, but common sense has prevailed. Best producers: A Bonhomme★★, Bret Brothers★, Cave de Viré★, Ch. de Viré★, Chaland★★, E Gillet★, Roally★, Thévenet★★. Best years: (2009) **08 07 06 05**.

VIRGINIA *USA* Virginia has a rapidly growing and improving wine industry, with more than 160 wineries and 6 AVAs. Aromatic Viognier and earthy Cabernet Franc show most promise, and varietal Petit Verdot produces some enticingly aromatic reds. Many growers continue to tinker with other varieties such as Petit Manseng, Nebbiolo and Tannat, and Sauvignon Blanc can be surprisingly good. Virginia is also producing some distinguished fizz. Best producers: BARBOURSVILLE★, Breaux, Chrysalis, HORTON★, Keswick, Kluge, LINDEN★, Pearmund★, Michael Shaps★, Rockbridge, Veritas★, White Hall (Viognier★).

VIVIANI *Valpolicella DOC, Veneto, Italy* Claudio Viviani's 9ha (22-acre) site is turning out some beautifully balanced VALPOLICELLA. The top AMARONE, Casa dei Bepi★★★, is a model of enlightened modernity, and the Valpolicella Classico Superiore Campo Morar★★ and RECIOTO★★ are of a similar quality. Best years: (2009) (08) 06 **04 03 01 00**.

ROBERTO VOERZIO *Barolo DOCG, Piedmont, Italy* One of the best of the new wave of BAROLO producers. Dolcetto (Priavino★) is successful, as is Vignaserra★★ – barrique-aged Nebbiolo with a little Cabernet – and the outstanding BARBERA D'ALBA Riserva Vigneto Pozzo dell'Annunziata★★★. Barriques are also used for fashioning his Barolo, but such is the quality and concentration of fruit that the oak does not overwhelm. Single-vineyard examples made in the best years include Brunate★★, Cerequio★★★, La Serra★★ and Riserva Capalot★★★. Best years: (Barolo) (2009) (08) (07) 06 **04 03 01 00 99 98 97 96 95 93 91 90 89 88 85**.

COMTE GEORGES DE VOGÜÉ *Chambolle-Musigny, Côte de Nuits, Burgundy, France* De Vogüé owns substantial holdings in 2 Grands Crus, BONNES-MARES★★★ and MUSIGNY★★★, as well as in Chambolle's top Premier Cru, les Amoureuses★★★. It is the sole producer of minute quantities of Musigny Blanc★★, but because of recent replanting the wine is currently being sold as (very expensive) BOURGOGNE Blanc. Best years: (Musigny) (2009) 08 07 06 05 03 **00 99 98 97 96 93 91 90**.

VOLNAY AC *Côte de Beaune, Burgundy, France* Some of the most elegant red wines of the CÔTE DE BEAUNE; attractive when young, good examples can age well. The top Premiers Crus are Caillerets, Champans, Clos des Chênes, Santenots and Taillepieds. Best producers: M Ampeau★★, d'ANGERVILLE★★, H Boillot★, J-M Boillot★★, J-M Bouley★, COCHE-DURY★★, V GIRARDIN★★, LAFARGE★★★, LAFON★★, Matrot★★, MONTILLE★★★, N POTEL★★, J Prieur★★, N Rossignol★★, J Voillot★★. Best years: (2009) 08 07 05 03 **02 99 98 96 95 91 90**.

CASTELLO DI VOLPAIA *Chianti Classico DOCG, Tuscany, Italy* One of the first great estates to emerge into quality production in the 1970s, making some elegant, relatively perfumed reds from grapes grown on high, steep, south-facing, rather sandy vineyards. CHIANTI CLASSICO★ is light, intense, exceeded by the fine Riserva★★, Coltassala★★ (95% Sangiovese 5% Mammolo) and Balifico★★ (Sangiovese-Cabernet). Good but not great VIN SANTO★. Riccardo Cotarella (see FALESCO) is consultant enologist.

VON SIEBENTHAL *Aconcagua, Chile* Tiny boutique winery situated almost opposite the gates of ERRÁZURIZ founded by Swiss lawyer Mauro von Siebenthal, who fell in love with the region. Eclectic range of reds of which the Carabantes (Syrah), Montelig★ (Cabernet) and Parcela #7★★(Cabernet-Merlot-Cabernet Franc) are consistently good. New addition Toknar★★ is a rich and vibrant 100% Petit Verdot.

VOSNE-ROMANÉE AC *Côte de Nuits, Burgundy, France* The greatest village in the CÔTE DE NUITS, with 6 Grands Crus and 13 Premiers Crus (notably les Malconsorts, aux Brûlées and les Suchots) that are often as good as other villages' Grands Crus. The quality of Vosne's village wine is also high. In good years the wines need at least 6 years' aging, but 10–15 would be better. **Best producers:** R Arnoux★★★, Cacheux-Sirugue★★, S CATHIARD★★★, B Clavelier★★, Eugénie★★ (formerly Engel), GRIVOT★★★, Anne GROS★★★, A-F GROS★★, M GROS★★★, F Lamarche★★, Dom. LEROY★★★, LIGER-BELAIR★★★, MÉO-CAMUZET★★★, Mugneret-Gibourg★★, RION★★★, Dom. de la ROMANÉE-CONTI★★★, E Rouget★★★. **Best years:** (2009) 08 07 06 05 03 **02 01 00 99** 98 97 96 95 93 90.

VOUGEOT AC *Côte de Nuits, Burgundy, France* Outside the walls of CLOS DE VOUGEOT there are only 11ha (27 acres) of Premier Cru and 5ha (12 acres) of other vines. Look out for Premier Cru Les Cras (red) and the Clos Blanc de Vougeot, first planted with white grapes in 1110. **Best producers:** Bertagna★, Chopin★★, C Clerget★, VOUGERAIE★★. **Best years:** (reds) (2009) 08 07 06 05 **03 02 00 99**.

DOM. DE LA VOUGERAIE *Côte de Nuits, Burgundy, France* An estate created by Jean-Claude BOISSET in 1999 out of the numerous vineyards – often excellent but under-achieving – that came with Burgundy merchant houses acquired during his rise to prominence since 1964. Wines have been generally outstanding, notably Clos Blanc de VOUGEOT★★★, GEVREY-CHAMBERTIN les Évocelles★★, le MUSIGNY★★★ and Vougeot les Cras★★ reds. **Best years:** (reds) (2009) 08 07 06 05 **03 02**.

CH. LA VOULTE-GASPARETS *Corbières AC, Languedoc, France* CORBIÈRES with flavours of thyme and baked earth from old hillside vines. Cuvée Réservée★ and Romain Pauc★ can be drunk young, but age well. Also a white Corbières. **Best years:** (Romain Pauc) (2009) 08 07 06 **05 04 03 01**.

VOUVRAY AC *Loire Valley, France* Dry, medium-dry, sweet and sparkling wines from Chenin grapes east of Tours. The dry wines acquire beautifully rounded flavours after 6–8 years. Medium-dry wines, when well made from a single domaine, are worth aging for 20 years or more. Spectacular noble-rot-affected sweet wines can be produced when conditions are right. The fizz, Mousseux and Pétillant (bottled at lower pressure) is some of the LOIRE's best. **Best producers:** Aubuisières★★, Bourillon-Dorléans★★, C & P Breton, Champalou★★, F CHIDAINE★★, CLOS NAUDIN★★, la Fontainerie★, Gaudrelle★, Gautier★★, P Gendron★, Haute Borne/V Carême★, HUET★★★, Pichot★, F Pinon★★, Taille aux Loups★★/BLOT, Vigneau Chevreau★. **Best years:** (dry) 2008 **07 06**; (sweet) (2009) **04 03 02 01** 99 97 96 95 90 89.

VOYAGER ESTATE *Margaret River, Western Australia* Originally planted in 1978, owned since 92 by mining magnate Michael Wright and now run by his daughter, Alex. One of the most impressive cellar-door complexes in MARGARET RIVER. Stellar, oatmealy Chardonnay★★★, vibrant Sauvignon Blanc-Semillon★★ and grassy Sauvignon Blanc★. The Cabernet Sauvignon-Merlot★★ and Shiraz★ are regularly some of WESTERN AUSTRALIA's best.

WACHAU *Niederösterreich, Austria* This stunning 1500ha (3700-acre) stretch of the Danube is Austria's top region for dry whites, from Riesling and Grüner Veltliner. **Best producers:** Alzinger★★, F HIRTZBERGER★★★, Högl★★, Jamek★, KNOLL★★★, NIKOLAIHOF★★, F X PICHLER★★★, Rudi PICHLER★★, PRAGER★★★, Schmelz★★, Domäne Wachau★. **Best years:** (2009) 08 07 **06 05 04 03 02 01 00 99 98 97**.

WACHENHEIM *Pfalz, Germany*   Wine village made famous by the BÜRKLIN-WOLF estate, its best vineyards can produce rich yet beautifully balanced Rieslings. Best producers: Josef Biffar, BÜRKLIN-WOLF★★, Karl Schaefer★, J L WOLF★★. Best years: (2009) 08 07 **05 04 03 02 01 99**.

WAGRAM *Niederösterreich, Austria*   2800ha (7000-acre) wine region on both banks of the Danube, stretching from just north of Vienna west to S Pölten. Previously known as Donauland – the name changed in 2007 – Wagram is the source of fine Grüner Veltliners. Best producers: J Bauer★, K Fritsch★, Leth★, Bernhard Ott★★, Wimmer-Czerny★.

WAIHEKE ISLAND *North Island, New Zealand*   Goldwater pioneered wine-making on this island in Auckland harbour in the early 1980s; it is now home to over 30 wineries. Hot, dry ripening conditions make high-quality Cabernet-based reds that sell for high prices. Chardonnay, Sauvignon and Pinot Gris are now appearing, together with experimental plots of stunning Syrah and Viognier. Best producers: Goldwater★, MAN O'WAR★★, Mudbrick★, Obsidian★, Passage Rock★, STONYRIDGE★★★, Te Whau★. Best years: (reds) (2009) 08 07 **05 02**.

WALKER BAY WO *South Africa*   This maritime district on the south coast is home to a mix of grape varieties, but the holy grail of the majority is Pinot Noir, with the hub of activity in the Hemel en Aarde (heaven and earth) valley. Also steely Sauvignon Blanc, minerally Chardonnay and refined Pinotage. Best producers: Ashbourne★, Beaumont★, BOUCHARD FINLAYSON★, HAMILTON RUSSELL★★, Hermanuspietersfontein★, Newton Johnson★. Best years: (Pinot Noir) 2009 08 **07** 06 05 04 03 02 01.

WALLA WALLA VALLEY AVA *Washington State, USA*   Walla Walla has over 100 of WASHINGTON's wineries, but 55 have only been producing wine since 1999. Similarly, vineyard acreage, although only 5% of the state total, has trebled since 99 – and is still growing. If you think there's a gold-rush feel about this exciting area you wouldn't be far wrong. Best producers: ABEJA★, CAYUSE VINEYARDS★★, DUNHAM CELLARS★, K Vintners★, L'ECOLE NO. 41★★, LEONETTI CELLAR★★★, LONG SHADOWS VINTNERS★★, Northstar★, PEPPER BRIDGE WINERY★, Reininger★, WOODWARD CANYON★★.

WARRE *Port DOC, Douro, Portugal*   Part of the Symington group, with top-quality Vintage PORT★★ and a good 'off-vintage' port from Quinta da Cavadinha★★. LBV★★ is in the traditional, unfiltered style. Warrior★ is a reliable ruby and Otima a solid 10-year-old tawny; Otima★ 20-year-old is much better. Best years: (Vintage) 2007 **03 00 97 94 91 85 83 80 77 70 66 63**; (Cavadinha) 2001 **99 98 96 95 92 90 88 87 86 82 78**.

WARWICK *Stellenbosch WO, South Africa*   Warwick produces the complex Trilogy★ BORDEAUX-style blend and a refined, fragrant Cabernet Franc★. The Three Cape Ladies★ red blend includes Pinotage along with Cabernet Sauvignon, Merlot and 'fourth' lady, Shiraz. Whites are represented by an unwooded Sauvignon Blanc and full-bodied, lightly oaked Chardonnay★. Best years: (Trilogy) 2007 06 **05 04 03 02 01 00**.

WASHINGTON STATE *USA*   The second-largest premium wine-producing state in the US (after California), with more than 650 wineries. The chief growing areas are in irrigated high desert, east of the Cascade Mountains, where the COLUMBIA VALLEY AVA encompasses the smaller AVAs of YAKIMA VALLEY, WALLA WALLA VALLEY, Wahluke Slope, Horse Heaven Hills, Rattlesnake Hills, Red Mountain, Columbia Gorge, Snipes Mountain and Lake Chelan. Although the heat is not as intense as in California, long

ummer days with extra hours of sunshine due to the northern latitude seem
o increase the intensity of fruit flavours and result in both red and white
vines of great depth. Cabernets Sauvignon and Franc, Merlot, Syrah,
Chardonnay, Semillon and Riesling can produce very good wines here.

GEOFF WEAVER *Adelaide Hills, South Australia* Low-yielding vines at Geoff
Weaver's Lenswood vineyard produce top-quality fruit, from which he
crafts limy Riesling★★, crisply gooseberryish Sauvignon★★ and stylish
cool-climate Chardonnay★★. Pinot Noir is promising.

WEGELER *Bernkastel, Mosel; Oestrich-Winkel, Rheingau; Deidesheim, Pfalz, Germany*
The Wegeler family's 3 estates are dedicated primarily to Riesling, and
dry wines make up the bulk of production. Whether dry or naturally
sweet Auslese, the best merit ★★ and will develop well with 5 or more
years of aging. Best years: (Mosel) (2009) 08 07 **06 05 04 02 01 99 98**.

WEHLEN *Mosel, Germany* Village whose steep Sonnenuhr vineyard
produces some of Germany's most intense Rieslings. Best producers:
Kerpen, Dr LOOSEN★★★, MOLITOR★★, J J PRÜM★★★, S A PRÜM★, Max Ferd
RICHTER★★, SELBACH-OSTER★★, Studert-Prüm, WEGELER★, Dr Weins-Prüm★.
Best years: (2009) 08 07 **06 04 03 02 01 99 98 97**.

ROBERT WEIL *Kiedrich, Rheingau, Germany* Huge investment from Japanese
drinks giant SUNTORY, coupled with Wilhelm Weil's devotion to quality,
has clearly paid off, showing particular flair with majestic sweet Auslese,
Beerenauslese and Trockenbeerenauslese Rieslings★★★. Other styles are
★, sometimes ★★, but less remarkable than the sweet wines. Best years:
(2009) 08 07 **06 05 04 03 02 01 99 98**.

WEINBACH *Alsace AC, Alsace, France* This Kaysersberg estate is run by the
Faller family. The extensive range (which includes cuvées Théo, Ste-
Catherine and Laurence) is complicated, with Théo★★ being the
lightest; Laurence wines are from the non-cru Altenbourg; Ste-
Catherine★★ bottlings come from the Grand Cru Schlossberg. The top
dry wine is the Ste-Catherine Riesling Grand Cru Schlossberg
L'Inédit★★★. Quintessence★★★ is an SGN from Pinot Gris or
Gewurztraminer. All the wines are exceptionally balanced and, while
delightful on release, can age for many years. Best years: (Grand Cru
Riesling) (2009) 08 07 **05 04 02 01 00 99 98 97 96 95 94 93 92 90**.

WEISSBURGUNDER See PINOT BLANC.

WELSCHRIESLING Unrelated to the great Riesling of the Rhine, this grape
makes some of the best sweet wines in Austria, but tends to be rather dull
as a dry wine. It is highly esteemed in Hungary as Olasz Rizling. As
Riesling Italico it has virtually disappeared in northern Italy.

WENDOUREE *Clare Valley, South Australia* Small winery making enormous,
ageworthy reds★★★ from paltry yields off its own very old Shiraz,
Cabernet, Malbec and Mataro (Mourvèdre) vines, plus tiny amounts of
sweet Muscat★. Some of Australia's best reds, they can, and do, age
beautifully for 30 years or more. Best years: (reds) (2008) 06 (05) 04 03 02
01 **99 98 96 95 94 92 91 90 86 83 82 81 80 78 76 75**.

WESTEND *Riverina, New South Wales, Australia* The Calabria family winery
(established in 1945) has dramatically increased production and
improved quality in recent years. Their latest addition is a Cool Climate
series, with whites from CANBERRA and reds from HILLTOPS. The 3 Bridges
range includes a powerful yet scented Durif★ and the lush, honeyed

Golden Mist Botrytis Semillon★. Richland is one of Australia's best budget ranges (especially Pinot Grigio and Sauvignon Blanc).

WESTERN AUSTRALIA Only the south-west corner of this state is suited to vines, the SWAN DISTRICT and Perth environs being the oldest and hottest area, with present attention (and more than 260 producers) focused on GREAT SOUTHERN, MARGARET RIVER, Geographe and PEMBERTON. The state produces just over 4% of Australia's grape crush but about 20% of its premium wines.

HERMANN J WIEMER *Finger Lakes AVA, New York State, USA* Wiemer's family has 300 years' experience of winemaking in the MOSEL; it is natural that he would play a role in establishing the FINGER LAKES as a premier region for Riesling. He worked with local pioneer Dr Konstantin FRANK before establishing his own winery in 1979. Wiemer excels in the sweeter style, including an Auslese-style Late Harvest Riesling★, though in recent years the dry wines have shown more pizazz. The sparkling wines are not to be missed.

WIEN *Austria* 700ha (1730-acre) wine region within the city limits of Wien (Vienna). The best wines come from south-facing sites in Grinzing, Nussdorf and the Bisamberg hill east of the Danube. The wines are mostly consumed young in the growers' Heurigen (wine inns). The local 'Gemischter Satz' tradition of field-blend vineyards is being revived by many growers. Best producers: Christ, Edlmoser, Mayer, Schilling, WIENINGER★★, Zahel. Best years: (2009) 08 **07 06 05 04**.

WIENINGER *Stammersdorf, Wien, Austria* Fritz Wieninger has risen above the parochial standards of many Viennese growers to offer a range of elegant, well-crafted wines from Chardonnay and Pinot Noir. The best range is often the Select★★, the pricier Grand Select★ being sometimes over-oaked. Recent additions are brilliant white wines from the renowned Nussberg★★ vineyard. Best years: (2009) 08 **07 06 05 04**.

WILLAMETTE VALLEY AVA *Oregon, USA* Wet winters, generally dry summers, and a so-so chance of long, cool autumn days provide sound growing conditions for cool-climate varieties such as Pinot Noir, Pinot Gris and Chardonnay. Dundee Hills, with its volcanic hillsides, is considered the best sub-region. Best producers: ADELSHEIM★, ARGYLE★, BEAUX FRERES★★, BERGSTROM★★, Cristom★, DOMAINE DROUHIN★★, DOMAINE SERENE★★, ELK COVE★, Evesham Wood★, Patricia GREEN★, PONZI★, ST INNOCENT★, Sineann★, SOTER★, WillaKenzie★, Ken WRIGHT★. Best years: (reds) 2008 **06 04 03 02**.

WILLIAMS SELYEM *Russian River Valley AVA, California, USA* Exemplary Pinot Noirs (Rochioli Riverblock★★, Westside Road Neighbors★★) from various regions, including RUSSIAN RIVER VALLEY, SONOMA COAST and ANDERSON VALLEY. Zins are good too. Best years: (Pinot Noir) 2008 07 06 05 04 **03 02 01 00 99 98**.

WINKEL *Rheingau, Germany* RHEINGAU village whose best vineyard is the large Hasensprung but the most famous one is Schloss Vollrads – an ancient estate that does not use the village name on its label. Best producers: Hamm, Prinz von Hessen, Johannishof★★, SCHLOSS VOLLRADS★, Spreitzer★, WEGELER★. Best years: (2009) 08 07 **06 05 04 03 02 01 99 98**.

WINNINGEN *Mosel, Germany* The steep slopes of this village, particularly the Ühlen and Röttgen sites, can produce excellent Rieslings, especially in a rich dry style. Best producers: Fries, HEYMANN-LÖWENSTEIN★★, Reinhard Knebel★★, Richard Richter★. Best years: (2009) 08 07 **06 05 04 03 02**.

WIRRA WIRRA *McLaren Vale, South Australia*   Outstanding producer with fine ADELAIDE HILLS whites – well-balanced and tangy Sauvignon Blanc★ and Riesling★ and tight, fine yet creamy Chardonnay★★ – and soft MCLAREN VALE reds led by delicious The Angelus (Dead Ringer outside Australia) Cabernet★★, chocolatey RSW Shiraz★★, rich, balanced Catapult Shiraz-Viognier★ and stylish, concentrated Woodhenge Shiraz★. In 2007 purchased outstanding Rayner vineyard in the McLaren Vale. **Best years:** (RSW Shiraz) 2009 08 06 05 04 **03 02 01 98 96 94 91 90**.

WITHER HILLS *Marlborough, South Island, New Zealand*   Large winery now owned by Lion Nathan breweries and struggling to hold on to its cult reputation created by founder Brent Marris (departed in 2007 to run his new Marisco Vineyards/'The Ned'). Sauvignon Blanc★ sadly seems to get sweeter every vintage, but the Chardonnay★ and Pinot Noir★ still do their best to maintain the original Wither Hills style.

WITTMANN *Westhofen, Rheinhessen, Germany*   Philipp Wittmann has worked wonders at his family's biodynamic estate, succeeding equally with bold dry Rieslings★★, Chardonnay★★ and voluptuous Trockenbeerenauslese ★★★. **Best years:** (2009) 08 07 **06 05 04 03 02**.

J L WOLF *Wachenheim, Pfalz, Germany*   Ernst Loosen, of Dr LOOSEN, took over this underperforming estate in 1996. A string of concentrated, mostly dry Rieslings★★ have won it a place among the region's top producers. **Best years:** (2009) 08 07 **06 05 03 02**.

WÖLFFER ESTATE *Long Island, New York State, USA*   One of the few wineries in LONG ISLAND's Hamptons, Wölffer created a sensation in the early 2000s when it released a 'Premier Cru' Merlot priced at a lofty $100. It is good – but overshadowed by the more modestly priced Estate Selection Merlot★, a rich Pinot Gris and a spritely rosé. Wölffer died in 2008, but quality remains consistent under winemaker Roman Roth.

WOODWARD CANYON *Walla Walla Valley AVA, Washington State, USA*   Big, barrel-fermented Chardonnays were the trademark wines for many years, but today the focus is on reds, led by Artist Series★★ Cabernet Sauvignon and Old Vines★★ Cabernet Sauvignon. Merlot★★ is rich, velvety and deeply perfumed. Red BORDEAUX-style blend is labelled Charbonneau★, the name of the vineyard where the fruit is grown. **Best years:** (top Cabernet Sauvignon) (2008) 07 06 05 **04 03**.

KEN WRIGHT CELLARS *Willamette Valley AVA, Oregon, USA*   Ken Wright produces more than a dozen succulent, single-vineyard Pinot Noirs. Bold and rich with new oak flavour, they range from good to ethereal, led by the Carter★★, Savoya★★, Guadalupe★★, McCrone★★ and Shea★★. Fine WASHINGTON Chardonnay from the Celilo Vineyard★★ and a crisp Freedom Hill Vineyard Pinot Blanc★ are made in very small quantities. **Best years:** (Pinot Noir) 2008 07 06 **05 04 03 02**.

WÜRTTEMBERG *Germany*   11,500ha (28,415-acre) region centred on the river Neckar. Seventy percent of the wine made is red, and the best comes from Lemberger (Blaufränkisch) or Spätburgunder (Pinot Noir) grapes. Massive yields are often responsible for pallid wines, especially from the locally popular Trollinger grape. A few top steep sites are now producing perfumed reds and racy Riesling. **Best years:** (reds) (2009) (08) 07 **06 05 04 03**.

WÜRZBURG *Franken, Germany* The centre of FRANKEN wines. Some Rieslings can be excellent, but the real star is Silvaner. Best producers: Bürgerspital★, JULIUSSPITAL★★, Staatlicher Hofkeller, Reiss, Weingut am Stein★. Best years: (2009) 08 07 06 05 **04 03 02 01**.

WYNNS *Coonawarra, South Australia* Wynns' name is synonymous with COONAWARRA. It is now part of the giant Foster's Wine Group, but its personality seems to have suffered less than most of the group's other brands and, even at the top end, prices remain fair. Investment in vineyard rejuvenation is paying off. Wynns is best known for reds, such as Shiraz★ and Black Label Cabernet Sauvignon★. Top-end John Riddoch Cabernet Sauvignon★★★ and Michael Shiraz★★★ were deep, ripe, oaky styles, but latest releases show more restraint and elegance. Also attractive Chardonnay★ and delightful Riesling★. Best years: (John Riddoch) 2009 08 06 **05 04 03** 99 96 94 91 90 88 86.

YAKIMA VALLEY AVA *Washington State, USA* Important valley within the much larger COLUMBIA VALLEY AVA. Yakima is planted mostly to Chardonnay, Merlot and Cabernet Sauvignon and has more than 65 wineries. Best producers: Chinook★, DELILLE CELLARS★★, Hogue Cellars, Wineglass Cellars★.

YALUMBA *Barossa Valley, South Australia* Robert Hill Smith has taken his distinguished family firm to the pinnacle of Australian winemaking. There's an increasingly wide range under the Yalumba label, as well as a labyrinthine group under the banner of Hill Smith Family Vineyards. The latter includes Heggies (minerally Riesling★★, plump Merlot★★, opulent Viognier★★), Hill Smith Estate (Sauvignon Blanc★), Pewsey Vale (Riesling★★★) and TASMANIA's Jansz★ (vintage★★, non-vintage★). Flagship reds are The Signature Cabernet-Shiraz★★, Octavius Shiraz★★, Tri-Centenary Grenache★★ and The Menzies Cabernet★★, and all age well. Bush Vine Grenache★★, Virgilius Viognier★★ and Shiraz-Viognier★ are good too. High-quality Y Series varietals★ (sometimes ★★) are among Australia's finest quaffers. Budget-priced Redbank , Mawson's, Oxford Landing (Sauvignon★) and Angas Brut are enjoyable. Museum Reserve fortifieds (Muscat★★) are excellent, but rare. Best years: (The Signature) (2009) (08) 07 06 05 **04 03** 02 01 00 99 98 97 96 95 93.

YARRA VALLEY *Victoria, Australia* With its cool climate, the Yarra is asking to be judged as Australia's best Pinot Noir region, but superb Chardonnay, fascinating Cabernet-Merlot and small amounts of world-class Shiraz are even more exciting. Fizz is also very good. The disastrous bushfires of February 2009 affected only 3% of the vineyards, and any smoke-tainted wines haven't been released. Best producers: Arthur's Creek★, COLDSTREAM HILLS★★, CARLEI★★, DE BORTOLI★★, Diamond Valley★★, DOMAINE CHANDON/Green Point★, Gembrook Hill, Giant Steps, Jamsheed★★, Leayton Estate★, Mac Forbes★, Timo Mayer★, Métier, MOUNT MARY★★, OAKRIDGE★★, St Huberts, Seville Estate★, TARRAWARRA★★, Toolangi, The Wanderer★, Wantirna Estate, Yarrabank★, Yarra Yering★★, Yeringberg★, Yering Station★★.

YATIR *Judean Hills, Israel* Rising star, whose winery is situated in the north-east Negev desert. Rich, full reds from high-altitude vineyards within Israel's largest forest: top red, Yatir Forest★★, has ripe dark fruit backed by Mediterranean herbs; also a silky Cabernet Sauvignon★ and aromatic Viognier. Best years: (reds) 2006 05 **04 03** 02 01.

YELLOWTAIL *Riverina, New South Wales, Australia* Yellowtail, Australia's fastest-growing export brand ever, has made the RIVERINA family winery, Casella, a major world player. Artfully crafted but overly sweet wines.

[yellow tail]

CH. D'YQUEM★★★ *Sauternes AC, 1er Cru Supérieur, Bordeaux, France* Often rated the most sublime sweet wine in the world, Yquem's total commitment to quality is unquestionable. Despite a large vineyard (100ha/250 acres), production is tiny. Only fully noble-rotted grapes are picked, often berry by berry, and low yield means each vine produces only a glass of wine! This precious liquid is then fermented in new oak barrels and left to mature for 30 months before bottling. It is one of the world's most expensive wines, in constant demand because of its richness and exotic flavours. Quality took a step forward during the 1990s and seems to have gone even further during the 2000s. A dry white, Ygrec, is made most years. In 1999 LVMH won a takeover battle with the Lur-Saluces family, owners for 406 years. **Best years:** 2007 06 05 04 03 **02 01 00 99 98 97 96 95 94 90 89 88 86 83 81 79 76 75 71 70 67 62**.

ZILLIKEN *Saarburg, Mosel, Germany* Estate specializing in steely Rieslings★★ (Auslese, Eiswein often ★★★) from the Saarburger Rausch. **Best years:** (2009) 08 07 06 05 **04 03 02 01**.

ZIND-HUMBRECHT *Alsace AC, Alsace, France* Olivier Humbrecht is one of France's outstanding winemakers, with an approach that emphasizes the individuality of each site and each vintage. Wines from 4 Grand Cru sites – Rangen, Goldert, Hengst and Brand – are superlative (Riesling★★★, Gewurztraminer★★★, Pinot Gris★★★ and Muscat★★), the Rangen in particular producing wines unlike any others in Alsace. Wines from specific non-Grand Cru vineyards such as Clos Windsbuhl and Clos Jebsal are also exceptional. Vendange Tardive and Sélection de Grains Nobles wines are almost invariably of ★★★ quality. Even basic Sylvaners★ and Pinot Blancs★★ are fine. Wines often have some residual sugar, but it's all natural. **Best years:** (Grand Cru Riesling) (2009) 08 07 05 **04 03 02 01 00 99 98 97 96 95**.

ZINFANDEL CALIFORNIA's versatile red grape can make big, juicy, fruit-packed wine – often farmed from very old vines – or insipid, sweetish 'blush' labelled as White Zinfandel, or even late-harvest dessert wine. Some Zinfandel is now made in other countries, with notable examples in Australia and South Africa. **Best producers:** (California) Brown★★, Cline Cellars★★, Dashe★★, DRY CREEK VINEYARD★★, DUTTON GOLDFIELD★★, Gary Farrell★★, FETZER★, HARTFORD★★, MARIAH★, Martinelli★★, Michael-David (Earthquake), Nalle★★, Preston★★, Rafanelli★★, RAVENSWOOD★, RIDGE★★★, Rosenblum★★, Saddleback★★, St Francis★★, SEGHESIO★★, Trinitas★★, TURLEY★★; (Australia) CAPE MENTELLE★★, Kangarilla Road, Nepenthe★★, Smidge, Tscharke. See also PRIMITIVO DI MANDURIA.

ZUCCARDI *Mendoza, Argentina* As engaging as they are experimental, the Zuccardi family have forged a global reputation for the unexpected and delicious. The Santa Julia range and above it the Zuccardi 'Q'★ varietals represent excellent value. Top of the range Zeta★, a Malbec-Tempranillo blend, is getting into its stride. Port-style Malamado from Malbec (and a white version from Viognier) and sparkling red Bonarda★ are among the more eclectic offerings.

GLOSSARY OF WINE TERMS

AC/AOC (APPELLATION D'ORIGINE CONTRÔLÉE)
The top category of French wines, defined by regulations covering vineyard yields, grape varieties, geographical boundaries, alcohol content and production method. Guarantees origin and style of a wine, but not its quality.

ACID/ACIDITY
Naturally present in grapes and essential to wine, providing balance and stability and giving the refreshing tang in white wines and the appetizing grip in reds.

ADEGA
Portuguese for winery.

AGING
An alternative term for maturation.

ALCOHOLIC CONTENT
The alcoholic strength of wine, expressed as a percentage of the total volume of the wine. Typically in the range of 7–15%.

ALCOHOLIC FERMENTATION
The process whereby yeasts, natural or added, convert the grape sugars into alcohol (Ethyl alcohol, or Ethanol) and carbon dioxide.

AMONTILLADO
Traditionally dry style of sherry. *See* Jerez y Manzanilla in main A–Z.

ANBAUGEBIET
German for growing region; these names will appear on labels of all QbA and QmP wines. There are 13 Anbaugebiete: Ahr, Baden, Franken, Hessische Bergstrasse, Mittelrhein, Mosel, Nahe, Pfalz, Rheingau, Rheinhessen, Saale-Unstrut, Sachsen and Württemberg.

AUSBRUCH
Austrian Prädikat category used for sweet wines from the town of Rust.

AUSLESE
German and Austrian Prädikat category meaning that the grapes were 'selected' for their higher ripeness.

AVA (AMERICAN VITICULTURAL AREA)
System of appellations of origin for US wines.

AZIENDA AGRICOLA
Italian for estate or farm. It also indicates wine made from grapes grown by the proprietor.

BARREL AGING
Time spent maturing in wood, usually oak, during which wine takes on flavours from the wood.

BARREL FERMENTATION
Oak barrels may be used for fermentation instead of stainless steel to give a rich, oaky flavour to the wine.

BARRIQUE
The *barrique bordelaise* is the traditional Bordeaux oak barrel of 225 litres (50 gallons) capacity.

BAUMÉ
A scale measuring must weight (the amount of sugar in grape juice) to estimate potential alcohol content.

BEERENAUSLESE
German and Austrian Prädikat category applied to wines made from 'individually selected' berries (i.e. grapes) affected by noble rot (*Edelfäule* in German). The wines are rich and sweet. Beerenauslese wines are only produced in the best years in Germany, but in Austria they are a regular occurrence.

BEREICH
German for region or district within a wine region or *Anbaugebiet*. Bereichs tend to be large, and the use of a Bereich name, such as Bereich Bingen, without qualification is seldom an indication of quality – in most cases, quite the reverse.

BIODYNAMIC VITICULTURE
This approach works with the movement of the planets and cosmic forces to achieve health and balance in the soil and in the vine. Vines are treated with infusions of mineral, animal and plant materials, applied in homeopathic quantities. An increasing number of growers are turning to biodynamism, with some astonishing results, but it is labour-intensive and generally confined to smaller estates.

BOTTLE SIZES

CHAMPAGNE
Magnum	1.5 litres	2 bottles
Jeroboam	3 litres	4 bottles
Rehoboam	4.5 litres	6 bottles
Methuselah	6 litres	8 bottles
Salmanazar	9 litres	12 bottles
Balthazar	12 litres	16 bottles
Nebuchadnezzar	15 litres	20 bottles

BORDEAUX
Magnum	1.5 litres	2 bottles
Marie-Jeanne	2.25 litres	3 bottles
Double-magnum	3 litres	4 bottles
Jeroboam	4.5 litres	6 bottles
Imperial	6 litres	8 bottles

BLANC DE BLANCS
White wine made from one or more white grape varieties. Used especially for sparkling wines; in Champagne, denotes wine made entirely from the Chardonnay grape.

BLANC DE NOIRS
White wine made from black grapes only – the juice is separated from the skins to avoid extracting any colour. Most often seen in Champagne, where it describes wine made from Pinot Noir and/or Pinot Meunier grapes.

BLENDING
The art of mixing together wines of different origin, style or age, often to balance out acidity, weight etc. Winemakers often use the term *assemblage*.

BODEGA
Spanish for winery.

BOTRYTIS
See noble rot.

BRUT
French term for dry sparkling wines, especially Champagne.

CARBONIC MACERATION
Winemaking method used to produce fresh fruity reds for drinking young. Whole (uncrushed) bunches of grapes are fermented in closed containers – a process that extracts lots of fruit and colour, but little tannin.

CHAMPAGNE METHOD
Traditional method used for all of the world's finest sparkling wines. A second fermentation takes place in the bottle, producing carbon dioxide which, kept in solution under pressure, gives the wine its fizz.

CHAPTALIZATION
Legal addition of sugar during fermentation to raise a wine's alcoholic strength. More necessary in cool climates where lack of sun produces insufficient natural sugar in the grape.

CHARMAT
See cuve close.

CHÂTEAU
French for castle: widely used in France to describe any wine estate, large or small.

CHIARETTO
Italian for a rosé wine of very light pink colour from around Lake Garda.

CLARET
English for red Bordeaux wines, from the French *clairet*, which was traditionally used to describe a lighter style of red Bordeaux.

CLARIFICATION
Term covering any wine-making process (such as filtering or fining) that involves the removal of solid matter either from the must or the wine.

CLONE
Strain of grape species. The term is usually taken to mean laboratory-produced, virus-free clones, selected to produce higher or lower quantity, or selected for resistance to frost or disease.

CLOS
French for a walled vineyard – as in Burgundy's Clos de Vougeot – also commonly incorporated into the names of estates (e.g. Clos des Papes), whether they are walled or not.

COLD FERMENTATION
Long, slow fermentation at low temperature to extract maximum freshness from the grapes. Crucial for whites in hot climates.

COLHEITA
Aged tawny port from a single vintage. *See* Port in main A–Z.

COMMUNE
A French village and its surrounding area or parish.

CO-OPERATIVE
In a co-operative cellar, growers who are members bring their grapes for vinification and bottling under a collective label. In terms of quantity, the French wine industry is dominated by co-ops. They often use less workaday titles, such as Caves des Vignerons, Producteurs Réunis, Union des Producteurs or Cellier des Vignerons.

CORKED/CORKY
Wine fault derived from a cork which has become contaminated, usually with Trichloroanisole or TCA. The mouldy, stale smell is unmistakable. Nothing to do with pieces of cork in the wine.

COSECHA
Spanish for vintage.

CÔTE
French word for a slope or hillside, which is where many, but not all, of the country's best vineyards are found.

CRÉMANT
French term for traditional-method sparkling wine from Alsace, Bordeaux, Burgundy, Die, Jura, Limoux, Loire and Luxembourg.

CRIANZA
Spanish term for the youngest official category of oak-matured wine. A red Crianza wine must have had at least 2 years' aging (1 in oak, 1 in bottle) before sale; a white or rosé, 1 year.

CRU
French for growth, meaning a specific plot of land or particular estate. In Burgundy, growths are divided into Grands (great) and Premiers (first) Crus, and apply solely to the actual land. In

Champagne the same terms are used for whole villages. In Bordeaux there are various hierarchical levels of Cru referring to estates rather than their vineyards. In Italy the term is used frequently, in an unofficial way, to indicate a single-vineyard or special-selection wine.

CRU BOURGEOIS
French term for wines from the Médoc that in 1932 were ranked immediately below the Crus Classés. The list was revised in 2003, but annulled in 2007; the name is no longer seen on labels.

CRU CLASSÉ
The Classed Growths are the aristocracy of Bordeaux, ennobled by the Classifications of 1855 (for the Médoc, Barsac and Sauternes), 1955, 1969, 1986, 1996 and 2006 (for St-Émilion) and 1953 and 1959 (for Graves). Curiously, Pomerol has never been classified. The modern classifications are more reliable than the 1855 version, which was based solely on the price of the wines at the time of the Great Exhibition in Paris, but in terms of prestige the 1855 Classification remains the most important. With the exception of a single alteration in 1973, when Ch. Mouton-Rothschild was elevated to First Growth status, the list has not changed since 1855. It certainly needs revising.

CUVE CLOSE
A bulk process used to produce inexpensive sparkling wines. The second fermentation, which produces the bubbles, takes place in tank rather than in the bottle (as in the superior Traditional Method). Also called Charmat.

CUVÉE
French for the contents of a single vat or tank, but usually indicates a wine blended from either different grape varieties or the best barrels of wine.

DEGORGEMENT
Stage in the production of Champagne-method wines when the sediment, collected in the neck of the bottle during *remuage*, is removed.

DEMI-SEC
French for medium-dry.

DO
Spanish quality wine category, regulating origin and production methods. *See* page 36.

DOC
Italian quality wine category, regulating origin, grape varieties, yield and production methods. *See* page 29.

DOC
Portugal's top regional wine classification. *See* page 37.

DOCA
Spanish quality wine category, intended to be one step up from DO. *See* page 36.

DOCG
The top tier of the Italian classification system. *See* page 29.

DOMAINE
French term for wine estate.

DOSAGE
A sugar and wine mixture added to sparkling wine after *dégorgement* which affects how sweet or dry it will be.

EDELZWICKER
Blended wine from Alsace, usually bland.

EINZELLAGE
German for an individual vineyard site which is generally farmed by several growers. The name is preceded on the label by that of the village; for example, the Wehlener Sonnenuhr is the Sonnenuhr vineyard in Wehlen. The mention of a particular site should signify a superior wine.

EISWEIN
Rare, chiefly German and Austrian, late-harvested wine made by picking the grapes and pressing them while frozen. This concentrates the sweetness of the grape as most of the liquid is removed as ice. *See also* Icewine.

ERSTE LAGE
In Germany's Mosel, this term is used to indicate outstanding sites.

ERSTES GEWÄCHS
An official classification used in the Rheingau in Germany. Top sites were chosen by a kind of popular vote. Growers tend to use the label only for their best wines. *See also* Grosses Gewächs.

ESCOLHA
Portuguese for selection.

EXTRACTION
Refers to the extraction of colour, tannins and flavour from the grapes during and after fermentation. There are various ways in which extraction can be manipulated by the winemaker, but over-extraction leads to imbalance.

FEINHERB
Disliking the term Halb-trocken, some producers prefer to use Feinherb. It lacks legal definition but usually applies to wines with 9–25g per litre of residual sugar.

FILTERING
Removal of yeasts, solids and any impurities from a wine before bottling.

FINING
Method of clarifying wine by adding a coagulant (e.g. egg whites, isinglass) to remove soluble particles such as proteins and excessive tannins.

FINO
The lightest, freshest style of sherry. *See* Jerez y Manzanilla in main A–Z.

FLOR
A film of yeast which forms on the surface of fino sherries (and some other wines) in the barrel, preventing oxidation and imparting a tangy, dry flavour.

FLYING WINEMAKER
Term coined in the late 1980s to describe enologists, many Australian-trained, brought in to improve the quality of wines in many underperforming wine regions.

FORTIFIED WINE
Wine which has high-alcohol grape spirit added, usually before the initial fermentation is completed, thereby preserving sweetness.

FRIZZANTE
Italian for semi-sparkling wine.

GARAGE WINE
See vin de garage.

GARRAFEIRA
Portuguese term for wine from an outstanding vintage, with 0.5% more alcohol than the minimum required, and 2 years' aging in vat or barrel followed by 1 year in bottle for reds, and 6 months of each for whites. Also used by merchants for their best blended and aged wines. Use of the term is in decline as producers opt for the more readily recognized Reserva as an alternative on the label.

GRAN RESERVA
Top category of Spanish wines from a top vintage, with at least 5 years' aging (2 of them in cask) for reds and 4 for whites.

GRAND CRU
French for great growth. Supposedly the best vineyard sites in Alsace, Burgundy, Champagne and parts of Bordeaux – and should produce the most exciting wines.

GROSSES GEWÄCHS
A vineyard classification in Germany, devised by the VDP growers' association and now widely adopted. Wines must meet both quality and stylistic criteria: essentially for Riesling, dry and very sweet wines.

GROSSLAGE
German term for a grouping of vineyards. Some are not too big, and have the advantage of allowing small amounts of higher QmP wines to be made from the grapes from several vineyards. But sometimes the use of vast Grosslage names (e.g. Niersteiner Gutes Domtal) deceives consumers into believing they are buying something special. Top estates have agreed not to use Gross-lage names on their labels.

HALBTROCKEN
German for medium dry. In Germany and Austria medium-dry wine has 9–18g per litre of residual sugar, though sparkling wine is allowed up to 50g per litre. *See* Feinherb.

ICEWINE
A speciality of Canada, produced from juice squeezed from ripe grapes that have frozen on the vine. *See also* Eiswein.

IGT
Italian classification of regional wines. Both premium and everyday wines may share the same appellation. *See page 29.*

IPR
The second tier in the Portuguese wine classifications. *See page 37.*

KABINETT
Term used for the lowest level of QmP wines in Germany.

LANDWEIN
German or Austrian 'country' wine; the equivalent of French vin de pays. The wine must have a territorial definition and may be chaptalized to give it more alcohol.

LATE HARVEST
See Vendange Tardive.

LAYING DOWN
The storing of wine which will improve with age.

LEES
Sediment – dead yeast cells, grape pips (seeds), pulp and tartrates – thrown by wine during fermentation and left behind after racking. Some wines are left on the fine lees for as long as possible to take on extra flavour.

MACERATION
Important winemaking process for red wines whereby colour, flavour and/or tannin are extracted from grape skins before, during or after fermentation. The period lasts from a few days to several weeks.

MALOLACTIC FERMENTATION
Secondary fermentation whereby harsh malic acid is converted into mild lactic acid and carbon dioxide. Normal in red wines but often prevented in whites to preserve a fresh, fruity taste.

MANZANILLA
The tangiest style of sherry, similar to fino. *See* Jerez y Manzanilla in main A–Z.

MATURATION
Term for the beneficial aging of wine.

MERITAGE
American term for red or white wines made from a blend of Bordeaux grape varieties.

MESOCLIMATE
The climate of a specific geographical area, be it a

vineyard or simply a
hillside or valley.

à

MIDI
A loose geographical term,
virtually synonymous with
Languedoc-Roussillon,
covering the vast, sunbaked
area of southern France
between the Pyrenees and
the Rhône Valley.

MOELLEUX
French for soft or mellow,
used to describe sweet or
medium-sweet wines,
particularly in the Loire.

MOUSSEUX
French for sparkling wine.

MUST
The mixture of grape juice,
skins, pips and pulp
produced after crushing
(but prior to completion
of fermentation), which
will eventually become
wine.

MUST WEIGHT
An indicator of the sugar
content of juice – and
therefore the ripeness of
grapes.

NÉGOCIANT
French term for a merchant
who buys and sells wine.
A *négociant-éleveur* is a
merchant who buys, makes,
ages and sells wine.

NEW WORLD
When used as a
geographical term, New
World includes the
Americas, South Africa,
Australia and New
Zealand. By extension, it
is also a term used to
describe the clean, fruity,
upfront style now in
evidence all over the
world, but pioneered in
the USA and Australia.

NOBLE ROT
(*Botrytis cinerea*) Fungus
which, when it attacks
ripe white grapes, shrivels
the fruit and intensifies
their sugar while adding a
distinctive flavour. A vital
factor in creating many of
the world's finest sweet
wines, such as Sauternes
and Trockenbeerenauslese.

OAK
The wood used almost
exclusively to make barrels
for fermenting and aging
fine wines. It adds flavours
such as vanilla, and tannins;
the newer the wood, the
greater the impact.

OECHSLE
German scale measuring
must weight (sugar
content).

OLOROSO
The darkest, most heavily
fortified style of sherry.
See Jerez y Manzanilla in
main A–Z.

OXIDATION
Over-exposure of wine to
air, causing loss of fruit and
flavour. Slight oxidation,
such as occurs through the
wood of a barrel or during
racking, is part of the aging
process and, in wines of
sufficient structure,
enhances flavour and
complexity.

PASSITO
Italian term for wine made
from dried grapes. The
result is usually a sweet
wine with a raisiny intensity
of fruit. The drying process
is called *appassimento*. *See
also* Moscato Passito di
Pantelleria, Recioto della
Valpolicella, Recioto di
Soave and Vin Santo in
main A–Z.

PERLWEIN
German for a lightly
sparkling wine.

PÉTILLANT
French for a lightly
sparkling wine.

PHYLLOXERA
The vine aphid *Phylloxera
vastatrix* attacks vine
roots. It devastated
vineyards around the
world in the late 1800s
soon after it arrived from
America. Since then, the
vulnerable *Vitis vinifera*
has generally been grafted
on to vinously inferior, but
phylloxera-resistant,
American rootstocks.

PRÄDIKAT
Grades defining quality
wines in Germany and
Austria. These are (in
ascending order) Kabinett
(not considered as Prädikat
in Austria), Spätlese,
Auslese, Beerenauslese,
the Austrian-only category
Ausbruch, and
Trockenbeerenauslese.
Strohwein and Eiswein are
are also Prädikat wines.
Some Spätleses and even a
few Ausleses are now
made as dry wines.

PRÄDIKATSWEIN
The new term for QmP.

PREMIER CRU
First Growth; the top
quality classification in
parts of Bordeaux, but
second to Grand Cru in
Burgundy. Used in
Champagne to designate
vineyards just below
Grand Cru.

PRIMEUR
French term for a young
wine, often released for
sale within a few weeks of
the harvest. Beaujolais
Nouveau is the best-
known example.

**QBA (QUALITÄTSWEIN
BESTIMMTER
ANBAUGEBIETE)**
German for quality wine
from designated regions.
Sugar can be added to
increase the alcohol
content. Usually pretty
ordinary, but from top
estates this category offers
excellent value. In Austria
Qualitätswein is equivalent
to German QbA.

**QMP (QUALITÄTSWEIN
MIT PRÄDIKAT)**
German for quality wine
with distinction. A higher
category than QbA, with
controlled yields and no
sugar addition. QmP
covers 6 levels based on
the ripeness of the grapes:
see Prädikat. The term will
be replaced by Prädikats-
wein from August 2007.

QUINTA
Portuguese for farm or
estate.

RACKING
Gradual clarification of wine; the wine is transferred from one barrel or container to another, leaving the lees behind.

RANCIO
Fortified wine deliberately exposed to the effects of oxidation, found mainly in Languedoc-Roussillon and parts of Spain.

REMUAGE
Process in Champagne-making whereby the bottles, stored on their sides and at a progressively steeper angle in *pupitres*, are twisted, or riddled, each day so that the sediment moves down the sides and collects in the neck of the bottle on the cap, ready for *dégorgement*.

RESERVA
Spanish wines that have fulfilled certain aging requirements: reds must have at least 3 years' aging before sale, of which one must be in oak barrels; whites and rosés must have at least 2 years' age, of which 6 months must be in oak.

RÉSERVE
French for what is, in theory at least, a winemaker's finest wine. The word has no legal definition in France.

RIPASSO
A method used in Valpolicella to make wines with extra depth. Wine is passed over the lees of Recioto or Amarone della Valpolicella, adding extra alcohol and flavour, though also extra tannin and a risk of higher acidity and oxidation.

RISERVA
An Italian term, recognized in many DOCs and DOCGs, for a special selection of wine that has been aged longer before release. It is only a promise of a more pleasurable drink if the wine had enough fruit and structure in the first place.

SAIGNÉE
Rosé wine takes its colour from the skins of red grapes: the juice is bled off (*saignée*) after a short period of contact with the skins.

SEC
French for dry. When applied to Champagne, it means medium-dry.

'SECOND' WINES
A second selection from a designated vineyard, usually lighter and quicker-maturing than the main wine.

SEDIMENT
Usually refers to residue thrown by a wine, particularly red, as it ages in bottle.

SEKT
German for sparkling wine. The best wines are made by the traditional Champagne method, from 100% Riesling or 100% Weissburgunder (Pinot Blanc).

SÉLECTION DE GRAINS NOBLES (SGN)
A superripe category for sweet Alsace wines, now also being used by some producers of Coteaux du Layon in the Loire Valley. *See also* Vendange Tardive.

SMARAGD
The top of the three categories of wine from the Wachau in Austria, the lower two being Federspiel and Steinfeder. Made from very ripe and usually late-harvested grapes, the wines have a minimum of 12% alcohol, often 13–14%.

SOLERA
Traditional Spanish system of blending fortified wines, especially sherry and Montilla-Moriles.

SPÄTLESE
German for late-picked (riper) grapes. Often moderately sweet, though there are dry versions.

SPUMANTE
Italian for sparkling. Bottle-fermented wines are often referred to as *metodo classico* or *metodo tradizionale*.

SUPER-TUSCAN
Term coined in the 1980s for top-quality wines that did not conform to local DOC regulations (usually Chianti) and were therefore classed as vini da tavola. Many are now sold under the regional IGT Toscana.

SUPÉRIEUR
French for a wine with a slightly higher alcohol content than the basic AC.

SUPERIORE
Italian DOC wines with higher alcohol or more aging potential.

SUR LIE
French for on the lees, meaning wine bottled direct from the cask/fermentation vat to gain extra flavour from the lees. Common with quality Muscadet, white Burgundy, similar barrel-aged whites and, increasingly, bulk whites.

TAFELWEIN
German for table wine.

TANNIN
Harsh, bitter, mouth-puckering element in red wine, derived from grape skins and stems, and from oak barrels. Tannins soften with age and are essential for long-term development in red wines.

TERROIR
A French term used to denote the combination of soil, climate and exposure to the sun – that is, the natural physical environment of the vine.

TRADITIONAL METHOD
See Champagne method.

TROCKEN
German for dry. In most parts of Germany and

327

Austria Trocken matches the EU definition of dryness – less than 9g per litre residual sugar.

TROCKENBEEREN-AUSLESE (TBA)
German for 'dry berry selected', denoting grapes affected by noble rot (*Edelfäule* in German) – the wines will be lusciously sweet although low in alcohol.

VARIETAL
Wine made from, and named after, a single or dominant grape variety.

VDP
German organization recognizable on the label by a Prussian eagle bearing grapes. The quality of estates included is usually – but not always – high.

VDQS (VIN DÉLIMITÉ DE QUALITÉ SUPÉRIEURE)
The second-highest classification for French wines, behind AC. Being phased out after the 2010 vintage. *See* page 22.

VELHO
Portuguese for old. Legally applied only to wines with at least 3 years' aging for reds and 2 years for whites.

VENDANGE TARDIVE
French for late harvest. Grapes are left on the vines beyond the normal harvest time to concentrate flavours and sugars. The term is traditional in Alsace. The Italian term is *vendemmia tardiva*.

VIEILLES VIGNES
French term for a wine made from vines at least 20 years old. Should have greater concentration than wine from younger vines.

VIÑA
Spanish for vineyard.

VIN DE GARAGE
Wines made on so small a scale they could be made

in a garage. Such wines may be made from vineyards of a couple of hectares or less, and are often of extreme concentration.

VIN DE PAILLE
Sweet wine found mainly in the Jura region of France. Traditionally, the grapes are left for 2–3 months on straw (*paille*) mats before fermentation to dehydrate, thus concentrating the sugars. The wines are sweet but slightly nutty.

VIN DE PAYS
The term gives a regional identity to wine from the less renowned districts of France. Many are labelled with the grape variety. Now being converted to new IGP classification. *See* page 22.

VIN DE TABLE
French for table wine, the lowest quality level; now being phased out. *See* page 22.

VIN DOUX NATUREL (VDN)
French for a fortified wine, where fermentation has been stopped by the addition of alcohol, leaving the wine 'naturally' sweet, although you could argue that stopping fermentation with a slug of powerful spirit is distinctly unnatural.

VIN JAUNE
A speciality of the Jura region in France, made from the Savagnin grape. In Château-Chalon it is the only permitted style. Made in a similar way to fino sherry but not fortified and aged for 6 years in oak. Unlike fino, *vin jaune* ages well.

VINIFICATION
The process of turning grapes into wine.

VINO DA TAVOLA
The Italian term for table wine, officially Italy's lowest level of production,

is a catch-all that until relatively recently applied to more than 80% of the nation's wine, with virtually no regulations controlling quality. Yet this category also provided the arena in the 1970s and 80s for the biggest revolution in quality that Italy has ever seen, with the creation of innovative, DOC-busting Super-Tuscans.

VINTAGE
The year's grape harvest, also used to describe wines of a single year. 'Off-vintage' is a year not generally declared as vintage. *See* Port in main A–Z.

VITICULTURE
Vine-growing and vineyard management.

VITIS VINIFERA
Vine species, native to Europe and Central Asia, from which almost all the world's quality wine is made.

VQA (VINTNERS QUALITY ALLIANCE)
Canadian equivalent of France's AC system, defining quality standards and designated viticultural areas.

WEISSHERBST
German rosé wine, a speciality of Baden.

WO (WINE OF ORIGIN)
South African system of appellations which certifies area of origin, grape variety and vintage.

YIELD
The amount of fruit, and ultimately wine, produced from a vineyard. Measured in hectolitres per hectare (hl/ha) in most of Europe and in the New World as tons per acre or tonnes per hectare. Yield may vary from year to year, and depends on grape variety, age and density of the vines, and viticultural practices.

WHO OWNS WHAT

The world's major drinks companies are getting bigger and, frankly, I'm worried. As these vast wine conglomerates stride across continents, it seems highly likely that local traditions will – for purely business reasons – be pared away, along with individuality of flavour. It's not all bad news: in some cases wineries have benefited from the huge resources that come with corporate ownership, but I can't help feeling nervous knowing that the fate of a winery rests in the hands of distant institutional investors. Below, I have listed some of the names that crop up again and again – and will no doubt continue to do so, as they aggressively pursue their grasp of market share.

Other wine companies – which bottle wines under their own names and feature in the main A–Z – are spreading their nets. GALLO has agreements with, among others, Leonardo Da Vinci winery in Tuscany, MCWILLIAM'S of Australia and Whitehaven of New Zealand. The HESS COLLECTION in California owns Peter LEHMANN in Australia, GLEN CARLOU in South Africa and Colomé in Argentina. As well as Ch. MOUTON-ROTHSCHILD, the Rothschild family have other interests in France, co-own OPUS ONE and, in partnership with CONCHA Y TORO, produce ALMAVIVA in Chile.

The never-ending whirl of joint ventures, mergers and takeovers shows no signs of slowing down: the following can only be a snapshot at the time of going to press.

AXA MILLÉSIMES
The French insurance giant AXA's subsidiary owns Bordeaux châteaux PETIT-VILLAGE, PICHON-LONGUEVILLE, Pibran and SUDUIRAUT, plus Dom. de l'Arlot in Burgundy, Mas Belles Eaux in the Languedoc, TOKAJI producer Disznókö and PORT producer Quinta DO NOVAL.

CONSTELLATION BRANDS
The world's largest wine company is a major producer not only in the USA, but also in Australia, New Zealand and Canada. The US-based company merged with Australia's BRL Hardy in 2003 and its portfolio now includes Amberley, Banrock Station, BAROSSA VALLEY ESTATE, BAY OF FIRES, Brookland Valley, Goundrey, HARDYS, HOUGHTON, LEASINGHAM, Moondah Brook, Chateau Reynella, Starvedog Lane, Stonehaven and Yarra Burn. BRL Hardy had already acquired New Zealand's NOBILO (Selaks, Drylands). In 2004 Constellation bought the prestigious Robert MONDAVI Winery and all its entities, including OPUS ONE (a joint venture with the Rothschild family of Ch. MOUTON-ROTHSCHILD). Robert Mondavi Winery is now part of Constellation's Icon Estates division, along with FRANCISCAN, Estancia, Mount Veeder Winery and SIMI in California. Other US brands include Blackstone, CLOS DU BOIS, RAVENSWOOD and Wild Horse in California. Constellation acquired Canadian drinks giant Vincor in 2006; the deal included Le CLOS JORDANNE, INNISKILLIN, JACKSON-TRIGGS, SUMAC RIDGE in Canada, as well as Kim Crawford in New Zealand, Kumala in South Africa, Toasted Head in California and Hogue Cellars in Washington State. In South Africa, Constellation brands include Flagstone, Fish Hoek, and joint venture partner Ses'fikile. One of the UK's top-selling brands, Stowells, is part of Constellation, which also has a 40% stake in Italy's RUFFINO.

FOSTER'S GROUP
The wine division of Foster's, the Australian brewing giant, was founded on the twin pillars of Australia's Wolf BLASS and BERINGER in California. In 2005 Foster's won control of Southcorp, Australia's biggest wine conglomerate. It currently controls around 60 different brands and producers. In California it

owns, among others, CHATEAU ST JEAN, Etude, Meridian, Souverain, St Clement and Stags' Leap Winery. Australian brands include Annie's Lane, Baileys of Glenrowan, Leo Buring, COLDSTREAM HILLS, Devil's Lair, Heemskerk, Jamiesons Run, LINDEMANS, Metala, Mildara, Greg Norman, PENFOLDS, ROSEMOUNT ESTATE, Rothbury Estate, Rouge Homme, St Huberts, Saltram (Mamre Brook), Seaview, SEPPELT, T'Gallant, Tollana, WYNNS, Yarra Ridge and Yellowglen. Foster's also owns MATUA VALLEY and Secret Stone in New Zealand, and Castello di Gabbiano in Tuscany.

FREIXENET

This famous CAVA producer remains a family-owned business, with winery estates and interests around the world. In Spain, alongside FREIXENET Cavas, the portfolio includes Castellblanch, Segura Viudas, Conde de Caralt, René Barbier, Morlanda and Valdubón. Further afield it includes Bordeaux *négociant* and producer Yvon Mau, the Champagne house of Henri Abelé, Gloria Ferrer in California, Viento Sur in Argentina and Australia's Wingara Wine Group (Deakin Estate, KATNOOK ESTATE).

JACKSON FAMILY WINES

Jess Jackson, founder of California's KENDALL-JACKSON, has a large portfolio in California, including: ARROWOOD, Atalon, Byron, Cambria, Cardinale, Edmeades, Freemark Abbey, HARTFORD, La Crema, La Jota, Lokoya, MATANZAS CREEK, Murphy-Goode, Pepi, Stonestreet and Vérité. Further afield, Jackson also owns Calina (Chile), Yangarra Estate (Australia), Château Lassègue (ST-EMILION) and Villa Arceno (Tuscany).

LVMH

French luxury goods group Louis Vuitton-Moët Hennessy owns Champagne houses MOËT & CHANDON (including Dom Pérignon), KRUG, Mercier, RUINART and VEUVE CLICQUOT, and has established DOMAINE CHANDON sparkling wine companies in California, Australia and Argentina. It also owns Ch. d'YQUEM, CAPE MENTELLE in Australia, CLOUDY BAY in New Zealand, NEWTON in California, Numanthia-Termes in TORO, Spain, and TERRAZAS DE LOS ANDES in Argentina.

PERNOD RICARD

The French spirits giant owns Australia's all-conquering JACOB'S CREEK brand, along with Wyndham Estate and the Orlando, Gramp's, Poet's Corner and Richmond Grove labels. Pernod Ricard's empire also encompasses New Zealand's mighty MONTANA, CHURCH ROAD, Corbans, Lindauer and Stoneleigh brands, as well as Champagne producers G H MUMM and PERRIER-JOUËT, Californian fizz MUMM NAPA, Long Mountain in South Africa and a number of Argentinian producers, including Etchart and Graffigna. In Spain, Pernod Ricard controls CAMPO VIEJO, Alcorta, Azpilicueta, Marqués de Arienzo, Siglo and Ysios, among others, and in Georgia it has a 75% stake in Georgian Wines & Spirits.

INDEX OF PRODUCERS

Numbers in **bold** refer to main entries.

338

344

358

359

OLDER VINTAGE CHARTS *(top wines only)*

FRANCE										
Alsace (vendanges tardives)	98	97	96	95	90	89	88	86	85	82
	9◇	8◆	8◆	9◆	10◆	9◆	8◆	8◇	9◆	10◆
Champagne (vintage)	99	98	97	96	95	90	89	88	85	82
	7◇	7◇	6◆	9◇	8◆	9◆	8◆	9◆	8◆	9◆
Bordeaux	99	98	97	96	95	94	90	89	88	86
Margaux	7◆	7◆	6◇	8◆	8◆	6◇	9◆	8◆	7◆	8◆
St-Jul., Pauillac, St-Est.	7◆	7◆	6◇	9◇	8◆	7◇	9◆	9◆	8◆	9◆
Graves/Pessac-L. (red)	7◆	8◆	6◇	8◆	8◆	6◇	8◆	8◆	8◆	6◇
St-Émilion, Pomerol	7◆	9◆	6◇	7◆	9◆	6◇	9◆	9◆	8◆	7◇
Bordeaux (cont.)	85	83	82	81	75	70	66	61	59	55
Margaux (cont.)	8◆	9◇	8◇	7◇	6◇	8◇	7◇	10◇	8◇	6◇
St-Jul. etc. (cont.)	8◆	7◇	10◆	7◇	8◇	8◇	8◇	10◇	9◇	8◇
Graves/P-L (red) (cont.)	8◆	8◆	9◇	7◇	6◇	8◇	8◇	10◇	9◇	8◇
St-Émilion etc. (cont.)	9◆	7◇	9◇	7◇	8◇	8◇	6◇	10◇	7◇	7◇
Sauternes	99	98	97	96	95	90	89	88	86	83
	8◆	7◆	9◆	9◆	7◆	10◆	9◆	9◆	9◆	9◆
Sauternes (cont.)	80	76	75	71	67	62	59	55	53	49
	7◇	8◇	8◇	8◇	9◇	8◇	9◇	8◇	8◇	10◇
Burgundy										
Chablis	99	98	97	96	95	92	90			
	7◇	7◇	7◇	8◆	8◆	7◇	9◇			
Côte de Beaune (wh.)	99	98	97	96	95	93	92	90	89	
	8◆	5◇	7◇	6◇	8◆	7◇	8◇	7◇	9◇	
Côte de Nuits (red)	99	98	97	96	95	93	90	89	88	85
	9◇	7◆	7◇	9◇	7◆	8◆	9◆	7◇	8◇	9◇